Aspects of the Morphology and Phonology of Kɔnni

SIL International and
The University of Texas at Arlington
Publications in Linguistics

Publication 141

Publications in Linguistics are published jointly by SIL International and the University of Texas at Arlington. The series is a venue for works covering a broad range of topics in linguistics, especially the analytical treatment of minority languages from all parts of the world. While most volumes are authored by members of SIL, suitable works by others will also form part of the series.

Series Editors

Donald A. Burquest
University of Texas at Arlington

Mary Ruth Wise
SIL International

Volume Editor

Rhonda Hartell-Jones

Production Staff

Bonnie Brown, Managing Editor
Karoline Fisher, Compositor
Hazel Shorey, Graphic Artist
Barb Alber, Cover design

Aspects of the Morphology and Phonology of Kɔnni

Michael C. Cahill

SIL International
and
The University of Texas at Arlington

© 2007 by SIL International
Library of Congress Catalog No: 2006-940459
ISBN-13: 978-155671-184-8
ISSN: 1040-0850

Printed in the United States of America

All Rights Reserved

No part of this publication may be reproduced, stored in a retrieval system, or transmitted in any form or by any means—electronic, mechanical, photocopy, recording, or otherwise—without the express permission of the SIL International. However, short passages, generally understood to be within the limits of fair use, may be quoted without written permission.

Copies of this and other publications of the SIL International may be obtained from

International Academic Bookstore
SIL International
7500 W. Camp Wisdom Road
Dallas, TX 75236-5699

Voice: 972-708-7404
Fax: 972-708-7363
Email: academic_books@sil.org
Internet: http://www.ethnologue.com

This book is dedicated to my SIL colleagues around the world.

Contents

Acknowledgements xiii

Abbreviations xvii

1 Introduction 1
  1.1 The people and language 1
    1.1.1 The Koma people 1
    1.1.2 The Kɔnni language and its relatives 3
    1.1.3 Resources and literature on Gur languages. 5
    1.1.4 The sources of the data 7
    1.1.5 Inventories of Kɔnni consonants, vowels, and tones. . 7
  1.2 Sketch of syntax 9
    1.2.1 Clause structure. 9
    1.2.2 Interrogatives 11
    1.2.3 Pronouns 13
    1.2.4 The noun phrase 15
    1.2.5 The verb phrase. 18
    1.2.6 Preverbal particles. 21
    1.2.7 Obliques 23
  1.3 Theoretical foundations and assumptions. 25
    1.3.1 Optimality/Correspondence Theory 25
    1.3.2 Features and their organization. 31

2 Morphology. 35
  2.1 Nominal morphology. 36
    2.1.1 Noun classes 36
    2.1.2 Noun-adjective complexes 45

	2.1.3 Derived nouns and adjectives.	48
	2.1.4 Compound nouns	54
	2.2 Verbal morphology.	58
	2.2.1 Aspectual and modal suffixes.	59
	2.2.2 Derived verbs and verbal extensors	68
	2.3 Modifiers	70
	2.4 Concluding observation.	73
3	Phonotactics and Syllables.	75
	3.1 Relative frequency of phonemes.	75
	3.2 Co-occurrences	78
	3.2.1 Vowels and consonants	78
	3.2.2 Consonants and consonants	84
	3.3 Distribution of consonants and vowels	85
	3.3.1 Word-final position	85
	3.3.2 Roots versus suffixes.	87
	3.3.3 Noun and verb structure.	89
	3.4 Consonant clusters.	91
	3.5 Syllable structure	93
	3.6 Minimality of nouns and verbs	95
4	Consonantal Phonology	97
	4.1 Consonant inventory, contrasts, and measurements	97
	4.1.1 Justification of contrasts.	97
	4.1.2 Phonetics: aspiration, prevoicing, and duration.	99
	4.2 Assimilatory processes	103
	4.2.1 Nasal place assimilation	105
	4.2.2 Intervocalic weakening.	117
	4.2.3 The case of [d] and [r] – one phoneme or two?	119
	4.2.4 Total assimilation of /r/	123
	4.2.5 Voicing assimilation of consonants	129
	4.2.6 Labialization	135
	4.2.7 Palatalization.	135
	4.3 Deletion	136
	4.3.1 The ŋ~g~k alternation and g-deletion.	136
	4.3.2 n-deletion.	141
	4.4 Dissimilation	144
	4.4.1 Data	144
	4.4.2 Analysis	148
	4.5 Epenthesis	161
	4.5.1 Data	161
	4.5.2 Analysis	163

4.6 Conclusion		170
4.6.1 Summary of constraints		170
4.6.2 Coronal review		172
4.6.3 Other comments.		173
5 Vocalic Phonology		**175**
5.1 Vowel inventory, contrasts, and measurements		175
5.1.1 Justification of phonemes		176
5.1.2 Vowel duration measurements		178
5.1.3 Vowel formant frequency measurements.		181
5.2 ATR vowel harmony		184
5.2.1 Vowel harmony within words		185
5.2.2 Vowel harmony across words.		205
5.2.3 A syntax-phonology interface.		217
5.3 Diphthongization		226
5.3.1 Diphthongization—data		226
5.3.2 Diphthongization—analysis.		228
5.4 Vowel assimilation I		244
5.4.1 Agreement of place across [g]		244
5.4.2 Coronal agreement across coronals		250
5.4.3 Assimilation of vowels to following glide		254
5.4.4 Backing of front vowels before ŋ		258
5.5 Vowel epenthesis		262
5.5.1 Data		262
5.5.2 Analysis		266
5.6 The agentive prefix.		275
5.7 Vowel shortening		278
5.7.1 Data		279
5.7.2 Analysis		281
5.8 Epenthesis or elision? Vowels after [g]		284
5.9 Vowel assimilation II: Total assimilation in vowel hiatus		288
5.9.1 Data		288
5.9.2 Analysis		292
5.10 Summary and discussion.		299
6 Tone		**303**
6.1 Introduction to Kɔnni tone		305
6.1.1 Tone inventories and distribution.		305
6.1.2 Representation and tone-bearing units.		307
6.1.3 High-toned nominal suffixes		310
6.1.4 Downstep from underlying Low tone		312
6.1.5 Floating associative morpheme		313
6.1.6 The absence of the OCP in Kɔnni		314

- 6.2 Basic tonal constraints 316
  - 6.2.1 Beginning constraints 316
  - 6.2.2 More complex constraints—*HLH, etc. 321
  - 6.2.3 Tone on epenthetic vowels 324
- 6.3 Nominals 331
  - 6.3.1 Simple singulars, plurals, definites 331
  - 6.3.2 The -sI suffix 339
  - 6.3.3 Class 1 tone polarity 342
  - 6.3.4 Derived nouns 353
  - 6.3.5 Adjectival extensions 356
  - 6.3.6 Associative noun phrases 364
  - 6.3.7 Compound nouns 378
  - 6.3.8 Postnominal modifiers 381
  - 6.3.9 Nonfinal contours 384
- 6.4 Verbal tone 386
  - 6.4.1 Aspectual tone 386
  - 6.4.2 Preverbal particles 407
- 6.5 Tone on conditionals 413
- 6.6 Yes/no question intonation 416
- 6.7 A note on stress 419
- 6.8 Concluding remarks 422

7 Conclusion 425
- 7.1 Data highlights 425
  - 7.1.1 Consonants 426
  - 7.1.2 Vowels 426
  - 7.1.3 Tones 427
- 7.2 Theoretical highlights 428
  - 7.2.1 Optimality Theory 428
  - 7.2.2 Consonants 428
  - 7.2.3 Vowels 429
  - 7.2.4 Tones 430
- 7.3 A "complete" tableau 430

Appendix A 435
 Perturbation of target nouns in tone frames 435

Appendix B 439
 Nouns, plurals, and definite articles 439

Appendix C 457
 Compound nouns 457

Appendix D 463
   Noun-adjective complexes 463

Appendix E 469
   Associative noun phrases. 469

Appendix F 473
   Verb aspects 473
      Imperfective 473
      Perfective 476
      Future 479
      Future imperfective. 481
      Imperative 483
      Imperative imperfective 484
      Iterative 485

Appendix G 487
   Preverbal particles. 487
      Single particles 488
      Interaction of 2 particles 490
      Interaction of three particles 491

References 493

Subject Index 511

Index of Constraints 515

Acknowledgements

Traditionally, an author acknowledges the support of his or her spouse through the trauma of writing such a document, and rightly so. This often comes as the final acknowledgment, perhaps on the theory that we should save the best for last. I want to break that pattern here and make the first proclamation, quite loudly and fervently, of thanks and gratitude to my wife Ginia. Her love has been constant, her support never ending, and the household management tasks that she has relieved me of are many. She has made it truly possible for this work to be finished, first as a dissertation and now in revised form. Ginia is the best partner, friend, and wife I could ever hope for. I am also very thankful for my children, Deborah, Laura, and Stephen, whose presence always reminds me that yes, there are more important things in the universe than even linguistics. Now we can play more!

I am overflowingly grateful to dozens of people who have contributed to the finishing of this degree. Here goes!

I was fortunate in having great members of my dissertation committee: David Odden, Beth Hume, and Brian Joseph. They have all been instrumental in shaping me as a linguist, each in a unique way. David Odden is the walking encyclopedia of phonological data, always ready with an answer to "Do you know of a language that has XYZ phenomena?" He has reinforced in me a healthy respect for firsthand data and a healthy (I hope) skepticism of second- and thirdhand data. He has read more versions of this too-hefty volume than anyone and has been incredibly helpful with many very specific suggestions. I am grateful to Beth Hume for her phonological expertise in teaching several seminars which were indispensable in the theoretical development of the topics in this study and her humane and gentle spirit in communicating that expertise to her students—may they sing her praises more loudly! Brian Joseph was especially instrumental in shaping my development in historical linguistics, and I very much appreciate the extra time he takes to give encouraging comments. His influence is evident in the many historical sidebars I have included here, even without his specific instigation. To Brian also must go much of the credit for maintaining a pleasant atmosphere in the Linguistics Department at Ohio State University during his tenure as Chair for most of my time there.

Other faculty members at Ohio State University made a significant impact on me and this study. Thanks to Arnold Zwicky for a number of valuable suggestions on the morphology chapter, clarifying the obscure, and offering alternate ways of looking at the data. To Keith Johnson for always being approachable and willing to offer advice on the phonetic side of things. His influence is present, though not explicitly recognized, in much of the instrumental work presented in this study. To Mary Beckman, who through the "Laboratory Phonology" course, instilled a great respect for phonology which can be supported by experimental evidence, and who redefined for me the term "rigor!" To Sam Rosenthall for discussion of Optimality Theory in general, and especially issues pertaining to vowels. Even when we could not solve the problems on the spot, he was always a friendly and stimulating influence. To Bob Kasper for discussion of syntactical relations pertaining to vowel harmony and for friendship.

Many thanks to members of the "Phonies" group and their lively discussions of Kɔnni data I threw out with a "How do you explain this?" challenge. Especially to Mary Bradshaw, fellow Africanist, for being willing to stop in the hallways of Oxley on the way to wherever she was going to discuss data and theory. My gratitude also to Frederick Parkinson, Rebecca Herman, Robert Poletto, No-Ju Kim, Hyeon-Seok Kang, Kevin Cohen, Bettina Migge, Nasiombe Mutonyi, Amanda Ockhuizen-Miller, and Jenn Muller. And to my fellow residents of 204 Oxley Hall, thanks for many discussions of matters linguistic and nonlinguistic, especially to Andy Saperstein, Steve Hartman-Keiser, Panos Pappas, Peter Wagner, Eun-Jung Yoo, Sun-hee Lee, and Michelle Ramos-Pellicia. Thanks to non-OSU scholars who have offered comments on various bits of this work, including Doug Pulleyblank, Linda Lombardi, and Keiichiro Suzuki. Even when I did not follow their suggestions, however, their discussion and ideas stimulated me in directions I would not necessarily have gone otherwise.

Many, many thanks to my colleagues of SIL International, in particular Don Burquest (also of the University of Texas at Arlington), one of the most encouraging teachers I have ever known, for really turning me on to

Acknowledgements

phonology in a series of classes in 1984–1985. My colleagues in Ghana, especially Rod Casali, have been a constant source of stimulation and encouragement. Cheri Black took my naive ideas on Principles and Paramaters syntax and helped make some sense out of them. Thanks to Fraser Bennett and Paul Thomas for listening and offering suggestions on vowels and consonants. Lou Hohulin and my co-workers in the International Linguistics Department of SIL were a great source of support, encouragement, and friendship in the last months of writing.

Thanks to all the people who prayed this project through to a conclusion, in Columbus, Dallas, and scattered throughout five continents. Only eternity will reveal how big a part you played. I am also grateful to churches and individuals who supported my wife and me financially while we were working in Ghana and continued to support us during my studies.

Our very great thanks to the Koma people, for years of hospitality and many bowls of *sààŋ*, for our friends Ali, Braimah, Tanni, and Seitu for being incredibly patient as we mangled their tongue. And to the late Pastor Martin Amoak, who helped us through the initial stages of adjusting to the language and culture, we owe an incredible debt.

Finally, I truly have saved the best for last. I thank God, my heavenly Father, the ultimate sina qua non, for making all things possible. In Ghana and the USA, he has taken me through language learning, culture stress, malaria, hepatitis, various and sundry parasites, a car wreck, unexpectedly home-delivering one of my daughters, rigorous courses and exams, and now, this work. As Bach initialed every one of his musical pieces "SDG" (soli Dei gloria), I also would like to mark this book, more understandably to a non-Latin-speaking audience, with

To God alone be the glory.

Abbreviations

1s	first-person singular pronoun
1p	first-person plural pronoun
2s	second-person singular pronoun
2p	second-person plural pronoun
3s	third-person singular pronoun
3p	third-person plural pronoun
Abd.	Abdulai
AFF	affirmative
Am.	Amadu
ATR	advanced tongue root
AGR	agreement
ART	article
C	consonant
CPZR	complementizer
def	definite
DET	determiner
EMPH	emphatic
F	format
FG	Feature Geometry
FUT	future tense
Hs	Hausa
IDEO	ideophone
IMPER	imperative
IMPF	imperfective
intrans.	intransitive

LOC	locative
NC	noun class
NEG	negative
nh	nonhuman
NP	noun phrase
Ns	noun stem
NUM	number
OCP	Obligatory Contour Principle
OT	Optimality Theory
PBK	Proto-Buli-Kɔnni
PERF	perfective
PL	plural
PP	Principles and Parameters
PRN	pronoun
RED	reduplicant
ROA	Rutgers Optimality Archive
SD	standard deviation
Sfx	suffix
SG	singular
sp.	species
SPE	The Sound Pattern of English
TBU	tone-bearing unit
TNS	tense
trans.	transitive
UR	underlying representation
V	vowel
Vb	verb
VOT	voice onset time

1
Introduction

1.1 The people and language

1.1.1 The Koma people

No language exists in a vacuum. Neighboring cultures, the physical environment, and the people's history all play a role in shaping the language. The people have hopes and dreams, fears and anxieties, joys and sorrows; they are not mere language machines. It is with deep respect for the speakers of Kɔnni that I offer this brief sketch of their life situation.

People who speak the Kɔnni language are called Koma or Kɔma. Kɔnni is a small language group by African standards, spoken by approximately 2,500 people, who live on the western edge of the Northern Region of Ghana. At the time I gathered the majority of my language data (1986–1993), the Koma people lived in the five villages of Yikpabongo, Tantuosi, Wontobiri, Nangurima, and Barisi. The Nangurima speech constitutes a slightly different dialect from the others (see section 1.1.2). In recent years, the hundred or so people in Barisi all moved to Yikpabongo, and a small group of people from Nangurima split off to form a new village called Senta. Yikpabongo itself is a divided village, including Yikpabongo proper (the "lower village") and Nagbiasi (the "upper village," on higher ground). Nagbiasi moved next to Yikpabongo perhaps 100 years ago, and retains its own chief and set of elders and traditional positions, separate from Yikpabongo.

The Koma are almost entirely subsistence farmers, growing millet, sorghum, corn, yams, sweet potatoes, cassava, peanuts, beans, and rice.

Hunting provides an occasional antelope or other animal to supplement the diet, and the Koma also keep cattle, sheep, goats, chickens, and guinea fowls to eat, to pay the bride-price (payment from the groom's family to the bride's family), and to sacrifice to various spirits.

The land is relatively fertile. It is fairly level, with rolling hills and large flat areas alternating. The Koma area is part of the African Sahel, with short trees and grasses that grow tall during the rainy season. Several small rivers run throughout the area. The rivers have been a barrier to wider communication of the Koma with others; there is no path into the Koma area that does not cross at least one river, and the Koma area is sometimes referred to by Ghanaians as "overseas." Even today, there is no road, paved or gravel, into the area, but only tractor trails which are a muddy morass during the rainy season.

The rainy season is from May to November. This is farming season, when both men and women work on farms. In the dry season, approximately December to April, no rain falls, the grasses dry out, and the men have less work to do. That is the time to build new mud-block houses or repair old houses damaged by the rains. Women fetch water and plaster the walls of the houses, and men make the blocks, build the walls, and put on the thatch or corrugated aluminum roofs. New farms are cleared and old ones maintained.

Though both Christians and Muslims are present among the Koma people, over 90 percent of the people follow the traditional Koma religion. The Koma, like many peoples in sub-Saharan Africa, speak of one good creator God, but in everyday experience they have more to do with spirits of ancestors and certain trees, rocks, and hills, to which they offer regular animal sacrifices and libations.

Western-style education has been slow in coming to the Koma due to their location and the corresponding fact that educated Ghanaians are reluctant to serve in such an isolated area. Attempts at elementary schools have been less than successful, hampered by the fact that trained teachers have not been Koma people and have communicated mostly in Mampruli and English. Several boys have been sent out of the area for education up to middle school level. I devised the first writing system for Kɔnni in 1987, and trial literacy classes in Kɔnni were begun. Since then, Konlan Kpeebi, of the Ghana Institute of Linguistics, Literacy, and Bible Translation, has to date (January 2006) successfully helped teach over 600 Koma people basic reading skills, and ninety-six have also received advanced reading certificates. Mr. Kpeebi is producing a growing body of literature in Kɔnni, and the expectation is that in the next several years the Koma people themselves will start authoring materials in their own language.

1.1 The people and language

The Kɔnni area is bordered by speakers of Sisaala-Pasaale, Buli (called Builsas), and Mampruli (called Mamprusis). The Koma people relate quite closely to these neighbors through marriage and trade. Some Koma people have knowledge of these neighboring languages sufficient for trade and everyday contacts, but very few have any knowledge of the languages of wider communication of Ghana: English, Hausa, and Twi (Akan). The Koma have a traditional system of government with a chief and elders and are under the dominion of the Mamprusis, reporting to the Mamprusi paramount chief. House architecture and much of the culture also resembles Mamprusi more than it does Builsa. However, Kɔnni is most closely related to Buli (Naden 1988, 1989), as shown both by lexical similarities and grammatical features such as the noun class system.

1.1.2 The Kɔnni language and its relatives

Kɔnni is a Gur language, of the Oti-Volta branch. Earlier surveys of Gur, such as Swadesh et al. (1966), Bendor-Samuel (1971), and Manessy (1975, 1979), do not include Kɔnni, since it was documented as a distinct language (though sketchily) only when J. Binnington transcribed a Swadesh 100-word list in a Builsa town in the early 1970s. Andrew Ring and Tony Naden gathered Kɔnni data in a four-day survey on foot in 1979. Naden summarized his findings on phonology, morphology, and syntax in Naden (1986). My findings are largely consistent with his preliminary report, although especially in the area of tone and vowels, my transcriptions differ from his in numerous places.

The language family tree in (1) shows the relationships of Kɔnni to its neighbors, extracted from Naden (1988, 1989). There are branches not shown in (1) and many more than the languages listed. Kɔnni and the languages which border it are shown bolded. Of these, Buli is both adjacent to Kɔnni and is the nearest genetic relative; it will be mentioned for comparative purposes several times in this work. Mampruli is more distantly related, and Sisaala-Pasaale is in a different branch of Gur altogether. But all have influenced Kɔnni (Naden 1986).

(1)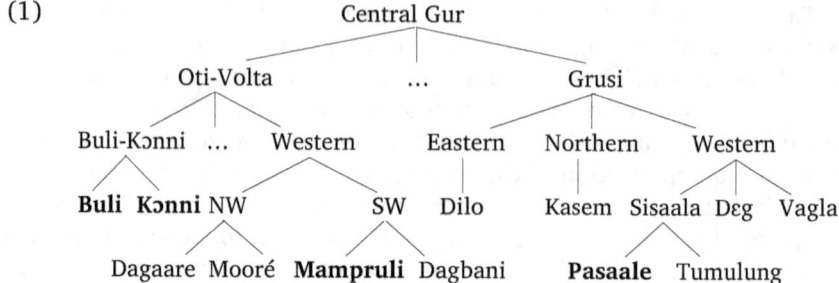

Kɔnni has two main dialects, the "Nangurima" dialect, spoken in Nangurima and Senta, and the "Yikpabongo" dialect, spoken in Yikpabongo and the other villages. The Nangurima dialect differs from the central, or Yikpabongo, dialect in at least three ways. First, lexically, Nangurima uses different words for some items than Yikpabongo.

(2) | Yikpabongo | Nangurima | |
| --- | --- | --- |
| bàllí | bàsí | 'children' |
| kpʊ̀ŋkpáŋ | nàŋkpàlìgíŋ | 'fish (sp.)' |
| mìmàáŋ | sììbúŋ | 'lungfish' |

Second, there are systematic sound differences between Yikpabongo and Nangurima, the most obvious one being that Nangurima has no /h/. Wherever Yikpabongo has [h], Nangurima has [ŋ] most often, and [w] sometimes.

(3) | Yikpabongo | Nangurima | |
| --- | --- | --- |
| hààgíŋ | ŋààgíŋ | 'bush' |
| hàgìtí | ŋàgìtí | 'shells' |
| hɔ̀gú | ŋɔ̀gú | 'woman, wife' |
| haarı | ŋaarı | 'to reach' |
| hʊ̀ʊ̀tí | wʊ̀ʊ̀tí | 'grasses' |

These differences connect to a larger pattern of historical development examined in Cahill (1995a, 1999b).

A third way that Nangurima speech differs from Yikpabongo is the regular use of pronouns such as *bʊ̀* 'it' (noun class 4), which connect to the noun class of the referent noun, rather than the more general *kà* 'it'.

In this work, I focus on the Yikpabongo dialect.

1.1.3 Resources and literature on Gur languages

Gur languages are spoken in Burkina Faso, Mali, northern Ghana, Togo, Benin, and Côte d'Ivoire. Due to the geographical location in the interior of Africa, as well as the relative poverty and unfavorable living situations of many of the Gur-speaking peoples, this African language family has not been as thoroughly described as some. Since all the Gur-speaking countries except Ghana are francophone, much of the research done has been published in French. Several German scholars have been active in Gur research as well. In this work, although I will mention some of the French work, I confine myself mostly to what is available in English. I do not list works which focus exclusively on Gur syntax, since that is not the focus of this book.

A good general overview of the Gur family is given in Naden (1989), and a survey limited to Gur languages within Ghana is in Naden (1988). In these works, Naden lays out general facts of Gur classification, phonology, morphology, syntax, and discourse, and also has a bibliography which concentrates on classificatory references.

At least three web sites have been established which focus on Gur languages. As a result of the first International Colloquium on Gur languages held in Ouagadougou, Burkina Faso, in 1997, a Gur web page now exists on the Internet, located at www.univie.ac.at/linguistics/gur. This contains a newsletter and announcements, a "Who's Who" in Gur linguistics, and a bibliography of papers put out since 1992. A web page devoted to a single Gur language, Dagaare, is maintained by Adams Bodomo at www.hku.hk/linguist/staff_ab.DagaareLinguist.html. This also has a "Who is Who" in Dagaare studies, a bibliography of Dagaare materials, and even the UN Declaration of Human Rights in Dagaare. Another web page devoted to a single Gur language is a dictionary of Koromfe with English, French, and German equivalents, found at www.univie.ac.at/linguistics/personal/john/kd_main.htm.

The six volumes of Gur Papers *(Cahiers Voltaïques)* published to early 2003 (send correspondence to Afrikanistik I, Universität Bayreuth, D-95440 Bayreuth, Germany) give a variety of papers on Gur, with the majority being classificatory or phonological. This journal promises to be a continuing source of useful information on Gur linguistics.

Several books aim to give a comprehensive description of phonology, morphology, and syntax of a Gur language. These include the Sénoufo language Supyire (Carlson 1994), the nontonal Koromfé (Rennison 1997), Kabiyé (Lébikaza 1999), and Cɛfɔ (Winkelmann 1998). Somewhat less extensive than these are works on Dagaare (Bodomo 1998—see also the review of this in Cahill 1999a), Gulmancema (Naba 1994), and Kar

(Wichser 1994). Russell (1985) has a comprehensive overview of Moba phonology. Olawsky (1996) has an introductory look at Dagbani phonology.

There are a number of dictionaries published on Gur languages. These languages include Buli (Kröger 1992, Melançon and Prost 1971), Sisaala-Tumulung (Blass 1975), Vagla (Crouch and Herbert 1981), Konkomba (Langdon and Breeze 1981), Supyire (Carlson 1992), Gulmancema (Ouba 1994), and Mooré (Nikiema and Kinda 1994).

Dissertations and theses done on morphology and phonology, or phonology alone, of Gur languages include those on morphology and phonology of Yom (Beacham 1968), tone in Sénoufo (Sucite dialect; Garber 1987), tone in Dagbani (Issah 1993), morphology and phonology of Lama (Ourso 1989), and tone and syntax of Mooré (Peterson 1971).

Preliminary phonological sketches have been published for several Gur languages through the Collected Field Notes series of the Ghana Institute of Linguistics, Literacy, and Bible Translation (GILLBT, formerly called the Institute of Linguistics), including Kasem (Callow 1965), Konkomba (Steele and Weed 1966), Vagla (Crouch and Smiles 1966), Dagaare (Kennedy 1966), Kusaal (Spratt and Spratt 1968), Tampulma (Bergman, Gray, and Gray 1969), Frafra (Schaefer 1975), Nafaanra (Jordan 1980), Hanga (Hunt 1981), Kɔnni (Cahill 1992a), Birifor (Kuch 1993), Sisaala-Pasaale (Toupin 1995), and Dɛg (Crouch 1994).

A more thorough monograph on Kasem phonology and phonetics is in Awedoba (1993), and a detailed phonology of Sénoufo is in Mills (1984). A syntax of Nateni by Neukom (1995) has information on noun classes. Finally, a collection of articles on Buli, with one on tone and several on syntax, is in Akanlig-Pare and Kenstowicz (2003).

A number of individual articles have appeared in various journals and will be referred to when appropriate, but the above are all the book-length publications known to me which describe a Gur language, in general, or its morphology or phonology.

Also relevant to Kɔnni morphology and phonology are comparative/historical works on the common ancestor of Buli and Kɔnni, reconstructing the consonants (Cahill 1995a), vowels (Cahill 1995b), and noun class system (Cahill 1997b) of Proto-Buli-Kɔnni. At times the synchronic morphology or phonology will be illumined by comparison with the closely related Buli.

With the exception of tone in Dagaare by Anttila and Bodomo (1996, 2000), no work within Optimality Theory has been done on a Gur language to my knowledge.

1.1.4 The sources of the data

The data used in this project came from a multitude of Kɔnni speakers, mostly from the village of Yikpabongo. My family and I spent five dry seasons there from 1986 to 1993, and one dry season with a language consultant (Abudlai Sikpaare) in Tamale. If linguistics had been the only matter at hand, we would soon have gathered all the information needed not only for this study, but for several others in syntax, discourse, semantics, etc. However, other concerns, such as learning to speak the language, developing an orthography, building furniture and a house, keeping it in repair, attending funerals and other social obligations, battling malaria in ourselves and our children, giving health care to the Koma, and taxiing them to the nearest clinic (three hours' drive) for the not-uncommon emergencies, were all part of the total living situation in the village. Collecting linguistic information was not always the highest-ranked constraint.

Though bits of data were gathered on the fly from many people in every Koma village in our ever-present data notebooks, most of my data comes from five men, and the bulk of that from two. From Juaŋ in Nagbiasi and Kwabena Joseph in Yikpabongo proper, I taped Swadesh 200-word lists and a number of paradigms and stories. From Benni in Yikpabongo I got many individual words and noun-adjective paradigms. Tahiru of Nangurima provided verbal and noun-adjective paradigms. For most of our time in Yikpabongo, our main language consultant was Mr. Abdulai Sikpaare, the town crier, who has a wonderfully clear voice for recording. Mr. Sikpaare is a farmer, probably in his late 30s at that time, and was born and raised in Yikpabongo. He belongs to the chief's clan, has had some primary education, and can identify English letters and speak some English. In our last visit to Ghana in 1997 our language consultant was Mr. Salifu James Amadu, who is in the same clan as Mr. Sikpaare. Mr. Amadu has been through middle school level, and his English is fairly good. The data from these two men is the most organized and comprehensive and is the source for a majority of the data cited in this volume.

1.1.5 Inventories of Kɔnni consonants, vowels, and tones

The following are the phonemic inventories of Kɔnni. Each will be discussed more fully, and evidence for contrast will be given in the respective chapters on consonants, vowels, and tones.

Kɔnni consonants occur in six places of articulation, with each place having several consonants, with the exception of the glottal place having only *h*. Nasals occur in every place except glottal.

(4)   Kɔnni consonants

	labial	alveolar	palatal	velar	labial-velar	glottal
stops	p, b	t, d		k, g	kp, gb	
affricates			ch, j			
fricatives	f, v	s, z				h
liquids		l, r				
nasals	m	n	ɲ	ŋ	ŋm	
glides			y	w		

The symbols *ch* and *j* are used throughout this work rather than the IPA tʃ and dʒ for typographical convenience. Likewise, the symbol *y* is used to symbolize a palatal glide, not a high front rounded vowel as in IPA

Kɔnni has a nine-vowel system typical of the Gur family and other languages in the area with the vowels dividing into two sets based on the ATR feature.

(5)   Kɔnni Vowels

	+ATR		−ATR	
high	i	u	ɪ	ʊ
mid	e	o	ɛ	ɔ
low			a	

These short vowels all have long counterparts, with the long mid vowels usually being manifested as diphthongs (discussed in section 5.3). Transcriptions of vowels in this work are phonetic except that the centralization of front vowels before [ŋ], as in /tɪŋ/ → [tɪ̆ŋ] 'village, town' (cf. *tɪkká* 'the village'), /keŋ/ → [kəŋ] 'come' (cf. *kenne* 'is coming'), is usually abstracted out. Except when focusing on this process, in section 5.4.4, I will write the front vowels preceding *ŋ* without noting this centralization.

The tonal system of Kɔnni has two levels of tone, High and Low, and a Downstepped High as well, symbolized by acute accent, grave accent, and raised exclamation mark before acute accent, as exemplified in (6).

(6)   Kɔnni tones
     High-High   kpááŋ   'oil'
     Low-High   kpààŋ   'back of head'
     High-Downstepped High kpá!áŋ   'guinea fowl'

1.2 Sketch of syntax

I include here a brief sketch of Kɔnni syntax, especially as it will relate to constructions with vowels and tone. I will start with the basic SVO structure of clauses, then treat interrogatives, the pronoun system, and noun phrases, with nouns and various modifiers, including noun + modifier, associative noun phrases, compound noun phrases, and relative clauses. Verb phrases are next presented, though this section is not as complete as the nominal syntax. The tense/aspect system will be mainly reserved for chapter 2, but preverbal particles will be mentioned here. Kɔnni has no prepositions or postpositions, so I also describe how Kɔnni handles various oblique relations.

Kɔnni has three words which are all translated 'and'. The first, *ta*, joins clauses, actions which are distinctly separate. The second, *a*, joins verbs in actions which are intimately tied together and could be considered one complex action. The third, *aŋaŋ*, joins noun phrases. These are discussed under the sections on clause structure, verb phrase, and noun phrase, respectively.

In the data below, if a sentence is unmarked for tone, it is because it was transcribed from a tape-recorded text by Mr. Ben Saibu, who did not mark tone.

1.2.1 Clause structure

Kɔnni is an SVO language, as illustrated by the sentences in (7).

(7) Unmarked sentence order—SVO

    a. ù yùàr-á !ɲááŋ
       3s fetch-IMPF water
       'S/he is fetching water.'

    b. ù dìgì-wó ɲúà
       3s cook-PERF yams
       'S/he has cooked yams.'

    c. Ali nàŋ gá tígíŋ
       Ali FUT go house
       'Ali will go to (his) house.'

    d. ù ká gá !kúáŋ
       3s NEG go farm
       'S/he didn't go to the farm.'

    e. m̀ mí   !ń tígírú wó !bínní-má
       1s build 1s house ?   year-LOC
       'I built my house last year.'

Though objects, including temporal and locative phrases, are postverbal in normal sentence order, direct objects or locational/temporal elements may be fronted for emphasis.

(8)   Fronting of an element (direct object, temporal, locative)

    a. tígím mám   mí-à
       house 1s.EMPH make-IMPF
       'a house, I'm making'

    b. mèmìé ò   yàlá mìŋ
       rice   3s like AFF
       'rice, s/he likes'

    c. jìnnɛ́ Amina nàŋ kéŋ
       today Amina FUT come
       'today Amina will come'

    d. Bɪyaŋsɪ   ma wʊ-rɪaŋ wʊ waa kalɪ
       Nangurima LOC 3s-also 3s now sit
       'at Nangurima, s/he also is now living'

Fronting of an object noun phrase is done for contrastive emphasis, as in 'I'm making a *house*, not a basket'. Perhaps because temporal elements tend to be one-word expressions, when these temporal elements are mentioned at all, they are almost always fronted. In contrast, it is quite rare to find locative phrases fronted; they are almost always postverbal.

Clauses may be joined by the coordinating conjunctions *yaa* 'or', *amaa* 'but', or *ta* 'and'. In the course of a multi-sentence discourse, *amaa* or *ta* may begin a sentence.

(9)   a. nɪ   yala m vuorewo Yisa Ju   vuosi   naawa **yaa**, m
       2p want 1s remove Jesus Jew people chief   **or**,   1s

1.2 Sketch of syntax

       vuore   Barabas vuo-kuruwa
       remove Barabas person-killer
       'Do you want me to release Jesus the King of the Jews, or release Barabas, a murderer?'

  b. dɪ   n   tim   ba   nawa jaaŋ   **amaa** n   daya   miŋ
     that 1s PAST want pick thing **but** 1s forgot AFF
     'I intended to bring something, but I forgot.'

  c. n   naŋ   ga **ta**   ŋ   keŋ
     1s FUT go **and** 1s come
     'I will go and come (back).'

1.2.2 Interrogatives

Polar interrogatives (yes/no questions) are exactly the same syntactically as the corresponding statements. The difference is that in questions, the initial pitch range is higher, and the last segment, whether vowel or nasal, is lengthened and has a slow fall in pitch. This contrasts with English in which the question "You're going to the park?" has a rise in pitch at the end. A sample is given in the display in (10).[1]

(10) Pitch traces for
     A. tì díè sààbú 'we are eating porridge'
     B. nì díè sààbʋ̀ʋ̀ 'are you (pl) eating porridge?'

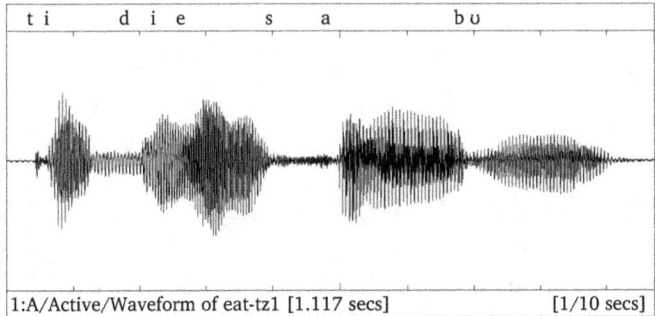

---

[1] These graphs were produced by the WinCECIL program, version 2.2, distributed by SIL International.

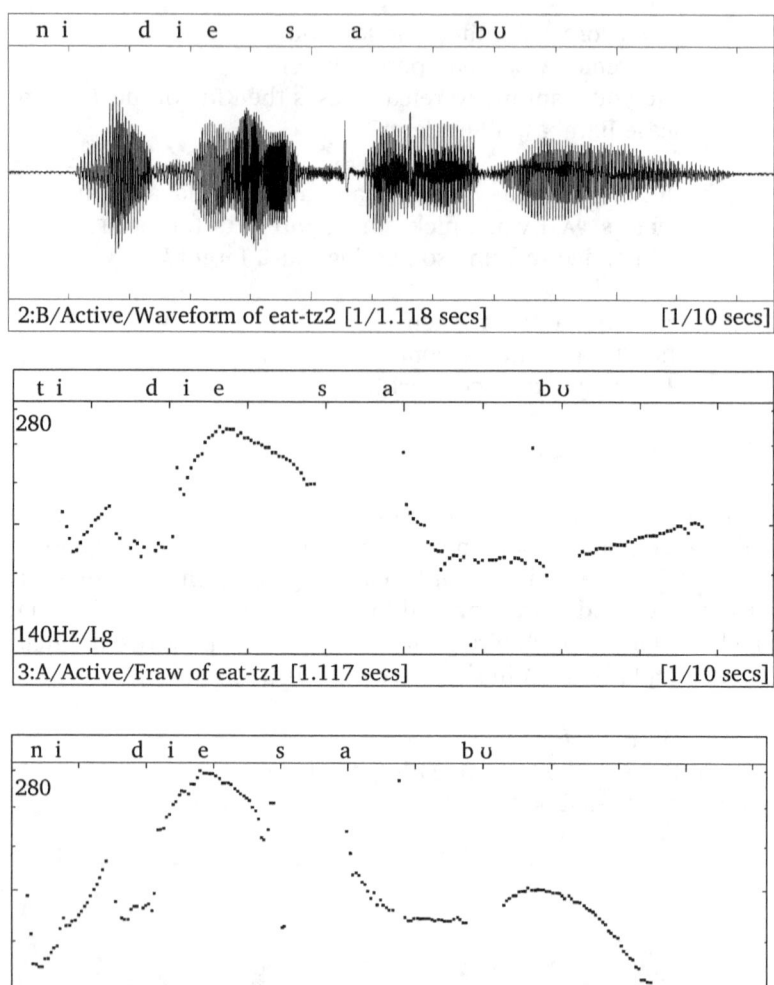

Content questions, on the other hand, use interrogative particles rather than a distinctive intonation pattern to indicate a question.

(11) a. **sìá** fí gâ
where 2s go
'Where did you go?'

1.2 Sketch of syntax

    b. fı̀ chʊ̀rʊ̀-wá   !gá !síá
       2s husband-the go where
       'Where did your husband go?'

    c. **dɛ̀bíyá** !fí gá
       why   2s go
       'Why did you go?'

    d. **bìyá** fí yíɛ̀
       what 2s doing
       'What are you doing?'

    e. a   mana yiwo **bıya**
       3p.nh all   be   what
       'What are all these?'

    f. **tam bıya** naŋ ga
       time what FUT go
       'When will you go?'

    g. **mìnná** !fí gbɛ́
       who   2s touch
       'Who did you touch?'

    h. bà wásì fʊ̀ **làlíà**
       3p call 2s how
       'How do they call you?' (i.e., 'What is your name?')

As seen in (11), it is possible for the question word to be either fronted or to be in the normal position of the NP that would answer the question. This may be related to the size of the subject NP (simple pronoun versus longer NP), but I have not investigated this in any detail.

1.2.3 Pronouns

Kɔnni has first-, second-, and third-person pronouns, singular and plural, with no distinction between masculine and feminine. The third-person pronouns have both human and nonhuman forms, with vowels alternating according to ATR vowel harmony (see section 5.2). Capital letters indicate this variation, with I = [i, ɪ], U = [u, ʊ], and A = [e, a].

(12) Kɔnni simple pronouns

	Subject pronouns				Object pronouns			
	1	2	3	3nh	1	2	3	3nh
SG	N	fI	U	kA[2]	mIŋ	fU	wA	kA
PL	tI	nI	bA	a	tI	nI	bA	hA

The first-person singular pronoun is a syllabic nasal with its own tone, Low in most constructions, e.g., ŋ̀ gáwà… 'I have gone…'. This pronoun is desyllabified after a vowel, e.g., dɪ́n !tíírí 'I should stretch' (lit., 'that I stretch'); this desyllabification is discussed in section 3.5. The subject pronouns are also used as pronominal possessives, e.g., bà kúáŋ 'their farm', ǹ chùrú 'my husband'. The third-person singular subject pronoun U also has an allomorph wU which may sometimes be used utterance initially, but more often in the middle of a sentence, presumably to avoid vowel hiatus, e.g., dʋʋ baa **wʋ** wa nɪɪ-kʋ miŋ 'that he said *he* calls the rain'.

Emphatic pronouns are basically formed by adding -niŋ to those in (12), except mán, mánɪ́ŋ for first-person singular.

(13) Kɔnni emphatic pronouns

	1	2	3	3nh
SG	mán, mánɪ́ŋ	fínɪ́ŋ	wúnɪ́ŋ	kánɪ́ŋ
PL	tínɪ́ŋ	nínɪ́ŋ	bánɪ́ŋ	(ánɪ́ŋ)

These emphatic pronouns are also the isolation forms, when affirming a statement or answering a question, as in (14a–b). They are also used for emphasis, in appositional phrases, to address someone in statements or to emphasize the pronoun, as in (14c–d).

(14) a. ʋ̀ gàrá kúáŋ   'S/he's going to the farm.'
        wúnɪ́ŋ   'him/her?'

     b. mìnná nàŋ gà   'Who will go?'
        mánɪ́ŋ   'me!'

     c. **nɪnɪŋ**   nɪ   ko   kiere
        2p.EMPH 2p just come
        'you, you just come'

---

[2]Occasionally in Yikpabongo and more commonly in Nangurima, one hears bU as a nonhuman third-person independent subject pronoun when referring to a noun in noun class 4 (see chapter 2).

1.2 Sketch of syntax

    d. ta waa tıalı-wa **fınıŋ**
       and now remain-PERF 2s.EMPH
       'and now you [and only you] have remained'

The reflexive property is marked by a possessive construction with *gbáŋ* 'self, skin' and is used when the object of the sentence has the same referent as the subject.

(15) Reflexive construction
    a. ŋm̀ gbáŋ   'myself'   tì gbáŋ   'ourselves'
       fı gbáŋ   'yourself'   nì gbáŋ   'yourselves'
       ʊ̀ gbáŋ   'him/herself' bà gbáŋ 'themselves'

    b. ǹ yínà ŋm̀ gbáŋ
       1s gave 1s self
       'I gave (it) to myself.'

       yie fı gbaŋ kpaa
       see 2s self much
       'Look at yourself well! (esp. when fighting)'

1.2.4 The noun phrase

Noun phrases consist of either adjacent nouns (in an appositional or associative construction), nouns joined by a conjunction, a noun followed by modifiers, or a noun modified by a relative clause. These are all illustrated in (16)–(21).

Appositional noun phrases consist of two adjacent nominals having the same referent. They can be either two pronouns or a noun and a pronoun, but in my data, a pronoun is always at least one of the nominals.

(16) a. **nınıŋ**   **nı** ko kiere
       2p.EMPH 2p just come
       'you, you just come' (repeated from 14c)

    b. jinne **wʊnıŋ** Nenchinaaŋ dii tʊgı mıŋ
       today 3s.EMPH Nenchinaa eat reach AFF
       'today, he, Nenchinaa, reached the age he should die' (free translation)

Simple juxtaposition of nominals in which the nominals do not have the same referent constitutes an associative or genitive construction. Embedding is common.

(17) a. ʋ̀ hɔ́!gʋ̀   'his wife'

    b. bʋ̀àwá dá!áŋ   'child's stick'

    c.   ʋ̀   chɔ́ŋ   !kʋ́á-kʋ́   síéŋ
        3s   father   farm-the   path
    [[[Pro Noun] Noun]   Noun]
    'his father's farm's path' (i.e., 'the path to his father's farm')

The second nominal of an associative construction always has a High tone on its first syllable if the possessor is a third-person pronoun or a noun, but not for first- or second-person pronominal possessors. This is discussed in detail in terms of a floating High tone associative morpheme in section 6.3.6.

Nouns may be joined by conjunctions to produce a larger noun phrase. The conjunctions illustrated are *aŋaŋ* 'and' or one of its reduced variants, or *yaa* 'or', the same conjunction used to join clauses and verbs.

(18) a. hɔ́wwá **ŋám** !bʋ́á   'woman **and** child'
    b. sʋrʋŋ **yaa** vʋntʋŋ   'tomorrow **or** the day after tomorrow'

There is more than one type of modifier in Kɔnni. True adjectives are bound morphemes, suffixed to noun stems; these are discussed under noun morphology. However, there are also other modifiers of nouns: quantifiers or demonstratives, which are separate words, since they occur after the suffix that marks the boundary of the noun.

(19) a. nembi-si mana
       bird-PL   all
       'all birds'

    b. dembi-si ba-ta
        man-PL   AGR-three
        'three men'

    c. kpall-a   halɪ
        calabash-PL many
        'many calabashes'

1.2 Sketch of syntax

    d. dàà-wá !géé
       man-the this
       'this man'

    e. dàá-ŋ   !káání
       stick-SG one
       'a certain stick'

These modifiers are also distinguished from adjectives in that they may stand alone as the subject or object of a sentence, while adjectives are always bound to a noun.

(20) a. **kààní** wóndè
        one   this.is
        'this is (another) one'

     b. **bataŋ** dɪ   chɪga
       some then run
       'others then run'

     c. be   yiwo **bu-lie**
       they are AGR-two
       'they are two (there are two of them)'

Nouns may also be modified by relative clauses. In the first two examples of (21), the subject noun phrase is appositional, with the pronoun *ka* 'it' or *wʊ* 's/he' as the second nominal. It is not known whether this pronominal presence is obligatory or not. Relative clauses are enclosed in brackets. Note that the low-toned relative pronoun *dì* 'that/who' is present in (21a) and (21d), but not (21b) and (21c).

(21) a. buubuge dɪ   bene fi juoku me ka yɪna fʊ gbɪgbararɪ
        fetish   [that exist 2s room LOC] it give 2s sleeplessness
        'The fetish/god that is in your room, it gives you sleeplessness.'

     b. bʊa-ɲaalɪka wʊ mɪɪrnawa wʊ nan dɪ   kʊma
       child-new [3s delivered] 3s FUT FUT.IMPF cry
       'The new child she delivered, s/he will be crying.'

c. naa yɪ vɔrɪka fɪ   yala
   pick give person [you want]
   'Give it to the person you want.'

d. be ken tɪan ɲɪn zie a   naa mafaasɪ daansɪ ye
   3p come pass exit stand and take guns   look see

   votamba dɪ   tanana ɲindeŋe
   people [that throwing things]
   'They came out and took their guns to see the people who were shooting.'

1.2.5 The verb phrase

The syntax of the verb phrase is more complex than that of the noun phrase, but my presentation of it here is less complete. More than one verb in a verb phrase is possible. We will examine verbs joined by conjunctions, serial verb constructions, and reduplication.

Verbs may be joined by the conjunctions *a* 'and' and *yaa* 'or'. As previously mentioned, *ta* and *a* are both translated 'and', the difference seemingly being that verbs joined by *a* are more closely tied together, being perhaps one complex action. The conjunction *yaa* 'or', besides joining clauses and noun phrases, may also join verbs and verb phrases.

(22) a. ba daa yasɪ **a**   yalɪ keŋ
     3p buy salt and have come
     'They bought salt and brought it.'

   b. fɪ hagɪ **a** digi daaŋ **yaa** yaalɪ kpɪaŋ **a** yaa ga
      2s get.up and cook drink or   find chicken and have go

      kaabɪ   ka
      sacrifice it
      'You get up and make alcohol or find a chicken and take (it) to sacrifice to it.'

Serial verb constructions are relatively common in everyday speech, and both sentences in (22) have them. There is quite a lot of debate on the semantics and syntax of serial verb constructions, or whether they even exist as a distinct syntactic construction (e.g., see articles in Joseph and Zwicky 1990 and references therein). I will assume the existence of serial

1.2 Sketch of syntax

verb constructions in Kɔnni and define them as two or more verbs in a sentence which are either adjacent or have a common object between them but with no conjunction between. Serial verb constructions generally denote a single complex action. Some actions which are expressed as single verbs in English are serial verb constructions in Kɔnni, as with *yaa ga* 'have go' = 'take (somewhere)' and *yaa keŋ* 'have come' = 'bring'. Additional examples follow, with the verbs in serial construction in bold. Note the shared object pronouns or nouns occurring between the serial verbs in (23c–g).

(23) a. **naa**   yɪ   mɪŋ
pick.up give 1s
'Give (it) to me.'

b. n   nan **yaa ga yɪ**   wa tigim me
1s FUT have go give 3s house LOC
'I will bring (it) to his/her house.'

c. **yaa** tasɪŋ   **keŋ**
have headpan come
'Bring the headpan!'

d. tɪ **yaa** ba **kieŋ**
1p have 3p come
'We brought them.'

e. da **kpaŋ** wa **taa**
NEG push 3s throw
'Don't push her/him down'

f. **na** bɔlɪka **yɪ**   wa
take ball   give 3s
'Give him/her the ball.'

g. nɪ **yaa** ligiri   bʊa **ken** n **ya**   **ga** tamalɪ a   daa keŋ
2p have money's child come I have go Tamale and buy come
'You(PL) give me a little money and I'll take it to Tamale to buy and come.'

In the last example (23g), there are two clauses and two instances of serial verb constructions. In the first, **yaa** *ligiri bʋa* **ken,** there is a multi-word noun phrase 'money's child' (= 'a little money') between the verbs.

Reduplication of verbs is used to indicate an action repeated several times, and can occur with various aspects, each aspect having its own tonal pattern. A few samples follow.

(24) a. ʋ̀ nàn súgúrí !súgúrî
    3s FUT wash wash
    'S/he will wash (repeatedly).'

   b. ù sùgùrè súgú!ré mìŋ
    3s wash.IMPF wash.IMPF AFF
    'S/he is washing (repeatedly).'

   c. ù sùgùrí !súgúrí mîŋ
    3s wash wash AFF
    'S/he washed (repeatedly).'

The *mìŋ* in (24b–c) is an extremely common particle, the meaning of which I have not yet been able to pin down precisely. Bodomo (1997) extensively discusses a particle in Dagaare which seems to function in a similar way and which he calls a factitive or affirmative marker. In Kɔnni, *mìŋ* seems to be used most commonly in the imperfective aspect of verbs normally thought of as intransitive, such as 'run', 'cry', 'sit', 'sleep', etc. It also can be used with verbs normally thought of as transitive, such as 'wash' in (24b–c). If there is no object in the imperfective aspect, *mìŋ* is obligatory. Consistent with its being a marker of affirmation, *mìŋ* never occurs in negative sentences, and very rarely in a sentence which has an object, as in (25e).

(25) a. ʋ̀ làm-á mìŋ   'S/he is tasting.'
   b. ʋ̀ làm-áá !jítí   'S/he is tasting soup.'
   c. ʋ̀ ká lám-à   'S/he is not tasting.'
   d. ʋ̀ ká lám-à jìtí   'S/he is not tasting soup.'
   e. ni tuo ni kpiinehe mìŋ   'You(PL) got your guinea fowls.'

The verbal system makes a basic distinction between completed and incomplete actions, which can be seen in future, present, and imperative forms. Most of the aspects are marked with suffixes and these are discussed under verbal morphology in section 2.2. The future tense is marked by a preverbal particle and is discussed in section 1.2.6.

1.2.6 Preverbal particles

Several preverbal particles add meanings like 'at that time', 'still/yet', FUTURE, PAST(?), 'again', 'just', 'must', and NEGATIVE. The following are all the particles I am aware of. Note that the particles in (26a–f) have differing tones depending on the preceding pronoun, while the tone on the particles in (26g–k) is constant. The glosses of some particles are not easily summarized, as noted by "?" after them.

(26) a. yA   'still/yet'   ù **yá** bɔ̀b-á mìŋ   'S/he is still tying.'
                            ŋ̀ **yá** bɔ̀b-á mìŋ   'I am still tying.'

    b. ŋaaN   'BEEN'   ù **ŋààm** mí-à mìŋ   'S/he has been building.'
                               ŋ̀ **ŋáám** mí-à mìŋ   'I have been building'

    c. waa   'now, then'   ù **wàà** bɔ̀b-à mìŋ   'S/he is now tying.'
                                  ŋ̀ **wáá** bɔ̀b-à mìŋ   'I am now tying.'

    d. vii   'again'   ù **vìì** mí-à mìŋ   'S/he is again building.'
                             m̀ **víí** mí-à mìŋ   'I am again building.'

    e. ko   'just'   ù **kò** bɔ́b-à mìŋ   'S/he is just tying.'
                         ŋ̀ **kó** bɔ́b-à mìŋ   'I am just tying.'

    f. won   'already'   ù **wòn** dág-à mìŋ   'S/he is already showing.'
                              ŋ̀ **wón** dág-à mìŋ   'I am already showing.'

    g. nÀn   FUT   ù **nàŋ** wí   'S/he will break'
                        ǹ **nàŋ** wí   'I will break'

    h. ká   NEG   ù **ká** láà   'S/he is not laughing.'

    i. kááN   NEG.FUT   ù **káán** díí   'S/he will not eat.'

    j. tíN   PAST?   ù **tín** sí-à mìŋ   'S/he was bathing.'

    k. dí   FUT.IMPF   ù nàn **dí** dá!g-à   'S/he will be showing.'

The last particle *dí* is unique in that it only appears in conjunction with the future particles *nàn* and *kááN*. The four particles listed in (26h–k)—NEGATIVE,

NEGATIVE FUTURE, PAST, and FUTURE IMPERFECT—have a consistent High tone, while the FUTURE (26g) has a consistent Low tone. With the others (26a–f), the tone varies with context, as shown by the Low tone when preceded by a third-person singular pronoun and High when preceded by a first-person singular. These particles are also High when preceded by another High-toned particle, as in (27), where *ya* is preceded by the hightoned *tín*.

(27) a. ù **tín yá** bɔ̀b-á mìŋ
       3s PAST still tie-IMPF AFF
       'S/he was still tying.'

   b. ŋ̀ **tín yá** bɔ̀b-á mìŋ
       1s PAST still tie-IMPF AFF
       'I was still tying.'

The gloss of some particles depends on the context. The particle *waa* is a temporal deictic particle, meaning 'at that time', and is translated either 'now' or 'then' depending on the temporal context. The particle *ya/ye* can likewise be translated either 'yet' or 'still'. The following sentences give examples of how the preverbal particles can be combined with each other. Note that the negative particle *ká* in (29) may occur in different positions, and this changes the scope of negation.

(28) Affirmative sentences (verb is bolded)
   ù tíŋ ŋáám **mía** mìŋ   'S/he had been building.'
   ù tíŋ yá **mìá** mìŋ   'S/he was still building.'
   ù tíŋ wáá **!mía** mìŋ   'S/he was then building.'
   ù tíŋ ŋáán yè **dígè** mìŋ   'S/he was still cooking.'
   ù wáá !víí **mía** mìŋ   'S/he is now again building.'
   ù yé !víí **mía** mìŋ   'S/he is yet again building.'
   ù nàŋ wáá **mì**   'S/he will then build.'
   ù wáá kò **dágà** mìŋ   'S/he is just now showing.'
   ù tín yé kò **dágà** mìŋ   'S/he was still just showing.'

(29) Negative sentences—note variable position of negative particle *ká*
   ù **ká** wáá mía   'S/he is not now building.'
   ù yà **ká** mía   'S/he is not yet building.'
   ù **ké** víí mía   'S/he is not again building.'
   ù ŋààŋ **ká** mía   'S/he has not been building.'
   ù tíŋ **ká** mía   'S/he was not building.'
   ù tín yá **ká** mía   'S/he was not still building.'

ù tín wáá **ká** mîà	'S/he was not then building.'
ù tín ŋááŋ **ká** mîà	'S/he had not been building.'
ù yé **ké** víí mîà	'S/he is not yet again building.'
ù wàà **ké** víí mîà	'S/he is not now again building.'
ù **ká** wáá !víí mîà	'S/he is not now again building.'
ù wáá **ká** !víí mîà	'S/he is not now again building.'

From the data in (28) and (29), certain ordering patterns emerge. The particles *vii* 'again', and *ko* 'just', and *won* 'already' are closest to the verb, and no other particles occur between them and the verb. They do not seem to co-occur. Similarly, the particles *ya* 'still/yet', *waa* 'then/now', and *ŋaaN* 'has/had' group in order and non-co-occurrence, and *tiN* PAST, *nàN* FUTURE, and *kááN* NEG.FUTURE also group together. The negative particle *ká* may occur in different positions, but does not co-occur with *kááN* NEG.FUTURE. These ordering relationships are summarized in the chart in (30). Note that all the particles in the rightmost column are [+ATR], and all the particles in the leftmost column are specified for tone. I have no explanation for these patterns, but note them here.

(30) Order of preverbal particles

tíN	yA		vii	
nÀN	waa	kÁ$_2$	ko	verb
kááN	ŋaaN		won	
kÁ$_1$				

1.2.7 Obliques

There are no prepositions or postpositions in Kɔnni, with the possible exceptions of *aŋaŋ* 'and/with' and *ma* LOCATION. However, *aŋaŋ* seems to function more as a conjunction than a preposition, and *ma* seems to function more as a dummy noun than a postposition. Several constructions are used to perform the functions of English prepositions. A sampling is given in (31); the "of" associative construction is covered in detail in chapter 6.

(31) a. SOURCE/GOAL—often uses "bare" verb
 ù ɲìn-ná Wontobiri
 3s leave-IMPF Wontobiri
 'S/he comes **from** Wontobiri.'

ŋ gá-!rá múgúŋ
1s go-IMP river
'I'm going **to** the river.'

ŋ̀ tá-!wá gbáá-ká
1s throw-PERF dog-the
'I have thrown (something) **at** the dog.'[3]

b. BENEFACTIVE—uses *yɪ* 'give'
bà nàn kú yí!síŋ á yì tì
3p FUT kill sheep and give 1p
'They will kill a sheep **for** us.'

c. ACCOMPANIMENT/INSTRUMENT—use *àŋáŋ* 'with/and'
ǹ nàn nígí fʊ̀ ŋán !dááŋ
1s FUT beat 2s with stick
'I will beat you **with** a stick.'

ǹ nàŋ gá Támàlè àŋám fíníŋ
1s FUT go Tamale with you/EMPH
'I will go to Tamale **with** you.'

d. LOCATION—use noun phrases, body parts, or the general locative *ma/me*
ù bìé tígírí mé
3s exist house LOC
'S/he is **at** the house.' ("at home")

ù bìé lʊ́ʊ́rì mà
3s exist lorry LOC
'S/he is **at** the lorry (truck).'

kà bìé kóŋ!kóŋ síkpéŋ
3s.nh exist can head
'It is **on top of** the can.'

The locative particle *ma/me* appears as a likely candidate to be a postposition, but its syntactic slot can be filled by a full noun. Its tone is the same as the final tone of the noun to which it is attached, and so this may be phonologically attached to the noun (see discussion in section 6.3.8).

---

[3] In an appropriate context, this could also be interpreted in a more literal sense: 'I have thrown the dog'.

1.3 Theoretical foundations and assumptions

The focus of this study is the Kɔnni language as analyzed through the window of Optimality Theory. This section lays out the theoretical basis on which I will analyze Kɔnni phonology. Though the primary focus of this work is not theoretical, in examining an entire language in depth, one unavoidably encounters phenomena which have implications for phonological theory. These will be appropriately noted.

1.3.1 Optimality/Correspondence Theory

The theory of choice of many phonologists today is Optimality Theory (OT). There are many reasons for this, among them a conceptual simplification of phonology. In recent years it has become apparent that constraints, whether labeled "constraints," "filters," "templates," or "well-formedness conditions," are necessary in addition to phonological rules. It seems impossible for phonology to do without constraints; is it possible to do without rules? The program which seeks to answer that question in the affirmative has produced Optimality Theory, a theory which uses only constraints to account for phonological patterns and alternations. For more discussion of the state of linguistics that led to Optimality Theory, see Archangeli (1997).

Much of the work in OT has been published electronically instead of in paper form. The biggest repository of such papers is the Rutgers Optimality Archive website, found at http://roa.rutgers.edu/. Each paper on this site has been given its own unique reference number. In the references of this study, when a reference has been taken directly from the Rutgers Optimality Archive, the source is given as ROA-###.

In Optimality Theory, as expounded in Prince and Smolensky (1993), McCarthy and Prince (1993, 1995), and McCarthy (2002), a function GEN produces an infinite set of output candidates. These candidates are judged by a function H-EVAL as to how well they conform to a set of constraints CON. The candidate which best satisfies the constraints is the form which is actually pronounced. This is the "winning" or "optimal" candidate. The phrase "best satisfies the constraints," however, must be explained in more detail.

Constraints have the potential to conflict with each other, and with many output forms it is impossible to satisfy *all* the constraints. For example, assuming an input of /dadp/ in a hypothetical language, several constraints might potentially apply. One constraint may prohibit consonant clusters (*CC). Another may prohibit deleting a consonant (MAX(C), "MAX" for "*max*imize output"), and yet a third may prohibit inserting a vowel (DEP(V),

"DEP" for "output *dep*ends on input"). If the surface form is identical to the underlying representation, then *CC is violated, but the other constraints are satisfied. On the other hand, to satisfy *CC, either a consonant must be deleted, giving [dap] or [dad], or else a vowel may be inserted, giving perhaps [dadap]. The first possibility violates MAX(C), and the second possibility violates DEP(V). Different languages resolve this conflict in different ways by differing in the *ranking* of the constraints. It is more important to satisfy a highly ranked constraint in a language than a lower-ranked constraint. So if we know that a surface form violates DEP(V) but does not violate *CC, then *CC must be more highly ranked than DEP(V). The candidates and constraints which apply to them are commonly displayed in a tableau, with constraints listed in columns and candidates in rows. The most highly ranked constraints are in columns to the left of the tableau. A tableau with these constraints, an input of /dadp/, and an output of [dadap], would be (32).

(32) Sample tableau illustrating /dadp/ → [dadap]

dadp	*CC	MAX(C)	DEP(V)
☞ a. dadap			*
b. dad		*!	
c. dap		*!	
d. dadp	*!		

The winning or optimal candidate, the actual surface form, is usually marked with a "pointing finger" (☞), as is candidate (32a). Each violation of a constraint is marked with an asterisk, or "star" (*). A "fatal violation" is one which removes the candidate from the running and is marked with an exclamation point (!) after the fatal violation. As seen in (32), even the winning candidate (32a) violates DEP(V); it has inserted a vowel. Other candidates have violated other constraints. Since they are not the winning candidate, the constraints that they violate are deduced to be more highly ranked than DEP(V). A further notational device is that constraints whose ranking cannot be determined with respect to each other have their columns separated by a dotted line, as between *CC and MAX(C) in (32). A solid line separates columns of constraints whose ranking can be determined, as between DEP(V) and the others in (32). The shaded area in (32) is a visual aid only; the shading is to the right of the constraint which is fatally violated for each candidate and so draws attention to the constraints which are fatal.

Though GEN theoretically generates an infinite number of candidates, in practice only the most likely candidates, or the ones pertinent to the

1.3 Theoretical foundations and assumptions

constraints under discussion at that point, are displayed. In the tableau in (32), for example, other likely candidates could be [dat], [dab], [dadip], [dadep], etc. The first two of these could be ruled out by fatal violations of MAX(C), but ruling out [dadip] and [dadep] in favor of the optimal candidate [dadap] would require the introduction of other constraints besides those listed.

Several other characteristics of the tableau and OT as contrasted with a rule-based approach deserve comment. First, all candidates are evaluated and the constraints are applied simultaneously. This parallel operation of constraints contrasts with the serial, or stepwise, application of rules that is characteristic of generative rules. Second, a candidate may be optimal and still violate one or even many constraints. In a rule-based system, a rule applies without exception within its domain (unless a form was lexically marked as an exception to that rule), but in OT, *any* constraint can in principle be violated. This leads to the third characteristic, that in a particular language, a constraint may be "undominated" or "top-ranked," but in another language, that same constraint may be outranked by other constraints. The usual assumption of Optimality Theory is that all constraints are present in all languages, and that the difference between languages is not the presence of a constraint but the relative ranking of the constraints. In the example in (32), if a language switched the rankings of DEP(V) and MAX(C), the optimal output form would be either [dad] or [dap], the choice depending on still other constraints.

This reranking of constraints across languages provides a fruitful field of cross-linguistic inquiry. The *typology* of constraints within OT will predict specific patterns across languages, depending on the ranking of the constraints under examination and is one check on whether the proposed constraints have any connection with reality. If, for example, three independently rankable constraints—A, B, and C—are proposed, then there are six possible rankings, assuming it is possible to clearly determine the ranking of each with respect to the others. (Indeterminate ranking expands the number of possibilities.) If these constraints are all actually valid, then languages should be found which exhibit all six rankings. The search for all these languages is quite time-consuming, of course, which is likely the reason so few wide-ranging cross-linguistic studies have actually been done.[4]

Constraints are of many forms but fall into two major types. One type is the so-called "faithfulness" constraints; the other type is well-formedness constraints.

---

[4]One cross-linguistic study is Casali (1997), who surveys eighty-seven languages examining vowel elision phenomena. Another ongoing attempt at a wide sampling of languages is Cahill (2000), who to date has examined twenty-nine languages which have floating tonal associative morphemes.

The "faithfulness" constraints enforce faithfulness to an underlying representation, or to some other representation. Though the assumption of underlying representations has come under fire from Russell 1995, Flemming 1995, Hammond 1995, Burzio 1996, and Hualde and Cole 1997, who abandon the idea of underlying representations, many others work with them as a fruitful concept, and I will assume their existence in this work. The PARSE and FILL constraints of the original OT (Prince and Smolensky 1993) have been replaced by the IDENT, MAX, and DEP constraints of the Correspondence Theory version of OT (McCarthy and Prince 1995). In this work, I assume Correspondence Theory. In Correspondence Theory, a correspondence exists between two representations. These representations may be underlying and surface representations, or in the case of reduplicated forms, it may be a base form and its reduplicant. Correspondences have also been proposed between one form in a paradigm and another (output-output constraints). Some of the more oft-used faithfulness constraint families are summed up in (33).

(33) IDENT(F): a feature has the same value in the input as in the output.
MAX I-O(S): a segment present in the input has a corresponding segment in the output.
DEP I-O(S): a segment present in the output has a corresponding segment in the input.

We call these "families" of constraints because each of these may have different variables. For example, the IDENT(F) family refers to various features, and so may have members IDENT([sonorant]), IDENT([nasal]), IDENT([voice]), etc. The IDENT(F) family of constraints generally assumes the view that features are binary and can thus have different "values." Thus the IDENT(F) family prohibits changing [+cont] to [−cont], or [−lateral] to [+lateral]. When referring to privative or monovalent features, IDENT(F) refers to changing the presence of that feature on the segment in question.

The constraint MAX-IO(S) prohibits deletion of a segment (i.e., a segment present in the input would *not* have a corresponding segment in the output). Likewise, DEP-IO(S) prohibits insertion of a segment (i.e., a segment in the output does not have a corresponding segment in the input). These constraints, originally applied only to segments, have been extended to other entities, such as moras (Itô, Kitagawa, and Mester 1996) and tones (Myers and Carleton 1996). Furthermore, under the assumption that features are unary rather than binary, the point is if a feature is present or not. In this case,

MAX-IO and DEP-IO constraints may apply to features as well as larger entities such as segments, as in fact Lombardi (1998c, 2001) does with [voice]. Since many features are assumed to be unary, in this study (see section 1.3.2), I often will not use the IDENT family of constraints to deal with these features but will use the MAX-IO and DEP-IO constraints. Unless otherwise noted, all correspondences examined in this work are input-output ones, so I will use the simpler MAX and DEP notations without the -IO, as in (34).

(34) **DEP[dors]:** every [dorsal] feature in the output has a correspondent in the input
MAX[dors]: every [dorsal] feature in the input has a correspondent in the output

The DEP[dors] constraint will prohibit insertion of the [dorsal] feature and has the effect of penalizing the change of a segment from anything to a [dorsal] place of articulation. The MAX[dors] constraint prohibits deletion of the [dorsal] feature, which must appear in the output, either on the segment on which it resided in the input or perhaps on some other output segment.

The other major types of constraints deal with the well-formedness of surface forms. These constraints may be formulated in either positive or negative terms. For example, a language may only allow CV syllables. This could be formulated as a constraint disallowing codas (abbreviated NOCODA). A language may require that a vowel feature (ATR, height, etc.) be manifested on all vowels of a word. Depending on one's view of features and their organization (see section 1.3.2), one may posit an AGREE(F) or ALIGN(F) which may require the feature to be manifested on all vowels in the word.

One of the principles relating to ranking of constraints deserves special mention here, since it is applicable in several areas in the remainder of this work. This is what has been termed "Paṇini's Theorem" by Prince and Smolensky (1993). Roughly, the idea is that if one constraint G is more general than another more specific one S—i.e., that the set of input forms that S applies to is a subset of the forms that G applies to-then the more specific constraint S must be ranked above the more general constraint G (S>>G). This is somewhat self-evident upon reflection; if the more specific constraint were ranked below the general constraint, its effects would never be observed.

Three other topics relating to OT deserve comment: the assumed universality of constraints, what criteria are used to evaluate a constraint as a principled or "good" one, and the phonetic versus phonological approach to constraints.

Constraints are generally assumed to be universal, that is, all constraints exist in all languages, though they may be ranked so low that their effects are not visible (Prince and Smolensky 1993, McCarthy and Prince 1995, McCarthy 2000). However, Russell (1997) maintains that constraints which refer to categories specific to a particular language cannot be part of Universal Grammar and presents several such cases. This seems irrefutable, since a morpheme of a particular language cannot possibly be universal. In the present volume, we shall see more such examples of constraints which must refer to specific Kɔnni morphemes in section 4.3.1 (*$g_{NC2/3}$), section 4.3.2 (*n_{NC1}), and in section 6.3.3 (POLAR). Interestingly, all of these constraints refer to properties of noun classes, especially noun class 1.

The matter of what makes a constraint "good" or "principled" is still an open question. Most researchers do not explicitly discuss the issue, but some have. Eisner (1997) has proposed primitive constraints of two main types (Implication and Clash). Work by several researchers (e.g., Beckman 1997, Casali 1997, Steriade 1994, 1995b, 1997, Jun 1995, Kaun 1995, Flemming 1995, Kirchner 1998) suggests a functional, phonetics-based motivation for many constraints. Hayes (1999), while acknowledging the phonetic basis for many constraints, points out the difficulty of translating experimental phonetic results, which typically give gradient results, into phonological terms which are typically categorial. He suggests two types of "principled" constraints: those based on typological, cross-linguistic evidence and those motivated by phonetic functionalism. In this work, as far as possible, I attempt to motivate the constraints I use by either referring to cross-linguistic commonality or inherent phonetic plausibility. (The exception is the families of MAX, DEP, and IDENT constraints, which I judge to have been sufficiently motivated in the literature.) However, some constraints, as noted above, are language-specific and refer to largely idiosyncratic contexts.

In seeking plausibility for constraints, the question arises of how much phonetic detail to include. Are constraints to be based on phonetics, or is it possible or desirable to incorporate the phonetic motivation directly into the constraints? An approach to Optimality Theory which seeks explanation for phonological patterns in detailed articulatory and acoustic mechanisms has been on the rise in recent years, particularly at UCLA by Steriade and her students. Let us take a specific example.

In OT, there are at least two general approaches to intervocalic lenition of voiced stops. The more phonological approach is to posit a constraint that simply forbids the occurrence of [d] intervocalically, such as *VdV. Though not explanatory, this accounts for the surface pattern and is attested cross-linguistically. Combined with other constraints, this produces the desired output. The other approach, used by Steriade and her students, is to

1.3 Theoretical foundations and assumptions

posit a constraint that attempts to get more directly to the phonetic motivation, as Kirchner's (1998) LAZY constraint does ("minimize articulatory effort"). Either approach can be made to work, and so the choice between the two approaches must be made on the basis of what one's view of the task of phonology is. In my view, phonology is about patterns of sounds and not about details of physiological articulatory force. So in this work, I take the more abstract phonological approach using *VdV rather than LAZY. While the distinction between the two approaches can sometimes be blurred, when possible I come down on the more abstract side, phonology, rather than the more concrete physical side, phonetics, in accounting for patterns of sounds. So while acknowledging a debt to Kirchner, Jun, Steriade, and others who are rigorously elucidating the physiological and acoustic basis for phonology, I focus on the less physical side of phonology and abstract the patterns away from the physiological.

1.3.2 Features and their organization

In the background for much of this study is the assumption of Feature Geometry (Clements 1985, Clements and Hume 1995) as an organizing principle of features, though this will not play as major a role in the OT analysis here as in a rule-based analysis.[5] The constriction-based place features and basic geometry of Clements and Hume (1995) are assumed here where relevant, with the addition of an oral node, the addition of [ATR] as a place feature, and the replacement of their [open] vowel height feature with the [closed] of Parkinson (1996a, b). Rationale for the [closed] feature is discussed in chapter 5. The organization of a feature tree of a vocoid is given in (35), with all features in place as a sample of a Feature Geometry representation. Not all these would co-occur, of course. There is no vowel which would have all of the V-place features simultaneously, for example.

---

[5] See, e.g., Cahill (1999c) in which the feature geometry of vowels is crucial to account for vowel diphthongization patterns.

(35)

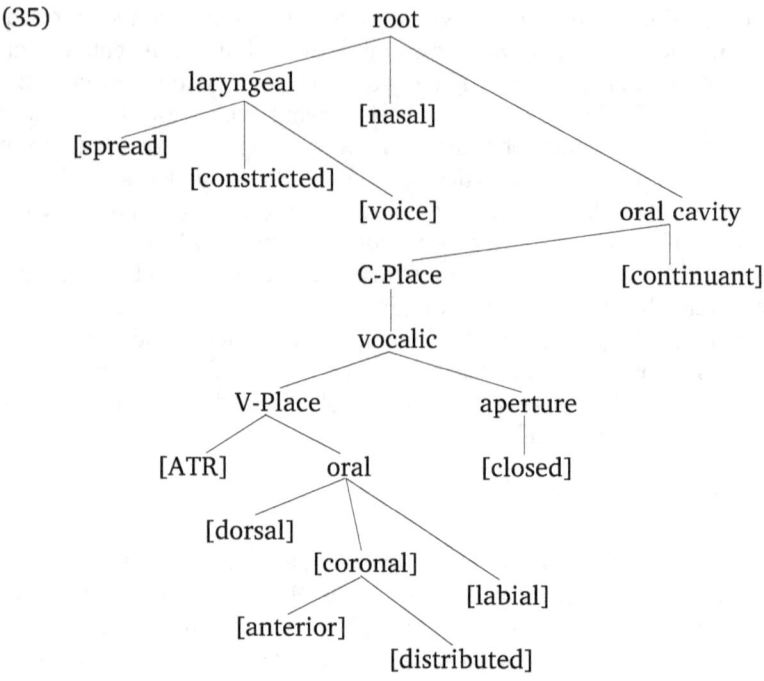

Most features which are active in Kɔnni and discussed in this work are assumed to be monovalent. These include the V-Place features [ATR], [closed], [dorsal], [coronal], [labial], as well as [voice] and [nasal]. In chapter 4, we see the binary features [±continuant] and [±anterior]. The features [distributed], [spread], and [constricted] are also assumed to be binary but play no part in this study.

An autosegmental representation is assumed throughout and will be particularly crucial in the tone chapter.

In the generative tradition of phonology, influential works and changes in trends have risen every several years. *The Sound Pattern of English* was published in 1968. Autosegmental Phonology got its big push with Goldsmith's dissertation in 1976. In 1982 came Lexical Phonology, in 1985 Feature Geometry, and in 1993 the first published works on Optimality Theory. This, of course, only includes some major trends within the generative tradition; I have omitted many other subtheories and different traditions such as natural phonology, dependency phonology, etc. Judging from the history of recent phonological theories, one may expect a major change in theories every decade or less, and I have no delusions that Optimality/Correspondence Theory in its present form will be an exception to this. One of my goals in this

1.3 Theoretical foundations and assumptions

study is to not only present an analysis of Kɔnni phonology, but to present the data in such a way as to make the pertinent facts readily accessible to future researchers in search of data for comparative purposes or simply data to test whatever theory happens to develop in the next decades. Because of this, in most sections I have clearly divided the data from the analysis of it. Of course, even in presentation of data, some theoretical assumptions must be made, e.g., how to organize and label the data. However, I trust this will cause minimal interference to future researchers, and I welcome you the reader, whether in 2007 or much later in the twenty-first century, to the Kɔnni language.

2
Morphology

Morphology in Kɔnni is manifested on three categories of words: nouns, verbs, and nominal modifiers. Nominal morphology includes suffixes which mark number and definiteness and varies according to the noun class. Adjectives are always suffixed to a noun and take a subset of the same suffixes from the noun class system that nouns take, and so are considered under nominal morphology. Verbal morphology includes suffixes marking the aspectual system, while other areas of the tense-aspect system indicated by separate particles were discussed in the syntax section of chapter 1. Nominal modifiers (demonstratives and numbers) have the only prefixes in Kɔnni; these agree with the class of the modified noun. These categories are discussed in turn below.

Various linguists have viewed morphemes as either "things" or "rules," in part depending on what is a more appropriate and useful approach to the data at hand. The "morphemes as things" approach views morphemes as entities stored in the lexicon which combine with other entities, either by simple concatenation of whole segments or, in an autosegmental representation, perhaps as a string of subsegmental features such as tone. The attachment of affixes to a stem is an example of this. (Also see the "nonconcatenative morphology" of McCarthy 1981.) The "morpheme as rule" approach views morphemes as processes, most easily illustrated by a morpheme that consists of a phonological change, e.g., stress that marks a word as a noun or a verb (*cóntrast* versus *contrást*). See Spencer (1991) for more discussion of the two perspectives. Since this work is not an exercise in theoretical morphology, I do not argue for one or the other view here. In the background, however, will be an assumption of the "morpheme as thing" model here, because the data seems to adequately fit this model.

2.1 Nominal morphology

A minimal noun in Kɔnni contains a noun stem and a singular/plural suffix (with the exception of noun class 5, which has a zero suffix). Adjectival morphemes, which are suffixed to the noun stem (section 2.1.2) may occur between the noun stem and the suffix, and a definite suffix may occur as the last element in the word. The structure of the noncompound noun in Kɔnni is laid out in (36), with optional elements in parentheses.

(36) Noun → Noun stem (Adj1) (Adj2) (Adj3) Suffix (Article)

The formulation of (36) is inadequate in one respect. The behavior of the singular suffix differs from the plural suffix in that the plural definite article is *added* to the plural suffix, but the singular definite article *replaces* [-ŋ].

(37) díí-ŋ   díí-rí   dí-è   dí-é-!hé
      forehead-SG   forehead-the   forehead-PL   forehead-PL-the
      Ns   Sfx   Ns   ART   Ns   Sfx   Ns   Sfx ART
      'forehead'   'the forehead'   'foreheads'   'the foreheads'

The suffix -ŋ may be regarded as an indefinite suffix in contrast to the definite suffixes. It is the form that appears on a noun in citation form.[1]

2.1.1 Noun classes

The noun class system of Kɔnni is manifested on the definite article and plural suffixes, as in (38). The numbering of the classes is arbitrary; no attempt has been made to connect these with the noun class system of Niger-Congo or other Gur languages. My database includes 989 nouns, of which I can identify the noun class of 728. (The class is unidentified for those nouns for which I lack a definite or plural form.) The approximate percentage that each noun class comprises of this total is indicated in the table in (38). Vowels in the suffixes given with capital letters indicate that

---

[1] The singular *definite* suffix in Kɔnni seems to correspond to the indefinite noun class suffix in other Gur languages. Proto-Buli-Kɔnni has undergone a restructuring of the noun class system, and Kɔnni uniquely has merged almost all singular indefinite forms into the suffix -ŋ (Cahill 1997b).

2.1 Nominal morphology

that vowel harmonizes in ATR value with the root, so /Í/, for example, is realized as either [í] or [ɪ́]. (See section 5.2.1 for use of /A/.)

(38)
Nouns	Singular	Singular definite	Plural	Plural + definite	% of nouns
Class 1 'bee'	/-ŋ/ síébíŋ	/-rÍ/ síébírí	/-A/ síébìè	/-A-hÁ/ síébíé!hé	26
Class 2 'courtyard'	/-ŋ/ gbààŋ	/-kÚ/ gbààkú	/-tÍ/ gbààtí	/-tÍ-tÍ/ gbààtítí	12
Class 3 'man'	/-ŋ/ dèmbíŋ	/-kÁ/ dèmbìké	/-sÍ/ dèmbìsí	/-sÍ-sÍ/ dèmbìsísí	31
Class 4 'meat'	/-ŋ/ nɔ̌ŋ	/-bÚ/ nɔ̀mbú	/-tÍ/ nɔ̀ntí	/-tÍ-tÍ/ nɔ̀ntítí	7
Class 5 'child'	/-Ø/ bùá	/-wÁ/ bùàwá	irreg. bàllí	irreg. bàllílí	13
Mixed	(singular definite from one class, plural from a different one)				11
'goat'	bìŋ	bííkú	bìé	bìèhé	

As noted in the preceding table, the noun classes are differentiated by means of the definite or plural suffixes. The indefinite singular suffix -ŋ is common to all classes except noun class 5. Noun class 4 consists of mass/abstract nouns, and class 5 consists of humans, but apart from these, assignment of a noun to the other classes appears to be arbitrary, with little semantic basis for assigning a noun to one noun class versus another.

There is a strong tendency for the plural definite suffix to be a reduplicated form of the plural indefinite. This is seen most clearly in classes 2, 3, and 4, where the plural definite is an exact reduplication of the plural indefinite /-tI,-tI-tI/ and /-sI,-sI-sI/. For class 1, the plural definite suffix /-A-hÁ/ is quite close to being a reduplicant of /-A/. In the class 5 example given in the preceding chart, the reduplication pattern holds in the particular sample word given /-lɪ,-lɪlɪ/, but most of the class 5 nouns have /-ba/ for a plural definite suffix (see 43). So in most forms, the definite plural may be looked on as RED, a reduplicated form of the indefinite plural suffix. Except for the definite plurals, most nouns have a single suffix which combines the markings of number and definiteness: singular/indefinite, singular/definite, and plural/indefinite.

Discussion of noun classes in the Gur family may be found in Manessy (1979), Nicole (1998), and Naden (1989), while noun classes of specific Gur languages are discussed in Carlson (1994), Kröger (1992), Bodomo (1997), Nicole (1998), Neukom (1995), Ourso (1989), Garber (1987), Beacham (1968), Peterson (1971), and Naden (1988). See Welmers (1973) for a discussion of noun classes in a larger African context. A reconstruction of the noun class system of Proto-Buli-Kɔnni is found in Cahill (1997b). Each of the Kɔnni classes is discussed in more detail below, with representative examples. A fuller set of nouns grouped by class is found in appendix B.

Noun class 1 is unique in Kɔnni in having a plural suffix which consists of only a vowel.

(39) Noun class 1

		Singular	Singular definite	Plural	Plural + plural definite
		/-ŋ/	/-rÍ/	/-A/	/-A-hÁ/
a.	'bee'	síébíŋ	síébírí	síébíè	síébíé!hé
	'breast'	bììsíŋ	bììsìrí	bììsá	bììsáhá
	'chin'	bítí!éŋ	bítíé!rí	bítíè	bítíé!hé
	'forehead'	dííŋ	díírí	díè	díé!hé
	'gr.stone'	nííŋ	níírí	nìà	níá!há
	'house'	tígíŋ	tígírí	tígè	tí!géhé
	'log'	dàmpàlí	dàmpàllí	dàmpàlá	dàmpàláhá
	'problem'	wííŋ	wíírí	wìà	wíá!há
	'shade'	jágíŋ	jágírí	jágâ	jágá!há
	'stump'	dààgbúgíŋ	dààgbúgírí	dààgbúgê	dààgbúgé!hé
b.	'knee'	dŭŋ	dùnní	dùné	dùnéhé
	'stone'	tăŋ	tànní	tàná	tànáhá
c.	'nail/arrow'	yí!íŋ	yí!rí	yíímà	yíí!máhá
	'seed'	bíŋ	bínní	bíè	bíé!hé
d.	'chest'	ɲóóŋ	ɲóórí	ɲúrà	ɲú!ráhá
	'day'	dààŋ	dààrí	dàrá	dàráhá
	'heart'	sìkpááŋ	sìkpáárí	sìkpárà	sìkpár!ráhá
	'hoe'	kòóŋ	kóórí	kúrá	kúráhá
	'name'	sààŋ	sààrí	sàrá	sàráhá

As in most nominal suffixes, the suffixes of noun class 1 are High-toned, with the notable exception of the plural morpheme /−A/, which is either

2.1 Nominal morphology

High or Low toned, having the opposite tone of the preceding tone. This tonal polarity is discussed in section 6.2.2.

Several alternations are apparent in (39). The singular article, given as /-rÍ/, is realized as [-rÍ], [-lÍ], or [-nÍ], the first occurring between vowels, and the latter two by assimilation to the final stem consonant. These alternations are discussed in section 4.2. Also, although every singular indefinite form ends with -ŋ, this masks the fact that some noun stems end with a nasal, which is evident on the definite and plural forms in (39b). There are a few words, as in (39c), which have an unexpected nasal in the plural which is not present in the singular definite (e.g., yíí!rí 'the nail', yíímà 'nails') or have a nasal in the singular which seems to be missing from the plural form (e.g., bínní 'the seed', bȋè 'seeds'). At least some of these are due to historical developments which produced synchronically different roots for singular and plural forms (Cahill 1997b). Suppletive forms occur in Kɔnni with even more drastic differences, e.g., náá!gíŋ/nííge 'cow/s', in which the stem vowels, the ATR, and the noun class is different in the singular and plural. Also, forms with [aa] or [ʊʊ] as the final vowel in the noun stem, as in (39d), shorten that vowel in the plural, and insert [r] preceding the expected suffix [-a] (see analysis in section 4.5.2).

Examples of noun class 2 nouns are presented in (40).

(40) Noun class 2

	Singular	Singular definite	Plural	Plural + plural definite
	/-ŋ/	/-kÚ/	/-tÍ/	/-tÍ-tÍ/
'baboon'	fááŋ	fáákú	fáátí	fáátítí
'farm'	kúáŋ	kúákú	kúátí	kúátítí
'hawk'	kpíí!líŋ	kpíí!líkú	kpíí!lítí	kpíí!lítítí
'inside'	sʊ̀ŋ	sʊ̀kú	sʊ̀tí	sʊ̀títí
'path'	síéŋ	siékú	síétí	síétítí
'shoulder'	bìŋkpíáŋ	bìŋkpìàkú	bìŋkpìàtí	bìŋkpìàtítí
'skin, book'	gbáníŋ	gbáŋkú	gbántí	gbántítí
'vulture'	zùúŋ	zùùkú	zùùtí	zùùtítí
'wood, stick'	dààŋ	dààkú	dààtí	dààtítí
'worm'	gbáríáŋ	gbáríákú	gbáríátí	gbáríátítí

Nouns in class 2 are quite regular, with largely transparent morphology and very few phonological alternations. An exception to this is vɔ́rítí ~ vɔ́ttí 'holes', with optional vowel deletion and assimilation of the [r]. Stem-final nasals are uncommon, with /gbán-/ 'skin' being the only example in my data. The plural morphemes -tí/-tí-tí are shared with noun class 4 as well.

Examples of noun class 3 nouns are presented in (41).

(41) Noun class 3

	Singular	Singular definite	Plural	Plural + plural definite
	/-ŋ́/	/-kÁ/	/-sÍ/	/-sÍ-sÍ/
'axe'	lí!áŋ	líá!ká	líásî	líá!sísí
'back'	kòáŋ	kòàká	kòàsí	kòàsísí
'chicken'	kpíáŋ	kpíáká	kpíásí	kpíásísí
'comb'	zúúchásíŋ	zúúchásíká	zúúchásá	zúúchásísí
'cookpot'	kúrúbâ	kúrúbá!ká	kúrúbá!sí	kúrúbá!sísí
'dog'	gbááŋ	gbààká	gbààsí	gbààsísí
'fly'	nánjúŋ	nánjúká	nánjúsí	nánjúsísí
'hat'	síbúbúŋ	síbúbúké	síbúbúsí	síbúbúsísí
'headpan'[2]	tá!síŋ	tásí!ká	tásísí	tásí!sísí
'knife'	jìbíŋ	jìbìká	jìbìsí	jìbìsísí
'lamp'	pópólí	pópólíké	pópólsí	pópólsísí
'man'	dèmbíŋ	dèmbìké	dèmbìsí	dèmbìsísí
'mussel'	káláŋgbí!áŋ	káláŋgbíá!ká	káláŋgbíá!sí	káláŋgbíá!sísí
'person'	vúóŋ	vúóké	vúósí	vúósísí
'tree (sp.)'	sěŋ	sèké	sènsí	sènsísí

Though most of the nouns in class 3 follow the usual pattern of having -ŋ in the citation form, a few do not (e.g., 'cookpot', 'lamp'). These seem to be mostly, perhaps all, borrowed words, e.g., *pópólí* 'lamp' is from Buli *polipoli*, *dúníá* 'world' is from Hausa *duniya,* and *bɔ́lî* 'ball' is from English 'ball'. Noun class 3 seems to be the default class in which to place borrowed words.

One other slight aberration is that the plural suffix -*sí* occurs with a falling instead of the usual High tone in several cases. These are all nouns in which there is a downstep in the citation form, and will be discussed in section 6.3.2.

Examples of noun class 4 nouns are presented in (42).

---

[2] A headpan is a large, two- to three-foot rounded pan which is used to carry water and heavy loads on the head.

2.1 Nominal morphology

(42) Noun class 4

	Singular	Singular definite	Plural	Plural + plural definite
	/-ŋ́/	/-bÚ/	/-tí/	/-tí-tí/
'ash'	táɲéé!líŋ	táɲéélí!bú	táɲéélí!tí	
'funeral'	kǔŋ	kùmbú	kùntí	kùntítí
'hunger'	kóŋ	kómbú	kóntí	kóntítí
'meat'	nɔ̌ŋ	nɔ̀mbú	nɔ̀ntí	nɔ̀ntítí
'medicine'	tììŋ	tììbú	tììtí	tììtítí
'oil'	kpááŋ	kpáábú	kpáátí	kpáátítí
'peanut'	sìŋkpááŋ	sìŋkpáábú	sìŋkpáátí	sìŋkpáátítí
'porridge'	sààŋ	sààbú	sààtí	sààtítí
'sleep'	gbíí!íŋ	gbíí!bú	gbíí!tí	gbíí!títí
'thing'	jààŋ	jààbú	ɲìntí	ɲìntítí
'water'	ɲááŋ	ɲáábú	ɲáátí	ɲáátítí
'wind'	bùlɔ̀gsíŋ	bùlɔ̀gsíbú		

The plural morphemes -tí/-tí-tí of noun class 4 are shared with noun class 2. Noun class 4 is one of the two noun classes in Kɔnni which has a consistent semantic basis. Nouns in this class are mass or possibly abstract nouns and therefore sometimes have no commonly used plural form. Kröger (1992) also notes that in Buli, the "-bu class," which corresponds to noun class 4 here (Cahill 1997b), refers to liquids, masses, and abstracts and often has no plural form. Two issues arise from the claim of semantic unity for this class: first, how can a mass noun, by definition uncountable, have a plural form, and second, how can words like 'peanut', 'funeral', 'thing', which are definitely countable, be considered mass nouns or abstract?

Mass nouns may have plural forms when they refer to a portion or share of the noun ("how many coffees did you order?") or different types of the noun ("the wines there are fantastic"). These plural forms would be severely restricted as to the circumstances in which they could be used.

As for 'peanut', 'funeral', and 'thing' not being mass nouns, I suggest this may be a function of worldview as much as any inherent qualities of the nouns, and also that the semantic matchups of the words may not be identical. 'Peanut' is not a mass noun in English, but in Kɔnni it functions in a way similar to 'corn' in American English. One does not count individual peanuts in Kɔnni, just as one does not count individual grains of corn in English. Thus for sentences glossed as 'the peanuts are in front of you', 'I'm eating/planting/shelling peanuts', the morphologically singular form is used.[3] The word *kǔŋ*, glossed 'funeral', also means 'death, dying' in Kɔnni. It is a broader and

---

[3]When one wants to refer to a single peanut, one may say 'single peanut' or 'one peanut'.

more abstract idea than conveyed by the simple English gloss 'funeral', but 'funeral' is the single word which comes closest to the most common situation in which kŭŋ is used. The word 'thing' is used in Kɔnni for physical items, actions, events, situations, even people. 'Funeral' and 'thing' are in this noun class in Buli as well, and seem to be more abstract in Ghanaian minds than in Western ones.[4]

Examples of noun class 5 nouns are presented in (43).

(43) Noun class 5

		Singular /-Ø/	Singular definite /-wÁ/	Plural irreg.	Plural + plural definite irreg. /-bÁ/
'child'		bùá	bùàwá	bàllí	bàllílí
'cook'		dìdìgìrú	dìdìgìrùwó	dìdìgìríŋ	
'daughter'		lìà	líá!wá	lí!áŋ	
'father'	a.	chùá	chùàwá	chùá!líŋ	chùálí!bá
	b.	chɔ̆ŋ	chɔ̀ŋwá	chùá!líŋ	chùálí!bá
'friend'		zùá	zùàwá	zùá!líŋ	zùálí!bá
'husband'		chùrú	chùrùwá	chùrú!líŋ ~ chŭl!líŋ	chùllíbá
'mother'	a.	nàá	nààwá	níí!líŋ	nììlí!bé
	b.	nŭŋ	núŋ!wó	níí!líŋ	nììlí!bé
'sister'		táà	táá!wá	táá!líŋ	táálí!bá
'older sibling (same sex)'		mî	míí!wá	míí!líŋ	míílí!bá
'woman/wife'		hɔ̀gú	hɔ̀gùwá ~ hɔ̀wwá	hùáŋ	hùàbá

Noun class 5 is a semantically based class, containing only human nouns. Not all humans, however, are contained in noun class 5, as shown by *dèmbíŋ* 'man' in noun class 3. Noun class 5 is the only one which does not systematically have -ŋ as a singular indefinite suffix. It instead adds no overt suffix to the noun stem. This noun class is also the only one in which most plurals end in -ŋ, generally as a part of a larger suffix (contrasting with most nouns in which -ŋ is a singular suffix). The singular definite suffixes are regular, with

---

[4]This is probably widespread in West Africa and perhaps further. In Adioukrou (Côte d'Ivoire), the word for 'thing' behaves morphologically as a mass noun (Ralph Hill, personal communication). In Gichode (Kwa, Ghana), 'a bad thing', morphologically singular, can refer to either a singular or plural object, or an action (Linda Neeley, personal communication). In Kɔnni and these languages, 'thing' is quite broad in application and is used for physical items, actions, events, situations, even people. The wide range of meaning of a word like 'something' in English catches some of this flavor.

2.1 Nominal morphology

-wÁ on all forms. However, the plural forms are not constant. Most have -líŋ as the plural suffix, but forms that have another suffix are not uncommon, e.g., bàl-lí 'children', líǃá-ŋ 'daughters', hùá-ŋ 'women', the latter two having -ŋ as the suffix. For the plural definite, almost all forms have a -bÁ suffix. The only ones which do not are 'child' and compounds derived from it.

The -bÁ plural definite suffix is so strongly associated with humans that it is often added as the plural definite suffix even when, on the grounds of the basic noun class of the noun or adjective stem, a different suffix would be expected, as in hɔ̀gù-kpíǃmá-bá 'the large women', where the plural adjective kpíímà 'large' generally takes the definite suffix -há (cf. jàà-kpíǃmá-há 'the big things').

Nouns of class 5 make up thirteen percent of the total nouns in my database (see 38). This is probably an overrepresentation, since approximately two-thirds of the nouns I have in this class have the -rU agentive suffix (discussed in section 2.1.3), which I actively elicited.

This noun class contains the only forms I am aware of which have a contour tone on a non-final syllable, found always in the plural forms such as 'friends', 'fathers'. They are always followed by a downstepped High in the next syllable.

Noun class 5 is also unique in containing some members, 'father' and 'mother', which have different forms for a word according to the person possessing it. First-person and second-person singular possessors take one form, and second-person plural and third-person possessors take another form, as in (44). The forms 'father' and 'mother' are also distinguished by being the only nouns in which the first- and second-person singular possessive pronouns are High toned.

(44) Possessed forms of 'father' and 'mother'

1s	ń ǃnáá	'my mother'	ń ǃchúá	'my father'
1p	tí ǃnáá	'our mother'	tí ǃchúá	'our father'
2s	fí ǃnáá	'your mother'	fí ǃchúá	'your father'
2p	nì nŭŋ	'your(PL) mother'	nì chɔ̌ŋ	'your(PL) father'
3s	ù nûŋ	'his mother'	ù chɔ̂ŋ	'his father'
3p	bà nûŋ	'their mother'	bà chɔ̂ŋ	'their father'
3s nh	kà nûŋ	'its mother'	kà chɔ̂ŋ	'its father'
3p nh	à nûŋ	'their mother'	à chɔ̂ŋ	'their father'

Though most nouns fit into the classes described above, about eleven percent of nouns have singulars from one class and plurals from another, as exemplified in (45). Note that the singulars are assigned to a class based on the singular definite forms.

(45) Mixed class nouns

	Classes (SG, PL)	Singular	Singular definite	Plural	Plural + plural definite
'goat'	2, 1	bììŋ	bììkú	bìé	bièhé
'guinea fowl'	2, 1	kpá!áŋ	kpáá!kú	kpíínè	kpíí!néhé
'room'	2, 1	jùóŋ	jùòkú	jùné	jùnéhé
'block'	2, 1	wáríŋ	wáríkú	wárà	wá!ráhá
'cow'	4, 1	náá!gíŋ	náágí!bú	níígè	níí!géhé
'horse'	4, 1	dùúŋ	dùùmbú	dùùné	dùùnéhé
'rope'	4, 1	gú!úŋ	gúúm!bú	gúúnê	gúúné!hé
'blindness'	2, 3	yîî	yíí!kú	yíísí	yíísísí
'chair'	2, 3	chîàŋ	chíá!kú	chíásî	chíá!sísí
'antelope'	3, 1	yìsíŋ	yìsìké	yìsé	yìséhé
'tree (sp.)'	3, 1	hààríŋ	hààrìká	hààrá	hààráhá
'rubbish heap'	1, 3	tàŋgúúŋ	tàŋgúúrí	tàŋgúúsí	—
'vulture'	3, 2	zùúŋ	zùùké	zùùtí	zùùtítí

Though several combinations of noun classes are attested, almost half of the "mixed class" nouns in my data have plurals in noun class 1.

Some nouns may have more than one acceptable form of the definite article, and so may be classed in more than one noun class. For example, 'the vulture' may be either *zùùké* as in (45), or *zùùkú*. Whether this is a true variation or represents confusion on the part of Mr. Amadu, who is not as intimately acquainted with wildlife as some, remains to be seen.

Also, for some fruit-bearing trees, one singular indefinite form is used for both the tree and its fruit or product, but a different plural form may sometimes be used for the tree and the fruit.

(46) kàmbùntáá!míŋ 'papaya (tree or fruit)' dùúŋ 'dawadawa (tree or fruit)'
kàmbùntáán!sí 'papaya trees' dùùsí 'dawadawa trees'
kàmbùntáámà 'papaya fruits' dùùtí 'dawadawa fruits'

The plural suffix for most species of trees (twenty-six out of thirty-four I have data for) is the *-si* noun class 3 plural suffix, as is the suffix for the general word for 'trees' *tíísí*. When there is a distinction between the fruits of a tree and the trees themselves, the trees themselves always take the *-si* plural suffix.

2.1.2 Noun-adjective complexes

Welmers (1973:250) writes that "in almost all Niger-Congo languages which have a class of adjectives, the class is rather small, and many concepts expressed by adjectives in European languages are expressed by other kinds of constructions using nouns or verbs or both." Carlson (1994) gives the exhaustive list of adjectives in Supyire as "small, big, good, first, new, hot, white, same, red, all, last, beautiful." Kɔnni, in common with these languages, has very few underived adjectives, about a dozen. These basic adjectives include: big, small, white, black, red, short, long, new, old, bad, wide, thin, while concepts of "good, heavy, sweet, bitter, hot, cold, rotten, tired," etc. are expressed by verbs, e.g., *ù gbàlīgá mìŋ* 's/he is tiring', i.e., getting tired. Adjectives derived from these and other verbs are fairly common.

Adjectives are discussed under nominal morphology, since they are always bound to nouns; try to elicit 'white' and you will get the response 'white *thing*'. (This is in contrast to numbers and other quantifiers, which can stand alone.) Qualitative adjectives are bound morphemes in many other Gur languages, and this seems to be the usual pattern for this language family. See Kröger 1992 for Buli, Carlson 1994 for Supyire, Bodomo 1997 for Dagaare, Nicole 1998 for Nawdm, and Naden 1988 for Vagla, Mampruli, and Gur languages in general.

Adjectives resemble nouns in that each adjective also has its own class suffixes, taken from the set of noun class suffixes discussed above. The adjective suffix may or may not be the same as the root noun would take by itself, as shown by examples in (47). The suffix is determined by the last adjective or noun stem present.

(47) a.   kpíá-**sí**   kpíá-yèèl-**à**
       fowl-PL   fowl-white-PL
       'fowls'   'white fowls'

    b.   dùùm-**bú**   dùùŋ-ŋmìŋ-**ká**
        horse-the   horse-red-the
        'the horse'   'the red horse'

    c.   hɔw-**wá**   hɔgù-kpíí-**ká**
        woman-the   woman-big-the
        'the woman'[5]   'the big woman'

---

[5]From /hɔgù-wá/.

Additional evidence that the suffix of a form does not depend on the noun, but on the adjective is given in the set of data in (48). Here, the noun is constant, but the suffix varies according to the adjective present. More adjectives have singular suffixes from class 3 and plurals from class 1 than other patterns, but this is by no means universal.

(48)

'X thing'	'the X thing'	'X things'		Class (SG/PL)
jà-kʊ̀ʊ́ŋ	jà-kʊ̀ʊ̀-rí	ɲìŋ-kù-rá	'old'	Class 1
jè-góbíŋ	jè-góbí-rí	ɲìŋ-gób-è	'short'	Class 1
jà-wɔ́ŋ	jà-wɔ́k-kú	ɲìŋ-wɔ́gí-tí	'long'	Class 2
jà-bìáŋ	jà-bìà-kú	ɲìm-bìà-tí	'bad'	Class 2
jè-bíŋ	jè-bì-ké	ɲìm-bì-sí	'small'	Class 3
jà-kpí!íŋ	jà-kpíí-!ká	ɲìŋ-kpíím-à	'big'	Class 3/1
jà-yèèlíŋ	jà-yèèlì-ká	ɲìn-yèèl-á	'white'	Class 3/1
jà-sɔ́bí!líŋ	jà-sɔ́bílí-!ká	ɲìn-sɔ́bíl-à	'black'	Class 3/1
jà-ŋmùníŋ	jà-ŋmùŋ-ká	ɲìŋ-ŋmùn-á	'red'	Class 3/1
jà-háá!líŋ	jà-háá!lí-ká	ɲìŋ-háál-à	'new'	Class 3/1

In (48) with 'thing', the suppletive plural noun stem *ɲìN-* 'things' occurs with plural adjective forms, not the singular form *jà* 'thing'. This situation is almost unique in Kɔnni. Few nouns have suppletive plural forms, but with most nouns which have suppletive plural forms, the singular stem is used even when a plural form of the adjective occurs, as in (49a and 49b).

(49) a. náá!gíŋ 'cow'
　　　　 níígè 'cows'
　　　　 náá-kpí!íŋ 'large cow'
　　　　 náá-kpíímà 'large cows'

　　 b. kpá!áŋ 'guinea fowl'
　　　　 kpíínè 'guinea fowls'
　　　　 kpé-!bíŋ 'small guinea fowl'
　　　　 kpé-!bísí 'small guinea fowls'

　　 c. bʊ̀á 'child'
　　　　 bàllí 'children'
　　　　 bʊ̀ò-bíŋ 'small child'
　　　　 bàllì-bìsí 'small children'

The singular noun stem *naag-* 'cow' generally shortens to *naa-* in compounds, and it is this singular stem which is used in the plural adjectival

2.1 Nominal morphology

form. Similarly, the singular noun stem *kpaa-* 'guinea fowl' (shortened and with a vowel change for ATR harmony) is used for the plural as well as the singular adjectival form. The noun 'child', as in (49c), is the only other one besides 'thing' in my data which takes the suppletive plural stem when in a plural adjectival form.

Kɔnni does not allow the infinite addition of adjectives to nouns. Three adjectives in a word is the most I have in my data, and even these are quite infrequent. Mr. Amadu was able to produce a word with four adjectives, but said it was "never heard."

(50) a. jà-kù-yèèlì-kpíí-!ká
   thing-old-white-big-the
   'the old big white thing'

   b. jà-háálí-yèèlì-kpíí-!ká
   thing-new-white-big-the
   'the new big white thing'

A similar situation exists in the Gur language Dagaare, but in that language it is possible to have four or even more adjectives after the noun stem (Bodomo 1997).

The order of the adjective stems is at least somewhat restricted. If the adjective 'new' or 'old' is present, it precedes any other adjective, attaching directly to the noun stem, as in (50) and (52a–c). Then if a color adjective is present, the color adjective precedes any adjectives other than 'new' or 'old'. Other adjectives come next, and adjectives derived from verbs, discussed below, occur last. In a few cases, Mr. Amadu gave mixed reactions to the ordering of color and other adjectives, while two less educated Kɔnni speakers, Taahiru and Benni, consistently put the color adjectives before other ones. I speculate that Mr. Amadu's extensive exposure to English may have affected the responses he gave in these cases.

The order, then, of adjectives in Kɔnni is:

(51) Noun stem – 'old/new' – color – other – derived adjectives

These are exemplified in (52).

(52) a. jà-kù-sɔ́bí!líŋ
   thing-old-black
   'old black thing'

b. jà-kù-yèèlì-ká
   thing-old-white-the
   'the old white thing'

c. jà-háálí-!yéélí-ká
   thing-new-white-the
   'the new white thing'

d. jà-yèèlì-bíŋ
   thing-white-small
   'small white thing'

e. jà-sɔ́bílí-!bíŋ
   thing-black-small
   'small black thing'

f. jà-yèèlì-kpí!íŋ
   thing-white-big
   'big white thing'

g. jà-sɔ́bílí-kpí!íŋ
   thing-black-big
   'big black thing'

h. jà-yèèlì-wɔ́ŋ
   thing-white-long
   'long white thing'

i. hɔ̀gù-sɔ́bílí-bí!áŋ
   woman-black-bad
   'bad black woman'

j. hɔ̀gù-sɔ́bílí-kpíí-bíá!ká
   woman-black-big-bad
   'big bad black woman'

2.1.3 Derived nouns and adjectives

Both nouns and adjectives can be derived by the addition of suffixes to verb stems. Nouns have a greater variety of these derivational suffixes, and will be considered first.

2.1 Nominal morphology

Several suffixes can derive nouns from verbs. These include:

(53) a. -ŋ   'thing that has been Xed'   jʊʊsɩŋ   'prayer' (jʊʊsɩ 'ask for something')
     b. -sI   'act of Xing'   dʊa-sɩ   'lying down' (dʊa 'lie down')
     c. -sIŋ   'place of Xing'   dʊágí-!síŋ   'lying-down place' (dʊagɩ 'lie down')
     d. -rU   'one who does X'   tì-tàà-rʊ́   'thrower, shooter' (taa 'throw')

The simplest way to nominalize a verb is with the suffix -ŋ. This gives a noun whose meaning is approximately 'something that has been Xed'. In (54), I give the noun and the verb from which it is derived, and also the noun class and whether a plural exists (marked by "y" or "n" for "yes" or "no"). In many of these, for which the only data I have is the citation form of the noun, the noun class and possibility of plural formation are not known to me.

(54) a.

Noun		Class	PL	CV-	Verb root
chììtí	'headload'	2/4	y	chi	'carry on head'
kʊ́áŋ	'farm'	2	y	kɔ	'farm'
nììŋ	'rain'	2	y	nɩ	'rain'
wííŋ	'flute'	3	y	wɩ	'blow on instrument'

b.

Noun		Class	PL	CVC-/CVCVC-	Verb roots
bàlíŋ	'talking, language'	2	y	bal-	'speak, talk'
bɔ̀bíŋ	'scarf, tying'	3	y	bɔb-	'tie'
chààríŋ	'winnowing'	?	?	chaar-	'winnow'
chìsìmíŋ	'sneeze'	4	n	chɩsɩm-	'sneeze'
dɔ̀míŋ	'thunder, shaking'	4	?	dɔm-	'shake, stir'
gàlìmíŋ	'blaming'	?	?	galɩm-	'blame'
gèrèntéŋ	'burp'	?	?	gerent-	'burp'
hìèsíŋ	'yawn'	2	n	hies-	'yawn'
làmíŋ	'taste'	?	?	lam-	'taste'
ɲʊ̀ʊgíŋ	'smell'	4	?	ɲʊʊg-	'smell'
pɔ̀gìlíŋ	'holding'	4	n	pɔgɩl-	'hold'
pʊ̀ʊsíŋ	'whisper'	?	?	pʊʊs-	'whisper'
sìbíŋ	'knowing'	2	n	sɩb-	'know'

sɔ̀bíŋ	'excreting, laying'	?	?	sɔb-	'excrete'
tʊ̀ʊlíŋ	'heat'	4	n	tʊʊl-	'be hot'

Verbs have no inherent tone in Kɔnni, but surface tones on verbs are a function of their syntactic and phonological contexts (see section 6.4). Thus it is not surprising that tone of nouns derived from verbs is also predictable. As seen in (54), such a derived noun has Low tone in the stem, with a High on the final syllable.[6]

The second and third morphemes, -sI and -sIŋ (in 53b and c), are the most poorly attested in my data, and it may be that they are actually alternate forms of the same morpheme. The form dʊasɪ 'lying down' is most often heard in the morning greeting dʊasɪ vɪɪna? '(your) lying down was good?' An alternate often heard is dʊasɪ-rɪ vɪɪna? It is quite likely that the first form is an informal shortening of the second, which has the -ri definite suffix. If this is so, then the "full" form of the first would be dʊasɪŋ vɪɪna? taking nasal place assimilation into account. The same account holds for kasɪ/kasɪŋ 'sitting'. (e.g., fɪ ká!sírí vìnáà 'your sitting is good?'). I have no other nouns which end in -si when no other suffixes are present. So very tentatively, I subsume the -si suffix under -siŋ.

The morphology of (53d), the agentive noun, is particularly interesting, in that besides the suffix, there is generally a reduplicative prefix consisting of the first consonant of the stem and a high vowel that generally agrees in roundness (or the [dorsal] feature, used in chapter 5) and ATR with the following stem. The vowel of the reduplicant prefix may thus be either [i, ɪ, u, or ʊ]. Rounding of the prefixed vowel occurs when the first stem vowel is rounded, as in (55f–j), but also occurs when the initial noun stem consonant is [w], as in (55j–k). This is a consequence of a general process in Kɔnni in which high vowels agree in place with a following glide, discussed in section 5.4.3.

(55) a. tɪ̀-tààrú 'thrower, shooter' (taa 'throw')
    b. dì-dìgì-rú 'cooker' (digi 'cook')
    c. dí-dàà-rú 'buyer, seller' (daa 'buy/sell')
    d. mì-mìì-rʊ̀ 'builder' (mɪɪ 'build')
    e. sì-sìè-rú 'dancer' (sie 'dance')
    f. bʊ̀-bʊ̀rì-tú 'sower' (bʊrɪ 'sow')

---

[6]The exceptions are the two nouns in (54a), that have a simple High tone pattern: kúáŋ 'farm' and wíŋ 'flute'. Whether these involve historical simplification of the LH contour, a back formation of the verb from the noun (in which case these nouns are not truly derived), or are simply exceptional is not known.

2.1 Nominal morphology

  g. gù-gùù-rú   'burier' (guu 'bury')
  h. jù-jùàlì-tú   'climber' (jʊalɪ 'climb')
  i. kù-kɔ̀lìn-tú   'mover, migrator' (kɔlɪŋ 'move')
  j. wù-wɔ̀sì-rú   'caller' (wɔsɪ 'call')
  k. wù-wàsì-rú   'greeter' (wasɪ 'greet')
  l. yì-yùòrìtú   'opener' (yuori 'open')

  The tonal pattern of these derived nouns is predictable; both the prefix and noun stem are Low toned, with the -tú/-rú suffix[7] always High toned. Again, since verbs are inherently toneless, this is not surprising.

  Productive formation of the agentive noun includes the prefix. However, there are a few very common words with [-rU] which lack a prefix. These include the following, most of which are common roles in Koma society.

(56) kpáá-!rú   'farmer' (cf. kpa 'pick')
   gáá-rú   'thief' (cf. ga 'deceive')
   bùgù-rú   'soothsayer' (cf. bugu 'earn')
   yàlì-tú   'hunter' (cf. yaalɪ 'find')
   wàsì-rú   'greeter' (as an alternative to wù-wàsìrú in 55k)

  Alternatively, a noun stem can replace the reduplicative prefix, making a compound, as in (57). The reduplicative prefix and the noun stem do not co-occur. This appears to be a productive process, in which an object of the verb can be compounded with the derived agentive noun.

(57) a. tɔ̀n-tàà-rú   'warrior (lit., bow thrower)'
   b. yílí-chíá-!rú   'singer (lit., song cutter)'
   c. hán-díí-rù   'debtor (lit., debt eater)'
   d. dɔ̀ŋ-kù-rú   'butcher (lit., animal killer)'
   e. náá-!yágí-rú   'cowherd (lit., cow driver)'
   f. tàm-mìì-rú   'mason (lit., dirt builder)'
   g. gbìèm-mìì-rú   'potter (lit., pot builder)'
   h. tíí-jùàlì-tú   'tree climber'

  I have no explanation of why the tone of the agentive suffix in *hándíí-rù* 'debtor' is Low rather than the usual High. Tones on the verbal stems above vary according to the preceding noun stems and are discussed in section 6.3.7.

---

[7]The alternation of *t* and *r* in this suffix is discussed in section 4.4.

I have no cases in my data of a noun being combined with a verb following, as in the unattested *tɔn-taa, which would mean 'to bow-throw' or figuratively 'make war'. Since there are no verbal compounds of this sort, I assume that the first noun in the compounds in (57) are added to the already-formed noun with -ru suffix, thus the morphological bracketing would be [[tɔ̀n][[tàà]rù]], not [[[tɔ̀n][tàà]]rú].

Since the forms in (57) are definitely compounds, combining lexical items, it is tempting to speculate that the normal agentive forms with reduplicative prefixes are also compounds. A supporting fact is that there are no other nominal prefixes in Kɔnni.

Agentive nouns may also take definite and plural suffixes. Not surprisingly, since these agentive nouns refer to humans, they are members of noun class 5. Gaps in the data in (58) reflect accidental gaps in my data, not any systematic pattern.

(58)
	Singular	Singular definite	Plural	Plural + definite	
a.	dì-dìgì-rú	dì-dìgì-rù-wó	dì-dìgì-ríŋ	—	'cook'
b.	dì-dàà-rú	dì-dàà-rù-wá	dì-dàà-ríŋ	—	'buyer, seller'
c.	yàlì-tú	—	yalɪ-tɪŋ	yalɪ-tɪ-ba	'hunter'
d.	chàkùt-tú	chàkùt-tú-wó	chàkùt-tíŋ	chàkùt-tì-bé	'blacksmith'

The plural morpheme for agentives is -ríŋ/-tíŋ, similar but not identical to the common -líŋ for noun class 5 plurals. The other suffixal morphology, -wa/-wo for singular definite and -ba/-be for plural definite, is identical to the usual noun class 5 pattern in (43). The word chàkùt-tú 'blacksmith' is a compound, from chǎŋ 'forge' and kʊ̀tí 'iron' (cf. Buli chuok 'forge', kutuk 'iron', but choa-biik 'blacksmith', literally, 'forge's child' in Kröger 1992).

Some adjectives are also derived from verbs, either by adding the simple nominalizing suffix -ŋ 'something that has the quality of X' or -kíŋ 'something that has gotten Xed'.

(59) a. kà vììná mìŋ   'it is good'   jà-vììníŋ   'good thing'
     b. kà chʊ̀ʊ̀sìyá   'it has spoiled'   jà-chʊ̀ʊ̀sìkíŋ 'a spoiled thing'

Adjectives derived from nouns differ from underived adjectives in at least three ways. First, underived adjectives are never used as verbs, while a morpheme such as "good" can be used both in an adjectival context and a verbal

2.1 Nominal morphology

one.[8] Second, while underived adjectives resemble nouns in having a variety of tonal patterns as in (48), the tone of adjectives derived from verbs is always predictable, as Low on the stem, ending in High ('wet/cold' and 'dirty' in (60) are the only exceptions to this pattern in my data). Third, while underived adjectives are members of a variety of classes, derived adjectives are consistently class 3 for the singular forms and class 1 for the plural forms (see (38) for table of all noun class suffixes).

(60)
	Singular	Singular definite	Plural	Plural + plural definite	
a.	jà-vììnɨ́ŋ	jà-vììŋká	ɲìm-vììná	ɲìm-vììnáhá	'good thing/s'
b.	jà-nànsɨ́ŋ	jà-nànsɨ̀ká	ɲìn-nànsá	ɲìn-nànsáhá	'sweet thing/s'
c.	jà-dòmsɨ́ŋ	jà-dònsɨ̀ká	ɲìn-dònsá	ɲìn-dònsáhá	'heavy thing/s'
d.	jà-hàgɨ̀rɨ́ŋ	jà-hàgɨ̀rɨ̀ká	ɲìŋ-hàgɨ̀rá	ɲìŋ-hàgɨ̀ráhá	'strong thing/s'
e.	jà-sún!súŋ	jà-sún!súká	ɲìn-súnsà	ɲìn-sún!sáhá	'wet thing/s'
f.	jà-dígín!tíŋ	jà-dígíntí!ká	ɲìn-dígíntà	ɲìn-dígín!táhá	'dirty thing/s'

The *-ŋ* suffix discussed above is for stative verbs. The singular form of another suffix that derives adjectives from verbs is *-kɨ́ŋ/-kɨ́ŋ*, which means roughly, 'something that has gotten Xed', or 'has become X', as seen in (61).

---

[8]Compare forms with the derived adjective *-vììnɨ́ŋ* 'good' (from the verb *vɯn-*) and the underived adjective *-kpɨ́!ɨ́ŋ* 'fat, big'.

    kè yìwó jà-vììnɨ́ŋ
    it make thing-good
    'it is good (lit., a good thing)'

    kà vììná mìŋ
    it good AFF
    'it is good (lit., it goods)'

    ù   yìwó jà-kpɨ́!ɨ́ŋ
    she make thing-big
    's/he is big (lit., a big thing)' (no verbal form)

(61)

	Singular	Singular definite	Plural	Plural + plural definite	
a.	jà-chʋ̀ʋ̀sì-kíŋ	jà-chʋ̀ʋ̀sì-kìrí	ɲìn-chʋ̀ʋ̀sì-ká	ɲìn-chʋ̀ʋ̀sì-káhá	'spoiled thing/s'
b.	jà-gìlìgì-kíŋ	jà-gìlìgì-kìrí	ɲìŋ-gìlìgì-ké	ɲìŋ-gìlìgì-kéhé	'round thing/s'
c.	jà-mɔ̀rì-kíŋ	jà-mɔ̀rì-kìrí	ɲìm-mɔ̀rì-ká	ɲìm-mɔ̀rì-káhá	'swollen thing/s'
d.	jà-fìàlì-kíŋ	jà-fìàlì-kìrí	ɲìm-fìàlì-ká	ɲìm-fìàlì-káhá	'cool thing/s'

The suffixes in (61) are broken up in more detail in (62). The real morpheme that makes verbs into this type of adjective is a bare -k-, with appropriate class suffixes added. This set of suffixes follows exactly the pattern of noun class 1 (see 39).

(62)
SG	-kíŋ	→	k + ŋ́	([i] is epenthetic)
SG.DEF	-kìrí	→	k + rí	([i] is epenthetic)
PL	-ká	→	k + á	
PL+PL.ART	-káhá	→	k + á + há	

2.1.4 Compound nouns

Compound nouns in Kɔnni consist of a noun stem and another lexical item which function together as one noun. I have found four possible types of compound nouns: noun-noun, noun-adjective, verb-noun, and noun-ideophone. Noun-noun compounds are by far the most common, and the last two are marginal. Compound words also exist in which only one component can be identified. These are all exemplified in (63), then each is considered in more detail.

(63)
a. Noun-noun: núágbámvááŋ 'lip'
      cf. núáŋ 'mouth', gbánɩ́ŋ 'skin', vààŋ 'leaf'
b. Noun-adjective: jàà-kúúŋ 'elder'
      cf. jààŋ 'thing' -kúúŋ 'old'
c. Verb-noun: bùgìrìtăŋ 'bird (sp.)'
      cf. bʋgɩrɩ 'learn', tăŋ 'stone'
d. Noun-ideophone: bìndúdù 'dung beetle'
      cf. bìn-tí 'feces'
e. ?-noun: sánúáŋ 'entrance'
      cf. sá '?', núáŋ 'mouth'

2.1 Nominal morphology

Noun-noun compounds are the result of joining two or more noun stems to make a more complex noun, as in (64) and (65). The suffix of the whole word is that of the last noun in the compound. This type of compound is fairly common, but I have not tested the productivity by attempting to make new words with this process. Compound agentive nouns derived from verbs are included in (64c, g and i), since I analyze these as noun + derived noun, rather than nouns derived from noun + verb.

(64) Noun-noun compounds
    a. bììsìnúáŋ   'nipple' (breast-mouth)
                           cf. bììsíŋ 'breast', núáŋ 'mouth'
    b. bììsìɲááŋ   'breast milk' (breast-water)
                           cf. bììsíŋ 'breast', ɲááŋ 'water'
    c. búntòòɲììrú   'hoodless cobra' (toad-swallower)
                           cf. búntòóŋ 'toad', ɲɪɪ 'to swallow'
    d. chíídèmbǐŋ   'brother-in-law' (sibling.in.law-man)
                           cf. chǐí 'sibling-in-law', dèmbǐŋ 'man'
    e. hánììdèmbǐŋ   'father-in-law' (in.law-man)
                           cf. hánìì 'in-law', dèmbǐŋ 'man'
    f. dááchúáŋ   'alcohol pot' (alcohol-pot)
                           cf. dááŋ 'alcohol', chúáŋ 'pot (sp.)'
    g. gbágíchíárù   'fisher' (lake-cutter)'
                           cf. gbágíŋ 'lake', chɪa 'cut'
    h. hàŋgbàáŋ   'leopard' (bush-dog), also hààgìŋgbàáŋ
                           cf. hààgíŋ 'bush', gbàáŋ 'dog'
    i. hɔ̀gùfààrìtú   'groom' (woman-marrier)
                           cf. hɔ̀gú 'woman, wife', faarɪ 'marry a wife'
    j. kààŋkpíŋ   'cheekbone' (cheek-shea.nut)
                           cf. kààmíŋ 'cheek', kpíŋ 'shea nut'
    k. nììtǎŋ   'hail' (rain-stone) cf. nííŋ 'rain', tǎŋ 'stone'
    l. lɔ̀lìwííŋ   'larynx' (voice-flute)
                           cf. lɔ̀líŋ 'voice', wííŋ 'flute'
    m. ɲáámbún!dááŋ   'catfish (sp.)' (water-donkey-male)
                           cf. ɲááŋ 'water', bún!íŋ 'donkey', -rááŋ 'male'

Compound nouns differ from the associative noun construction, in which two nouns are also conjoined, in at least two ways. First, in associative noun constructions, each noun possesses its own suffix, while in compound nouns, only the last noun does. The first noun of a compound, and if present, any other non-final nouns, have only their stems present. Second, associative constructions always manifest a High tone on the first syllable of the second noun and any subsequent noun, while in compound nouns, the second noun's first syllable is High toned only if lexically so or a result of usual tonal processes discussed in section 6.1. The differences are illustrated below in the following pairs, the first of each is a compound and the second an associative noun phrase; both use the same noun stems.

(65) a. hánìì-nǔŋ   'mother-in-law'
        cf. há!n?ííŋ 'in-law', nǔŋ 'mother'
    há!níín nûŋ   'in-law's mother'
  b. hààgìn-tììsí   'bush-trees'
        cf. hààgíŋ 'bush', tììsí 'trees'
    hààgín tíí!sí   'bush's trees'

Comparing the pair in (65a and b), we see that the suffix /-ŋ/ (surfacing as [-n] by place assimilation) of the first noun hanuŋ is present in the associative form but not in the compound where there is only the bare stem of the first noun hanu-. Also, the second noun nuŋ starts with a High tone in the associative construction, but not in the compound.

Compound nouns do not necessarily have a semantic difference from the corresponding associative construction. For example, the compound náá!bíísíŋ 'cow milk' has the same basic meaning as the associative phrase náá!gíŋ bíí!ísíŋ 'cow's milk'. On the other hand, they are often quite different in meaning, as in (63a), where 'mouth-skin-leaf' means 'lip', not the leaf of the skin of a mouth!

Noun-adjective compounds, however, are distinguished from the usual noun-adjective composites (e.g., tígí-yéé!líŋ 'white house') chiefly by a lexicalized meaning which is different from the meaning of their individual components. Perhaps these are lexicalized versions of ordinary noun-adjective composites.

(66) Noun-adjective compounds
    a. jàà-kùúŋ   'elder (lit., old thing)'
        cf. jàáŋ 'thing', -kùúŋ 'old'
    b. ŋmáríyéé!líŋ   'red-eyed turtle dove (lit., white dove)'
        cf. ŋmáríŋ 'dove', -yéélíŋ 'white'

2.1 Nominal morphology

c. ɲìnɲìŋká   'fruit (lit., things that have come out)'
   cf. ɲìn-tí 'things', ɲìŋ 'come out'
d. ɲìndìkké   'food (lit., things cooked)'
   cf. ɲìn-tí 'things', digi 'cook'

These do not seem to be as common as noun-noun compounds. When another adjective is added to these compounds, normally prohibited orders of adjectives may be allowed. Normally -kòóŋ 'old' would precede -yèèlíŋ 'white', but in 'old red-eyed turtledove', the form is ŋmarı-yɛɛlı-kʋʋŋ. This order indicates that ŋmarı-yɛɛlı- has been lexicalized; it is in the lexicon as one lexeme rather than two.

Examples (66c and d) show that derived adjectives may participate in noun-adjective compounds. As mentioned, noun-verb compounds do not seem to exist independently, so I propose that a noun is only compounded with the verbal adjective when it displays the adjectival morphology, not with the verb alone. Thus the morphological bracketing of (66c) would be $[[[(ɲìn]_{NS}[ɲìŋ]_V k]_{Adj}]_{NS}á]_N$, not $[[[[ɲìn]_{NS}[ɲìŋ]_V]_{NS}k]_{Adj}]_{NS}á]_N$.

Although nú!bíŋ 'finger' would seem to be related to nú-bí!ŋ́ 'small arm', the tonal pattern shows that bíŋ in 'finger' is not 'small' (see discussion in section 6.3.5). The bíŋ here is likely 'seed, child', which combines with many nouns, e.g., nòò-bíŋ 'small intestine (lit., stomach-child)', gàmbíŋ 'front rib (lit., rib-child)'.

Verb-noun compounds are the most dubious of the types listed above and may actually be non-existent. The only possibility of an example I have in my data is:

(67) Verb-noun compound ?
    bʋ̀gìrìtăŋ   'bird (sp.)' (learn?-stone?)
        cf. bʋgırı 'learn', tăŋ 'stone'

People sometimes catch this kind of bird, cut it open, and count the number of stones in the crop. That is supposed to be the number of years they have left to live. One "learns from the stones." This has the ring of a folk etymology, especially since the name of this bird is precisely homophonous with bʋ̀gìrìtăŋ 'anklebone'. I conclude that the evidence for this type of compound is not sufficient to justify it as a separate type of compound.

The noun-ideophone class of compounds seems to be more securely founded, though it, too, only has one definite candidate, in (68).

(68) Noun-ideophone compound
 bìndúdù 'dung beetle'
  cf. bìn-tí 'feces'

Amadu informed me that the *dudu* of the above described "the way that the beetle rolls" the dung ball. The form *dudu* is also seen to act as an ideophone phonologically in that it contains an intervocalic *d*, which is only found in ideophones or at the beginning of lexical items.

Besides the compounds in which all components may be identified, there are some nouns which are evidently compounds, which have a component which cannot be readily identified, as the following:

(69) Compounds with an unknown component
 a. sánúáŋ   'entrance'
   cf. sá '?', núáŋ 'mouth'
 b. chìàkólí   'buttock'
   cf chìáŋ 'waist, bottom', kólí '?'
 c. ɲíncháásí   'front teeth'
   cf. ɲíŋ 'tooth', cháásí '?'
 d. chínchàgìmbíŋ 'kidney'
   cf. chínchàgìm '?', bíŋ 'child, seed'

It would not be surprising if some of these unknown morphemes could be identified in the future, and I merely lack the data to do so at present. Comparison with related languages may also eventually shed light on some of these. For example, 'buttock' in Buli is *bitakoli*. The *-koli* is identical to Kɔnni, and is evidently at least historically a separate morpheme. Kröger 1992 also gives *bitagi* as another word for 'buttock', and a scenario yielding *bitakoli* from *bitagi* + *koli* is plausible. However, Kröger gives no indication of the components of *bitakoli* in his dictionary, and the meaning of *koli* is still unknown. It is likely that a good number of the unknown components of these compounds are "cran morphs" in which one component, like "cran-" in "cranberry," is and will remain unknown in meaning.

2.2 Verbal morphology

The area of tense, aspect, and mood in Kɔnni verbs is partly marked in the syntax and partly in the morphology. The syntax was sketched in section 1.2,

2.2 Verbal morphology

with various pre-verbal particles. In this section I discuss the morphology of verbs in Kɔnni.

There are two areas of interest in Kɔnni verbal morphology. The first is that various aspects and modes (imperfective, perfect, imperative, imperfective II, "neutral") are signaled by suffixes on the verb stem, and each has its own tonal melody. For some aspects and modes, this melody is partly dependent on the subject pronoun. Since tone is entirely predictable on the basis of the grammatical construction, it is evident that verbs in Kɔnni have no lexical tone, unlike nouns and adjectives. The second area of interest is that of derived verbs. A few verbs in Kɔnni are derived from other lexical categories, but many verbs are derived, at least historically, from other verbs by means of various suffixes which are attested cross-linguistically within the Gur family. Each of these areas will be examined in turn.

2.2.1 Aspectual and modal suffixes

While some parts of the tense/aspect/mode system, such as future, are coded syntactically in Kɔnni with preverbal particles, as noted earlier, most expressions of the aspectual-modal system in Kɔnni are expressed morphologically. Inflectional suffixes are used for the imperfective, perfective, imperative, imperfective II, and "neutral" aspects in Kɔnni, as summarized in (70).

(70) Verbal suffixes

Imperfective	-A	ù kùr-é !sáán̋	'S/he is pounding porridge.'
Perfective	-yA	ù kùr-ì-yé	'S/he has pounded.' (intransitive)
	-wA	ù kùr-ù-wó !kápálí	'S/he has pounded fufu.' (transitive)[9]
Imperative	-Ø	kùr-í	'pound!'
Imperative imperfective	-mA	kùr-ì-mé	'keep pounding!'
Imperfective II	-nA	túú!lím bé-nè	'Heat exists (i.e., it is hot).'
Neutral	-Ø	ù nèŋ kúr-í	'S/he will pound.'

The apparent [-I] suffix in the perfective, imperative, and neutral forms of 'pound' is epenthetic. Nicole (1998) notes that in Gur languages in general, the basic aspectual distinction is between incomplete and complete

---

[9]Fufu is a staple food of southern Ghana, less common in northern Ghana, made by pounding boiled yams, cassava, or plantains in a mortar. One forms this into grapefruit-sized balls and eats it with soup on it.

(or sometimes neutral). This is supported also in Kɔnni, with the imperfective and imperative imperfective bearing an incomplete function, and the others an implication of completeness (except imperfective II; see below). Each aspect of the verb has its distinctive tone pattern (discussed in chapter 6); all verbal tone is grammatical.

2.2.1.1 Imperfective aspect

The imperfective aspect indicates an action that is ongoing or continuous at the time it is occurring. In context, this could be either past, present, or future. The additional preverbal particles *nan dí* indicate future imperfective. Without them, the imperfective is either past or present, depending on context. Thus the glosses in this section could be '*was* Xing' as well as the explicitly glossed '*is* Xing'.

The tonal patterns for imperfective depend on which person is subject. All first- and second-person pronouns pattern together, and third-person pronouns pattern together, as illustrated in (71).[10]

(71) All pronouns for imperfective /sɪ/ 'bathe'
    a. ǹ sí!á mìŋ   'I am bathing.'
       tì sí!á mìŋ   'We are bathing.'
       sí!á mìŋ   'You (SG) are bathing.'
       nì sí!á mìŋ   'You (PL) are bathing.'

    b. ù sì-á mìŋ   'S/he is bathing.'
       bà sì-á mìŋ   'They are bathing.'[11]

Therefore in this presentation, first- and third-person singular forms are taken as representative of the entire pattern. Several verbs with variable syllable length and final stem vowels are given in (72).

(72) Imperfective (past or present)
    /la/   ù là-á mìŋ   'S/he is laughing.'   ǹ lá-!á mìŋ   'I am laughing.'
    /di/   ù dì-é mìŋ   'S/he is eating.'   ǹ dí!é mìŋ   'I am eating.'
    /tu/   ù tù-ó mìŋ   'S/he is digging.'   ǹ tú!ó mìŋ   'I am digging.'

---

[10]The particle *mìŋ*, as discussed in chapter 1, seems to be an affirmative or emphatic particle, similar to the Dagaare particle *lá* discussed in Bodomo 1997. It is obligatory in imperfective, but prohibited in the negative imperfective.

[11]The same tonal pattern holds with nouns as with third-person pronouns, but tonal perturbations due to the common final High tone on the noun may mask this. For example, the surface nìikkú !nía mìŋ 'the rain is raining' comes from underlying /nìikkú nìá mìŋ/, with the verb having the same tone as the other CV verbs above.

2.2 Verbal morphology

/kpat-/ ù kpàt-á mìŋ 'S/he is finishing.' ŋ̀m kpá!tá mìŋ 'I am finishing.'
/sulis-/ ù sùlìs-é mìŋ 'S/he is polishing.' ǹ súlí!sé mìŋ 'I am polishing.'

The imperfective suffix, as illustrated in (72), may take various forms, either [-a], [-e], or [-o], depending on the phonological context. It is [-a] in a [−ATR] word, [-o] in a [+ATR] word when adjacent to [u],[12] and [-e] in other [+ATR] words. This is discussed more fully in section 5.2.

In third-person forms, the tone is Low on the entire stem, whether the stem has one or two syllables, and High on the suffix. In contrast, in first- and second-person forms, a High tone appears on the first syllable of the verb, and a downstepped High on the final suffix syllable. This pattern is abstracted into a LH pattern and discussed in section 6.4.1.

The future imperfective has no tonal variation on the verb due to subject person, although as seen (73) and (74), the future particle *nan* is High toned in second-person singular. The third-person singular will adequately represent the range of possibilities on the verb itself.

(73) All pronouns for future imperfective /sɪ/ 'bathe'
    ǹ   nàn dí sí-!á   'I will be bathing.'
        nàn dí sí-!á   'You will be bathing.'
    ù   nàn dí sí-!á   'S/he will be bathing.'
    tì   nàn dí sí-!á   'We will be bathing.'
    nì   nàn dí sí-!á   'You(PL) will be bathing.'
    bà nàn dí sí-!á   'They will be bathing.'

(74) Future imperfective
    /la/   ù nàn dí lá-!á   's/he will be laughing'
    /tu/   ù nàn dí tú!ó   's/he will be digging'
    /di/   ù nàn dí dí!é   's/he will be eating'
    /kpat-/ ù nàn dí kpát-!á   's/he will be finishing'
    /sulis/ ù nàn dí súlís-!é   's/he will be polishing'

The verb in the future imperfective always has a High on the first syllable and a downstepped High on the final syllable. This appears to be a pattern quite different from the other imperfective, but the difference is illusory. The first High in the future imperfective is a consequence of the High-toned *dí* preceding the verb, and this High has spread to the verb, displacing the Low, thus creating downstep. When the surface Highs at the beginning of the verb are abstracted away, what remains is the

---

[12]The imperfective suffix is also [-o] when adjacent to underlying /o/, but the combination of these two vowels diphthongizes to [uo], only rarely giving a surface [oo]. See discussion in section 5.3.

Low-High pattern of the third-person subjects in (72), and we see that the LH pattern of imperfective is manifested on both the normal imperfective in (72) and the future imperfective in (73) and (74).

Consistent tone patterns on verbs are also found in transitive constructions and with negatives of the preceding. These and the above tonal patterns are discussed and analyzed in section 6.4.1.

2.2.1.2 Perfective aspect

The perfective aspect morpheme is -yá/-yé in intransitive clauses (ones with no overt object) and -wá/-wó in clauses with an overt direct object. It denotes a completed action, whether in the recent or distant past. It can also be used to describe the condition of a person or object, as in *ù yì-wó jà-kpí!íŋ* 'he is a big person', literally, 'he has been/made big-thing'. Like the imperfective, the tonal pattern in the perfective aspect depends in part on the subject pronoun, with the same division into first- and second-person subjects versus third-person subjects, as shown in (75). Therefore, first- and third-person subjects are again used in (76) and (77) to represent the two patterns.

(75) All pronouns for perfective intransitive with /sɪ/ 'bathe'
    a. ǹ sí!yá mìŋ 'I have bathed.'
       tì sí!yá mìŋ 'We have bathed.'
       sí!yá mìŋ 'You have bathed.'
       nì sí!yá mìŋ 'You(PL) have bathed.'

    b. ù síyá mìŋ 'S/he has bathed.'
       bà síyá mìŋ 'They have bathed.'

(76) Perfective intransitive
    ù là-yá 'S/he has laughed.'   ǹ lá-!yá 'I have laughed.'
    ù dìì-yé 'S/he has eaten.'   ǹ díí-!yé 'I have eaten.'
    ù kpàtì-yá 'S/he has finished.'   ŋm kpátí-!yá 'I have finished.'
    ù sùlìsì-yé 'S/he has polished.'   ǹ súlísí-!yé 'I have polished.'

The similarity to the imperfective tone pattern is that the first tone-bearing unit (TBU) of the verb after a first-person subject is High, while after third person it is Low. The perfective suffix morpheme -yá (alternating with -yé as a result of ATR harmony) is always High, and so is assumed to have a High tone lexically.

Unlike the imperfective, the perfective aspect is signaled by a different allomorph when in a transitive clause. This is -wa, alternating with -wo as a

2.2 Verbal morphology

result of ATR harmony (see section 5.2.1), and shows the same tonal alternations due to subject person.

(77) ù là-wá !búá   'S/he has laughed at a child.'
      ǹ lá-!wá bùàwá   'I have laughed at the child.'

      ù dù-wó !sááŋ   'S/he has eaten porridge.'
      ǹ dú-!wó sààŋ   'I have eaten porridge.'

      ù kpàtù-wá !júóŋ   'S/he has finished a room.'
      ŋ̀m kpátú-!wá !júóŋ   'I have finished a room.'

      ù sùlìsù-wó gbíá!bíŋ 'S/he has polished a door.'
      ǹ súlísú-!wó gbíá!bíŋ 'I have polished a door.'

Locatives act syntactically as objects in Kɔnni and thus also occur with the /-wA/ allomorph. Other components such as adverbs and embedded sentences may also follow it. Though these are scarce in my elicited data, they occur fairly commonly in texts. The /-wA/ in discourse may have a further discourse function and needs more study. (Tone was not transcribed for most of the texts and so is not marked in most of the following examples.)

(78) a. m baa-m   balı-**wa**   wunsie
        1s intend-1s say-PERF   be.true.IMPF
        'I'm going to speak the truth.'

    b. dìènó   fı   bá!lí-**wá** kà vììná
       yesterday 2s say-PERF   it good
       'Yesterday you said it's good.'

    c. ba kalı-**wa** kɔbga   kɔbga
       3p sit-PERF   hundred hundred
       'They sat in [groups of] hundreds.'

    d. a-rıaŋ   a   yi-**wo**   sıba jagıŋ naa
       they-too they make-PERF   like shade like.this
       'They had also erected a shade like this one.'

2.2.1.3 Imperative mode

The imperative mode is used for direct commands. Pragmatically, it is not used as often as in English, since imperatives are considered too direct and disrespectful to equals or elders. The more polite way of making requests is, literally, 'that you X', e.g., *dí !fí díí* 'that you eat! (you should eat)'. These forms will be discussed later. Also, imperatives may denote either a single or a continuing action, labeled here as simple imperative and imperative imperfective. These two types of imperatives in Kɔnni are represented by the following forms.

(79) Imperative, imperative imperfective
làá	là-má	'laugh!, be laughing!'
tùú	tù-mé	'dig!, be digging!'
sìé	sè-mé	'dance!, be dancing!'
lǎŋ	làm-má	'taste!, be tasting!'
kpàtí	kpàtì-má	'finish!, be finishing! (?!)'
bɔ̀bí	bɔ̀bì-má ~ bɔ̀m-má	'tie!, be tying!'
dìgí	dìgì-mé	'cook!, be cooking!'
tììrí	tììrí-má	'stretch!, be stretching!'
sùlìsí	sùlìsì-mé	'polish!, be polishing!'

When giving commands to more than one person, the second-person plural pronoun is placed before the verb, as in *nì sìé* 'you(PL) dance!' The verb undergoes no segmental or tonal changes in this context.

The imperative forms are the most basic form of the verb that can be uttered in isolation, segmentally consisting of the stem alone, along with final epenthetic /-I/ in consonant-final stems to avoid these final nonnasal consonants being word final. (Nasals are the only consonants allowed stem finally which do not require epenthesis, as in *lǎŋ, làm-má* 'taste!, be tasting!' in (79). For more on vowel epenthesis, see section 5.5.) The final TBU of the verb has a High tone to end the word, and a Low must also be present. In monosyllabic verbs this gives a rising contour tone. In disyllabic verbs, this yields a LH pattern, while in trisyllabic verbs, this yields a LLH pattern. The High is thus always on the right edge, and Lows are to the left of this.

A similar tonal pattern is found in the imperative imperfective forms, with a High on the rightmost TBU, and Lows elsewhere. However, the High in this case is always associated to the segmental morpheme *-má/-mé,* and there are no contour tones in imperative imperfective.

The entire tonal register is generally higher for imperatives (of either sort) than for nonimperatives. A typical rise in fundamental frequency of a sentence-initial Low-High sequence in a nonimperative sentence would be from 170 to 260 Hz for Amadu, but for an imperative, it is typically about 240 to 290 Hz.

As mentioned, the more polite form to request something is, literally, 'that you X'. This can also be used with other pronouns, having the force of 'you should X'. It can have the -má/-mé imperfective suffix as well. This may be termed an "indirect imperative" or perhaps "hortative."

(80) Indirect imperative, with /di/ 'eat'
dín !díí	dín !dímé	'that I eat, I should eat'
dí tí !díí	dí tí !dímé	'that we eat, we should eat'
dí !fí díí	dí !fí dímé	'that you eat, you should eat'
dí !ní díí	dí !ní dímé	'that you(PL) eat, you(PL) should eat'
dú!ú díí	dú!ú dímé	'that s/he eat, s/he should eat'
dí !bé díí	dí !bé dímé	'that they eat, they should eat'

First person has a different tonal pattern from second or third person in (80); note the position of the downstep (!) after the pronoun in first-person forms, but before the pronoun in second- and third-person forms. First- and third-person singulars are taken as representative of the two patterns, with a variety of verbs in (81).

(81)
	1s subject	3s subject	
a.	dín !síé	dú!ú síé	'I, s/he should dance.'
	dín !sémé	dú!ú sémé	'I, s/he should be dancing.'
b.	dín !tíírí	dú!ʊ̀ tíírí	'I, s/he should stretch.'
	dín !tíírímá	dú!ʊ̀ tíírímá	'I, s/he should be stretching.'
c.	dím !búgúrí	dú!ʊ̀ búgúrí	'I, s/he should learn.'
	dím !búgúrímá	dú!ʊ̀ búgúrímá	'I, s/he should be learning.'

On each of these, the verb has all High tones, and there is a downstep present in the whole phrase; the location of the downstep is after the first-person pronoun but before the third-person pronoun.

2.2.1.4 Imperfective II: "na"

In Kɔnni the suffix -na/-ne is used in a variety of contexts, as seen in (82). The Gur languages of Sisaala-Pasaale (Toupin 1997), Supyire (Carlson 1994), and Buli (Kröger 1992) have two types of imperfective suffixes or markers (Kröger labels the more marked one as "continuous aspect"). The Kɔnni pattern follows these languages: /-nA/ seems to be another type of imperfective suffix, though much less common than the /-A/ discussed above.[13] In different contexts it may be past or present, and when past is indicated by context, I have glossed this as a simple past rather than the more complex past progressive. It may often represent being in a state of doing the verb. The samples in (82) show that person makes no difference in the tonal pattern for this aspect.

(82) ǹ yí-**ná** !wá !bííkú,... 'when I **was giving** him/her the goat...'
ù yí-**ná** !wá !bííkú,... 'when s/he **was giving** him/her the goat...'

This morpheme is often reduplicated, uniquely among verbal suffixes. When the verb stem itself is reduplicated with other tenses or aspects, it indicates a repetitive action; and the reduplication of this suffix likely also indicates a repeated action, as the verb stem itself is not reduplicated with this suffix (as it is in the imperfective, e.g., ù dàg-á dág-à mìŋ 's/he is showing repeatedly').

(83) ù ɲúó!té dɔ́n-**nà**   'His/her stomach **is stirring** (i.e., rumbling).'

ù ɲúó!té dɔ́n-!**náná**   'His/her stomach **is stirring** (i.e., rumbling).'

ù dí-**nè** sààbú wá...   'when s/he **ate** porridge,...'
ù dí-**né!né** !sáábú wá...   'when s/he **was eating** porridge,...'

ù tá-!**ná** ném!bíké, ú kù kà   'When s/he **threw** at the bird, s/he killed it.'
ù tá-!**náná** ném!bíké, ká hàgì 'When s/he **was throwing** at the bird, it flew away.'

The data in (84) give the morpheme in a variety of other contexts.

(84) ù nínnè tùòlín-**nè**   'His/her eyes are **turning** (i.e., s/he is confused).'

ǹ sún chúúsí-**nâ**   'My heart is **spoiled** (i.e., I am sad).'

---

[13]Comments from both Mary Esther Kropp-Dakubu and Alain Delplanque lead me to tentatively suggest a historical tie-in to a morpheme -ni which is combined with the normal -a imperfective to form the present -na. More comparative work is needed to evaluate the merits of such a suggestion.

2.2 Verbal morphology

ù ɲìŋgbánɪ́ŋ kpɪ́-**nè**	'His/her body is **dying** (i.e., s/he is dizzy).'
ǹ ɲìŋgbánɪ́ŋ ŋmɪ́ɪ́gɪ́-**nâ**	'My body **is weak**.'
túú!lím bé-**nè**	'Heat **exists** (i.e., it is hot).'
wɪ́ɪ́ŋ kágá-**nà** mìŋ	'problem **missed** me'
bɪ́á kú-!**ná** !fɪ́ !nááwá	'What **killed** your mother?'
ù kɪ́é-**néné**	'S/he **is coming**!'
nàáŋ vɪ́ɪ́!tɪ́ dɪ́-**nè** bòlɪ́ŋ	'Chief's sheds are **eating** fire (i.e., chief is dead).'
ǹ náŋ wɪ́-**nà**	'My leg **is broken**.'
ǹ nán lɪ́gɪ́rɪ́-**nè**	'My leg **is sprained**.'
mìná wɔ́rà-**nà** sààŋ	'Who **stirs** porridge?'
mìná dɪ́gɪ́-**nè** jìtɪ́	'Who **cooks** the soup?'
ù hɔ́gʋ̀ yɪ́-**nè** mìnɪ̂a	'His wife **is** who?'
koburu yɪ-**na** ballɪ saraha	'Koburu **gives** the children names.'
sɪ́ŋkpáábʋ́ dɔ́n-**nà** nì kìrì	'Groundnuts are **lying** at your(PL) front.'
bìtá-!bɪ́tá yɪ́gɪ́!-**néné** ŋmààmɪ́ŋ jʋ́!ŋ	'small-small **catches** monkey's tail'
jìidɪ́éké dɪ́ chɪ́á-!**ná** yɪ́!sɪ́kʋ́ bɪ́é !géé	'The snake that **bit** the sheep is here.'
ŋmɪ́ŋ yɪ́-!**náná**	'God **gives** (is the one who gives, the giver).'

2.2.1.5 "Neutral" form

What I have labeled the "neutral" form is the form of the verb with no suffixal material. Verbs with CV or CVN stems remain unchanged segmentally, while verbs with CVC or CVCVC stems add an epenthetic /-I/. The neutral form actually has no aspectual content, but takes the time frame from the surrounding context, and its use seems to be confined to those larger contexts; one does not find it in an isolated sentence. It often can be translated with a simple past tense in English. The example in (85) is the third sentence from a folk story, where the setting has already been given. The bolded verbs below have no morphemes added to the verb stem.

(85) lɛlɛ   naachɪgɪ-kpɪɪŋ dɪ   **ga** **magsɪ**   sɪba daboziesi a   **kalɪ**
     now   lion-big   then   **go** **measure** like Daboziesi and **sit**
     'Now a big lion went and lived at a village like Daboziesi.'

The tone of this aspect has not been studied adequately enough to give a detailed account, but it seems to vary depending not only on the phonological context, but whether it is in a serial verb construction or not.

To sum up, each aspect has not only segmental morphology associated with that aspect, but a particular tonal melody as well. For some aspects, the person of the subject pronoun makes a difference in the surface tonal pattern, with first and second person adding a High tone to the verb.

2.2.2 Derived verbs and verbal extensors

Verbs derived from other lexical categories are rare in Kɔnni, although verbs can commonly serve as the base for deriving either adjectives or nouns. Verbs derived from other verbs by means of verbal extensions are not as rare.

In a database of 460 verbs, I have only three definite examples of verbs derived from other lexical categories. Two adjective-based verbs are *wɔgɪrɪ* 'to be long' from the adjective *-wɔ́g-* 'long' (the *ɪ* is epenthetic after the *g*), and *kʋrɪm* 'to grow old' from *kʋʋ* 'old'.

(86) a. jà-wɔ́ŋ   'long thing' (from /-wɔ́g-ŋ/)
     ɲìŋ-wɔ́gí-í   'long things'
     jà-wɔ̀gí-!vííŋ-ká   'long good thing'
     ʋ̀ wɔ̀gìrí mìŋ   'He is tall ("long").'
   b. jà-kʋ̀ʋ́ŋ   'old thing, elder'
     jà-kʋ̀ʋ̀-rí   'the old thing'
     kʋ̀ríŋ   'grow old'
     ʋ̀ kʋ̀rìm-á mìŋ   'He is growing old.'[14]

Both of these verbs have [-rɪ] as an extension, with *kʋrɪm* also having a stem-final nasal. With this limited amount of data, firm conclusions are hazardous, but in these cases, a suffix *-rɪ* meaning approximately 'to be/become X' is present in Kɔnni. Judging from the paucity of data with this pattern, it is likely that *-rɪ* is not synchronically active, but was active at an earlier stage of Kɔnni or its ancestor (though this apparent paucity may be attributable to a gap in my data).

The only other instance I have of a derived verb is *kpaalɪ* 'to be fatty' from *kpaaŋ* 'oil, fat'.

---

[14]Buli, the language most closely related to Kɔnni, has a similar situation, with two related but distinct adjectives meaning 'long': *wɔŋ, wɔgli,* and corresponding verbs *wɔŋa, wɔgla* (Kröger 1992). Also, there is the adjective 'old' *-kpak* with corresponding verb *kpagim.* In Buli as well as Kɔnni, derived verbs appear to be rare.

2.2 Verbal morphology

(87) kpáá-bú   'the fat'
    nɔ̀mbú **kpàà-lì**-yá mìŋ 'The meat is fatty.'

Whether the -*li* suffix is related to the -*ri* suffix above cannot be determined with this limited data.

In verbs, the final syllables -*ri*, -*li*, -*gi*, and -*si* are very common, and in at least some cases may be regarded as suffixal material. For example, *zie* and *zieli* are both used for 'stand,' with no obvious difference in meaning.

Comparative work with other Gur languages shows this is not an unusual situation. In Buli, Kröger (1992) surmises that di- and trisyllabic verbs are derived from monosyllabic ones, on the basis of the extremely limited range of final syllables in verbs (including the same -*ri*, -*li*, and -*si* as in Kɔnni), though he cannot assign a definite meaning to any "suffix." For Yom, Beacham (1968) notes that many polysyllabic verbs have /l/ or /g/ as final consonants, seemingly identical to some derivational suffixes, but cannot extract a clear pattern from the few examples in his data. Nawdm also has many verbs with suffixes which change the meaning to causative, inversive, or others (Nicole 1998), but there does not seem to be a consistent meaning per suffix there either. More specifically, for Mooré, Peterson (1971:46–48) gives examples of suffixes -*se*, -*ge*, -*le*, -*di* which can change a verb to causative, transitive, repetitive, and so forth. Natɛni, discussed in Neukom (1995), has a much more extensive and coherent system of verbal extensions with -*k*- being ingressive/inchoative, -*n*- being transitive, -*t*- being reversative, and so on.[15]

In a discussion of Gur languages in general, Naden (1989) labels these added verbal segments as "consonantal extensors," which may derive categories such as causative, reversative, or repetitive in various Gur languages. He notes the system is well developed in some but not all Gur languages. He also comments that the meanings associated with a particular extensor are not very consistent between languages. The Kɔnni examples below show that there is no systematic relationship between the extensors and their meaning.

(88) a. Roots and extended roots with same meanings
    dʊa, dʊagɪ   'lie down'
    lagɪŋ, lagɪsɪ   'gather'
    ŋmɪ, ŋmɪlɪ   'make rope'
    tuu, tuuli   'dig'
    zie, zieli   'stand'

---

[15]Brian Joseph reminds me that this situation also has a parallel in Indo-European, where so-called "root extensions" exist which are synchronically purely formal elements, but which are assumed to have had some real function at an earlier stage.

b. Roots and extended roots with related meanings
ba, balɪ	'say, tell'
bʊgɪ, bʊgʊrɪ	'soothsay, learn'
gɪrɪ, gɪrɪgɪ	'surround/fence in, be crowded'
hagɪ, hagɪrɪ	'get up, be strong'
la, lalɪ	'smile/laugh, play'
lam, lansɪ	'taste, lick'
mʊgɪ, mʊgɪsɪ	'suck (object wholly within mouth, partly within)'
ɲmʊ, ɲmʊrɪ	'squeeze/wring, dent/bend'
ɲɪɪ, ɲɪɪsɪ	'swallow, show teeth (not smile)'
puo, puori	'divide, cut open'
su, sugi, suguri, suuli	'put inside, dip, wash, be full'
vii, vigi, viiri, vili, visi	'repeat, shake, return, weave, fan'

These "verbal extensors" are quite likely not synchronically productive morphemes in present-day Kɔnni, but judging from the comparative data they were productive suffixes at some stage in Proto-Gur.

2.3 Modifiers

Modifiers, specifically demonstratives and numbers, seem to be the only class of words in Kɔnni which have any sort of agreement with another class of words. Besides the difference in morphosyntactic behavior, these modifiers differ from adjectives in that the modifiers are all quantitative, referring to specific numbers or quantitative concepts such as 'all' or 'some' rather than qualitative concepts like adjectives 'big', 'white', etc. (Recall that adjectives are suffixes—not independent words.) These are separate words, as shown by their occurrence in the subject or object position of sentences where noun phrases normally occur.

(89) a. **kààní** wóndè
 one this.is
 'This is (another) one.'

  b. **bataŋ** dɪ chɪga
 some then run
 'Others then run.'

2.3 Modifiers

    c. be   yiwo **bu-lie**
       they are   AGR-two
       'They are two (there are two of them).'

Since these modifiers can fill the syntactic positions of noun phrases as above, it is reasonable to ask if these may in fact be nouns. The modifiers differ from the usual Kɔnni nouns in at least two systematic ways. First, they take none of the morphology of normal nouns, that is, the suffixes. Second, a sequence of two nouns in Kɔnni will be either in an appositional relationship, as the pronouns in *ŋgbáŋ ǹ dígí ɲìndìkké* 'myself, I cooked food', or in an associative relationship, as in *gbàáŋ náŋ* 'dog's leg'. The appositional relationship is not tenable for a noun-modifier phrase, since the modifier limits its connected noun rather than repeating the same referent, as the appositional phrase does. In an associative relationship, the second noun always has a High tone on its first syllable. The forms here do not exhibit this tonal pattern. In short, if these modifiers are nouns, they are a different type than the usual nouns. We may just call them "eccentric nouns," with some but not all the properties of nouns, or we may say the constructions in (89) include modifiers in headless noun phrases.[16]

The specific form of the demonstrative 'a certain', and its plural 'some' is somewhat related to the form of the definite article of the noun class of the noun it modifies. Recall that the singular determiner 'the' has several forms depending on its noun class.

(90) | Noun class | Singular determiner | | |
| --- | --- | --- | --- |
| 1 | -rI | dàà-rí | 'the day' |
| 2 | -kU | dàà-kú | 'the stick' |
| 3 | -kA | gbàà-ká | 'the dog' |
| 4 | -bU | sàà-bú | 'the porridge' |
| 5 | -wA | bùà-wá | 'the child' |

The word 'one, a certain' does not have five distinct forms, corresponding exactly to the articles in (90), but it does have three forms which differ in the prefix attached to the root *-ní/-ɲí*. The first three noun classes all take the same form *kaa-nɪ*, while the forms for noun classes 4 and 5 have prefixes *bU-* and *wU-* which closely resemble the singular definite articles for words in their noun class *bU-* and *-wA* (compare 90 and 91).

---

[16]An example of a headless NP in English is the bolded portion of "You take the red pen and I'll take **the blue**." My thanks to Arnold Zwicky for these possible alternative ways of viewing these modifiers.

(91) NC 1   dàáŋ !káá-ní   'a certain day' (kàà-ɲí in Nagbiasi section)
     NC 2   dàáŋ !káá-ní   'a certain stick'
     NC 3   gbàáŋ !káá-ní 'a certain dog'
     NC 4   sàám !bʊ́-ɲí   'a certain porridge'[17]
     NC 5   bʊ̀á !wʊ́-ɲí   'a certain child'

Similarly, the plurals translated 'some' have forms which vary. The plural definite articles, however, do not correspond to the prefixes in 'some' at all, with the exception of noun class 5 -ba.

(92) Noun class   Plural determiner
     1   -hA-   yí!sé-hé   'the sheep (PL)'
     2   -tI   dàátì-tí   'the sticks'
     3   -sI   gbààsí-sí   'the dogs'
     4   -tI   kpáátí-tí   'the oils'
     5   -bA   zʊ̀àlí-!bá   'the friends'

(93) NC 1   yísè à-tâŋ   'some sheep'
     NC 2–3 *no nonhuman data available*
     NC 4   kpáám !bʊ́-tâŋ   'some oils'
     NC 5   bàllí !bá-tâŋ   'some children'
     NC 3   vʊ̀òsí !bá-tâŋ   'some people'

The only correlation between the prefix for 'some' and definite plural suffixes is the -ba suffix of noun class 5. This correlates with the ba- prefix used with humans, either in noun class 5 or in another noun class if the referent is human, as in *vʊ̀òsí !bá-tâŋ* 'some people' in (93), where *vʊ̀òsí* 'people' is a member of noun class 3. The semantics of humanness requires *ba-taŋ* independent of morphological noun class.

Although nouns fall into five basic classes, there is only a three-way distinction in agreement prefixes in Kɔnni modifiers. Furthermore, of these three, the prefix *bʊ-* is not heard much and may be disappearing from the language. For example, *tííŋ* 'medicine' is a class 4 mass noun, but one usually hears *tííŋ !káání* rather than *tíím !bʊ́ɲí*, the more specific modifier. What remains common in Kɔnni is a basic distinction between human and nonhuman in these modifiers. In the same way, the independent pronoun *bU* is quite uncommon, even when the noun used comes from the appropriate

---

[17]The close resemblance between the demonstratives *bʊ́-ɲí* and *wʊ́-ɲí*, together with the former's occurrence after a nasal in the data in (91), may lead to speculation that the former is a case of postnasal hardening, but this is not the case. There is no such process in the Kɔnni language.

noun class. The more neutral *ka* is generally used as the third-person nonhuman singular pronoun.[18]

Numbers also have agreement prefixes which differ according to whether the noun under consideration denotes a human or nonhuman referent. There are two prefixes used for nonhuman subjects. At this point, I do not know what determines the use of *a-* rather than *aba-*, or if they are in free variation. The prefix *ba-*, however, is always used with human referents. The prefixes are:

(94) **a-** as in: gbààsá !á-nísà 'four dogs'
 aba- as in: kpíbíè **àbá**-tà 'three lice'
 ba- as in: dembisi **ba**-ta 'three men'

I also have two cases of *bu-* used as prefix to a number (*bu-lie* 'two') in my database of texts. These are both from the village of Nangurima, which tends to be more conservative in its language use, preserving older forms.

2.4 Concluding observation

One interesting observation from the preceding sections is that the pronoun system exhibits divisions which are different in different subsystems. In the imperfective aspect, first- and second-person subjects have one tonal pattern, and third-person subjects have another. (See also (75) for the same pattern for the perfective aspect.) This may be summarized as third person versus nonthird person.

The indirect imperative, on the other hand, splits the forms into first-person subjects versus second- and third-person subjects, each exhibiting its distinctive tonal pattern, as in (80). This may be summarized as first person versus nonfirst person.

Finally, in noun class 5, the words for "father" and "mother" have different forms according to the person of the possessor. First-person and second-person singular possessors take one form, and second-person plural and third-person possessors take another form, as in (44).

To sum up, there are at least three different classes of person/number splits.

---

[18]The noun class system of the closely related Buli has retained a much closer correlation between definite suffixes, independent pronouns, and demonstrative prefixes. See Kröger (1992) for a survey of Buli noun classes and their morphology, and Cahill (1997b) for a reconstruction of the Proto-Buli-Kɔnni noun class system.

(95) Construction: Person/number split
    imperfective and perfective aspects   3 versus non-3
    indirect imperative   1 versus non-1
    'father/mother' possessor   2s and 1s versus 2p and 3

3
Phonotactics and Syllables

Goldsmith (1997:135) makes the point that phonologists, in their concentration on selected aspects of a language, often do not attempt to develop a complete description of a language, which would include, for example, the most commonly occurring phonemes and sequences of a language. This chapter is devoted to at least partially rectifying this situation for one language. The data presented in this chapter is also relevant to discussions about markedness and positional faithfulness.

3.1 Relative frequency of phonemes

Here I present the relative frequency of occurrence of the phonemes of Kɔnni. To tabulate this information, I extracted all words in my SHOEBOX lexical database, with the exception of ideophones and interjections; this gave a database of 1,650 words. (Ideophones and interjections often have different phonologies than other words, e.g., *pabap* 'quickly', which has a [p] word finally, and *pai* 'hard', which has an otherwise unattested diphthong.) I used citation forms only, with no duplication due to plural and definite forms of nouns, for example. So these counts are a measure of how productive each phoneme is in forming distinct words. I inserted spaces between each character, re-combining digraphs such as *kp, ie, aa*. Finally, I ran a word count using SIL's WDL (WORDLIST) program. The results with vowels are presented in (96).

(96) Vowel frequency
Short vowels			Long vowels/diphthongs	
952	ɪ	(325 are word final)	248	aa
651	a		105	ɪɪ
435	i	(142 are word final)	84	ʊʊ
286	ʊ		80	ɪa
127	u		71	ʊa
110	ɔ		46	ie
104	e		43	ii
74	o		41	uo
27	ɛ		39	uu

Because [-ɪ/-i] is the epenthetic vowel (see section 5.5), this affects the high number of occurrences of ɪ and i which are word final. In my count of "word final," I did not include monosyllabic stems such as di 'eat', for which the final -i is part of the stem. If one is looking for frequency in stems, these word-final occurrences, almost all in verbs, would be winnowed out. Since ATR is a morpheme-level feature (see section 5.2), combining vowels which differ only in ATR gives a slightly different view of the frequencies and reveals an additional pattern.

(97) Vowel frequency, combining ATR values
Short vowels			Long vowels/diphthongs	
1387	ɪ/i	(467 are word final)	248	aa
651	a		148	ɪɪ/ii
413	ʊ/u		126	ɪa/ie
184	ɔ/o		123	ʊʊ/uu
131	ɛ/e		112	ʊa/uo

Examining the short vowels, the vowel /I/ (that is, [ɪ/i]) is clearly the most frequent, even if we subtract the word-final epenthetic occurrences. The vowels /a/ and /U/ are next, with the mid vowels /O/ and /E/ trailing far behind. For short vowels, then, the high and low vowels, which occupy the extremes of the vowel space, are by far the most frequent in Kɔnni. However, we find a distinctly different pattern for the long vowels. For these, /aa/ is definitely the most frequent, but the others are packed fairly close together, with /ɪɪ/ perhaps having a slight lead. Obviously, lengthening the vowels largely neutralizes the frequency differential found in short vowels. Presumably the extra duration of long vowels allows time for the more marked ones to be correctly perceived by the listener. When duration is shorter, the vowel has a greater chance of being

3.1 Relative frequency of phonemes

mis-perceived and reinterpreted as one of the less-marked vowels, a high or low one.

Another bit of information we can extract from (97) is the relative frequency of [+ATR] versus [−ATR] vowels. [+ATR] vowels are *i, e, o, u,* with long vowels/diphthongs *ii, ie, uo, uu,* while [−ATR] vowels and diphthongs are *ɪ, ɛ, a, ɔ, ʊ, ɪɪ, ɪa, ʊa, ʊʊ*. For short vowels, there are 2,026 [−ATR] vowels and 740 [+ATR] vowels. For long vowels, there are 588 [−ATR] vowels and 169 [+ATR] vowels. Totaling these, the 2,614 [−ATR] vowels are 74.2 percent of the total, and the 909 [+ATR] vowels are 25.8 percent of the total number of vowels.

We turn next to consonants. These results were obtained with the same methodology as the vowels.

(98) Consonant frequency

808	ŋ	(712 are word final, 620 in nouns)	114	w
383	n		110	y
329	s		110	kp
318	t		89	j
302	r		76	ɲ
298	l		73	gb
297	g		70	p
282	b		59	v
238	m		57	h
211	k		42	ŋm
160	d		33	f
117	ch		31	z

Similar to the case with the vowels *ɪ/i*, I note here the number of occurrences of *ŋ* which are word final. This is important because *ŋ* is the singular suffix for four of the five noun classes in Kɔnni (see section 2.1.1). Also, *ŋ* is the only consonant allowed utterance finally (the dictionary form of the word is the citation form, which is utterance final). Again, if one is looking for frequency in roots, these occurrences would be winnowed out, leaving *ŋ* as one of the less-frequent phonemes of Kɔnni.

Also relevant to the nasal counts are prevocalic versus preconsonantal positions, since a nasal assimilates in place to whatever consonant follows it. Of the ninety-six occurrences of *ŋ* which are not word final, only thirty-three are prevocalic; the other sixty-three are a result of place assimilation. Other nasals do not occur word finally, so all their occurrences have either a vowel or consonant following. For *n*, of the 383 occurrences, 207 are prevocalic and the other 176 are a result of place assimilation. For *m,* of the 238 occurrences, 148 are prevocalic and the other ninety are a result of place assimilation.

One noteworthy pattern is the frequency of coronal consonants. With *ŋ* removed from top position, the top five positions on the list are occupied by coronals, and if the frequencies of *d* and *r* are combined,[1] then every coronal except *z* is more frequent than any non-coronal. The high frequency of coronals cross-linguistically has been frequently noted and connected to the view that coronals are the most unmarked place of articulation (Paradis and Prunet 1991, Hume 1992, extensive discussion of the issues in Rice 1999, and arguments for pharyngeal as more unmarked than coronal in Lombardi 2002).

3.2 Co-occurrences

In this section, I present charts of co-occurrences for both consonants and vowels. These will include vowels co-occurring with consonants and consonants with consonants. The main story with vowel co-occurrences is in the area of vowel harmony, which is discussed in section 5.2.

3.2.1 Vowels and consonants

In this section, I present tables showing which vowels can occur with which consonants. I have broken this into two categories: word-initial syllable, and noninitial syllable of a word. Since there are more disyllabic words in Kɔnni than other polysyllabic words, in most cases noninitial is the second and word-final syllable.

Each cell in the following tables gives the absolute number of cases of that co-occurrence, and in a smaller italicized font, the ratio of actual to expected cases. For example, the cell that indicates cases of word-initial *pi* is at the top left corner of the table in (99). There are 111 cases of word-initial short *i* in Kɔnni, as shown by the total at the bottom of the column. If these were evenly distributed over the twenty-three word-initial consonants, we would expect $111/23 = 4.83$ cases of short *i* per consonant. For *pi*, there are only 2. So the actual 2 divided by the expected 4.83 gives 0.414, which I round to the nearest tenth and record as 0.4. All ratios are rounded to the nearest tenth. If a ratio is nonzero but would round to zero, I record it as 0.1 to distinguish it from the absolute zeros. A number greater than 1.0 indicates greater than expected frequency, while a number less than 1.0 indicates less than

---

[1] Though I analyze *d* and *r* as separate phonemes in this work, they were almost certainly allophones of /d/ in an earlier stage of Kɔnni. See discussion in section 4.2.3.

3.2 Co-occurrences

expected frequency. These ratios must be interpreted with caution, especially when the total number of occurrences of the vowel in question is low, as in the extreme case of ɛ, which has only thirteen occurrences. Any actual occurrence will be higher than the expected 0.56 instantiations of ɛ per consonant, and so while the presence or absence of a co-occurrence may be important, the actual numbers are not.

Since some of the borrowed words and ideophones were culled from this set, the total numbers of vowels in these tables are slightly smaller than the totals in (96). Some patterns are distinguishable: /ch, j, kp, gb, y/ occur more frequently before front vowels, /k, v, w/ more frequently before back vowels, /h/ almost exclusively before /a/. In noninitial position, the patterns are consistent with these, but not so clear. One difference is that /r/ is most frequent before front vowels.

(99) Occurrences of short vowels with consonants
   a. Word-initial position (since *r* is never word-initial, it is omitted here)

	i	ɪ	e	ɛ	a	ɔ	o	ʊ	u
p	2	2	2	–	16	4	3	1	5
	0.4	0.3	1.0	0	0.7	1.2	1.9	0.2	1.5
b	14	11	2	–	36	10	3	12	6
	2.9	1.4	1.0	0	1.7	3.0	1.9	2.0	1.7
t	8	16	2	1	40	6	4	11	7
	1.7	2.0	1.0	1.8	1.9	1.8	2.5	1.9	2.0
d	4	6	6	2	66	6	–	7	4
	0.8	0.8	3.1	3.5	3.1	1.8	0	1.2	1.2
ch	6	13	1	2	8	3	–	5	4
	1.2	1.6	0.5	3.5	0.4	0.9	0	0.8	1.2
j	7	20	2	1	11	1	1	3	–
	1.5	2.5	1.0	1.8	0.5	0.3	0.6	0.5	0
k	1	1	4	–	36	17	5	14	7
	0.2	0.1	2.1	0	1.7	5.1	3.1	2.4	2.0
g	4	14	4	–	19	–	2	7	2
	0.8	1.8	2.1	0	0.9	0	1.2	1.2	0.6
kp	9	3	7	2	29	–	2	2	–
	1.9	0.4	3.7	3.5	1.3	0	1.2	0.3	0
gb	4	7	1	–	16	–	–	–	–
	0.8	0.9	0.5	0	0.7	0	0	0	0
f	–	5	1	–	2	–	3	1	1
	0	0.6	0.5	0	0.1	0	1.9	0.2	0.3

Word-initial position (continued)

	i	ɪ	e	ɛ	a	ɔ	o	ʊ	u
s	14	23	5	–	12	3	4	28	7
	2.9	2.9	2.6	0	0.6	0.9	2.5	4.7	2.0
z	–	3	2	–	3	–	–	2	2
	0	0.4	1.0	0	0.1	0	0	0.3	0.6
h	–	–	–	–	29	4	1	–	–
	0	0	0	0	1.3	1.2	0.6	0	0
l	3	–	1	1	13	4	–	2	1
	0.6	0	0.5	1.8	0.6	1.2	0	0.3	0.3
m	2	14	1	–	10	2	–	12	6
	0.4	1.8	0.5	0	0.5	0.6	0	2.0	1.7
n	11	13	1	–	39	2	–	3	9
	2.3	1.6	0.5	0	1.8	0.6	0	0.5	2.6
ŋ	–	–	–	–	1	1	–	–	–
	0	0	0	0	0.1	0.3	0	0	0
ŋm	3	7	–	–	7	–	–	1	–
	0.6	0.9	0	0	0.3	0	0	0.2	0
ɲ	4	14	–	–	5	–	–	3	1
	0.8	1.8	0	0	0.2	0	0	0.5	0.3
y	9	9	2	4	15	6	–	4	3
	1.9	1.1	1.0	7.1	0.7	1.8	0	0.7	0.9
w	1	1	–	–	18	6	6	14	11
	0.2	0.1	0	0	0.8	1.8	3.7	2.4	3.2
Total	111	182	44	13	496	76	37	136	79

b. Noninitial syllable position

	i	ɪ	e	ɛ	a	ɔ	o	ʊ	u
p	–	–	–	–	14	1	1	1	2
	0	0	0	0	1.2	1.0	0.8	0.3	1.0
b	42	2	3	1	24	3	8	13	2
	3.1	0.1	1.2	3.0	2.0	3.0	6.6	3.7	1.0
t	21	62	4	–	23	1	–	3	4
	1.6	2.0	1.6	0	1.9	1.0	0	0.8	2.0
d	8	3	6	1	7	–	–	–	3
	0.6	0.1	2.5	3.0	0.6	0	0	0	1.5
r	47	165	6	1	21	1	1	7	9
	3.5	5.3	2.5	3.0	1.7	1.0	0.8	2.0	4.6

3.2 Co-occurrences

Noninitial syllable position (continued)

	i	ɪ	e	ɛ	a	ɔ	o	ʊ	u
ch	1	9	–	1	5	1	–	–	–
	0.1	0.3	0	3.0	0.4	1.0	0	0	0
j	2	3	1	–	6	–	–	–	1
	0.1	0.1	0.4	0	0.5	0	0	0	0.5
k	10	16	6	–	15	8	6	9	6
	0.7	0.5	2.5	0	1.2	8.0	5.0	2.5	3.1
g	45	115	7	–	20	–	6	28	6
	3.4	3.7	2.9	0	1.7	0	5.0	7.9	3.1
kp	2	–	6	–	16	–	–	1	–
	0.1	0	2.5	0	1.3	0	0	0.3	0
gb	2	2	–	–	19	–	–	–	1
	0.1	0.1	0	0	1.6	0	0	0	0.5
f	–	1	–	–	4	–	1	–	1
	0	0.1	0	0	0.3	0	0.8	0	0.5
v	1	1	–	–	1	1	3	1	1
	0.1	0.1	0	0	0.1	1.0	2.5	0.3	0.5
s	48	127	4	–	16	2	–	8	1
	3.6	4.1	1.6	0	1.3	2.0	0	2.3	0.5
z	–	–	–	–	–	–	–	1	2
	0	0	0	0	0	0	0	0.3	1.0
h	–	–	–	–	6	2	–	–	–
	0	0	0	0	0.5	2.0	0	0	0
l	63	144	9	2	15	4	–	–	2
	4.7	4.7	3.7	6.0	1.2	4.0	0	0	1.0
m	13	39	1	–	18	–	–	1	3
	1.0	1.3	0.4	0	1.5	0	0	0.3	1.5
n	4	34	3	1	22	–	–	4	1
	0.3	1.1	1.2	3.0	1.8	0	0	1.1	0.5
ŋ	10	8	–	–	8	–	–	1	–
	0.7	0.3	0	0	0.7	0	0	0.3	0
ŋm	1	4	–	1	5	–	–	–	–
	0.1	0.1	0	3.0	0.4	0	0	0	0
ɲ	–	3	1	–	1	–	–	–	–
	0	0.1	0.4	0	0.1	0	0	0	0
y	1	5	1	–	11	–	–	–	–
	0.1	0.2	0.4	0	0.9	0	0	0	0
w	–	–	–	–	13	–	3	5	2
	0	0	0	0	1.1	0	2.5	1.4	1.0
Total	321	743	58	8	290	24	29	85	47

(100) Co-occurrences of long vowels with consonants
   a. Word-initial position

	ii	ıı	ie	ıa	aa	ʋa	uo	ʋʋ	uu
p	4 3.0	– 0	– 0	1 0.4	4 0.5	1 0.5	3 2.2	3 1.3	– 0
b	1 0.7	6 1.8	– 0	5 2.2	3 0.4	3 1.5	– 0	2 0.9	2 1.3
t	1 0.7	9 2.7	1 0.7	8 3.5	15 2.0	5 2.5	3 2.2	6 2.6	9 5.9
d	5 3.7	2 0.6	6 4.5	2 0.9	30 3.9	4 2.0	– 0	4 1.7	3 2.0
ch	4 3.0	8 2.4	– 0	12 5.2	8 1.0	4 2.0	– 0	3 1.3	2 1.3
j	1 0.7	4 1.2	– 0	– 0	5 0.7	2 1.0	4 2.9	2 0.9	– 0
k	– 0	– 0	2 1.5	– 0	9 1.2	7 3.5	2 1.4	4 1.7	1 0.7
g	– 0	– 0	1 0.7	– 0	7 0.9	1 0.5	2 1.4	1 0.4	3 2.0
kp	1 0.7	4 1.2	– 0	5 2.2	10 1.3	– 0	1 0.7	– 0	– 0
gb	– 0	2 0.6	2 1.5	1 0.4	4 0.5	1 0.5	– 0	– 0	– 0
f	– 0	– 0	– 0	3 1.3	1 0.1	1 0.5	– 0	1 0.4	– 0
v	2 1.5	5 1.5	– 0	– 0	3 0.4	– 0	5 3.6	4 1.7	2 1.3
s	1 0.7	1 0.3	6 4.5	1 0.4	12 1.6	1 0.5	2 1.4	– 0	2 1.3
z	– 0	2 0.6	1 0.7	– 0	4 0.5	1 0.5	3 2.2	1 0.4	1 0.7
h	– 0	– 0	2 1.5	– 0	6 0.8	1 0.5	– 0	4 1.7	– 0
l	2 1.5	– 0	5 3.7	5 2.2	3 0.4	2 1.0	– 0	1 0.4	2 1.3
m	2 1.5	6 1.8	1 0.7	– 0	8 1.0	1 0.5	– 0	3 1.3	– 0
n	1 0.7	12 3.5	– 0	3 1.3	19 2.5	4 2.0	– 0	– 0	3 2.0
ŋ	– 0	– 0	– 0	– 0	2 0.3	– 0	– 0	– 0	– 0

3.2 Co-occurrences

Word-initial position (continued)

	ii	ɪɪ	ie	ɪa	aa	ʋa	uo	ʋʋ	uu
ŋm	–	4	–	–	5	–	–	1	–
	0	1.2	0	0	0.7	0	0	0.4	0
ɲ	3	5	2	1	6	1	–	9	–
	2.2	1.5	1.5	0.4	0.8	0.5	0	3.8	0
y	3	4	2	3	5	5	5	3	–
	2.2	1.2	1.5	1.3	0.7	2.5	3.6	1.3	0
w	–	4	–	3	7	1	2	2	5
	0	1.2	0	1.3	0.9	0.5	1.4	0.9	3.3
Total	31	78	31	53	176	46	32	54	35

b. Noninitial syllable position

	ii	ɪɪ	ie	ɪa	aa	ʋa	uo	ʋʋ	uu
p	–	–	–	–	–	1	2	–	–
	0	0	0	0	0	1.2	2.7	0	0
b	1	1	2	1	1	1	–	3	2
	3.0	1.3	5.3	0.9	0.4	1.2	0	3.1	8.0
t	1	1	1	1	7	4	3	–	2
	3.0	1.3	2.7	0.9	2.8	4.8	4.0	0	8.0
d	1	2	–	–	10	2	–	1	–
	3.0	2.5	0	0	4.0	2.4	0	1.0	0
r	–	–	–	–	2	–	–	–	–
	0	0	0	0	0.8	0	0	0	0
ch	2	1	–	9	1	1	2	1	–
	6.0	1.3	0	8.0	0.4	1.2	2.7	1.0	0
j	–	–	–	–	5	4	2	2	–
	0	0	0	0	2.0	4.8	2.7	2.1	0
k	–	–	–	–	3	3	4	4	–
	0	0	0	0	1.2	3.6	5.3	4.2	0
g	–	–	–	–	2	–	–	2	1
	0	0	0	0	0.8	0	0	2.1	4.0
kp	–	2	–	4	6	–	–	–	–
	0	2.5	0	3.6	2.4	0	0	0	0
gb	–	–	–	2	3	–	–	–	–
	0	0	0	1.8	1.2	0	0	0	0
f	–	1	–	1	1	–	–	–	–
	0	1.3	0	0.9	0.4	0	0	0	0
v	–	–	–	–	1	–	1	1	–
	0	0	0	0	0.4	0	1.3	1.0	0

Noninitial syllable position (continued)

	ii	ɪɪ	ie	ɪa	aa	ʋa	uo	ʊʊ	uu
s	–	–	3	1	1	–	–	–	–
	0	0	8.0	0.9	0.4	0	0	0	0
z	–	–	–	1	–	–	2	–	–
	0	0	0	0.9	0	0	2.7	0	0
h	–	–	–	–	2	–	–	1	–
	0	0	0	0	0.8	0	0	1.0	0
l	1	–	–	3	2	–	1	–	1
	3.0	0	0	2.7	0.8	0	1.3	0	4.0
m	–	1	1	–	3	–	–	2	–
	0	1.3	2.7	0	1.2	0	0	2.1	0
n	1	1	–	1	–	3	–	1	–
	3.0	1.3	0	0.9	0	3.6	0	1.0	0
ŋ	–	–	–	–	1	–	–	–	–
	0	0	0	0	0.4	0	0	0	0
ŋm	–	–	–	–	4	–	–	–	–
	0	0	0	0	1.6	0	0	0	0
ɲ	–	6	1	1	2	1	–	3	–
	0	7.6	2.7	0.9	0.8	1.2	0	3.1	0
y	1	2	1	2	–	–	1	1	–
	3.0	2.5	2.7	1.8	0	0	1.3	1.0	0
w	–	1	–	–	2	–	–	–	–
	0	1.3	0	0	0.8	0	0	0	0
Total	8	19	9	27	59	20	18	23	6

3.2.2 Consonants and consonants

In this section, I give co-occurrences of consonants separated by a vowel. For which consonant clusters are allowed, see section 3.4. The table in (101) excludes forms with the reduplicative prefix CV which replicates the first consonant of a verb stem. In this table, the presence of the relevant co-occurrence is marked with "x" and no attempt has been made to make finer distinctions.

Not many patterns of co-occurrences or restrictions reveal themselves in this table. One, however, is that the labial-velars /kp, gb, ŋm/ never follow a labial consonant (including other labial-velars), though they can follow a velar one. Since labial-velars are not common in C_2 position, this pattern must be interpreted cautiously.

3.3 Distribution of consonants and vowels

(101) Co-occurrences of consonants C_1VC_2
(C$_1$ is in the left column; C$_2$ is read from the top line)

	p	b	t	d	r	ch	j	k	g	kp	gb	f	v	s	z	h	l	m	n	ŋ	ŋm	ɲ	y	w
p		x	x			x							x				x	x	x	x			x	x
b	x	x		x	x		x	x					x				x	x	x	x		x	x	x
t		x	x	x	x			x	x	x		x					x	x	x	x			x	
d		x	x		x			x	x						x		x	x	x	x			x	x
ch		x	x				x	x					x				x	x	x	x	x		x	
j		x	x	x	x			x	x	x	x	x	x				x	x	x	x	x		x	
k	x	x	x			x	x	x	x	x			x				x	x	x	x		x		x
g		x	x			x	x	x	x	x	x		x				x	x	x	x	x	x	x	
kp		x	x			x	x	x					x				x	x	x	x				x
gb		x	x	x				x									x		x	x		x		
f		x		x				x						x			x							
v		x	x	x				x	x					x	x	x	x	x	x					
s		x		x			x	x	x				x				x	x	x	x	x	x		x
z		x	x					x						x	x			x	x	x			x	
h			x	x				x						x			x	x	x	x		x		
l		x	x				x		x					x				x	x	x	x			
m			x	x				x						x	x		x	x	x	x				
n		x	x		x	x		x	x	x				x		x		x	x	x				
ŋ		x												x			x	x	x	x				
ŋm		x		x										x				x	x					
ɲ			x				x							x				x	x	x			x	
y		x		x				x						x			x		x	x				x x
w		x	x	x				x						x		x	x		x			x	x	x

The co-occurrences listed are within single stems; since verbs can take suffixes beginning with *n, m, y, w*, and the noun class suffixes begin with *b, r, t, s, k, ŋ*, all consonants can be followed by these sounds in these cases.

3.3 Distribution of consonants and vowels

In this section, the restrictions on consonants and vowels within words are presented.

3.3.1 Word-final position

One restriction which is pervasive in Kɔnni is that the only utterance-final consonant allowed in the language is [ŋ] (except for a few ideophones). Nasals are the only consonants allowed word finally, and if they are followed by another word, then the nasal assimilates in place to the initial consonant of that word. Alternations in some verbal forms show that the verb stem ends in /m/, as in (102a), where the imperfective suffix /-a/ has been added to the verb stem. However, the verb in isolation surfaces with a final [ŋ].

(102) a. ʊ̀ tʊ̀m-á mìŋ   'S/he is working.'
      b. tʊŋ   'work (verb)'

We have two distinct but interrelated patterns to account for here: that nasals are the only consonants allowed word finally, and that ŋ is the only nasal allowed utterance finally. In Optimality Theory terms, various faithfulness constraints would come into play to prevent the deletion of a word-final nasal or its change to a nonnasal. I assume the existence of such constraints, but will not discuss them here. What I will discuss in this volume is the change of place of the word-final nasal. Assimilation of the nasal to the place of the following consonant is discussed in section 4.2.1, and in this section I discuss the neutralization of word-final nasals to ŋ when they occur utterance finally. To account for this in Optimality Theory, a constraint that bans all consonants except ŋ from utterance-final position is needed.

(103) ŋ//: ŋ is the only consonant licensed utterance finally

This constraint is a shorthand for a number of constraints banning all other consonants from utterance-final position. Thus ŋ// should be understood as a conflation of the constraints *p// (where // stands for utterance boundary), *b//, *m//, *t//, etc. These other constraints would all be undominated, while *ŋ// is ranked low, allowing ŋ to occur utterance finally.

A question that arises is, why ŋ in this position and not some other nasal? The [coronal] place is generally regarded as the most unmarked one (and both consonantal and vowel epenthesis in Kɔnni generally support this-see sections 4.5 and 5.5); why a [dorsal] nasal rather than the [coronal] nasal *n*? Rather than framing the question in terms of features, the acoustic properties may be more relevant. As Ohala and Ohala (1993) point out, ŋ is a less distinct nasal than *n* or *m* by virtue of its having the tongue dorsum as articulator. The dorsum moves more slowly than lips or tongue tip and produces a less distinct transition in both amplitude and spectrum between vowels and the nasal. For this reason, in several languages ŋ postvocalically is confused with or alternates with nasalized vowels (Ohala and Ohala give references to Mixtec, Mbay, and French loanwords in Vietnamese). In an

3.3 Distribution of consonants and vowels

earlier work, Ohala (1975) also notes that the antiformant or zero of ŋ is located in the more attenuated higher frequencies of the spectrum, which makes it less perceptible as a nasal. The phonetic characteristics of ŋ, then, single it out as a more nondescript nasal than others.[2] It is key that it is only in word-final or postvocalic position that ŋ is so cross-linguistically common. Word initially it is rare in Kɔnni and nonexistent in English, but word finally it is common in both languages. The indistinct phonetic qualities of ŋ seem therefore to be most compatible with a noninitial position and thus provide at least the start of an explanation of why ŋ// is a reasonable constraint. Perception experiments might also shed additional light on this issue, but I have not investigated this area.

An illuminating tableau for /tUm/ → [tʊŋ] would also need at least the following constraints.

(104) MAX[lab]: a [labial] feature in the input has a correspondent in the output
DEP[dors]: a [dorsal] feature in the output has a correspondent in the input

(105) tʊŋ 'work' (verb)

tUm	ŋ//	MAX[lab]	DEP[dors]
☞ a. tʊŋ		*	*
b. tʊm	*!		

The winning candidate (105a) has replaced the [labial] place of the underlying /m/ with the [dorsal] ŋ. This involves deletion of the [labial] feature, violating MAX[lab], and insertion of a [dorsal] feature, violating DEP[dors]. However, the losing candidate (105b) violates the undominated ŋ//. Another way to avoid violating ŋ// is to delete the nasal altogether; this would violate faithfulness constraints prohibiting deletion of a consonant.

3.3.2 Roots versus suffixes

Affixes typically draw from a more restricted set of phonemes than roots do, and Kɔnni illustrates this cross-linguistic tendency. The suffixes of

[2] These phonetic characteristics also seem inconsistent with the phonological claim in Chomsky and Halle (1968) that of the nasals n, m, ŋ, that ŋ is the most marked. Foley (1975) argues that ŋ is the least marked consonant (not just least marked nasal) in Palauan, supporting it with several lines of evidence, including the fact that ŋ is the epenthetic consonant inserted to satisfy the constraint that words must begin and end in a consonant. For Japanese, it has been argued that word-final ŋ is actually placeless. (Vance 1987 gives several pages of discussion to this "moraic nasal" whose articulation is quite variable.)

Kɔnni listed exhaustively in (106) are far from containing all the consonants of the language.

(106) Suffixes in Kɔnni
  a.

Noun class	1	2	3	4	5
Singular	ŋ́	ŋ́	ŋ́	ŋ́	—
Singular definite	rí/rí	kú/kú	ké/ká	bú/bú	wó/wá
Plural	e/o/a	tí/tí	sí/sí	tí/tí	*irreg.*
Plural definite	hé/há	tí/tí	sí/sí	tí/tí	bé/bá

  b. Derivational suffixes (deriving nouns/adjectives from verbs)
        ŋ́   sí/sí   síŋ/síŋ rú/rú   kíŋ/kíŋ

  c. Verb aspects
     Perfective Imperfective Imperative imperfective Imperfective II
     yé/yá,   e/o/a   mé/má   ne/na
     wú/wá

One gap that stands out in the vowels is that the mid vowels [ɛ, ɔ] are not represented in any of the suffixes. As we will see in section 5.2.1, the cases of [e, o] in the a~e~o alternations above are derived from underlying /a/, and so the occurrences of *e, o* are not underlying. The result is that only high and low vowels, not mid ones, are present underlyingly in Kɔnni suffixes.

The consonantal inventory of affixes is also smaller than the full Kɔnni set. The suffixes above draw their consonants from the eleven-member set /b, r, h, k, m, n, ŋ, s, t, w, y/. Since Kɔnni has twenty-four consonantal phonemes, this is a considerable reduction. Probably not coincidentally, these eleven consonants are among the most common ones which occur as C_2 in the C_1VC_2 sequences tabulated in (101), and also in overall consonant frequencies tabulated in (98). Suffixal consonants are drawn only from the set /ŋ, r, b, t, s, k, h/ for nominals and /y, w, m, n/ for verbs. Interestingly, these are disjoint sets; the consonantal inventory in suffixes may be one way of distinguishing nouns and verbs.

These restrictions on vowel and consonants in roots and affixes can be captured by constraints which must refer crucially to position in the word as well as lexical category (N, V) and morphological category (stem, suffix). The common constraints referring to prohibition of individual segments (e.g., *g), will need to be divided into families as specifically as *g_{Nsuff}, *z_{Nsuff}, *kp_{Nsuff}... >> *$ŋ_{Nsuff}$, *d_{Nsuff}, *k_{Nsuff}... >> for noun suffixes and *g_{Vsuff}, *$ŋ_{Vsuff}$, *d_{Vsuff}... >> *y_{Vsuff}, *w_{Vsuff}, m_{Vsuff}, *n_{Vsuff} for verb suffixes. These constraints will account for distribution of sounds

3.3.3 Noun and verb structure

About half of the nouns in my database are monosyllabic or disyllabic, but I have found apparently monomorphemic nouns of up to five syllables and one of six syllables. Every consonantal phoneme in Kɔnni is found both word initially and word medially. This bare statement, however, conceals as much as it reveals. There seem to be no positional restrictions on vowels or consonants in nouns, but the situation is obscured by synchronic and diachronic compounding, in which the compound noun consists of two or more noun stems. For these compounds, one might more accurately speak of a particular consonant as being lexeme initial though not word initial.

For example, *gbágíchíá!rú* 'fisherman' is composed of the noun stem *gbagɪ* 'lake' and *chɪa* 'cut' plus the agentive suffix *-ru*. A fisherman, then, is literally a 'lake-cutter' ("cutting the lake" refers to a specific method of fishing). The sound *ch* is word internal but lexeme initial in this compound. This is the case with almost all instances of word-internal /ch/. Of the 116 words I have in my database containing *ch*, eighty-six have word-initial [ch]. Of the thirty which are word internal, eighteen can be identified as compounds through identification of at least one nominal component, as in *gbágíchíá!rú* 'fisherman'. Another one is borrowed, and two can be identified as historical compounds by the mix of ATR values, as in *mànchíŋ* 'blade of grass', which has both [−ATR] and [+ATR] vowels present. There is a good chance that the remaining nine words with internal *ch* were, at one time, compounds as well.

Even when the component parts of a noun cannot be identified at the present time, two diagnostics can show they were at one time compounds. The first is a mix of ATR values in vowels as above; *gaalluuŋ* 'cat' also has mixed ATR values. The second diagnostic is comparative work with Buli. Kröger (1992) lists the Buli cognate of Kɔnni *sùŋkpááŋ* 'peanut' as a compound, and one can see the components are also reasonable in Kɔnni: *sùmíŋ* 'Bambara bean' and *kpááŋ* 'oil'.[3] However, even with these tools, some suspect cases do not have any evidence to support their identity as a compound, past or present. Thus the picture of which consonants or vowels may occur stem internally in Kɔnni nouns has some unavoidable uncertainty. In addition, it is doubtful that the present-day Kɔnni speakers are aware of the etymology of words that were historically compounds; for present-day Kɔnni speakers, they are single lexemes.

---

[3] The Buli forms Kröger lists are *sumi* 'Bambara bean', *kpaam,* 'oil', and *suŋkpaam* 'peanut'.

The situation with verbs is clearer. The vast majority of verbs are mono- or disyllabic (420 out of 461 in my database), with none more than trisyllabic. There are no compound verbs, though the "extensors" /-rI, sI, lI, gI/ may have at one time been separate morphemes (see section 2.2.2 for discussion). There is an interesting pattern with vowels in verbs: almost all the vowels in the second and third syllables are *I*.

(107) Vowels in verbs (lexical form)

	Monosyllabic		Disyllabic		Trisyllabic	
a	ga	'go'	batɪ	'trap'	garɪsɪ	'pass'
ɛ	yɛ	'be small'	yɛsɪ	'carve'	——	
e	ye	'see'	kpesi	'observe'	kpegiri	'snap'
ɪ	yɪ	'give'	chɪgɪ	'run'	ɲɪgɪsɪ	'flash'
i	di	'eat'	pili	'unroll'	chigisi	'sift'
ɔ	dɔ	'lie down'	bɔbɪ	'tie'	mɔgɪsɪ	'measure'
o	to	'take'	fogi	'take apart'	forisi	'untie'
ʊ	kʊ	'kill'	bʊrɪ	'plant'	sʊrɪsɪ	'rub'
u	gu	'bury'	kuri	'pound'	furisi	'slurp'
					suguri	'wash'
					bʊgʊrɪ	'learn'

Any of the nine phonemic vowels may occur with monosyllabic verbs, as seen above. In disyllabic verbs, any of these vowels may occur in the first syllable, but the second is always *I*. In the trisyllabic verbs, almost any vowel (excepting *ɛ*, which is probably an accidental gap due to its low frequency in the language as a whole) may occur in the first syllable, and like disyllabic verbs, only *I* occurs in the last syllable. The only vowel that occurs in the middle syllable is also *I*, with the exception of the two forms at the bottom of (107) which have *U*. This *U* is analyzed in section 5.4.1 as a spreading of the [dorsal] feature across *g*. V_2 of the verb is *U* only when V_1 of the verb is *U* and there is an intervening *g*. It is thus predictable, and the final vowel in polysyllabic verbs is predictably *I*. The middle vowel of trisyllabic verbs is predictably either *I* or *U*. This leaves the first vowel of a verb as the only distinctive vowel, no matter what the length of the verb. A verb is thus specified in the lexicon for only one vowel.

Any consonant may occur word initially in a verb, but the set of consonants in C_2 or C_3 position is quite limited.

(108) Frequency of consonants in noninitial position in verbs
a. Consonants in C_2 position in verbs

	total	2-syllable	3-syllable
g	74	53	21
r	74	62	12
s	56	55	1
l	48	40	8
t	21	18	3
b	18	17	1
ŋ	6	6	0
m	3	0	3

b. Consonants in C_3 position in verbs

s	22
r	8
g	5
l	2

c. NC clusters in verbs (all in disyllabic ones)

ns	14
nt	10
ŋŋ	2

The consonants in C_3 position are the same ones discussed as verbal "extensors" not only in Kɔnni, but in related languages as well (see section 2.2.2). Note that these are also the ones which are by far most frequent in C_2 position in (108a). These were therefore quite likely multimorphemic at an earlier stage of Kɔnni or its ancestor language, but are not at the present day.

Besides the above, there are ten verbs in my data which in citation form all end in -ŋ, but when followed by the imperfective suffix /-A/, manifest themselves as [m], e.g., tʋŋ 'work', ʋ̀ tʋ̀má mìŋ 's/he is working'. These are nasal-final verbs. There is also at least one case where there is an n~ŋ alternation: (ɲʋŋ 'go out' ʋ̀ ɲùná mìŋ 's/he is going out'. All three cases of m in (108a) are in trisyllabic verbs, e.g., kpamɪsɪ 'fold'.

3.4 Consonant clusters

Vowel clusters are limited to two vowels and these follow the patterns for diphthongization given in section 5.3. The situation with consonant clusters is more involved. Consonant clusters occur in two situations. The first is a nasal-consonant cluster, which may occur either within a morpheme or across a morpheme boundary (although I am starting to suspect that at some point in the historical development of Kɔnni all NC clusters were across morphemes). If a cluster does not involve a nasal, it is almost always a result of concatenation of morphemes. The exceptions to this are a few words with [ll], as in bùllɔ̀gìsíŋ 'wind', and the one case of [pp] I have found.[4] In the data in (109), in most cases a speaker can insert a vowel between the consonants of the cluster even in the cases I have labeled "obligatory," but this is only in very careful speech. In these cases of vowel insertion there is of course no consonantal assimilation. All obligatory clusters I am aware of are listed in (109a), while a sample of optional clusters is listed in (109b).

(109) Possible nonnasal consonant clusters in Kɔnni
    a. Obligatory clusters

r-t	→	tt	vɔ́t-tí	'holes' (cf. vɔ́ríŋ 'hole')
b-b	→	bb	kɔ̀b-bìŋ	'small bone'
g-k	→	kk	ɲìndìk-ké	'food'
g-g	→	gg	bɔ̀g-góbè	'long fibers'
N-r	→	nn	yàn-ní	'the frog'
l-r	→	ll	dàmpàl-lí	'the log'
g-kp	→	kkp	hɔ̀k-kpí!íŋ	'big woman'

    b. Optional clusters

g-h	→	kh	tìgì-háá!líŋ ~ tìk-háá!líŋ	'new village'[5]
g-b	→	gb[6]	tìgì-bíŋ ~ tìg-bíŋ	'small village'
g-s	→	ks	bùllɔ̀gìsíŋ ~ bùllɔ̀ksíŋ	'wind'
b-s	→	ps	bɔ́bísí ~ bɔ́psí	'head scarves'

---

    [4]There are two reasons for the scarcity of [pp]. The first reason is that *p in Proto-Buli-Kɔnni split into synchronic Kɔnni /y, w, h/. The phoneme /p/ does occur in present-day Kɔnni but as a result of borrowing (Cahill 1992b, 1995a, 1999b). Second, and possibly related to the first reason, many of the geminates [ll, kk, tt] appear in definite forms of nouns as a result of adding definite suffixes /-kU, -kA, -rI/ to nouns with consonant-final stems. There are no suffixes in Kɔnni containing /p/.

    [5]A discrepancy exists between the behavior of the words for 'village' and 'house', in that 'village' tolerates consonant clusters while 'house' does not.

tígí-háá!líŋ	'new house'	versus	tìk-háá!líŋ	'new village'
tígí-!kúúŋ	'old house'		tìk-kúúŋ	'old village'

This is an idiosyncratic property of the noun classes to which these belong. Noun class 3, to which 'village' belongs, does not epenthesize a vowel in these circumstances, while noun class 1, to which 'house' belongs, does. See discussion in section 4.3.1.

    [6]The [g-b] cluster here is phonetically distinct from the labial-velar stop [gb]. See footnote 21, chapter 4.

Concentrating on the obligatory clusters, the clear pattern is that clusters are obligatory in cases in which the consonants have the same place. They may differ in voicing or other features in the input, but the output is almost always a cluster of identical consonants. The exception is the *k-kp* cluster. In this cluster, *k* is [dorsal], and *kp* is both [dorsal] and [labial]. So even in this case, the consonants both have a place feature in common. That there is an ordering of the place features of *kp* is shown by the form *kɔ̀bì-kpí!íŋ* 'large bone', in which [b-kp] (or [p-kp] by voicing assimilation) is an impossible cluster. (Unfortunately, *kp* does not occur stem finally, so testing the consequences of a *kp* + *C* sequence is impossible.) This is summed up in the following constraint.

(110) $C_{iPL}C_{iPL}$: adjacent consonants must have the same place values

In a Feature Geometry (FG) framework, this constraint could be interpreted as requiring the two consonants to be multiply linked to a single place node, but I know of no specific evidence relating to this configuration, and in terms of FG, two identical place nodes linked to the adjacent consonants will also satisfy the constraint. This constraint will be violated in several specific contexts, which we will see later. The optional nonhomorganic clusters in (109b) are regarded as fast-speech phenomena and will not be discussed further. At this point, I will not demonstrate a tableau using this constraint, but it will be important in the discussion of vowel epenthesis in section 5.5.

3.5 Syllable structure

Surface syllable types are V, N, CV, CVC, CVN, CVV, and CVVN. The last three can stand as independent words in citation; the others need additional phonological material to be pronounceable.

(111) Syllable types

V	àlìbésà	'onion' (Hausa)	ànísà	'four'
N	ǹ dyààyá	'I forgot'	m̀ bììŋ	'my goat'
CV	bʊrɪ	'plant, sow'	bítíéŋ	'chin'
CVC	hàkkó	'the shell, the bark'	vɔ́ttí	'the hole'
	tìg-bíŋ	'small village'	yàltó	'hunter'
CVN	káŋ	'roan antelope'	dèmbíŋ	'man'
CVV	bùá	'child'	tʊʊsɪ	'pluck'
CVVN	dààŋ	'wood, stick'	gúúm!bú	'the rope'

The syllable types V and N are extremely limited in distribution. N is the first-person singular pronoun, used as either a subject pronoun or possessive pronoun. V comprises some subject pronouns, is the agreement marker on some numbers, and begins some borrowed words. CVC is found only at the concatenation of morphemes. The other syllable types are all common.

The nasals in the forms like *gúúm!bú* 'the rope' and others are shown to be codas rather than onsets to the next syllable (prenasalized stops) by several lines of evidence. First, the pitch on the nasal is always the same as the preceding vowel, showing that it does not comprise a tone-bearing unit (TBU) distinct from the preceding vowel (the syllable is shown to be the TBU in chapter 6). Second, prenasalized stops are never found in an unambiguous word-initial position. Third, syllable types like CVVN are found in isolation, as single words, as in the left column above, and thus coda nasals are shown to be possible.

When a syllabic nasal, as in (112a), follows another syllable, that nasal is desyllabified. (The difference in tonal patterns is discussed in section 6.4.1.7.) The hyphenated *-m* in (112b) is phonologically attached to the preceding word, but syntactically a separate word, as are all pronouns.

(112) a. m̀ búgó!r-á mìŋ
1s learn-IMPF AFF
'I am learning.'

b. dí-m !búgúrí
that-1s learn
'I should learn.'

c. dí !fí búgúrí
that 2s learn
'You should learn.'

Syllables with long vowels, including diphthongs, have a restricted distribution, in that there is usually a maximum of only one of these, either CVV or CVVN, allowed per word. A long vowel may be either in the first syllable, as in (113a), or later in the word, as in (113b). A long vowel is not required, of course; many words have no long vowel at all. In my database, I do have fifty-two words with two long-voweled syllables, as in (113c), but fifty-one of these words are compound, and the other one is borrowed. Thus a monomorphemic stem may contain only one long vowel.

(113) a. Long vowel or diphthong in first syllable
    bìíŋ   'goat'   dààŋ   'day, stick'
    bɪɪsɪ   'count'   haarɪ   'meet, reach'
    háá!gíŋ   'bush'   gbíábíŋ   'door'
    yíí!gíŋ   'tree (sp.)'   làálíŋ   'cockroach'
    chìàkùríŋ   'scorpion'   wúútúlíŋ   'stomach'

  b. Long vowel or diphthong in second syllable
    gbáríáŋ   'earthworm'   gbìɲùáŋ   'duck'
    há!nííŋ   'in-law'   dàyùúŋ   'rat'
    gùrá!áŋ   'lizard'   súkúúŋ   'morning'
    nánjúúŋ   'fly'   sìŋkpááŋ   'peanut'
    sìɲíí!ríŋ   'anger'   kùjààgíŋ   'sore'
    gàɲìàrà   'weaver bird'   jínjáámíŋ   'bat'

  c. Two long vowels or diphthongs
    dáá-chúáŋ   'alcohol pot (alcohol-pot)'
    júò-mììrú   'mason (room-builder)'
    níí-!búá   'upper grinding stone (grinding.stone-child)'
    wáá-kpí!íŋ   'python (snake-big)'

3.6 Minimality of nouns and verbs

Nouns and verbs in citation form in Kɔnni have a minimal size of one syllable with two moras, that is, either CVV or CVŋ. CVVŋ is also allowed. This and a constraint on tonal contours (section 6.4.1.1) is the only area I know of in which the mora has any relevance at all in Kɔnni. (In light of the lack of activity of a moraic unit elsewhere in Kɔnni, one might be excused for wondering if the mora is in fact the relevant quantity here.) With nouns, this is demonstrated by a simple lack of citation forms with fewer than two moras, while with verbs, there are actual alternations in vowel length.

Most nouns in citation form have a suffix -ŋ with the systematic exception of those in noun class 5 and a few forms in other noun classes (see section 2.1.1). Monosyllabic nouns which do not have this suffix all are CVV. A light syllable CV is attested as the final syllable of polysyllabic nouns such as kúrúbâ 'pot (sp.)' and gbárà 'bath sponge', as well as the derived agentive nouns such as dìdììrú 'eater', so there is no general prohibition against light syllables to end a noun in Kɔnni, but there does seem to be a prohibition against light syllables in isolation. Although many nouns have stems which consist of /CV-/, these all add the suffix -ŋ. So monosyllabic nouns in Kɔnni in citation form are all either CVŋ or CVV. There are no alternations of any of the nouns as far as the number of moras; the minimality requirement is shown by the simple lack of any forms which are less than CVV or CVŋ.

In contrast to nouns, monosyllabic verbs do show alternations in vowel length when in different morphosyntactic frames. When the verb stem stands alone as a word, either in citation form or in the future tense (e.g., ù nàn síé 's/he will dance'), the verb always surfaces as CVV; there are no cases of CV in this context. However, when a suffix is added, as in the imperfective II or perfective aspects, the verb stem is only CV-; there are no cases of CVV- in these contexts.

(114) Vowel length alternations in verbs in different contexts

Citation	Future	Impf. II	Perfective	
sie[7]	sie	se-ne	se-ye	'dance'
puo	puo	po-ne	po-ye	'divide'
dii	dii	di-ne	di-ye	'eat'
mɪɪ	mɪɪ	mɪ-na	mɪ-ya	'build'
taa	taa	ta-na	ta-ya	'throw'
hʊʊ	hʊʊ	hʊ-na	hʊ-wa	'swear'
tuu	tuu	tu-ne	tu-wo	'dig'

Monosyllabic verbs thus do not have a contrast in vowel length, although Kɔnni in general does have a contrast between long and short vowels (see section 5.1.1). Verbs can exhibit a contrast in long and short vowels (e.g., pili 'to roof' versus piili 'to start'), but this contrast is always in polysyllabic verbs.

---

[7]In 'dance' the lengthening of /e/ produces [ie] by a diphthongization process discussed in section 5.3. Likewise, a lengthened /o/ becomes [uo] in 'divide'.

4

Consonantal Phonology

4.1 Consonant inventory, contrasts, and measurements

4.1.1 Justification of contrasts

The phonemic consonants of Kɔnni are listed in (115). In this work, the symbols *r, ch, j,* and *y,* are used for typographical convenience, rather than the corresponding IPA symbols [ɾ, tʃ, ʤ, j].

(115) Consonantal phonemes of Kɔnni

	labial	alveolar	palatal	velar	labial-velar	glottal
stop	p b	t d		k g	kp gb	
affricate			ch j			
fricative	f v	s z				h
liquid		l r				
nasal	m	n	ɲ	ŋ	ŋm	
glide			y	w		

The phone [ɾ], an alveolar tap or flap, is in complementary distribution with [d] but is considered a separate phoneme for reasons discussed in section 4.2.3.

I group /w/ under the velar place of articulation because a nasal assimilates as [ŋ] before [w] (section 4.2.1). The glottal stop [ʔ] is not contrastive, but it occurs sometimes at the beginning of a vowel-initial utterance to keep vowels distinct in hiatus (sections 4.5 and 5.9) and often at the end of an emphatic utterance. There are five basic places of articulation (excluding h) as evidenced by the nasals in those places. Interestingly, stops occur at all these places except palatal, where the affricates *ch* and *j* occur. This is consistent with the assertion of many (e.g., Jakobson, Fant, and Halle 1952, Chomsky and Halle 1968, Rubach 1994, Steriade 1993, and Clements 1998) that affricates function as simple stops at the phonological level.

The consonants in (115) are shown to be contrastive by the following minimal and near-minimal pairs.

(116) Contrasts of consonants

	#Caa		#CII		#CUU	
p	páálíŋ	'swamp'	piili	'start'	pʊ̀ʊsíŋ	'a whisper'
b	baaŋ	'show'	bìíŋ	'goat'	bùúŋ	'fetish, god'
t	tá!áŋ	'shea tree'	tìíŋ	'tree'	tuuri	'mark a line'
d	dààŋ	'stick'	dííŋ	'forehead'	dùúŋ	'horse'
k	kááŋ	NEG.FUT	—	—	kùúŋ	'hoe'
g	gààŋ	'land'	—	—	gú!úŋ	'rope'
kp	kpááŋ	'oil'	kpììlíŋ	'thigh'	—	—
gb	gbààŋ	'dog'	gbìíŋ	'catfish'	—	—
ch	cháánʊ̀	'stranger'	chííŋ	'moon'	chùùríŋ	'diarrhea'
j	jààŋ	'thing'	jí!íŋ	'tree (sp.)'	jʊʊsi	'ask, request'
f	fááŋ	'baboon'	—	—	fʊʊsi	'blow'
v	vááŋ	'leaf'	viigi	'carry'	vuugi	'wriggle'
s	sààŋ	'porridge'	sí!íŋ	'a cold'	sʊʊŋ	'get down'
z	záá	'millet'	zììgíŋ	'center pole'	zùúŋ	'vulture'
l	làálíŋ	'cockroach'	lɪɪrɪ	'remove'	luuli	'break up'
m	maagi	'draw, write'	mìíŋ	'biting ant'	mʊʊlɪ	'announce'
n	nàáŋ	'chief'	nìíŋ	'net' or 'rain'	núúŋ	'arm'
ŋ	ŋaaŋ	BEEN	—	—	—	—
ŋm	ŋmáá!níŋ	'okra'	ŋmɪɪgɪ	'be weak'	ŋmʊʊrɪ	'dent, bend'
ɲ	ɲááŋ	'water'	ɲììlíŋ	'guinea worm'	ɲúúŋ	'chest'
w	waalɪ	'broadcast'	wííŋ	'problem'	wú!úŋ	'gennet'
y	yaalɪ	'find'	yí!íŋ	'nail, arrow'	yʊʊrɪ	'remove bark'
h	hààgíŋ	'bush'	—	—	hʊ̀úŋ	'grass'

All consonants contrast before *aa*, and most before *II* and *UU* as well. I regard the gap in the chart above where *fII* should be as accidental; /f/ is a relatively rare phoneme (see section 3.1). Similarly, the gap for *ŋUU* may be accidental, given the rarity of word-initial [ŋ]. However, the other gaps under *CII* and *CUU* can be traced to various historical developments. A sound change from Proto-Buli-Kɔnni to Kɔnni of *ŋII > ɲII removed any potential cases of ŋII. Almost every Kɔnni word containing the phoneme /h/ is a product of historical development from either *ŋ or *y before /a/. All these are documented in Cahill (1999b). The lack of kII and gII is also attributable to historical changes, though the picture here is not as clear. In the development of many Ghanaian languages, *k, g changed to ch, j before front vowels (e.g., the frozen spellings of {ky, gy} in Akan represent [tʃ, dʒ]). I assume something similar to this happened in the history of pre-Kɔnni, probably prior to Proto-Buli-Kɔnni (since Buli also has no kII or gII). The gap of kpUU and gbUU can be accounted for by the historical development of labial-velar stops from KU > Kw > KP, where KUU does not participate in such a change (languages having a gap of KPU are not unusual for this reason—see Cahill 1997a, 1999d). As expected from this scenario, kUU and gUU sequences are not uncommon in Kɔnni.

Some consonants have a contrast between singletons and geminates within words. These are limited to nasals, [l], and voiceless stops.[1] Geminate nasals and laterals are fairly common, as is the stop [kk], but I have only one case of [pp] and a few of [tt]. Geminate stops seem to occur only at morpheme boundaries, or what appear to have been boundaries at one time. These are discussed in the section on assimilation (4.2).

(117)	Geminates			Singletons	
k	súnǃsúkkú	'the middle'	kpààlì-kú	'the handle'
t	chàkùttú	'blacksmith'	gʊtɪ	'help'
p	ŋmárichíáǃppúríŋ	'speckled dove'	náǃpɔ̀ríŋ	'calf (leg)'
n	kàànní	'the cheek'	tàná	'stones'
m	chùmmá	'walk...'	kààmíŋ	'cheek'
ŋ	níŋŋá	'front'	gàŋìsí	'ribs'
l	búllɔ̀gíŋ	'bag'	kalɪ	'sit'

4.1.2 Phonetics: aspiration, prevoicing, and duration

Though this work is not a treatise on phonetics, in the interest of a fuller picture of Kɔnni, I note a few observations on the phonetics of stops in Kɔnni. Similar observations could be made of other consonants, but stops are the only consonant types which have variable aspiration, prevoicing, and gemination.

---

[1] I also have cases of an occasional voiced stop geminate, e.g., kɔ̀b-bíŋ 'small bone', but the more usual pronunciation is with an epenthetic vowel between the stops. The examples in (117) are consistent in their pronunciation, i.e., there is never an epenthetic vowel in these.

Voiceless stops are generally lightly aspirated, except for the labial-velar [kp], which is unaspirated. The phones [t] and [p] have weaker aspiration than [k], but definitely have aspiration, unlike [kp]. This is illustrated in (118) for [kpa__], [ka__], [pa__], and [ta__] sequences which are utterance initial.

(118) Aspiration versus nonaspiration on voiceless stops

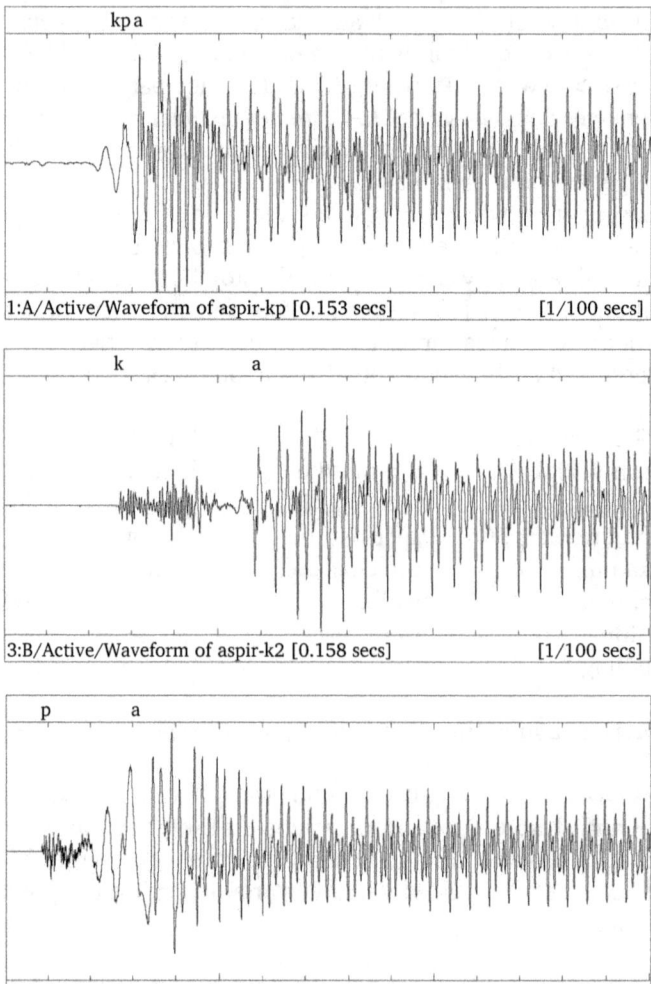

4.1 Consonant inventory, contrasts, and measurements

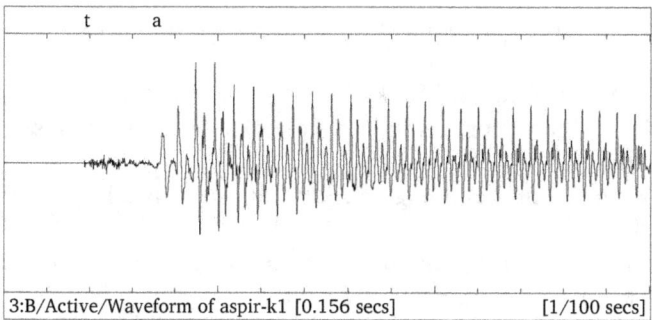

Voiced stops, at least utterance initially, have prevoicing. This is not prenasalization; no air flows though the nasal passages. This can be seen in the waveforms in (119).

(119) Prevoicing on voiced stops

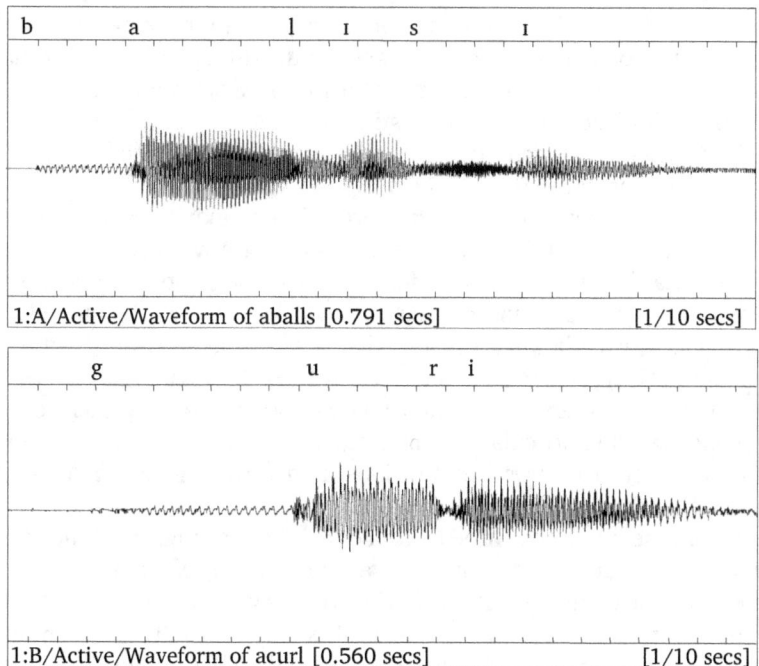

The duration of consonants varies not only according to whether they are singletons versus geminates, but also with their position in a word and whether they are lexeme initial or not. Average measurements, with standard deviations (SD) are given below for [k].

(120) Nine measurements of each type, except eleven measurements for (d)
  a. [k] in a suffix, e.g., fàà-kú 'the baboon'   ave. 93 ms, SD = 8
  b. [k] within a morpheme, e.g., tókóró 'window'   ave. 91 ms, SD = 7
  c. [k] in a compound, e.g., lee-kuŋ 'axe handle'   ave. 116 ms, SD = 7
  d. [k] across words, e.g., ù kàlì 's/he sat...'   ave. 113 ms, SD = 9
  e. [kk] in a word, e.g., súnsúk-kú 'the middle'   ave. 141 ms, SD = 5

These five measurements can be combined into three groups based on their duration. The first group, consisting of (120a and b), has [k] within a word, whether across a morpheme boundary or not. The second group, consisting of (120c and d), has [k] across a word boundary; this can be in a compound word or across independent words. Finally, the third group consists only of (120e), in which adjunction of morphemes has produced a geminate consonant [kk]. These systematic differences suggest that consonant duration may be a cue for determining word boundaries, as well as a simple single/double length distinction.

This pattern of longer consonant duration in word-initial position is not unique to Kɔnni. As part of a general phonetic pattern, [p] and [m] are observed to have greater duration in word-initial than in word-final position in Taiwanese (Hsu 1996). A significant pressure rise was also detected for the word-initial but not the word-final positions. Fougeron and Keating (1995) give several examples and references to works in which the magnitude of a consonantal articulation is greater when the consonant is word initial. These include English (Browman and Goldstein 1992, Byrd 1994) and Korean (Jun 1993), among others. Furthermore, Fougeron and Keating themselves give evidence relating articulatory magnitude not only to position in the word, but to higher-level prosodic positions, and further investigation of Kɔnni may well uncover such a pattern.[2]

A test case involving three instances of /b/ in a single sentence suggests there may be at least one other level of duration relevant to consonants. The first case of /b/ in (121) is in the verb bá which is probably on its way to becoming an auxiliary. The second is word initially in the main verb bɔ́bí, and the third, which actually surfaces as [β], is word internally in the same verb.

---

[2] My thanks to Keith Johnson for the Fougeron and Keating reference as a starting point for this topic.

(121) ʊ̀ yà **bá** !ʊ́ bɔ́bɪ́
    3s yet will 3s tie
    's/he is yet to tie'

(122) Three cases of /b/:

	b1	b2	b3
	78	96	43
	80	109	42
	74	113	31
average	77	106	39

As expected from previous results, the word-initial /b/ in bɔ́bɪ́ has the longest duration, and the word-internal one has the shortest. But from the measurements, it seems that the auxiliary has a duration intermediate between the other two, and this category deserves further investigation which is beyond the scope of the present work. The comparative brevity of consonants intervocalically within a word also suggests they may be more vulnerable to further weakening and even elision, as in fact happens in Kɔnni.

4.2 Assimilatory processes

Assimilation between consonants, although a very common phenomenon, has not been a major research emphasis within Optimality Theory. One looks in vain for it in major works such as Kager (1999). Three works which have dealt with it in some detail are Pulleyblank (1997), who gives a general schema for assimilation of adjacent consonants, and Jun (1995) and Kirchner (1998), who do the same. Padgett (1996) deals with the more limited topic of nasal place assimilation and gives a constraint SPREADPLACE, but in the context of OT this must be regarded as a shorthand for several constraints which give the effect of spreading, rather than a single constraint. McCarthy and Prince (1995) mention two constraints which have the effect of assimilation, but are not explicit on details. For example, they give a constraint PAL (p. 341), not actually defining it, but characterizing it as "a kind of CV-linkage of the coronal feature." McCarthy (2002) mentions nasal place assimilation in passing, but again is not explicit in his discussion. The major approaches are Pulleyblank, who gives a family of simple phonological constraints, and Jun and Kirchner, who give more phonetically based accounts.

Jun (1995) views assimilation between consonants as a reduction or loss of the gesture of the target consonant and a corresponding lengthening of the gesture of the triggering consonant. Jun sums this up in a WEAK constraint, which is basically the same constraint as the LAZY constraint of Kirchner (1998, see also Steriade 1995b).

(123) WEAK: "conserve articulatory effort" (Jun 1995:121)
     LAZY: "minimize articulatory effort" (Kirchner 1998:37)

The term "conserve" in this context is identical to "minimize," that is, to "avoid use of." WEAK is violated by any gesture, so any consonant will violate it once. In a consonant cluster, if the cluster has two different places of articulation, WEAK will be violated twice, but if the cluster has only one place of articulation, WEAK is only violated once. This gradient violation of WEAK is the motivation for place assimilation.

The other main conception of assimilation within OT abstracts away from the phonetics and is more strictly phonological. Pulleyblank (1997) accounts for various assimilations between adjacent consonants in terms of "identical-cluster constraints" (ICCs), which say that consonant clusters must be identical in some feature. The general form of his constraint is:

(124) **ICC[F]**: adjacent consonants must be identical for the feature F

The general feature F would be replaced by the specific feature under discussion. So ICC[nas] mandates that adjacent consonants be identical in nasality, ICC[cor] mandates that adjacent consonants be identical in the feature [coronal], etc. As stated, this constraint family is fully compatible with an autosegmental representation, but is not dependent on it. An autosegmental representation would make a distinction between inserting a feature and spreading one:

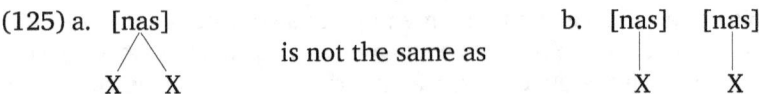

(125) a. [nas]   b. [nas] [nas]
     / \   is not the same as | |
    X X   X   X

However, the ICC formula is indifferent to the distinction. Within the Feature Geometry framework, assimilations are regarded as spreadings (Clements and Hume 1995) and would give the result in (125a). Constraints could be formulated which are explicit in distinguishing (125a) and (125b). In the general sense, one would have to weigh the costs of introducing a new feature, as in (125b), which would violate a DEP[nas] constraint, against the cost of having a multiply linked feature as in (125a), which may violate a constraint against multiply linked features. On the other hand, for some features, there may be a constraint *against* having singly linked features in the

4.2 Assimilatory processes

context of adjacent consonants. This constraint would be the equivalent of the ICC family in explicit autosegmental terms and would force either spreading of the feature or deletion of it.

In this work, to motivate assimilation of features, I employ the general strategy of prohibiting adjacent segments from having differing features. As Pulleyblank (personal communication) has pointed out, the general OT strategy is to prohibit ill-formed sequences, and so I propose the following as a general schema.

(126) *F_iF_j: adjacent segments with differing feature values are prohibited

Depending on the phenomenon being discussed, this may prohibit differing place values or differing values of a binary feature. As stated, this type of constraint, like the ICC family above, makes no prediction as to whether an assimilation would insert a feature or spread it, and as far as I am aware, Kɔnni has no crucial evidence to determine single versus multiple linking of features. In principle, evidence to distinguish these configurations may be possible (by analogy with tones, as in L versus LL linked to two TBUs in chapter 6), but I know of no such test for Kɔnni.

Both Pulleyblank's and the WEAK/LAZY conceptions converge on the same concept, though they are formulated quite differently. Jun's WEAK refers directly to the phonetics, and so has its motivation explicit in its formulation. However, the term "articulatory effort" must be interpreted in specific terms. Pulleyblank's ICC[F] constraints are a family and comprise as many constraints as there are features. They include a level of abstraction not present with Jun's WEAK, but refer to phonological features. The *F_iF_j family I will use is presumably motivated by phonetic considerations, but it shares the same level of phonological abstraction as Pulleyblank's ICC[F] constraints.

4.2.1 Nasal place assimilation

4.2.1.1 Data

Kɔnni exhibits the very common process of nasals assimilating to the place of articulation of the following consonant. Three places are illustrated below. Based on this pattern, I presume that a nasal will assimilate as [ɲ] before a palatal [y, ch, j], but have not verified that it is in fact [ɲ] rather than [n] in this environment. Note that although [w] is phonetically both back and round ([dorsal] and [labial] in terms of the features used here), a nasal assimilates to it as [ŋ], not [m] or [ŋm]. Only the backness ([dorsal]) place assimilates.

(127) Nasal place assimilation:
    a. ǹ díè mìŋ   'I am eating.'
       ǹ láà mìŋ   'I am laughing.'
       m̀ bɔ́bà mìŋ   'I am tying.'
       ŋ̀ gárà mìŋ   'I am going.'
       ŋ̀ wáálà mìŋ   'I am broadcasting (seed).'
    b. náá!gín náŋ   'cow's leg'
       náá!gíŋ kɔ́!bíŋ   'cow's bone'
       náá!gím !búá   'cow's child'
    c. bà **sún** dí fìàlì   'They were happy. (lit., Their heart was cool.)'
       ù **súm** fìàlìyá   's/he is happy.'
       ù **súŋ** ká fìàlìyá   's/he is not happy.'
    d. tè**m**-bíŋ   'small stone'
       tà**n**-sɔ́bílíŋ   'black stone'
       tà**ŋ**-kpí!íŋ   'big stone'

Kɔnni has an interesting twist to nasal place assimilation, in that a nasal is pronounced as [ŋ] before labial-velar stops within words, and [ŋm] before labial-velars across words. This last is variable across speakers, and also depends on speech carefulness; more careful speech can give [ŋ] across words.

(128) Nasal assimilation type 1: [ŋ] before a labial-velar *within* words:
    a. Single-morpheme words:
       tìŋgbáŋ   'floor'
       bìŋkpìáŋ   'shoulder'
    b. Compound nouns:
       hàŋ-gbàáŋ   'hyena (bush-dog)'
       ɲìŋ-gbáníŋ   'body (front-skin)'
    c. Noun-adjective:
       dùùŋ-kpí!íŋ   'big horse (horse-big)'
       bíŋ-kpí!áŋ   'dry seed (seed-dry)'

(129) Nasal assimilation type 2: [ŋm] before a labial-velar *across* words:
    a. Pronoun (possessive and subject):
       ŋ̀m gblèŋ   'my pot'   ŋ̀m kpàllí   'my calabash'
       ŋ̀m gbálígí-yà   'I'm tired.'   ŋ̀m kpátí-yà   'I've finished.'
    b. Noun Phrases:
       sìŋkpááŋm kpááŋ   'peanut oil' (cf. sìŋkpááŋ 'peanut')

c. Verb Phrases:
    kéŋm kpátì   'come finish'
    kéŋm gbírígì   'come kneel'

Since a distribution of [ŋKP] and [ŋmKP] (KP is a cover term for *kp* and *gb*) is undocumented in phonological literature for any language but Kɔnni up to this time, I will take some space to justify my transcriptions.[3] As I discuss in more detail in Cahill (1999d), the difference between [ŋ] and [ŋm] before a labial-velar stop is not always easy to distinguish by ear alone, especially for the nonnative speaker. Ward (1933:10), in discussing nasal place assimilation in Efik, writes:

> The question as to which nasal consonant is used with **kp** is interesting, since in this plosive, labial and velar articulations occur together....It is, however, extremely difficult to *hear* which is being said without *seeing* the presence or absence of lip-articulation.

The auditory difference between [ŋmkp] and [ŋkp] is not very great, and the reason for this is not hard to find. [ŋm] has two places of articulation: a front [m] and a back [ŋ]. In the resonating cavity which is composed of the oral and nasal tracts, [ŋm] has one of its complete constrictions at the same place as [ŋ]. It is this rearmost constriction that defines the length of the oral part of the resonating cavity for [ŋm]. As Ohala and Ohala (1993:236) comment, "Any additional constriction forward of that point is acoustically irrelevant." To distinguish [ŋmkp] and [ŋkp] reliably, it is indeed crucial to use one's eyes as well as ears, as Ward notes above. This is especially crucial in utterance-initial contexts, when there is no vowel transition into the nasal; such vowel transitions, of course, aid the task in those contexts immensely.

That being said, it is possible to reliably distinguish the two, especially in a live situation, once one is aware of the differences and is on the lookout for them and has had some experience with the language. In *ŋ̍m gbálígí-yà* 'I'm tired', the lips are closed during the nasal portion of the utterance, while in *tùŋbáŋ* 'floor' the lips are open for the preconsonantal nasal.

4.2.1.2 Analysis

I will first offer an analysis of nasal assimilation in general, then deal with the special case of the two types of nasal assimilation before labial-velars.

---

[3]Padgett (1996) claims that Gã has [ŋKP] across morphemes and [ŋmKP] within morphemes, but neither the sources he cites nor my own first-hand investigation support this (Cahill and Parkinson 1997). Efik (Ward 1933, Cook 1969, Ohala and Ohala 1993) seems to have both [ŋKP] and [ŋmKP], but the distribution or possibly variation is not clear.

The two crucial patterns that one must deal with are first, that a nasal and a consonant following it have the same place of articulation, and second, that cross-linguistically, nasals assimilate in place to stops, but not the reverse. For the first pattern, we will use a constraint of the *F_iF_j family discussed above:

(130) *Cpl_iCpl_j: adjacent consonants may not have differing place features

In terms of OT constraints and place features, in an NC cluster, it is more important to preserve the place features of C than it is to preserve those of N. Since there are two differences (nasal versus nonnasal and first versus second position), we must determine which of these is the crucial factor, if possible. Though the nasal/nonnasal distinction is crucial in many languages, we shall see that it cannot account for all the Kɔnni facts.

As has been noted (e.g., Ohala and Ohala 1993, Padgett 1996), in many cases it is the difference between nasal and obstruent that is the crucial difference as to which one retains its place. This is because the acoustic cues for place in nasals are not as prominent as those for obstruents (this holds for any post-vocalic stops versus nasals—see Jun 1995 and references therein, as well as Steriade 1994). The robustness of cues for obstruents makes them less susceptible to change, and conversely, the less robust cues for nasals make them more susceptible to change. Therefore, there would be a universal constraint ranking $\text{MAX[pl]}_{\text{OBST}} >> \text{MAX[pl]}_{\text{NAS}}$, with place features for obstruents being more highly ranked than place features for nasals.[4]

(131) $\text{MAX[pl]}_{\text{OBST}}$: for every input place feature in an obstruent, there is a correspondent in the output
$\text{MAX[pl]}_{\text{NAS}}$: for every input place feature in a nasal consonant, there is a correspondent in the output

Padgett notes the German *haben ~ habm* as a case in which the nasal has the release cues, but still assimilates to the preceding stop. To his German example I can add the case of Gwari (Rosendall 1992), which has CNV syllable types, and the /n/ assimilates to a preceding labial obstruent:

---

[4]The internal place cues for glides and liquids are also more salient than those for nasals. Johnson (1997) notes that nasal murmurs are not very good indicators of place of articulation, drawing on experiments by Repp showing that vowel formant transitions give a much more accurate identification of place. Jun (1995) places all continuants above nasals in preservation of place features, and presumably the place features for these are also more faithful to the input than nasal place features. Jun's constraints use Pres for "preserve" place values rather than the MAX constraints used here.

4.2 Assimilatory processes

(132) Postobstruent nasal assimilation in Gwari (Rosendall 1992)[5]
tnútnúnù   'rubbish'   ɓmà   'break'
dnásò   'river'   gbmínà   'feather'

The Tyebaara dialect of Senoufo (Mills 1984) and the Mada language (Price 1989) also have a similar pattern.

To this point, nasal place assimilation for every case in Kɔnni, the other languages cited, and cases like English word-final *chant, camp,* and *thi[ŋ]k* can be accounted for by the universal constraint ranking of MAX[pl]$_{OBST}$ over MAX[pl], the latter applying to nasals. When a nasal and obstruent come together and differing places are not allowed, it is universally the nasal that assimilates in place to the obstruent, never the reverse. However, cases such as *náá!gín náŋ* 'cow's leg' from (127b), in which both members of the consonant cluster are nasals, shows that an additional factor must be taken into account. The crucial factor in this case is the position, not only whether one member of the cluster is nasal. There is also an underlying phonetic motivation for this, in that release cues are important in identifying a consonant. In a consonant cluster, the first consonant is not released into a vowel and so has no cues characteristic of release such as burst or formant transitions. Its perceptual salience is less than that of the second consonant, which does have these characteristics, and so it is more likely to lose its characteristic gesture of place. These phonetic motivations could be directly translated into constraints, as indeed has been done by Steriade and her students (see very similar constraints in Padgett 1996).[6]

(133) **MAX[Cpl]:** a C-Place feature in the input has a correspondent in the output
MAX[Cpl]$_{rel}$: a C-Place feature on a released consonant in the input has a correspondent in the output

We also must include a constraint or constraints to preserve the nasality of the first consonant in a cluster. Either an IDENT[nas] or a MAX[nas] constraint (in combination with other constraints) could conceivably account for preserving an underlying nasal into the output. However, later we will see cases of /n-r/ → [nn], in which a segment gains a [nasal] specification. With the understanding that [nasal] is a privative feature, there is a contradiction in

---

[5]CNV is a normal syllable pattern in Gwari. A postconsonantal nasal does not assimilate in place to that consonant if the consonant is velar, e.g., *kná* 'send'. As far as I know, the evidence for assimilation is distributional rather than alternational.

[6]Similarly, Hume (1998) in her accounting for cross-linguistic patterns of consonant-consonant metathesis shows that it is the relative perceptibilities of the consonants which is crucial.

ranking if IDENT[nas] applies both in cases which preserve underlying nasality and in cases in which nasality is spread. A nasal input never loses its nasality, so in analyzing nasal inputs, IDENT[nas] is undominated. However, in the /n-r/ → [nn] case, the /r/ gains a [nasal] specification, IDENT[nas] is violated and it must be ranked low. For this reason, I use a MAX[nas] constraint here to account for the retention of nasality by an input nasal and consider the assimilation of nasality in /n-r/ → [nn] a violation of a lower-ranked IDENT[nas]. I discuss the IDENT[nas] constraint more in section 4.2.4.

(134) **MAX[nas]:** a [nasal] feature in the input has a correspondent in the output

In nasal place of assimilation, there is a question in some morphemes of what the underlying place value of the nasal actually is. None of the alternations exists in a "neutral" context, but the nasal always occurs before a consonant to which it assimilates. In such cases whether one underspecifies place or assigns a place arbitrarily makes no difference; the assimilation of the nasal will give the same result either way. For the tableau in (135), I use a case in which the assimilating nasal can unambiguously be labeled /n/ on the evidence of the plural form tàn-á 'stones'. (The stem vowel A of 'stone' is realized as [e] in tèm-bíŋ due to ATR spread from the adjective, discussed in section 5.2.)

(135) tèm-bíŋ 'small stone' *Cpl_iCpl_j, MAX[Cpl]$_{rel}$, MAX[nas], MAX(C) >> MAX[Cpl]

tAn-biŋ	*Cpl_iCpl_j	MAX[nas]	MAX[Cpl]$_{rel}$	MAX(C)	MAX[Cpl]
☞ a. tembiŋ					*
b. tenbiŋ	*!				
c. tebiŋ				*!	*
d. tendiŋ			*!		*
e. tebbiŋ		*!			*

The optimal candidate (135a) violates MAX[Cpl] by changing the place of articulation of the nasal, but other candidates violate more highly-ranked constraints. Candidate (135b) violates *Cpl_iCpl_j, since the nasal/stop sequence [nb] has two places of articulation. Candidate (135c) violates MAX(C) by deleting the nasal consonant altogether. (This constraint is not undominated, since consonant deletions do occur in Kɔnni; see section 4.3.) Candidate (135d) is internally well-formed, but is unfaithful to the input, fatally violating MAX[Cpl]rel. Finally, candidate (135e) has denasalized the input segment and fatally violates MAX[nas].

In the tableau in (135), the additional constraints MAX[pl]$_{OBST}$ and MAX[pl]$_{NAS}$ could also be inserted, and they would also force the choice of the correct candidate. However, as discussed, in the case of *náá!gín náŋ* 'cow's leg', the use of MAX[Cpl]$_{rel}$ is crucial, and for generality's sake, I use this in (135) as well.

The matter of place assimilation of a nasal to a labial-velar adds an additional level of complexity. In this work I use KP as a cover symbol for both [kp] and [gb].

Nasal place assimilation to labial-velars in a nonlinear framework has been considered explicitly in Sagey (1990), Ryder (1987), Padgett (1996), and Cahill (1997a, 1998a, 1999d). Sagey (1990), in a Feature Geometry framework, dealt only with languages in which a nasal assimilated as [ŋmKP] and exhibited no awareness that in some languages the product of assimilation is [ŋKP]. Accounting for [ŋmKP] is relatively simple and is done in Clements and Hume's 1995 version of Feature Geometry by spreading the C-Place node from consonant to the preceding nasal. Ryder (1987), working in an autosegmental framework but not Feature Geometry, specifically considered Gã, which has (at least sometimes) [ŋKP]. In Cahill (1998a), both the [ŋKP] and [ŋmKP] of Kɔnni were analyzed using two separate rules which accounted for the data, but these rules were arbitrary. Padgett (1996) is the first OT analysis of the phenomenon, and he, like Ryder, also worked with Gã. In his account, Gã reportedly manifests [ŋmKP] within morphemes and [ŋKP] across morphemes (but see footnote 3, chapter 4). He does not satisfactorily account for the lack of [mKP] and treats [dorsal] and [labial] as crucially phonologically ordered.[7]

---

[7]If [labial] and [dorsal] are phonologically ordered, then the total assimilation of a nasal as [ŋmKP] is problematic. This ordering would entail that part of the nasal assimilates to one place feature, and another part of the nasal skips over that place feature to assimilate to the next place feature, giving a representation as below, with line-crossing configuration necessary.

[dors] [lab]

Also, there are several cross-linguistic lines of evidence strongly suggesting that the [labial] and [dorsal] place features are unordered. These include co-occurrence restrictions in Kukú and Ngbaka, where KP cannot occur in the same word with other labial consonants (in either direction). Also, the phoneme /kp/ in Nzima and Dagbani has an allophone [tp] before front vowels, an assimilation of the [coronal] place. If the places were ordered, the [coronal] place of the vowel would have to skip over the [labial] place of /kp/, leaving it untouched, in order to reach and displace the [dorsal]. For details, see Cahill (1999d).

To review the Kɔnni situation, a nasal will assimilate as [ŋ] before KP within words, and as [ŋm] before KP across words (see (128)–(129) for more data).

(136) a. Nasal assimilation type 1: [ŋ] before a labial-velar within words:
tìŋgbáŋ   'floor'
b. Nasal assimilation type 2: [ŋm] before a labial-velar across words:
kéŋm gbírígí   'come kneel'

The problems at hand are first, how can a nasal assimilate partially to the places of assimilation of KP? Second, why does a partial assimilation yield [ŋKP] and not [mKP]? Third, why does a nasal assimilate totally to both of the places of articulation of KP in (136b), but only to one of them in (136a)? Part of the answer to these questions as well as cross-linguistic patterns of labial-velar behavior lies in the specific feature geometric configuration of KP, but the rest may lie in the phonetics of labial-velars.

Specific feature geometries for labial-velars have been proposed in Sagey (1986), Clements (1991), Lahiri and Evers (1991), and Clements and Hume (1995), but these have not taken the full range of cross-linguistic behavior of labial-velars into consideration. Cahill (1997a) proposes that individual languages may have their own representation, consistent with a proposal in Clements (1991), who argues for a diachronic change in featural geometric configuration to account for historical developments. The three most likely geometries for labial-velars are shown in (137).[8]

(137) Possible labial-velar geometries

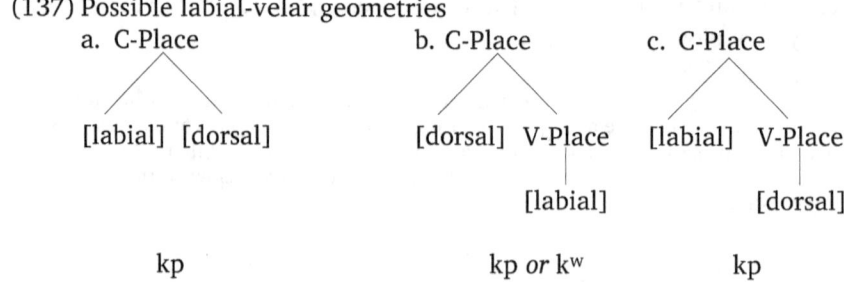

The representation in (137c) explains why KP patterns with labial but not dorsal consonants in many languages; the primary articulation is labial. It

---

[8]The configurations in (137b) and (137c) have some conceptual resemblance to the notion of labial-velars in Chomsky and Halle (1968) and Anderson (1976), as either dorsals with extreme rounding, or labials with extreme velarization. The feature system of SPE did not allow simultaneous major articulators. The configuration in (137a), of course, fits neither of these conceptions.

4.2 Assimilatory processes

also explains [tp] as an allophone of /kp/ which precedes front vowels in languages such as Dagbani and Nzima: we assume a [coronal] feature under V-place of the following vowel, and this [coronal] spreads to the V-place node of the KP, displacing the [dorsal]. The representation of (137c) can also account for neutralization to P word finally in languages such as Amele and Efik (see Cahill 1997a, 1999d), on the notion that complex consonants are not allowed word finally, and it is the secondary articulation which disappears rather than the primary one. Representation (137b) can aid in explaining the historical origins of KP and the cross-linguistic absence of /KP^w/ (Clements 1991). For quite a few languages, there is no evidence for one feature versus the other to be primary, and this would yield configuration (137a). For more detailed discussion of how Feature Geometry relates to cross-linguistic behavior of labial-velars, see Cahill (1997a, 1998b). The representation in (137c) may be argued to be not the one for Kɔnni, on the basis that [w], which is similar in having [dorsal] as its active feature under V-place, has a prohibition against a following [e], but [kpe] exists (see section 5.2.1.2).

Nonetheless, neither Feature Geometry nor any principled set of constraints in Optimality Theory seems capable of giving a strictly phonological solution to the partial nasal assimilation yielding [ŋKP]. If the [dorsal] and [labial] features of KP are phonologically unordered (see footnote 7, chapter 4), a rule or constraint referring to [dorsal] rather than [labial] as the trigger for partial nasal assimilation yielding [ŋKP] is arbitrary rather than principled; a rule or constraint could equally well select [mKP] as the surface form. An answer to why a nasal before KP is [ŋKP] and not [mkp] may be found in the phonetics of labial-velars, and the remainder of this section will be devoted to exploring some of these phonetic properties.

For several decades, /kp/ has usually been transcribed as [kp] and not [pk]. This is no accident; perceptually, a vowel transition into KP sounds like a transition into a velar component, and the release sounds labial. This is supported by spectrograms from Dedua (from Papua New Guinea) and Efik (Ladefoged and Maddieson 1996) as well as Ibibio (Connell 1994). This is also supported by the more direct means of electromagnetic articulography measurements from Ewe (Maddieson 1993a, b). The diagram below is from Ladefoged and Maddieson (1996), also Maddieson (1993a, b).

(138) Electroarticulagraphic measurements of Ewe [kp]

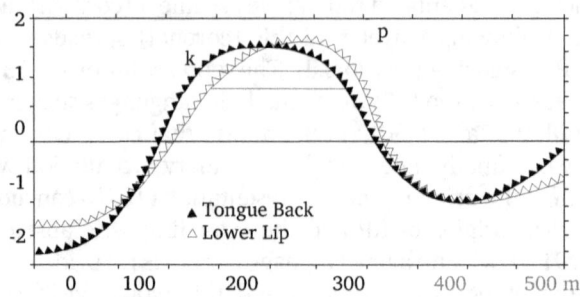

Coordination of lower lip and tongue back movements in the Ewe word *akpa*. Y-axis is vertical displacement; horizontal lines indicate the likely duration of actual contact of the articulator.

This phonetic pattern of a velar articulation preceding (but mostly overlapping) the labial articulation makes sense not only of the observation that there is no [mKP] but also that there is no [KPŋ] in languages having postconsonantal nasals (as Gwari). A nasal assimilates either to the place of articulation of the nearest edge, or alternatively, to the entire articulation, since both articulations are present in the majority of the stop. This can be schematized in terms of the articulatory phonology model of Browman and Goldstein (1989, 1990, 1992), in which the primitive units of phonology are gestures.

139. a. Gestural score for **ŋKP**

VELUM	▬▬▬		
T. BODY	▬▬▬▬▬▬▬▬		
LIPS		▬▬▬▬▬▬▬	
	[ŋ]	KP	]

4.2 Assimilatory processes

b. Gestural score for **ŋm-KP**

VELUM			
T. BODY			
LIPS			
	[ŋm	KP	]

The crucial parameter is which gestures the VELUM overlaps with. In (139a), the VELUM overlaps only with the TONGUE BODY, and the nasal is [ŋ]. In (139b), the VELUM overlaps with the TONGUE BODY for its entire duration, but also with the LIPS for a majority of its duration. Overlapping with both gestures, the nasal may be legitimately transcribed as [ŋm].

This representation of the phonetics illustrates why in Kɔnni and other languages there is [ŋKP] but not [mKP]. However, it does not at all explain why in some languages there is [ŋKP], in others there is [ŋmKP], and in Kɔnni there is both. If a language chose exclusively one pattern or the other, it would be possible to attribute it to the different phonetic patterns of different languages: just as one language has a longer VOT than another, so one language could have a different timing pattern of the gestures above. However, the case of Kɔnni explodes this option.

The gestural score in (139) is not to be taken as being an accurate scale of relative durations, but one way it can be interpreted is that in [ŋmKP], the nasal gesture is longer than in [ŋKP], and so the nasal gesture overlaps both the labial and velar gestures. If this is so, then in the positions in which the difference is found (within words versus across words), we would expect to find a systematic difference in duration of nasals as a general pattern.[9] The lengthening of phonetic components before a boundary is a pattern that is cross-linguistically common (Maddieson 1996). However, this is just what we do not find in Kɔnni. I measured the duration of nasals in various contexts for both Sikpaare and Amadu, with the results in (141) and (142).

(140) Contexts for measuring durations of nasals
    a. within words   kàlìmbàànì   'pride'
    b. across words   dá kén tígíŋ   'don't come (to) house'
    c. syllabic nasal   m̀ búgùrà mìŋ   'I am learning.'
    d. desyllabified nasal   ǹ yálà dí-ŋ !gá   'I want to go. (lit., I want that I go.)'

---

[9]Thanks to David Odden for suggesting this test.

(141) Sikpaare: Durations of nasals in various contexts (ms)

	n	m	ŋ
a. within words	69 n = 14, SD = 14	68 n = 20, SD = 6	68 n = 16, SD = 14
b. across words	74 n = 11, SD = 13	87 n = 7, SD = 26	73 n = 4, SD = 5
c. syllabic nasal	155 n = 7, SD = 21	152 n = 10, SD = 17	151 n = 13, SD = 26
d. desyllabified nasal		79 n = 6, SD = 13	

(142) Amadu: Durations of nasals in various contexts (ms)

	n	m	ŋ
a. within words	58 n = 31, SD = 15	77 n = 36, SD = 10	77 n = 19, SD = 13
b. across words	61 n = 21, SD = 9	81 n = 6, SD = 5	77 n = 18, SD = 16
c. syllabic nasal	134 n = 30, SD = 19	132 n = 24, SD = 22	141 n = 27, SD = 14
d. desyllabified nasal		73 n = 15, SD = 9	

The syllabic nasals and the "desyllabified nasals" are the first-person singular pronoun. In present-day Kɔnni, we see that nasals before word boundaries have approximately the same duration as nasals within words; the small differences are not statistically significant. The exception is the first-person singular pronoun, which is a syllabic nasal. This nasal is significantly longer than the others. The reason for this is presumably the requirement that syllables must have a certain minimum phonetic duration to be perceived as syllabic (tonal qualities may also enter into this). That it is syllabification that makes the difference is seen by the results of (140d), in which the same morpheme N occurs, but postvocalically, where the nasal is desyllabified (cf. ŋ̀ gárà mìŋ 'I am going', ǹ yálà dí-ŋ !gá 'I want to go'). In the desyllabified context, the nasal pronoun has the same duration as other nasals.

Mr. Amadu's and Mr. Sikpaare's measurements for nasal durations are comparable, with the slight exception that Sikpaare's syllabic nasals are definitely longer than Amadu's. This similarity in measurements is all the more striking when considering the fact that the tapes that Sikpaare's speech were recorded on were recorded over a period of about three years, with fewer controls than Amadu's speech. Sikpaare had more of a variation in his speech than Amadu, and this shows up occasionally in the standard deviation values. Fewer measurements were taken for Sikpaare because the taped data for him is less organized.

The conclusion from this is that the duration of nasals in various positions is not related to the ŋKP versus ŋmKP alternation.

Another way that the gestural score in (139) can be interpreted is that the duration of the labial gesture of the labial-velar stop KP itself is greater in (139b) than in (139a). This may well be integrated with greater total duration of the labial-velar stop in this position. If the duration is greater in word-initial position, this would agree with measurements of others (e.g., Fougeron and Keating 1996, Browman and Goldstein 1992, Byrd 1994, Jun 1993) that word-initial stops are more forcefully articulated, because more perceptually salient, than noninitial stops.[10] This also is consistent with my own measurements of [k] in various positions (see (120)), showing that consonants in word-initial position have greater duration than in word-internal position. This seems to be a promising explanation for the variable assimilation of nasals to labial-velar stops.

4.2.2 Intervocalic weakening

/g/ weakens to [ɣ] intervocalically, as in hɔ̀yú 'woman'. In rapid speech it sometimes deletes altogether, as in tuguri ~ tuuri 'be bright'. /g/ also weakens and assimilates to /w/ in at least one case, the very common hɔ̀wwá 'the woman', from /hɔgu-wa/. Intervocalic /b/ also often weakens to [β], as in /gobi/ → [gòβí] 'to cut grass', or in the sole intervocalic /b/ which is also intramorphemic ù yà bá !ú bɔ́bí [bɔ́βí] 's/he is yet to tie' from (121). As suggested in the discussion in section 4.1.2, the weakening that occurs within words is a natural result of less duration than when the consonant is in word-initial position.

The case of [d] and [r] appears to be parallel to the above, and probably was in an earlier stage of Kɔnni, but it has special complexities and will be considered separately in section 4.2.3.

The difference between [g, b] and [ɣ, β] is the feature [continuant]. Lombardi (1990) argues convincingly on the basis of the phonology of affricates that two values of [cont] are necessary; it cannot be a unary feature (she advocates using the opposing unary features [stop] and [cont],

---

[10]One may wonder if word-initial stops are more perceptually salient because of the forceful articulation, that is, whether the causation goes in the other direction. (One could imagine a physiological basis for word-initial position being more forceful.) Psycholinguistically, word-initial position is the position which influences word recognition more than word-internal position. But is this because of the greater forcefulness of the articulation, or solely the position? I myself know of no experiments in which duration, amplitude, or other correlates of "forcefulness" are controlled for.

but translates these into the more familiar [+cont] and [−cont], which she treats as separate autosegments). Here I assume the traditional binary values for [cont]. For a binary-valued feature, the IDENT family of constraints comes into play.

(143) IDENT[cont]: the value of the feature [continuant] on a segment is the same in the output as in the input

Accounting for intervocalic lenition of consonants in a principled way has been a challenge in the generative tradition. Intuitively and in most conceptualizations, weakening of /g/ to [ɣ] is viewed as an assimilation to the surrounding vowels. In SPE, a rule could be formulated to express this (or any) generalization, but distinguishing natural or common processes from impossible ones was not a part of the formalism; it had to be sought in the metatheory outside the rule itself. The advent of Feature Geometry brought an inherent naturalness to assimilation by viewing assimilation as spreading of features (e.g., Hayes 1986a, Clements 1985). However, in the case of intervocalic lenition, both vowels are necessary in the environment, and there would need to be a spread from both vowels of the [+continuant] feature, as discussed by Flemming (1995). Indeed, Inouye (1995) formulates such a process. However, this is foreign to the Feature Geometry approach, in which a rule incorporates only one process, not two as the spreading from both vowels would.

In OT terms, there can be at least two general approaches to intervocalic lenition of voiced stops, as there were for consonant assimilation in general. One is to posit a constraint that simply forbids the occurrence of [d, g, b] intervocalically, such as *VDV. This accounts for the surface pattern and is widely attested cross-linguistically. Combined with other faithfulness constraints, this produces the desired output. The other approach is to posit a constraint that goes more deeply to the phonetic motivation behind the lenition, as Kirchner's LAZY constraint explicitly does. Either approach can be made to work. As discussed in section 1.3.1, in this work I take the more abstract phonological approach rather than refer directly to phonetic constraints, and so I use *VDV rather than LAZY.

(144) *VDV: voiced stops are disallowed intervocalically

Another constraint preserves the voicing of the consonant.

(145) IDENT[voi]: every instance of [voice] in the input has the same value in the output

4.2 Assimilatory processes

This constraint is shown (146) below as ranked below MAX(C); the tableau showing this specific ranking is in (164).

(146) hɔ̀yú 'woman' *VDV, MAX(C), IDENT[voi] >> IDENT[cont]

hɔgʊ	*VDV	MAX(C)	IDENT[voi]	IDENT[cont]
☞ a. hɔyʊ				*
b. hɔgʊ	*!			
c. hɔʊ		*!		
d. hɔkʊ			*!	

The winning candidate (146a) violates only the low-ranked IDENT[cont]. Candidate (146b) violates *VDV by retaining the voiced stop [g]. Candidate (146c) satisfies *VDV but violates MAX(C) in deleting a consonant. Candidate (146d) also satisfies *VDV but in deleting the voicing specification of the consonant, loses by violating IDENT[voi].

The special case of [d] occurring intervocalically is considered in the next section.

4.2.3 The case of [d] and [r] – one phoneme or two?

The phones [r] and [d] are in completely complementary distribution, and also alternate in some morphemes. All cases of [r] are intervocalic within words, and [r] never occurs word initially. [d] normally appears either word initially or after [n]; it occurs intervocalically only in very restricted contexts. These intervocalic contexts are limited to ideophones, borrowed words, or within a word when [d] is morpheme initial and that morpheme is a noun, verb, or adjective derived from a verb. The distribution of [r] and [d] is illustrated in (147) and (148).

(147) Distribution of [r]
    a. [r] intervocalically within words, morpheme internal
        sàŋkpàríŋ   'navel'   háá!ríŋ   'boat'
        kúrúbâ   'bowl'   yʊʊrɪ   'flay'
        chùrú   'husband'   péríŋ   'button'

    b. [r] intervocalically within words, morpheme initial (but not lexeme initial)
        dàà-rí   'the day'
        ga-ra   'is going'

gàà-rú 'thief (lit., deceiver)'
zùù-ràáŋ 'male vulture (lit., vulture-male)'
ba-rıaŋ 'they-also'

(148) Distribution of [d]
    a. [d] word initially
      ù **d**ìé mìŋ 'S/he is eating.'
      dá !**d**áá **d**ááŋ 'Don't buy alcohol!'
      ù bá **d**í !fí kêŋ 'S/he said that you (should) come.'
      bìé **d**í ɲíŋ 'Goats then left.'
    b. [d] intervocalically within word, lexeme initial
      jùò-**d**ìkkíŋ 'cooking room' (cf. digi 'cook')
      dì-**d**àà-rú 'buyer'
      chìì-**d**èmbíŋ 'brother-in-law (lit., sibling.in.law-man)'
    c. [d] after [n] within a word
      ŋmààn-**d**ààŋ 'male monkey'
      ŋmín**d**áríŋ 'spider'
      tàn**d**úŋ 'pestle'
    d. [d] intervocalically within a word in borrowed words
      kò**d**ú 'banana' (Twi)
      ya**d**a 'belief' (Hausa)
      gá**d**ámà 'trouble' (Hausa)
      sí**d**í 'cedi' (Ghanaian national currency)
    e. [d] intervocalically within a word, in ideophones
      bìn-**d**ú**d**ù 'dung-beetle'
      sáá!bá**d**índì 'black scorpion'

The data in (148a) shows that it is not necessary for a word to be a major category lexical item to have word-initial [d] rather than [r]. The last two sentences in (148a) have the particles *dí* 'that' and *dí* 'then' which both have [d]. The data in (148b) is especially interesting because [d] is preserved in lexical items. In *jùò-dìkkíŋ* 'cooking room', the adjective *-dìkkíŋ* suffixed to the noun stem is derived from the verb *digi*. It appears, then, that there is morpheme-initial [d] in nouns and verbs, but not adjectives. The data in (148c) is also interesting, in that virtually all cases of [nd] in my data involve identifiable compound words. These are not always compounds in present-day Kɔnni, but some, as *tàndúŋ* 'pestle' are readily identifiable as at least historical compounds because of their mix of [−ATR] and [+ATR] vowels (see section 5.2).

Whether [d] and [r] belong to separate phonemes or a single one is a nontrivial question. In favor of a single phoneme /d/ is the distributional

4.2 Assimilatory processes

evidence: [r] is always intervocalic, while [d] is intervocalic only in the case of compounds, borrowed words, or ideophones. The last two categories are prime candidates for inclusion in a phonological system separate from the native vocabulary. It has been known for some time (e.g., Pike and Fries 1949) that separate phonologies may coexist in the same language, with borrowed words participating in a different phonology than native words. The partially disjunct phonology of Latinate words in English is another example.[11] Also, ideophones in African languages are often characterized by phonemes not found in other words, or unique sequences of phonemes, or tonal aberrancies (Welmers 1973). Thus Newman (1968) is able to distinguish ideophones in Hausa on the basis of their phonological properties. Compound words may be regarded as comprising two phonological words and thus the distribution of [d] as word initial may be maintained. Thus with a fine-grained look at the distribution patterns, we may say that [d] and [r] are in complete complementary distribution.

It is still possible, however, that there exist two separate phonemes /d/ and /r/, with quite limited distributions, as with the case of English h and $ŋ$, which exist in complementary distribution but are not generally considered to be members of the same phoneme. Positive support for this comes in three areas. First, there is a surface contrast between intervocalic [d] and [r]. It is true that intervocalic [d] occurs only in certain restricted cases, but the naive language speaker might not take account of whether a word has been borrowed or not. Some of these borrowed words quite possibly have been in the language long enough so that Kɔnni speakers do not think of them as "foreign" anymore. When borrowed words have been adopted to this point, then a contrast exists in the minds of the speakers. Borrowed words can thus be the point of entry of a new contrast in a language.[12] Second, native Kɔnni speakers react to the difference between [d] and [r] as if they were separate phonemes. In the traditional view, native speakers are generally unaware of subphonemic differences, except to think of them as "a funny accent." But Kɔnni speakers are highly aware of the difference between [d] and [r], readily correcting my pronunciation if I tried to substitute [d] for an [r] intervocalically. Third, unlike the case of [g]/[ɣ], in which intervocalic [ɣ] is pronounced [g] in more careful speech, an intervocalic [r] has no careful-speech pronunciation of [d]; a careful pronunciation still gives [r].

Writers on other Gur languages have split on whether /d/ and /r/ are separate phonemes or not. Naden (1989) in a survey of Gur languages,

---

[11]Itô and Mester (1995) discuss Japanese morpheme classes which behave differently with respect to phonological processes, and also refer to a number of other languages which have similar phenomena.

[12]Thanks to David Odden for bringing up this point.

states that [r] is "regularly a non-initial allophone of /d/." Gur languages for which researchers have written that [d] and [r] are members of a single phoneme /d/ include Supyire (Carlson 1994), Dagaare (Kennedy 1966, Bodomo 1997), Nafaara (Jordan 1980), Hanga (Hunt and Hunt 1981), Dilo (Jones 1987), Birifor (Kuch 1993), Sisaala-Pasaale (Toupin 1997), Kasem (Awedoba 1993), Mampruli (Naden 1988), Dagbani (Wilson and Bendor-Samuel 1969, Olawsky 1996), Dɛg (Crouch 1994), and Buli (Poulter 1984), as well as my earlier write-up on Kɔnni (Cahill 1992a). However, for other languages, researchers have concluded that /d/ and /r/ are separate phonemes; these include Kusaal (Spratt and Spratt 1968), Konkomba (Steele and Weed 1966), Vagala (Crouch and Smiles 1966), Tampulma (Bergman, Gray, and Gray 1969), Buli (Kröger 1992), and Frafra (Schaefer 1975). The difference seems to be largely one of differing interpretations of very similar sets of data, Buli being analyzed in both ways by different writers, for example. In none of these languages does [r] appear word initially, and in most cases the distribution of [r] and [d] is quite similar to Kɔnni, with intervocalic [d] only appearing in loanwords and compounds (no one else mentions ideophones). Interestingly, {r} is represented in all orthographies of these languages as separate from {d}, even for the languages in which [r] is analyzed as an allophone of /d/. For Supyire, Carlson is explicit that this is to facilitate bridging into the national language (French). Poulter specifically notes that Buli speakers react to [d] and [r] as separate phonemes, as I have noted for Kɔnni.

In light of the above, and especially the fact that [r] cannot have an alternate pronunciation as [d] even in careful speech, it is likely that /r/ and /d/ are separate phonemes in Kɔnni, and I will treat them as such in this work, though they were undoubtedly a single phoneme at some previous point in time. If there were one phoneme /d/ today, all occurrences of [r] would have their source in that /d/, and this adds more complexity to the analysis, in that not only do intervocalic [r]s have to be generated from /d/, but cases of intervocalic [d] must be allowed in specific instances, and the dissimilation effects involving [r] are not as transparent. With /d/ and /r/ being separate phonemes, most cases of [d] and [r] may be merely considered as faithful to the input forms. The exception to this is the morpheme in which [r] alternates with [d], considered in section 4.4.

The crucial feature distinguishing [d] and [r] is here considered to be [sonorant]. Another possibility for distinguishing [d] and [r] might be [continuant], which in a previous stage of Kɔnni, would unify the treatment of *d/r* with *g/y* and *b/β* considered above as intervocalic weakening of all

4.2 Assimilatory processes

voiced stops /d, g, b/.[13] The feature [rhotic] or [retroflex] is also sometimes mentioned (Suzuki 1998, Steriade 1995b, Walsh-Dickey 1997, though the last concludes that [rhotic] is not necessary as a distinctive feature). Since the [r] in Kɔnni is an alveolar flap with no retroflexion, the [retroflex] feature does not seem appropriate for Kɔnni, but we will use [rhotic] as a cover term to account for dissimilation.

In spite of the constraint *VDV prohibiting intervocalic voiced stops, some do surface in compounds such as *chǐidèmbíŋ* 'brother-in-law'. The [d] is preserved here by a top-ranked constraint IDENT[son]$_{LEX}$ which maintains the value of [sonorant] in lexical items. It is discussed more fully in section 4.4.2.

4.2.4 Total assimilation of /r/

Suffix-initial /r/ totally assimilates to a preceding nasal or [l], yielding [nn] or [ll]. The driving force behind this is, in this analysis, a desire to avoid clusters of nonidentical sonorants. Interestingly, the same constraints used here to force assimilation will be used in section 4.4 to force dissimilation of /r/ in other suffixes.

For two suffixal morphemes, there is an alternation between [r] and either [n] or [l], the latter two occurring when the stem to which it is suffixed ends with a nasal or [l], respectively.

The first morpheme I consider here is the singular definite suffix of noun class 1, which has the surface variants [-rI, -nI, -lI]. In (149a), when the stem ends in a consonant other than N or [l], an epenthetic vowel appears, and the morpheme appears as [-rI]. In (149b) below, when the stem ends in a nasal, the suffix is [-nI] rather than [-rI]. The place assimilation of the nasal is explained in section 4.2.1. In (149c), the suffix after a stem-final [l] is [-lI] rather than [-rI].

---

[13]It is difficult to find a writer to commit to the value of [continuant] with respect to flapped *r*. This is possibly because, as Chomsky and Halle (1968:318) note, there may be two extremely similar sounds with different airflow distinctions. The first is the "tap [r]" in which the tongue tip temporarily strikes the palate as a result of the Bernoulli effect produced by the rapid flow of air through a narrow cavity. In this sound, the contact of the tongue tip and the palate is merely a by-product of the articulation, and this sound may be classed [+cont]. The other sound is the "tongue flap [D]" which is a less forceful and more rapid form of [d]. This sound is [−cont]. Since the articulation of [r] in Kɔnni is not known to this level of phonetic detail, I will not discuss [cont] in relation to [r].

(149)

		Singular	Definite	Plural
a.	'breast'	bìıs-íŋ	bìısì-rí	bìıs-á
	'river'	múg-úŋ	múgú-rí	múg-à
	'corn'	káwún!t-íŋ	**káwún!tí-rí**	káwúnt-à
b.	'sparrow'	gìm-íŋ	gìn-ní	gìm-é
	'frog'	yàn-íŋ	yàn-ní	yàn-á
c.	'log'	dàmpàl-í	dàmpàl-lí	dàmpàl-á
	'tortoise'	kùl-í	kùl-lí	kùl-é

Exactly the same set of alternations occurs with the morpheme for 'also', which alternates between [-rıaŋ, -lıaŋ, -nıaŋ]. After a vowel, as in (150a), it is [-rıaŋ]. After a noun-final nasal, as in (150b), it is [-nıaŋ], and after a stem-final [l], as in (150c), it is [-lıaŋ].

(150) a. tı-rıaŋ 'we-also'
    bie-rıaŋ 'goats-also'
 b. gbigimin-nıaŋ 'lion-also'
    jaan-nıaŋ 'thing-also'
    nıın-nıaŋ 'rain-also'
    ŋmin-nıaŋ 'God-also'[14]
 c. bital-lıaŋ 'male.goat-also'
    kul-lıaŋ 'tortoise-also'

In both of these morphemes, /r/ assimilates to a preceding nasal as [n], and to a preceding /l/ as [l].

One may wonder if this total assimilation of [r] to a preceding consonant is a general property of suffixes in Kɔnni. As seen in (147b), there are three other suffixes which are [r] initial when intervocalic. One of these, the imperfective [-ra], occurs only with the verb ga 'go' (ga-ra 'going'); no further forms are available. The others, the agentive suffix [-rU] (gàà-rú 'thief' and [-raaŋ] 'male' (zùù-rááŋ 'male vulture'), show dissimilatory effects in certain contexts, quite different behavior from the suffixes considered in this section. The two suffixes considered here may, however, both be classed as inflectional suffixes, in contrast to the others. The [r] in this type of suffix is "weaker" than the others in terms of keeping its articulations; it assimilates completely while the others do not. [r] as a voiced coronal tap is largely unmarked and this also correlates with its being the only epenthetic consonant within words (see section 4.5).

---

[14]In my data from the village of Nangurima, I have ŋmin-dıaŋ 'God also', where 'also' is [-dıaŋ] after a nasal rather than [-nıaŋ] as in the Yikpabongo dialect I am dealing with in this book.

4.2 Assimilatory processes

The total assimilation of /r/ is one area in which the advantages of having a separate phoneme /r/ are apparent, rather than having [r] derived from /d/. For one thing, there is no [d] ever occurring in these morphemes; /r/ is a less abstract analysis than /d/. Second, prohibiting an [nd] sequence, which would be the predicted output of /nd/, is an additional complication if r in these morphemes came from /d/.

Our analysis must account for two patterns: first, why there is assimilation to [n] and [l] only, rather than vowel epenthesis as with other preceding consonants, and second, why the assimilation is limited to the morphemes /-rI/ and /-rIAŋ/, and excludes /-rU/ and /-raaŋ/.

As shown above, [r] assimilates only to [n] and [l]. It is possible to generalize this and say "nasals" instead of [n], but the surface form is always [n] due to place assimilation of the nasal. The nasal is both coronal and sonorant. The question is, which of these qualities, or both, is crucial? If we examine the data for other coronals in this position, we find there are plenty of stems which have [s] in this position, e.g., bɪ̀s-ɪ̀rɪ́ 'the breast' (the ɪ between the s and r is epenthetic). The only word in my data with [t] in this position is káwún!tíŋ 'corn', listed in (149), which happily takes káwún!!tí-rí as its definite. The coronal place, then, is not the crucial factor for assimilation of suffixal /r/. Consider now the possibility that sonorants are crucial. These sonorants would include not only n, l as above, but also r, w, y. The latter two (w and y) do not occur stem finally, so there is no chance to test these with an r-initial suffix. However, nouns do occur with stem-final r, and there are no cases of rr or rVr in Kɔnni. There is more than one strategy to avoid such sequences; one is historical. Several nouns with stem-final r take the plural form of noun class 1, but the singular form, without exception, is in another class.[15] Thus there is not a form such as XXXXri-ri. For example, wár-íŋ 'block' has a plural form wár-à which has the noun class 1 suffix, but the singular definite does not have the expected noun class 1 form /warɪ-rɪ/, but a noun class 2 form wárí-kú. Examples could be multiplied (see the "Mixed Classes" sections of appendix B). It is likely that mixing the noun class was a way to avoid rVr sequences. Nouns may switch from one class to another diachronically (Cahill 1997b).

Thus it appears that the class of sonorants is adequate to characterize the consonants to which [r] assimilates. Geminate sonorants are allowed in Kɔnni, but sequences of nonidentical sonorants are not. More specifically, one may say that any consonant except a sonorant requires an epenthetic vowel between it and the suffix [-rI] or [-rIaŋ], e.g., bɪ̀sɪ̀-rɪ́ 'the breast'.

---

[15]There are many r-final nouns in noun classes 2 and 3, a few in noun class 4, and none in class 1 or 5. The lack of such in class 5 is not surprising, given that almost all the noun stems in that class are vowel final, but the lack in noun class 1 suggests a more systematic gap.

Viewing the underlying /r/ as assimilating in features of nasality (or in the case of *dampal-lɪ* 'the log', laterality) may be possible, but this would view these as two logically independent assimilations, when analyzing these as total assimilation unites them.[16]

Considering the sonorant types of nasals and liquids, sequences of [rr], [nr], [lr], [rl], [rn] are not attested in Kɔnni, while [ll], [nn], [mm], [ŋŋ], and [nl][17] are attested (there is no combination of morphemes that would be expected to yield the [ln] sequence). Kɔnni therefore does not exhibit a prohibition against adjacent sonorants, but against [r] occurring adjacent to sonorants. More generally, [r] does not occur as a member of any consonant cluster. When a sequence of *r* and a consonant would arise though morpheme concatenation, the /r/ always either assimilates, as with the sonorants here, or an epenthetic vowel surfaces between [r] and the other consonant.

(151) *[son]r: no [sonorant]-[r] or [r]-[sonorant] clusters are allowed

It is possible to have epenthetic vowels in many places in Kɔnni; what prevents that in this case? This would give forms like the unattested *duni-ri, *kuli-ri. However, these sequences would be virtually unique in Kɔnni. There are no *nVr* sequences in Kɔnni,[18] and only a very few *mVr* ones. Anticipating the discussion of the OCP and dissimilation in section 4.4, we can propose a constraint that prohibits a nasal-vowel-r sequence:[19]

(152) *NVr: no nasal-vowel-[r] sequences are allowed

This describes the general pattern in the language. The few forms in which there is a *mVr* sequence may be allowed by ranking the appropriate faithfulness constraints above *NVr. Vowel epenthesis is also penalized by DEP(V), and it is indeterminate which constraint crucially rules out epenthesis. The similar constraint *[liq]V[liq], discussed in section 4.4.2 (203) is also included in the tableau in (157). As we shall see, *NVr and *[liq]V[liq] must have different rankings and so cannot be combined into

---

[16] Also, Walsh-Dickey (1997) presents compelling arguments that [lateral] is not a valid phonological feature, and argues that assimilations involving [l], as here, are best viewed as total assimilations rather than spreading of [lateral].

[17] The [nl] sequence occurs only in a few words, and all of these are compounds, with *n#l*.

[18] There are no nouns which have an underlying /-nV-/ sequence to which [r] could be suffixed. Any apparent stem-final vowel after [n] is epenthetic.

[19] In this work, I have not proposed conjoining of constraints to account for dissimilation, as Suzuki (1998) and others have done. To do so may replace the unnatural-looking *NVr by a more natural-looking set of constraints. For the present, however, I leave the surface-true *NVr in place.

4.2 Assimilatory processes

a unitary constraint such as *[son]Vr. Another constraint which we shall see is necessary is a faithfulness to the feature [sonorant]:

(153) IDENT[son]: a segment's value of [sonorant] is the same in the output as in the input

Since the second consonant is [nasal] in the output but not the input, we will discuss faithfulness constraints for [nasal]. Two types of constraints are possibly violated (also see the discussion in section 4.2.1.2 on IDENT[nas] versus MAX[nas]).

(154) DEP[nas]: a [nasal] feature in the output has a correspondent in the input
IDENT[nas]: a segment will have the same value of nasal in the output as in the input

The /r/ in the suffix gains a nasal specification which was lacking in the input, and we may state that in terms of either inserting a [nasal] segment or spreading the nasal which is present in the input stem. If a [nasal] is inserted, then there is a violation of DEP[nas], since there is a [nasal] feature present in the output which was not present in the input. IDENT[nas] is also violated, since the second segment bears a [nasal] specification in the output which it did not in the input. On the other hand, if the underlying nasal is spread, then there is no new [nasal] feature inserted, so no violation of DEP[nas], but the second consonant bears a [nasal] specification in the output which it did not have in the input, which is a violation of IDENT[nas]. This is diagrammed in (155).

(155) Possible configurations and violations

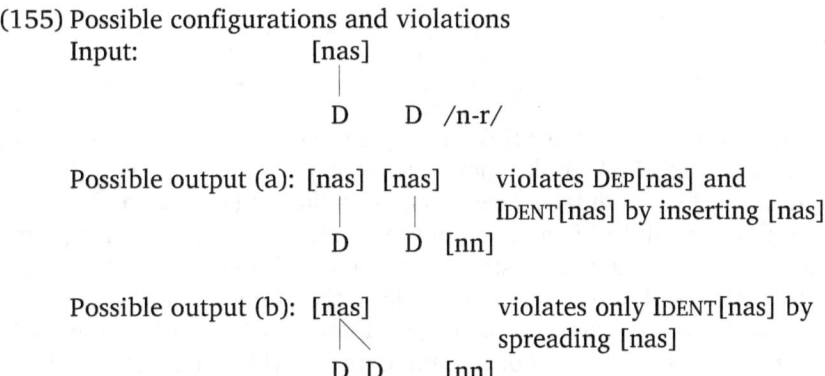

In previous autosegmental approaches, an assimilation in nasality as here would be assumed to be a spreading of the feature [nasal], as in the possible output (155b). This would violate only IDENT[nas]. As it turns out, there is additional support within this OT approach which necessitates using IDENT[nas] for this situation, and thus supports configuration (155b). This additional support comes from considering constraint rankings and avoiding a paradox in ranking. The constraint IDENT[son] must dominate whatever nasal constraint is violated, since any potential candidates in which the value of [son] is changed in C_2 are failed candidates. We shall see this in tableau (156). However, when we discuss dissimilatory effects in section 4.4, it becomes apparent that the constraint DEP[nas] unambiguously dominates IDENT[son] (see tableau 199). If the configuration in possible output (155a) is correct, however, then IDENT[son] would outrank both IDENT[nas] and DEP[nas]. To avoid a ranking paradox, as well as to be consistent with previous analyses of [nasal] assimilation, I consider the possible output (155b), with a single [nasal] feature shared between two segments, as being correct.

With these in place, we account for the total assimilations discussed here.

(156) gìnní 'the sparrow' *[son]r, IDENT[son] >> IDENT[nas]

gim-ri	*[son]r	MAX [Cpl]$_{rel}$	*NVr	IDENT [son]	DEP(V)	IDENT [nas]	MAX [Cpl]
☞ a. gin-ni						*	*
b. gin-di				*!			*
c. gin-ti				*!			*
d. gin-ri	*!						*
e. gimi-ri			*!		*		
f. gim-mi		*!				*	*

The winning candidate (156a) changes the input *r* to *n*, and so violates IDENT[nas] and MAX[Cpl] by changing the place of the input nasal from *m* to *n*, but other candidates fare worse. Candidates (156b and c) lose by changing the value of [sonorant] of the input. The latter also changes the value of [voice], but the constraint this violates is not shown above. Candidate (156d) with its *nr* sequence violates the undominated *[son]r, and candidate (156e) with its *mir* sequence violates *NVr (if *NVr were not in place, DEP(V) would rule it out). Candidate (156f) fails because the direction of assimilation was progressive instead of regressive. A tableau

4.2 Assimilatory processes

which is similar, but omits the constraints which are included to account for nasal place assimilation in (156), accounts for *kùl-lí* 'the tortoise'.

(157) kùl-lí 'the tortoise'

kul-ri	*[son]r	*[liq]V[liq]	IDENT [son]	DEP(V)
☞ a. kul-li				
b. kul-di			*!	
c. kul-ri	*!			
d. kul-ti			*!	
e. kuli-ri		*!		*

For the sake of completeness, I mention here the one example I have in which /r/ assimilates to a following [l] when adjacent. This is [chʊ̀rʊ́-!lɪ́ŋ] 'husbands' which has a pronunciation in fast speech as [chʊ̆l!lɪ́ŋ] (the tone marked as rising on the [ʊ] actually rises into the [l]). This is the mirror image case of /kul-ri/ → [kùllí] 'tortoise' given in the tableau in (157). Either /r-l/ or /l-r/ will result in surface [ll]. The same constraints that force [ll] in (157) will force [ll] in *chʊ̆l!lɪ́ŋ*, with the complication that the /ʊ/ of *chʊ̀rʊ́* is deleted.

4.2.5 Voicing assimilation of consonants

Both voiced and voiceless consonants occur stem finally in verbs and nouns, e.g., *gbarɪ* 'watch' versus *gbatɪ* 'force' and *jèvùkíŋ* 'snake' versus *mʊ́gʊ́ŋ* 'river'.[20] An underlying voiced consonant may devoice if it is brought into contact with a following voiceless consonant, as in:

(158) a. ɲin-di**g**-**k**e → ɲìndìkké 'food'
(cf. digi 'to cook')
jà-wɔ́**g**-**k**ʊ́ → jàwɔ́kkʊ́ 'the long thing'
(cf. ɲìŋ-wɔ́gítí 'long things')
tì**g**-**k**á → tìkká 'the village'
(cf. tìgìsí 'villages')
tì**g**-**k**ʊ̀ʊ́ŋ → tìkkʊ̀ʊ́ŋ 'old village'
kpàɲì**g**-**k**pí!íŋ → kpàɲìkkpí!íŋ 'large tick'
(cf. kpàɲìgìsí 'ticks')

---

[20]Stem-final /k/ is rare in Kɔnni, due to a historical change that changed intervocalic *k* to *g*. Most present-day instances of intervocalic *k* are morpheme initial in a compound. Also, stem-final *p* is nonexistent, and *p* as a whole is relatively rare, because of a historical change of *p to *h, y*, or *w*. See Cahill 1992b, 1995a, 1999b.

b. chìàkùr-tí → chìàkùttí 'scorpions'
(cf. chìàkùríŋ 'scorpion')
jɔ́r-tí → jɔ́ttí 'ladders'
(cf. jɔ́ríŋ 'ladder')

In very careful speech, most of the above have alternates in which there is an epenthetic vowel between the bolded consonants on the left, e.g., *jɔ́rí-tí*.

A common pattern cross-linguistically is that sonorants are the only consonants allowed as codas. In Kɔnni, though there are a variety of consonant clusters across morpheme boundaries, within morphemes, nasals and [l] are the only allowed codas. This is expressed as the following coda condition constraint.

(159) **CODACOND**: only sonorants are allowed as codas

A strong pattern in Kɔnni is that the consonants in consonant clusters agree in voicing. This is always the case with obstruents and is violated only when the first member of the cluster is a lateral or nasal.

(160) *C[αvoi]C[−αvoi] (*CC ± voi): adjacent consonants with differing voice values are prohibited

In the case in which voiced consonants are brought into contact with other voiced consonants, and there is no epenthesis, both retain their voicing. This happens only in casual speech and is much less common than the devoicing above.

(161) tìg-bíŋ 'small village'
kɔ̀b-bíŋ 'small bone'
kág-bíŋ 'small roan antelope'[21]
bɔ̀g-góbè 'short fibers'

If both members of the cluster are underlyingly voiced as in (161), the cluster retains its voicing, but if the second member is voiceless, then the entire cluster surfaces as voiceless. (The case in which a voiceless

---

[21]There is a phonetic distinction between the sequence [g-b] and the single labial-velar stop [gb]. Average duration measurements of [g-b] in *kág-bíŋ* 'small roan antelope' and *kɔ́g-bíŋ* 'small cleared area' give 166 ms (n=6, SD = 17), while measurements of the duration of [gb] in *kàgbá* 'straw hat' gave 73 ms (n = 10, SD = 8). An additional factor in the duration of [g-b] is that it is at a morpheme boundary, where duration may be expected to be longer. The Niger-Kordofanian language Eggon of Nigeria has clusters [bg] which contrast with the labial-velar [gb], and even has clusters [gb-g]. In these "clusters," unlike Kɔnni, there is always a slight vocalic transition (Ladefoged and Maddieson 1996).

4.2 Assimilatory processes

consonant is adjacent to a following voiced one does not arise; there is always a vowel between, sometimes as a result of epenthesis.) In both cases above, the voicing in the consonant cluster must be identical. But a nasal never devoices, and in the rare case in which *l* is adjacent to a voiceless consonant, it does not devoice either (e.g., *yàltʊ̀~yàlītʊ́* 'hunter'). A sonorant almost never devoices in Kɔnni (the sole exception is the *-rU/-tU* alternation of the agentive suffix discussed in section 4.4), and we state the highly ranked constraint in terms of sonorants.

(162) IDENT[son]: a [sonorant] feature in the input has the same value in the output

The final consideration before we are ready to present a tableau on these words is why the geminate clusters in (158a) are voiceless rather than voiced. Lombardi (1998b, 1999) notes that voicing assimilation in obstruent clusters is overwhelmingly regressive. She notes that the first obstruent is in coda position while the second is in the onset position and proposes that it is these positions which are the crucial factor; it is more important for an onset obstruent to retain its voicing specification than for a coda obstruent. The constraint IDOnsLar is used to express this.

(163) **IDOnsLar:** Onsets should be faithful to underlying laryngeal specification[22]

A tableau illustrating the regressive voicing assimilation is given in (164).

---

[22]This approach has been termed Licensing by Prosody. Another approach is the Licensing by Cue schema of Steriade (1997). In Licensing by Cue, the nature and number of the phonetic cues available are taken as the crucial factor, while prosodic positions such as onset, coda, and word final are taken as less basic. In Steriade's approach, a pair of relevant constraints might be *voice/V_[−son] >> Preserve voice. The former constraint would rule out both candidates in tableau (164c and d), rather than the two separate constraints needed in the tableau. In this work, however, I am favoring the more abstract phonological approach rather than an approach which refers more directly to phonetics and so retain and apply the constraints in tableau (164).

(164) tɪ̀kká 'the village' MAX(C), IDOnsLar, *CC±voi, DEP(V) >>
CODACOND, IDENT[voi]

tɪg-ka	MAX(C)	IDOnsLar	*CC ±voi	DEP(V)	CODA COND	IDENT [voi]
☞ a. tɪk-ka					*	*
b. tɪgɪ-ka				*!		
c. tɪg-ka			*!			
d. tɪg-ga		*!				
e. tɪ-ka	*!					

The winning candidate (164a) violates IDENT[voi], since the voicing feature of the input *tig-* is deleted. However, these constraints are ranked lower than the other relevant ones which apply here. Candidate (164b) loses by inserting a vowel. The DEP(V) constraint is ranked rather low, as will be examined in more detail in chapter 5 when epenthesis is discussed. Nevertheless, it is ranked high enough to disqualify candidate (164b). Candidate (164c) is ruled out by a violation of *CC±voi. Candidate (164d), changing the [voice] of the suffix consonant, is ruled out by a violation of IDOnsLar, and candidate (164e) is ruled out by deleting a consonant and so fatally violating MAX(C). The constraint IDENT[son] is not active in ruling out any candidates in (164) but is active in (165) when a nasal precedes the voiceless stop.

(165) bʊ̀ŋká 'the donkey' MAX[nas], IDOnsLar >> *CC±voi

bʊŋ-ka	MAX [nas]	IDENT [son]	MAX(C)	IDOnsLar	*CC ±voi	DEP(V)
☞ a. bʊŋ-ka					*	
b. bʊg-ka	*!				*	
c. bʊk-ka	*!	*				
d. bʊg-ga				*!		
e. bʊɲɪ-ka						*!
f. bʊ-ka		*!				
g. bʊŋ-a		*!				

4.2 Assimilatory processes

In similar fashion, IDENT[son] prevents any change of [l] when it is adjacent to a voiceless stop, in the casual pronunciation *yàltʊ́* 'hunter' (~*yàlĭtʊ́*).

(166) yàltʊ́ 'hunter' **IDOnsLar** >> *CC±voi

yal-rʊ	IDENT[son]	MAX(C)	IDOnsLar	*CC±voi	DEP(V)
☞ a. yal-tʊ				*	
b. yat-tʊ	*!				
c. yal-dʊ				*!	

The general IDENT[voi] constraint plays no active role in (166) and is omitted here as well as in the tableau in (167).

(167) tɩ̀g-bɩ́ŋ 'small village' MAX[pl], MAX(C), IDOnsLar, *CC±voi, DEP(V) >> CODACOND

tɩg-bɩŋ	MAX [pl]$_{obs}$	IDOns Lar	*CC ±voi	MAX(C)	DEP(V)	CODA COND
☞ a. **tɩg-bɩŋ**						*
b. tɩk-bɩŋ			*!			*
c. tɩg-pɩŋ		*!	*			*
d. tɩb-bɩŋ	*!					*
e. tɩ-bɩŋ				*!		
f. tɩgɩ-bɩŋ					*!	

Candidates (167a-d) all violate CODACOND by having nonsonorant codas. The *CC±voi is the crucial constraint in ruling out candidate (167b), since the [kb] cluster has dissimilar voicing. Candidate (167c) is ruled out by violating IDOnsLar, since the onset consonant has lost its voicing. Candidate (167d) is ruled out by violating MAX[pl]$_{obs}$. Candidate (167e) or any other that deletes a consonant is ruled out by violating MAX(C). Candidate (167f) is interesting in that this is often the pronunciation heard. For an epenthetic vowel not to be inserted then, CODACOND must be crucially ranked below DEP(V), as in the tableau in (167). In the more usual case, where an epenthetic vowel is present, the rankings of these two must be reversed. Here is a case where optionality of pronunciation involves re-ranking of two constraints.

Optionality is treated in OT with variable rankings or floating constraints. Antilla (1995) and Kiparsky (1994) are early accounts of variability within an OT approach. Kang (1997) treats variability in Korean glides using such variable rankings, using Reynolds' (1994) model of floating constraints, as do Nagi and Reynolds (1997) for Faetar. Zubritskaya (1997) also uses a similar model to account for historical sound changes. For a criticism of OT's ability to account for language variation, see Guy (1997). Variable ranking in these papers is used to account for intra- and inter-speaker variation as well as historical change. Here I am interested only in variation in one speaker, and the constraints CODACOND and DEP(V) are ranked below in the reverse order from the above tableau.

(168) tɪ̀g-bíŋ 'small village' with CODACOND >> DEP(V)

tɪg-biŋ	MAX [pl]$_{obs}$	MAX(C)	IDOnsLar	*CC ±voi	CODA COND	DEP(V)
a. tɪg-biŋ					*!	
☞ b. tɪgɪ-biŋ						*

The optional re-ranking of constraints in (168) makes no difference when the input adjacent consonants have the same place, as in kɔ̀b-bíŋ 'small bone'. Since the consonants are identical, CODACOND is violated for neither, and thus the deciding constraint is DEP(V), which is violated by inserting a vowel. This accounts for clusters of obstruents with identical place values being acceptable, never having vowel epenthesis, but clusters with nonidentical place having optional epenthesis.

The one case not covered above is the one in which two underlyingly voiceless stops adjoin, as in the hypothetical /bak-ka/. For cases in which the voiceless stops are of different places, there is always an epenthetic vowel present, as discussed in section 5.5. For cases in which adjacent underlying voiceless stops are identical in place, we would predict no epenthesis from the attested patterns in this work. Such cases, however, are exceedingly rare, because of an unfortunate combination of two patterns. First, suffixes which begin with a voiceless stop, including adjectival suffixes, almost always begin with /k/ or /kp/, as in -kʊ̀ʊ́ŋ 'old', -ká 'the (NC3)', -kpí!íŋ 'big'. However, due to the historical change of *k to g intervocalically, there are no underived noun stems which end in /k/. Thus the circumstances that bring these two together are extremely uncommon, and there are none in my database.

4.2.6 Labialization

Labialization of a consonant before a round vowel is a common cross-linguistic phenomenon, whether or not the labialization is clearly audible. Connected to this is the fact that the [dorsal] (and possibly [labial]) specifications of an underlying [dorsal] vowel are preserved even when the vowel itself loses those specifications. Consider the following data, in which an underlying back round vowel is fronted when before the glide [y]. Here we merely note the preservation of the [dorsal] feature; see section 5.4.3 for details.

(169) /kʊ/ 'dry'   kà kʷìyá 'it has dried'
      /po/ 'divide'   pʷeye   'has divided'

4.2.7 Palatalization

/s/ and /z/ optionally palatalize before /I/, varying with speaker and rate. Both of the alternants below are common.

(170) zììgíŋ ~ ʒììgíŋg 'center pole' (for shelter)
      sìá ~ ʃìá   'where'

The constraint enforcing this palatalization makes use of the [anterior] feature which is a dependent of [coronal] (Hume 1992, Clements and Hume 1995). Front vowels are [−anterior], and [ʃ, ʒ] are also [−anterior], while [s, z] are [+anterior].

(171) *[+ant]$_{fric}$[−ant]$_{vow}$ (= *[+ant][−ant]): a coronal fricative adjacent to a front vowel cannot be [+anterior]

Since the value of [anterior] alternates for consonants but not for vowels, we may assume that IDENT[ant] for vowels is undominated in Kɔnni.

(172) IDENT[ant]$_C$: consonants have the same value for [anterior] in the input as in the output
      IDENT[ant]$_V$: vowels have the same value for [anterior] in the input as in the output

The optionality or variability is accounted for by variable ranking of the constraints *[+ant][-ant] and IDENT[ant]$_C$. If *[+ant][−ant] >> IDENT[ant]$_C$, then the sibilants are palatalized as below.

(173) ʒìιgíŋ 'center pole' with *[+ant][−ant] >> IDENT[ant]_C

zιιgιŋ	IDENT[ant]_V	*[+ant][−ant]	IDENT[ant]_C
☞ a. ʒιιgιŋ			*
b. zιιgιŋ		*!	

However, if these two rankings are reversed, then the unassimilated forms surface, as in (174).

(174) ʒìιgíŋ 'center pole' with IDENT[ant]_C >> *[+ant][−ant]

zιιgιŋ	IDENT[ant]_V	IDENT[ant]_C	*[+ant][−ant]
a. ʒιιgιŋ		*!	
☞ b. zιιgιŋ			*

4.3 Deletion

Deletion of consonants in Kɔnni is fairly rare and, as we shall see, restricted to certain specific noun classes. We shall see two cases of constraints which may be classed as morphological rather than strictly phonological, since they apply only to a certain class of morphemes.

4.3.1 The ŋ~g~k alternation and g-deletion

In quite a few nouns, /g/ assimilates to a following /k/ in voicing, e.g., kúk-ká, 'the tree (sp.)'. From the plural form kúg-ísí, we deduce that the stem is /kúg-/. However, this /g/ deletes before the singular suffix -ŋ́, giving /kúg-ŋ́/ → kúŋ 'tree (sp.)'. However, in other noun stems which end in /g/, e.g., múg-úrí 'the river' (cf. múg-à 'rivers'), the /g/ does not delete, but an epenthetic vowel surfaces, giving /múg-ŋ́/ → múgúŋ 'river'. The environments for the /g/ in these two patterns are virtually identical; there is no factor in the environment that can account for the differences. The synchronic pattern here can be traced back to the historical sources of these nouns, and a synchronic explanation must refer to the noun class to which the noun belongs.

4.3.1.1 Data

In my database, there are twenty-two nouns which have a /g/ as the last consonant in the stem. However, this /g/ only surfaces as [g] in the plural forms. This /g/ assimilates in voicing to a /k/-initial suffix, as discussed in the previous section. Thus in the singular definite, with a definite suffix /-kA/ or /-kU/ (depending on noun class), the /g/ surfaces as [k]. In the singular citation form, however, there is no trace of the /g/; when the /g/ is adjacent to a nasal, it deletes, as in 'fiber', that is, /bɔ̌g-ŋ́/ → [bɔ̌ŋ]. A sample of forms is given in (175). The forms in (175a) are from noun class 2, and the ones in (175b) are from noun class 3.[23]

(175) g-final nouns from noun classes 2 and 3

	Singular	Singular definite	Plural	
a.	bɔ̌ŋ	bɔ̀k-kú	bɔ̀g-ìtí	'fiber (used for rope)'
	hǎŋ	hàk-kú	hàg-ìtí	'shell, bark'
	zàmpúŋ	zàmpúk-kú	zàmpúg-ítí	'hedgehog'
b.	kúŋ	kúk-ká	kúg-ísí	'tree (sp.)'
	kpàjìŋ	kpàjìk-ká	kpàjìg-ìsí	'wart'
	gbígbáŋ	gbígbák-ká	gbígbág-ísí	'tree (sp.)'

This general picture of g-deletion is complicated, however, by forms like *múgúŋ* 'river', which should also be analyzed with a C-final stem /múg-/, based on the plural *múg-à*. If it followed the same pattern as *kúŋ* in (175b), the citation form should be *múŋ*. But here there is an epenthetic vowel, in this case [ʊ] (for discussion of why it is not the usual epenthetic *I*, see section 5.4.1). Based on the plurals, there are forty nouns in my data which have a nondeletable /g/ as a stem-final consonant. A sample of these is given in (176). Nouns in (176a) are from noun class 1; those in (176b), which are much less frequent, are either from noun class 4 or a mixed noun class.

(176) g-final nouns from noun classes 1 and 4

	Singular	Singular definite	Plural	
a.	múg-úŋ	múg-úrí	múg-á	'river'
	tíg-íŋ	tíg-írí	tíg-è	'house'
	kònchìàg-íŋ	kònchìàg-írí	kònchìàg-á	'cornstalk'
	kpàlìg-íŋ	kpàlìg-írí	kpàlìg-á	'hawk'

---

[23]Interestingly, three nouns do have [g] in the citation form, e.g., *yíŋ!gíŋ, yíŋk!ká, yíŋ!gísí* 'tree (another species), the tree, trees'. The difference here may be that these three have an underlying stem-final vowel: /yŋgɪ-/, while the noun stems in (175) end in consonants. This is supported by the fact that *yíŋk!ká* has a variant pronunciation *yíŋgɪ!ká*, but *kúkká* is never pronounced with a vowel between the consonants.

	Singular	Singular definite	Plural	
b.	náá!g-íŋ	náá!g-íbú	níí!g-è	'cow'
	wàg-íŋ	wàg-ìbú	wàg-ìtí	'fight'

To sum up, nouns which are identical in all relevant ways act one way when they are members of noun classes 2 and 3, and another way when from noun classes 1 and 4. (There are no nouns in noun class 5 which end in /g/.)[24] There is epenthesis in /wàg-ŋ́/ → wàgíŋ 'fight' (176b), but deletion of /g/ in /hàg-ŋ́/ → hăŋ 'shell, bark' (175a). Any synchronic solution to this must refer to the noun classes as a phonological arbitrary label (though the fact that both noun classes 2 and 3 have k in the definite suffix is historically related). However, we can gain insight as to how this situation arose by examining the common ancestor of Buli and Kɔnni.

4.3.1.2 Historical excursus

The noun class system of Buli is quite similar to Kɔnni, but preserves more features of the system from Proto-Buli-Kɔnni (Cahill 1997b). The Buli data below is all from Kröger's (1992) Buli-English dictionary. Many nouns belong to the corresponding noun classes in both languages, but it is also quite common to find cognate nouns which belong to one noun class in Kɔnni and to a different one in Buli. Unsurprisingly, the exact glosses for the cognates may differ slightly, e.g., Kɔnni múgúŋ 'river' has the Buli cognate mogi, which is restricted to large rivers or a reservoir. The Kɔnni gloss is used below for consistency with the rest of this volume, as is my numbering of noun classes rather than Kröger's.

In the previous section, the presence or absence of stem-final [g] in the singular citation form of a noun was shown to be dependent on its noun class. In (177) and (178) forms are given from two of these classes which have divergent behavior, Kɔnni noun class 1 and noun class 2. In noun class 1 in (177), the stem-final /g/ is present in all forms in both Buli and Kɔnni.

(177) Noun class 1

Kɔnni: Singular, Singular definite, Plural	Buli: Singular, Singular definite, Plural	
jígíŋ, jígírí, jígê	jìgī, jigini, jiga	'place'
múgúŋ, múgúrí, múgà	mógí, mógní, moga	'river'
hààgíŋ, hààgírí, —	sagi, sagni, saga	'bush'

---

[24]The only exception may be hɔ̀gú 'woman', but it is uncertain whether the final vowel is underlying or not. The definite form can be pronounced hɔ̀gùwá, but is almost always heard as hɔ̀wwá.

4.3 Deletion

With the *g* always present in every form in (177), there is no question of its being part of the stem in Proto-Buli-Kɔnni (PBK). But this is not the case in forms from noun class 2 in (178). In these noun stems, there is no *g* present in the Buli forms at all, but only *k*.

(178) Noun class 2
Kɔnni: Buli:
Singular, Singular definite,   Singular, Singular definite,
  Plural   Plural
yʊ́ŋ, yʊ́kkʊ́, yʊ́gítí   yok, yoku, yokta   'night'
bɔ̌ŋ, bɔ̀kkʊ́, bɔ̀gítí   bok, boku, bokta   'fiber'
bʊ̀llɔ́ŋ, bʊ̀llɔ̀kkʊ́, bʊ̀llɔ̀gìtí   buluk, buluku, bulukta   'armpit'
hǎŋ, hàkkʊ́, hàgìtí   pak, paku, pakta[25]   'bark, shell'

The *g* in the Kɔnni nouns in (178) only surfaces in the plural forms, as noted before. In terms of historical development, all these *g*s are the result of a sound change in which intervocalic [k] changed to [g] in Kɔnni (Cahill 1995a).[26]

(179) Posited historical development of 'night' from Proto-Buli-Kɔnni (from Cahill 1997b)

	Kɔnni:				Buli:	
PBK	*yʊk	yʊkkʊ	yʊktɪ	PBK	*yʊk	yʊkkʊ	yʊkʊ
	↓	↓	↓		↓	↓	↓
	yʊŋ	yʊkkʊ	yʊgɪtɪ		yok	yoku	yokta

The [g] has thus been present in all stages of development from PBK in noun class 1, but has only come about relatively recently in noun class 2. This is a case of synchronic analysis being clearly different from historical development, since we analyze the present input form of 'night' in Kɔnni as /yʊg-/, but historically the root is *yʊk-.

4.3.1.3 Analysis

Although historically there was no *g* in the Kɔnni noun classes 2 and 3 words like *yʊ́ŋ* 'night', it is consistent with the rest of Kɔnni phonology to analyze them with a *g* in present-day Kɔnni, and this *g* deletes in the citation form of

---

[25]The Buli form has an alternate *pauk*. The sound change of Proto-Buli-Kɔnni *p > Kɔnni *h* before *a* is documented in Cahill (1992b, 1999b).

[26]This had the result, as noted in chapter 3, that all cases of intervocalic *k* within words in present Kɔnni are in morpheme-initial position in compounds, or begin a nominal suffix, or are in borrowed words.

the noun. This cannot be a general process in Kɔnni, for as we have seen the noun class 1 and 4 stems which end in g regularly insert a vowel before the singular citation form, as in tígíŋ 'house'. Therefore, in noun classes 2 and 3 nouns, a stem-final g deletes before the singular suffix -ŋ, though not in the plural when it is prevocalic. The motivation for this may be expressed by a morphologically-based constraint as follows. (The "citation form" is taken to be the singular indefinite, in isolation.)

(180) *$g_{NC2/3}$: a g is disallowed stem-finally in citation forms of nouns of noun classes 2 and 3

This is an extremely specific constraint and cannot be regarded as universal, since it refers specifically to noun classes 2 and 3 of Kɔnni, which of course no other language possesses. It expresses a pattern which is not strictly phonological, but must refer to morphology. It is undominated.

(181) yʋŋ 'night' shows *$g_{NC2/3}$ >> MAX(C)

yʋg-ŋ	*$g_{NC2/3}$	MAX(C)	CODACOND	DEP(V)	IDENT[voi]
☞ a. yʋŋ		*			*
b. yʋgŋ	*!		*		
c. yʋgɪŋ	*!			*	

The undominated constraint *$g_{NC2/3}$ is what rules out the nonoptimal candidates (181b–c), although all candidates violate other constraints as well. But this constraint does not apply at all to nouns outside noun classes 2 and 3, and so constraints which take no part in ruling out candidates in (181) are crucial in determining the optimal candidate in a member of noun class 1, as in (182).

(182) mʋgʋŋ 'river' MAX(C), CODACOND >> DEP(V)

mʋg-ŋ	*$g_{NC2/3}$	MAX(C)	CODACOND	DEP(V)	IDENT[voi]
a. mʋŋ		*!			*
b. mʋgŋ			*!		
☞ c. mʋgʋŋ				*	

The constraints MAX(C) and CODACOND were unimportant in ruling out candidates in (181), but they rule out candidates (182a and b). Similar candidates in (181) and (182) violate the same constraints in the same

4.3.2 *n*-deletion

While nouns with stem-final *m* or *ŋ* always add an epenthetic vowel before the singular suffix *-ŋ*, nouns with stem-final *n* sometimes epenthesize a vowel and sometimes delete the *n*. In a pattern similar to the *g* case above, whether epenthesis or deletion takes place depends on the noun class of the target noun.

4.3.2.1 Data

When the nasals /m/ or /ŋ/ are stem final in nouns, there is always an epenthetic vowel inserted between that nasal and the singular nominal suffix /-ŋ/. Nouns with /m/ stem finally are quite common, while those with /ŋ/ stem finally in my data are limited to the four listed in (183b). The nouns belong to noun classes 3 or 1 or a mix of the two.

(183) a. Retention of stem-final *m*

Singular	Singular definite	Plural	
bímbélím-íŋ	bímbélíŋ-ké	bímbélín-sí	'bells'
bùrìm-íŋ	bùrìn-ní	bùrìn-sí	'oryx'
chàm-íŋ	chàn-ní	chàm-á	'castanets'
dòm-íŋ	dòŋ-ká	dòn-sí	'mosquito'
gìm-íŋ	gìn-ní	gìm-é	'sparrow'
gùm-íŋ	gùŋ-ká	gùn-sí	'kapok tree'
gbégím-íŋ	gbégín-ní	gbégím-è	'lion'
	and many more		

b. Retention of stem-final *ŋ* (complete list of examples in my database)

bíɲí!líŋ-íŋ	bíɲí!líŋ-ké	bíɲí!lín-sí	'tree (sp.)'
gbíŋgbí!ŋ-íŋ	gbíŋgbíŋ-!ké	gbíŋgbín-sì	'chicken (sp.)'
kàmbòŋ-íŋ	kàmbòŋ-ké	kàmbòn-sí	'Twi language'
ɲìŋ-íŋ	ɲìŋ-ké	ɲìŋ-é	'driver ant'

---

[27]Ideally, I would show that noun stems historically ending in both [_k] and [_g] delete before *ŋ*. However, all relevant cases had word-final *k* in Proto-Buli-Kɔnni, as they do in present-day Buli. This was a noun class marker which was reinterpreted in Kɔnni as part of the stem. The result is that there are no word-final *g*s in these classes in Proto-Buli-Kɔnni.

The constraints CODACOND and DEP(V) can be re-ranked, as shown in tableaus in (167) and (168). If re-ranked here with no other constraints, this would give the incorrect output *mugŋ*. A constraint disallowing this form, perhaps allowing syllabic nasals only utterance initially, or disallowing complex codas, would rule this out.

In contrast, nouns which demonstrably have stem-final /n/, as seen by the pre-vocalic form of the noun stem, show two patterns of behavior. In some nouns, the /n/ acts as the other nasals above, and an epenthetic vowel is inserted between the /n/ and the singular suffix /-ŋ/, as in the examples in (184a). However, the majority of nouns with /n/ stem finally delete that /n/ before the suffix /-ŋ/, as in the examples in (184b). The lists in both (184a and b) include all the examples I have in my database.

(184) a. Retention of stem-final *n*

Singular	Singular definite	Plural	
bùùn-íŋ	bùùm-bú	bùùn-é	'boundary'
yàn-íŋ	yàn-ní	yàn-á	'frog'
bòn-íŋ	bòŋ-ká	bòn-sí	'donkey'
gá!n-íŋ	gáŋ-!ká	gán-sì	'thin rope'
gbán-íŋ	gbáŋ-ká	gbán-sí	'skin'
pón-íŋ	póŋ-ké	pón-sí	'tree (sp.)'

b. Deletion of stem-final *n*

bĕŋ	bèn-ní	bèn-é	'tribal face scar'
bǐŋ	bìn-ní	bìn-á	'year'
dààkpăŋ	dààkpàn-ní	dààkpàn-á	'bachelor'
dŭŋ	dùn-ní	dùn-é	'knee'
gìŋgáŋ	gìŋgàn-ní	gìŋgàn-á	'drum (sp.)'
jìŋmíŋ	jìŋmín-ní	jìŋmín-à	'evening'
ɲíŋ	ɲín-ní	ɲín-à	'tooth'
tăŋ	tàn-ní	tàn-á	'stone'
tàŋbáŋ	tàŋbàn-ní	tàŋbàn-á	'land god'
wú!tágbáŋ	wútàgbàn-ní	wútàgbàn-á	'lizard (sp.)'
dùúŋ	dùùm-bú	dùùn-é	'horse'
gú!úŋ	gúúm-!bú	gúún-è	'rope'
níŋ	ním-bú	nín-è	'eye'
wú!úŋ	wúúm-!bú	wúún-è	'genet'

4.3.2.2 Analysis

The pattern of deletion seems to be related to the noun classes, as was *g*-deletion in the previous section, but the pattern here is not quite so obvious. One pattern to note is that every single one of the nouns in which /n/ deletes in (184b) has a plural form showing the noun class 1 suffix -*a*/-*e*, but only two of the forms in (184a) do. Of the nine Buli forms which I have been able to connect as cognates to the above forms, the seven

4.3 Deletion

corresponding to nouns in (184b) also have noun class 1 endings, and both the Buli nouns corresponding to nouns in (184a) have noun class 3 endings. As a general pattern, then, nouns which are in noun class 1, or at least partially so, as evidenced by the plural suffix, delete the /n/. However, this leaves the words for 'boundary' and 'frog' in (184a) as anomalies; they both have noun class 1 plural suffixes, but do not delete the /n/. Thus we will have to either mark these two as true exceptions to the generalization of noun class 1 *n*-deletion, or else abandon the idea of connecting *n*-deletion to any morphological *or* phonological class, and just mark all the nouns in either (184a or b) arbitrarily as undergoing the process or not. On the theory that it is better to have a generalization connected to an already-motivated entity (noun classes) with a little residual data rather than create two arbitrary classes, I will propose a constraint similar to the one in the previous section, which prohibits the stem-final *n* in noun class 1 nouns.

(185) *n_{NC1}: *n* is disallowed stem-finally in citation forms of nouns which belong partially or wholly to noun class 1

This is another language-specific constraint, referring to the Kɔnni noun class 1, which does not occur in any other language. With this constraint in place, we may account for all the nouns above except for *bùùnɩ́ŋ* 'boundary' and *yànɩ́ŋ* 'frog', which must remain exceptional. Truly there is no way in the same set of constraints to account for the fact that *yànɩ́ŋ* 'frog' does not delete the stem-*n*, while *tằŋ* 'stone' does, without an arbitrary marking of one or the other. Tableaus for forms exhibiting *n*-deletion and no *n*-deletion are shown in (186) and (187).

(186) n-deletion: bɪŋ 'year' *n_{NC1} >> MAX(C)

	bĭn-ŋ	*n_{NC1}	MAX(C)	CODACOND	DEP(V)	IDENT[voi]
☞ a.	bɪŋ		*			*
b.	bɪn-ŋ	*!		*		
c.	bɪnɪŋ	*!			*	

Very similar to the cases of *g*-deletion in the previous section, the constraint *n_{NC1} crucially eliminates candidates (186b and c) where the *n* in the stem is retained. The winning candidate (186a) is optimal although it violates the relatively highly-ranked MAX(C). However, when the noun does not belong to noun class 1, *n_{NC1} does not apply, and MAX(C) and CODACOND emerge as the most highly ranked relevant constraints, as in (187).

(187) no n-deletion: bùnɩ́ŋ 'donkey'

bɩn-ŋ	*n_NC1	MAX(C)	CODACOND	DEP(V)	IDENT[voi]
a. bʊŋ		*!			*
b. bʊn-ŋ			*!		
☞ c. bʊnɩŋ				*	

4.4 Dissimilation

Dissimilation in Kɔnni is limited to two morphemes which contain the coronal /r/: the agentive suffix /-rU/, and /-raaŋ/ 'male', which exhibit two distinct patterns.[28]

4.4.1 Data

The /-rU/ agentive suffix, which turns verbs into agentive nouns, has allomorphs [-rU] and [-tU]. The variant [-rU] is the default case, occurring in various intervocalic contexts.

(188) dáwʊ̀rì-nìgà-rʊ́   'village crier (lit., gong-beater)'
     bʊ́ntʊ̀ʊ̀-ɲìì-rʊ́   'hoodless cobra (lit., toad-swallower)'
     yìlì-chìà-rʊ́   'singer (lit., song-cutter)'
     mì-mì-rʊ̀   'builder'
     wʊ̀-wɔ̀sì-rʊ́   'caller'
     tì-tàà-rʊ́   'shooter, thrower'
     gù-gùù-rʊ́   'burier'
     pʊ̀-pʊ̀ntì-rʊ́   'splasher'
     bʊ̀gʊ̀-rʊ́   'soothsayer'
     dì-dàà-rʊ́   'buyer'
     dì-dìgì-rʊ́   'cook'
     hʊ̀-hʊ̀ʊ̀-rʊ́   'swearer'
     dì-dàgì-rʊ́   'teacher (lit., show-er)'
     gbì-gbàtì-rʊ́   'robber'
     gàà-rʊ́   'thief (deceiver)'

The variant [-tU], on the other hand, has quite limited distribution. [-tU] occurs with verbs whose last root consonant is either [l] or [r], as in

---

[28]Thanks to Keiichiro Suzuki for useful comments and encouragement on this section.

4.4 Dissimilation

(189a and b). It also occurs when adjacent to a root-final [n], as in (189c), and is optional when the last consonant is [ŋ], as in (189d).

(189) a. gbì-gbàrì-tú   'watcher'   fí-fààrí-tú   'groomsman (lit., marrier)'
         bù-bùrì-tú   'sower'   bìm-vààrí-tú   'feces collector'

     b. bì-bàlì-ú   'talker'   jù-jùàlì-tú   'climber'
         yàlì-tú   'hunter'   mù-mùlì-tú   'announcer'

     c. chì-chɛ̀n-tú   'fryer' (chɛm-)   kù-kɔ̀lìn-tú   'migrator' (kɔlɪm-)
         dì-dààn-tú   'forgetter' (daaN)   síé-chún-!tú   'traveller (road-walker)' (chún-)
         tù-tùn-tú   'worker' (tʊm-)

     d. pì-pàŋì-tú   'borrower' (paŋɪ)²⁹
         ~ pìpàŋì-rú
         kpì-kpàŋì-tú   'pusher' (kpaŋɪ)
         ~ kpì-kpàŋì-rú

Note that the first example in (188) has an [r] earlier in the word, but since it is not the last consonant preceding the suffix, that suffix surfaces with [r]. In keeping with Odden's (1994) typology of adjacency patterns, this dissimilation requires that the relevant segments be in adjacent syllables.

This is quite possibly part of a larger pattern. There are no cases in my data of words containing *rVL* or *rVVL*. There are no cases of *lVr* within a morpheme, and only three morphemes with *lVVr*, one of which is borrowed. There are no nouns in noun class 1 (which takes -*ri* as the definite suffix) which have *r* as the last stem consonant, though there are in other noun classes.³⁰

So the pattern seems to be that there is a long-distance voicing dissimilation in voicing for nasal or liquid + [r], producing [t].

---

[29] Given the pervasiveness of word-final epenthetic vowels, one might wonder if the final vowels here are also epenthetic. However, verbs with final nasals are fairly common (43 in my database). Whatever the underlying nasal is, it surfaces as *ŋ* when the verb is in citation form, rather than adding a vowel as with other consonants. So for a verb to surface in citation form with [__ŋɪ], we can conclude that the final [ɪ] is underlying and not epenthetic.

[30] There is the one possible exception of *gbú!bárárí* 'the sleeplessness', which I have only heard once, from a younger middle-school student. The more usual pronunciation is *gbú!báráká*, with a definite suffix from a different noun class.

The pattern producing [nt] in (189c) may be somewhat surprising, given the prevalence of voicing after nasals and the phonetic motivation for doing so (Pater 1996, 1999, Hayes and Stiver 1996, Hayes 1999). From general principles and cross-linguistic comparisons, we would expect [d] postnasally rather than [t]. (But see Hyman (1999) and Archangeli, Moll, and Ohno (1998) for a number of exceptions to this pattern.)

However, this, too, is part of a larger pattern in Kɔnni. I find only eighteen Kɔnni words with [nd] in them. They are all nouns. Of these, fourteen are definitely compounds, one is a place name, one is borrowed, one is ideophonic, and the last I am not sure about. The compounds have the word break between *n* and *d*, e.g., *ɲín-dá!áŋ* 'front tooth (lit., tooth-stick)'. However, I find forty-nine nonagentive words with [...nt...], most are not compounds, and there are ten verbs among them, e.g., *dantɪ* 'greet in morning'. It appears possible that [nd] is not a permissible combination *word internally* in Kɔnni, but [nt] is. Let us compare this to other nasal + obstruent sequences.

The [nt] sequence stands out as the only one which may occur in verbs. This is likely a result of the historical development of Kɔnni; *-rI* was probably a verbal suffix at one point in Kɔnni history. If so, then we have at some point in history the same alternation and dissimilation with the verbal extensor *-rI* as with the agentive suffix *-rU* here: [r] intervocalically, and [t] postnasally.

The only consonant clusters found in verbs are word final and are [__nsI], [__ntI], [__llI], and [__ŋŋI]. (The last two, namely [__llI] and [__ŋŋI], are quite rare, with two cases of [__ŋŋI] and only one of [__llI].) It is no coincidence that the verbal extensors discussed in section 2.2.2 were *-sI, -rI, -lI,* and *-gI;* these correlate with the consonant clusters of present Kɔnni with a nasal as the first member. That is, *n-sI → [__nsI], *n-dI → [__ntI], *n-lI → [__llI], and *n-gI → [__ŋŋI].

With this historical pattern as well as the synchronic pattern in (190), it seems likely that an [nd] cluster currently signals a compound.

(190) Word-internal nasal + obstruent sequences in Kɔnni[31]

	Number	Type of words	
nd	18	nouns (almost all compounds)	*ɲín-dá!áŋ* 'front tooth (lit., tooth-stick)'
nt	49	verbs, nouns	*dantɪ* 'greet in morning'

---

[31]In comparison to the 186 NC clusters listed in (190), I have only thirty-eight CC clusters in my data which do not include a nasal. At least half of these are borrowed. These do not include the CC clusters produced as a result of suffixation such as *hak-ka* 'the bark'. It seems that CC clusters which do not include a nasal are unusual at best, and perhaps prohibited in native Kɔnni vocabulary altogether.

4.4 Dissimilation

	Number	Type of words	
ŋg	12	nouns (most are compounds), ideophones	ɲíŋ-góli̋ŋ 'molar (lit., tooth-back)'
ŋk	17	nouns (most are compounds), ideophones	náŋ-kúáŋ 'top of foot (lit., foot-back)'
mb	36	nouns (many compound)	dèmbíŋ 'man'
mp	7[32]	nouns (most borrowed)	tàmpáŋ 'drum (sp.)' (Twi)
ŋgb	10	nouns (some compound)	tíŋgbáŋ 'floor, ground'
ŋkp	16	nouns (many compound)	bìŋkpìáŋ 'shoulder'
nch	12	nouns (most compound)	màn-chíŋ 'blade of grass'
nj	9	nouns (some compound)	nánjúúŋ 'fly'

The other morpheme of Kɔnni which exhibits dissimilatory effects is /-raaŋ/ 'male', which has allomorphs [-daaŋ, -raaŋ]. Normally, it is [-raaŋ] which occurs, as in (191a). However, when the final consonant of the noun is [l], my language consultant pronounced both, as in (191b). When the nouns ended in [r] or a nasal, it always surfaces as [d], as in (191c–d). The nasal is the only consonant which is adjacent to the /-daaŋ/; any other consonant of the noun always has a vowel between it and the /-raaŋ/, whether an underlying stem vowel or an epenthetic one.

(191) a. kpá-!rááŋ   'male guinea fowl'
         ná-!rááŋ   'male cow'
         dù-rààŋ   'male horse'
         dàkúá-rááŋ   'male parrot'
         zùù-rààŋ   'male vulture'

     b. kùlì-rààŋ ~ kùlì-dààŋ   'male tortoise'
         gáán!lù-rààŋ ~ gáán!lù-dààŋ   'male cat'
         jùlà-rààŋ ~ jùlà-dààŋ   'male whydah'
         wàlì-rààŋ ~ wàlì-dààŋ   'male oribi'

     c. ŋmárí-dá!áŋ   'male dove'
         gàɲìàrà-dááŋ   'male weaver-bird'

     d. ŋmààn-dááŋ   'male monkey'
         bùn-dááŋ   'male donkey'
         bùrìn-dááŋ   'male oryx'

---

[32]This very small number of occurrences of [mp] can be traced to the triple split of Proto-Buli-Kɔnni *p into h, y, w (Cahill 1992b, 1995a, 1999b).

There is some question about the independence and underlying representation of /-raaŋ/. There is an independent word dàá 'man', much less common than the normal dèmbíŋ 'man', and /-raaŋ/ is probably derived historically from this. At the present time, however, it is quite likely that there are two lexical forms, a noun /daa/ and an adjective /-raaŋ/. The latter is established as an adjective (rather than a noun which forms compounds) by analogy with /-niiŋ/ 'female'. This /-niiŋ/ not only does not occur independently, but has the property characteristic of adjectives of spreading its ATR value into a preceding noun stem, unlike a compound noun (section 5.2.1). It is possible that the underlying representation of the adjectival 'male' might be analyzed as /-daaŋ/, with /d/ rather than /r/. There is no empirical evidence I am aware of that would decisively settle the question. However, an underlying representation of /-daaŋ/ would complicate the analysis in that a distinction would be needed between lexical items which are nouns and lexical items which are adjectives. In nominal compounds where the second noun has an intervocalic /d/, such as chìi-dèmbíŋ 'brother-in-law (lit., in.law-man)', the /d/ always surfaces as [d], but in the case of 'male' here, the default surfacing of the morpheme-initial consonant is [r] intervocalically. If the underlying representation were /-daaŋ/, then the constraint IDENT[son]$_{LEX}$ which preserves the /d/ of dèmbíŋ would need to be split into two constraints, a highly ranked one applying to the noun dèmbíŋ and a lower-ranked one applying to the adjective /-daaŋ/ which would be commonly violated. For the sake of analytical simplicity, then, I choose /-raaŋ/ as the underlying representation.

A crucial difference between the intervocalic [d] of [-daaŋ] 'male' and the agentive suffix [-tU], with intervocalic [t] in the same phonological environment, is that [-daaŋ] is a lexical item.

4.4.2 Analysis

I will organize my account of the dissimilation of these two morphemes according to the various environments: first I will discuss dissimilation after a stem r, then after a stem l, and finally after nasals.

The analysis here must account for why the two morphemes have allomorphs with different coronal alternants (r/t for the agentive suffix versus r/d for 'male'). This should also connect to the language-wide absence of [rVr] and [lVr], and the absence of [nd] intramorphemically. It should also differentiate between these morphemes and the assimilating /-rI/ definite suffix.

A review of recent approaches to dissimilation is in order here. Dissimilation has in recent years been viewed as a consequence of a violation of the Obligatory Contour Principle (OCP). A form of the OCP was originally proposed for tones (Leben 1973), but is currently used for other elements as well, and in its most general form was stated by McCarthy (1988) simply as:

(192) **OCP:** Adjacent identical elements are prohibited

In a dissimilatory context, one of the adjacent elements is deleted, and a default value which has the opposite value is inserted. The definition of "adjacent" then becomes highly relevant and has been a subject of much discussion. Clements and Hume (1995) point out that the Classical Arabic restriction against having two consonants of the same place value in a word crucially depends on the definition of adjacency. The consonant sequence *dbt, for example, is disallowed in a word, presumably because both d and t are [coronal]. These consonants are not adjacent on the segmental level; they are separated by the b and whatever vowels occur. But by assuming that each place feature occupies its own tier, Clements and Hume can maintain that the [coronal] features of the d and t are adjacent on the [coronal] tier. In a similar way, Odden (1994) reviews many cases of what may be called nonlocal assimilatory and dissimilatory phenomena and proposes a Locality Condition, essentially that any material intervening between a target and trigger node in a process must lie on a distinct plane from these nodes.

Ní Chiosáin and Padgett (1997) demand strict locality in spreading, by which they mean on the segmental level that consonants will participate in spreading of vowel features across them, rather than the feature "skipping" the consonant. But it is interesting that they note that dissimilation cannot be subject to the same locality requirements as assimilation, as evidenced by OCP effects which are long-distance, and they admit they cannot hope for a unified theory of locality to explain both.

Suzuki (1998), in a study which focuses on dissimilation, has proposed the "Generalized OCP" (GOCP) which is a violable, ranked constraint schema under OT. The general schema for the GOCP is:

(193) **Generalized OCP** (Suzuki 1998)
 *X...X: A sequence of two Xs is prohibited, where $X \in \{PCat, GCat\}$, and "..." is intervening material

This abstract form represents a schema in which specific elements can be inserted.[33] Suzuki asserts that the elements allowable as X are features, segments (i.e., root nodes), prosodic units, or morphemes (1998:65). The GOCP deliberately does not make reference to autosegmental tiers, and the notion

---

[33] In this it resembles the ALIGN schema, which is not properly a family of constraints but a formula for generating such constraints.

of adjacency with respect to a particular tier or plane which was crucial in Feature Geometry approaches is irrelevant in the GOCP. The crucial thing is an identity of some sort between elements, not the specific representation. The GOCP can be exploded into a hierarchy of constraints which are universally ranked according to the distance between the elements under consideration (the "identicals," to use Suzuki's terminology).

(194) **GOCP + Proximity Hierarchy** (Suzuki 1998)
 *X...X: = {*XX » *X-C_0-X » *X-μ-X » *X-μμ-X » *X-σσ-X » ...» *X-∞-X}

By ranking the relevant Faithfulness constraints in the appropriate position in this hierarchy, an OCP constraint may apply only when the "identicals" are strictly adjacent, or separated by some other specified amount of material. The hierarchy entails that elements which are disallowed at some specific distance are also disallowed at any closer distance.[34]

Suzuki does not deal with notions of representation at all, nor issues of adjacency as applied to transparency, blocking, assimilation, and so forth. It seems that he and Ní Chiosáin and Padgett would agree that there may be an entirely different set of principles which apply to dissimilatory phenomena than to other processes such as assimilation.

Suzuki also provides a list of languages which undergo dissimilation of various sorts, including dissimilation of liquid segments, which is of interest to us for the Kɔnni cases here. Besides the well-known Latin case, he divides these into dissimilations of the features [LIQUID] (Javanese), [lateral] (Kuman, Latin, Yidiɲ, and Yimas), and [rhotic] (or [retroflex]) (Ainu, Georgian, Modern Greek, Sundanese, and Yindjibarndi). Most of these liquid dissimilations are dealt with in more depth in Walsh-Dickey (1997). The cases considered to be dissimilations [rhotic] all have inputs of /r...r/, and most have outputs of [l...r] or [r...l].

In Suzuki's survey, the language which appears closest in input and output to Kɔnni, with input of /r...r/ and output [r...t], is Yimas. Yimas (Foley 1991) is a Papuan language of Papua New Guinea. It has dissimilation of an

---

[34]Suzuki also claims that this GOCP is able to capture a gradient quality of dissimilations or co-occurrence restrictions, unlike the traditional formulation of the OCP. This is that dissimilations are more likely when the elements are closer together. Thus he cites Pierrehumbert's (1993) study of Arabic showing that besides the near-total lack of adjacent consonants with identical place, there is a much lower frequency than expected of consonants with identical place within a word even when these consonants are not adjacent. I do not see how this constraint ranking could generate this lower frequency. In a tableau, it is an individual word that is examined, not the entire language. Unless there is a separate ranking for each word (or perhaps class of words), an additional mechanism besides what Suzuki proposes is necessary.

4.4 Dissimilation

inchoative suffix -*ara* which surfaces as -*ata* when preceded by an [r] ([r] is described as an alveolar tap, as in Kɔnni). Odden (1994), Walsh-Dickey (1997), and Suzuki (1998) all analyze this as a dissimilation in [lateral], the reason for this being that Foley writes that [r] is in free variation with the lateral [l]. This seems to be a general restriction in Yimas; there are no *rVr* sequences, and Suzuki proposes a general GOCP constraint on the [lateral] feature to cover this. This analysis will not work for Kɔnni, however, since [lateral] has nothing to do with [r] in Kɔnni; there are no variations between *r~l*, and the only alternation involving these is the total assimilation of *r* to *l* in the noun class 1 definite suffix discussed in section 4.2.4.

Walsh-Dickey (1997) finds that rhotic consonants do comprise a natural class, but is able to define them in phonological terms without using the specific feature [rhotic]. All rhotics in her proposal have the structure in (195) in common.

(195)
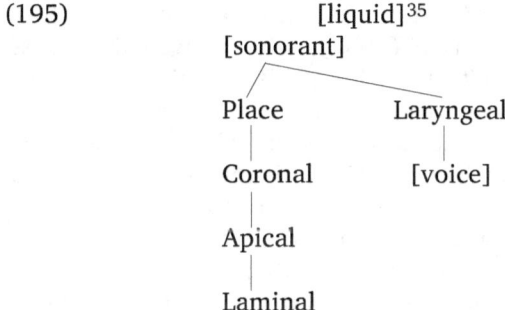

Suzuki, on the other hand, assumes [rhotic] to be a feature and presents several cases of avoidance of sequences of rhotics. Whether there is a feature [rhotic] or whether there is a configuration as above which all rhotics have in common is a debate beyond the scope of this work. In terms of Suzuki's GOCP constraints, it is possible to have the "identical element" be a node or a feature, but if [rhotic] is best viewed as a configuration rather than as a single feature, then the list of types of elements in Suzuki's GOCP would need to be extended to specific configurations. Whatever the representation, it is evident that cross-linguistically a prohibition against consecutive rhotic elements is common. In Kɔnni, the general constraint producing dissimilation will be such a prohibition against [rhotic] sequences. (Note that I use *rVr as an abbreviated form of *[rhotic]V[rhotic] in the tableaus.)

---

[35] One of the major claims in Walsh-Dickey (1997) is that there is a natural class of [liquid]. This is a major class feature and is a feature of rhotics and sonorant laterals.

(196) *[rhotic]V[rhotic] (*rVr): a sequence of [rhotic] features separated by only a vowel is disallowed

In the tableaus below, I do not consider outputs with [n] or [l] as alternants to the optimal candidates. Cross-linguistically, from Suzuki's (1998) survey, seven of the ten languages which have dissimilation of some liquid feature produce a nasal or lateral in the output. However, this does not happen in Kɔnni, and there is no spontaneous lateralization or nasalization. I will therefore regard candidates with [n] or [l] to be ruled out by high-ranking DEP[nasal] and DEP[lateral] constraints.

Assuming the input form of the -rU/-tU suffix is /-rU/, some of the constraints relevant in section 4.2.4.2 for assimilation of /r/ are also applicable here. However, the IDENT[son] constraint needs to be expanded into a family of constraints, to reflect the pattern that if there are two cases of /r/ in a word, one in the stem and one in a suffix, it is the suffixal /r/ that dissimilates, while the stem /r/ surfaces as [r]. I propose a distinction similar to that proposed by Casali (1997), who showed that cross-linguistically, vowels in lexical items are less subject to elision than vowels in affixes. Though at this point the relevant constraint could be stated in terms of a lexical versus nonlexical distinction, when we discuss the fact that the adjectival suffix, which is lexical, dissimilates, we note that the distinction between stem and nonstem is more crucial. (The distinctions between stem and lexical item are an area where more research could prove fruitful.) McCarthy and Prince (1995:364) also noted that universally Root Faithfulness outranks Affix Faithfulness. In keeping with these, I propose a member of the IDENT[son] family specific to stems. In keeping with the notion that more specific constraints are ranked more highly than the general constraint (see discussion of "Panini's Theorem" in section 1.3.1) IDENT[son]$_{STEM}$ will be ranked higher than the general IDENT[son] constraint which applies to all positions.[36]

(197) IDENT[son]$_{STEM}$: the value of the feature [sonorant] in a stem is the same in the output as in the input

In similar fashion, I propose that IDENT[voi] is expanded into a family of constraints which includes at least a distinction in lexical and nonlexical items:

---

[36]Alternatively, both IDENT[son]$_{STEM}$ and IDENT[son]$_{LEX}$ could be proposed, but the latter is redundant in Kɔnni.

4.4 Dissimilation

(198) IDENT[voi]_LEX: the value of the feature [voice] in a lexical item is the same in the output as in the input

(199) bù-bùrì-tʊ́ 'sower' *rVr, IDENT[son]_STEM, DEP[nas] >> IDENT[son]

bʊ-bʊr-ʊ	*rVr	IDENT [voi]_LEX	IDENT [son]_STEM	DEP [nas]	IDENT [son]	*VDV	IDENT [voi]
☞ a. bʊ-bʊrɪ-tʊ					*		*
b. bʊ-bʊrɪ-dʊ					*	*!	
c. bʊ-bʊrɪ-rʊ	*!						
d. bʊ-bʊrɪ-nʊ				*!			
e. bʊ-bʊtɪ-rʊ		*!	*!		*		*

The constraint IDENT[voi]_LEX is listed as undominated in (199) because there is never a case in Kɔnni where it is violated to my knowledge. The winning candidate (199a) violates IDENT[son] by changing the [+son] of the suffixal input r to [−son] of the output t, violating IDENT[voi] at the same time. Candidate (199b) also violates IDENT[son], but in addition violates the low-ranked constraint *VDV. Candidate (199c) violates the top-ranked *rVr, while candidate (199d) violates DEP[nas] by introducing a new nasal segment. Candidate (199e) differs from the winning candidate in that the r of the root rather than that of the suffix is changed.

Note that losing candidate (199d), introducing a new nasal, shows that DEP[nas] outranks IDENT[son], and this is part of the evidence that shows both DEP[nas] and IDENT[nas] are necessary in Kɔnni.

Another possible candidate bʊ-bʊr-rʊ is ruled out not only by the previously discussed *[son]r, but by the *rr constraint that is implied in Suzuki's GOCP proposal. Recall that his universal hierarchy in (194) entails that elements which are disallowed at some specific distance are also disallowed at any closer distance.

Applying this principle, the *rVr constraint entails a *rr constraint which outranks the first. Actually, since *rVr is never violated, it is difficult to see empirically how another constraint could outrank it, but if *rVr is never violated, Suzuki's hierarchy would predict that *rr would never be violated either, and that is indeed the case.

The fact that /-rU/ is a nonlexical item and /-raaŋ/ is a lexical item is what makes the difference in their dissimilation patterns. The voicing may change on the nonlexical morpheme /-rU/, but not on the lexical item /-raaŋ/.

(200) dù-rààŋ 'stallion' (horse-male)

du-raaŋ	*rVr	IDENT [voi]$_{LEX}$	IDENT [son]$_{STEM}$	*VDV	IDENT [voi]
☞ a. du-raaŋ					
b. du-daaŋ			*!	*	
c. du-taaŋ		*!	*!		*

In the case of *ŋmárí-dá!áŋ* 'male dove' (201), the question is why the /r/ of the adjectival 'male' changes to [d] rather than the /r/ of the noun stem 'dove'. The differences between them are first, morpheme-initial versus morpheme-medial position, and second, stem versus suffix (or head versus dependent). Regarding position in the morpheme, we would expect that morpheme initial would be a position of greater faithfulness to underlying representation than morpheme medial. If so, then the morpheme-medial position would be the one expected to change, yielding the unattested *ŋmádí-rá!áŋ*. Position within the morpheme thus is not a sufficient criterion to predict the attested results. Though both 'dove' and 'male' are lexical items, 'dove' is a stem and 'male' is a suffix. We expect consonants of a stem to be more faithful than consonants of a suffix, and the constraint referring to faithfulness of [son] in a stem is what makes the difference in (201). The crucial difference between candidates (201a and d) is that in (201d) the stem consonant is unfaithful, while in (201a) the suffixal consonant is.

(201) ŋmárí-dá!áŋ 'male dove' *rr, *rVr >> DEP(V)

ŋmar-raaŋ	*rr	*rVr	IDENT [voi]$_{LEX}$	IDENT [son]$_{STEM}$	DEP (V)	*VDV
☞ a. ŋmarɪ-daaŋ					*	*
b. ŋmarɪ-raaŋ		*!			*	
c. ŋmarɪ-taaŋ			*!		*	
d. ŋmadɪ-raaŋ				*!	*	*
e. ŋmar-raaŋ	*!					

The cases in which the last consonant in the stem is [l] or [n] have yet to be considered and bring additional complexities. A stem that has [l] as the last consonant yields the following forms (see (189c), (191b) for additional data).

4.4 Dissimilation

(202) a. yàlì-tó 'hunter'
b. kùlì-ràáŋ ~ kùlì-dàáŋ 'male tortoise'

Recall that there are no cases of [lVr] within a single morpheme in Kɔnni. We then have a constraint penalizing such sequences. Because of (202b) we know it cannot be undominated. This separates it from the constraint *rVr, which is undominated. In Suzuki's terms, this will be a constraint prohibiting sequences of [liquid].

(203) *[liquid]V[liquid] (*[liq]V[liq]): a sequence of [liquid] features separated by only a vowel is disallowed

Since *rVr refers to a subset of the forms referenced by *[liq]V[liq], we would expect by Pāṇini's Theorem that *rVr outranks *[liq]V[liq] (see discussion in section 1.3.1). Indeed, this is the case, since *rVr is undominated, while *[liq]V[liq] can be violated in Kɔnni, as shown in (204b). It is also violated in the few lexical cases where [lVl] occurs, as in the verb root /lal-/ 'play'. In the case of underlying /lVl/, the relevant faithfulness constraints outrank *[liq]V[liq] and preserve the two liquids. The *[liq]V[liq] constraint is ranked below the undominated IDENT[voi]$_{LEX}$ but relatively high in (204) and (205), though the only ranking justified here is above IDENT[voi]. The ranking of *[liq] V [liq] with respect to other constraints will be justified in (206) and (207).

(204) yàlì-tó 'hunter' CODACOND >> DEP(V)
     *[liq]V[liq], *VDV, CODACOND >> IDENT[voi]

	yal-rʊ	IDENT [voi]$_{LEX}$	*[liq]V[liq]	*VDV	CODA COND	DEP(V)	IDENT [voi]
☞ a.	yalı-tʊ					*	*
b.	yal-tʊ				*!		
c.	yalı-dʊ			*!		*	
d.	yalı-rʊ		*!			*	

The winning candidate (204a) violates no constraints except IDENT[voi] by devoicing the /d/ and DEP(V) by inserting a vowel. The other candidates violate restrictions on particular sequences. Candidate (204b) fatally violates CODACOND by having a non-ŋ coda. Candidate (204c) violates *VDV and candidate (204d) violates *[liq]V[liq]. The constraints applying to lexical morphemes, in particular IDENT[voi]_LEX, do not apply here to the nonlexical agentive suffix /-rU/, though they will be crucial below.

The word yàlì-tʊ́ 'hunter' also has the alternate pronunciation yàl-tʊ́. The sonorant l is allowed next to t since they have the same place of articulation. Here the alternate pronunciation is accounted for by a switch in the rankings of DEP(V) and CODACOND from above.

(205) yàl-tʊ́ 'hunter' DEP(V) >> CODACOND

yal-rʊ	IDENT [voi]_LEX	*[liq]V[liq]	*VDV	DEP(V)	CODA COND	IDENT [voi]
☞ a. yal-tʊ					*	*
b. yalɪ-tʊ				*!		
c. yalɪ-dʊ			*!			
d. yalɪ-rʊ		*!		*		

Since there is variability in the pronunciation of 'male tortoise' (Amadu went back and forth between the two with equal fluency), we account for this also by variable ranking of constraints, this time of *VDV and *[liq]V[liq]. These were coranked in (205) above, and we see in (206) that it is their variability in ranking which decides between the pronunciations of kùlì-ràáŋ ~ kùlì-dààŋ 'male tortoise'.

(206) kùlì-ràáŋ 'male tortoise' with variable ranking *VDV >> *[liq]V[liq]

kuli-raaŋ	IDENT [voi]_LEX	*VDV	*[liq]V[liq]	IDENT [cont]_LEX	IDENT [voi]
☞ a. kuli-raaŋ			*	*	
b. kuli-daaŋ		*!			
c. kuli-taaŋ	*!				*

In (206), with *VDV outranking *[liq]V[liq], *[liq]V[liq] is reduced to irrelevance by higher-ranking constraints; the winning candidate (206a) violates it. The losing candidate (206b) is now eliminated by violating *VDV. Candidate (206c) has lost [voice], which was not serious in (204), since the morpheme involved was nonlexical. However, here the morpheme is lexical and, so devoicing it violates the top-ranked IDENT[voi]_LEX.

4.4 Dissimilation

(207) kùlì-dàáŋ 'male tortoise' with variable ranking *[liq]V[liq] >> *VDV

kuli-daaŋ	IDENT [voi]$_{LEX}$	*[liq]V[liq]	*VDV	IDENT [cont]$_{LEX}$	IDENT [voi]
a. kuli-raaŋ		*!		*	
☞ b. kuli-daaŋ			*		
c. kuli-taaŋ	*!				*

In (207), with *[liq]V[liq] outranking *VDV, it is the turn of *VDV to be reduced to irrelevance by higher-ranking constraints; the winning candidate (207b) violates it. The losing candidate (207a) is now eliminated by violating *[liq]V[liq]. Again, candidate (207c) is eliminated by losing its specification of [voice].

The final environment for these two morphemes to dissimilate is following a nasal. (For more data, see 189c and 191d.)

(208) a. tù-tùn-tú   'worker' (from tʊm-)
     b. ŋmààn-dàáŋ   'male monkey'

As noted previously, virtually all words in Kɔnni with [nd] are compounds. Many of the ones which synchronically cannot be identified as such, such as *tàndúŋ* 'mortar', are shown to be such by their mixing of [−ATR] and [+ATR] vowels in the same word. We propose a constraint prohibiting the sequence [nd] in Kɔnni. The same constraint will also apply to [ld] sequences, of which there are none in Kɔnni, so we generalize this to sonorants. This will be violated in several circumstances, as in (208b), as well as across word boundaries and in compound words of present-day Kɔnni.

(209) *[son]d: the sequence [sonorant] + [d] is prohibited

As seen in the table of nasal-stop clusters in (190), most of these clusters are in compounds, with the exception of [nt], which appears not only in monomorphemic nouns but in verbs as well. It is quite possible that the *[son]d constraint is only one instantiation of a larger pattern. Taken by itself, it does not appear to have any phonetic motivation; on the contrary, languages in general tend to voice stops after nasals, not devoice them as in Kɔnni (as in Pater 1996, 1999, Hayes and Stiver 1996, Hayes 1999). However, Hyman (1999) presents a number of languages in which a constraint *ND seems to be active; in Tswana, for example, there are numerous instances of [nt, mp, ŋk], but [mb, nd, ŋg] are almost nonexistent. There is thus some cross-linguistic evidence for *ND, and in Kɔnni it extends to all sonorants, not just nasals, and I leave the constraint as *[son]d. In the tableaus in (212) and (213), outputs with [r] are not considered. [r] never occurs after a nasal or any consonant, and I will consider it ruled out by an undominated constraint to that effect. The choice then becomes between [d] and [t], and the different morphemes in question choose differently. Again, the difference becomes that between a nonlexical morpheme and a lexical one.

The final area we must consider is why the *nd* sequence with the definite article and 'also' totally assimilates to a stem, giving *nn* (e.g., *gìn-ní* 'the sparrow', *nʊn-nʊaŋ* 'rain also', but here the same *nd* sequence yields *nt* or *nd* (e.g., *tʊ̀-tʊ̀n-tʊ́* 'worker', *ŋmààn-dááŋ* 'male monkey', from 208). The distinctiveness of the affix is preserved here but not in the definite article. We have made reference to the distinction between lexical item and affix in this phonology in constraints on [voice]. Here we find that we must make a finer-grained distinction than that, that we must distinguish between inflectional and derivational suffixes. The constraint that prevents the derivational suffix /-rU/ from totally assimilating to a preceding nasal, as the inflectional suffix /-rI/ did, must be a constraint that refers to the derivational status of the affix. I conceive that there is a scale of "wordhood," for lack of a better term, that starts with inflectional affixes on the low end, and then continues to derivational affixes, particles, and independent lexical items. In general, the lower a morpheme is on the scale, the more likely it is to assimilate and lose its own identity. Universally, then, we should have a constraint family with universal rankings as in (210). There may be more members on the cline; these are given as representative.

(210) IDENT[F]$_{LEX}$ > > IDENT[F]$_{PART}$ > > IDENT[F]$_{DER}$ > > IDENT[F]

So to account for the lack of assimilation to a preceding nasal by the agentive suffix /-rU/, I propose a constraint referring to the derivational level of the above hierarchy.

(211) IDENT[nas]$_{DER}$: a derivational affix will have the same value of nasal in the output as in the input

This constraint will be ranked above the corresponding constraint which applies to inflectional suffixes. Indeed, that constraint will be ranked low enough to make no difference in a tableau yielding *nn* from the definite suffix as in (156). But in the tableau below it does make a distinct contribution.

4.4 Dissimilation

(212) tʊ̀-tʊ̀n-tʊ́ 'worker' *[son]d, IDENT[nas]_der >> IDENT[voi]

tʊ-tʊm-rʊ	IDENT [voi]_LEX	*[son]d	IDENT [nas]_der	IDENT [voi]
☞ a. tʊ-tʊn-tʊ				*
b. tʊ-tʊn-dʊ		*!		
c. tʊ-tʊn-nʊ			*!	

In (212), the losing candidate (212b) loses by virtue of violating *[son]d. The winning candidate is unfaithful to the input by losing voicing, but the relevant constraint IDENT[voi] is low-ranked. The other losing candidate (212c) violates IDENT[nas]_der by gaining a [nasal] specification in the derivational suffix.

(213) ŋmààn-dààŋ 'male monkey' IDENT[voi]_LEX, IDENT[nas]_LEX >> *[son]d

ŋmaan-raaŋ	*[son]r	IDENT [voi]_LEX	IDENT [nas]_LEX	*[son]d	IDENT [voi]
☞ a. ŋmaan-daaŋ				*	
b. ŋmaan-taaŋ		*!			*
c. ŋmaan-naaŋ			*!		
d. ŋmaan-raaŋ	*!				

In (213), the winning candidate (213a), like the losing candidate in (212), violates *[son]d. However, the losing candidate (213b) violates the higher-ranked IDENT[voi]_LEX, since /-raaŋ/ is a lexical item. The losing candidate (213c) loses by violating IDENT[nas]_LEX, and the last loser (213d) violates the undominated *[son]r.

The total assimilation of /mr/ → [nn] as in *gìnní* 'the sparrow' is repeated from (156) to exemplify the differences in treatment of nasals.

(214) gìnní 'the sparrow' *[son]r, *NVr, MAX[Cpl]_{rel}, IDENT[son]
      >>IDENT[nas]

gim-ri	*[son]r	MAX [Cpl]_{rel}	*NVr	IDENT [son]	DEP(V)	IDENT [nas]	MAX [Cpl]
☞ a. gin-ni						*	*
b. gin-di				*!			*
c. gin-ti				*!			*
d. gin-ri	*!						*
e. gimi-ri			*!		*		
f. gim-mi		*!					*

The IDENT[nas] constraint in (214) does not refer to a lexical item or a derivational affix, as the two previous tableaus did. This is because the relevant morpheme /-rI/ is an inflectional suffix, and the IDENT[nas] constraint referring to it is ranked lower than the others. In the tableau in (214), IDENT[nas] is violated by the winning candidate, but the constraint is ranked low enough not to rule it out. An unlisted candidate *gir-ri is ruled out by the undominated constraint MAX[nas] (see 134).

The last nasal-related data here is pì-pàŋí-tú ~ pìpàŋì-rú 'borrower', in which there is free variation between -tú/-rú after the nasal vowel sequence [ŋV]. We have already noted the constraint *NVr (152) similar to the *[liq]V[liq] and *rVr. Thus, this looks like we may be able to combine all into one constraint *SON-V-r. This would also include the other nasals, and indeed there are few cases of [mVr] and none of [nVr]. However, there is an absolute absence of rVr in Kɔnni, but lVr is found as one option in kuli-raaŋ 'male tortoise'. Since the prohibition against rVr is absolute but NVr and lVr do occur, the rankings must be separate and they are distinct constraints.

An interesting point about dissimilation in Kɔnni is that both cases involve coronals, and /r/ is indeed arguably the least marked consonant in Kɔnni, since [r] is the only epenthetic consonant within words (section 4.5). This goes against the tendency noted by Alderete (1997) and Suzuki (1998) that it is marked structures that tend to dissimilate, though Suzuki notes exceptions to this tendency and differs from Alderete's approach.

4.5 Epenthesis

There are two epenthetic consonants in Kɔnni. First, glottal stop [ʔ] occurs between words in some but not all vowel hiatus situations, depending on the syntactic context. Second, [r] seems to be inserted in certain plural nouns of noun class 1. We will see that these insertions follow from cross-linguistically motivated constraints.

4.5.1 Data

The only glottal stops in Kɔnni occur at word edges; there are no word-internal glottal stops.[37] Glottal stop insertion in Kɔnni is closely tied to vowel assimilation in hiatus, and the whole phenomenon, including a more detailed examination of syntactic conditions under which it occurs, is examined in section 5.8. The syntactic environment determines whether assimilation of the vowels occurs or not.

(215) a. No assimilation
    tí   ʔàlívésà   N'→NP-N
    1p onion
    'our onion'

    ǹ nàn lígí ʔáŋ!kúríká   V'→V-NP
    1s FUT cover barrel.the
    'I will cover the barrel.'

  b. Assimilation
    gbààsá !átà   NP→N-NUM
    dog.PL 3
    'three dogs'

    dʋ́! ʋ́ tíírí   C'→ C-IP
    that 3s stretch
    'S/he should stretch!'

The waveform in (216) shows an example of glottal stop. Note the lack of periodic energy the duration of the glottal, followed by an abrupt rise in amplitude of the waveform for the following vowel, characteristic of stops.

---

[37] At least some glottal stops occur utterance initially when the first word of the utterance begins with a vowel, but I have not studied this enough to know if this is consistent.

(216) Waveform of tí ʔàlívɛ́sà 'our onion', showing glottal stop

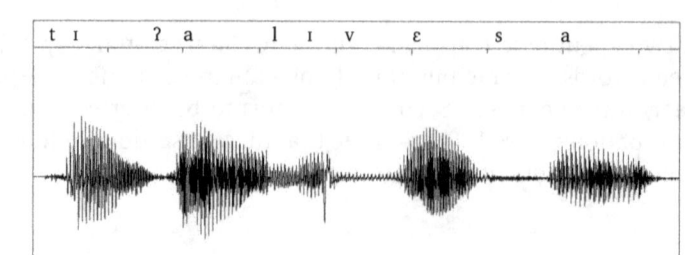

Anticipating the discussion in section 5.8, it appears that total assimilation does not take place between a lexical item (noun or verb) and a maximal projection XP. This is the environment in which a glottal stop is inserted.[38]

The other epenthetic consonant in Kɔnni is [r], which occurs only in some plural forms of noun class 1 nouns. While the usual plural suffix for noun class 1 is [-a] or [-e], depending on vowel harmony, for some class 1 nouns the plural suffix is [-ra], as in dà-rá 'days'. Samples are given of the "normal" plural suffix in (217a), and a list of the seventeen words in my data which exhibit [-ra] are in (217b).

(217) Noun class 1

		Singular /-ŋ/	Plural /-A/
a.	'bee'	síébí-ŋ	síébí-è
	'breast'	bìs-íŋ	bìs-á
	'chin'	bítíé-ŋ	bítí-è
	'forehead'	díí-ŋ	dí-è
	'grinding stone'	níí-ŋ	ní-à
	'house'	tíg-íŋ	tíg-è
	'mouth'	núá-ŋ	nú-à
	'problem'	wíí-ŋ	wíí-à
	'shade'	jág-íŋ	jág-â
	'stump'	dààgbúg-íŋ	dààgbúg-ê
	'yam'	ɲú-ŋ	ɲú-à

---

[38]James Amadu was consistent in inserting glottal stops before nouns. However, two other speakers, Tahiru and Kwabena Joseph, did not insert glottal stops, but they did keep the vowels distinct. This is discussed more in chapter 5.

4.5 Epenthesis

b.
'back of head'	kpàá-ŋ	kpà-rá
'chest'	ɲóó-ŋ	ɲó-rà
'cloud'	nììŋmàá-ŋ	nììŋmà-rá
'day'	dàá-ŋ	dà-rá
'duck'	gbìɲʊ́á-ŋ	gbìɲɔ̀-rá
'elder'	jàkʊ́ʊ́-ŋ	ɲìŋkʊ̀-rá
'grasshopper'	sàŋkpàá-ŋ	sàŋkpà-rá
'heart'	sìkpáá-ŋ	sìkpá-rà
'hoe'	kʊ̀ʊ́-ŋ	kʊ̀-rá
'hyena'	gbàànchʊ́ʊ́-ŋ	gbàànchʊ̀-rá
'land'	gàá-ŋ	gà-rá
'mouse'	hàŋkʊ̀ʊ́-ŋ	hàŋkʊ̀-rá
'name'	sàá-ŋ	sà-rá
'rat'	dàyʊ̀ʊ́-ŋ	dàyʊ̀-rá
'thumb'	núkpáá-ŋ	núkpá-rà
'toad'	bʊ̀ntʊ̀ʊ́-ŋ	bʊ̀ntʊ̀-rá
'tree (sp.)'	ɲʊ̀ŋ-ŋ	ɲʊ̀-rá

The variant [-ra] occurs only if the final underlying vowels of the noun stem are /aa/, /ʊʊ/, or in one case, /ɔɔ/.[39] Note there are four cases of stem-final [ii], [ɪɪ], or [ie] in (217a), with a resulting lack of [r]-insertion. [r]-insertion does not occur with any [+ATR] vowels. This could be an accident of the data (80 percent of nouns are [−ATR]), but I will argue below that there are plausible phonetic reasons for this pattern.

4.5.2 Analysis

The analysis of epenthesis in Kɔnni must account for several patterns. First is the epenthesis of [ʔ] between vowels which are across words, but epenthesis of [r] within members of noun class 1. An account of [r]-insertion must account for insertion of [r] rather than another consonant, its insertion only in nouns with /aa/, /ʊʊ/, or /ɔɔ/ in their stems, and its complete lack in [+ATR] nouns. The first and last patterns are relatively easy to account for; the second is more complex.

The insertion of [r] and [ʔ] rather than other consonants can be accounted for on the basis of markedness. The special behavior of coronals has been noted for some time; see Paradis and Prunet (1991) for discussion of several aspects. The assumption in that volume was that the behavior of coronals which differentiates them from consonants with other

---

[39]For discussion of the diphthongization by which /ɔɔ/ → [ʊa] in *gbìɲʊ̀áŋ* 'duck', see section 5.3.

places of articulation was explained by the notion that coronals were unspecified for place. McCarthy and Taub (1992) in their review of the volume, raised substantial objections to the underspecification assumption. Steriade (1995a) and others have also raised objections to parts or all of the approach that uses underspecification as a major explanatory tool of phonology. Within an Optimality Theory approach the special properties of coronals are assumed to be a consequence of their unmarkedness, such unmarkedness being directly expressed by universal ranking of *Cor below *Dor and *Lab as in Smolensky (1993). But Lombardi (1998a, 2002) notes that glottal stop is the most common epenthetic segment cross-linguistically and extends this hierarchy to include a low ranking of the ban on pharyngeal place to account for glottal stop insertion as well.

(218) *Dor, *Lab >> *Cor >> *Phar

In the context of epenthesis, and in keeping with our conception of place features as privative to which the MAX and DEP family of constraints apply, we can restate the above hierarchy as:

(219) DEP[Dor], DEP[Lab] >> DEP[Cor] >> DEP[Phar]

These constraints ensure that it is better to insert a pharyngeal place feature than a coronal one and that both of these are better than inserting a dorsal or labial feature. If no other factors were involved, the above constraint ranking would always favor glottal stop over a coronal as an epenthetic consonant. However, there are a number of factors which Lombardi notes are relevant to coronal epenthesis, e.g., a need for codas to be sonorants. This last factor in constraint form would rule out glottal stop in coda position. All cases that Lombardi (1998a, 2002) has found in which epenthetic coronal sonorants are onsets (as in Kɔnni) are restricted to particular morphological contexts (as in Kɔnni). While she does not give detailed analyses of languages with this pattern, it is clear that such analyses may depend on morphologically based constraints.

The first epenthesis we consider, however, depends on a particular syntactic and lexical environment. A glottal stop is inserted to clearly separate the noun from a preceding word. These are illustrated below with two hiatus situations, both with input /ɪ # a/.

4.5 Epenthesis

(220) a. Glottal stop epenthesis[40]
tì àlǐvésà → tì ʔàlǐvésà   'our onion'   N' → NP-N

b. No glottal epenthesis—vowel assimilation
gbààsì !átà → gbààsá !átà   'three dogs'   NP → N-Num

I assume that in this syntactic situation, a consonant must be present to prevent vowel assimilation, which would blur the boundaries between the two syntactic divisions. In terms of a constraint, this would mandate that the word beginning the second division must have an onset in its initial syllable.

(221) **ONS-lex**: a lexical item must have an onset

This general ONS constraint is familiar from many OT accounts; here I assume that it is, like many constraints, explodable into a family of constraints. This member of the family specifically refers to initial syllables in lexical items. Numbers, pronouns, and conjunctions in Kɔnni are not considered lexical items and may or may not have initial onsets.

The hierarchy in (218) will ensure a pharyngeal epenthetic consonant in such cases, but we must bear in mind that [h] is also pharyngeal. To decide between [h] and [ʔ], we note that stops in general are less marked than fricatives. Cross-linguistically, some languages occur with stops but no fricatives, but there is no language which has fricatives in its inventory but no stops (see Maddieson 1984 for a representative sample of languages). In featural terms, [+continuant] is more marked than [−continuant] for obstruents. Also, in languages with an epenthetic laryngeal consonant, that epenthetic consonant is [ʔ], not [h], even when the languages have both in their inventory (as in Arabic and Sundanese).[41] So I propose a universal ranking of constraints for this feature. In general, a faithfulness constraint for a binary feature will be expressed with an IDENT constraint, as indeed I have done earlier in this chapter. However, in an epenthesis situation, when either value of the feature is present in the output, that value has been inserted and not present in input, so again DEP is the appropriate family of constraints here.

(222) **DEP[+cont] >> DEP[−cont]**

---

[40]Not all Kɔnni speakers insert a glottal under these circumstances, though they all do keep the vowels distinct, with no assimilation. In this section I consider the speakers who do insert the glottal consistently, as James Amadu did.

[41]My thanks to David Odden for bringing this point to my attention.

Also I have noted that [ʔ] only occurs at the edges of words. The same restriction applies to [h] as well. Except for a few borrowed words and compounds, [h] is always word initial.

(223) **[phar]-edge:** [pharyngeal] consonants are not permitted word internally

This will play no role in glottal stop epenthesis, but will rule out candidates with inserted pharyngeal place in [r]-epenthesis in the discussion below. With these constraints in place, I propose the following tableau for insertion of [ʔ].

(224) tì ʔàlĩvέsà 'our onion' ONS-lex, DEP[+cont], DEP[cor] >> DEP[−cont], DEP[phar]

tɪ alɪvɛsa	ONS-lex	DEP [+cont]	DEP [cor]	DEP [−cont]	DEP [phar]
☞ a. tɪ ʔalɪvɛsa				*	*
b. tɪ alɪvɛsa	*!				
c. ta alɪvɛsa	*!				
d. tɪ halɪvɛsa		*!			*
e. tɪ dalɪvɛsa			*!	*	

The optimal candidate (224a) violates both DEP[−cont] and DEP[phar], but other candidates violate more highly-ranked constraints. Note that candidates (224b and c) violate only ONS-lex, since àlĩvέsà is a noun. This is the difference between tì ʔàlĩvέsà 'our onion' with glottal insertion and gbààsá !átà 'three dogs' in (225) with no insertion.

(225) gbààsá !átà 'three dogs'

gbaasɪ ata	ONS-lex	DEP [+cont]	DEP [cor]	DEP [−cont]	DEP [phar]
☞ a. gbaasa ata					
b. gbaasa ʔata				*!	*!
c. gbaasa data			*!		

Continuing on to [r]-insertion, let us consider the lack of [+ATR] nouns in this pattern first. The lack of [-re], the [+ATR] counterpart of [-ra], in this situation may be an accidental gap, since [−ATR] vowels are in an 80

4.5 Epenthesis

percent majority in nouns. On the other hand, since [-re] is acoustically quite similar to the definite suffix [-rí, -rí],[42] there may be another factor at work here, which is the functional pressure to avoid confusion of the definite and plural suffixes. It is possible for nouns to change the membership of the noun class they belong to over time (Cahill 1997b), and this may help explain the high proportion of nouns in a "mixed" class (a singular from one class and a plural from another) which have the plural from noun class 1. Even more striking is that about 75 percent of these mixed nouns with plural from noun class 1 are [+ATR], much higher than the 20 percent expected from the general distributional percentage. This seems to indicate that [+ATR] nouns which had the potential for confusion of definite and plural suffixes have avoided this by historically moving into a mixed noun class.[43]

Besides the functional desire to avoid confusion of plural and singular definite forms, there may be a more direct phonetic explanation as well. In Chumburung (Snider 1984),[44] the phoneme /l/ is realized as [l] intervocalically only when preceded by [l] in the previous syllable and if it is in a [+ATR] word. If in a [−ATR] word, then intervocalic /l/ is always [r]. Thus [l] is linked with [+ATR], and [r] is linked with [−ATR]. In West African languages studies by Ladefoged (1964), [l] is articulated with a raising of the dorsum, while [r] is not. The [−ATR] vowels are pronounced with the dorsum low and pulled back, and [+ATR] vowels are pronounced with the tongue pushed forward and the dorsum raised. So the dorsum is lowered for both [r] and [−ATR] vowels, and raised for [l] and [+ATR] vowels. (Further references are found in Snider 1984). There is a phonetic incompatibility between [r] and [+ATR] vowels, and that is just the vowel set which does not have [r]-insertion in Kɔnni.

Both the functional and phonetic connections point in the same direction: that [r] is to be avoided in [+ATR] contexts. Obviously, there are some [+ATR] nouns which do take the [-rI] singular definite suffix, but the factors mentioned above have historically shifted nouns of class 1 into different classes in order to avoid potentially confusing or phonetically incompatible situations.

The insertion of [r] here is connected with the shortening of the vowel in the plural forms above. As we will discuss more fully in section 5.6,

---

[42] See section 5.1.3 for formant measurements of the vowels.

[43]Consider as an example nín 'eye'. The plural form, showing the noun class 1 suffix, is nínè. If the singular definite form were also from noun class 1, this would give *nínní. The potential for confusion between plural and singular definite clearly exists. The actual singular definite form is nímbú, showing the noun class 4 definite suffix. The Buli forms show the same mixed noun class suffixes (numu, nina for singular definite and plural, respectively), showing that the migration of the singular to noun class 4 morphology must have taken place in Proto-Buli-Kɔnni or a previous stage.

[44]My thanks to David Odden for steering me to this reference.

there is a constraint in Kɔnni disallowing triple-length vowels, *VVV. But there is also obviously a constraint which penalizes deleting a segment, such a segment being defined in terms of a root node.

(226) MAX-SEGMENT (MAX-S): a segment (root node) in the input has a correspondent in the output

The idea I will propose is that the triple length input vowel must change, and directly deleting one of the vowel segments is suboptimal. The optimal solution is to change the middle vowel to a consonant. These constraints can account for the "epenthesis" of [r]. Epenthesis is in quotes because there is not an epenthetic segment as such in this view, but there is an epenthetic set of features.

In other words, [r] is the surface correspondent of V_2 of the vowel sequence, e.g.,

(227) /d a_1 a_2 a_3/ → [d a_1 r_2 a_3]

(228) dàrá 'days' *VVV, [phar]-edge, MAX-S >> DEP[+cont], DEP[cor]

	daa-a	*VVV	[phar]-edge	*VDV	MAX-S	DEP [+cont]	DEP [cor]
☞ a.	dara					?	*
b.	daaa	*!					
c.	daa				*!		
d. daʔa			*!				
e.	dada			*!			*

If we consider [r] as [+continuant], there may be an insertion of such in the optimal candidate (228a), violating DEP[+cont]. That is, if we assume that the long vowel /aa/ is a geminate, one feature set linked to two timing units, then the change from input to output above involves delinking the feature set from the second timing unit of the geminate. The features that characterize [r] are all inserted. In this view, we go from one occurrence of [+cont] which covers the geminate [aa] to two, one for the vowel [a] and one for [r]. On the other hand, if the two vowels comprising [aa] are considered as a sequence, with each having its own feature [+cont], then the number of [+cont] occurrences is constant from input to output and the [+cont] in the input may be said to have a correspondent in the output. Candidate (228a), besides the possible violation of

4.5 Epenthesis

DEP[+cont], also violates DEP[cor] by inserting [r]. Candidate (228b) loses by violating the undominated *VVV. Candidate (228c) loses by deleting a vowel and so violating MAX-S. Candidate (228d) loses by inserting [ʔ] rather than [r]. If the inserted position were at the edge of a word, inserting the glottal stop would be optimal, but word internally, it violates [phar]-edge. Candidate (228e) loses by violating *VDV.

Other candidates with coronal consonants inserted would be ruled out by other constraints, for which there is no room in (228). A form [dana] would be ruled out by DEP[nas], which we have seen is undominated in Kɔnni. Similarly, a form [dala] would be ruled out by DEP[lateral], which we have not needed to consider in this work.[45] Insertion of [y] in the candidate [daya] would be ruled out by DEP[−ant], assuming it is better to insert a [+ant] than a [−ant] segment, since a gesture involving the tongue tip would involve less articulatory effort than one involving the tongue body.

There are several words with long stem vowels, however, which do not insert [r], as repeated below from (39a).

(229) Singular   Plural
      bítíé-ŋ   bítí-è   'chin'
      díí-ŋ   dí-è   'forehead'
      níí-ŋ   ní-à   'grinding stone'

The vowels in these cases are all front *(ɪɪ, ii, ie)*, and so, in our feature system, are [coronal]. What this amounts to is that a [coronal] consonant cannot be inserted in a position adjacent to a [coronal] vowel. This looks like a good case of an OCP-type instantiation.

(230) *[cor][cor]: adjacent coronals are disallowed

In the typology of Suzuki's (1998) Generalized OCP, there can be no intervening material of any sort here, and that is our desired outcome. In the case of a noun with /ɪɪ/ as the final stem vowels, *[cor][cor] will rule out the otherwise well-formed candidate with [r]-insertion, candidate (231c).

---

[45]In light of Walsh-Dickey's (1997) assertion that [lateral] as a feature is unnecessary, it is possible that the appropriate constraint would refer to a specific configuration of features, similar to what I have assumed with [rhotic] as a cover term for a slightly different configuration of features (195).

(231) wíà 'problems' *VVV, [phar]-edge, *[cor][cor] >> MAX-S

wII-a	*VVV	[phar]-edge	*[cor][cor]	MAX-S	DEP [+cont]	DEP [cor]
☞ a. wIa[46]				*		
b. wIIa	*!					
c. wIIra			*!		*	*
d. wIra			*!		*	*
e. wII-ʔa		*!				

The optimal candidate in (231a) violates MAX-S by deleting a segment present in the input. This would be enough to disqualify a candidate with noncoronal vowels, but with the coronal /II/ as input, inserting [r] as in (231c and d) violates the higher-ranked constraint *[cor][cor]. Candidates (231b and e) are ruled out by violations of the top-ranked constraints *VVV and [phar]-edge. The candidate wII, not listed above, would be ruled out by Casali's (1997) constraint MAXMS, prohibiting deletion of a morpheme consisting of a single segment.

Obviously, there do exist cases of adjacent coronals in Kɔnni; a word such as bítíéŋ 'chin' has coronal vowels surrounding a coronal consonant. We can account for these in a straightforward way. The MAX[cor] constraint is ranked above *[cor][cor]. Any occurrence of [coronal] present in the input will surface in the output, but an inserted [coronal] is disallowed when adjacent to another one.

A more complicated factor to be discussed in the next chapter is that the epenthetic vowel /I/ is [coronal], and this is inserted next to [coronal] consonants, both before and after a coronal consonant, e.g., kpatɪ 'finish', tígírí 'the house' (see section 5.5).

4.6 Conclusion

4.6.1 Summary of constraints

All the constraints discussed in relation to Kɔnni consonants in this chapter are listed in (232), with rankings indicated by arrows. The top three lines contain constraints which are never violated, as far as I am aware. Variable rankings, indicating optional pronunciations, are indicated by

---

[46]The diphthong ɪa also occurs as a product of the underlying long mid vowel /εε/. See section 5.3 for discussion.

4.6 Conclusion

two-headed arrows between constraints on the same line. This display shows that there are no contradictions in ranking. The constraints are given in three groups; with the data at hand, I have no way of relating these groups to each other.

(232) Constraint ranking summary
   a.

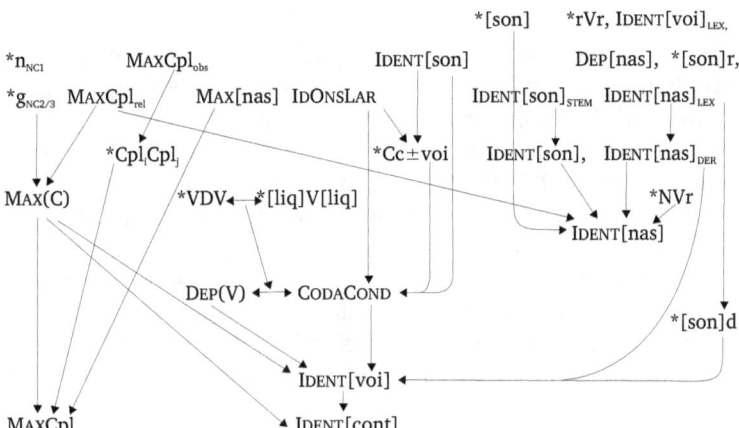

   b.

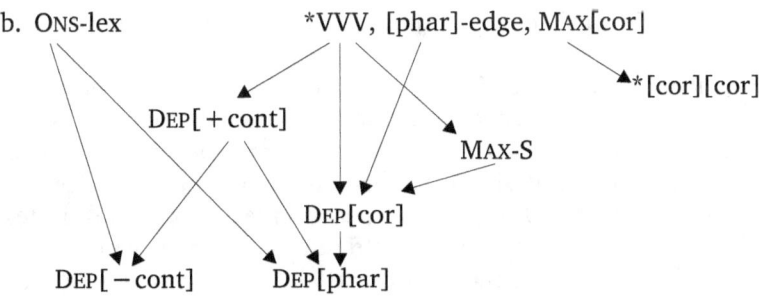

   c. IDENT[ant]$_V$, *[+ant][−ant] ⟷ IDENT[ant]$_C$

There are three pairs of constraints which have variable ranking in the set of constraints in (232). These pairs can switch ranking, giving alternate pronunciations of the same word.[47] One of the properties of these pairs is that they are adjacent in ranking in the tableaus in which they appear. In the diagram in (232), this is manifested in the configurations in which each of the pair of constraints in question is dominated by the

---

[47]For an extensive examination of phonological variation explained by variable ranking of constraints, see Kang (1997).

same constraints and dominates the same constraints. Intuitively, it makes sense that if two constraints will be reranked, it will be constraints which are adjacent in ranking. This will make for minimal disturbance of the communicative function by changing the form in a minimal fashion.

4.6.2 Coronal review

Much of the consonantal phonology of Kɔnni involves coronals, and here I briefly review and connect one set of illustrative phenomena.

Much of the phonology of coronals in Kɔnni is driven by co-occurrence restrictions, particularly with *r* and other sonorants. One of the points that Suzuki (1998) discusses is that the OCP, referring to different features or other elements, is stronger when the elements are more similar to each other. We see this at work in Kɔnni, where there is never a case of *rVr* or *nVr* and very rarely of *lVr*, but a few of *mVr*, *ŋVr*, and *ŋmVr*.

We see that we need to refer to the morphological classes of lexical item versus derivational versus inflectional suffix in coronal phonology. All these factors emerge in examining three different outputs of /nr/:

(233) a. yàn-rí   → yàn-ní   'the frog'
      b. chì-chèn-rú → chì-chèn-tú 'fryer'
      c. ŋmààn-ràáŋ   → ŋmààn-dàáŋ   'male monkey'

In none of these cases do we have an epenthetic vowel between n and *r*; they are too similar to each other and, as we shall discuss more in section 5.5, epenthesis generally requires the adjacent consonants to be of different place values. Besides, an epenthetic vowel would produce the ill-formed *nVr*. The difference in the assimilation or lack of it lies in the morphological identities of the different morphemes which contain the /r/. In (233a), /-rI/ is the definite article, an inflectional morpheme. In (233b), the agentive suffix /-rU/ is derivational, and in (233c), the morpheme /-raaŋ/ is a lexical item, though bound.

The constraint *[son]r motivates change in all the forms of (233). The difference in (233a) and (233b) is the IDENT[nas] family, which is ranked higher for lexemes than for derivational affixes and higher for derivational than inflectional affixes. Thus it is more important for a morpheme to keep its [nasal] specification if it is a lexical item or derivational affix than if it is an inflectional affix. So the inflectional affix totally assimilates to the preceding nasal in (233a), but the others in (233b and c) are protected from this.

Similarly, the difference between (233b) and (233c) depends on the analysis with IDENT[voi]$_{LEX}$ ranked higher than the general IDENT[voi]. The voicing of /r/ is preserved in the lexical item /-raaŋ/ while it is not in the derivational affix /-rU/. The constraint *[son]r which forces change in /-rU/ is ranked below IDENT[voi]$_{LEX}$, so the voicing may remain.

4.6.3 Other comments

The consonantal phonology of Kɔnni gives two examples of constraints which refer to morphemes particular to Kɔnni, specifically the noun classes. These are the constraints *g$_{NC2/3}$ and *n$_{NC1}$. The constraint *g$_{NC2/3}$ was proposed in (180) to account for forms such as /yʊg-ŋ/ → [yʊ́ŋ] 'night', in which members of noun classes 2 and 3 do not have a stem-final g in the citation form (though nouns of other classes do, e.g., tíg-íŋ 'house'). Similarly, the constraint *n$_{NC1}$ was proposed in (185) to account for words such as /bɪn-ŋ/ → [bɪ̆ŋ] 'year', in which members of noun class 1 do not have a stem-final n in the citation form though nouns of other classes do, e.g., yàníŋ 'frog'. These are extremely specific constraints and cannot be regarded as universal, since they refer specifically to noun classes 1, 2, and 3 of Kɔnni, which of course no other language has.

Both IDENT and DEP/MAX constraints are necessary for [nasal]. In (199), losing candidate (199d), introducing a new nasal, shows that DEP[nas] outranks IDENT[son], and this is part of the evidence that shows both DEP[nas] and IDENT[nas] are necessary in Kɔnni.

As noted in section 4.2.1, nasal place assimilation for almost every case in Kɔnni can be accounted for by the universal constraint ranking MAX[pl]$_{OBST}$ >> MAX[pl]$_{NAS}$. However, with the examination of more data, such as náá!gín náŋ 'cow's leg', it is clear that another set of constraints is necessary, MAX[Cpl]$_{rel}$ >> MAX[Cpl], referring to the release of a sound. This shows clearly that in Optimality Theory, more than one set of constraints, and valid constraints at that, can account for the same data. The natural question is then, which set of constraints is really crucial to the analysis, or is it possible that both coexist? Two possibilities arise. First, it could be possible that further examination of the language confirms that both sets of constraints are vital, and that one cannot decide which is more important in determining the optimal outputs. In this case, there are *many* reasons for the output being what it is, and one would predict such outputs to be very stable with respect to historical change, that speech errors would be less likely in these forms, and that speech rate would have less influence on these. On the other hand, it is possible that further investigation of the language would uncover forms that would require one set of constraints but not the other to account for it, as in the case above. The point is, as with any theory, more than a fraction of a language must be examined if one is to have any confidence in the proposed analysis.

5
Vocalic Phonology

5.1 Vowel inventory, contrasts, and measurements

Kɔnni has a nine-vowel system typical of the Gur family and other languages in the area, with the vowels dividing into two sets based on the ATR feature. +ATR

(234) Short vowel phonemes

	+ATR		−ATR
i	u	ɪ	ʊ
e	o	ɛ	ɔ
		a	

(235) Long vowel phonemes

	+ATR		−ATR
ii	uu	ɪɪ	ʊʊ
ee~ie	oo~uo	ɛɛ~ɪa	ɔɔ~ʊa
		aa	

The alternations between the long mid vowels and the noted diphthongs are the result of a diphthongization process which results in the near absence of phonetic long mid vowels in Kɔnni. This is discussed in section 5.3.

The transcriptions of vowels in this chapter are phonetic except in two areas. First, phonemic front vowels are phonetically centralized before [ŋ], as in /tĭŋ/ → [tɨŋ] 'village, town' (cf. tɪkká 'the village'), /keŋ/ → [kəŋ] 'come' (cf. kenne 'is coming'). Except when focusing on this process, in section 5.4.3, I will write the front vowels preceding ŋ without noting this centralization. Second, vowels preceding a nasal consonant are phonetically nasalized, but this is never contrastive, and I have not marked this in the transcriptions.

5.1.1 Justification of phonemes

While high and low long vowels are unambiguously attested, as seen in (237), long mid vowels are rare, and various "vowel combinations" are quite frequent. My contention is that the long mid vowels almost invariably are manifested as diphthongs, discussed in section 5.3. Data showing contrasts of short and long vowels are given in (236) and (237), respectively. Verbs are listed without tones, since the tone depends on syntactic context (see section 6.4). Since the mid vowels /e, o, ɛ/ are relatively rare, fewer tokens of these were found that exhibited direct contrast with other vowels.

(236) Contrasts of short vowels

/u/	/ʊ/	/o/	/ɔ/	/a/
dúŋ 'knee'	dʊŋ 'bite'		dɔ̃ŋ 'animal'	dámá 'power'
kúŋ 'handle'	kʊ́ŋ 'funeral'	kóŋ 'hunger'	kɔ́!ŋ́ 'farmed area'	káŋ 'antelope (sp.)'
buli 'spring up'	bʊrɪ 'sow'	bòlíŋ 'fire'	bɔ́lì 'ball'	balɪ 'tell'
ju 'enter'	jʊ 'light'	jòlíŋ 'jackal'	jɔ́ríŋ 'ladder'	jalɪŋ 'lean against'
tuŋ 'pay'	tʊŋ 'work'	tòbíé 'tobacco seeds'	tɔbɪ 'pierce'	tabaarɪ 'traitor'
wúsíŋ 'tamarind'	wʊsɪ 'waste time'	woliŋ 'be first'	wɔsɪ 'call'	wasɪ 'greet, thank'

5.1 Vowel inventory, contrasts, and measurements

/i/	/ɪ/	/e/	/ɛ/	/a/
bíŋ 'seed'	bǐŋ 'year'	běŋ 'tribal scar'		báŋ 'ten'
chigisi 'sift'	chɪgɪ 'run'		chɛŋ 'fry'	chagɪ 'be satisfied'
digi 'cook'	dɪgɪntɪ 'be dirty'	densi 'balance on head'	dɛbɪya 'why?'	dansɪ 'look at'
giligi 'be round'	gɪrɪgɪ 'be crowded'	gerenti 'burp'		garɪsɪ 'pass'
gbiŋ 'tie'	gbígbáŋ 'tree (sp.)'			gbágíŋ 'lake'
jigiŋ 'place'	jìtí 'soup'	je 'fish (w/ basket)'		jatɪ 'spread'
niŋkogiŋ 'eyebrow'	nìmbúá 'younger sibling'	ném!bíŋ 'bird'		nánjʋ́ʋ́ŋ 'fly'
yi 'make, do'	yɪ 'give'	ye 'see'	yɛ 'be small'	ya 'still, yet'

(237) Contrasts of long vowels

/uu/	/ʋʋ/	/uo/	/ʋa/	/aa/
chuuri 'have diarrhea'	chʋʋsɪ 'spoil'		chʋarɪ 'be taboo'	chaar 'winnow'ɪ
	kʋʋrɪ 'snore'	kùòlíŋ 'water calabash'	kʋarɪ 'gather'	kaarɪ 'rush'
suuli 'be full'	sʋʋŋ 'get down'	suo 'swim'	súá!míŋ 'rabbit'	sààmíŋ 'porcupine'
tuuri 'mark a line'	tʋʋlɪ 'take down'	tùóŋ 'baobab tree'	tʋ̀áŋ 'share'	tá!áŋ 'shea tree'
gú!úŋ 'rope'	gʋ́ʋ́!líŋ 'pit'	goori 'separate'	gʋarɪ 'bend'	gáárú 'thief'
	yʋʋrɪ 'strip fiber'	yuori 'open'	yʋarɪ 'fetch'	yaalɪ 'find'
zùúŋ 'vulture'	zʋʋrɪ 'bend down'	zùóŋ 'hair'	zʋ̀á 'friend'	záá 'millet'

/ii/	/ɪ/	/ie/	/ɪa/	/aa/
diisi	dìɪsíŋ	die	dɪanʊ	dààŋ
'put on top'	'spoon'	'long ago'	'yesterday'	'wood, stick'
chììtí	chɪɪrɪ		chìàrʊ́	chaarɪ
'headload'	'tear'		'singer'	'winnow'
kpììlíŋ	kpíí!líŋ		kpíásí	kpààlíŋ
'ancestor'	'hawk (sp.)'		'chickens'	'handle'
ɲiisi	ɲɪɪsɪ	ɲìé	ɲɛɛlɪ	ɲááŋ
'bite off'	'show teeth'	'neck'	'hope'	'water'
sììmé	sí!íŋ	sìé	sìá	sààmíŋ
'beans (sp.)'	'a cold'	'honey'	'where?'	'porcupine'
	tìíŋ	tìéŋ	tìáŋ	tá!áŋ
	'tree'	'owner'	'sleeping mat'	'shea tree'

Evidence of contrast between short and long vowels is given in (238).

(238) Contrast between short and long vowels
    Short vowels   Long vowels
  a. High and low vowels

dúŋ	'knee'	dùúŋ	'horse'
kúŋ	'tree (sp.)'	kòóŋ	'hoe'
pili	'to roof'	piili	'to start'
síŋ	'fish (sp.)'	sí!íŋ	'a cold'
náŋ	'leg'	nààŋ	'chief'

  b. Mid vowels

kóŋ	'hunger'	kùòlíŋ	'water calabash'
sĕŋ	'tree (sp.)'	síéŋ	'path'
chɛŋ	'fry'	chìàŋ	'waist'
chɔ̀ŋ	'father'	chùáŋ	'small pot'

5.1.2 Vowel duration measurements

To contribute to the general knowledge on vowel duration, the following measurements are presented, based on the speech of Mr. Amadu and Mr. Sikpaare. Duration was measured using the WINCECIL program, version 2.2, produced and distributed by SIL International. In any duration measurements, care must be taken as to variation in speech rate. (For example, a dramatic story is not an ideal candidate for comparing vowel durations, since

5.1 Vowel inventory, contrasts, and measurements

the speech rate is a function of factors such as the tension level in the story, whether the material is foreground or background, etc.) All measurements presented here were of single words repeated in lists. In this situation, the speech rate was fairly constant.

Another variable to be taken into account is the vowel quality, which affects duration. Different vowels have differing inherent duration, which have been measured for a number of languages (Maddieson 1997 and Lehiste 1970). In general, the height of a vowel is inversely correlated with vowel duration: all else being equal, a higher vowel will have shorter duration than a lower vowel. The physiological basis for this is that the articulators, especially the hinge of the jaw, must move a greater distance for lower vowels than for higher. Unsurprisingly, this pattern is also borne out in Kɔnni, as the average measurements in (239) show (SD = standard deviation).

For ease and accuracy in measurement, most vowel durations were measured only between stops or affricates. In the case of some vowels, however, my recordings did not include enough of such cases, so vowels before /l/ were also included. The vowels were measured from the point at which the spikes of the waveform were higher than the consonantal ones, a clear point in almost all cases. A preponderance of the words measured were disyllabic and had the target vowel in the first syllable. The vowels /ɛ/ and /ɪa/ are not included below due to lack of disyllabic words containing /ɛ/.

(239) Vowel duration measurements—Amadu

	Short vowels				Long vowels				Ratio of
	Sample word	# of trials	Ave. (ms)	SD	Sample word	# of trials	Ave. (ms)	SD	long/short
i	sibi	12	65	9	siimiŋ	12	144	9	2.2
ɪ	dìdààrú	22	78	10	tɪ̀jʋàlɪ̀tú	12	141	14	1.8
u	kúgè	12	81	13	tuuri	9	164	9	2.0
ʋ	bʋ̀gʋ̀rʋ́	12	80	12	jàkʋ̀ʋ̀rí	12	166	9	2.1
e	kpesi	9	94	14	gbieri	12	172	20	1.8
o	kosiŋ	15	99	9	puosi	12	180	14	1.8
ɔ	bɔbɪŋ	18	114	15	pʋasɪ	15	189	27	1.7
a	dìdàgìrú	15	114	11	dìdààrú	18	229	24	2.0

Consistent with Lehiste (1970) and Maddieson (1997), the higher vowels have shorter durations, and the lower ones have longer. Within the high vowels, it can also be seen that the front vowels are shorter than the back ones. There is less data on the mid vowels, but what there is is also consistent with front mid vowels being shorter than back ones.

The average duration of a long vowel is approximately 1.9 times the duration of a short vowel. This is consistent with the findings of Hubbard (1998), who notes that languages in which vowel quality plays no part in quantity contrasts show a 2:1 ratio or longer in duration ratio, while those languages in which quality and quantity are linked tend to show smaller ratios.

To test for consistency across speakers, similar measurements were made for Sikpaare's speech. These words were recorded under less controlled conditions than those of Amadu, being recorded over a period of years rather than weeks. Some of the same patterns as above were found, but some were different. The pattern of all high vowels consistently having shorter duration was not found here, although the long diphthong ʊa is longer than higher vowels, and the low vowel /a/ is consistently longer than any others. What is fairly consistent between speakers is the ratio of long to short vowels, which still averages approximately 1.9 to one. This is in spite of the lower-than-average 1.6 to one ratio of a:aa.

(240) Vowel duration measurements—Sikpaare

	Short vowels				Long vowels				
	Sample word	# of trials	Ave. (ms)	SD	Sample word	# of trials	Ave. (ms)	SD	Ratio of long/short
i	tigiŋ	8	88	17	niige	3	167	5	1.9
ɪ	jɪbɪŋ	10	85	13	bɪɪkʊ	27	155	26	1.8
u	dune	4	74	6	zuuti	6	152	19	2.1
ʊ	kʊra	4	87	29	kʊʊrɪ	8	176	19	2.0
e	sekke	6	86	14	gbieke	12	153	18	1.8
o	—	—	—		juoku	4	155	17	—
ɔ	—	—	—		kʊakʊ	12	184	16	—
a	dara	17	116	23	daatɪ	24	188	23	1.6

In a more extensive phonetic study of vowel duration in Kɔnni, other factors would also be studied and appropriate statistical analysis presented. One factor is total word length: in the course of taking these measurements I found that the length of the word in terms of syllables affects the absolute vowel duration. For example, in Amadu's speech, the short vowel (averages 114 ms as the first syllable of disyllabic words, but only 91 ms in the first syllable of trisyllabic words. Different prosodic positions in the word may affect absolute duration as well, with the vowel of the reduplicative agentive prefix CV- being shorter in duration than a short vowel in a stem. The relation of tone and duration in Kɔnni, if any, is totally unexplored at present. Also, the effect on duration of the consonants surrounding the target vowel is an area I have not explored, although there may be a tendency for fricatives preceding the vowel to have a shortening effect. These are all matters for future study.

5.1.3 Vowel formant frequency measurements

Phonetic measurements of vowel formants in languages which contrast an ATR feature are relatively rare (see McCord (1989), Hess (1992), and Maddieson (1998) for three such studies). I am not aware of any such studies which have been done on Gur languages.

Studies by Makashay (1998) and others cited in his study have shown that a better characterization of vowels is obtained by measuring not only the formant values at the midpoint of the steady-state portion of the spectrogram, but also the values toward the beginning and end of the vowel as well. This is useful because in normal speech, vowels are quite often not in a steady state, and it is not only the static F_1, F_2, and F_3 values that assist in identifying them, but also the movement and direction of movement of those values in the course of pronouncing the vowel which assists the hearer in identifying the vowel. Makashay also suggests that for a nonnative speaker of a language, it is the unfamiliar trajectory of the formants over time as much as the static part of the spectrogram which inhibits correct identification of the vowel.

Nonetheless, in this study, as a pragmatic matter, I present only measurements taken at the midpoint of the steady-state portion of the vowel, or as close to the midpoint as the display allowed. The main focus of this study is phonology rather than phonetics, and measurements of three places of the vowel formants is a matter of more phonetic complexity than is necessary for our purposes here, though I hope to perform and report on these more detailed measurements at a later date.

Measurements were done using SIL International's WINCECIL program, version 2.2. In this version, formant tracking within a spectrogram is one of the options, and the numerical value of the formants is displayed at the location of the cursor. All the measurements below were done with Mr. Amadu's speech. The ellipses represent the average of the measurements plus and minus one standard deviation (SD).

Two sets of measurements were taken. The first, in (241), presents measurements of vowel formants in suffix and utterance-final position.

(241) Vowel formant measurements—vocalic suffixes

Vowel	n	F_1	SD	(F_2-F_1)	SD
u	25	396	43	500	61
ʊ	14	440	64	470	49
i	24	450	57	1335	105
ɪ	24	460	56	1170	88
e	24	463	43	1205	142
a	24	730	46	595	56

(242) Vowel formant chart—vocalic suffixes

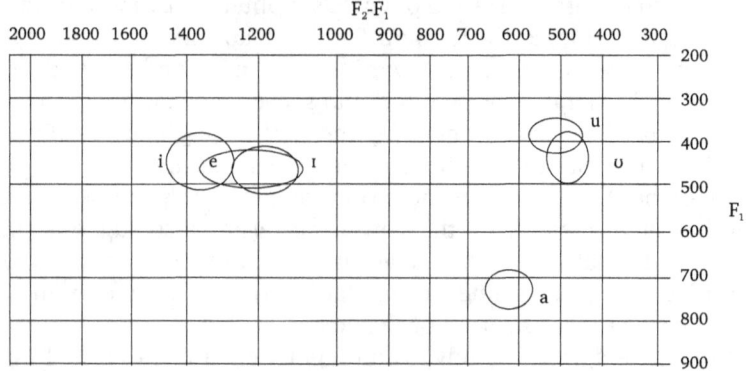

The measurements in (242) were taken of vowels at the end of words, usually suffixes, in an attempt to avoid coarticulatory effects from following consonants. However, taking measurements at this position had two drawbacks. First, this limited the vowels it was possible to measure, since ɛ and ɔ are never found in suffixes, and o was rare enough so only a few cases were available. Second, the front vowels especially tended to neutralize in this position, as seen by the overlap in the plots for [i, ɪ, e].

Therefore, another set of measurements was taken (shown in 243), and these were of the vowel in the first syllable of an utterance, with this first syllable belonging to a stem. The vowels were also usually followed by a consonant.

5.1 Vowel inventory, contrasts, and measurements

(243) Vowel formant measurements—word-initial syllables

Vowel	n	F_1	SD	(F_2-F_1)	SD
u	27	410	46	570	110
ʊ	22	440	45	610	104
i	25	370	45	1400	140
ɪ	24	420	49	1270	165
o	23	470	40	620	76
e	23	470	56	1080	114
ɛ	15	650	69	910	267
ɔ	22	610	67	460	80
a	24	730	80	620	140

(244) Vowel formant chart—word-initial syllables

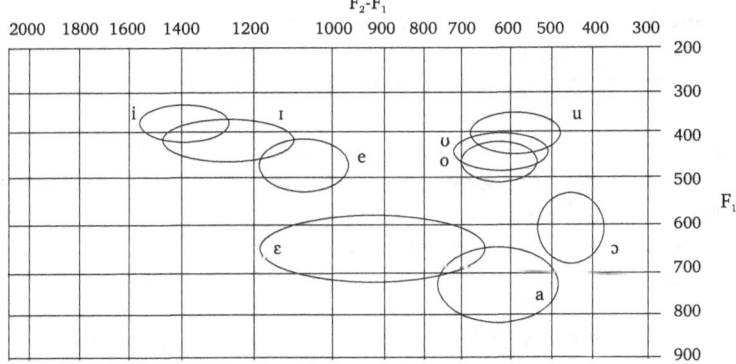

There is better separation of the front vowels in word-initial position (shown in chart 244) than in utterance-final position (242). In light of recent studies on positional contrast, this should come as no surprise. Word-initial position is more important in word recognition than noninitial position (Cutler 1995 and references therein), so it is more important for vowels in the initial syllable to be distinct than vowels in noninitial positions. Consistent with this, Beckman (1997) gives examples of a number of languages in which the initial syllable of a word contains more contrasts than a noninitial syllable.

In spite of this cross-linguistic pattern to which the front vowels of Kɔnni conform, the back vowels are grouped just as closely in the second chart as the first. In particular, the second chart shows an almost complete overlap of the sounds [o] and [ʊ]. This offers some explanation for the personal difficulty I have had and still have in distinguishing these vowels on a purely auditory basis.

Also above, the area covered by [ɛ] is disproportionately larger than the others. I assume this is primarily due to the smaller sample size; [ɛ] is a relatively uncommon vowel, and the presence of some outliers has proportionately more influence than if there were more samples. There are not many words I have taped with this vowel in the initial syllable.

5.2 ATR vowel harmony

Like many languages within the Gur family, Kɔnni has a system of cross-height vowel harmony based on the ATR feature. For example, simple words (those containing only one lexical item) contain either all phonetically [+ATR] vowels or [−ATR] vowels.

(245)   [+ATR] words   [−ATR] words
    súúlì   'to be full'   jʊ́ʊ́lì   'to climb'
    bítíéŋ   'beard'   tɔ́bì   'to pierce'
    tókórósí 'windows'   kʊ́rʊ́bâ   'cooking pot'

Words from the [−ATR] set are far more numerous than those from the [+ATR] set, comprising approximately 80 percent of nouns and 70 percent of verbs in Kɔnni. Though below I will contend that ATR is a privative feature, and thus the real contrast is between the presence and lack of ATR, in this section I will use [+ATR] and [−ATR] for expositional convenience, as above.

This system, though not perhaps the distributional percentages, is similar to the well-known system of Akan (in e.g., Clements 1981). Other Gur languages for which ATR-based harmony has been documented include Kasem (Awedoba 1993), Birifor (Kuch 1993), Sisaala (Toupin 1995), and Dagaare (Bodomo 1997). As Dakubu (1997) observes, ATR-based vowel harmony has generally been under reported in the group, and is quite likely present in several languages where it has not been explicitly noted by earlier investigators.[1]

The vowel harmony system of Kɔnni is mentioned in Cahill (1992a), but a more extensive analysis is presented in terms of Feature Geometry in Cahill (1996).

---

[1] Naden (1989) expresses doubt that ATR vowel harmony is widespread in Gur languages, but these more recent studies show that it is more common than previously assumed.

5.2.1 Vowel harmony within words

5.2.1.1 Data

ATR vowel harmony in Kɔnni is shown most clearly by alternations in suffixes, which depend solely on the ATR specification of the root to which they are attached. The ATR specification of the suffix agrees with that of the root. This is illustrated in (246) and (247) with the definite and plural suffixes for nouns (more forms are given in appendix B) and aspectual suffixes for verbs.

(246) Nouns

[+ATR]		[−ATR]	
tígí-rí	'the house'	kʊ̀ʊ̀-rí	'the hoe'
sìè-kú	'the path'	nɪ̀ɪ̀-kʊ́	'the rain'
kùm-bú	'the funeral'	nɔ̀m-bʊ́	'the meat'
yìsì-ké	'the antelope'	nánjʊ́-ká	'the fly'
dùn-é	'knees'	tàn-á	'stones'
dùn-é-hé	'the knees'	tàn-á-há	'stones'
tú-ò	'beans (sp.)'	nʊ́-à	'mouths'
tú-ó-hé	'the beans (sp.)'	nʊ́-á-há	'the mouths'
tókóró-sí-sí	'the windows'	nánjʊ́-sí-sí	'the flies'
yìsì-tí-tí	'the antelopes'	váá-tí-tí	'the leaves'

(247) Verbs

[+ATR]		[−ATR]	
kùrì-yé	'has pounded'	pàsì-yá	'has peeled'
sùgùr-é	'is washing'	pɔ̀gìl-á	'is holding'
tù-ó	'is digging'	kʊ̀-á	'is killing'
dígí-wó	'cooked'	gá-!wá	'went'
chìì-mé	'carry!'	dʊ̀m-má	'bite!'

Note the alternations based on ATR of i~ɪ, u~ʊ, e~a, and o~a. The [o] in suffixes occurs only when adjacent to [u] or [w]. No suffixes in Kɔnni contain [ɔ] or [ɛ].[2]

---

[2] Interestingly, if /-a/ is taken to be the basic form from which [-a, -e, -o] are derived, then there are no underlying mid vowels in suffixes. This would account for the absolute absence of [-ɛ, -ɔ] in suffixes, and that the only mid vowels in suffixes are the [+ATR] vowels [e, o] which alternate with [-a]. It has long been noted that there are fewer contrasts in affixes than in roots, and this would be another case in point: Kɔnni allows only underlying high and low vowels in suffixes.

Though [o] follows [w] in [+ATR] suffixes (and in the personal pronoun *wa/wo* 'him/her' discussed in section 5.2.3), other vowels may follow [w] in roots, with the exception of [we]. This may be an accidental gap in the data, given the relative scarcity of [e] in Kɔnni as a whole, but it is possible that this is a systematic gap instead.

(248) wíŋ, wɩ́è   'tribal scar/s'   wɔɔrɪ   'stir'
      wɪ   'break in two'   wuri   'take off clothes'
      wɪɪ   'blow on instrument'   wʊʊrɪ   'peel, shell (vb)'

While mono-stem words contain either all [+ATR] vowels or [−ATR] vowels, poly-stem words may mix the two. These words are either noun-adjective complexes or compound nouns, both of which are illustrated in (249). The part of the word which is [+ATR] is bolded for ease of reference.

(249) a. Noun-adjective complexes
      jùò-háá!líŋ   'new room (room-new)'
      ném!bí-kúlíŋ   'big bird (bird-big)'
      dùùŋ-ŋmìŋká   'red horse (horse-red)'
      tígí-!kúúŋ   'old house (house-old)'
      ɲìm-bʊ̀ʊ̀rá   'seeds (things-planted)'

   b. Compound nouns
      nɩ̀ɩ̀m-**bó!líŋ**   'lightning (rain-fire)'
      sɩ̀ɲɪ́ɪ́rɪ́-**!tíéŋ**   'angry person (anger-owner)'
      nɪ́ŋmáárɪ́-**!vúóŋ**   'jealous person (jealousy-person)'
      ɲá-sɪ́ɪ́rɪ́-**!júóŋ**   'bath-room (water-bathing-room)'
      ɲá-**líírítú**   'kingfisher (water remover)'
      gbìèm-mɩ̀ɩ̀rú   'potter (pot-builder)'
      ɲìn-ɲìŋká   'fruit (things-that have come out)'
      túú-vááŋ   'bean-leaf'
      tígí-ŋmáríŋ   'house-dove'
      bítíé-gbáríŋ   'jaw (beard- ?)'
      núú-kúáŋ   'back of hand (hand-back)'

Note that while either the first or the second member of a compound noun may be [+ATR], all the examples above of noun-adjective complexes are those in which the first element, the noun, is [+ATR], and the adjective is [−ATR]. This is no accident of the data. When an adjective which is [+ATR] follows a noun stem which is [−ATR], the last vowel of

5.2 ATR vowel harmony

the noun stem becomes [+ATR] for many, but not all, nouns.[3] This apparent leftward spread of [+ATR] is one of the reasons for positing ATR as a privative feature; [−ATR] is never active.

(250) a. Spreading of ATR from adjective into noun stem
 jè-vùkíŋ 'snake (lit., thing wriggling)' (cf. jààŋ 'thing')
 jè-góbíŋ 'short thing (thing short)'
 fé-bîŋ 'small baboon' (cf. fááŋ 'baboon')
 né-ní!íŋ 'female cow' (cf. ná-!rááŋ 'male cow')
 gbè-góbíŋ 'short dog' (cf. gbààŋ 'dog')
 jù-bíŋ 'small tail' (cf. jŭŋ 'tail')
 kùù-bíŋ 'small hoe' (cf. kùúŋ 'hoe')[4]
 tìì-bíŋ 'small tree' (cf. tìì-ká 'the tree')
 kpíé-!bíŋ 'small chicken' (cf. kpíáŋ 'chicken')
 léé-!bíŋ 'small axe' (cf lí!áŋ 'axe')
 kúó-bí!ké 'the small farm' (cf. kúáŋ 'farm')
 gbùò-bíŋ 'small bark' (cf gbùáŋ 'bark')
 chòm-bíŋ 'small father' (cf. chɔ̆ŋ 'father')
 tòŋ-góbíŋ 'short bow' (cf. tɔ̆ŋ 'bow')
 bùn-ní!íŋ 'female donkey' (cf. bòn-dááŋ 'male donkey')
 wàlì-ní!íŋ 'female oribi' (cf. wàlì-dááŋ 'male oribi')
 bòrìn-ní!íŋ 'female oryx' (cf. bòrìn-dááŋ 'male oryx')
 jùlè-ní!íŋ 'female whydah' (cf. jùlà-rááŋ 'male whydah')
 ŋmárí-ní!íŋ 'female dove' (cf. ŋmárí-dááŋ 'male dove')
 dàkúó-ní!íŋ 'female parrot' (cf. dàkúá-!rááŋ 'male parrot')
 bòntùù-bíŋ 'small toad' (cf. bòntòò-kpí!íŋ 'big toad')
 kɔ́ŋkòm-bĭŋ 'small tin can' (cf. kɔ́ŋkòŋ 'tin can')
 kàréntìè-bĭŋ 'small cutlass' (cf. kàréntìà 'cutlass')
 gàɲìàrè-ní!íŋ 'female weaver-bird' (cf. gàɲìàrà-dááŋ 'male weaver-bird')
 múgú-bíŋ 'small river' (cf. múgúŋ 'river')
 túgú-bîŋ 'small termite hill' (cf. túgúŋ 'termite hill')

 b. No spreading
 ŋmààn-ní!íŋ 'female monkey'
 kàgbàà-bĭŋ 'small hat'
 ná!ráá-bíŋ 'small male cow'
 gùráá-ní!íŋ 'female lizard'

---
[3]In Cahill (1996), I reported that ATR spreads leftward from an adjective into a noun stem, without any qualification as to how far. The present work represents a more complete set of data.

[4]I have this also recorded as kù-bíŋ, with a short vowel, in the same recording session.

dàà-**bîŋ** 'small stick'
táá-!**bíŋ** 'small sister'
kág-**bíŋ** ~ 'small roan antelope'
kágí-**bíŋ**

Though the presence of ATR is sometimes not auditorily clear on short vowels (especially i/ɪ), it appears that [+ATR] generally spreads only one syllable to the left into the noun stem, with the clear exceptions of two words (representative of a larger sample) in which it spreads two syllables in (250a): 'small river' and 'small termite hill'; these both have /ʊgV/ which surfaces as [ugu].[5] However, ATR does not spread at all if the noun stem vowel is aa, or if the final noun stem syllable is closed as a result of lack of vowel epenthesis, as in kág-bíŋ ~ kágí-bíŋ.[6] With many words, as in (250a), an underlying /aa/ shortens in the noun-adjective complex, and when this happens, the short a undergoes ATR spread and surfaces as e. The /aa/ is the only long vowel to resist ATR spread; long ɪɪ, ʊʊ, ɪa, and ʊa (the last two being manifestations of /ɛɛ/ and /ɔɔ/) all undergo ATR spread.

ATR appears to spread only from adjectives into noun stems, and not from one noun stem to another in compound nouns or from adjective into other adjectives, as shown in (251).

(251) a. Compound nouns
nììm-**bó**!**líŋ** 'lightning (rain-fire)'
chìì-**dèmbíŋ** 'brother-in-law (sibling.in.law-man)'
hánìì-**nŭŋ** 'mother-in-law (in.law-mother)'
gàm-**bíè** 'front ribs (rib-children)'
ɲʊ̀ʊ̀-**bíŋ** 'small intestine (stomach-child)'
chìà-**kólè** 'buttocks (waist-?)'
kààŋ-**kpíè** 'cheekbones (cheek-shea nuts)'
ná-!**kémé** 'heels (foot-?)'
líá-**díírú** 'beautiful woman (daughter-eater)'

b. Noun-adjective-adjective
tígí-yéélí-!**bísì** 'small white houses (house-white-smalls)'

---

[5]It is not often reported that ATR spreads only one syllable into another word. This does occur in Akan (Dolphyne 1988), Nawuri for rightward ATR spreading only (Casali 1988), and Lango (Woock and Noonan 1979). Thanks to David Odden for the last reference. Casali for Nawuri and Jones (1987) for Dilo both also note that the leftward ATR spreading effect tends to diminish with distance from the trigger.

[6]For analysis showing this alternation illustrates lack of epenthesis versus epenthesis, see sections 4.3.1 and 5.5.

5.2 ATR vowel harmony

The noun-adjective-adjective case is actually unclear, since the position where a spread ATR would be expected, on the *i* of -*yééli-*, is very short, and it is difficult to determine its ATR quality. Other adjectives in my data suffer the same difficulty, and I do not have a case like /jà-kòò-bíŋ/ 'small old thing' in my data, where the ATR spread would be obvious if present.

The ATR behavior is one way to tell the difference between *bíŋ* 'child' and -*bíŋ* 'small'. The latter, as an adjective, spreads its ATR value to a preceding noun, and the former, as a noun within a compound, does not spread its ATR. Some present-day monomorphemic nouns seem to be historically compounds on the basis of the mixing of ATR specifications within a word, such as *gààŋlúúŋ* 'cat' and *kpàŋvólí* 'small entrance to compound through wall'.

5.2.1.2 Analysis

As mentioned in section 1.3.2, I assume that ATR is a monovalent feature. For this reason, when I refer to the phonological absence of ATR in a word, I will label it "non-ATR" rather than the more phonetic label of [−ATR].

In the vowel harmony system of Kɔnni, there are two main patterns which must be accounted for. The first is the alternation of suffixal vowels between ATR and non-ATR, especially the [a] ~ [e] and [a] ~ [o] alternations, which involve more feature differences than the simple ATR alternations in [i] ~ [ɪ] and [u] ~ [ʊ]. The second is the agreement of suffixes in ATR with the adjacent stems, but the preservation of the ATR specification of the lexical stems. The special case of spreading ATR from an adjective into a noun stem will also be analyzed.

The case of ATR spreading in Kɔnni is consistent with Beckman's (1997) succinct statement "Bad vowels spread." By "bad vowels" she means the vowels or features that are less perceptually salient. Spreading such features increases their duration and thus gives the hearer a greater opportunity to correctly identify them. Whether ATR in general makes a vowel a "bad feature" in perceptual terms is an open question awaiting more detailed studies, but the graph of formants in (244) is suggestive as far as Kɔnni. The separation between the [−ATR] vowels [ɪ, ɛ] is much greater than the separation between their [+ATR] counterparts [i, e]. Likewise, the separation between the [−ATR] vowels [ʊ, ɔ] is much greater than the separation between their [+ATR] counterparts [u, o]. The [+ATR] vowels in Kɔnni are thus closer together on formant charts and are more likely to be confused with each other than the [−ATR] vowels. We may also extend the notion of "bad features" to "marked features" and further to monovalent features. Again, the fact that approximately 80 percent of nouns and verbs are phonetically [−ATR] is consistent with the markedness of [+ATR].

Vowel features in Kɔnni are assumed here to be monovalent rather than binary, with [dorsal], [coronal], and [ATR] features for place and [closed] for height. The [dorsal] and [coronal] features have been well-discussed (Clements and Hume 1995 and references therein), but the monovalent features [ATR] and [closed] deserve some discussion.

Cross-linguistically, African languages generally have only one value of ATR which is active. This is typically shown by spreading this value of ATR, while the other value never spreads. Casali (1998), in a survey of forty-six Niger-Congo and Nilo-Saharan languages, found twenty-eight with active [+ATR], fifteen with active [−ATR], and three which actually showed both [+ATR] and [−ATR] active.[7] In almost all languages, then, either [+ATR] or [−ATR] (also called RTR) can be viewed as monovalent. The nonactive value can be treated as simply absent (underspecified), as indeed Casali (1998) proposes to do with a constraint PRIVATIVITY, which allows only one of the values to be employed in a language. In Kɔnni, ATR is assumed as the monovalent feature, since it is only the "[+ATR]" value that is active in spreading.

In the presentation below, the additive height feature [closed] will be used rather than the more common [±high] and [±low]. Since it plays an important role below, but is not as well known as other features, some introduction of the rationale behind [closed] and its properties is in order. The feature [closed] was introduced in Parkinson (1996a, b). It is an additive feature, in that a segment may have multiple instances of it to represent different vowel heights. So rather than a combination of [high] and [low], there are simply different numbers of [closed]. A low vowel has no instances of [closed], and for each degree of height, one [closed] feature is added. A three-height vowel system will have [closed] features as in (252a), and a four-height vowel system will have [closed] features as in (252b).[8]

---

[7]These cases with both values of ATR active seem quite unusual in light of the prevalence of only one value of ATR being active in most languages. Casali notes Turkana (Dimendaal 1983, also Vago and Leder 1987), Toposa (Schröeder and Schröeder 1987), and Kalabari Ijo (Jenewari 1973), the last being a possible rather than a certain case. Noske (1996) notes that Turkana has some suffixes which are invariably [+ATR], some which are invariably [−ATR], and some which are variable. Her conclusion is that +ATR, −ATR, and ØATR are all necessary for lexical specification of suffixes.

[8] Though [±high] and [±low] are still the most commonly referred to features for vowel height, two alternative height feature systems have been relatively recently proposed besides Parkinson's [closed]. The [closed] feature is close to being the converse of the [±open] feature proposed in Clements (1991) and Clements and Hume (1995). One of the differences is the binary nature of [open], and another is that each occurrence of [open] is posited to be on its own tier, rather than being "stacked" as the [closed] is above. The real converse of [closed] is the |a| particle of Particle Phonology (Schane 1984, 1995), which indicates the lowness of the vowel.

5.2 ATR vowel harmony

(252) Occurrences of [closed] in 3- and 4-height systems

a.   3-height system

vowel	i	e	a
[closed]	•	•	
[closed]	•		

b.   4-height system

vowel	i	e	ɛ	a
[closed]	•	•	•	
[closed]	•	•		
[closed]	•			

In the three-height system of (252a), the low vowel *a* has no instances of [closed], the mid vowel *e* has one instance of [closed], and the high vowel *i* has two instances of [closed]. In the four-height system of (252b), the low vowel *a* still has no instances of [closed], while ɛ has one, *e* has two, and the high vowel *i* has three. Thus this schema of using [closed] has the result that languages with different numbers of height levels will have different numbers of [closed] features for their maximally high vowel. One can see that if n is the number of height levels that a language contrasts, then $n-1$ will be the number of [closed] features that the maximally high vowel has.

The main argument for a [closed] feature in Parkinson (1996a, b) comes from the phenomenon of partial height assimilation, in which vowels partially assimilate in height to a neighboring vowel. Total height assimilation can be handled by a number of frameworks equally well, but Parkinson, in looking at a variety of languages, found a remarkable asymmetry in partial height assimilations: they are all one-step raisings. There are no partial lowerings, and only two types of assimilatory processes: a vowel raises either one step higher or totally assimilates in height. If partial height assimilation is in fact an assimilatory phenomenon, a feature that has the effect of raising rather than lowering height and raising it one step only, is needed. This is the [closed] feature. Parkinson also examines a number of other vowel phenomena using [closed], including coalescence and diphthongization, showing that his model can account for a wide range of phenomena.

The assumed feature specifications of Kɔnni vowels are in (253).

(253)

	i	ɪ	e	ɛ	a	ɔ	o	ʊ	u
ATR	•		•				•		•
[dorsal]						•	•	•	•
[coronal]	•	•	•	•					
[closed]	•	•	•	•		•	•	•	•
[closed]	•	•						•	•

Note that in this schema, /a/ has no feature specifications at all.

The active feature of the back round vowels [ɔ, o, ʊ, u] is considered to be [dorsal] here rather than [labial] (this is the only difference in feature specifications from those assumed for Kɔnni in Parkinson 1996b). A [dorsal] specification as the active feature for these is based on two lines of evidence. The first is based on the assumption that these vowels and [w] have the same place features. As noted in chapter 4, a nasal assimilates in place to [w] as [ŋ], not [m] or [ŋm]. Since [ŋ] is only [dorsal], but not [labial], this assimilation supports [w] as being [dorsal]. Recall that a nasal assimilates in place to [KP] as [ŋm], with both [dorsal] and [labial] features active, in the same conditions in which a nasal assimilates to [w] as [ŋ]: *ŋm kpati* 'I finish' versus *ŋ wo* 'I lack'. If [w] has only [dorsal] as an active feature, then we assume the same for the corresponding back round vowels. The second line of evidence is that high vowels must be identical across [dorsal] consonants. If the active feature of the vowels is itself [dorsal], then this becomes a more natural process (see section 5.4.1 for data and discussion). In contrast, the [labial] feature, which is no doubt present in phonetic articulation, does not seem to play any role in any phonological phenomena in the round vowels of Kɔnni.

Several basic constraints are necessary to account for ATR vowel harmony in Kɔnni. Let us start with the basic cases of single monomorphemic words, in which all the vowels agree in ATR (see also 245). Though ATR associates to vowels, ATR is not lexically a feature of a single vowel, but rather of a morpheme. I propose that the morpheme is stored in the lexicon with or without an ATR feature. There is at most one ATR feature per morpheme.

(254) without ATR: sUgUrI → sʊgʊrɪ 'wake (someone)'

                      ATR
    with ATR: sUgUrI → suguri 'wash'

Since ATR is considered monovalent, being only present or absent, the Faithfulness constraints MAX(ATR) and DEP(ATR) are relevant here:

5.2 ATR vowel harmony

(255) MAX(ATR): every ATR occurrence in the input has a correspondent in the output (prohibits deleting ATR)
DEP(ATR): every ATR occurrence in the output has a correspondent in the input (prohibits inserting ATR)

Also relevant are constraints similar to those Akinlabi (1994) uses for ATR in Kanembu.[9]

(256) ALIGN[ATR]μ: ALIGN (ATR, Morpheme): any occurrence of ATR is aligned to both the left and right edges of its sponsoring morpheme
NOGAP: gapped configurations are prohibited

A "gapped" configuration is one in which an autosegment is associated to two feature-bearing units, and unassociated to a feature-bearing unit between these two. In the illustration below, for example, the ATR feature could potentially be associated to all three vowels, but is not associated to the middle one.

(257) gapped configuration for ATR:

$$\begin{array}{c} \text{ATR} \\ \diagup \quad \diagdown \\ \text{V} \quad \text{V} \quad \text{V} \end{array}$$

The results of the ALIGN[ATR]μ constraint are first, to force all syllables of an ATR morpheme to manifest ATR, and second, to prohibit ATR spreading beyond the morpheme with which it occurs in the lexicon. At this point, the constraint could be formulated in terms of alignment to the word, but when compound nouns and noun-adjective complexes of the type in (249) are considered, it is evident that the generalization in Kɔnni is that ATR is a characteristic of the morpheme and not an entire word. Actually, this constraint is a conflation of constraints aligning ATR to the left and to the right edges of the morpheme. In Kɔnni, there is no distinction needed between the two. ALIGN[ATR]μ is shown in the tableaus below as dominated by other constraints. This is because ALIGN[ATR]μ may be violated in some cases, as we shall see throughout this chapter, while the others are all undominated and never violated. The tableau in (258) shows the application of these constraints on an ATR word.

---

[9]Akinlabi's actual constraints are ALIGN[+ATR], aligning a [+ATR] incompletive morpheme to both edges of the stem (since he assumes ATR to be a binary feature), and *Gapped, which is merely a different label for NOGAP.

(258) ATR-related constraints for suguri 'wash'

sUgUrI, ATR	Max(ATR)	Dep(ATR)	NoGap	Align[ATR]μ
☞ a. suguri				
b. sʊgʊrɪ	*!			
c. ATR / \ sugʊri			*!	
d. sʊguri				*!
e. sugʊrɪ				*!
f. sugurɪ				*!
g. sʊguri				*!

The winning candidate (258a) violates no constraints at all. In (258b) the ATR feature has been deleted, fatally violating Max(ATR). In (258c) the middle vowel is non-ATR while the vowels on either side are ATR, violating NoGap. Candidates (258d–g) violate Align[ATR]μ in one way or another. The tableau for a non-ATR word is given in (259).

(259) ATR-related constraints for sʊgʊrɪ 'wake someone'

sUgUrI	Max(ATR)	Dep(ATR)	NoGap	Align[ATR]μ
☞ a. sʊgʊrɪ				
b. suguri		*!		
c. sugʊri		*!	*!	
d. sʊguri		*!		*
e. sugʊrɪ		*!		*
f. sugurɪ		*!		*
g. sʊguri		*!		*

The winning candidate (259a) again violates no constraints. In each of the losing candidates, however, Dep(ATR) is violated, since an ATR has been inserted.

Candidates with more than one ATR vowel may be regarded as multiply linked to one ATR, as assumed in tableau (258), or each linked to its own ATR autosegment. In the latter case, not represented above, there would be multiple violations of Dep(ATR) which remove these candidates from consideration.

5.2 ATR vowel harmony

Let us continue with two types of polymorphemic cases. In the first, a suffix agrees with its root in ATR, with [i] ~ [ɪ] and [u] ~ [ʊ] alternations, which involve only the ATR feature. In the second, the lexemes in noun-noun and most noun-adjective complexes retain their lexical value of ATR (see 246, 247, 249).

(260) a. Suffixes alternate to agree with the root in ATR value
  tígí-**rí**   'the house'   kʊ̀ʊ̀-**rɪ́** 'the hoe'
  sìè-**kú**   'the path'   nɪ̀ɪ̀-**kʊ́** 'the rain'

  b. Lexical items retain their distinctive ATR values
  hánɪ̀ɪ̀-**dèmbíŋ** 'father-in-law (in.law-man)'
  jùò-háá!líŋ   'new room (room-new)'

In other words, affixes (and, as we will see in section 5.2.2, most particles) alternate in ATR value, while lexical morphemes generally do not. The suffix -rI has the ATR version -ri when following the ATR stem *tigi-*, but the non-ATR adjective *haalŋ* remains non-ATR even when following the ATR stem *juo-*. The generalization that suffixes agree with the stem to which they are attached can be expressed as the constraint AGR(ATR).

(261) AGR(ATR): an affix and the stem to which it is affixed must agree in ATR

Though only suffixes occur in Kɔnni, the constraint is expressed in terms of the more general "affix." Since affixes are not lexically specified for ATR in Kɔnni, AGR(ATR), in conjunction with the MAX(ATR) and DEP(ATR) constraints, ensures that the ATR value of a suffix will agree with the lexical value of ATR in a stem. It expresses the cross-linguistically widespread pattern of "stem-controlled" harmony, in which stems are invariant for some vowel feature, but the affixes alternate so as to agree with the stem for that particular feature (see van der Hulst and Weijer 1995 and references therein).[10] This constraint will also apply when there is more than one affix attached to a stem, as in *dun-e-he* 'the knees', in which both suffixes are ATR because of the noun stem being ATR (cf. *tan-a-ha* 'the stones'). This constraint is only violated in one case that I am aware of (in the case in which the suffix vowel totally assimilates to a following vowel; see section 5.9), but as a result it is not top-ranked. The tableaus for ATR and non-ATR single

---

[10] In languages in which affixes may have lexical values of ATR, additional Faithfulness constraints ranking Faithfulness of ATR in stems above ATR in affixes would also need to be active.

stems with suffixes are shown below. The ATR specification is written under its sponsoring morpheme.

NoGap is irrelevant for disyllabic forms, since a minimum of three syllables is necessary for a "gap" to potentially occur. Since it is never violated, NoGap and candidates which violate it will not be presented in tableaus in the remainder of this chapter.

(262) ATR-related constraints for sie-ku 'the path' Agr(ATR), Max(ATR) >> Align[ATR]μ

sIE-kU ATR	Max (ATR)	Dep (ATR)	Agr (ATR)	Align [ATR]μ
☞ a. sie-ku				*
b. sie-kʊ			*!	
c. sɪa-ku			*!	*
d. sɪa-kʊ	*!			

In the winning candidate (262a), note that Align[ATR]μ is violated, since the right edge of ATR is not aligned with the right edge of its sponsoring morpheme, but one morpheme further to the right. Candidate (262b) fatally violates Agr(ATR) by having ATR on the stem but not the suffix, while (262c) also violates it by having ATR on the suffix but not on the stem. (I assume here that the input ATR is the one present in the output. If the stem ATR is deleted and another ATR is inserted on the suffix, this would violate both Max(ATR) and Dep(ATR).) Candidate (262d) has deleted the ATR feature altogether and so fatally violates Max(ATR). This tableau shows Agr(ATR) and Max(ATR) outrank Align[ATR]μ.

The same constraints also account for non-ATR stems, but in quite a different way:

(263) ATR-related constraints for níí-kʊ́ 'the rain'

nII-kU	Max(ATR)	Dep(ATR)	Agr(ATR)	Align[ATR]μ
☞ a. nɪɪ-kʊ				
b. nɪɪ-ku		*!	*	
c. nii-kʊ		*!	*	
d. nii-ku		*!		

5.2 ATR vowel harmony

Starting with a non-ATR noun stem, any occurrence of ATR fatally violates DEP(ATR), as candidates (263b, c, and d) do. Candidates (263b and c) also violate AGR(ATR), since stem and affix have different ATR values. The constraint ALIGN[ATR]μ is not violated by any of these candidates, since there is no morpheme present which has sponsored an ATR feature.

The constraints already in place are sufficient to account for all compound nouns as well as those noun-adjective complexes in which the adjective is non-ATR. In particular, the ALIGN[ATR]μ constraint penalizes a single ATR feature when realized on any morpheme other than its sponsoring morpheme. However, another constraint will be necessary later, when discussing ATR spread to particles. This expresses the generalization that lexical items almost always retain their value of ATR, in contrast to affixes and particles. This constraint will be:

(264) IDENT(ATR)$_{Lex}$: the value of ATR in the input of a lexical item is identical with its value in the output

We see the effect of this constraint below. The only time when this is violated is in the case of adjectives spreading ATR into a preceding noun, while ALIGN[ATR]μ is violated in a number of cases. For these reasons, IDENT(ATR)$_{Lex}$ is not top-ranked, but it is ranked above ALIGN[ATR]μ.

(265) ATR-related constraints for jùò-háá!lɪ́ŋ 'new room'

juo-haalɪŋ ATR	MAX (ATR)	DEP (ATR)	IDENT (ATR)$_{Lex}$	ALIGN [ATR]μ
☞ a. juo-haalɪŋ				
b. juo-heeliŋ			*!	**
c. jʊa-haalɪŋ	*!		*	

(266) ATR-related constraints for hánɪ́í-dèmbíŋ 'father-in-law'

hanɪ-dembiŋ ATR	MAX (ATR)	DEP (ATR)	IDENT (ATR)$_{Lex}$	ALIGN [ATR]μ
☞ a. hanɪɪ-dembiŋ				
b. henii-dembiŋ			*!	**
c. hanɪɪ-dɛmbɪŋ	*!		*	

DEP(ATR) is never violated in (265) or (266), since no new ATR feature is introduced that was not present in the input. This assumes that both candidates (265b) and (266b), which have ATR on both morphemes, share a single ATR feature. The same phonetic result would occur if a new ATR feature were introduced, and this candidate would be ruled out by its violation of DEP(ATR).

The IDENT(ATR)$_{Lex}$ and DEP(ATR) constraints (and ALIGN[ATR]μ in this case) thus rule out any spreading of ATR from one lexical morpheme to another. However, such spreading does occur in a noun-adjective complex when the adjective is ATR, as shown in the data in (267) selected from (250).

(267) Spreading of ATR
    a. **gbè-góbíŋ**   'short dog' (cf. gbààŋ 'dog')
    b. **kù-bíŋ**   'small hoe' (cf. kʋ̀ʋ́ŋ 'hoe')
    c. **kpíé-!bíŋ**   'small chicken' (cf. kpɪ́áŋ 'chicken')
    d. **hògù-bǐŋ**   'small woman' (cf. hɔ̀gʋ́ 'woman')
    e. **dàkúó-ní!íŋ**   'female parrot' (cf. dàkʋ́á-!rááŋ 'male parrot')
    f. **kàréntìè-bǐŋ**   'small cutlass' (cf. kàréntɪ̀à 'cutlass')
    g. **bùntùù-bíŋ**   'small toad' (cf. bʋ̀ntʋ̀ʋ̀-kpɪ́!ɪ́ŋ 'big toad')
    h. **múgú-bíŋ**   'small river' (cf. mʋ́gʋ́ŋ 'river')
    i. **túgú-bîŋ**   'small termite hill' (cf. tʋ́gʋ́ŋ 'termite hill')

    No spreading
    j. **dàà-bîŋ**   'small stick'
    k. **ŋmààn-ní!íŋ**   'female monkey'
    l. **kàgbàà-bǐŋ**   'small hat'
    m. kág-**bíŋ** ~   'small roan antelope'
       kágí-**bíŋ**

The shortening of certain long noun stem vowels will be discussed in section 5.7. In this specific morphological context and no other, ATR spreads from one lexical morpheme to another within a word. In most cases, the ATR of the final syllable only of the noun stem is ATR, with three types of exceptions. First, in (267h-i), the ATR is in both syllables of the noun stem, when there is an input /ʋgʋ/ sequence. Second, in (267j-l), there is no spreading at all when the final noun stem vowel is [aa]. Third, in (267m), there is no spreading of ATR when there is an optional epenthetic vowel between the target and the ATR source.

For the majority of cases, in which ATR spreads one syllable into the noun stem, the constraint ALIGN[ATR]μ is violated. A rather specific constraint prohibiting a noun stem which has no ATR associations being adjacent to an ATR adjective must be proposed:[11]

---

[11] Thanks to Doug Pulleyblank for suggesting the basic idea behind this constraint.

5.2 ATR vowel harmony

(268) *]$_{\text{N-Adj}}$[ATR: a noun stem which has no ATR associations is prohibited adjacent to an ATR adjective

To satisfy this constraint when given an input of a non-ATR noun and an ATR adjective, one can either spread the ATR from the adjective to the noun, or delete the ATR. Since MAX(ATR) is undominated, deleting ATR is not an option, so ATR will spread. In the cases presently being considered, there will be a conflict between *]$_{\text{N-Adj}}$[ATR which forces ATR to spread onto the noun, and IDENT(ATR)$_{\text{Lex}}$ (as well as ALIGN[ATR]μ) which prefers that ATR not be spread onto the noun at all. The compromise is a minimal spreading: one syllable. Any more spreading than that incurs multiple violations of ALIGN[ATR]μ, but does not improve the situation with respect to *]$_{\text{N-Adj}}$[ATR. The relative ranking between these two constraints can be seen easily in the forms in which the noun stem is monosyllabic.

(269) fè-bíŋ 'small baboon': *]$_{\text{N-Adj}}$[ATR >> IDENT(ATR)$_{\text{Lex}}$

fAA-bIŋ ATR	MAX (ATR)	*]$_{\text{N-Adj}}$[ATR	IDENT (ATR)$_{\text{Lex}}$	ALIGN [ATR]μ
☞ a. fe-biŋ			*	*
b. fa-biŋ		*!		
c. fa-bɪŋ	*!		*	

ATR spreads into the noun stem in the winning candidate (269a), violating IDENT(ATR)$_{\text{Lex}}$. However, it does not violate the higher-ranked *]$_{\text{N-Adj}}$[ATR, as the losing candidate (269b) does. Deleting the ATR specification altogether fatally violates MAX(ATR), as in candidate (269c).

A disyllabic noun shows the gradient nature of the constraint ALIGN[ATR]μ.

(270) bʊ̀ntʊ̀ʊ̀-bíŋ 'small toad'

bUntUU-bIŋ ATR	MAX (ATR)	*]$_{\text{N-Adj}}$[ATR	IDENT (ATR)$_{\text{Lex}}$	ALIGN [ATR]μ
☞ a. bʊntuu-biŋ			*	*
b. bʊntʊʊ-biŋ		*!		
c. buntuu-biŋ			*	**!
d. bʊntʊʊ-bɪŋ	*!		*	

The multiple violations of ALIGN[ATR]μ are what makes the difference in the winning candidate (270a) and the losing candidate (270c). Candidate (270a) only has one violation, while candidate (270c) has two.

Several factors could be responsible for the spreading of ATR through two syllables in (267h) *múgú-bíŋ* 'small river'. That it is not round vowels in general or the presence of *g* alone is shown by (267d) *hɔ̀gù-bǐŋ* 'small woman', in which the ATR spreads only one syllable left. The hypothesis most compatible with the data is that high round vowels must be identical across *g*. Other possibilities could no doubt also be proposed. This phenomenon is also related to the fact that V_2 in trisyllabic verbs is always i/ɪ, with the sole exception that V_2 can be u/ʊ only if V_1 is also u/ʊ and the intervening consonant is *g*. I will defer discussion of these until section 5.4.1.

The lack of ATR spread in (267j–l), e.g., in *dàà-bǐŋ* 'small stick', is accounted for as part of a larger pattern in Kɔnni, that long /aa/ is resistant to change, to the point of a total lack of alternation. If /aa/ shortens, however, the short vowel is subject to ATR sharing with the adjective, as in *fè-bíŋ* 'small baboon' (from *fááŋ* 'baboon'), appearing in the tableau in (269). At this point, why shortening of /aa/ occurs in some words but not in others which are apparently phonologically identical in the relevant aspects is unknown.

However, it is evident that a constraint preserving all features (or lack of them) of /aa/ is active. Though preserving /aa/ may be possible with the DEP constraints for [dorsal], [coronal], and [closed], we shall see that these are ranked too low to have the desired result. So I propose the general descriptive constraint below.

(271) FAITH[aa]: a long [aa] retains its identity

This is a combination of both the identity of the vowel, i.e., /a/, and its duration, which is long. From a phonetic viewpoint, this is an expected outcome. If a sound is longer, the speaker has more time to hit the intended articulatory target.

(272) dàà-bǐŋ 'small stick', showing MAX(ATR), FAITH[aa] > > SHARE[ATR]$_{ADJ-N}$

dAA-bIŋ ATR	MAX (ATR)	FAITH[aa]	*]$_{N-Adj}$[ATR	IDENT (ATR)$_{Lex}$
☞ a. daa-biŋ			*	
b. dee-biŋ		*!		*
c. daa-bɪŋ	*!			*

5.2 ATR vowel harmony

In (272), the winning candidate (272a) violates *]$_{\text{N-Adj}}$[ATR, but does not violate FAITH[aa]. Candidate (272b) loses by violating FAITH[aa], and candidate (272c), which shows no ATR at all, thus loses by violating MAX(ATR).

The discussion above has dealt only with alternations in which the only difference between ATR and non-ATR vowels was the presence of ATR itself. However, as noted above, when an affix has [a] in a non-ATR context, it may be either [e] or [o] in an ATR context. Both of these alternants have feature differences from [a] besides the ATR difference. As seen in (253), [e] also has a [coronal] place and a [closed] feature, while [o] has a [dorsal] place feature and a [closed] feature. It is to this alternation that we now turn, using the examples *dùn-é* 'knees' and *tu-o* 'is taking' to illustrate these patterns.

A constraint common among ATR-harmony languages is often formulated as *ATR/Low, prohibiting co-occurrence of ATR and the [+Low] feature (e.g., Archangeli and Pulleyblank 1994). However, in light of the [closed] height feature assumed here, I reformulate it as a positive constraint ATR/[closed], saying if ATR is present, at least one [closed] feature must also be present, or in other words ATR must co-occur with at least one [closed]. This constraint is satisfied if an ATR vowel co-occurs with one or two instances of [closed] and violated if an ATR vowel has no instance of [closed].[12]

(273) **ATR/[closed]:** if a vowel is ATR, then it has at least one occurrence of [closed]

Central vowels are placeless in the feature system used here, and /a/ is the only central vowel. Nonlow vowels must have a place feature, either [dorsal] or [coronal].

(274) **[closed]/PLACE:** a vowel with a [closed] feature must also have a place feature

/I/ is the epenthetic vowel, with a [coronal] place. It is consistent with this to propose that [coronal] is the default place value in vowels in Kɔnni, consistent with Hume (1992) and the rather large literature on coronals. In OT terms, it is less costly to insert a [coronal] than a [dorsal] or any other place feature. Translating this into ranked constraints, DEP[dors] >> DEP[cor]. We must also consider the DEP[closed] constraint in these examples.

---

[12] Parkinson (1996b) uses a constraint PL → cl which has similarities to (273) and (274). He subsumes ATR under place features. His analysis of Kɔnni diphthongization will be discussed in section 5.3.2.1.

(275) DEP[dors]: every [dorsal] in the output has a correspondent in the input
　　　 DEP[cor]: every [coronal] in the output has a correspondent in the **input**
　　　 DEP[closed]: every [closed] in the output has a correspondent in the input

Tableaus for both ATR stems and non-ATR stems are shown below. The two constraints to the left in (276) are top-ranked; they are never violated in Kɔnni. The two constraints to the right can both be violated, but their relative ranking is unknown. The assumption in the tableau below is that if the suffix has a feature [closed], then that is a distinct occurrence from a [closed] on the stem. There is no height assimilation, which would be evidence for spreading of [closed], in Kɔnni.

(276) dùn-é 'knees'

dUn-A ATR	ATR/ [closed]	[closed]/ PLACE	AGR (ATR)	DEP [dors]	DEP [cor]	DEP [closed]
☞ a. dun-e					*	*
b. dun-i					*	*!*
c. dun-a			*!			
d. dun-ɛ			*!		*	*
e. dun-ə		*!				*
f. dun-æ	*!				*	
g. dun-o				*!		*

The candidates in which all vowels are non-ATR are not considered above due to space considerations. They would all be ruled out by violating MAX(ATR). Likewise, all candidates in which the noun stem surfaces as [dʊn-] and the suffix has ATR are ruled out by violations of ALIGN[ATR]μ, also not shown in (276).

In (276), candidate (a) is optimal, since it violates only DEP[closed] and DEP[cor] once each, by adding a [closed] and a [coronal] feature. Candidate (276b) is ruled out by its multiple violations of DEP[closed]. Candidates (276c and d) are ruled out by violating AGR(ATR), since the suffix does not agree with the root in ATR value. Candidate (276e) is ruled out by having a vowel [ə] which has a [closed] but not a place feature. Candidate (276f) is ruled out by having a vowel [æ] which has ATR but not a [closed] feature,

5.2 ATR vowel harmony

and candidate (276g) is ruled out by inserting a [dorsal] feature. We can account for non-ATR forms by use of the same constraints. Several constraints used in (276) are irrelevant in (277) and are not included in the tableau.

(277) tàn-á 'stones'

tAn-A	Dep [ATR]	Agr (ATR)	Dep [cor]	Dep [closed]
☞ a. tan-a				
b. tan-ɛ			*!	*!
c. tan-e	*!	*	*	
d. ten-e	*!			

The winning candidate (277a) violates no listed constraints. Candidate (277b), by having [ɛ] in the output which was not in the input, adds both a [coronal] and a [closed] feature and is so ruled out. Candidates (277c and d) and any other candidates with an ATR vowel are ruled out by the violation of Dep[ATR], as well as possibly other constraints.

Since suffixal [o] occurs only adjacent to [w, u], there is evidently a sharing of the [dorsal] feature (recall /w/ was specified as [dorsal] on the basis of nasal assimilation). However, this is restricted to an ATR context; -*wa* occurs as a non-ATR suffix. This pattern is not limited to suffixes; there is never a case of [...we...] anywhere in my data, though there are cases of [kpe...], [gbe...], [ke...], and [ge...]. It is the [dorsal] under V-place that is the crucial configuration. Other front vowels do occur after [w] (see 248), although I have only one case each of [wi...] and [wɛ...]. All vowels are attested after [w] except for [e]. This gap may be argued to be an accidental one, given the relative scarcity of [e] in general. On the other hand, it could conceivably be systematic. If it is systematic, then the pattern is that a mid ATR vowel following [w] (or [u]) must share its [dorsal] feature, not only in suffixes but across the board. This view predicts that [we] never occurs anywhere in Kɔnni, but any other vowel after [w] is allowed. Similarly, when we discuss diphthongization, we shall see that [uo] is present in an ATR context, but [ʊa] in a non-ATR context. The constraint to express this generalization must be quite specific, as below.

(278) **[dors]-Agr:** a nonhigh ATR vowel must agree in [dorsal] specification with an adjacent vocoid.

The condition of "adjacent" vocoid is needed since the [dorsal] feature is not shared across an intervening consonant (recall *dùn-é* 'knees' above, where the stem vowel is [dorsal], but *n* intervenes between it and the suffixal vowel *e*). The term "vocoid" rather than "vowel" is used since the relevant sounds are [u] and [w], a vowel and a glide. Tableaus for words with an ATR (279) and a non-ATR (280) stem are given.

(279) tù-ó 'is taking'

tU-A ATR	MAX [ATR]	[dors]-AGR	AGR (ATR)	DEP [dors]	DEP [cor]	DEP [closed]
☞ a. tu-o						*
b. tu-e		*!			*	*
c. tu-a			*!			
d. tʊ-a	*!					

In (279), the winning candidate violates none of the listed constraints except DEP[closed]. Candidate (279b) has a fatal violation of [dors]-AGR by having the *u-e* sequence in which the vowels do not agree in [dorsal]. Candidate (279c) has a fatal violation of AGR(ATR) since the vowels in the *u-a* sequence do not share the same ATR value. Candidate (279d) is ruled out by deleting the [ATR] feature altogether and thus fatally violating MAX[ATR]. The constraint DEP[dors] is not violated at all in (279) and so does not rule out any candidates. A new [dorsal] feature is not introduced in the output, but a single [dorsal] feature is shared between root and suffix.

(280) kʊ-a 'is killing'

kU-A	DEP [ATR]	[dors]-AGR	DEP [dors]	AGR (ATR)	DEP [cor]	DEP [closed]
☞ a. kʊ-a						
b. kʊ-ɛ					*!	*!
c. kʊ-ɔ			*!			*
d. ku-a	*!	*!		*		
e. ku-e	*!	*!			*	*
f. ku-o	*!					*

In (280), again the winning candidate (280a) violates no listed constraints. Candidate (280b) violates DEP[cor] by inserting a [coronal] feature. All other candidates incur a fatal violation of DEP[ATR] by introducing an [ATR] feature, as well as fatal violations of other constraints.

5.2.2 Vowel harmony across words

5.2.2.1 Data

Particles of various sorts (pronouns, complementizers, the negative particle, the future particle, etc.) also harmonize with the nearest stem, with "nearest" to be discussed more explicitly below. As will be shown, the span of vowel harmony partly depends on syntactic structures. For the syntactic structures below, I rely largely on my preliminary analysis within a GB framework in Cahill (1993). Many more syntactic structures could be elicited than what I have in my data, but those I do have will be sufficient to propose some significant generalizations.

Before giving examples of where vowel harmony does occur across words, below are examples in which vowel harmony does not occur across words. When nouns or verbs with differing ATR values are adjacent, each retains its own value of ATR.[13] The [+ATR] words are bolded for ease of reference.

(281) a. Noun-noun
  níí!gé kɔ́bà   'cows' bones'
  múlé júŋ   'bird's (sp.) tail'
  dààwá **gílìnsìèlé** 'man's dance'
  vúó-kpíí!má **jú!né** 'big-people's rooms'

 b. Noun-verb
  nàáŋ **jùó !júóŋ** 'chief is entering room'
  wàlím **bénnè**   'It's warm. (sweat exists)'
  ù **ɲúó!té** dɔ́nnà 'His/her stomach is rumbling. (shaking)'
  víví !yá!lá mɪ́ŋ 'I'm feeling shy. (shyness is holding me)'

 c. Verb-verb
  yáá **kêŋ**   'bring! (have come)'
  nagɪ **chii**   'carry! (take carry)'
  díí chagɪ   'Eat 'til you're satisfied! (eat satisfy)'
  ken saŋɲɪ   'come help!'

---

[13]The sole exception I have found to this is cases in which the verb *ga* 'go' sometimes becomes the ATR *ge* before another ATR verb, as in *ù nèn gé zíe* 's/he will go stand'. However, this pattern is not consistent; it varies with speakers and even with a single speaker. It is possible that in some contexts the verb *ga* is being re-interpreted as a particle. This is a common historical process (see Hopper and Traugott 1993, and especially for African languages, Heine and Reh 1984). As a particle, it is vulnerable to ATR spread, but as a lexical verb, it is not.

d. Verb-noun
   ù dàgá **!júókú**   'S/he is showing the room.'
   ù chɔ̀gìsá **!bólíŋ**   'S/he is fetching fire.'
   ù gbɪ̀èré !sááɲ   'S/he is cutting porridge.'
   ù tùlìmé !dáákú   'S/he is turning a stick.'

e. Verb-nominal[14]
   ù bɪ̀é !sɪ́á   'S/he is where?' (cf. ù gá !sɪ́á 'S/he went where?')
   ù nèn díí súrúŋ   'S/he will eat tomorrow.'

In examples in (282), the entire sentence, with several particles, agrees with the bolded verb in ATR.

(282) a. bè ké **yé** wò
       3p NEG see 3s
       'They did not see him/her.'

   b. bà ká **yí** wà
      3p NEG give 3s
      'They did not give him/her.'

   c. ù yá ká **dágà**
      3s yet NEG show
      'S/he is not yet showing.'

   d. ù yé ké **dígè**
      3s yet NEG cook
      'S/he is not yet cooking.'

Examples in (283) show two or three distinct [(ATR] spans in a sentence, with the [+ATR] spans bolded.

(283) a. ←[−ATR]——→ ←[+ATR]→
         dí ká yɪ̀à kà **kè ɲìndííké**
         that NEG give it it food
         'that (you) do not give it its food'

---

[14]Interrogatives such as *bɪ̀á* 'what?' and *sɪ́á* 'where?' act syntactically as nouns as far as sentence position, as well as phonologically in retaining their ATR value in all contexts. Likewise, words which function as adverbs as far as time, location, manner, etc. follow the same pattern of retaining their underlying value of ATR. Most of the time interrogatives and adverbials occur sentence initially, but occasionally they occur postverbally, as in the examples above.

5.2 ATR vowel harmony

b. ù yì ká !ké tígíŋ
   3s give it its house
   'S/he gave it its house.'

c. ù yàllí bá !bé yísè
   3s sell 3p 3p sheep(PL)
   'S/he sold them their sheep (PL).'

d. bà gá !bé tígíŋ
   3p go 3p house
   'They went to their house.'

e. **bè díí** !bá sá!áŋ
   3p eat 3p porridge
   'They ate their porridge.'

f. **bè chíí** wú záá
   3p carry 3s millet
   'They carried his/her millet.'

g. bà bá !bé gúú wó síá
   3p will 3p bury 3s where
   'Where will they bury him/her?'

h. **bè nèn gúú wó** tàn-jààlím má
   3p FUT bury 3s rock-wide at
   'They will bury her in a wide rock.'

The difference between (282) and (283) is that the sentences in (282) have only one lexical item, the verb. All other words are particles which are, I propose, underlyingly unspecified for ATR and only surface as ATR when in the domain of an ATR word. In contrast, those in (283) have two lexical items of opposite ATR values in them, and these result in two ATR spans (or in (283g), three). Most of the rightmost ATR spans in (283) happen to be noun phrases, but note in (283g) that the same pattern may happen with embedded sentences. The span of ATR is limited to the largest constituent, including intonational phrase, that does not contain another lexical item. The connection between syntax and ATR span will be examined more closely below.

Examples in (284) and (285) show the result when a pronoun, unspecified for ATR, occurs between verbs with different values of ATR. The pronouns in the examples in (285) are both coreferential with the subject pronouns; it is not expected that this is germane to the analysis here.

(284) a. tɪ   yaa   **ba** *kieŋ*
        1p have   3p come
        'We brought them.'

   b. *be*   *to*   **be**   *dʊa*
      3p   take   3p   lie.down
      'They laid them down.'

(285) a. bà   báá   *!bé*   *díì*
        3p will 3p   eat
        'They are going to eat.'[15]
   b. ʊ̀   yàlá   *!ú*   *díì*
      3s want   3s   eat
      'S/he wants to eat.'

There are two distinct syntactic situations in (284) and (285). In (284), the two verbs are in a serial verb construction, and the pronoun harmonizes with the first verb in ATR. However, in (285) the second verb is embedded in a sentence which is a complement to the first verb, and the pronoun harmonizes with the second verb. (The set of verbs which requires a sentence as complement, as in (285), is quite limited and contains no verbs which are [+ATR]). Thus both examples in (285) have the main verb as [−ATR], and the [+ATR] span is to the right. It is evident from the above that a particle between lexical items (nouns, verbs) with differing values of ATR will agree with the lexical item to which they are most closely bound syntactically. This connection between phonology and syntax is examined more closely in section 5.2.3.

No particles except pronouns occur between verbs in serial constructions. However, the conjunction à 'and' may occur between verbs or begin a clause after a pause, as in à kèn dʊ́á 'and (s/he) came (and) lay down'. In these cases, the à retains its [−ATR] value.

Preverbal particles, which we may generally consider as adverbial in nature, may or may not have their own lexical values of ATR. If such a particle is lexically [+ATR], the particle to the left also generally is [+ATR]. Particles with their own lexical value of ATR include *ko* 'just, only', *woŋ* 'already', and *vii* 'again'. Particles with /a/, e.g., *ká* 'NEG' and *yá* 'still, yet', are lexically unspecified for ATR. They undergo spreading of ATR, which also can spread through them, while particles with /aa/, e.g., *wáá* 'now, then', remain as [aa].

---

[15]The verb *baa* that I have glossed 'will' here is almost certainly derived from *ba* 'say'. It is not an auxiliary verb, but does not exhibit all the variation of a full lexical verb either. Aaron (1996/1997) has documented the grammaticalization of a full verb 'say' through a phase of intentionality to a phase of future tense. The Kɔnni construction illustrated here is in the second stage of this process.

(286) a. **be ko** taa mɪŋ
   3p just throw EMPH
   'They just fired [guns].' (cf. bà tàá mìŋ)

b. **be woŋ** kpatɪ tɪ bʊʊrɪkʊ
   3p already finish 2p tribe
   'They'd already destroyed our tribe.' (cf. bà kpàtí !túúmá)

c. **ù yé !kó** dágà mìŋ
   3s still just show EMPH
   'S/he's still just showing.' (cf. ʊ̀ yà dàgá mìŋ)

d. kááŋ **kó kèŋ**
   NEG.FUT UST COME
   'Won't you just come?'

e. **ù ké víí** dágɪ
   3s NEG again show
   'S/he has not again shown.' (cf. ʊ̀ ká dágà)

f. **ù yè ké víí** dágà
   3s still NEG again show
   'S/he is not yet again showing.' (cf. ʊ̀ yà ká dágà)

g. ʊ̀ wáá **víí** dágà mìŋ
   3s now again show EMPH
   'S/he is now again showing.'

h. ʊ́ ká wáá !**víí** dágà
   3s NEG now again show
   'S/he is not now again showing.'

i. ʊ́ wàà **súgùrè** mìŋ
   3s now wash EMPH
   'S/he is now washing.'

Thus preverbal particles, either pronouns or adverbs, take their ATR specification from the verb or preverbal particle to the right. Some preverbal particles are invariant in their ATR value. There is never a particle with a short vowel which is invariant as [−ATR], but there are at least three particles which are invariant as [+ATR], and these all immediately precede the verb; there are no other particles following them.

(287) Order of preverbal particles (repeated from (30) in chapter 1)

tÍN	yA		vii	
nÀN	waa	kÁ$_2$	ko	verb
kááN	ŋaaN		won	
kÁ$_1$				

Finally, I have two cases of contrasting ATR value in my data in which the direct object pronoun agrees in ATR with the following numerical quantifier.

(288) ú nìgì-wá **wó !búlíè**   'S/he beat him/her twice.'
   ú nìgì-wá **wá !bútáà**   'S/he beat him/her three times.'

Since I have only these two sentences in my data, I will not venture an analysis of these at this time.

5.2.2.2 Analysis

The main generalization from all the above is that lexical items (N, V, A) keep their underlying values of ATR, and nonlexical items around them agree in ATR value with them. In particular, ATR lexical items never lose ATR, the few ATR particles never lose ATR, and non-ATR lexical items only rarely become ATR (the sole exception is ATR spreading from adjective to noun), but non-ATR particles consistently become ATR when in an ATR domain.

The faithfulness of lexical items in phrases to their underlying ATR value is accounted for by the same constraint which maintained their faithfulness in compounds: the previously-proposed constraint IDENT(ATR)$_{Lex}$, here repeated from (264).

(289) IDENT(ATR)$_{Lex}$: the value of ATR in the input of a lexical item is identical with its value in the output

Again, this constraint assumes the monovalency of ATR. We are able to account for the stability of ATR in adjacent lexical items with this constraint and others already in place.

5.2 ATR vowel harmony

(290) **múlé** júŋ 'bird's (sp.) tail'

mUlE jUŋ ATR	MAX[ATR]	IDENT(ATR)_Lex	ALIGN[ATR]μ
☞ a. mule juŋ			
b. mulɛ juŋ	*!	*	
c. mʊle juŋ		*!	*
d. mule juŋ		*!	**

(291) dààwá **gílìnsìèlé** 'man's dance'

dAAwA gIlInsIEla ATR	MAX [ATR]	IDENT(ATR)_Lex	ALIGN [ATR]μ
☞ a. daawa gilinsiele			
b. daawa gɪlɪnsɪala	*!	*	
c. diewo gilinsiele		*!	**

In the tableaus in (290) and (291), when a vowel belonging to a non-ATR lexical item is pronounced with ATR, agreeing with an adjacent ATR lexical item, this is interpreted as autosegmental spreading, with no new ATR feature being introduced. For this reason, the candidates' (c) in both tableaus above fatally violate IDENT(ATR)_Lex (and ALIGN[ATR]μ), and not the DEP(ATR) constraint that would be violated if a new occurrence of ATR were introduced. In both candidates' (b) above, of course, the ATR present in the input is not present in output, fatally violating MAX[ATR].

In the cases in which ATR does spread from a lexical item to various particles, the simplest case is that in which only one lexical item is present in a sentence. In such a case, that lexical item must be a verb, as illustrated in (292).

(292) a. bè ké **yé** wò
 3p NEG see 3s
 'They did not see him/her.' (all ATR)

b. bà ká **yí** wà
 3p NEG give 3s
 'They did not give him/her.' (all non-ATR)

The basic principle here is that an ATR feature will spread or be aligned to any particle in the same utterance. We will see that this pattern (and the constraint expressing it) is far from undominated; the idea is that ATR spreads until some other factor stops it, and there are several such factors.

(293) ALIGN[ATR]$_{UTT}$: an occurrence of ATR is aligned to both the left and right edges of the utterance containing it[16]

As with ALIGN[ATR]μ, the above is a conflation of the constraints aligning ATR to the left and to the right; the distinction is not necessary in Kɔnni. In the case of an ATR verb and several particles, ALIGN[ATR]$_{UTT}$ has the effect of spreading ATR to all particles in a sentence, as the tableau in (294) illustrates. A strict interpretation of the constraint will count a violation for every syllable in which ATR is not manifested, but a display based on this will get awkward as the size of the sentence increases. As a practical matter, I will list a maximum of four violations per constraint per candidate.

(294) bè ké **yé wò** 'they did not **see** him/her' ALIGN[ATR]$_{UTT}$ >> ALIGN[ATR]μ

	BA kA yE wA ATR	MAX [ATR]	NO GAP	[dors] -AGR	DEP [ATR]	ALIGN [ATR]$_{UTT}$	ALIGN [ATR]μ	DEP [cor]
☞ a.	be ke ye wo						***	**
b.	ba ka yɛ wa	*!						
c.	ba ka ye wa					*!**		
d.	ba ke ye wa					*!*	*	*
e.	be ka ye wo		*!		*!	**?	*	*
f.	ba ka ye wo					*!	*	
g.	be ke ye wa					*!	**	
h.	be ke ye we			*!			***	***

The winning candidate (294a) violates the constraints DEP[cor], since the particles *be* and *ke* each have an instance of [coronal] not present in the input, and ALIGN[ATR]μ, since the ATR has spread beyond the edges of its sponsoring morpheme *ye*. Candidate (294b) fatally violates MAX[ATR], since the ATR in the input is now absent altogether. Candidates (294c–g) have one or more particles which do not manifest ATR which has its source in the verb. Candidate (294e) is actually a conflation

---

[16] I have not explored multi-clausal sentences, nor multi-sentence utterances. In light of the syntactic conditions on vowel harmony explored below, it is quite possible that a more accurate formulation of this constraint might refer to intonational or phonological phrases. Since the maximum span considered here is a sentence which is coterminous with an utterance, a constraint referring to an utterance will yield the correct outputs in this work.

5.2 ATR vowel harmony

of two phonetically identical candidates which have different representations. If the ATR on *be* is considered to be a distinct inserted ATR, the fatal condition is the violation of DEP[ATR]. Alternatively, if one views the ATR on *be* as a result of spreading from the ATR verb *ye*, then NOGAP would be the constraint that is fatally violated. Finally, in (294f), the constraint [dors]-AGR is fatally violated.

Example (295) is a sentence in which the verb, the only lexical item, is non-ATR.

(295) bà ká yí wà 'they did not give him/her'

bA kA yI wA	MAX[ATR]	DEP[ATR]	ALIGN[ATR]$_{UTT}$
☞ a. ba ka yɪ wa			
b. ba ka yi wa		*!	***
c. be ke yi wo		*!	

Candidate (295a) violates none of the listed constraints. Candidates (295b and c), or any other candidate which has an ATR present in the output, fatally violate DEP[ATR].

In the case of two lexical items of differing ATR values with no particles between, the situation is still straightforward. Particles on the left and the right will assume the ATR value of the lexical item adjacent to them. The tableau illustrating this is in (296).

(296) ʊ̀ dàgá !jùòkú 's/he is showing the room'

U dAgA jUO-kU ATR	MAX [ATR]	DEP [ATR]	IDENT (ATR)$_{Lex}$	ALIGN [ATR]$_{UTT}$	ALIGN [ATR]μ
☞ a. ʊ daga juoku				***	*
b. u daga juoku		*!		***	*
c. ʊ daga juakʊ	*!		*!		
d. ʊ dage juoku			*!	**	**
e. u dege juoku			*!		****

Candidate (296a) above wins because it violates no highly ranked constraints. Candidate (296b) has the pronoun *u* as ATR. I view this as due to the introduction of an additional ATR feature, thus incurring a fatal violation of DEP[ATR]. (Alternatively, if the ATR feature is viewed as linked to two syllables without being linked to the syllable(s) between them, then

NoGap is fatally violated.) Candidate (296c) loses because it has no ATR in the output, though it does in the input. Candidate (296d) has the ATR from the noun *juoku* spread to the last syllable of /daga/, and so violates IDENT(ATR)$_{Lex}$. Candidate (296e) perfectly satisfies ALIGN[ATR]$_{UTT}$, but like (296d), fatally violates IDENT(ATR)$_{Lex}$.

Two types of particles add complexity to this view. Particles which have [aa] systematically violate ALIGN[ATR]$_{UTT}$, that is, when adjacent to an ATR word, they do not agree in ATR. Also, some particles have underlying ATR. We consider both of these next.

Though most particles are assumed to lack ATR in input form, as shown by their alternation between ATR and non-ATR forms, a few particles consistently are ATR and are assumed to have an ATR specification in input form. These are the particles *vii* 'again', *ko* 'just', and *woN* 'already'.[17] If present, these particles occur immediately adjacent to the verb, with no possibility of other particles intervening (see 287). Particles which occur to their left will agree with these ATR particles in ATR (with the exception of the [aa] particles discussed below), exactly as if there were an ATR verb in that position. In the data below, the verb is non-ATR, but the particles preceding the ATR particle are also ATR.

(297) a. ù yé !kó dágà mìŋ
       3s still just show EMPH
       'S/he's still just showing.'
       (cf. ʊ̀ yà dàgá mìŋ 's/he's still showing')

   b. **be woŋ** kpatɪ tɪ buurɪku
      3p already finish 1p tribe
      'They'd already destroyed our tribe.'
      (cf. bà kpàtɪ́ !túúmá 'they finished work')

   c. ù yè ké víi dágà
      3s still NEG again show
      'S/he is not still again showing.'
      (cf. ʊ̀ yà ká dágà 's/he's not still showing')

These patterns can be accounted for by the constraints already in place. In particular, the tableau in (298) shows the importance of multiple violations of constraints we have previously discussed. One pattern in particular shows the need for IDENT(ATR)$_{Lex}$, which up to this point has been

---

[17]The particle *woN* is listed with a coda unspecified for place because it is impossible to tell the underlying place of the nasal; a consonant-initial word always follows it, and the nasal has the same place as that consonant.

5.2 ATR vowel harmony

almost redundant (candidates that it eliminates in preceding tableaus could also be ruled out by violations of ALIGN[ATR]μ). This is the asymmetric relationship that lexical items never become ATR when adjacent to an ATR particle, although particles commonly become ATR when adjacent to an ATR lexical item. It is worse for an ATR particle to spread ATR to a lexical item than to another particle. That is, *be ko daga* is fine, but *ba ko dega* is not. Lexical items do not receive ATR specifications from a nonlexical source.

(298) be ko daga 'they are just showing'

bA kO dAgA ATR	MAX [ATR]	IDENT (ATR)_{Lex}	ALIGN [ATR]_{UTT}	ALIGN [ATR]μ
☞ a. be ko daga			**	*
b. ba ko daga			**!*	
c. ba ko dega		*!	**	*
d. ba kɔ daga	*!			

The winning candidate (298a) violates ALIGN[ATR]_{UTT} by not having the verb *daga* agree in ATR with the preceding particle *ko*, and also violates ALIGN[ATR]μ by having the ATR from *ko* spread to the preceding particle. Candidate (298b) loses by having more violations of ALIGN[ATR]_{UTT} than (298a) does. Candidate (298c) loses by violating the highly-ranked IDENT(ATR)_{Lex}, and (298d) loses by deleting the ATR altogether.

Another tableau, this time showing two preverbal particles, is in (299).

(299) ù yé !kó dágà 's/he's still just showing'

U yA kO dAgA ATR	MAX [ATR]	IDENT (ATR)_{Lex}	ALIGN [ATR]_{UTT}	ALIGN [ATR]μ
☞ a. u ye ko daga			**	**
b. ʊ ya ko daga			***!*	
c. ʊ ye ko daga			***!	*
d. ʊ ya kɔ daga	*!			
e. u ye ko dega		*!	*	***
f. ʊ ye ko dege		*!	*	***

Candidate (299a) wins despite violating two key constraints. It violates ALIGN[ATR]_{UTT} twice, by the fact that the particle *ko* disagrees with the verb *daga* in ATR. It also violates ALIGN[ATR]μ twice, since the ATR from *ko* has spread two syllables to the left. Candidates (299b and c) lose by violating ALIGN[ATR]_UTT three (or four) times, as compared to (299a), which only has two violations. Candidate (299d) loses by dropping the ATR feature altogether, violating MAX[ATR]. Candidates (299e and f) lose by violating IDENT(ATR)_Lex.

Just as nouns with [aa] were immune to ATR spread from a following adjective (see 272), so particles with [aa] are immune to ATR spread. These include *kááN* 'NEGATIVE FUTURE', *waa* 'now, then', and *ŋaaN* 'has been'. These may occur adjacent to either lexical or nonlexical ATR words and retain the [aa] quality.

(300) a. ʊ̀   wàà   **súgùrè** mìŋ
       3s now   wash   EMPH
       'S/he is now washing.'

   b. kááŋ   **kó**   **kèŋ**
      NEG.FUT just   come
      'Won't you just come?'

   c. ʊ̀ wáá **víí**   dágà   mìŋ
      3s now again   show   EMPH
      'S/he is now again showing.'

To account for this, we again invoke the highly-ranked constraint FAITH[aa], repeated from (271).

(301) **FAITH[aa]**: a long [aa] retains its identity

(302) ʊ̀ wáá víí dágà 's/he is now again showing'

	U wAA vII dAgA ATR	MAX [ATR]	FAITH[aa]	IDENT (ATR)_Lex	ALIGN [ATR]_UTT	ALIGN [ATR]μ
☞ a.	ʊ waa vii daga				****	
b.	ʊ waa vıidaga	*!				
c.	ʊ wie vii daga		*!		***	*
d.	u wie vii daga		*!		**	**
e.	ʊ waa vii dega			*!	***	*
f.	ʊ waa vii dege			*!	***	**

5.2 ATR vowel harmony

Candidate (302a) wins, though it violates ALIGN[ATR]$_{UTT}$ because *vii* does not spread its ATR to the words on either side of it. Candidate (302b) loses by deleting the ATR feature. Candidates (302c and d) both change the vowel [aa] and thus fatally violate FAITH[aa]. Candidates (302e and f) both lose by spreading the ATR into the following verb and thus violating IDENT(ATR)$_{Lex}$. The additional candidate *u waa vii daga* would be ruled out by either NOGAP or by DEP[ATR], depending on whether the ATR value of *u* is a spreading of ATR or an insertion.

5.2.3 A syntax-phonology interface

5.2.3.1 Data

Up to this point, all cases of vowel harmony involving particles have involved particles adjacent to a lexical item, or other particles with a lexical ATR specification. There has been no possibility of influence from another lexical item without violating NOGAP. However, when particles occur between lexical items, the lexical item they agree with in ATR is a function of the syntax and not simply linear order. In cases such as those below, a conflict arises when a particle occurs between two lexical items with differing ATR values. The conflict, of course, comes from the fact that the particle is adjacent to both an ATR lexical item and a non-ATR lexical item. In such a case where a target occurs between differing ATR values, there are two possibilities. There could either be a gradient effect on the particle, and it will have phonetic characteristics of ATR transitioning into non-ATR (or the reverse), or else the particle will clearly agree with one or the other lexical items. If the latter, which is the actual case in Kɔnni, then we hope to find some principle by which to predict which lexical item the particle agrees with. In the examples in (303), the particle (bolded for emphasis, while ATR spans are in italics) occurs between a verb and a noun. The particle agrees in (303a) with the noun on its right, but in (303b) agrees with the verb on its left.

(303) a. *bé díí* **!bá** sá!áŋ
   3p eat 3p porridge
   'They ate their porridge.'

   b. *bè nèn gúú* **wó** tàn-jààlím má
   3p FUT bury 3s rock-wide place
   'They will bury her in a wide rock.'

Nothing in the linear word structure of the sentences can explain the difference in ATR agreement of the verb. An equal number of violations of ALIGN[ATR]μ occur in both. While multiple violations of ALIGN[ATR]$_{UTT}$ correctly predict the winning candidate in (304), they predict the wrong winner in (305).

(304) *be nen guu wo tan-jaalim ma* 'they will bury her in a wide rock'

Guu wA tAn...ATR	ALIGN[ATR]$_{UTT}$	ALIGN[ATR]μ
☞ a. guu wo tan...	*	*
b. guu wa tan...	**!	*

(305) *bé díí !bá sá!áŋ* 'they ate their porridge'

...dII bA sAAŋ ATR	ALIGN[ATR]$_{UTT}$	ALIGN[ATR]μ
a. be dii ba saaŋ	**!	*
💣 b. be dii be saaŋ	*	**

Similarly, in (306), a particle occurs between two verbs but differs in which verb it agrees with. In (306a, b) it agrees with the left verb, but in (306c) it agrees with the verb to the right. Again, nothing in the linear structure or the constraints heretofore proposed can account for the difference in direction of agreement of the interverbal particle.

(306) a. tɪ   yaa   **ba**   *kieŋ*
         1p   have   3p   come
         'We brought them.'

   b. *be   to*   **be**   dʊa
      3p   take   3p   lie.down
      'They laid them down.'

   c. ʊ̀   yàlá   *!ú*   *dîi*
      3s   want   3s   eat
      'S/he wants to eat.'

The key is in recognizing that the sentences considered above have differing syntax, and the particle will agree with whichever lexical item is more closely related. However, the notion of "closely related" must be examined in more detail.

5.2.3.2 Analysis

There have in general been two approaches to the relation of syntax and phonology. For general overviews see Inkelas and Zec (1995) and the articles in the journal *Phonology,* Volume 4. One is the "direct reference" theory espoused by Kaisse (1985) and Odden (1987, 1990a, 1996), in which the phonology makes direct reference to syntactic structure and syntactic relations between words such as c-command. The other main approach, which I will term "indirect reference," uses prosodic structures created on the basis of the syntactic structure, but does not refer to the syntactic structure directly. This has been posited in works such as Napoli and Nespor (1979), Nespor and Vogel (1986), and Selkirk (1986). Interestingly, Poletto (1998a) presents data from Runyankore which necessitates using *both* approaches for two different tonal phenomena. In contrast to all the above, we will see that neither approach is totally successful with Kɔnni, and the nonstructural syntactic notion of theta-marking will be proposed instead.

The "indirect reference" approach constructs prosodic phrases built on either words or maximal projections, and then refers to the left or right edges of these. For Kɔnni, since we are dealing with multi-word units, the maximal projection parameter is the appropriate one. Below are two cases in which a pronoun occurs between two verbs, and the terminal nodes are identical, but the sentences have quite different structures. The serial verb structure in (307a) is patterned after Baker (1989) (also see discussion by several researchers in Joseph and Zwicky 1990, and an identical structure for the related Gur language Dagaare in Bodomo 1998).

(307) a.

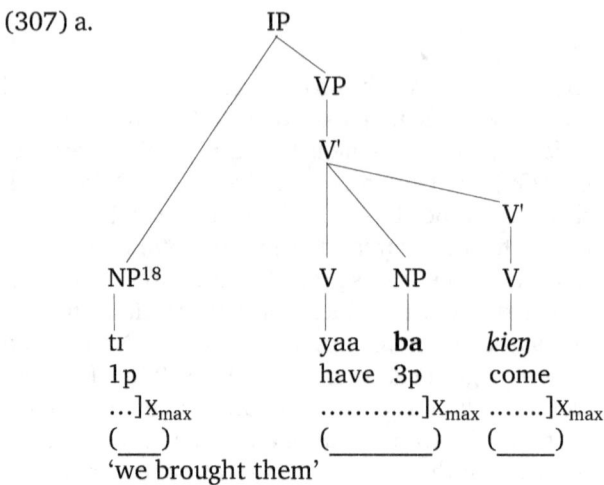

'we brought them'

b.

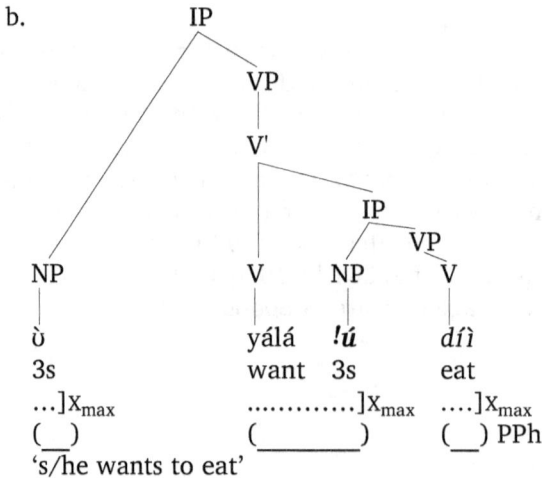

's/he wants to eat'

In keeping with the strategy of Selkirk (1986), I have placed $]x_{max}$ labels to mark the right edges of maximal projections. The pronouns in all the sentences under consideration may be replaced by nouns, and so are labeled as NP nodes. The prosodic domains, labeled prosodic phrases, are

---

[18] It is possible that only an N rather than an NP dominates pronouns. It is true that if syntactic structure were the only determining factor in ATR harmony, a pronoun as NP would not be expected to harmonize with a following verb in the indirect reference approach. However, in the theta-marking approach discussed below, the subject pronoun is theta-marked by the verb no matter if it is a full NP or not, so nothing here hinges on this theory-internal question.

5.2 Vowel harmony

the spans between the $]x_{max}$ labels and are marked with parentheses. In (307a), the pronoun *ba* is at the end of a prosodic domain which includes the preceding verb. For this case, we may say that the pronoun agrees in ATR with the lexical item in its prosodic domain. However, (307b) shows this cannot be generalized. In (307b), there are the same prosodic domains as in (307a), but here the pronoun agrees with the lexical item in the *adjacent* prosodic domain. Thus constructing prosodic domains leads to conflicting directionality of ATR agreement. Reversing the parameter of the direction of the $]x_{max}$ to $x_{max}[$ does not improve the situation. The indirect reference approach thus fails with Kɔnni.

For a direct reference approach to be successful, a consistent structural relationship must hold between the variable-ATR pronoun and the lexical item it agrees with in ATR. The notion of c-command is often invoked in such cases. From Haegeman (1991), c-command is defined as follows, where A and B are nodes, including terminal nodes.

(308) **C-command:** A c-commands B iff A does not dominate B, and every X that dominates A also dominates B

When X is equated with the first branching node, then A strictly c-commands B, while if X is a maximal projection (e.g., NP or VP), then A *m-commands* B. The trees in (309) show a pronoun between a verb and a noun, with the pronoun and noun being one NP. In the construction in (309a and b), the pronoun agrees in ATR with the following noun, while in (309c), the pronoun agrees with the preceding verb. In terms of privative ATR, the ATR spreads from the right in (309a), does not spread from the left in (309b), but spreads from the left in (309c).

(309) a.

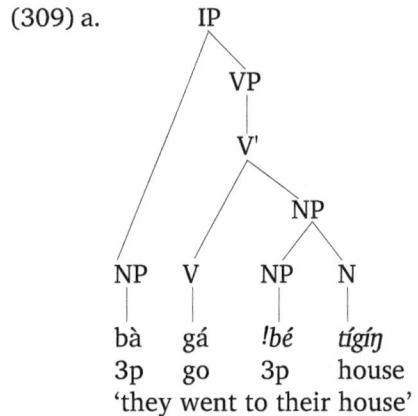

bà gá !bé tígíŋ
3p go 3p house
'they went to their house'

b.

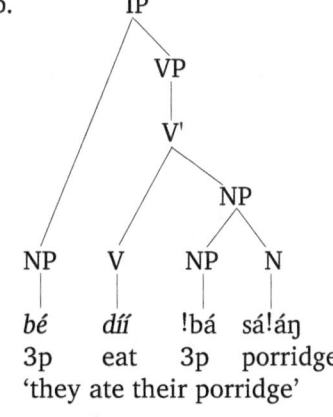

bé díí !bá sá!áŋ
3p eat 3p porridge
'they ate their porridge'

c.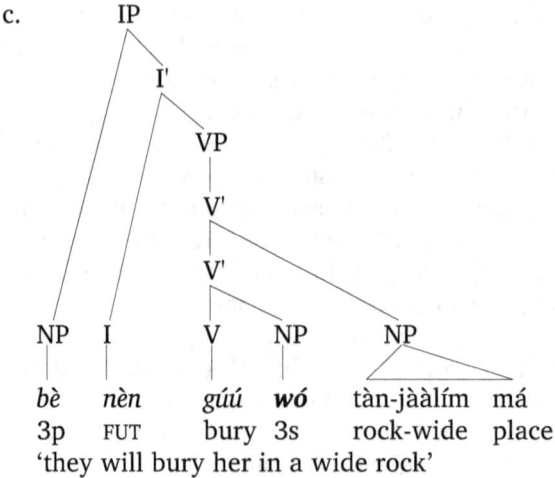

bè   nèn   gúú   wó   tàn-jààlím   má
3p   FUT   bury   3s   rock-wide   place
'they will bury her in a wide rock'

In terms of syntactic relations, the pronoun and noun in (309a–b) both c-command each other. (I assume the ATR spread in (309b) from the verb to the subject pronoun is analyzable in terms of the pronoun as particle being adjacent to the lexical item which is the verb.) In contrast, the verb preceding the pronoun c-commands the pronoun, but the relationship is not mutual; the pronoun does not c-command the verb. In (309c), the verb preceding the pronoun has a mutual c-command relation with it, but the NP following it does not. If all the data had a similar structure, the case for direct reference would be clear. However, the same set of data that was problematic for the indirect reference approach is also problematic for the direct reference approach.

5.2 Vowel harmony

(310)

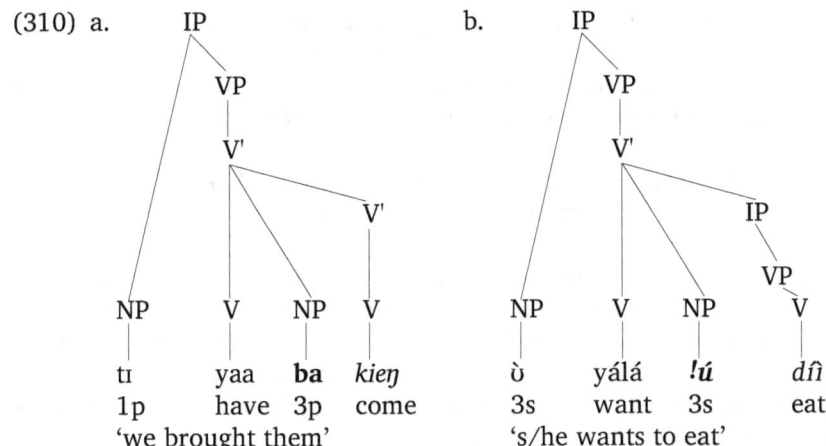

In (310b) the pronoun in question and the following verb do c-command each other, as in the data presented above. However, in (310a), *both* the verb preceding and the verb following mutually c-command the pronoun between them. Another principle is needed to describe why the pronoun in (310a) agrees with the verb on its left. Fortunately, the principles of syntax are not limited to structural ones, and a nonstructural syntactic principal will account for all the cases presented here.

Theta theory is the area we need to invoke here.[19] Lexical items—nouns and verbs, for our purposes here—assign thematic roles to their arguments. This is termed theta-marking. Crucially, a verb theta-marks its subject and object, while a noun theta-marks its possessor. In all the cases above, and others, the pronoun in question agrees in ATR with the lexical item, verb or noun, of which it is an argument, and which theta-marks it. In the case of the serial verb construction in (310a), Baker (1989) has argued on independent grounds that it is the first verb which directly theta-marks the pronoun object in this type of serial verb construction, in which the object is not shared by the two verbs.

In short, no single structural relationship is able to describe the domain of ATR spread to a pronoun trapped between lexical items of conflicting ATR values. Neither the "direct reference" nor the "indirect reference" approach is adequate to account for the Kɔnni facts. What is necessary is a

---

[19] My thanks to Cheri Black for first suggesting that the key to understanding this area was theta-marking rather than a strictly structural explanation.

syntactic relationship, theta-marking, which has not to my knowledge been proposed in the phonology/syntax literature.[20]

Now we must express the generalizations here in terms of Optimality Theory and integrate them with the previous analysis.

(311) **ATR-AGR(θ):** a nonlexical item must agree in ATR with the lexical item which theta-marks it

This is quite similar in spirit to AGR(ATR) (261), which stated that an affix must agree in ATR with the lexical item to which it is affixed. Indeed, the motivation is identical: nonlexical items, including both particles and affixes, obtain their ATR value from the lexical item in whose domain they lie. For affixes the domain was the word, and for particles the domain includes the lexical item to which it is an argument. However, there are differences, the one being that while AGR(ATR) is almost undominated, ATR-AGR(θ) may be violated in two cases: of particles with [aa] and particles with their own inherent ATR feature. For the first tableaus we examine, however, ATR-AGR(θ) is not violated for the winning candidate.

(312) *be to **be** dʊa* 'they laid them down'

	...tO bA dUA ATR	ATR-AGR(θ)	ALIGN [ATR]$_{UTT}$	ALIGN [ATR]μ
☞ a.	...to be dʊa		*	*
b.	...to ba dʊa	*!	**	

(313) tɪ yaa ***ba*** kiEŋ 'we brought them' ATR-AGR(θ) >> ALIGN[ATR]$_{UTT}$

	...yAA bA kIEŋ ATR	ATR-AGR(θ)	ALIGN [ATR]$_{UTT}$	ALIGN [ATR]μ
☞ a.	...yaa ba kieŋ		**	
b.	...yaa be kieŋ	*!	*	*

The constraint ATR-AGR(θ) rules out the losing candidate in both the above cases. In (312), the absence of ATR-AGR(θ) would not have been fatal; the winning candidate would have been selected without it. However, in (313), it is crucial. The moral is that a constraint which is not even

---

[20]The Nilo-Saharan language Bongo (Kilpatrick 1985) also has vowel harmony across words in some syntactic constructions but not others. This would be an interesting case to examine in more detail.

5.2 Vowel harmony

listed in a tableau may actually be the one that rules out losers, once a fuller picture of the language is known.

Below we see the cases in which ATR-AGR(θ) can be overridden by more highly ranked constraints. First is an utterance involving the particle *waa*, which never changes in ATR.

(314) ʊ̀ wàà súgùrè mìŋ 's/he is now washing'

U wAA sUgUrA ATR	FAITH [aa]	ATR-AGR(θ)	ALIGN [ATR]$_{UTT}$	ALIGN [ATR]μ
☞ a. ʊ waa sugure		*	**	
b. ʊ woo sugure	*!	*	*	*
c. u woo sugure	*!			**

Candidate (314a) wins even though violating ATR-AGR(θ) since the particles *ʊ* and *waa* are non-ATR though theta-marked by the ATR verb *sugure*. It is more important to preserve [aa] than for the subject pronoun to agree with a lexical item, as the failed candidates (314b and c) show.

The other case in which ATR-AGR(θ) is overridden is the one in which a particle has an inherent ATR feature.

(315) *be woŋ kpatɪ* 'they already finished' IDENT(ATR)$_{Lex}$ >> ATR-AGR(θ)

bA wOŋ kpAtI ATR	MAX [ATR]	IDENT (ATR)$_{Lex}$	ATR-AGR(θ)	ALIGN [ATR]$_{UTT}$	ALIGN [ATR]μ
☞ a. be woŋ kpatɪ			*	**	*
b. ba woŋ kpatɪ			*	**!*	
c. ba wɔŋ kpatɪ	*!				
d. be woŋ kpeti		*!			

The winning candidate (315a) violates ATR-AGR(θ) since its subject pronoun *be* disagrees in ATR with the verb which theta-marks it. It also violates ALIGN[ATR]$_{UTT}$ twice, since *woŋ* disagrees with the adjacent word *kpatɪ* in ATR. However, the other candidates are worse. Candidate (315b) violates ALIGN[ATR]$_{UTT}$ three times with the particle *woŋ* sandwiched between two non-ATR words. The only way to make the particles agree in ATR with the verb is to remove the ATR altogether as in (315c), which fatally violates MAX[ATR], or to spread ATR to the verb itself as in (315d), which fatally violates IDENT(ATR)$_{Lex}$.

The constraints needed to account for Kɔnni ATR vowel harmony are diagrammed below.

(316) Ranking of constraints

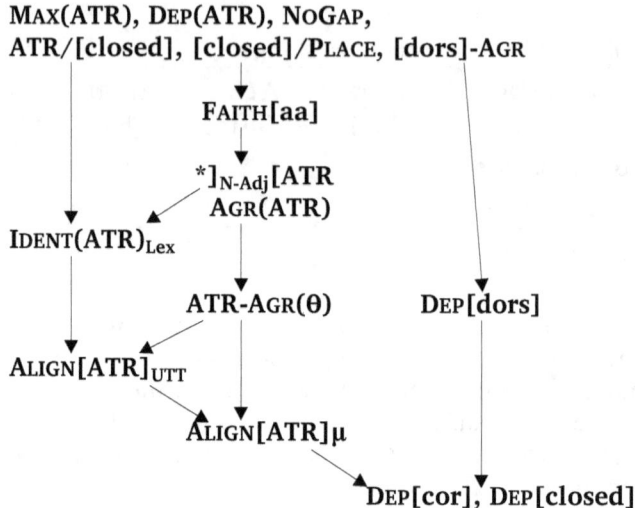

5.3 Diphthongization

5.3.1 Diphthongization—data

High and low long vowels ([aa], [ii], [ɪɪ], [uu], [ʊʊ]) are unambiguously attested, as seen in (237) and (317).

(317) dààŋ 'wood' wííŋ 'problem' dúúŋ 'horse'
 háá!gíŋ 'bush' kpɪ̀ɪlɪ́ŋ 'ancestor' bʊ̀ntʊ̀ʊ́ŋ 'toad'

Long mid vowels are quite rare. However, various "vowel combinations" are quite frequent:

(318) bítíéŋ 'beard'
 jùóŋ 'room'
 lí!áŋ 'axe'
 dùáŋ 'bush-pig'

5.3 Diphthongization

Here I will claim all the above phonetic vowel sequences come from underlying long mid vowels, that is:

(319) [ie] comes from /ee/
 [ɪa] comes from /ɛɛ/
 [uo] comes from /oo/
 [ʊa] comes from /ɔɔ/

A diphthongization process explains the distributional gap of no long mid vowels, showing that long mid vowels manifest themselves as diphthongs.[21]

Also, there are alternations in verbal and nominal forms which show diphthongization as a productive process. One verbal suffix which is still imperfectly understood but seems to deal with a type of Imperfective aspect is [-na/-ne] (see discussion in section 2.2.1.4); the surface form depends on vowel harmony. Another is the imperfective [-a/-e/-o]. These are illustrated in (320).

(320) Imperfective II   Imperfective
 be-ne   bi-e   'exist'
 dɔ-na   dʊ-a   'lie down'
 to-ne   tu-o   'get'
 ye-ne   yi-e   'see'
 ze-ne   zi-e   'stand'

The verb stem vowels in (320) are mid, as shown in the first column. When the imperfective suffix is added, as in the second column, it is pronounced as either [a], [e] or [o]. When a long mid vowel would be predicted on the basis of concatenating the vowel morpheme, what results is a set of diphthongs that is phonetically indistinguishable from the diphthongs above which occur in morphologically simple words.

Also relevant here is the one noun in my data which fills the two crucial conditions of (1) belonging to noun class 1 which takes /-A/ as the plural suffix and (2) having a stem ending in a mid vowel, which is bùmbó-ŋ/bùmbù-ó 'clay pot/s'. In (321a and b), the final stem vowel is -u and the plural suffix is -o, as expected from the dorsal vowel harmony noted in the constraint [DORS]-AGR (278) and illustrated in (279). However, in (321c), the final stem vowel is the mid o, but when the suffix is affixed, the result is the same [uo].

---

[21]Not direct evidence, but nonetheless interesting, is the evidence from related Gur languages (e.g., Mampruli). In several of these, /ɛ, ɔ/ becomes [ya, wa], very close to what I am proposing here (Naden 1988:22, 1989:154).

(321) Singular   Plural
  a. líékú-ŋ   líékú-ò   'ax handle'
  b. tàndú-ŋ   tàndú-ò   'pestle'
  c. bùmbó-ŋ   bùmbù-ó   'clay pot'

In this noun and the imperfective verbal forms above, not only does V_2 agree with V_1 in ATR and other features, but V_1 becomes a high vowel, and the result is a diphthong.

From the fact that there are very few surface long mid vowels, plus some productive alternations as in (114), I conclude that long mid vowels diphthongize in Kɔnni as an active process with outputs as follows:[22]

(322) Diphthongization
/ee/ → [ie]   /oo/ → [uo]   Note: all vowel "sequence"
                                      outputs are in the same
/εε/ → [ɪa]   /ɔɔ/ → [ʊa]   ATR harmony set

5.3.2 Diphthongization—analysis

Relative to other vocalic phenomena, diphthongization has not been the subject of many analyses. Surveys of diphthongization patterns are found in Donegan (1978), Hayes (1990), and Schane (1995). Analyses of diphthongization within OT are found in Rosenthall (1994), for several languages in Parkinson (1996b), for Korean and Portuguese in Suh (1998), and for Nakanai and Bella Coola in Carlson (1997).

5.3.2.1 Previous analyses of Kɔnni

Besides the reporting of Kɔnni diphthongization in Cahill (1992a) which uses a descriptive rule as in (322), three quite different analyses of Kɔnni diphthongization have appeared. These are Cahill (1994), Parkinson (1996b), and Cahill (1999c). These all share various insights, which I will summarize briefly.

Any analysis must come to grips with at least two key observations. First, V_1 of the diphthong is always a high vowel. Second, the height of V_2 alternates, as do its other features. In the [−ATR] cases (ɪa, ʊa), V_2 is always [a], but in the [+ATR] cases, V_2 is [e, o]. Not coincidentally, this is exactly the same alternation we saw in the suffixal ATR harmony in section 5.2.1. In vowel harmony of suffixes, Cahill (1996) posits /-a/ as the lexical vowel in

---

[22]The exception to this pattern is that a long mid vowel after a homorganic glide does not always diphthongize; I have cases of [woo...] and [wɔɔ...] but never [wuo...] or [wʊa...] in my data. The case after y is somewhat different; I have both [yεε...] and [yɪa...].

5.3 Diphthongization

suffixes that alternate with [-e, -o], and all the analyses discussed below connect diphthongization with this vowel harmony pattern.

Cahill (1994) used the coindexation approach of Hayes (1990), in which the association lines of autosegmental phonology were eliminated. Their functions were replaced by the two mechanisms of an outline format to indicate hierarchy, and coindexation to indicate relations of features to timing units. In this approach, SPE features were used, so mid vowels were specified as [−high, −low]. A single rule was proposed to deal with diphthongization, with the objectives being to remove the [−high] specification on V_1, remove the [−low] specification and [round] if present on V_2. This rule was formalized as follows.

(323) Diphthongization by coindexation (Cahill 1994)

	V_iV_j	CV tier
delete i	$[-\text{high}]_{ij}$	[high] tier
delete j	$[-\text{low}]_{ij}$	[low] tier
delete j		[round] tier

With an underlyingly long vowel specified as [−high, −low], and [+round] in the cases of /oo/ and /ɔɔ/, the results of this rule would be V_1 unspecified for [high], V_2 unspecified for [low], and V_2 unspecified for [round]. Later steps in the derivation filled in [+high] as default for V_1, [+low] for V_2, and [+ATR] and [+round] were spread by specific rules from V_1. These were the same rules needed to account for the vowel harmony system and there was thus a tight connection made between vowel harmony and diphthongization.

Besides the debate about the merits or lack thereof of the extensive underspecification and default rules used in this approach, one obvious shortcoming is that one rule here is performing several processes. Hays (1990) treated diphthongizations of similar complexity with more than one rule, and in retrospect, that would have been a better approach in this framework. However, that brings out an inherent weakness in SPE-style features applied to Kɔnni diphthongization. Using SPE features, it is impossible to describe Kɔnni diphthongization as a unitary process. To take a concrete example, in the case of /ɔɔ/ → [ʊa], V_1 changes [−high] to [+high], V_2 changes [−low] to [+low], and V_2 changes [+round] to [−round]. This is hardly a unitary process.

Within a derivational feature geometry approach, the diphthongization process has a somewhat neater solution in Cahill (1999c). This approach uses the Feature Geometry of Clements and Hume (1995), with the modifications proposed in the present work, especially that multiple occurrences of [closed] are used to represent vowel height. As in the previous approach, key features are that ATR influences the nature of the output, and the vowels in V_2 position exhibit the same a/e/o alternations as the vowel harmony system. Diphthongization is again intimately tied to the vowel harmony system; both use largely the same set of rules. The main distinctive characteristic of diphthongization is a transfer of [closed] from V_2 to V_1 of the sequence, accomplished by a rule that delinks the entire vocalic node of V_2.

The one constant of a long mid vowel is that each mora is specified for one occurrence of [closed]. After the long mid vowel has been split into two separate but featurally identical vowels, and separate feature trees on two V-slots can be independently dealt with, the vocalic node is delinked from V_2, leaving a bare vowel segment there. This process is formalized as:

(324) V_2 delinking

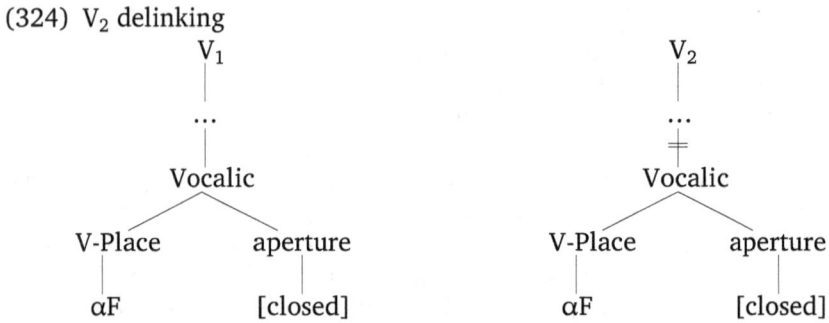

This rule leaves any place features of V_2, as well as the [closed] feature, floating. Since all features of V_2 are identical to V_1, there is no available slot for them to re-associate to, and they are stray erased. The [closed] feature, however, may have multiple occurrences on one vowel, and so the floating [closed] re-associates to V_1, giving V_1 two occurrences of [closed] and making it a high vowel. In the non-ATR diphthongs [ɪa, ʊa], this is all that happens, and we are left with V_1 as a high vowel and V_2 as the featureless [a]. In an ATR diphthong, however, rules linking ATR to [closed] and spreading [dorsal] if applicable, apply next to give the correct [ie, uo].[23]

Parkinson (1996b) gives an Optimality Theory account of Kɔnni diphthongization using many of the same insights as the above analyses. Since the analysis presented here will also be in the OT framework and

---

[23]This shifting of a [closed] autosegment has a close parallel in Schane's (1995) analysis of diphthongization in the framework of particle phonology. He treats some types of diphthongization as the delinking of a particle from one half of a diphthong and reattachment to the other half, as in [eu] → [io], where the height particle |a| has migrated from the left to the right half of the diphthong.

5.3 Diphthongization

similar in many respects to Parkinson's, we will review Parkinson's account in greater detail than the others above.

In any OT account of Kɔnni diphthongization, one must have constraints forcing the existence of a diphthong rather than a long mid vowel, requiring that the diphthong be an "opening" one, in which the height is less in V_2 than in V_1,[24] and that V_1 be high and V_2 be one of [a, e, o]. Parkinson reformulates some of the insights of previous analyses as constraints. The constraints he uses are:

(325) Constraints of Parkinson (1996b) to account for Kɔnni diphthongization

    DIPH = if two moras form the nucleus of a single syllable, then the two moras must be distinct

    *CLOSING = the second element of a diphthong may not be more constricted than the first (i.e., *ie* but **ei*)

    PL → [cl] = if a vowel is specified for a place feature (including +ATR), then that vowel must also be specified for [closed]

    HEIGHTPL = if a vowel is specified for an occurrence of [closed], it must also be a front or back vowel

    HILEFT = the left edge of a diphthong must be specified for the maximum number of occurrences of [closed] active in the language

    INTEG[cl] = no occurrence of [closed] has multiple output correspondences

    DEP[cl] = if a sound is specified for an occurrence of [closed] in the output, this feature must be present in its input correspondent

    ATRHARM = both moras in a domain are required to share an [ATR] value

---

[24]The traditional term "rising" may also be used to refer to the types of diphthong present in Kɔnni, where what actually "rises" is the relative prominence of the vowel (Crystal 2003). For example, in [ɪa], the [a] element is more prominent, so it is a rising diphthong. However, in the midst of a discussion of vowel height, this is potentially confusing, since the vowel height of [ɪa] actually falls. So following Parkinson, I use the more articulatory-based "opening" for the Kɔnni-type diphthongs.

(326) Ranking of constraints in Parkinson (1996b)
DIPH, *CLOSING, ATRHARM, HILEFT, PL → [cl], HEIGHTPL
↓
INTEG[cl]
↓
DEP[cl]

A few explanatory comments are in order concerning these constraints. The DIPH constraint prohibits long vowels in which the first and second moras are identical in featural content; they must be distinct as far as being different in at least one feature. As Parkinson formulates it, this constraint applies to all vowels, not only mid ones. For Kɔnni, this is too broad and this will require a narrowing so it applies to only mid vowels. The constraint *CLOSING ensures that the nature of the diphthong will be opening and not closing. The PL → [cl] and HEIGHTPL constraints are fairly direct translations of the Kɔnni rules in Cahill (1994, 1999c), as well as applying to other languages Parkinson analyzes. They express dependency relations of features which are a matter of surface truth. The HILEFT constraint also expresses a surface truth about Kɔnni (though it is possible to express this in another way, as we shall see below). The INTEG general constraint is taken from McCarthy and Prince (1995:372). With the [closed] specification, it accounts for the conservation of [closed] particles in the non-ATR diphthongs, and that the [closed] particle from the input V_2 is manifested on V_1 in the output diphthong. Parkinson describes the formulation of the constraint ATRHARM in his text with approximately the language above, but does not give a formal definition for it. Parkinson is not entirely explicit in marking dominance relations in the tableaus for Kɔnni, but the ranking above appears to be the intended one.

Parkinson presents tableaus for three of the four diphthongs in Kɔnni, omitting only /oo/ → [uo], which would require the additional complications of [dorsal] spread (or [labial], in his presentation). To see how his proposal works, I present below his tableau 4.23. Occurrences of [cl] in the normal square brackets are instances of the feature present in the input; [closed] features in parentheses are those not present in input, but inserted. Recall that /ɛ/ in the feature system here has the [coronal] feature and one occurrence of [closed] in input, and thus /ɛɛ/ has two occurrences of [closed], one linked to each /ɛ/.

5.3 Diphthongization

(327) Tableau 4.23, taken from Parkinson (1996b:115) (compare to mine in 332)

εε → ɪa	HiLeft	Pl → [cl] Integ[cl]	Dep[cl].

☞ a. ɪ   a
    | |
 [cl] <[cor]>
    |
 [cl]
			*

b. ε a | | [cl] <[cor]>	*!		
c. ε æ | | [cl] [cor]	*!	*	

d. ɪ   æ
   | |
 [cl] [cor]
   |
 [cl]
		*!	

e. ɪ   ɛ
   | |
 [cl] [cor]
   |
 [cl]
		*!	

f. ɪ   ε
   | |
 [cl] [cor]
   |
 [cl]
			**!*

In (327), the winning candidate (327a) incurs only a violation of Dep[cl]. This interpretation of Dep[cl] assumes that the span over which to consider violations is the segment (or mora) to which the feature is associated. However, if the question is not so much the location of [closed] but whether it is present somewhere in the output or not, then Dep[cl] has not been violated. There were two occurrences of [closed] in the input, one on each ε, and two in the output, both now on ɪ. Parkinson presents the [coronal] feature as present but unparsed in (327a and b), in keeping with earlier versions of Optimality Theory. Candidates (327b and c) both lose because they do not have V_1 being the highest vowel possible in Kɔnni. Candidate (327c) also violates PL → [cl], since [æ] has a place feature, but is low (i.e., it lacks a [closed]). Candidate (327d) loses for the same reason. The problem with losing candidate (327e) is the presence of an extra [closed]. This violates INTEG[cl], on the view that one of the [closed] features in the input has two correspondents in the output. The losing candidate (327f) is phonetically identical to (327e), but in (327f) all three occurrences of [closed] are inserted ones, triply violating DEP[cl].

However, when DEP[cl] is understood as simply prohibiting an insertion of [closed], the need for INTEG[cl] vanishes. On this view, candidate (327a) does not violate DEP[cl] at all, since no new [closed] features have been introduced (although one has shifted position). Candidate (327e) then loses, with a single violation of DEP[cl], because it has inserted an extra [closed]. The history of the [closed] features in candidate (327f) becomes irrelevant, if indeed there was any meaningful distinction in the first place between an inserted [closed] and one present in the input. If the [closed] features in (327f) are simply counted without regard to their source, then it is identical to (327e) and loses for the same reason: one violation of DEP[cl].

5.3.2.2 The current proposal

An OT account of diphthongization must have constraints that force a change in long mid vowels, and only long mid ones, into a diphthong, and this diphthong must be opening, have a high vowel in V_1 position, and have the same vowels [a, e, o] which were present as the suffixal realizations of /-a/ in the vowel harmony section. The proposal expounded here is more complete than either Parkinson's or the one in Cahill (1999c).

Note also that the two halves of the vowel must be treated as separate units, as is also the case of front vowel centralization before [ŋ]. Diphthongization inherently challenges the view that long vowels must always be represented by a single set of vocalic features linked to two timing units (see Perlmutter 1995, McCarthy 1981, Hayes 1986, and Schein and Steriade 1986 for discussion).

The constraint that motivates diphthongization of mid vowels could be something like DIPH as Parkinson proposed, or possibly a constraint *[VV]$_{mid}$, prohibiting long mid vowels. The DIPH constraint has the drawback noted above that it refers to all vowels, not only mid ones. The *[VV]$_{mid}$ constraint relates to the general markedness of mid vowels relative to high and low ones in vowel inventories of the world's languages. This has been remarked before with regard to underlying vowels in Kɔnni suffixes. With this

5.3 Diphthongization

in mind, I will use *[VV]$_{mid}$. The constraint *[VV]$_{mid}$ is defined in terms of the [closed] feature used here.[25]

(328) ***[VV]$_{mid}$:** adjacent identical vowels which each have exactly one occurrence of [closed] are prohibited

The constraint *[VV]$_{mid}$ taken alone does not force diphthongization. The constraint could be satisfied by either deleting one or both vowels, changing the quality of the entire long vowel in height (either raising or lowering), or changing the height of one (or both) of the vowels. Only the last would be a diphthongization.

To prevent deleting a vowel, a constraint prohibiting deletion of a mora and preserving vowel length needs to be in place. MAX-µ has been used by Itô, Katagawa, and Mester (1996) as well as others. However, the mora as such seems to play very little part in Kɔnni phonology, but the segment or root node does. The constraint that is relevant, then, is the same MAX-S which I invoked for the "epenthetic *r*" in chapter 4:

(329) **MAX-SEGMENT (MAX-S):** a segment (root node) in the input has a correspondent in the output (from (226) in chapter 4)

MAX-S is ranked highly, but not undominated (we will see deletions in section 5.7). Raising or lowering the long vowel as a whole is prohibited by MAX[cl] and DEP[cl]:

(330) **MAX[cl]:** every occurrence of [closed] in the input has a correspondent in the output (prohibits deletion of [closed])
   DEP[cl]: every occurrence of [closed] in the output has a correspondent in the input (prohibits insertion of [closed])

The above constraints will prohibit any satisfaction of *[VV]$_{mid}$ except for diphthongization. The specific instantiation of what type of diphthong depends on yet other constraints. I adopt Parkinson's *CLOSING constraint to prohibit closing diphthongs, ensuring a diphthong in which the constriction widens rather than narrows.

---

[25]This constraint has some resemblance to an OCP constraint, in that it forbids adjacent identical segments. However, in terms of the crucial feature [closed], it does not forbid adjacent instances of [closed] in general, since there can be two adjacent high vowels (e.g., *ii*, *uu*) or a high and a mid vowel (e.g., *ie*, *uo*). In this way, it is unlike what is normally expected in an OCP constraint.

(331) *CLOSING: the second element of a diphthong may not be more constricted than the first (e.g., *ie* but **ei*) (from Parkinson 1996b)[26]

These, together with the constraints already in place for vowel harmony, are sufficient to account for the Kɔnni diphthongs. In the tableaus below, I have represented the input long mid vowels as having separate feature trees. While a full discussion of this configuration versus a single set of features linked to two timing units will not be undertaken here, the operating assumption here is that in Kɔnni a long vowel, at least a long mid vowel, must be regarded as having a separate set of features for each mora or timing unit. This relates to the concept of Cloning as in Parkinson (1996b) and Hume (1992), in which a single set of input features spread over two moras splits itself into two identical feature sets. If the input were only one set of features for two moras, it is possible that the tableau below would end up more like that in (337).

---

[26]Rosenthall (1994) has a constraint which prohibits rising (or opening, in our terminology) diphthongs, also in Carlson *LHDIP: "diphthongs must not rise in sonority." This corresponds to Parkinson's *OPENING; the difference is not substantive, but in the labeling only.

5.3 Diphthongization

(332) εε → ıa (compare to Parkinson's tableau in 327)

	E E | | cl cl	*[VV]$_{mid}$	ATR/ [closed]	*Closing	Max[cl]	Dep[cl]
☞ a.	ı a | cl cl					
b.	ε | cl				*!	
c.	ε ε | | cl cl	*!				
d.	aa				*!*	
e.	ı ı | | cl cl cl cl					*!*
f.	a ı | cl cl			*!		
g.	εa | cl				*!	
h.	ı ε | | cl cl cl					*!
i.	ı æ | cl cl		*!			
j.	ε æ | cl		*!		*!	

For the sake of simplicity and space, candidates which violate *[VV]$_{mid}$, MAX(V), and *CLOSING, that is, long mid vowels, short vowels, and closing diphthongs, will not be considered in the tableaus in (333) and (334), and these constraints will not be listed either.

(333) ee → ie (to be updated in 341)

	ATR E E | | cl cl	ATR/[closed]	MAX[cl]	DEP[cl]
☞ a.	i e | | cl cl cl			*
b.	aa		*!*	
c.	ææ	*!*	*!*	
c.	i i | | cl cl cl cl			*!*
d.	i æ | cl cl	*!		
e.	e æ | cl	*!	*!	

5.3 Diphthongization

(334) ɔɔ → ʊa

	O O | | cl cl	ATR/[closed]	MAX[cl]	DEP[cl]
☞ a.	ʊa | cl cl			
b.	ɔa | cl		*!	
c.	ʊ ʊ | | cl cl cl cl			*!*
c.	aa		*!*	
d.	ʊ ɔ | | cl cl cl			*!

(335) oo → uo

	ATR O O | | cl cl	ATR/[closed]	MAX[cl]	DEP[cl]
☞ a.	u o | | cl cl cl cl			*
b.	u u | | cl cl cl cl			*!*

In none of the tableaus above was there listed a candidate in which the vowels disagreed in ATR value. This was a deliberate omission due to the fact that there are two situations covered with diphthongization: within a single morpheme and across morphemes and the constraints that rule out disagreeing vowels differ in the two situations. If a diphthong is within a morpheme, the constraint ALIGN[ATR]μ is the relevant one, forcing ATR to be realized everywhere within its sponsoring morpheme. If the diphthong is across morphemes, as in a nominal or verbal suffix added to a vowel-final stem, then AGR(ATR) enforces the agreement of the affix vowel, V_2 of the diphthong, with the stem vowel V_1.

Thus far no constraint of the type HILEFT proposed by Parkinson, which refers to the maximum vowel height in a language, has been needed. The fact that V_1 is the highest vowel possible in Kɔnni is a result of Kɔnni's vowel inventory and the constraints posed thus far. However, another set of data, not analyzed by Parkinson, does show the need for a constraint with this effect. These are the nouns and verbs which have a suffix /-A/ added to a stem with a final mid vowel (see 114 and 321).

(336) dɔ + A → dʊ-a   'lying down'
      be + A → bi-e   'existing'
      to + A → tu-o   'getting'
      bumbo + A → bumbu-o   'clay pots'

In each of these, the number of [closed] occurrences in the output is one more than in the input, and so DEP[cl] will be violated once for each of the above. The constraints proposed thus far give the wrong prediction for the optimal output:

(337) ε + A → ɪa

EA	*[VV]$_{mid}$	MAX[cl]	DEP[cl]
☞ a. ɪa			*
☛ b. εa			
c. εε	*!		
d. aa		*!*	
e. ɪε			**!

Candidate (337a) is the correct output above, but it violates DEP[cl], while candidate (337b), an incorrect output, violates no constraints listed. Similar tableaus can be presented for the other diphthongs. Therefore, a constraint is needed which will force the insertion of an extra [closed], and this constraint must be ranked above DEP[cl].

5.3 Diphthongization

Parkinson's HıLEFT (325) constraint would describe this function adequately, but it has the drawback of actually describing two conditions at once. First, it says that part of the diphthong must be the highest vowel height available in the language, and second, that this vowel must be V_1, to the left. A redundancy thus exists with *CLOSING, which entails that V_1 must be higher than V_2; the directionality expressed by HıLEFT is also expressed by *CLOSING. A constraint sufficient for the need, then, would express that one of the members of a diphthong must have the maximum number of [closed] occurrences allowed by the language. By making the observation that V_1 and V_2 of the diphthong are maximally different in height, one way of expressing the same generalization is evident. This observation of maximal differentiation may well be connected with the function of diphthongization. If one is going to differentiate adjacent vowels, the difference is perceptually more salient if it is a larger magnitude. Thus in [ɪa], a high and low vowel are present, the maximal difference possible, while in [ɪɛ], the height difference is not maximal. The two constraints we will consider to account for V_1 being high can be stated as in (338).

(338) possible constraints to account for V_1 being high
    HıDıPH: one of the members of a diphthong must have the maximum number of [closed] occurrences allowed by the language
    DıPHMAX: the members of a diphthong must be maximally different in height

These are not identical constraints. HıDıPH would never be violated in Kɔnni and so would be top-ranked. However, DıPHMAX must be violated in the diphthongs [ie, uo], since the [e, o] portions of the diphthong are not maximally different in height from [i, u], respectively. More importantly, DıPHMAX suffers from the same criticism leveled at HıLEFT above: it does two things at once, an allowed but less desirable situation. To be "maximally different" in height, one member of the diphthong must have the maximum number of [closed] occurrences allowed in the language, and the other must have the minimum number allowed. Thus DıPHMAX includes HıDıPH plus another condition. Also, the concept of "maximally different" must be defined with reference to the actual vowel inventory of the language. It is not clear how this would be done, but it clearly would add more complexity to the analysis. For these reasons, I will use HıDıPH as the simpler and more primitive constraint. Sample tableaus using HıDıPH are presented below.

(339) ɛ + A → ɪa

ɛa	*[VV]$_{mid}$	HIDIPH	MAX[cl]	DEP[cl]
☞ a. ɪa				*
b. ɛa		*!		
c. ɛɛ	*!			
d. aa			*!*	
e. ɪɛ				**!

Candidate (339a) wins, though it violates DEP[cl] by inserting a [closed] not present in the input. HIDIPH rules out candidate (339b), which was incorrectly picked as the optimal candidate in (337). Other candidates are ruled out by the same constraints as in (337). A tableau with an ATR stem is shown in (340).

(340) e + A → ie

eA	*[VV]$_{mid}$	HIDIPH	MAX[cl]	AGR(ATR)	DEP[cl]
☞ a. ie					**
b. ɪa				*!	*
c. ɛa		*!		*	
d. ee	*!				*
e. aa			*!		

In (340), the winning candidate (340a) has two violations of DEP[cl], but other candidates have violations of higher-ranked constraints. In candidate (340b), the suffix does not agree with the stem in ATR. Candidate (340c) is particularly bad in violating two top-ranked constraints, since V_1 is not high and [a] does not agree with the stem in ATR. Candidate (340d) is the illicit long mid vowel, and candidate (340e) has deleted the [closed].

The new constraint HIDIPH has little impact on the tableaus previously presented. It reinforces the badness of one candidate below and does the same with other diphthongs derived from long mid vowels. However, it does not change which constraint rules out a candidate.

5.3 Diphthongization

(341) a. ee → ie (from 333)

ee	ATR/[closed]	MAX[cl]	DEP[cl]
☞ a. ie			*
b. aa		*!*	
c. ææ	*!*	*!*	
c. i i			*!*
d. iæ	*!		
e. eæ	*!		*!

b. ee → ie, with new constraint HIDIPH

ee	ATR/[closed]	HIDIPH	MAX[cl]	DEP[cl]
☞ a. ie				*
b. aa			*!*	
c. ææ	*!*		*!*	
c. i i				*!*
d. iæ	*!			
e. eæ	*!	*!	*!	

Note that if the SPE-type features [high] and [low] were used, an additional level of complexity would be required. The present constraints *[VV]$_{mid}$, *Closing, and HIDIPH could easily be adapted to these features. However, these constraints by themselves would take an input of /εε/ and yield an output of [iε], since these constraints require no change in the second half of the long vowel. An additional constraint or constraints would be required to change V$_2$ from [−low] to [+low], and it is difficult to see how these would be motivated.

The new constraints needed for diphthongization, with their rankings, are:

(342) Constraints needed for diphthongization:
   *[VV]$_{mid}$, HIDIPH, MAX[cl], *Closing
   ↓
   MAX-S
   ↓
   DEP[cl]

5.4 Vowel assimilation I

In this section, assimilations of vowels to consonants or vowels across consonants are discussed. For assimilation of vowels in hiatus contexts, see section 5.9.

5.4.1 Agreement of place across [g]

5.4.1.1 Data

There are two patterns in which vowels across [g] act differently than they do across other consonants. First, recall that in section 5.2.1 (see discussion after 270) that ATR spreads across [g] as in (343a). This is unlike the usual pattern of ATR spreading only one syllable from an adjective into a noun stem, as in (343b) (data reproduced from 250a):

(343) a. **múgú-bíŋ** 'small river' (cf. múgúŋ 'river')
      túgú-bîŋ 'small termite hill' (cf. túgúŋ 'termite hill')
  b. **bùntùù-bíŋ** 'small toad' (cf. bùntʊ̀ʊ̀-kpí!íŋ 'big toad')

Second, all di- and trisyllabic verbs in citation form have [-i, ɪ] as the final vowel. Furthermore, as previously mentioned, in trisyllabic verbs, by far the most common vowels in V_2 position are [ɪ, i]. In six verbs, however, [ʊ, u] is in V_2 position. No other vowels occur in V_2 position in verbs. The verbs with [ʊ, u] in V_2 position are:

(344) Exhaustive list of Kɔnni verbs with /U/ as V_2
    bʊgʊrɪ 'learn'   mʊgʊsɪ 'suck'   ɲʊgʊsɪ 'sharpen'
    suguri 'wash'   sʊgʊrɪ 'wake'   tuguri 'be bright'

In all of these, V_1 is also /U/ and /g/ precedes V_2, i.e., a *CUgUCI* sequence. There are no verbs with /I/ as V_2 in trisyllabic verbs after the *Ug*, i.e., **CUgICI*. This is evidently the result of a spreading of the [dorsal] feature from /U/ over the /g/ to the next vowel. This does not happen with other nonhigh round vowels, as seen in (345a). It also does not happen with consonants other than [g], as seen in (345b). The final vowel of a verb is invariably [i, ɪ] in citation form, even if the sequence *-Ug-* precedes it, as seen in (345c).

5.4 Vowel assimilation I

(345) a. mid round V before /g/
    kpogiri 'break'
    mɔgɪsɪ 'be okay'
    pɔgɪlɪ 'hold'

b. non-/g/ consonants after /U/
    sʊrɪsɪ 'rub'
    furisi 'slurp'
    sulisi 'be full'

c. disyllabic verbs with /U/ as V_1
    bʊgɪ 'soothsay'
    hʊʊgɪ 'be rotten'
    mʊgɪ 'suck'
    ɲʊʊgɪ 'smell something'
    sugi 'dip in soup'
    tʊgɪ 'reach (a destination)'
    vugi 'swing arms'
    yʊgɪ 'weave'

In these verbs, then, if a sequence -*Ug*- occurs, the following vowel is *U* rather than the *I* present in any other circumstances. Note that at least one concrete alternation is available to illustrate this: the base verb *mʊgɪ* 'suck' and the verb derived from it, *mʊgʊsɪ* 'suck'. When *UgV* is nonfinal, it is *UgU*, and if it is final, it is *UgI*.

In nouns there is a similar but not identical situation. There are several forms in which the citation form ends in -*UgIŋ*. However, when the extra syllable of the definite suffix is added, there is a *U* on either side of the [g].

(346) Citation form   Definite form
    bàɲʊ̀ʊ̀gíŋ   bàɲʊ̀ʊ̀gʊ̀rí 'soup leaf'
    kúgíŋ   kúgúrí 'cooking place'
    ɲʊ̀ʊ̀gíŋ   ɲʊ̀ʊ̀gʊ̀bú 'smell'

Again we see the pattern that a nonfinal high vowel following a [Ug] must also be [U]. There is an agreement of [dorsal] feature in this situation. This does not happen with non-*g* consonants in a [UC] environment.

(347) Citation form   Definite form
- chʊ́ʊ́!sɪ́ŋ   chʊ́ʊ́!sɪ́rɪ́   'gecko'
- nʊ́!bɪ́ŋ   nʊ́!bɪ́ké   'finger'
- wʊ̀ʊ̀bɪ́ŋ   wʊ̀ʊ̀bɪ̀rɪ́   'liver'
- sàawùrɪ́ŋ   sàawùrìké   'porridge stirrer'
- tʊ́ʊ́!lɪ́ŋ   tʊ́ʊ́!lɪ́bʊ́   'heat'

The last example in (347) is particularly crucial in that it shows that a [UCICU] sequence is allowed. A high vowel between two instances of [U] is not automatically [U].

Data with respect to [k] is more sparse. There are no native Kɔnni verbs with intervocalic [k] at all, and very few monomorphemic nouns have [VkV],[27] one of the few being *sùkùlí* 'heart', and even this may be historically a compound. With the definite article /kÚ/ added, there is the possibility of high vowels agreeing on either side of [k], and that is what we in fact find, as seen in (348).

(348) Citation form   Definite form
- tùùrɪ́ŋ   tùùrùkú   'line, mark'
- chʊ̀bɪ́ŋ   chʊ̀bʊ̀kʊ́   'wing' (cf. chʊ̀bɪ̀tɪ́ 'wings')
- kpé!júsɪ́ŋ   kpé!júsúkú   'black kite' (cf. kpé!júsítí 'kites')
- bʊ̀asɪ́ŋ   bʊ̀asʊ̀kʊ́   'viper' (cf. bʊ̀asɪ̀tɪ́ 'vipers')
- chɪ̀akʊ̀rɪ́ŋ   chɪ̀akʊ̀rʊ̀kʊ́   'scorpion' (cf. chɪ̀akʊ̀rɪ̀tɪ́ 'scorpions')

In at least some of the above words, a gradient effect can be discerned, in that the vowel quality in *u* in *kpé!júsúkú* 'black kite' starts as more of an *i* sound and changes quality to *u* towards the end.

Of the handful of nouns which have /UkV/, the only one apparently inconsistent with the *g* pattern is *jèvùkìrí* 'the snake'. In this case the inconsistency is removed upon a closer examination. The word *jèvùkìrí* is derived from /ja-vug-kiri/, and the [k] in *jèvùkìrí* is actually a remnant of a dorsal consonant cluster. Again a dorsal consonant cluster reduces to a single consonant. So the data with [k], while not abundant, is consistent with the data for [g], and we may tentatively generalize that both voiced and voiceless velar stops have the same behavior of allowing [dorsal] spread over them in short open syllables.

---

[27]The lack of intervocalic [k], and the abundance of intervocalic [g], is likely due to a historical change voicing the [k] intervocalically and deriving present-day intervocalic [k] from ancestral *kk. This hypothesis is also supported by the fact that some short *ks* are derived at least historically from sequences of *k*, e.g., *jevukiŋ* 'snake' from /ja-vug-kiŋ/. For other evidence to support *k > g intervocalically, see Cahill (1995a).

I have only one case in my data of word-internal ŋ with high round vowels adjacent: *púŋú!lú!ŋ* 'fish (sp.)'. This also fits the pattern of dorsal consonants having high round vowels on both sides.

5.4.1.2 Analysis

In terms of Optimality Theory, constraints are needed which enforce the same value of [dorsal] and ATR for high vowels on either side of the [dorsal] stops /g, k/.

The facts of agreement of [dorsal] and of ATR across [g] can be combined in one generalization; that high vowels must agree in place features across [g], these features specifically including [coronal], [dorsal], and [ATR], the V-Place features. Though the data is less abundant for [k], it appears that the same generalization also holds for it. This will be formalized as the constraint in (349).

(349) **VgV-AGR:** high vowels must agree in V-place features across [g, k, ŋ]

In a more detailed examination of this phenomenon, it appears that [dorsal] for high vowels may spread across a consonant if that consonant is itself high and [dorsal] and so compatible with that spread. One may envision the process as spreading of the feature to the consonant and through it to the vowel. In this view, spreading of [dorsal] is segment-to-segment, not merely treating a consonant as transparent (see Ní Chiosáin and Padgett 1997 for extended discussion of locality). Nondorsal consonants block this spreading. In terms of features, this is quite plausible if we take the point of view that vocalic features spread only through consonants with which that feature is compatible. An explanation of the spread of [ATR] through a [dorsal] consonant (only documented by alternations in the case of *g*) is more speculative. One possibility is that it may be related to the fact that the tongue root is actively involved in the articulation of dorsal consonants. If there were opposite values of ATR on either side of the [g], the tongue root would have to move from one tongue root configuration to the other while the [g], which itself has an articulatory target involving the tongue dorsum, which carries the root along, is being pronounced. Rather than having the complex motion of the tongue dorsum both moving up to contact the velum to make the stop *and* simultaneously sliding backward or forward, the speaker opts for merely the former. It may be that this constraint should be split into two, one referring to [dorsal] and the other referring to ATR, but in Kɔnni these will co-occur and can be conflated into one constraint.

This spreading across a [dorsal] consonant is additional evidence that the active feature of back round vowels in Kɔnni is [dorsal] rather than [labial].

VgV-AGR is commonly violated in the case in which V_2 is the final vowel in the word, as exemplified by words in (350a).

(350) a. hʊʊgɪ   'be rotten'
       kpʊgɪ   'weave'
       kúgíŋ   'cooking place'
       baɲʊ̀ʊ̀gíŋ   'soup leaf'
       jèvùkíŋ   'snake'

   b. sʊ̀gɪ̀tàá   'sibling (same parents)'[28]
       múgílí!múgílí!ŋ   'tree (sp.)'
       mʊ́múgílíŋ   'tree (sp.)'

There are thus often cases of *UgI*, but never of *IgU*. The directional asymmetry in this pattern could be attributed to an inherent direction of spreading of [dorsal], but as noted, the cases of *UgI* are only when *I* is the last vowel in the word, or epenthetic. As we will see in section 5.5, the epenthetic vowel is *I*, and this quality of an inserted vowel takes precedence over the agreement of [dorsal] across [g].

In the 110 forms I have in my database where high vowels are on either side of [g], the three cases in which the vowels do not agree in [dorsal] are listed in (350b). The word *sʊ̀gɪ̀tàá* is a compound noun, from *sʊ̀g-* 'inside' and *tàá* 'sister'. The [ɪ] in this word is clearly epenthetic and at the end of a word (though that word is itself part of a larger compound word) and so actually fits with the generalizations above. The other forms in (350b) are names of specific trees. It is also quite likely that these are also compounds as well; names of trees often consist of compound forms, as in *kàmbòn-táá!mɪ́ŋ* 'papaya (lit., Ashanti shea nut)', *kpáámvááŋ* 'tree (sp.) (lit., oil-leaf)', and *dààkpàndíí!sɪ́ŋ* 'tree (sp.) (lit., bachelor-spoon)'. If so, then these are not truly exceptional either.

Cases where ATR has spread over [g] and [dorsal] has spread over [g] are shown below. In the first, the relevant constraints used in tableaus for ATR spreading from adjectives into nouns are used as before (e.g., in 269 and 270) with the addition of VgV-AGR.

---

[28]In a polygamous culture, such as that of the Koma, one can commonly have siblings who have the same father but a different mother.

5.4 Vowel assimilation I

(351) múgú-bíŋ 'small river'

mUgU-bIŋ ATR	MAX(ATR)	*]$_{\text{N-Adj}}$[ATR	VgV-AGR	ALIGN [ATR]μ
☞ a. mugu-biŋ				**
b. mʊgu-biŋ			*!	*
c. mʊgʊ-biŋ		*!		
d. mʊgʊ-bɪŋ	*!			

Candidate (351a) is the optimal one, even though it has two violations of ALIGN[ATR]μ, since the ATR has spread two syllables from the sponsoring morpheme -*bíŋ*. These two violations, one more than candidate (351b), would have been enough to eliminate this candidate under the previous listing of constraints. But the violation of VgV-AGR eliminates candidate (351b). Candidate (351c) is ruled out by violation of *]$_{\text{N-Adj}}$[ATR, since the ATR from the adjective is not shared with the noun stem, and (351d) is ruled out by deleting ATR altogether and so violating MAX(ATR). A candidate like *múgó-bíŋ*, with the second vowel lowered, would lose by deleting a [closed] feature.

The next word to analyze, *suguri* 'wash', has the *UgU* pattern in a trisyllabic verb rather than the usual *UgI*. The MAX[place]$_V$ constraint, prohibiting deletion of any vowel place feature, is introduced more fully in the next section.

(352) suguri 'wash'

sUgIrI ATR	MAX(ATR)	VgV-AGR	ALIGN[ATR]μ	MAX[place]$_V$
☞ a. suguri				*
b. sugiri		*!		
c. sʊgɪrɪ	*!			

The winning candidate (352a) violates only the low-ranked MAX[place]$_V$ by deletion of the [coronal] feature of the V$_2$ position.[29] Candidate (352b), which conforms to the usual pattern of verbs in Kɔnni, is ruled out by its violation of VgV-AGR. Candidate (352c) dies because it deletes ATR and so fatally violates MAX(ATR). Interestingly, the input could be *sUgUrI*, with V$_2$

---

[29]This is assuming that V$_2$ is indeed underlyingly specified for [coronal]. Since [coronal] is the default place feature, it is quite possible that V$_2$ has no underlying place specification and that verbs have only one inherent vocalic place feature, which is realized on V$_1$.

being U rather than I, and the same result would obtain, except that the winning candidate would not have a violation of MAX[place]$_V$ starting from that underlying representation.

A final form to submit to analysis is *huugɪ* 'be rotten', which violates the VgV-AGR constraint. The quality of the final epenthetic vowel *I* takes precedence over agreement of vowels across [g, k]. This is discussed in section 5.5.2, with a tableau in (395).

5.4.2 Coronal agreement across coronals

Frequently, /a/ fronts when followed by a syllable with a front vowel, e.g., /yalɪ/ → [yɛlɪ] 'have'. Also, the sequence [ɪɛ] may be heard as a variant of the diphthong [ɪa], e.g., *pɪasɪ* ~ *pɪɛsɪ* 'ask' when followed by *ɪ*.[30] This does not happen in careful speech; in Amadu's careful recordings, it is almost totally absent, but is frequent in other recordings. The first set of data below shows variation in the single short vowel *a*, while the second data set shows variation with the diphthong *ɪa*.

(353) Fronting of *a* (optional)

    a. balɪ ~ bɛlɪ   'speak'
       dalɪ ~ dɛlɪ   'be much'
       tasɪ ~ tɛsɪ   'kick'
       yalɪ ~ yɛlɪ   'have'
       gbalɪgɪ ~ gbɛlɪgɪ 'be tired'
       gbáríáŋ ~ gbéríáŋ 'earthworm'

    b. pɪasɪ ~ pɪɛsɪ   'ask'
       chɪasɪ ~ chɪɛsɪ   'contribute'
       tɪalɪ ~ tɪɛlɪ   'remain (be left)'
       fɪalɪ ~ fɪɛlɪ   'be cool'
       kpɪasɪ ~ kpɪɛsɪ   'chickens'

Not all the cases of *a* before *ɪ* front, however. In the words above, the *a* is always a short one, and the consonant between *a* is always [coronal] continuant. Below are words for which I have never heard the vowel preceding *ɪ* as fronted, grouped by pattern.

---

[30] I believe the same pattern would hold if the vowel following *a* were *ɛ*. However, *ɛ* is a relatively rare vowel to start with, and I have no cases in my data of *aCɛ*. Since *a* is phonetically [−ATR], *ɪ* and *ɛ* are the only front vowels possible in a monomorphemic root. The result of all this is that *aCɪ* sequences are the only ones which can be considered in this pattern.

5.4 Vowel assimilation I

(354) No fronting of *a*
    a. chagɪ   'be satisfied, sated'
       dagɪ   'show'
       hagɪ   'get up, rise'
       nagɪ   'pick up, take'
       bɪagɪ   'be able'
       hagɪrɪ   'be strong'
       naɲɪ   'melt'
       namɪsɪ   'suffer'
       ŋmabɪ   'shatter'

    b. waalɪ   'broadcast (seed)'
       taasɪ   'join, assemble'
       daarɪ   'wash dishes'
       kpaalɪ   'be fatty'
       gbaasɪ   'claim girl as wife'

    c. dʊarɪ   'take top part off'
       pʊasɪ   'strip bark from tree'
       yʊarɪ   'fetch'

    d. kalɪ   'sit'
       kalɪŋa   'sleeping mat'
       kagɪlɪ   'cross out'
       garɪsɪ   'pass'
       wasɪ   'greet'

In group (354a), the *C* of the *aCɪ* sequence is noncoronal. Most of these are *g*, but there are two labials as well. In group (354b), the vowel *a* is long, and in group (354c), the *a* is part of a [ʊa] diphthong. In (354d), the consonant before the *a* is [dorsal].[31] This last is interesting given the alternation *gbalɪgɪ* ~ *gbɛlɪgɪ* 'be tired' in (353a). From this pattern, the labial-velar does not pattern with velars.

In terms of our vowel features, this would be a spreading of [coronal] across a coronal continuant to a placeless preceding vowel. This pattern may be expressed in an OT approach with a constraint that penalizes a placeless vowel across a consonant from a [coronal].

---

[31] The case in which the intervening consonant is [t] has conflicting evidence. The very common *kpatɪ* 'finish' never fronts the *a*, and neither does *natɪ* 'shout', but *jatɪ* 'unroll' does have *jɛtɪ* as a variant. The verb *watɪ* 'split' also does not front the *a*, but would not be expected to independently of the issue of the *t*, because of the [dorsal] *w*.

(355) *VCV_[cor]: a placeless vowel in the syllable preceding a [coronal] vowel is disallowed

The consonant between the vowels must be coronal itself. This is consistent with Ní Chiosáin and Padgett's (1997) view of spreading as strictly local. If so, then the [coronal] would associate to the intervening consonant on the way to the placeless a. If a consonant has a [coronal] place, there is no conflict and the a assimilates. If, however, the intervening consonant has a [dorsal] or [labial] place, the spreading is blocked, presumably because the intervening consonant cannot bear both [coronal] and another place feature simultaneously. In the most general case, this would be due to a constraint forbidding multiple place associations on a single consonant.

(356) ***Complex**: more than one place specification on a consonant is disallowed[32]

Note that the labial-velars would keep their multiple places due to the high-ranked MAXCPl$_{obs}$, but *Complex mitigates against the creation of multiply-articulated consonants. In this characterization, the top-ranked NOGAP will rule out spreading which skips the intervening consonant. Presumably there would also be a constraint which penalizes the spreading of the [coronal] feature, or the configuration which has multiply-linked [coronals]. The exact formulation of this could take various forms, but it would be ranked at the bottom of the following tableaus, and I will thus neither include it in the tableaus nor attempt a formalization.

(357) dɛlɪ 'be much'

	dAlI	*Complex	*VCV$_{[cor]}$
☞ a. dɛlɪ			
b. dalɪ			*!

The intervening consonant g makes the difference in (358). The [coronal] feature cannot skip the intervening consonant, nor may it add the [coronal] to the [dorsal] already present, without violating highly-ranked constraints.

---

[32]Padgett (1996) notes a similar constraint when discussing labial-velar consonants.

5.4 Vowel assimilation I

(358) dagɪ 'show' NoGap, *Complex >> *VCV[cor]

dAgI	NoGap	*Complex	*VCV[cor]
☞ a. dagɪ			*
b. [cor] /\ d ɛ g ɪ	*!		
c. dɛgdɪ		*!	

The constraint Faith[aa], previously discussed, would prevent the long [aa] from fronting.

(359) taasɪ 'join, assemble' Faith[aa] >> *VCV[cor]

tAAsI	Faith[aa]	*Complex	*VCV[cor]
☞ a. taasɪ			*
b. tɛɛsɪ	*!		

The lack of fronting when the initial consonant is velar, as in the data in (354d), is the result of a constraint penalizing [coronal] vowels after velar consonants. As noted in section 4.4.1, there is a total lack of *kII* and *gII* in Kɔnni, due to historical changes. Though there are cases of [coronal] vowels after *k* and *g*, these are relatively uncommon, again due to the diachronic situation (Cahill 1995a). For this reason, I propose a constraint as follows.

(360) *$C_{dors}V_{cor}$: a sequence of dorsal consonant and coronal vowel is disallowed

Again, the faithfulness constraint Max[cor]$_V$, discussed in the next section, would preserve sequences as in *gílí* 'egg', but the above constraint exerts pressure against the creation of new $C_{dors}V_{cor}$ sequences.

(361) garɪsɪ 'pass' *$C_{dors}V_{cor}$ >> *VCV[cor]

gArIsI	Max[cor]$_V$	*$C_{dors}V_{cor}$	*VCV[cor]
☞ a. garɪsɪ			*
b. gɛrɪsɪ		*!	

The winning candidate (361a) violates only *VCV$_{[cor]}$, while the losing candidate (361b) fatally violates *C$_{dors}$V$_{cor}$. In the tableau below, I illustrate how an underlying C$_{dors}$V$_{cor}$ sequence would be preserved.

(362) gılı 'egg' MAX[cor]$_V$ >> *C$_{dors}$V$_{cor}$

	gIlI	MAX[cor]$_V$	*C$_{dors}$V$_{cor}$	*VCV$_{[cor]}$
☞ a.	gılı		*	
b.	galI	*!		*

The winning candidate (362a) violates *C$_{dors}$V$_{cor}$, but the losing candidate (362b) is worse by virtue of deleting an input [coronal] feature and so violating MAX[cor]$_V$.

To account for the variation in the pronunciation of words such as fıalı ~ fıɛlı 'be cool' in (353), the rankings of the constraints *VCV$_{[cor]}$ and the constraint preventing spreading of [coronal] would be reversed.

5.4.3 Assimilation of vowels to following glide

Nonlow vowels will usually assimilate to a following glide. The low vowel /a/, whether short or long, does not assimilate. The perfective aspect is a convenient testing ground for this, since the perfective intransitive aspect marker is /-yA/ and the perfective transitive marker is /-wA/.

(363) a. Assimilation to [w]
    /mı/ 'build'   muwa... 'has built...'
    /di/ 'eat'   duwo... 'has eaten...'
    /se/ 'dance'   sowo... 'has danced...'

  b. Assimilation to [y]
    /kʊ/ 'dry'   kà kʷìyá 'it has dried'
    /po/ 'divide'   pʷeye   'has divided'

  c. No assimilation with [a]
    /ga/ 'go'   gaya   'has gone'
    /ta/ 'throw'   tawa... 'has thrown...'

I also record cases where assimilation and no assimilation occur in back-to-back recitations of the same word, as in [ŋmʊ-ya] ~ [ŋmʷɪ-ya] 'has squeezed'. Speech rate and carefulness may also be involved, and I focus on the more casual speech style here. A constraint forcing a nonlow

5.4 Vowel assimilation I

vowel to have the same place as a following glide is needed here. One possibility is a constraint stating that "a nonlow vowel and a following glide must agree in place value." However, there is another more general possibility. In the feature system used here, the low vowel /a/ has no place features. As seen in (363c), /a/ does not assimilate in place to a following glide; it is inert to this process. I propose that this is a direct consequence of its having no place features to conflict with the place features of a following glide. With this in mind, the constraint can be expanded beyond "nonlow" vowels to all vowels.

(364) **VG-AGR:** a vowel and a following glide must not have conflicting place values

The nature of the constraint is not that vowel + glide must agree in place features, but that they must not conflict. Since *a* has no place value, it does not differ with the place value of a following glide. However, any other vowel does have a place value and there is a potential for conflicting place values. So *a* does not conflict in place with any vocoid, but a [dorsal] will conflict with a [coronal], for example.

It is the vowel which changes its place value from the input; the place value of the glide remains the same as in the input. So the MAX[dors] and MAX[cor] constraints applying to glides must be ranked higher than those applying to vowels. These constraints could be stated either in terms of glides versus vowels or syllable onsets versus nuclei, and as far as I can tell, it would make no difference. Since I have stated VG-AGR in terms of vowels and glides, I will do the same for the MAX constraints. The place feature of a glide is never deleted, since glides in Kɔnni never change their place, so I conflate the MAX[place] constraints for glides into one.

(365) **MAX[place]$_G$:** a [dorsal] or [coronal] feature in an input glide must have a correspondent in the output

However, the situation with place features for vowels is different.[33] The input [labial] vowel place is retained in the output in forms like *kà kʷì-yá* 'it has dried' (from /kʊ/ 'to dry', see 363b), but the [coronal] vowel place is not retained in *du-wo...* 'has eaten...' (from /di/ 'eat', see 363a). We do not find **dʸu-wo*. Since the [labial] place of a vowel is not deleted, but the [coronal]

---

[33]In the following discussion, I assume labialization of consonants is a function of the [labial] feature and not the [dorsal] one. So here the [labial] feature of vowels is in focus, unlike earlier sections, where back round vowels were argued to have the [dorsal] place only as the active feature. I assume the [labial] feature here is a redundant one, possibly not present in input forms of the vowels, but present in surface forms.

place is deleted in the same circumstances, the MAX constraints for vowel place must be separated according to the features involved, with the MAX[lab]$_V$ constraint ranked above the MAX[cor]$_V$ constraint. Also, since (derived) labialized consonants are allowed, but not palatalized ones, the constraint *Complex is assumed to be ranked between these.

(366) **MAX[lab]$_V$**: a [labial] feature in an input vowel must have a correspondent in the output
      MAX[cor]$_V$: a [coronal] feature in an input vowel must have a correspondent in the output
      *****Complex**: more than one place specification on a consonant is disallowed (repeated from 356) (*Comp)

Glides never change their place in Kɔnni, so MAX[place]$_G$ will be considered undominated. A [labial] vowel feature is never lost in Kɔnni, so MAX[lab]$_V$ is also assumed to be undominated.

(367) mʊwa… 'has built…'

mI-wA	VG-AGR	MAX [place]$_G$	MAX [lab]$_V$	*Comp	MAX [cor]$_V$
☞ a. mʊwa					*
b. mɪwa	*!				
c. mɪya		*!			
d. mʸʊwa				*!	

The winning candidate (367a) has lost the [coronal] vowel place feature and so violated MAX[cor]$_V$. However, other candidates fare worse. Candidate (367b) violates VG-AGR by the [ɪw] sequence disagreeing in place, and candidate (367c) violates MAX[place]$_G$ by losing the input place of the glide.

(368) kʷɪ-ya 'has dried'

kU-yA	VG-AGR	MAX [place]$_G$	MAX [lab]$_V$	*Comp	MAX [cor]$_V$
☞ a. kʷɪ-ya				*	
b. kɪ-ya			*!		
c. kʊ-ya	*!				
d. kʊ-wa		*!		*!	

5.4 Vowel assimilation I

The winning candidate (368a) violates only *Comp by creating a complex consonant. Since the vowel of the verb differs in input and output, there is a violation of some faithfulness constraint which keeps the place value of the value associated to that vowel; this would be ranked low and I do not discuss it further. But the [labial] autosegment present in the input on the vowel does indeed have a correspondent in the output—the labialization on [k^w]. Candidate (368b) loses because it deletes the vowel feature [lab] altogether. Candidate (368c) loses by the vowel and following glide disagreeing in place, and candidate (368d) loses by changing the place of the glide.

The agreement of a vowel with a glide overrides the otherwise robust generalization that high vowels across [g] have the same place value.

(369) múgí-yéélà 'white rivers' (cf. múgú-bíŋ 'small river')

The vowel í in *múgí-yéélà* is epenthetic and so not indicated in the input of the tableau in (370).

(370) múgí-yéélà 'white rivers' **VG-AGR, MAX[place]$_G$, *Comp** >> **VgV-AGR**

	mUg-yEElA	VG-AGR	MAX [place]$_G$	MAX [lab]$_V$	*Comp	VgV-AGR	MAX [cor]$_V$
☞ a.	mʊgɪ-yɛɛla					*	
b.	mʊgʊ-yɛɛla	*!					
c.	mʊgʊ-wɛɛla		*!				
d.	mʊg^{w}ɪ-yɛɛla				*!	*	

Candidate (370a) wins even though it violates VgV-AGR by having a UgI sequence word internally. The other most likely candidate, (370b), loses by violating VG-AGR with a [ʊy] sequence, and candidate (370c) loses by changing the place of the glide and so violating MAX[place]$_G$. The vowel before [y] is epenthetic and so incurs no violations of the MAX[lab]$_V$ or MAX[cor]$_V$ constraints. Candidate (370d), which is similar to the winning candidate *k^{w}ɪ-ya* in (368), is ruled out by *Comp since it creates a complex consonant. In *k^{w}ɪ-ya* the complex consonant is created to avoid deleting the [labial] feature, but in *múgí-yéélà* there is no such necessity, since the [labial] feature on a possible *g^w* would have its source in the preceding *ʊ*, and this [labial] feature is not deleted under any reasonable candidate. The geometric representations of these are illustrated in (371); for the sake of space, only the [labial] feature and not the [dorsal] one is shown on the *ʊ*.

(371) Input and output representations of *kʷɪ-ya* and *mʊgɪ-yɛɛla*

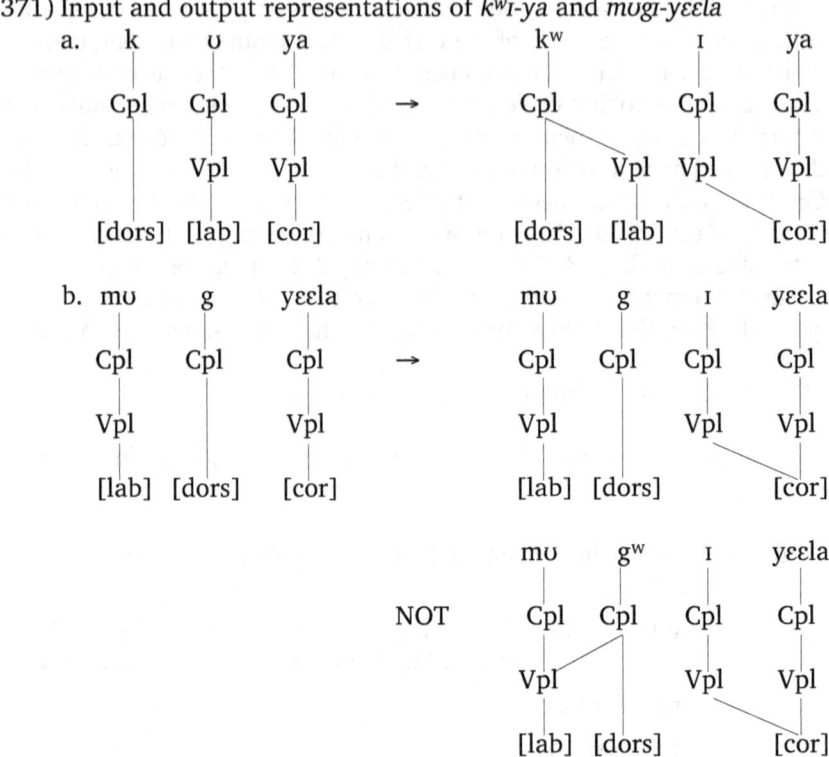

5.4.4 Backing of front vowels before *ŋ*

Although in most of this work, I have written front vowels before [ŋ] with their phonemic representation, this has obscured a pervasive phonetic pattern, which is that phonemic front vowels are centralized before [ŋ] and [ŋm] (but not other consonants, including [g, k, kp, gb]). For convenience I use [ɨ] and [ə] in the data in this section to represent both the ATR and non-ATR central high and mid vowels, respectively.

(372) a. /tɪ-ŋ/ → [tɪ̈ŋ] 'village'(cf. tìkká 'the village')
b. /tu-ŋ/ → [tɨ́ŋ] 'tree' (cf. tɨ́ká 'the tree')
c. /dembi-ŋ/ → [dèmbɨ́ŋ] 'man' (cf. dèmbìké 'the man')

5.4 Vowel assimilation I

d. /keŋ/ → [kəŋ] 'come' (cf. ken-ne 'is coming')

e. /bitie-ŋ/ → [bítíəŋ] 'chin, beard' (cf bítíérí 'the chin')

f. /gbiŋgbiɲi-ŋ/ → [gbíŋgbíˈɲíŋ] 'a type of chicken' (cf. gbíŋgbínsì 'chickens')

g. /tɪ ŋɔbaa ɲindikke/ → [tɨ̀ ŋɔ́báˈá ɲíndíkkè] 'We are chewing food.'

h. /ʊ nan dɪ ŋmʊa/ → [ʊ̀ nàn dɨ̀ ŋmʊ́ˈá] 'S/he will be squeezing.'

Almost all of the examples in (372) are within words, and the centralization occurs both within a morpheme, as in (372f), and across morpheme boundaries, as in the others. Since word-initial ŋ is quite rare, opportunities to test this pattern across words are quite rare; the only such verb in the Yikpabongo dialect is ŋɔbɪ 'chew', as in (372g). However, there are a handful of verbs beginning with ŋm, and these exhibit the same pattern. (This also implies a directional asymmetry for the structure of labial-velars.) It appears that centralization occurs across word boundaries.

Note that this centralization applies not only to a short front vowel, as in (372a, c, d, and f), but also to the second half of an underlying long vowel, in (372b and e). As with diphthongization, the two halves of a long vowel must be treated as separate units here. Centralization occurs not only in the last syllable of a word, but also when ŋ is intervocalic, as in (372f).

This appears to be an assimilation in backing, but it is unlikely to specifically be an assimilation of the [dorsal] feature of [ŋ]. Besides the fact that the centralization does not occur before other [dorsal] consonants, formant measurements do not indicate extensive backing. If we were to take measurements of the F_2-F_1 values of a [dorsal] vowel, e.g., the high back unrounded vowel [ɯ], we would expect these to be comparable to those of the back vowels [u/ʊ]. For the high centralized vowel I have transcribed as [ɨ], preliminary measurements actually give F_1 and F_2-F_1 values of (420, 750), almost exactly between [i/ɪ] and [u/ʊ] on the suffixal formant chart in (242), more consistent with a high central vowel [ɨ] than a high back unrounded vowel [ɯ]. If this is an assimilation, it would have to be a phonetic gradient process. Besides this phonetic interpretation, however, there is another account available as well.

If we retain the assumption of privative place features, we note that [ɨ] and [ə] are not [dorsal], as [ŋ] is, so this is not a sharing of place features.

Rather, [ɨ] and [ə] are placeless. The motivation for this change becomes clearer by noting what other phonetic vowels actually may occur before [ŋ].

(373) Vowels preceding [ŋ] (besides [ɨ] and [ə])
    [a]   [dàáŋ]   'stick'
    [u]   [dǔŋ]]   'knee'
    [ʊ]   [dʊ̀ʊ́ŋ]   'tree (sp.)'
    [ɔ]   [nɔ́ŋ]   'meat'
    [o]   [kóŋ]   'hunger'

In short, any vowel except the front vowels may occur before [ŋ]. So [dorsal] or placeless vowels may occur before [ŋ], but not [coronal] ones. In OT terms, this is expressed by a constraint that prohibits a surface [coronal] vowel before [ŋ], *[cor]ŋ.

(374) *[cor]ŋ: a [coronal] vowel is prohibited before [ŋ][34]

This does not prohibit underlying sequences of [coronal]ŋ, of course. An input [coronal][ŋ] sequence is resolved in a way that is maximally faithful to the input by deleting the feature [coronal], but not adding the other active place feature [dorsal]. DEP[dorsal], penalizing insertion of [dorsal], is undominated, as we have seen. Sharing of [dorsal] place between the vowel and the [ŋ] is avoided by a constraint prohibiting a VC sequence from sharing [dorsal].

(375) *[dors]SHARE: a vowel and consonant cannot share a single [dorsal] feature

This constraint cannot be extended to place features in general, since in palatalization a consonant and vowel share an [anterior] feature. This constraint *[dors]SHARE must be ranked below the undominated VG-AGR, since a vowel and a following glide share the same place feature. Therefore, *[dors]SHARE is dominated.

---

[34]With more research, I suspect this constraint could be transformed into one or more that relate to a limited prohibition of dissimilar features, but for this work I leave the above descriptive constraint in place.

5.4 Vowel assimilation I   261

(376) dèmbɨ́ŋ 'man' *[cor]ŋ, Dep[dors], *[dors]Share >> Max[cor]$_V$

dEmbIŋ ATR	*[cor]ŋ	Dep[dors]	*[dors]Share	Max[cor]$_V$
☞ a. dembɨŋ				*
b. dembiŋ	*!			
c. dembuŋ | d			*!	*
d. dembuŋ || dd		*!		*

In all candidates except (376b), Max[cor]$_V$ is violated, since the value of the input's vowel place [coronal] is not preserved in the output. This is the only constraint violated by the winning candidate (376a). Candidate (376b) fails through violating the undominated *[cor]ŋ. Candidates (376c and d) are phonetically identical, but differ structurally. In (376c), the [dorsal] feature is shared between [u] and [ŋ] and thus violates *[dors]Share. In (376d), [u] and [ŋ] each have their own [dorsal] feature, and by inserting a [dorsal], this candidate violates Dep[dors].[35]

New constraints and rankings in this section are:

---

[35] A possible alternative to *[dors]Share would be a constraint having the effect that dorsal sonorants ([ŋ, w]) determine the place of the preceding vowel. This approach would treat [ɨ] and [ə] as back vowels with [dorsal] specification. The advantage to this approach is that before the glide [w], [E] and [I] have the rounded [labial] variants [O] and [U], consistent with [w], while before the *un*rounded [ŋ], the variants of [E] and [I] are the unrounded [ɨ] and [ə], consistent with the [dorsal] but *not* [labial] specification of [ŋ]. One complication is that this would require treating the central [a] as a back [dorsal] vowel as well. A consequence of this is that the constraint would have to specifically mention nonlow vowels (or another constraint thrown in which would have that effect). Another consequence is that the diphthongization /ɛɛ/ → [ɪa] would have a more complicated analysis, since a [dorsal] feature would have to be introduced for the [a]. A further complication is that a variant of the same constraint VG-Agr would still be needed to account for /uy/ → [iy]. Still another complication is the pattern of nasal assimilation to [w] as [ŋ] rather than [ŋm]. If [w] has both [dorsal] and [labial] features active in the vowels assimilating to it, why does the nasal only assimilate to the [dorsal] place of [w]?

(377) 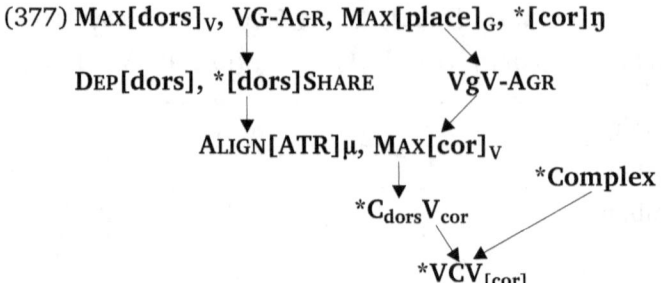 MAX[dors]$_V$, VG-AGR, MAX[place]$_G$, *[cor]ŋ

DEP[dors], *[dors]SHARE   VgV-AGR

ALIGN[ATR]μ, MAX[cor]$_V$

*C$_{dors}$V$_{cor}$ *Complex

*VCV$_{[cor]}$

5.5 Vowel epenthesis

5.5.1 Data

Data concerning epenthesis of vowels comes from borrowed words, nouns, and verbs, and we present each of these in order.

The most obvious evidence for epenthesis in Kɔnni is in borrowed words which end in consonants or in consonant clusters in the source language. When borrowed into Kɔnni, these have inserted vowels, bolded below.

(378) a. From English
bágìtí	'bucket'
pɔ́mpì	'pump'
bɔ́lì	'ball'
chénjì	'change'
sìpánì	'wrench' (British *spanner*)
sɔ́kìsì	'socks'
mílìkì	'milk'

b. From Hausa
Kɔnni	Hausa	
àlìbésà	albasa	'onion'
àlìbárìkà	albarka	'blessing'

Nouns are a fruitful area of investigation for epenthesis or the lack of it, due to the possibility of adding various suffixes, including adjectives. One pattern of evidence for epenthesis comes from alternations of singular and plural nouns in noun class 1. From previous discussion and the data in (379), we see that the plural suffix for noun class 1 is either [a] or [e],

5.5 Vowel epenthesis

depending on vowel harmony. This suffix adds to the noun stem, whether that stem ends in a vowel, as with /siebi-/, or a consonant, as in /dun-/. The singular suffix is -ŋ and the singular definite suffix is -rI (or -nI by assimilation to a stem nasal). If we strip these suffixes off the actual forms, we derive the stem listed in the leftmost column in (379). We arrive at the same stem no matter which suffix we strip off.[36]

(379) No epenthesis

Stem	Singular	Singular definite	Plural	
/siebi-/	síébí-ŋ	síébí-rí	síébí-è	'bee'
/dii-/	díí-ŋ	díí-rí	dí-è	'forehead'
/dun-/	dŭ-ŋ	dùn-ní	dùn-é	'knee'
/tan-/	tă-ŋ	tàn-ní	tàn-á	'stone'
/bɪn-/	bĭ-ŋ	bìn-ní	bìn-á	'year'

However, in the forms in (380), we obtain a different result for the stem if we strip the suffix off the plural than we do if we strip the suffixes off the singular and singular definite. In 'bag', for example, we obtain /bʊllɔg-/ if we strip the plural suffix, but /bʊllɔgɪ-/ if we strip off the singular or singular definite suffix. The difference is the vowel /ɪ/. This cannot be a vowel present in the stem, or the plural suffix would simply add to it as it does in the first two examples in (379). This vowel is epenthetic and inserted before the -ŋ and -rI suffixes to preserve the highly-valued CV and CVN syllable structures. To avoid proliferation of hyphens in (380), the epenthetic vowels are grouped together with the suffixes.

(380) Epenthesis in singular and singular definite

Stem	Singular	Singular definite	Plural	
/bʊllɔg-/	búllɔ́g-íŋ	búllɔ́g-írí	búllɔ́g-à	'bag'
/bɪɪs-/	bìɪs-íŋ	bìɪs-ìrí	bìɪs-á	'breast'
/chʊʊs-/	chʊ́ʊ́!s-íŋ	chʊ́ʊ́s-í!rí	chʊ́ʊ́s-à	'gecko'
/daagbug-/	dààgbúg-íŋ	dààgbúg-úrí	dààgbúg-ê	'stump'
/jag-/	jág-íŋ	jág-írí	jág-â	'shade'
/tig-/	tíg-íŋ	tíg-írí	tíg-è	'house'
/yis-/	yís-íŋ	yís-írí	yís-è	'sheep'

Besides the noun class 1 nouns above, the ʊ before the plural suffix -sI is sometimes epenthetic, as seen in the ŋ/k/g alternations previously discussed in section 4.3.

---

[36]The exception in this data is with /dii-/ 'forehead', which has a vowel shortening in the plural form. This shortening is discussed in section 5.6.

(381) kúŋ   kúkká   kúgúsí   'tree, the tree, trees (sp.)'

There are also some variations in forms in which an adjectival suffix is added to the noun stem. The epenthetic vowel may or may not be present, depending on speech rate. In casual speech, there is no epenthetic vowel, but in careful speech (sometimes it needs to be very careful), a vowel is inserted.

(382) bɔ̀gì-góbè   ~ bɔ̀g-góbè   'long fibers'
      kɔ̀bì-bíŋ   ~ kɔ̀b-bíŋ   'small bone'
      jùòdìgì-kíŋ ~ jùòdìk-kíŋ   'cooking room'
      vɔ̀rí-tí   ~ vɔ̀t-tí   'holes'[37]

The nature of the consonants largely determines whether epenthesis occurs or not. The consonant contexts where epenthesis does and does not occur are tabulated in (383) and (384). Nouns with the sequences in (383) are special cases; they exhibit consistent epenthesis or consistent deletion depending on the noun class they belong to (see section 4.3).

(383) a. Epenthesis
        g-ŋ   tíg-íŋ   'house' (cf. tígè
                           'houses')
        n-ŋ   yàn-íŋ   'frog' (cf. yàná 'frogs')

     b. No epenthesis
        g-ŋ → ŋ   kúŋ   'tree (sp.)' (cf. kúg-úsí 'trees')
        n-ŋ → ŋ   tăŋ   'stone' (cf. tàn-á 'stones')

The generalization taken from (384b) is that consonant clusters are allowed when the two consonants are either stops or sonorants and of the same place.

(384) a. Epenthesis[38]
        r-k   gàrù-kú   'the cloth' (cf. gàt-tí 'clothes')
        r-b   jíkkɔ̀rì-bĭŋ   'small basket' (cf. jík!kɔ́ttí 'baskets')
        r-s   gbàrìsì   'bath sponges' (cf. gbàrà 'bath sponge')

---

[37] I have six examples of [rIt] in my data, where [I] is epenthetic, and seven where no epenthesis occurs. Five of these seven examples in which [tt] is the preferred result, though, have [ɔ] as the preceding vowel, as in the [vɔ́ttʃ] 'hole' example in (382). The other two have [ʊ] as the preceding vowel.

[38] I am convinced that other examples exist, such as b-s, and b-k, but the alternations which would conclusively demonstrate these are absent, and the evidence for these two is absent. But they do fit the overall pattern.

5.5 Vowel epenthesis

r-ŋ	gàr-íŋ	'cloth' (cf. gàt-tí 'clothes')
l-k	kpììlìké	'the ancestor' (cf. kpììlé 'ancestors')
b-r	kpánjábírí	'the butterfly' (cf. kpánjáb-à 'butterflies')
b-t	yóbítí	'elephants' (cf. yóbà 'elephants', alt. form)
b-ŋ	kpánjábíŋ	'butterfly' (cf. kpánjáb-à 'butterflies')
b-kp	kɔ̀b-ìkpí!íŋ	'big bone' (cf. kɔ́b-á 'bones')
g-b	tígí-bí!ŋ́	'small house' (cf. tíg-è 'houses')
g-d	jígí-dík!ké	'cooking place' (cf. jíg-ê 'places')
g-s	gbígbágísí	'tree (sp.)' (cf. gbígbákká 'the tree')
g-r	tíg-írí	'the house' (cf. tíg-è 'houses')
g-t	bóg-ìtí	'fibers' (cf. bɔ̀k-kú 'the fiber')
g-ŋ	tígíŋ	'house' (cf. tíg-è 'houses')
m-ŋ	chàm-íŋ	'castanet' (cf. chàm-á 'castanets')
s-b	bììs-ìbú	'the milk' (cf. bììs-á 'breasts')
s-r	bììs-ìrí	'the breast' (cf. bììs-á 'breasts')
s-k	wúsí!ké	'the tree (sp.)' (cf. wúsè 'trees')
s-ŋ	bììs-ìŋ	'breast' (cf. bììs-á 'breasts')

b. No epenthesis

r-t	→ tt	vɔ́t-tí	'holes' (cf. vɔ́ríŋ 'hole')
b-b	→ bb	kɔ̀b-bíŋ	'small bone' (cf. kɔ̀bá 'bones')
g-k	→ kk	ɲìndìk-ké	'food'
g-g	→ gg	bɔ̀g-góbè	'long fibers' (cf. bɔ̀gìtí 'fibers')
g-kp	→ kkp	hɔ̀k-kpí!íŋ	'big woman' (cf. hɔ̀gú 'woman')
g-h	→ kh	tìk-háá!líŋ	'new village' (cf. tìgìsí 'villages')
n-r	→ nn	yàn-ní	'the frog' (cf. yàníŋ 'frog')
l-r	→ ll	dàmpàl-lí	'the log' (cf. dàmpàlá 'logs')

Verbs are another area in which epenthesis is evident. Verbs in citation form invariably end in [i, ɪ] if they are di- or trisyllabic, while monosyllabic verbs in citation may end with any vowel.

(385)
Citation	Perfective	Imperfective	Stem	
laa	la-ya	la-a	/la/	'laugh'
dii	di-ye	di-e	/di/	'eat'
tuu	tʷi-ye	tu-o	/tu/	'dig'
kpatɪ	kpatɪ-ya	kpat-a	/kpat-/	'finish'
tɪɪrɪ	tɪɪrɪ-ya	tɪɪr-a	/tɪɪr-/	'stretch'
sulisi	sulisi-ye	sulis-e	/sulis-/	'polish'
bʊgʊrɪ	bʊgʊrɪ-ya	bʊgʊr-a	/bʊgʊr-/	'learn'

In a way similar to the approach taken with members of noun class 1 in (380), we can see that stripping off the -*a, e, -o* imperfective suffix leaves the stem. An *I* is inserted in the citation and perfective (and other) forms when necessary to prevent illicit syllable-final consonants.

In almost all the noun examples above, the inserted vowel was /I/. The exceptions were *dààgbúg-úrí* 'the stump' in (380) and *kúgúsí* 'trees' in (381), where [u, ʊ] is epenthetic. In these cases, the usual /I/ surfaces as [u, ʊ] to agree in [dorsal] with the [u, ʊ] present across the [g] (see section 5.4.1 for details and analysis). Another exception is with the perfective aspect in a transitive sentence, in which the epenthetic vowel surfaces as [u, ʊ] before a [w] (see section 5.4.3 for details and analysis).

(386) /kpat-/   kpatʊ-wa...   'has finished...'
      /dag-/   dagʊ-wa...   'has shown...'
      /bʊgʊr-/   bʊ-gʊ-rʊ-wa...   'has learned...'
      /kpegir-/ kpegiru-wo...   'has broken...'

In both of these cases, the usual identity of the epenthetic vowel as /I/ is overridden by its assimilation to a neighboring [dorsal] vocoid. To sum up, the epenthetic vowel is always high and is [u, ʊ] when before a [w] or across a [g] from another [u, ʊ]. Otherwise, the epenthetic vowel is [i, ɪ].

We must also account here for the fact that the epenthetic vowel word finally is always [-I], even when across a [g] from a high round vowel, as in:

(387) hʊʊgɪ   'be rotten'
      kpʊgɪ   'weave'
      kúgíŋ   'cooking place' (see other data in 350)

5.5.2 Analysis

The goals of this section are to account for the fact that epenthesis occurs in Kɔnni and for the nature of the epenthesized vowel.

As discussed in chapter 3, the syllable structure of Kɔnni is most often CV or CVN. In some cases word-internal CVC may be allowed if the syllable-final consonant is identical to the adjacent consonant which begins the next syllable. The driving force for vowel epenthesis is assumed to be the avoidance of syllable-final consonants, specifically syllable-final consonants which do not share the place value of the consonant which begins the next syllable. One generalization which is never violated is that word-final consonants do not occur at all, except for [ŋ]. As repeated from (103) in chapter 3, we have a constraint disallowing almost

5.5 Vowel epenthesis

all consonants utterance finally. The constraint listed in (388) is actually a conflation of constraints, such as *b//, *k//, *z//, referring to all consonants in Kɔnni except ŋ. The constraint *ŋ// is ranked quite low, to the point of invisibility in Kɔnni, while the constraints referring to other consonants are top-ranked and can be combined for expository purposes into ŋ//.

(388) ŋ//: ŋ is the only consonant licensed utterance finally

To avoid a word-final consonant when one is present in the input, one may either delete the consonant or insert a vowel after it. (Other changes are also conceivable, such as changing the consonant to a vowel, but these do not seem to be commonly attested, are totally unattested in Kɔnni, and will not be considered here.) Cross-linguistically, both possibilities are attested; Kɔnni chooses the vowel epenthesis option. In terms of OT constraints regarding insertion and deletion, the constraint DEP(V), prohibiting insertion of vowels, would need to be ranked lower than MAX(C), which prohibits deleting a consonant. Below, however, I will propose that DEP(V) is too broad, and must be split into a family of constraints.

(389) MAX(C): every consonant in the input has a correspondent in the output (prohibits deleting consonants)
DEP(V): every vowel in the output has a correspondent in the input (prohibits inserting vowels)

The nature of the inserted vowel is also determined by appropriate constraints. Three approaches are worth considering as alternatives: one employs a markedness approach to features, and the other two use DEP constraints which refer either to whole vowels or to individual features.

The markedness approach would employ constraints such as *[dors], *[cor], *[closed], etc. By ranking *[dors] above *[cor], we can ensure a [coronal] epenthetic vowel, which is what we in fact get. However, ensuring the insertion of a high vowel is more problematic. Using [closed] to represent height as we do here, with multiple occurrences possible, a high vowel would incur more violations of *[closed] than a mid or low vowel. If the unary [closed] is used for a height feature, a markedness approach would always predict the insertion of a vowel with the fewest instances of [closed], that is, a low vowel. This is precisely what we do not get in Kɔnni. Also, assuming /a/ to be placeless, a markedness approach would penalize any place features and prefer [a] or a central vowel to any front or back vowel. To sum up, the markedness approach would predict [a] to be epenthetic and cannot be used here.

With DEP constraints, one approach is to deal with the vowel as a whole unit, and the other is to determine the epenthetic vowel by a combination of features. A modified form of the latter approach is the one I will use. To deal with the vowel as a whole unit would mean splitting the DEP(V) constraint into a family of constraints such that every vowel is listed. In this approach, there would be DEP(ɪ), DEP(i), DEP(o), and so forth, for all the nine phonemic vowels of Kɔnni as a minimum, and possibly all the phonetic qualities of vowels as well (e.g., DEP(ə)). Besides the listing of more constraints, this approach misses the generalization that in Kɔnni all epenthetic vowels are high. A mere listing of vowels would regard the ranking of DEP constraints for high vowels together, and nonhigh vowels together, as coincidence, with no more inherent probability than any other ranking of DEP constraints. A better approach will group high vowels together in a principled way.

Using faithfulness constraints which deal solely with features is not a workable approach, however. In the absence of high-ranked constraints, it is better not to insert a particular feature, since to do so would violate one of the constraints DEP[dors], DEP[cor], or DEP[closed], the relevant features for Kɔnni vowels (ATR, the other vowel feature, would be spread from the stem and would not incur a violation of DEP[ATR]). In an inserted vowel, the only way to avoid a violation of one of these constraints is to insert a vowel which contains none of these features, the vowel [a]. The vowel [a] is indeed the epenthetic vowel in some languages, but not in Kɔnni.

On the other hand, if there were a way to require that the epenthetic vowel have two occurrences of [closed], as indeed the epenthetic vowel in Kɔnni always does have, then other constraints already in place will ensure the correct output as [i, ɪ, u, ʊ] in the appropriate environments. Recall that if a vowel has an occurrence of [closed], it must also have a place feature. The ranking of DEP[dors] above DEP[cor] ensures that an inserted place feature will be [coronal].

(390) **[closed]/PLACE:** a vowel with a [closed] feature must also have a place feature (from 274)
DEP[dors]: every [dorsal] in the output has a correspondent in the input (from 275)
DEP[cor]: every [coronal] in the output has a correspondent in the input (from 275)

Of course, if the epenthetic vowel follows -Ug- or precedes the [dorsal] vocoid [w], the vowel will be [dorsal] as well, by constraints enforcing place agreement of high vowels across [g] or with a following glide.

5.5 Vowel epenthesis

To ensure that the maximum number of [closed] features are the ones inserted, I propose a constraint DEP(V$_{CL-CL}$). This would be part of a family of constraints on vowel insertion depending on the number of [closed] occurrences each has. The constraints DEP(V$_{CL}$), dealing with one occurrence of [closed], and DEP(V$_{ØCL}$), dealing with a vowel with no occurrences of [closed], would be ranked as undominated, since a mid or low vowel is never inserted in Kɔnni, while DEP(V$_{CL-CL}$) is ranked low, since the epenthetic vowel in Kɔnni is always high.[39]

(391) **DEP(V$_{CL-CL}$):** every vowel with two [closed] in the output has a correspondent in the input (prohibits inserting high vowels)
DEP(V$_{CL}$): every vowel with one [closed] in the output has a correspondent in the input (prohibits inserting mid vowels)
DEP(V$_{ØCL}$): every vowel with no [closed] in the output has a correspondent in the input (prohibits inserting low vowels)

The notation V$_{ØCL}$ is used to avoid possible confusion with another possible notation, DEP(V), which could also be interpreted as having no [closed] feature, but is generally used to refer to any vowel, regardless of height. A tableau with these constraints applied to a word-final epenthetic vowel on a verb is given in (392).

(392) kpatɪ 'finish'

	kpAt-	MAX(C)	DEP(V$_{CL}$)	DEP(V$_{ØCL}$)	[closed]/PLACE	ŋ//	DEP[dors]	DEP[cor]	DEP[closed]
☞	a. kpatɪ							*	**
	b. kpat					*!			
	c. kpa	*!							
	d. kpata			*!					
	e. kpatɛ		*!					*	*
	f. kpatɨ				*!				**
	g. kpatʊ						*!		**

---

[39] An alternative set of constraints might use DEP(V$_{MAX-CL}$) to refer to the highest vowel and DEP(V$_{0-CL}$) for the lowest vowel of a language. However, in Kɔnni, using these alone would force insertion of a mid vowel as epenthetic. A language which inserts a low vowel as epenthetic would have the same difficulty in eliminating a mid vowel as the winning epenthetic candidate. Thus, as awkward as it may seem, there seems to be a need for constraints which refer to specific heights.

The winning candidate (392a) violates DEP[cor] and DEP[closed], but other higher-ranked constraints knock out other plausible candidates. Even though inserting [closed] features is penalized, doing that is better than inserting another vowel which does not have two occurrences of [closed], as in (392d and e). It is also better to insert a high vowel than to leave the stem with a consonant in final position (392b) or to delete that consonant (392c). A high vowel must have a place feature, so candidate (392f) is eliminated, and it is better to insert a [coronal] than a [dorsal] feature, so candidate (392g) is eliminated.

If this analysis is on the right track, it has implications for vowel epenthesis in other languages as well. By splitting the DEP(V) into three constraints based on the number of occurrences of [closed], the claim is made that cross-linguistically, the height of the vowel is the key quality of an inserted vowel; other features are secondary in that they are dependent on the height of the vowel. Languages are known to epenthesize vowels of all heights; Axininca's (Ajyininka) epenthetic vowel is [a], a low vowel (Payne 1981, Black 1991, McCarthy and Prince 1993). The epenthetic vowel of Latin, Spanish, and Gengbe is [e], a mid vowel (Schane 1973, Harris 1969, Abaglo and Archangeli 1989). The epenthetic vowel in English and French is the mid vowel [ə]. The epenthetic vowel of Yoruba is [i] (Abaglo and Archangeli 1989), of Korean is [ɨ], and of Japanese and Modern Icelandic is [u] (Kenstowicz 1994), all high vowels. While there seems to be some preference cross-linguistically for high vowels as epenthetic ones, vowels of all phonetic heights can be found to epenthesize in various languages.[40] Typologically, this amounts to ranking the constraints DEP($V_{\emptyset CL}$), DEP(V_{CL}), and DEP(V_{CL-CL}) differently in the different languages. In the case of Axininca, DEP($V_{\emptyset CL}$) would be lowest ranked, so the low vowel [a] is inserted. In the case of Spanish, DEP(V_{CL}) would be lowest ranked. so the mid vowel [e] is inserted. Spanish would also have the constraint [closed]/PLACE, as Kɔnni does, to ensure that an epenthetic vowel must have place; otherwise the vowel would be [ə], as in English. Spanish would have the same rankings of DEP[dors] >> DEP[cor] as Kɔnni, so the epenthetic vowel would be [coronal]. In the case of Korean, DEP(V_{CL-CL}) would be lowest ranked, as in Kɔnni, so the high vowel [ɨ] could be inserted. The difference between Kɔnni and Korean is that Korean would not have the constraint [closed]/PLACE highly ranked. A high vowel would not need a place value, and the relevant DEP

---

[40]The vowel system of Axininca has only two heights, so /a/ as the epenthetic vowel is the lower of two heights, not three or more. This can, of course be accommodated in the family of constraints I propose here, with DEP(V_{CL}) outranking DEP($V_{\emptyset CL}$) to force the insertion of a vowel with no occurrences of [closed]. The need for three constraints referring to different heights comes with the existence of languages which insert a mid vowel.

5.5 Vowel epenthesis

constraints for place features would penalize insertion of such features. The result is the placeless high vowel [ɨ]. For Japanese and Icelandic which have epenthetic [u], the DEP(V_{CL-CL}) and [closed]/PLACE constraints would be highly ranked, and there would be the ranking DEP[cor] > > DEP[dors], the opposite of Kɔnni and Spanish. This is merely a sketch of possibilities, of course, but it does point to an area of future research.

Words which have [-I] as a word-final epenthetic vowel when preceded by [-Ug-] must now be accounted for, as in hʊʊgɪ 'be rotten'. If there is a UgV sequence, where V is high and it is nonfinal, that V agrees with the U in having a [dorsal] feature. There are no UgI sequences word internally, but there are many cases of UgI word finally. The features of an epenthetic vowel word finally are [I] and only [I]. We have seen previously that VgV-AGR is not undominated. It is the final position in the word that is the key factor in keeping the [dorsal] from being shared over the [g]. It is not merely that it is an epenthetic vowel, or alternations such as in 'cooking place' would not occur (see other data in 346).

(393) kúgíŋ 'cooking place'   kúgúrí 'the cooking place'

The prohibition against multiple linking of [dorsal] or [coronal] to the final vowel in a word is expressed by NONFINAL below. This is analogous to nonfinality in tonal patterns, in which a tone in some languages is prohibited from spreading to the final Tone-Bearing Unit.[41]

(394) **NONFINAL[dors]:** the place feature [dorsal] is prohibited on the final vowel of a word

This constraint marks the final vowel of a word as immune to spreading of [dorsal] (although of course ATR will spread into it). A tableau crucially using this constraint is given in (395).

(395) hʊʊgɪ 'be rotten' NONFINAL[dors] > > VgV-AGR

hUUg-	ŋ//	DEP [dors]	NONFINAL [dors]	VgV-AGR	DEP [cor]	DEP [closed]
☞ a. hʊʊgɪ				*	*	**
b. hʊʊgʊ			*!			**
c. hʊʊg	*!					

---

[41]Thanks to David Odden for pointing out the conceptual similarity of the featural pattern here to tonal constraints.

The winning candidate (395a) violates VgV-AGR by having *UgI*, and DEP constraints for [coronal] and [closed] as well by inserting the wordfinal [-I]. But other candidates fare worse. Candidate (395b) violates the NONFINAL[dors] constraint by having [dorsal] linked across the [g]. Note that by assuming that [dorsal] is linked to both vowels on either side of the [g] in (395b), the constraint DEP[dors] is unviolated, since no new occurrence of the [dorsal] feature has been introduced. This points out the necessity of NONFINAL[dors]; if this constraint were absent, then candidate (395b) would be optimal. Candidate (395c) fails because of a violation of ŋ//.

Note that the constraint NONFINAL[dors] refers to the last vowel in a word, but this does not necessarily refer to a word-final vowel. In *kúgíŋ* 'cooking place', the [i] is the last vowel of the word, but it is not word final. NONFINAL[dors] applies to this [i] as well as the [ɪ] in *hʊʊgɪ*.

Of course, [dorsal] vowels do occur in the final syllable of words, but these are underlyingly [dorsal], as in *bʊ̀ntʊ̀ʊ́ŋ* 'toad' and *zàmpʊ́ŋ* 'hedgehog'. This shows that it is more important to preserve an input [dorsal] than to not have a final [dorsal] present. This is illustrated by the tableau in (396), using a MAX[dors] constraint which must be undominated.

(396) zàmpʊ́ŋ 'hedgehog' **MAX[dors]** >> NONFINAL[dors]

zampʊg-ŋ	MAX[dors]	NONFINAL[dors]
☞ a. zampʊŋ		*
b. zampɪŋ	*!	

Next we turn to word-internal epenthesis. We need to review the circumstances in which epenthesis must take place, or to look at it another way, which consonant clusters are allowed in Kɔnni. As noted in chapter 3, consonant clusters are allowed only when they have the same place value, as formalized in the constraint *Cpl$_i$Cpl$_j$, repeated from (130) in chapter 4.

(397) ***Cpl$_i$Cpl$_j$**: adjacent consonants may not have differing place features

This is the key for why some input consonant clusters remain clusters in the output and others must epenthesize a vowel. For example, the forms *tígí-rí* 'the house' and *tìk-ká* 'the village' have very similar stems /tíg-/ and /tìg-/, respectively. However, when the definite suffixes are added, a vowel is epenthesized in *tígírí* but not in *tìkká*. This is due to the fact that in

5.5 Vowel epenthesis

tígírí, the [g] and the [r] have differing places ([dorsal] and [coronal]), while in *tìkká* the /g/ from the noun stem and the [k] from the suffix are both [dorsal].[42]

(398) tígírí 'the house'

tIg-rI ATR	Max(C)	*Cpl$_i$Cpl$_j$	Dep(V$_{CL\text{-}CL}$)
☞ a. tigiri			*
b. tigri		*!	

(399) tìkká 'the village'

tIg-kA	Max(C)	*Cpl$_i$Cpl$_j$	Dep(V$_{CL\text{-}CL}$)
☞ a. tɪkka			
b. tɪgɪka			*!

One might achieve an acceptable consonant cluster in the nonoptimal cases above by changing the place of one of the input consonants to avoid a violation of *Cpl$_i$Cpl$_j$, but this would involve a violation of the top-ranked Max[place]$_{cons}$, discussed in the last chapter and thus would be rejected.

This approach to epenthesis differs from some in that one of the main motivations for epenthesis is not just to preserve CV syllable structure, but to avoid nonidentical consonant clusters. To sum up the approach, let us return to the forms *kúŋ, kúkká, kúgúsí* 'tree, the tree, trees (sp.)' from (381).

From the alternations, especially the plural form, I assume an input noun stem of /kúg-/. In the citation form *kúŋ,* there is no epenthesis because the input consonants /g+ŋ/ are both [dorsal]. (The deletion of /g/ is discussed in section 4.3.) Likewise in the definite form *kúkká,* there is no epenthesis because the input consonants /g+k/ are both [dorsal]. However, in the plural form *kúgúsí,* epenthesis occurs because the adjacent input consonants /g+s/ have different place values [dorsal] and [coronal].

However, lack of agreement in place is not by itself sufficient to account for all cases of epenthesis. In cases like *digu-wa...* 'has eaten...', the *u* is epenthetic, in spite of the fact that both *g* and *w* are [dorsal]; **dig-wa* is not heard. The key here is not that obstruents are generally disallowed syllable finally (cf. *ɲìndìkké* 'food'), but that the only consonants appearing before glides are nasals, e.g., *lan-ya* 'has tasted (intrans.)', *laŋ-wa* 'has tasted (trans.)'. This is in keeping with the general pattern of nasals as the most usual codas, represented by the constraint CodaCond discussed in chapter 4.

---

[42]The voicing assimilation of /g/ to following /k/ is discussed in section 4.2.5.

(400) *CODACOND: only sonorants are allowed as codas (repeated from 159)

This will account for forms such as the perfective aspects in verbs such as /kpat-/ 'finish'.

(401) kpatɪya 'has finished' CODACOND >> DEP[cor], DEP[closed]

kpAt-ya	MAX (C)	DEP (VɸCL)	VG-AGR	CODA COND	DEP [dors]	DEP [cor]	DEP [closed]
☞ a. kpatɪya						*	**
b. kpatya			*!				
c. kpataya		*!					
d. kpaya	*!						
e. kpatʊya			*!		*		

(402) kpatʊwa 'has finished...'

kpAt-wa	MAX (C)	DEP (VɸCL)	VG-AGR	CODA COND	DEP [dors]	DEP [cor]	DEP [closed]
☞ a. kpatʊwa				?			**
b. kpatwa			*!				
c. kpatawa		*!					
d. kpawa	*!						
e. kpatɪwa			*!		*		

The constraints introduced in this section are summarized with rankings below.

(403) MAX[dors], MAX(C), DEP(V_{CL}), DEP(V_{ɸCL}), ŋ//

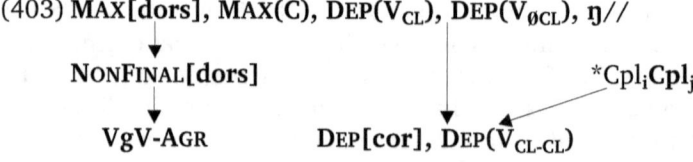

NONFINAL[dors]

VgV-AGR   DEP[cor], DEP(V̄_{CL-CL})   *Cpl_iCpl_j

5.6 The agentive prefix

As presented in section 2.1.3, an agentive noun derived from a verb has both a suffix [-rU/-tU] and a CV prefix,[43] a reduplicative form which includes the initial consonant of the verb and a high vowel. As seen in the data in (404) repeated from (55), the vowel of the reduplicant is either [i, ɪ, u, ʊ]. The vowel is [U] if the first vowel of the verb is back and rounded ([dorsal], in our feature specifications) or if the initial consonant of the verb is [w]. Otherwise, the vowel of the reduplicant is [I].

(404) a. tì-tàà-rú   'thrower, shooter' (taa 'throw')
  b. dì-dìgì-rú   'cooker' (digi 'cook')
  c. dì-dàà-rú   'buyer, seller' (daa 'buy/sell')
  d. mì-mìì-rú   'builder' (mɪɪ 'build')
  e. sì-sìè-rú   'dancer' (sie 'dance')
  f. bù-bùrì-tú   'sower' (bʊrɪ 'sow')
  g. gù-gùù-rú   'burier' (guu 'bury')
  h. jʊ̀-jʊ̀àlì̀-tú 'climber' (jʊalɪ 'climb')
  i. kù-kɔ̀lìn-tú   'mover, migrator' (kɔlɪŋ 'move')
  j. wù-wɔ̀sì-r   'caller' (wɔsɪ 'call')
  k. wù-wàsì-rú   'greeter' (wasɪ 'greet')
  l. yì-yùòrì-tú   'opener' (yuori 'open')

One question to be considered is the specific form of the reduplicant. I will assume a reduplicant with a CV template, rather than a bare C with a vowel epenthesized. The reduplicant vowel does follow the pattern of an epenthetic vowel in that it is always high and generally [coronal]. When the vowel is [dorsal], this can always be traced to the contextual factors of a following [w] or the stem vowel being [dorsal]. However, there is a difficulty in accounting for the [dorsal] in forms like *jʊ̀-jʊ̀àlì̀-tú* 'climber' if the vowel is epenthetic; there is no general process of [dorsal] spreading in Kɔnni; indeed, in section 5.4.1 we saw that [dorsal] did not spread across consonants in general.

A more promising approach is to treat the [dorsal] on the reduplicant vowel as part of the reduplication process. This is formally expressed in Correspondence Theory with a Base-Reduplicant (BR) constraint. McCarthy and Prince (1995) give a partial analysis of a very similar phenomenon in Akan,

---

[43]Though in chapter 2 I proposed that the CV added to the verb stem acts like a compounding process, for brevity's sake I will continue to refer to it as "prefix."

in which there is a CV reduplicative prefix of verbs in which the V is always high, and back/round when the vowel of the verb is back/round, giving the same four vowels [i, ɪ, u, ʊ] which are found in the Kɔnni reduplication. They deal only with the height of the reduplicated vowel and make no comment on the alternation between *I* and *U* in the reduplicated vowel. Their approach to height is an example of an "emergence of the unmarked" (McCarthy and Prince 1994), and I will follow their basic approach, modified by the different vowel features I am using here.

The fact that the reduplicant vowel is always high is intimately tied to the same fact about epenthetic vowels. A high vowel is inserted rather than a mid or low vowel by the interaction of constraints as in (392); a vowel with one or no occurrences of [closed] is dispreferred. The place features of the reduplicant are copied from the base, as expressed in the constraint.

(405) **MAX-BR[pl]:** a vowel place feature in the base has a correspondent in the reduplicant

If the base has a [coronal] or [dorsal] feature for the vowel, the same will be copied as the reduplicant feature. In the case of a base containing /a/, which in our view has no place features, constraints already in place force the reduplicant to have *I* in the output. Below I present five tableaus illustrating the different types of cases represented in the data: where [I] is the reduplicant vowel though /a/ is in the base, where [I] is the reduplicant vowel with a [coronal] vowel in the base, where [U] is the reduplicant vowel due to a [dorsal] vowel in the base, where [U] is the reduplicant vowel due to agreement with a following glide, and where [I] is the reduplicant vowel due to glide agreement even though there is a [dorsal] vowel in the base. The same constraints are presented in each of the tableaus to facilitate comparison, though some of them are not needed in all the tableaus.

(406) dɪ̀-dàà-rʊ́ 'buyer, seller'

	RED-dAA-rU	DEP (V_CL)	DEP (V_ØCL)	VG-AGR	MAX-BR[pl]	DEP [dors]	DEP [cor]	DEP [closed]
☞ a.	dɪ-daarʊ						*	**
b.	dʊ-daarʊ					*!		**
c.	dɛ-daarʊ	*!					*	*
d.	da-daarʊ		*!					

In (406), MAX-BR[pl] is not violated by any candidates, since the input /a/ is placeless. The winning candidate (406a) violates only low-ranked

5.6 The agentive prefix

constraints. The losing candidate (406b) is removed by its violation of DEP[dors]; it has inserted a [dorsal] feature. Candidates (406c and d) lose by not having the reduplicant vowel be high. Recall that DEP(V_{CL}) and DEP($V_{\emptyset CL}$), prohibiting the insertion of mid and low vowels, are undominated (section 5.5.2), while DEP(V_{CL-CL}), prohibiting insertion of high vowels, is ranked low. Any candidate with a mid or low vowel in the reduplicant will fatally violate one of these.

(407) mì-mìì-rú 'builder' MAX-BR[pl] >> DEP[cor]

	RED-mII-rU	DEP (V_{CL})	DEP ($V_{\emptyset CL}$)	VG-AGR	MAX-BR[pl]	DEP [dors]	DEP [cor]	DEP [closed]
☞ a.	mɪ-mɪɪ-rʊ						*	**
b.	mʊ-mɪɪ-rʊ				*!	*		**
c.	mɛ-mɪɪ-rʊ	*!					*	*
d.	ma-mɪɪ-rʊ		*!		*!			

The tableau in (407) differs mainly from (406) in that candidates which do not have [coronal] in the reduplicant vowel violate MAX-BR[pl]. The winning candidate (407a) violates only low-ranked constraints. The losing candidate (407b) would lose by its violation of DEP[dors], since it has inserted a [dorsal] feature, but the violation of MAX-BR[pl] is even more serious. Candidates (407c and d) lose by not having the reduplicant vowel be high, as in (406), but candidate (407d) also loses by violating MAX-BR[pl].

(408) jù-jùàlì-tú 'climber' MAX-BR[pl] >> DEP[dors]

	RED-jOOl-rU	DEP (V_{CL})	DEP ($V_{\emptyset CL}$)	VG-AGR	MAX-BR[pl]	DEP [dors]	DEP [cor]	DEP [closed]
☞ a.	jʊ-jʊalɪtʊ					*		**
b.	jɪ-jʊalɪtʊ				*!		*	**
c.	jɔ-jʊalɪtʊ	*!				*		*
d.	ja-jʊalɪtʊ		*!		*!			

Candidate (408a) wins, though it violates DEP[dors] which ruled out a candidate in the previous tableau. However, in this case, not inserting a [dorsal] feature violates the undominated constraint MAX-BR [pl], as with candidate (408b), which for this reason is ruled out. Candidates (408c and d) are ruled out by a violation of DEP(V_{CL}) or the equally highly-ranked DEP($V_{\emptyset CL}$). Candidate (408d) is also ruled out by not reduplicating the [dorsal] place of the base.

(409) wù-wàsì-rú 'greeter'

RED-wAsI-rU	DEP (V_CL)	DEP (V_ØCL)	VG-AGR	MAX-BR[pl]	DEP [dors]	DEP [cor]	DEP [closed]
☞ a. wʊ-wasɪrʊ				?			**
b. wɪ-wasɪrʊ			*!			*	**
c. wɔ-wasɪrʊ	*!			?			*
d. wa-wasɪrʊ		*!					

The output in (409) also has a [dorsal] vowel in the reduplicant; this is not because of any [dorsal] vowel in the base, but to agree with the initial [w] of the base. Candidate (409a) wins by having the reduplicant vowel agree with the [dorsal] feature of [w], presumably by spreading, but it makes no difference to the outcome if it is by insertion (the question marks under DEP[dors] indicate a conflation of the candidates which have a separate [dorsal] inserted and those which share the same [dorsal] feature as the [w]). Candidate (409c) loses by not having a high vowel in the reduplicant.

(410) yì-yùòrìtú 'opener' **VG-AGR > > MAX-BR[pl]**

RED-yUOrI-rU	DEP (V_CL)	DEP (V_ØCL)	VG-AGR	MAX-BR[pl]	DEP [dors]	DEP [cor]	DEP [closed]
☞ a. yi-yuoritu				*	*		**
b. yu-yuoritu			*!				**
c. ye-yuoritu	*!					*	*
d. ya-yuoritu		*!					

This is the tableau that shows the ranking of VG-AGR over MAX-BR[pl]. The winning candidate (410a) violates MAX-BR[pl] by having a different place in the reduplicant than in the base. However, the losing candidate (410b) violates VG-AGR and so loses by the fact that its reduplicant vowel is [dorsal] while the following glide is [coronal].

5.7 Vowel shortening

In this section, all the alternations involve shortening of a trimoraic sequence to bimoraic, or bimoraic to monomoraic.

5.7 Vowel shortening

5.7.1 Data

Trimoraic vowels are never found within a word in Kɔnni. When a suffix consisting only of a vowel is added to a stem which already ends in a long vowel, the result is a bimoraic vowel length. The noun class 1 suffix /-A/ is a case in point.

(411) Singular   Plural
 níí-ŋ   ní-à   'grinding stone'
 bítí!é-ŋ   bítí-è   'chin'
 díí-ŋ   dí-è   'forehead'
 jí!í-ŋ   jí-à   'tree (sp.)'
 bùntʊ́ʊ́-ŋ   bùntʊ́-rá   'toad'
 dàá-ŋ   dà-rá   'day'

The two-vowel limit in Kɔnni applies only within words. Across words, there may be three vowels, as seen in (410).

(412) Three vowels across words
 bìá !ánísà   'four goats'
 kʊ̀á !átá   'three hoes'

Another case of vowel shortening is found in noun-adjective complexes, where a long /aa/ in the noun stem will often shorten. Interestingly, many words with /aa/ in the input shorten in this environment, as in (413a), but a few do not, as in (413b). (See also (250) for more data; the shortening words outnumber the nonshortening words fourteen to five in my data.) As far as I can tell, there is no property of these words that will enable the prediction of vowel shortening or not, and these nouns must be marked with a diacritic to undergo shortening or not when followed by an adjective.[44]

(413) a. Shortening of /aa/, with ATR spread[45]
 jè-vùkíŋ   'snake (lit., thing wriggling)' (cf. jàà-bú 'the thing')
 fé-bîŋ   'small baboon' (cf. fáá-kú 'the baboon')

---

[44]Another possibility might be that the "variable-length /a/" nouns in (413a) are actually underlyingly short, and become lengthened before the singular indefinite, singular definite, and plural articles, but retain their short /a/ before adjectives. However, such an analysis would predict that all nouns with final short /a/ would lengthen this /a/ before articles, and this does not happen, e.g., bágábá 'forest squirrel', bágábáká 'the forest squirrel', kúrúbâ 'bowl', kúrúbá!ká 'the bowl'.

[45]Shortening of vowels does not occur with other modifiers, e.g., jàám mánà 'every thing', jààbú !géé 'this thing (lit., this-the-thing)'. Any other modifier besides an adjective will necessarily also include a nominal suffix as well.

    gbè-góbíŋ   'short dog' (cf. gbàà-sí 'dogs')
    sìŋkpé!bíŋ   'small peanut' (cf. sìŋkpáábʋ́ 'the peanut')

b. No shortening of /aa, with no ATR spread
    dàà-bîŋ   'small stick' (cf. dàà-kʋ́ 'stick')
    táá-!bíŋ   'small sister' (cf. táà 'sister')
    gùráá-!bíŋ 'small lizard' (cf. gùrá!áŋ 'lizard')

    As noted in chapter 2, some class 1 nouns form their plural not by adding the expected /-A/, as in (414a) (accompanied by shortening to avoid sequences of three vowels), but by shortening the stem vowel and adding [-ra], as in the forms in (414b).

(414) a. Singular   Plural
    bítí!é-ŋ   bítí-è   'chin'
    wíí-ŋ   wí-à   'problem'
    níí-ŋ   ní-à   'lower grinding stone'
    díí-ŋ   dí-è   'forehead'
    nʋ́á-ŋ   nʋ́-à   'mouth'

b. dàá-ŋ   dà-rá   'day'
    sìkpáá-ŋ   sìkpá-rà 'heart'
    sàá-ŋ   sà-rá   'name'
    dàyʋ̀ʋ́-ŋ   dàyʋ̀-rá   'rat'
    ɲʋ́ʋ́-ŋ   ɲʋ́-rà   'chest'
    kʋ̀ʋ́-ŋ   kʋ̀-rá   'hoe'
    gbìɲʋ̀á-ŋ   gbìɲɔ̀-rá 'duck'

    The presence of the shortening and [r]-insertion depends on the quality of the long vowel in the noun stem. Note that in (414a), the long vowels are all front, with the exception of *nʋ́áŋ* 'mouth', but in (414b), the shortening nouns, the vowels are all [aa] or [ʋʋ], as well as the single case of [ʋa] in *gbìɲʋ̀á-ŋ* 'duck'. One case of [ʋa] in my data shortens and one does not, and each of these words is a clear case. There are no cases in my data on noun class 1 of [ɪa], [uu], or [uo], the remaining long vowels. So with the one

5.7 Vowel shortening

exception of *núáŋ* "mouth', the generalization is that stem-final noncoronal long vowels of noun class 1 shorten in the plural form.[46]

5.7.2 Analysis

The apparent shortening of a vowel and insertion of *-r* in some plural forms of noun class 1 has been discussed under consonant epenthesis (section 4.5).

To account for the bimoraic limit on vowel quantity within words we need a constraint to prohibit trimoraic or longer sequences. The constraint could take the form of simply prohibiting three vowels in a row VVV, or alternatively could say that bimoraic VV is maximal; the effect would be the same in either case. I thus propose *VVV as follows:

(415) ***VVV:** trimoraic vowel sequences are prohibited within words

If VVV is prohibited, when such a sequence is present in input, several ways could be conceived of avoiding VVV in the output. The option that Kɔnni usually takes is to elide a vowel. This will rank *VVV above MAX-S. Of the vowels which could be elided, the suffix vowel is never elided. Casali (1997), in his extensive overview of elision phenomena, proposes constraints which I will adopt here. First is a constraint MAX-MS to ensure that the monosegmental suffix vowel is preserved. The vowel that is deleted is from the noun stem or verb, lexical items. Deletion of this vowel will violate the second constraint, MAXLEX, which prohibits deleting a segment from a lexical item.

(416) **MAXMS:** every input segment which is the only segment in its morpheme must have a corresponding segment in the output
MAXLEX: every input in a lexical word or morpheme must have a corresponding segment in the output.

In Kɔnni, it is better to delete a stem vowel than the vowel which is the only segmental content of the morpheme, so MAXMS, preserving the monosegmental morpheme vowel, will be ranked above MAXLEX, which preserves the vowel of the stem.

[46]I speculate that *núà* 'mouths' may be based on an older, fossilized form of Kɔnni. Some support for this comes from the closely related language Buli, in which there is no [-ra] form for some nouns. The plural in Buli for 'mouths' is *noa*, and either from a frozen form or by continuous influence from Buli, the present form has resisted the historical change that added [-ra] to such forms. It may also be relevant to note that 'mouth' is a high-frequency word, and such words tend to resist change more than low-frequency words.

(417) díɛ̀ 'foreheads' *VVV, MAXMS >> MAXLEX, MAX-S

dII-A ATR	*VVV	MAXMS	MAXLEX	MAX-S
☞ a. die			*	*
b. de			**!	**!
c. diie	*!			
d. dii		*!		*

The optimal candidate in (417a) violates MAXLEX and MAX-S once each by deleting one of the verb stem vowels. This is better than candidate (417b), which deletes both of them. Candidate (417c) has a triply-long vowel sequence and so violates *VVV, and the last candidate (417d) elides the suffix vowel and so violates MAXMS.

An interesting variation on the above comes when lexical items having diphthongs (from long mid vowels in the input) have the suffix added. For example, the noun *bítíé-ŋ* 'chin' in plural form *bítíɛ̀* still has the vowel sequence [ie], though the plural suffix has been added. When we combine the constraints above with those pertaining to diphthongization, the correct result is produced.

(418) bítíɛ̀ 'chins'

bItEE-A ATR	MAXMS	*VVV	*[VV]$_{mid}$	HIDIPH	MAX[cl]	MAXLEX	DEP[cl]
☞ a. bitie						*	*
b. bitie	*!						*
c. biteee		*!	*!				
d. bitiee		*!	*!				
e. bitee	*!		*!				
f. biteæ				*!	*!		

Most of the candidates in (418) have violations of more than one top-ranked constraint. The winning candidate, however, violates none except the lower-ranked MAXLEX and DEP[cl]. Candidates (418a and b) are phonetically identical; the difference is that the final vowel in (418a) has its source in the plural suffix /-A/ and a stem vowel is deleted, while the final vowel in (418b) has its source in the stem and the suffixal vowel is deleted, violating MAXMS. Candidates (418c and d) fatally violate *VVV and *[VV]$_{mid}$. Candidate (418e) violates two top-ranked constraints:

5.7 Vowel shortening

MAXMS by eliding the suffix vowel, and *[VV]$_{mid}$ by not diphthongizing. Candidate (418f) also violates two top-ranked constraints: HIDIPH by not having the left member of the diphthong be a high vowel, and MAX[cl] by eliding one of the vowels which has a [closed].

Some lessons can be drawn from this tableau that go beyond the particular candidates at hand. Most of the candidates violated more than one undominated constraint and thus were rejected for more than one reason. If we wanted to have a more concise tableau, it would be possible to omit any one of *[VV]$_{mid}$, *VVV, HIDIPH, or MAX[cl] (or even two of these, as long as one is from the first pair and one is from the last pair) without changing the results that *bitie* is the winning candidate. Two points at least may be noted from (418). First, a particular tableau may present an incomplete picture of the language and still work, correctly picking the winning candidate. Second, a constraint may be highly ranked in the language and relevant to a particular tableau, but not listed at all if the investigator has not examined a wide range of phenomena in that language. Such a tableau would be not only incomplete, but potentially misleading in that it implies that only the constraints listed are relevant.

Finally, the fact that /aa/ in some nouns shortens when followed by an adjective must be expressed by a very specific constraint.

(419) ***aa]-Adj**: an [aa] sequence is disallowed before an adjective

This constraint is surface true, but has no particular phonological or other motivation I can see. At this point, I will assume the constraint as is and leave investigation of its motivation for the future.

(420) jè-bíŋ 'small thing' *aa]-Adj >> FAITH[aa], ALIGN[ATR]μ

	jAA-bIŋ ATR	*aa]-Adj	FAITH[aa]	*]$_{N-Adj}$[ATR	ALIGN[ATR]μ
☞ a.	je-biŋ				*
b.	jaa-biŋ	*!		*	
c.	ja-biŋ			*!	
d.	jee-biŋ		*!		

Compare this with the tableau for *dàà-bîŋ* 'small stick' in (272). In this, the constraint *aa]-Adj is not listed. If it were, the actual optimal candidate *dàà-bîŋ* would violate it.

The conclusion to draw is that *dàà-bîŋ* in some way avoids the effect of *aa]-Adj. It will have to be marked with a diacritic marking it exceptional to this constraint. This is an undesirable result, but also unavoidable. There is no relevant phonological difference between words like *faaŋ*, which undergoes shortening, and *daaŋ*, which does not, so an arbitrary diacritic on one or the other is an unavoidable consequence. The *daaŋ* forms are truly exceptional.[47]

The additional constraints and rankings from this section are in (421).

(421) *VVV, MAXMS   *aa]-Adj
         ↓   ↓
      MAXLEX, MAX-S   FAITH[aa]
                                  ↓
                              ALIGN[ATR]μ

5.8 Epenthesis or elision? Vowels after [g]

In section 5.5, the lack of a vowel between identical consonants was analyzed as due to a failure to epenthesize. But in some words, whether the lack of a vowel between consonants is due to a failure to epenthesize or simply an elision is not so clear. Furthermore, in a good number of cases, the vowel "needs" to be present to block ATR spread. The /I/ after a /g/ seems to be the most common environment for this questionable vowel. In the examples in (422a), it is impossible to tell whether the vowel is part of a stem, or an epenthetic vowel within the stem. However, in the words in (422b), the vowel is epenthetic, based on singular and plural form alternations.

(422) a. bìllɔ̀gìsíŋ   ~ bìllɔ̀ksíŋ   'wind'
         chɔ́g!ísá   ~ chɔ́k!sá   'is making fire'

      b. kágí-bíŋ   ~ kág-bíŋ   'small roan antelope'
         kɔ́gí-!bíŋ   ~ kɔ́g-!bíŋ   'small cleared area'
         tìgì-vìiníŋ ~ tìg-vìiníŋ   'good village'
         tìgì-háá!líŋ ~ tìk-háá!líŋ 'new village'

It thus appears that an underlying vowel *I* is subject to deletion (422a) and a potentially epenthetic vowel fails to epenthesize (422b), under the

---

[47]Alternatively, the shortening words could be marked as exceptional. One set or the other must be. The nonshortening nouns are marked as exceptional on the basis of lexical frequency here: in my database, fifteen nouns undergo shortening of /aa/, while only five do not.

5.8 Epenthesis or elision? Vowels after [g]

same conditions: between [g] and a consonant. This also relates to the citation forms in which root-final *g* deletes altogether when adjacent to a final *-ŋ*, as in *káŋ* 'roan antelope', from /kag-ŋ/ (see section 4.3 for further discussion). There is a surface generalization that the *I* in a *gIC* sequence is not a highly valued vowel, and in OT terms, a constraint or constraints would be needed to penalize the *gIC* sequence.

Even when the vowel is phonetically deleted, however, it acts as if it were still present with respect to ATR spreading. Recall that an ATR adjectival suffix will spread its ATR one syllable into the noun stem (sections 5.2.1–5.2.2). This is illustrated in *kɔ́gí-!bíŋ* 'small cleared area' and *kágí-bíŋ* 'small roan antelope' in (423), with the ATR spreading from the adjective *-bíŋ* into the vowel preceding it. The first stem vowels, ɔ and a, respectively, do not surface as ATR vowels. When there is no phonetic *I* present, we would predict that the stem vowel would surface as ATR, since it would be the only vowel present. However, it does not. With regard to ATR spread from the adjective, the forms *kɔ́g-!bíŋ* and *kág-bíŋ* act as if the vowel were still present.

In a derivational model, of course, the solution would simply be to order a general rule of vowel epenthesis, then ATR spread, then deletion of *I* between *g* and another consonant. In OT, ordering of this type is not an option, and we must explore other possibilities.

One possibility, which is immediately rejectable, is that ATR spread does not occur across an obstruent cluster. Two difficulties with this present themselves. First, we see several cases in which ATR spreads across a NC cluster in (423).

(423) Spreading across NC cluster (repeated from 250)
    chòm-bíŋ 'small father' (cf. chɔ̌ŋ 'father')
    tòŋ-góbíŋ 'short bow' (cf. tɔ̌ŋ 'bow')
    bùn-ní!íŋ 'female donkey' (cf. bùn-dààŋ 'male donkey')
    bùrìn-ní!íŋ 'female oryx' (cf. bùrìn-dààŋ 'male oryx')
    kɔ́ŋkòm-bǐŋ 'small tin can' (cf. kɔ́ŋkɔ̀ŋ 'tin can')

It is not immediately obvious why a CC obstruent cluster should prevent ATR spread but an NC cluster should not. Second, in most cases vowel features spread freely across consonants, the exceptions being a vocalic feature which is blocked by a consonant bearing that same feature. But ATR is a feature that spreads freely across all consonants, and a consonant cluster of whatever type blocking it is not likely.

At least three other possibilities present themselves, to explain the lack of ATR spread in the forms *kɔ́g-!bíŋ* and *kág-bíŋ*, and at this point the advantage of one over the other is based more on simplicity than any other consideration. Part of the decision depends on whether the inaudible vowel is still in some sense present or not. If so, then it will absorb the ATR spread and prevent ATR from spreading further into the noun stem. A second possibility, in which the vowel is phonologically as well as phonetically deleted, is that ATR does not spread into the noun stem *of kág-bíŋ* on the basis of paradigm pressure from other surface forms with *kág-*. The third possibility is that there are two phonological levels in Kɔnni to which different constraints apply. I will briefly examine each of these.

The first possibility relates to the fact that the influence of the vowel remains even though it has no overt phonetic manifestation. In some sense the vowel is "still there" though inaudible. As evidence against the vowel with its timing slot being totally deleted, the duration of the *gIC* sequence and of the *gC* sequence are presented below for two words. Note that the "deletion" of the *I* makes essentially no difference in the duration of the sequence.

(424) 'small cleared area' kɔ́gí-!bíŋ   172 161 180   ave. 171 ms
                            kɔ́g-!bíŋ   152 189 170   ave. 170 ms

     'small roan antelope' kágí-bíŋ   182 182 174   ave. 179 ms
                            kág-bíŋ   142 161 164   ave. 157 ms

Waveforms for three repetitions each of *kɔ́gí-!bíŋ* and *kɔ́g-!bíŋ* are shown in (425), with essentially equal total times represented in each window. Note the presence of a vowel in the top waveforms, though its magnitude is quite variable. The actual duration measurements above were made by zooming in on the relevant portion, then the time of the displayed utterance is read directly from the display at the bottom of the screen.

(425) Waveforms for kɔ́gí-!bíŋ (1:A) and kɔ́g-!bíŋ (2:B), three repetitions each

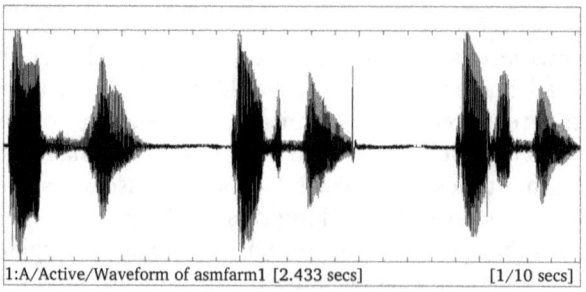

5.8 Epenthesis or elision? Vowels after [g]

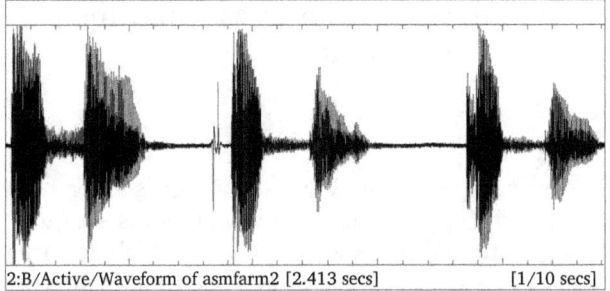

2:B/Active/Waveform of asmfarm2 [2.413 secs]   [1/10 secs]

To account for the influence that a phonetically inaudible vowel has, this proposal is that the vowel is still present but reduced. In this proposal, the moras are conserved, thus the constant duration whether the *I* is audible or not. The inaudible vowel is dissociated from the moraic tier and floats (an older version of OT might say it is not parsed). The ATR from the adjectival suffix does indeed spread to the last vowel of the noun stem, but this vowel is the floating one, inaudible, and the spreading stops at that point. This view assumes the presence of the epenthetic vowel in output. It is perhaps noteworthy that in the top window in (425), the audible presence of *I* is quite variable in *kɔ́gí-!bíŋ*. In the first sample, *I* is barely a blip on the waveform, but is stronger in the second sample and a full-length vowel in the third. This suggests a gradient phonetic elision, with the vowel present in all stages, but having variable phonetic manifestation, including complete phonetic inaudibility. This is the solution I favor.

A second possibility is that paradigmatic pressure from other related forms of *kɔg-*, including the form with vowel epenthesis *kɔ́gí-!bíŋ*, prevents ATR spread into the noun stem. In this scenario, there would be an output-output correspondence constraint regarding ATR which would outrank the constraint *]$_{\text{N-Adj}}$[ATR. The result is that *kɔ́g-!bíŋ*, with no epenthetic vowel, is modeled on the pattern of the form with the epenthetic vowel. Paradigmatic correspondences are an active force diachronically, and have been proposed synchronically in Optimality Theory.

The third proposal is that there are two levels of Kɔnni phonology. In this scenario, in the first level, epenthesis and the constraints to spread ATR are active, giving *kɔ́gí-!bíŋ*. At the second level, the vowel elides, but constraints such as *]$_{\text{N-Adj}}$[ATR are not active.[48] Optimality Theory in general has not adopted this approach, since the theory is largely based on simultaneous evaluation of candidates. But here, as in Roberts-Kohno (1998), there may be a good case made for more than one level.

---

[48]There is also some tonal evidence for two levels, in which a constraint barring HLH on the surface does not seem to apply if the first High tone is a result of spreading from a previous syllable. See section 6.3.2 for discussion and details.

5.9 Vowel assimilation II: Total assimilation in vowel hiatus

5.9.1 Data

Since the most common pattern in Kɔnni is for words and morphemes to be consonant initial, the opportunities for vowel hiatus are quite limited. Within words, there are two suffixal morphemes which consist only of a vowel: the imperfective suffix on verbs, and the plural suffix for class 1 nouns. When these are suffixed to vowel-final stems, the output follows the same patterns that were discussed under "Diphthongization" in section 5.3. Shortening was discussed in section 5.7.

(426) Word-internal vowel hiatus
    a. Imperfective suffix
        /yɪ-A/ → yɪa   'is giving'
        /di-A/ → die   'is eating'
        /su-A/ → suo   'is putting inside'
        /hʊ-A/ → hʊa   'is swearing'
        /to-A/ → tuo   'is taking'
        /ye-A/ → yie   'is seeing'
        /yɛ-A/ → yɪa   'is reducing'
        /dɔ-A/ → dʊa   'is lying down'
        /la-A/ → laa   'is laughing'

    b. Plural suffix
        /sɪ-A/ → sɪa   'fishes (sp.)'
        /bi-A/ → bie   'goats'
        /jʊ-a/ → jʊa   'tails'
        /leeku-A/ → leekuo   'ax handles'
        /bitie-A/ → bitie   'chins'

Similarly, few words in Kɔnni begin with a vowel. Words which are vowel initial include some particles, numbers, and a few nouns. The particles are the personal pronouns *u/ʊ* 'third singular human', *a* 'third singular nonhuman', and the conjunctions *a* 'and', *aŋaŋ* 'and/with', and *amaa* 'but'. Numbers which refer to nonhumans have prefixes *a-* or *aba-*. Finally, a few nouns and names which are borrowed are vowel initial, such as *Ali, áŋ!kʊ́rá* 'barrel'. All verbs are consonant initial. Since I have very little data on the conjunctions, the present study is limited to pronouns, vowel-initial nouns, and numbers occurring after other words.

5.9 Vowel assimilation II: Total assimilation in vowel hiatus

When a number with prefix a- or aba- occurs after a noun (which would need to be plural to take a number of this type), the last vowel of the noun totally assimilates to the a.[49] Note that if a noun ends with a diphthong, as with bìé 'goats', it is only the final vowel of the diphthong that assimilates to the following vowel, and the number of moras remains constant. This assimilation is characteristic of casual speech; in very careful speech there is no assimilation.

(427) a. Variable assimilation with number prefix a-:
    bìé   'goats'   bìá !átá (~ bìé !átâ) 'three goats'
    nííge   'cows'   nííga !átá   'three cows'
    gbààsí   'dogs'   gbààsá !átà   'three dogs'

    b. Variable assimilation with number prefix aba-:
    nííge ʔàbátà   'three cows'   níí!gá ábá!nísà   'four cows'
    bìé !ʔábátà   'three goats'   bìá ábánísà   'four goats'
    gbààsí !ʔábátà 'three dogs'
    múgà àbátà   'three rivers'
    táná !ábátà   'three stones'
    kpìbíè àbátà   'three lice'
    ~ kpìbíà àbátà

    c. Variable assimilation with ataŋ 'some (nonhuman)'
    yísè àtâŋ ~ yísà àtâŋ   'some sheep (PL)'
    nííge àtâŋ ~ níí!gá!átâŋ   'some cows'

This phenomenon is under the speaker's control and is largely dependent on speech rate, as Kɔnni speakers at normal conversational speed produce 'four cows' as níí!gá !ánísà but in careful speech can produce nííge ʔànísà. The phenomena of glottal stop insertion and nonassimilation co-occur; if a glottal stop occurs, the vowel of the first word does not assimilate to the second one. However, the lack of insertion of a glottal stop does not guarantee assimilation, as the variants kpìbíà àbátà ~ kpìbíè àbátà 'three lice' shows. Mr. Amadu almost always pronounced numbers with the aba- prefix with a glottal stop, but almost always did not pronounce a glottal stop with the a- prefix numbers.

---

[49]The phenomenon illustrated here has also been termed compensatory lengthening of the second vowel upon deletion of the first. The phenomenon can be approached in a number of ways, depending on one's theoretical framework. I use the term "total assimilation" here for convenience, not committing myself to any particular representational view by doing so.

A similar but not identical situation occurs with the complementizer *dI* 'that'. This complementizer surfaces as [dI] when followed by a consonant-initial pronoun, as in (428a). However, if *dI* is followed by a vocalic pronoun, its vowel *I* totally assimilates to the vowel of that pronoun, as in (428b).

(428) Vowel assimilation with 'that'
    a. dí !fíbúgúrí   'you(SG) should learn! (that you learn)'
       dí !bé díí   'they should eat'
       dí !tí díí   'we should eat'

    b. dú!ú súgúrí   's/he should wash! (that s/he wash)'
       dʋ́!ʋ́ tíírí   's/he should stretch!'
       dá!á díí   'they(nh) should eat!'

In the case of this complementizer /dI/, I have never heard an instance of nonassimilation, either with or without glottal stop insertion.

The question words which occur sentence initially may have a subject pronoun following, and in such cases there is assimilation.

(429) Vowel assimilation with question words and pronouns
    a. sìá ʋ̀ gáà → sì ʋ́ʋ́ !gáà   'where is s/he going?'
    b. bìá ʋ̀ yíè → bì ʋ́ʋ́ !yíè   'what is s/he doing?'

In some constructions, however, vowels occur in hiatus and there is never assimilation. In constructions having a possessive pronoun followed by noun, the vowels do not assimilate, as in (430a). Similarly, in an associative construction, there is no assimilation of vowels between the two nouns, as in (430b). The glottal stops are a constant feature of Amadu's recordings, but two other speakers (Kwabena Joseph and Tahiru) did not insert glottal stops, while maintaining the pattern of nonassimilation (e.g., *u alwɛsa* 'his/her onion'). Thus the glottal stops in (430) may be regarded as Amadu's insertion to emphasize the word breaks and not essential to the nonassimilation.[50]

---

[50]If Amadu's had been the only recording available, the temptation would have been to emphasize that nouns, perhaps all lexical items, must be consonant initial, and this would have led to a mistaken analysis. The lesson is that speech from more than one speaker is necessary if one is to have confidence in the results.

5.9 Vowel assimilation II: Total assimilation in vowel hiatus

(430) No assimilation: possessive construction
a.
1st person	2nd person	3rd person	
ǹ ʔàdùwá	tì ʔàdùwá	ù ʔá!dúwá	'my, etc. beans'
ǹ ʔàlìvésà	tì ʔàlìvésà	ù ʔàlìvésà	'my, etc. onion'
ǹ ʔáŋ!kúrá	tì ʔáŋ!kúrá	ù ʔáŋ!kúrá	'my, etc. barrel'

b.
ŋ̀ hɔ̀gú ʔá!lívésà	'my wife's onion'
ŋ̀ chùrú ʔáŋ!kúrá	'my husband's barrel'
ŋ̀ hɔ̀gú ʔá!dúwá	'my wife's beans'

When a vocalic pronoun or vowel-initial noun occurs after a verb, there is no assimilation of the hiatus vowels, with or without glottal stop insertion.

(431) No assimilation: after verbs
a. Embedded sentence follows verb
ù yàlá !ú gá	's/he wants to go (s/he wants s/he go)'
ù yàlá !ú díí	's/he wants to eat'
ù bá ù díí	's/he is going to eat'

b. Noun phrase follows verb
kà bíé !ú kúákú má	'it is at his/her farm'
à bíé !ú tígírí mé	'they(nh) are at his/her house'
ǹ nàn lígí ʔáŋ!kúríká	'I will cover the barrel'
ǹ yìé ʔàlìvé!síká	'I see the onion'
ǹ nàŋ ŋɔ́bí ʔàlìvésà	'I will chew beans'
ǹ nàŋ gúú ʔáŋ!kúríká	'I will bury the barrel'
ŋ̀ wó ʔàláámfìà	'I am not well (lit., I lack health)'

c. Pronoun follows noun in appositional NP
ŋ̀ káyí!yúúrì ù bíé síá 'where is Nkayiyuuri?'
Nkayiyuuri 3s exist where

In (431b), again the glottal stops are Amadu's insertions; Kwabena Joseph and Tahiru did not insert them, while maintaining a pattern of nonassimilation (e.g., ŋ̀ wó àlìvésà 'I lack onion').

To sum up, there are three situations with interword vowel hiatus for which I have data. First, vowels in hiatus may optionally (depending on speech rate and carefulness) have an assimilation in which V_1 totally assimilates to V_2, as in (427). Second, V_1 may obligatorily assimilate to V_2, as in (428). Third, with or without insertion of a glottal stop between the hiatus vowels, no assimilation occurs, as in (430) and (431). In all cases of assimilation, it is the final vowel of the first word that assimilates to the initial vowel of the second word. Also, it is noteworthy that vowel-initial nouns never participate in assimilation, but always surface with an initial glottal stop.

5.9.2 Analysis

An analysis of complete vowel assimilation in Kɔnni must account for several patterns. First, the direction of assimilation is always right-to-left. Second, in what appear to be identical phonetic environments, assimilation sometimes does and sometimes does not occur. Third, vowels assimilate rather than elide; the segment count is preserved.

The basic constraint that will drive assimilation is that vowels across words must have the same features (or lack of them). This may be expressed by a constraint $*V_{Fi}\#V_{Fj}$.

(432) $*V_{Fi}\#V_{Fj}$: adjacent vowels across words must be identical in features

The phonetic motivation for such a constraint, and for many assimilations, comes from economy of articulatory effort (Steriade's *Lazy* principle). This constraint is obviously not undominated, since several situations exist in which adjacent vowels across words are not identical.

The direction of assimilation in Kɔnni is always right-to-left, that is, it is the leftmost vowel, ending the first word, which loses its distinctive featural values. Casali (1997) reviews the psycholinguistic evidence for the prominence of word-initial segments and syllables and shows it plays a greater role in word recognition than later segments. I follow Casali in adopting a constraint which values word-initial vowels. Casali stated the constraint in terms of segments and referred to vowels which were prohibited from deleting. In Kɔnni, however, the mora count is almost always preserved, so what this constraint must refer to is the *featural content* of the vowel rather than the vowel itself. This constraint is never violated in Kɔnni; it is top-ranked.

(433) **IDENT(F)-WI:** the feature content of word-initial vowels in the output must be identical to that of the input

The constraint MAX-S is also necessary here and is repeated from (226).

5.9 Vowel assimilation II: Total assimilation in vowel hiatus

(434) MAX-SEGMENT (MAX-S): a segment (root node) in the input has a correspondent in the output

Armed with these constraints, we now present tableaus for *gbààsá !átà* 'three dogs' and *dʊ́!ʊ́ tíírí* 's/he should stretch!'.

(435) gbààsá !átà 'three dogs' IDENT(F)-WI, MAX-S, *V_{Fi}#V_{Fj} > > MAX[cor]$_V$

gbAA-sI AtA	IDENT(F)-WI	MAX-S	*V_{Fi}#V_{Fj}	MAX[cor]$_V$
☞ a. gbaasa ata				*
b. gbaasɪ ata			*!	
c. gbaas ata		*!		*
d. gbaasɪ ta	*!			
e. gbaasa ta	?	*!		*
f. gbaasɪ ɪta	*!			

The winning candidate (435a) violates MAX[cor]$_V$ by deleting the [coronal] place of the input /I/, but violates no others. Candidate (435b) is what is expected for each word pronounced individually, but when the words are in the phrase above, they violate *V_{Fi}#V_{Fj} by having separate vowel qualities across the word boundary. Candidates (435c–e) all have deleted a mora and so fatally violate MAX-S. Candidate (435d) also has lost a word-initial vowel, another fatal violation. Candidate (435e) may have violated IDENT(F)-WI if the featural content of *a* is regarded as lost, with the *a* present in *gbaasa* present independently. However, if this *a* is regarded as the "same" featural content as the elided vowel, then there is no violation. Since (435e) fatally violates MAX-S, it loses regardless of whether it violates IDENT(F)-WI or not. Finally, candidate (435f) fatally violates IDENT(F)-WI by losing the featural identity of the *a* in *ata*. The candidates in the tableau in (436) win and lose for reasons similar to the preceding.

(436) dú!ú tíírí 's/he should stretch!'

	DI U tIIrI	IDENT(F)-WI	MAXMS	MAX-S	*V_{Fi}#V_{Fj}	MAX [cor]_V
☞ a.	dʊ ʊ tɪɪrɪ					*
b.	dɪ ʊ tɪrɪ				*!	
c.	dɪ ɪ tɪrɪ	*!				*
d.	da a tɪɪrɪ	*!				**
e.	dɪ tɪɪrɪ	*!	*!	*		*
f.	dʊ tɪɪrɪ			*!		*

The winning candidate (436a) violates only the relatively low-ranked MAX[cor]_V. Candidate (436b), the one expected if there were no assimilation, fatally violates *V_{Fi}#V_{Fj}. In candidate (436c), assimilation has taken place, but in the wrong direction, violating IDENT(F)-WI. Candidate (436d), in which all vocalic features have been deleted, also fatally violates IDENT(F)-WI. Candidate (436e) has multiple fatal violations based on its deleting the monosegmental morpheme vowel. Finally, candidate (436f) loses by deleting a vowel also.

The form *bia ata* 'three goats' must also be accounted for, especially since on the basis of previous constraints we produced *bie* as output in citation form. There are several features we have not seen previously. For one, this (and others like it like *niiga ata* 'three cows') are the only cases in which a suffix does not agree with its root in ATR value. Thus AGR(ATR), which could have been regarded as undominated with all the data considered to this point, is not only not top-ranked, but is dominated by a constraint, *V_{Fi}#V_{Fj}, which itself is not top-ranked. Obviously, consideration of the full range of data available is necessary to establish the ranking of constraints with any confidence.

(437) bìá !átà 'three goats'

	bI-A AtA ATR	MAX [ATR]	IDENT (F)-WI	MAX-S	*V_{Fi}#V_{Fj}	AGR (ATR)
☞ a.	bia ata					*
b.	bɪa ata	*!				
c.	bie ata				*!	
d.	bie ta		*!	*		
e.	bi ata			*!	*!	

The winning candidate (437a) violates AGR(ATR) by a suffix not agreeing with the root in ATR value, but other candidates fare worse. Candidate (437b) loses by deleting ATR altogether. Candidate (437c) violates the highly-ranked *$V_{Fi}\#V_{Fj}$ by not having the vowels agree across the word boundary. Candidate (437d) loses by deleting the word-initial vowel, and candidate (437e) violates MAX-S and loses by deleting the word-final vowel.

The bigger challenge is to account for those forms which do *not* show total vowel assimilation. Recall that several contexts prevent assimilation, as listed below (data repeated from (430) and (431), with omission of phonetic glottal stops).

(438) a. associative construction
 tì àlìvésà 'our onion'
 ǹ chùrú áŋ!kúrá 'my husband's barrel'

b. embedded sentence follows verb
 ʊ̀ yàlá !ʊ́ gá 'S/he wants to go. (s/he wants s/he go)'

c. noun phrase follows verb
 kà bíé !ʊ́ kúákú má 'It is at his/her farm.'
 ǹ nàn lígí áŋ!kúríká 'I will cover the barrel.'

Since it has been established that it is the leftmost vowel which loses its features in Kɔnni total assimilation, some property of the leftmost vowels in (438) protects them from assimilation. Of course, the glottal stop, as a consonant, serves this function, but I regard this as a phonetic detail which helps implement the strategy of nonassimilation in these cases. As noted in the previous chapter, James Amadu consistently inserted glottal stop noun initially, but other speakers did not. He was implementing a constraint I noted as:

(439) **ONS-lex:** a lexical item must have an onset (repeated from (221) in ch. 4)

Even those speakers who did not insert a glottal stop kept the vowels distinct. That is why I regard the nonassimilation as the more basic phenomenon, and it is to reasons for assimilation versus nonassimilation that I now turn.

Some possibilities may be ruled out immediately. It is not the nature of the vowels involved: assimilation does not occur in *tì àlìvésà* and *lígí áŋ!kúríká* above, but it does occur in *gbaasa ata* (from *gbaasɪ ata*), as shown in (435).

Both have an *I-a* sequence in input, but one assimilates and the others do not. Invoking the constraint MAXMS to protect monosegmental morphemes could rule out assimilation when the potential target vowel is either (1) a vocalic pronoun *ʊ* or (2) the final vowel of a verb, which is always a tense/aspect morpheme. However, the cases in (438a) are not ruled out.

As with the domains associated with ATR spread across words, the solution here depends on the syntactic constructions of the utterances. Let us examine the syntax of the constructions which undergo assimilation compared to those which do not. In Kɔnni, it appears that associative noun phrases are head-final, but other phrases (VP, IP, CP, other NP) are head-initial (Cahill 1993). In the following examples, all glottal stops are omitted to emphasize the syntactic pattern.

(440) a. No assimilation

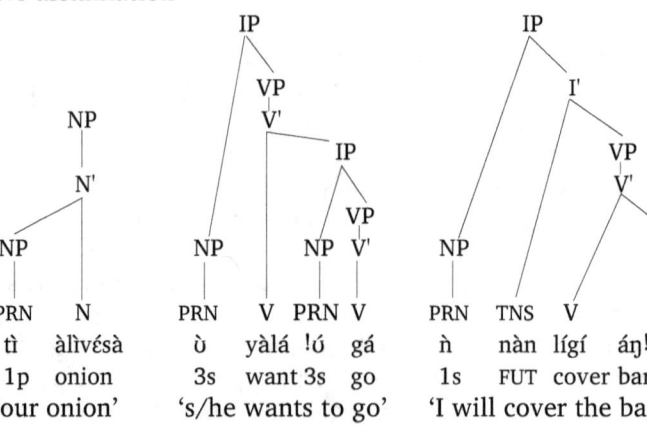

b. Assimilation

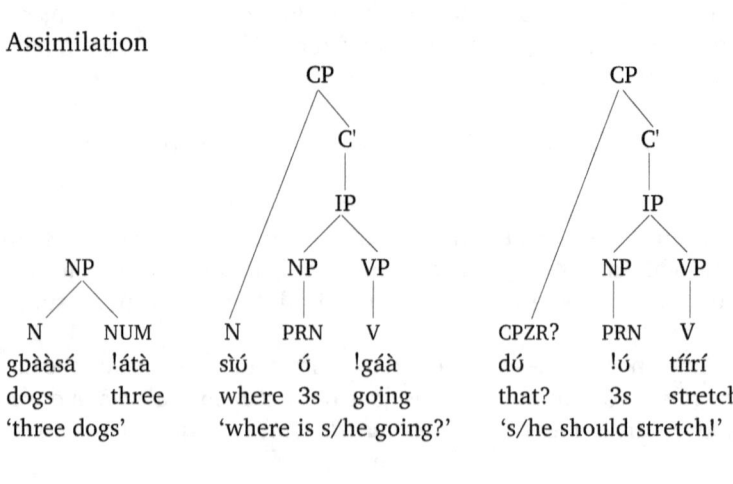

5.9 Vowel assimilation II: Total assimilation in vowel hiatus

There is some question regarding the category some of the words above should bear; for example the category of átà 'three' might be "number," "determiner," or some other possibility. However, the exact label is not crucial to the analysis; its syntactic relationship with the preceding noun is the same. Extracting the node (and its immediate constituents) that dominates the word boundaries in question, where assimilation does or does not take place, gives the following.

(441) a. No assimilation
    tì àlìvésà   'our onion'   N' → NP-N
    ù yàlá !ú gá   'S/he wants to go.'   V' → V-IP
    ǹ nàn lígí áŋ!kúríká 'I will cover the barrel.' V' → V-NP

  b. Assimilation
    gbààsá !átà   'three dogs'   NP → N-NUM
    dú !ú tíírí   'S/he should stretch!'   CP → CPZR-C'
    síú ú !gáà   'Where is s/he going?'   CP → N-C'

The common thread running through the cases in (441a) in which no assimilation occurs is that there is no assimilation between a head of X' and its complement, where the head is a lexical item. In (441b), where there is assimilation, the node immediately dominating the two words is a maximal projection, and none of the words themselves are a maximal projection. Note, however, that the head of C' is not a lexical item. While this generalization needs to be more fully specified, it appears that total assimilation does not take place between a lexical item and a maximal projection. This leads to a constraint which we can express as:

(442) **XP-distinct:** vowels across XP boundaries must be distinct

This constraint does not prevent sequences of identical vowels across XP boundaries, of course, but only requires that each vowel have its own set of features. XP-distinct, unlike ATR-AGR(θ), makes direct reference to the syntactic structure of the utterance and is consistent with the direct reference approach to the syntax/phonology interface espoused by Kaisse (1985) and Odden (1987, 1990a, 1996). Data for various syntactic constructions is quite limited, of course, but XP-distinct is undominated as far as I can tell. It must outrank $*V_{Fi}\#V_{Fj}$, as shown in (443) and (444).

(443) tì àlìvésà 'our onion' **XP-distinct** >> $*V_{Fi}\#V_{Fj}$

tI AlIvEsA	XP-distinct	MAX [ATR]	IDENT (F)-WI	MAX-μ	$*V_{Fi}\#V_{Fj}$
☞ a. tı alıvɛsa					*
b. ta alıvɛsa	*!				
c. tı ılıvɛsa	*!		*!	*	
d. t alıvɛsa				*!	

The winning candidate (443a) violates $*V_{Fi}\#V_{Fj}$ by having different vowels across the word boundary, but satisfies the higher-ranked XP-distinct. Candidate (443b), in contrast, loses by violating XP-distinct. Candidate (443c) fatally violates both XP-distinct, by having vowels with shared features, and also IDENT(F)-WI by changing the features of the input word-initial vowel. Candidate (443d) loses by deleting a vowel altogether. The next tableau repeats the tableau from (437), in which assimilation occurs, but also includes the new constraint XP-distinct, and we see that its inclusion does not change the results, since the syntactic configuration it refers to is not present in the utterance.

(444) bìá !átà 'three goats'

bI-A AtA ATR	XP-distinct	MAX [ATR]	MAX(F) -WI	MAX-μ	$*V_{Fi}\#V_{Fj}$	AGR (ATR)
☞ a. bia ata						*
b. bɪa ata	*!					
c. bie ata					*!	
d. bie ta			*!	*		
e. bi ata				*!	*!	

The new constraints for this section and rankings are presented in (445).

(445) MAX(F)-WI, MAXMS, XP-distinct
   ↓
   MAX-S, $*V_{Fi}\#V_{Fj}$
   ↓
   MAX[cor]$_V$

5.10 Summary and discussion

From the summaries of constraints and their rankings in (316), (342), (377), (403), (421), and (445), the following summary of constraint rankings discussed in this chapter may be compiled. Many of the constraints are represented as undominated, and will undoubtedly remain so even under further scrutiny. However, it would not be shocking if further research uncovered some circumstances in which a constraint listed as undominated is in fact violated. At this point in time, though, I know of no such circumstances; each undominated constraint represents an exceptionless pattern in Kɔnni. Some dominated constraints have been grouped together; this does not necessarily mean they have equal ranking, but it is convenient for display and consistent with the facts of Kɔnni. There are no contradictory rankings here or in the tableaus in this chapter.

(446) Ranking of constraints from (316), (342), (377), (403), (421), and (445)

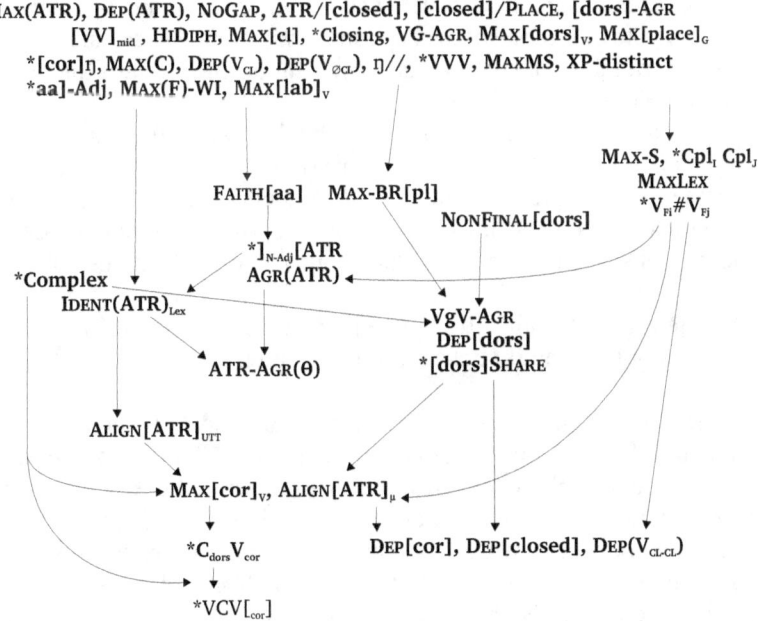

The analysis of Kɔnni vowels has brought to our attention several points about how constraints work in Optimality Theory. These have been noted in the preceding text; here I amplify on them.

In ordinary conversations, people speak in different manners in different circumstances. One speaks more precisely when teaching a child a new word than one does to a friend in a heated discussion, to take two extremes. I have made several references here to careful speech and casual, or normal speed speech, and the differences are significant between the two registers. (Even labeling them as only "two registers" oversimplifies the picture.) Two areas in Kɔnni where register makes a distinct difference is in the areas of total vowel assimilation in hiatus and vowel epenthesis/deletion.

(447) Careful speech   Casual speech
     bìé !átâ   bìá !átâ   'three goats'   (see 427)
     bìlɔ̀gìsíŋ   bìlɔ̀ksíŋ   'wind'   (see 422)

Obviously, the constraints cannot apply in the same way in different speech registers. In this work I have generally concentrated on the casual speech register. A more complete account of Kɔnni or any language must account for the difference between casual and careful speech and specify what subset of rankings of constraints is constant across registers and what varies according to that particular register.

Optimality Theory has been called "the theory that thrives on exceptions," and justifiably so. The principle of constraint violability and interaction can produce a principled account of what appears to be surface exceptions. Nonetheless, even OT must make room for truly exceptional cases, such as the lack of shortening in some /aa/ nouns before adjectives but not others.

(448) jè-bíŋ   'small thing'   (cf. jààŋ 'thing')   (see 420)
     dàà-bîŋ   'small stick'   (cf. dààŋ 'stick')

Some nouns with stem *Caa-* shorten the *aa*, and ATR spreads from an adjectival suffix, and some do not operate this way. There is apparently no relevant systematic phonological difference between those noun stems which shorten and those which do not. In this work, I have assumed that the ones which do not shorten are marked as exceptional; the constraints which force shortening simply do not apply to them. In effect, this is putting a diacritic mark on some words, in the same way as in rule-based models. Archangeli (1999) and Golston (1996) argue for "Direct Optimality Theory" (DOT), i.e., that exceptions have necessary constraint violations, and that seems to be the best approach here.

5.10 Summary and discussion

The matter of which constraint or constraints are most relevant to a particular form is a nontrivial and continuing matter of concern. How does one know if the constraints in the tableau are the "right" ones? In the tableau in (312), a violation of ATR-AGR(θ) rules out the major nonoptimal candidate. The absence of ATR-AGR(θ), however, would not have been crucial for that tableau; the winning candidate would have been selected without it. However, in (312) it is crucial. The moral is that a constraint which is not even listed in a tableau may actually be the one that rules out losers, once a fuller picture of the language is viewed. In (418) also, the same point may be made. A particular tableau may present an incomplete picture of the language and still work, correctly picking the winning candidate. A constraint may actually be highly ranked in the language and relevant to a particular tableau, but not listed at all if the investigator has not examined a wide range of phenomena in that language. Such a tableau would be not only incomplete, but potentially misleading in that it implies that only the constraints listed are relevant. This will always be a point of tension in any analysis, of course, but the uncertainty can be minimized by examining as large a sample of the language as possible. I predict that many OT analyses of small samples of languages will be found to have the relevant constraints not even listed in tableaus, or the rankings significantly changed. A case in point from this study is the constraint AGR(ATR), which is undominated with regard to most of the data in this chapter. It is only when the topic of total vowel assimilation is examined that we discover it can be violated. Obviously, considering the full range of data available is necessary to establish the ranking of constraints with any confidence.

This is a definite point of difference with a rule-based account. In a rule-based approach, omitting a rule has direct and definite consequences; some process does not occur which the rule would force to occur. In OT, there may be many constraints which rule out a particular candidate, and for a particular tableau, omitting one or more may not make any difference in selecting the correct output.

A final comment reaches beyond the theory of OT into the implications of underspecification. There have been claims that normally the maximally unspecified vowel is the epenthetic vowel. This is clearly not the case in Kɔnni, where *I* is epenthetic (or *U* if [dorsal] spread occurs), but these are not maximally unspecified. The high vowel which is inserted has the *most* number of occurrences of [closed]. The totally unspecified vowel /a/, is not the epenthetic one. Interestingly, the same point can be made even using SPE features, as in Cahill (1994). In that feature system, using Radical Underspecification, *I* was still not the most unmarked vowel. In the vowel height system of Clements (1991), in which multiple instantiations of the binary feature [open] are possible, all vowels would have the same number of height features on the surface, with the high vowels being [−open, −open], and /a/ being [+open, +open]. If a version of underspecification is chosen which takes [−open] as default, then /I/ could be unspecified for height features. However, /I/ is specified for [coronal] place, and thus both /A/ and /I/ have some underlying specification.[51] We conclude that claiming an epenthetic vowel is chosen as epenthetic because of its lack of underlying specification is not always a productive approach.

---

[51] Using the [±open] feature for vowel height rather than [closed] as I have done in this work has other implications for Kɔnni, largely due to its binary nature. Diphthongization, for example, would become much more complex, with the pattern /εε/ → [ɪa] involving V_1 changing a [+open] to [−open], and also V_2 changing [−open] to [+open], but only in this circumstance. This has the same drawbacks as using traditional [high] and [low] features discussed in section 5.3.2.2.

6

Tone

Gur languages, with the sole exception of Koromfe (Rennison 1997), are tonal, like most other sub-Saharan African languages. Not as much analysis has been done on tone in the Gur family as has been done in other African language families such as Kwa and Bantu, and within the OT framework, most African languages which have been analyzed have been Bantu languages (listed below). These have far different tonal characteristics than Gur languages. For example, Bantu languages may often be analyzed as having only a High tone that is phonologically present (e.g., Makonde in Odden 1990b, and discussion in Odden 1995). In contrast, Kɔnni requires a Low tone both in underlying and surface forms to account for the phenomena of downstep and contour tones on single TBUs. Also, as with any language, Kɔnni has its own unique characteristics and idiosyncrasies, e.g., a H!H contour on a single tone-bearing unit (TBU), a virtually unpublished phenomenon in African languages.[1] We will also see that disyllabic nouns with a citation LH tone pattern actually must have one of four distinct underlying tonal representations to account for differences in perturbational patterns.

Works having to do with Gur tone include those in this paragraph. The references noted are fairly comprehensive as far as what is available in English,

---

[1] I am aware of only two other published cases of H!H on a single TBU. Essien (1990:55) briefly reports for Ibibio a "type of falling tone consist[ing] of a sequence of high and downstepped tones rather than high and low tones." My thanks to Kevin Cohen for bringing this to my attention. Casali (1995) in his footnote 22 mentions the verb *naa* 'walk' is *náà* in the completive and *nálá* in the incompletive. Besides these published sources, Marj Crouch demonstrated to me in 1985 a H!H contour on a single TBU in Deg, another Gur language. It remains to be seen how many other languages of West Africa have this feature. What seems unusual at the present time may turn out to be more underreported than unique.

less so for French, but do not include material available in any other language. Two dissertations dealing largely with Gur tone are Garber (1987) for Sucite and Peterson (1971) for Mooré, as well as Issah's (1993) master's thesis. Articles dealing with tone in Gur languages include Akanlig-Pare (1997), Anttila and Bodomo (1996, 2000), Cahill (1998b), Carlson (1983), Hyman (1993), Kebikaza (1994), Kedrebéogo (1997), Kenstowicz, Nikiema, and Ourso (1988), Kinda (1997), Rialland (1981, 1983), Schaefer (1975), and Somé (1998). Monographs on Gur languages which include a discussion of tone are Awedoba (1993), Beacham (1968), Bodomo (1997), Carlson (1994), Kröger (1992), Mills (1984), Olawsky (1996), Ourso (1989), Russell (1985), and Winkelmann (1998). Issues of the Collected Field Notes Series of the University of Ghana always include some mention of tone, including contrastive levels and notes on tonal perturbations and downstep. Issues which include somewhat greater detail include Cahill (1992a), Callow (1965), Hunt (1981), and Steele and Weed (1966).

All Gur languages have either two or three contrastive tone levels, with a majority being two-tone systems in keeping with the cross-linguistic observation that two-tone languages are the most frequently encountered (Maddieson 1978). Consonant-tone interactions have been noted for Mooré (Kinda 1997) and Dagara (=Dagaare; Somé 1998), but do not seem to exist in Kɔnni.

Within an Optimality Theory framework, analyses of tone are available for a variety of non-African languages, including North Kyung-Sang Korean (Kim 1997), Chinese (Yip 1996), Min languages (Jiang-King 1998), Navajo (Fountain 1998), Mixteco (Tranel 1996), and Mamainde (Eberhard 2003). Most OT analyses of African tone have been with Bantu languages, including Chichewa (Myers and Carleton 1996), Runyankore (Poletto 1996, 1998a), Ekegusi and others (Bickmore 1996), Isixhosa and Shingazidja (Cassimjee and Kisseberth 1998), Venda (Reynolds 1997), Yao (Odden 1998), and Olusamia (Poletto 1998b). Non-Bantu African languages in which at least some tonal analysis has been done are far fewer, but include the Edoid languages Etsako and Bini (Akinlabi 1995, 1996) and the Khoisan languages Ju|'hoasi and !Xoo (Miller-Ockhuizen 1998). The only Gur language which has any tonal analysis available in OT is Dagaare (Anttila and Bodomo 1997, 2000).

Other analyses of tone in Bantu languages have used various versions of ALIGN constraints to account for spreading, but I have not found these to be the main driving force in Kɔnni. In the previous chapters of this book, though an autosegmental representation has been assumed with little comment, it has not been crucial in most of the analysis. However, with respect to tone, the association of tones with TBUs becomes critical.

In keeping with the general strategy of concreteness, with inputs identical to outputs unless there is good reason to posit otherwise, I will operate under the assumption that tones are linked to TBUs in the lexicon. This is consistent with the view of Lexicon Optimization in Inkelas, Orgun, and Zoll (1996), Inkelas (1994), and Prince and Smolensky (1993).

6.1 Introduction to Kɔnni tone

6.1.1 Tone inventories and distribution

Kɔnni has two basic tone levels, High and Low. A downstepped High tone also may occur after a High. I follow the usual conventions of marking a High tone with acute accent (á), a Low tone with grave accent (à), and downstepped High with superscripted exclamation point (!á). The minimal and near-minimal tone pairs (and the one triplet) below are all that occur in my data; there are undoubtedly more in the language, but Gur languages in general do not have the density of minimal tone pairs common in many languages of Nigeria and Cameroon, for example. Nouns are chosen to illustrate tonal contrasts, since verbs have no lexical tone and other categories of words are not as easily comparable. Choosing nouns in citation form does have the disadvantage that most of the forms below end with a High tone. This is the result of the word-final singular suffix -ŋ́ (see section 6.1.3).

(449) Monosyllabic
LH (rising) versus H

kǔáŋ	'back'	kúáŋ	'farm'
dǎáŋ	'stick, day'	dááŋ	'alcoholic drink'
nǐíŋ	'net, rain'	nííŋ	'lower grinding stone'
ɲǐŋ	'bush partridge'	ɲíŋ	'tooth'
ɲǔŋ	'market'	ɲúŋ	'yam'
sǔŋ	'inside'	súŋ	'broom'
ɲǔúŋ	'tree'	ɲúúŋ	'chest'

LH (rising) versus H!H

| jǐíŋ | 'spitting cobra' | jí!íŋ | 'tree (sp.)' |

H versus H!H

| chííŋ | 'moon, month' | chí!íŋ | 'squirrel' |
| gbííŋ | 'catfish' | gbí!íŋ | 'sleep' |

HL versus LH
chîàŋ	'chair'	chìáŋ	'bottom, waist'
mî	'older sibling' (same sex)	mìí	'biting ant'

HL versus H!H
lîà	'daughter'	lí!áŋ	'ax'
yî	'blind person'	yí!íŋ	'nail, arrow'

HL versus H
táà	'sister'	tá	'and (between verbs)'

a tone triplet
kpááŋ	'oil'	kpààŋ	'back of head'	kpá!áŋ	'guinea fowl'

Disyllabic
LH versus HH
kpìbíŋ	'louse'	kpíbíŋ	'shea nut'
nùámíŋ	'floor pounder'	núámíŋ	'scorpion'
ɲùùrí	'the tree (sp.)'	ɲúúrí	'the chest'
yìsíŋ	'duiker antelope'	yísíŋ	'sheep'

LH versus H!H
hààríŋ	'tree (sp.)'	háá!ríŋ	'boat'
kpììlíŋ	'thigh'	kpíí!líŋ	'hawk (sp.)'
lààlíŋ	'cockroach'	láá!líŋ	'playing'
'tùùlíŋ	'headpad'	túú!líŋ	'heat'

LLH versus HH
nànjùúŋ	'pepper'	nánjúúŋ	'fly'

The attested surface (or "phonetic") tones which are found on nouns are as follows (besides the forms in (449), see sample forms in appendix A). Contours on a single syllable are indicated by hyphens between the two tones.

(450) Phonetic sequences of tones on nouns in varying tonal contexts
One-syllable: H, L-H, H-L, H-!H
Two-syllable: HH, HL, LH, LL, H!H, LH-!H
Three-syllable: HHH, HHH-L, HHL, HH!H, H!HH, HLL, LHH, LH!H, LLH, LLL

Four-syllable: HHHH, HHH!H, H!HHH, LHLL, LLH!H
Five-syllable: LLHLL

It is noteworthy that the number of tonal possibilities actually realized is far fewer for longer nouns than for shorter ones. The four- and five-syllable nouns are mostly either compounds or borrowed. An examination of the patterns above and elsewhere leads to the following generalizations:

(451) Surface generalizations about Kɔnni tone
   a. There are very few Low-toned nouns; the only ones I have are di- and trisyllabic, and even these surface as Low in very restricted contexts
   b. There is no HLH sequence phonetically within a word, and only rarely across words.
   c. Contour tones are only found on the last syllable of a word, with very rare exceptions
   d. A contour in Kɔnni has a maximum of two pitch levels, H-L, L-H, or H-!H , i.e., a maximum of two tones associated to a TBU.

As we will see in the course of the analysis, there are other generalizations as well.

   e. High tones do not remain floating, but Low tones can float between Highs, causing downstep.
   f. High tones always remain associated to the TBU that sponsors them.

These generalizations will form the basis for several of the constraints in OT which are proposed here.

6.1.2 Representation and tone-bearing units

An autosegmental representation of tones is assumed in this work, with each tone acting as an entity which may be referred to independently of the segmental material accompanying it. Thus tones are represented on a tier separate from segmental features, as in Goldsmith (1976) and the extensive literature arising from that work. A more detailed representation of tonal features such as [±raised, ±upper] (e.g., Pulleyblank 1986), or the representation of pitch register and pitch height on separate tiers (e.g., Snider 1990, 1999) is not necessary for our purposes here. While the Kɔnni analysis is translatable into such systems, these extra enrichments of representation would not be illuminating, and the tones will be abbreviated simply as H for High tone and L for Low tone.

Odden (1995) cites evidence from different languages which seem to indicate that the unit to which tone relates (the tone-bearing unit or TBU) is apparently the mora in some languages and the syllable in others and concludes that more research is needed to definitively settle the question of what the TBU is. Until a theory which can unify these behaviors is developed, individual researchers will assume either the mora or the syllable as the TBU for the particular language under study. There are at least two lines of evidence in support of the syllable rather than the mora as the tone-bearing unit (TBU) in Kɔnni. First, tonal distribution patterns are described in terms of syllables rather than moras, and second, in spreading and other processes which change a tone, the tone of the whole syllable is affected, not just a mora.

Kɔnni tolerates a maximum of two pitch levels per syllable, as I noted in (451d): rising, falling-to-Low, or falling-to-downstepped High. Phonologically, this corresponds to two tones associated per syllable. These two associated tones may be either HL, LH, or in the case of [H!H], there are two Highs associated with a floating Low between (see section 6.1.4). This restriction holds for all syllable weights: CV, CVV, CVN, or CVVN.

(452) CV   kúrúbâ   'bowl'

      CVV   táà   'sister'
               bùá   'child'
               ù nàn dí lá!á   'S/he will be laughing.'

      CVN   tăŋ   'stone'
               á tôŋ   'to work'
               kàmbálú!ŋ́   'frog (sp.)'

      CVVN   gàáŋ   'land'
                chǐàŋ   'chair'
                tá!áŋ   'shea tree'

Not all these tonal patterns are attested in every grammatical context, but that is not the point. The data above shows what is possible on a single syllable (of course, besides the contours above, a level High or Low tone is possible on every syllable type as well).

For CV syllables, only the HL falling tone is attested. This is the only context in which the mora might be relevant in Kɔnni tonology; two moras are required for a LH rising or a H!H falling tone. However, whether the mora as a formal unit is relevant is still open to question, though there is no doubt that extra duration of the syllable is necessary to accommodate any contour tone other than HL falling. This is in accord with the observation that HL is the most common type of contour in tonal languages (Maddieson 1978, Yip 2002).

If in fact the mora were the TBU, then a vowel or a syllable-final nasal would each contribute to the mora count. This view would predict that the last syllable pattern, CVVN, would have three moras and could accommodate three tones (e.g., gàáǹ), but this pattern is completely unattested.[2] The pattern of contour tonal distributions is more evidence that the TBU is the syllable, no matter what the length.

Also, when a syllabic nasal follows a vowel, that nasal becomes desyllabified, and the V+N unit becomes one TBU (see examples in (80) and (589)). If the TBU depended on the mora count, there should be no change in the number of TBUs, but if the TBU is the syllable, this behavior is readily accounted for.

Another line of evidence that supports the syllable as the TBU is the behavior of words such as *kaanɪ* 'one' with respect to spreading of High tone. As we will discuss in greater detail later, a HLH underlying tone is realized as H!HH on the surface. Thus in *zàsíŋ* 'fish' and *ŋ̀ wó !zásíŋ* 'I lack fish', the High-toned *wó* verb preceding the LH of the noun creates an underlying HLH sequence which is realized as H!HH. However, if two Low-toned TBUs intervene between the High tones, the underlying HLLH also surfaces as HLLH, as in *ŋ̀ wó dàmpàlá* 'I lack bench'.[3] The question, then, is whether the first two moras of *kaanɪ* [ka-a] act like two TBUs, with two instances of Low, or one.

If *kaanɪ* is preceded by a Low tone on the head noun, the two first moras [aa] are on the same Low pitch, and the second syllable [nɪ] is High-toned, as in *kàgbà kààní* 'one hat'. However, if the preceding noun ends in a High tone, the entire word *kaanɪ* is pronounced on the same pitch, as a downstepped High tone, as in *zàsíŋ !káání* 'one fish'. The long vowel in *kaanɪ* acts as if it were a single TBU with a single Low tone, as in

---

[2]One might wonder about the possibility of a bimoraic maximum to a syllable, in which case *gaaŋ* would be one syllable divided into moras as *ga.aŋ*. Assuming a limit of one tone per mora, this would correctly predict the maximum two tones on *gaaŋ*. However, if *aŋ* were one mora, this schema would be incorrect in predicting a limit of one tone on a *CVŋ* word, whereas in fact there are multitudes of such words with rising tones, e.g., *tăŋ* 'stone', *jŭŋ* 'tail', etc.

[3]See discussion in section 6.1.6 for evidence that *dàmpàlá* has two Low tones rather than one.

zàsíŋ rather than *dàmpàlá* in the preceding paragraph. Therefore, the long vowel in *kààní* and other words might have a configuration something like the following (omitting a moraic tier):

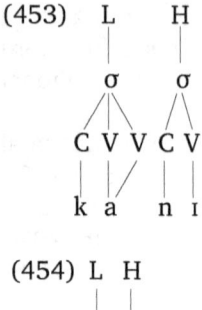

(454) L H
 | |
 kaanɪ

However, I will use (454) as a shorthand representation for (453), and the L tone is to be regarded as being linked to the whole syllable *kaa*. All vowel sequences in the same word, such as [ɪa] or [ʊa], are a result of diphthongization of long mid vowels and are likewise in the same syllable.

For completeness' sake, I also mention syllabic nasals here. These occur only in one morpheme, the first-person singular pronoun, and also bear tone, which may differ from the following syllable, as in [m̀ bʊ̀àwá] 'my child', [ń !náá] 'my mother', [ŋ̀ gá...] 'I went to...'.

It is perhaps also relevant to note that other Gur languages such as Mooré, Lama (both in Kenstowicz et al. 1988), Dagaare (Anttila and Bodomo 1997), Vagla (Crouch 1985), and Dagbani (Hyman 1993) all have been analyzed with the assumption that the syllable is the TBU. While no comprehensive survey has been done, it appears that the syllable as TBU may be a familial or at least areal characteristic of Gur languages.

6.1.3 High-toned nominal suffixes

The table in (455) is extracted from appendix B and contains a selection of various tone patterns by noun class. The most striking generalization to be noted is that an overwhelming majority of nouns, whether singulars or plurals, definite or not, end with a High tone, whether downstepped High or nondownstepped High. The exceptions are some plurals in classes 1 and 3 and a few singulars in class 3 and 5.

6.1 Introduction to Kɔnni tone

(455)

Nouns	Singular	Singular + definite	Plural	Plural + definite
Noun class 1	/-ŋ/	/-rÍ/	/-A/	/-A-hÁ/
'stone'	tăŋ	tànní	tàná	tànáhá
'chest'	ɲúúŋ	ɲúúrí	ɲúrà	ɲú!ráhá
'nail'	yí!íŋ	yíí!rí	yíímà	yíí!máhá
'bee'	síébíŋ	síébírí	síébíè	síébíé!hé
'breast'	bììsíŋ	bììsìrí	bììsá	bììsáhá
Noun class 2	/-ŋ/	/-kÚ/	/-tÍ/	/-tÍ-tÍ/
'courtyard'	gbààŋ	gbààkú	gbààtí	gbààtítí
'farm'	kúáŋ	kúákú	kúátí	kúátítí
'hawk'	kpíí!líŋ	kpíí!líkú	kpíí!lítí	kpí!lítítí
Noun class 3	/-ŋ/	/-kÁ/	/-sÍ/	/-sÍ-sÍ/
'person'	vúóŋ	vúóké	vúósí	vúósísí
'dawadawa tree'	dùùŋ	dùùká	dùùsí	dùùsísí
'axe'	lí!áŋ	líá!ká	líásî	líá!sísí
'fly'	nánjúŋ	nánjúká	nánjúsí	nánjúsísí
'man'	dèmbíŋ	dèmbìké	dèmbìsí	dèmbìsísí
'headpan'	tá!síŋ	tásí!ká	tásísí	tásí!sísí
'lizard'	gùrá!áŋ	gùráá!ká		
'cookpot'	kúrúŋbâ	kúrúbá!ká		
Noun class 4	/-ŋ/	/-bÚ/	/-tÍ/	/-tÍ-tÍ/
'water'	ɲááŋ	ɲáábú	ɲáátí	ɲáátítí
'meat'	nɔŋ	nɔmbú	nɔntí	nɔntítí
'sleep'	gbí!íŋ	gbíí!bú	gbíí!tí	gbíí!títí
'peanut'	sìŋkpááŋ	sìŋkpáábú	sìŋkpáátí	sìŋkpáátítí
'ash'	táɲéé!líŋ	táɲéé!líbú		
Noun class 5	/-Ø/	/-wÁ/	irreg.	irreg.
'child'	bùá	bùáwá	bàllí	bàllílí
'woman'	hɔgú	hɔwwá	hùáŋ	hùàbá
'sister'	táà	táá!wá	táá!líŋ	táálí!bá

So a reasonable hypothesis is that all the suffixes (with the systematic exception of the plurals [-a/-e] in noun class 1) are High toned. These will include the singular indefinite suffix /-ŋ/, the singular definite suffixes /-rÍ/, /-kÁ/, /-kÚ/, /-bÚ/, /-wÁ/, the plural markers /-tÍ/, /-sÍ/, /-lÍ, -líŋ, -ŋ/, and the plural definite suffixes /-hÁ/, /-tÍ/, /-sÍ/, /-bÁ/. The only singular indefinite nouns which end in a Low tone lack the -ŋ suffix; these are from noun classes 3 and 5 (see forms in appendix B). Every noun ending in -ŋ also ends in a High tone, whether in citation form or in a larger context, as shown by data in appendix A. Therefore, any noun with -ŋ will have a final High tone in underlying representation.

The plural suffixes of noun class 1, which consistently surface with a tone opposite to the previous stem tone, will be examined below in section 6.3.3, and the alternations in the -sI suffix of noun class 3 will be discussed in section 6.3.2, but all the other noun suffixes have a High tone lexically.

6.1.4 Downstep from underlying Low tone

In some languages, such as Supyire (Carlson 1983) and KiShambaa (Odden 1982), downstep occurs when two High autosegments are adjacent, and the downstep marks the boundary between the two. However, in Kɔnni, two adjacent Highs can peacefully coexist with no phonetic perturbation. For example, both noun stem and suffix in *díí-rí* 'the forehead' have High tones, and the result is [HH]. The downstep in Kɔnni, as in many languages, can be shown in many cases to have an underlying Low in that location through alternations with different suffixes. For example, when the plural definite suffix of noun class 1 (High-toned *-há*) is added to a plural noun ending in Low, a downstep results.

(456) ɲúrà   'chests'
      ɲú!ráhá   'the chests'

The existence of downstep will be explained by the presence of a floating Low tone, as has been done for many languages. The representations for 'chests, the chests' is given in (457). The Low that is present and associated in 'chests' is still present but floating in 'the chests', a result of a spreading explained in section 6.2.2.

(457) H L   H L   H
      | | | /|
      ɲʊ ra   ɲʊ ra ha

In this conceptualization, a word like *kpá!áŋ* 'guinea fowl' would be represented as having a HLH tone pattern, with the Low floating and causing downstep. Further examples will be seen as we progress through this chapter.

6.1.5 Floating associative morpheme

The morpheme which marks the associative construction for third person, as in 'his/her stone' or 'child's stick', is posited to be a segmentless High tone. The evidence for this is that the head noun of every such construction has a High tone on its initial syllable. Note in (458) that *daaŋ* in the third-person columns starts with a High tone, while the first- and second-person forms do not.

(458)
	1st	2nd	3rd	3rd nonhuman	
singular	ǹ dààŋ	fì dààŋ	ʊ̀ dá!áŋ	kà dá!áŋ	'my, etc. stick'
plural	tì dààŋ	nì dààŋ	bà dá!áŋ	à dá!áŋ	

If the head noun already has a High tone on its first syllable in citation form, then there is no change when it is placed in an associative construction. Examples are given in (459) with both pronouns and nouns as possessors. The examples in (459a) are taken from appendix A, and those in (459b) are taken from appendix E.

(459) a. tǎŋ ʊ̀ **tá!ŋ́** 'stone, his stone'
       zàsíŋ ʊ̀ **zá**!síŋ 'fish, his fish'
       dàmpàlá ʊ̀ **dám**!pálá 'bench, his bench'

    b. bʊ̀àwá **dá!áŋ** 'child's stick' (cf. bʊ̀àwá 'the child', dààŋ 'stick')
       bʊ̀á **káréntìà** 'child's cutlass' (cf. bʊ̀á 'child', kàréntìà 'cutlass')
       chʊ̀rú **dám**!pálá 'husband's bench' (cf. chʊ̀rú 'husband', dàm!pàlá 'bench')

The alternation between the initial Low for head nouns in citation form and the initial High in the associative construction is explained by the existence of a High tone between the two nouns (similar to the **'s** in English "child**'s** stick"). The High associates to the head noun, giving the observed pattern of a High tone on the first syllable (sometimes as part of a H!H contour on that syllable, as in 'stone' and 'stick' above). The matter of directionality as well as the entire associative tonal pattern will be discussed in more detail in section 6.3.6.

6.1.6 The absence of the OCP in Kɔnni

In words such as ɲúúrí 'the chest', I have indicated the tones as HH. There is no phonetic difference between two distinct High tones and one High multiply associated to the two syllables. In some languages, sequences of two identical tones are not allowed, and they either merge, as in HH → H, or one dissimilates, as in Meeussen's Rule HH → HL (Goldsmith 1984) or a downstep (possibly a floating Low) is inserted between them. However, in Kɔnni, it does not seem that the OCP is active with regards to tones. We can see cases for both High and Low tones in which sequences of LL or HH must be allowed.

For High tones, consider the case of *ják-â* 'shades' and *múg-à* 'rivers' (singulars are *jágŋ́* and *múgʊ́ŋ*, both with epenthetic vowels before the final *-ŋ*). Both are representative of several words, i.e., neither is a unique case, and both have the tonally "polar" plural suffix *-a*, to be further discussed in section 6.3.3, which in both of these words inserts a Low tone, since the previous tone is High. The question, of course, is how to explain the difference between the final Low tone in *múgà* and the final HL falling tone in *jágâ*. The fall cannot be the result of a spreading process, since it does not occur in *múgà*. The solution is that *jágâ* has two adjacent High tones in underlying representation, and *múgà* has one, as in (460).[4]

(460) H H L   H L
       | |/ | |
       ja ga   mʊ ga

Two adjacent High tones are thus allowed in Kɔnni, and I assume for the rest of this work that when two High tones adjoin, as in ɲúú-rí 'the chest', that the surface representation does contain two distinct High tones, not one.

(461) H H
       | | ɲúú-rí 'the chest'
       ɲʊʊ-rɪ

Evidence is available that shows two Low tones are also distinct from a single Low autosegment associated to two TBUs. The word *dàmpàlá*

---

[4]This argument establishes that the OCP is inactive at an underlying level, but it might be possible for the two high tones to fuse on the surface as a result of the OCP. The result would be phonetically identical to two separate High tones, and there is no empirical test to distinguish the two in Kɔnni. However, it is more consistent with the constraints proposed in this chapter for the two High tones to remain in output representation, chiefly due to the undominated constraint MAX(H) prohibiting deletion of a High tone. For the tableau of *jágâ*, see (502).

6.1 Introduction to Kɔnni tone

'bench (lit., logs)', contrasted with *bʊ̀rɪ̀mɪ́ŋ* 'oryx' shows the difference between words with a single multiply-linked Low and two adjacent Lows. Each of these words has two TBUs which bear Low tones. However, in a context in which *dàmpàlá* and *bʊ̀rɪ̀mɪ́ŋ* have a High-toned word preceding them, they exhibit different tonal behavior.

(462) dàmpàlá   ŋ̀ wó dàmpàlá   'bench, I lack bench'
      bʊ̀rɪ̀mɪ́ŋ   ŋ̀ wó !bʊ́rɪ́mɪ́ŋ   'oryx, I lack oryx'

As previously mentioned, and to be discussed in more detail in section 6.2.2, a HLH underlying tone is realized as H!HH on the surface. A single Low between Highs is not associated, but is always floating, resulting in downstep. However, if more than one Low is present between Highs, then these Lows are associated and pronounced with Low tone. My claim is that the difference in tonal behavior between 'bench' and 'donkey' is the result of the presence of two lexical Low tones versus one.

(463) a. Underlying representations

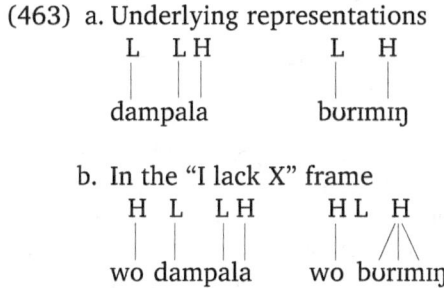

b. In the "I lack X" frame

Two Low tones, then, may also be adjacent without merging or otherwise changing in any way.[5]

Since identical adjacent tones may exist for both High and Low tones, it is evident that the OCP cannot be an all-pervasive constraint in Kɔnni. It is possible, of course, that the OCP is active in some restricted context, and that is one possibility for the polar plural suffix of noun class 1 discussed in section 6.3.3. But since the OCP is definitely not active in the contexts above, it is quite possible that it is never active in Kɔnni; empirically, it is never necessary to invoke the OCP to explain tonal phenomena in Kɔnni.

---

[5]The basic claim is two Low tones versus one in these examples. However, the picture is complicated when we consider the possibility that the *ɪ* in *bʊrɪmɪŋ* is epenthetic. If so, to be consistent with the constraint rankings developed in this chapter, the Low on it in citation form would be inserted and there would be two Lows in citation form, though not in the input. Still, only one Low would be present in the "I lack X" form for *bʊrɪmɪŋ*, contrasting with the two Lows present in the "I lack X" form for *dampala*.

6.2 Basic tonal constraints

6.2.1 Beginning constraints

From the beginning of autosegmental theory (Goldsmith 1976), it was seen that the optimal configuration, or at least the starting configuration in a derivational framework, was that there was one tonal autosegment associated to one TBU. It was when there were more tones than TBUs, more TBUs than tones, or some language-specific spreading rule, that this pattern was violated. But the one-to-one mapping of tones to TBUs is a general pattern in languages—one which is often violated, to be sure, but which is the general default case. The following constraints, taken from Anttila and Bodomo (1997), give the results of this mapping; let us consider them as a starting point.

(464) a. **1TONE/TBU:** every TBU is linked to exactly one tone
(= *CONTOUR, *TONELESS)

b. **1TBU/TONE:** every tone is linked to exactly one TBU
(= *FLOAT, *SPREAD)

In the case where both constraints are completely satisfied, there is one tone for every TBU, and one TBU for every tone, i.e., a one-to-one mapping of tones and TBUs. Each of these general constraints may be violated in two ways, a consequence of the term "exactly" having two parts to its interpretation, that is, "exactly" has the parts "at least" and "not more than."

Thus if two tones are linked to a single TBU, then 1TONE/TBU is violated by this contour tone. In complementary fashion, if there is a TBU which is not linked to any tone, then 1TONE/TBU is violated by this *toneless* TBU. Similarly, if a tone is not linked to a TBU, 1TBU/TONE is violated by this floating tone, symbolized as (T). And finally, if a tone is linked to more than one TBU, 1TBU/TONE is violated by the multiply-linked tone.

It is an empirical question if the functions need to be separated into their components, or whether the more general constraints of (464) are sufficient. Anttila and Bodomo do not separate the functions of (464) for Dagaare, but leave open the possibility that it may be necessary in some situations. In several languages it can be demonstrated that these functions act separately, where a language exhibits one of the pairs of behavior but not the other. For example, Shona disallows floating tones but has extensive tone spreading (Odden 1981, Myers 1987), Kikerewe has toneless syllables but no contours, and Kenyang has contours but no toneless

6.2 Basic tonal constraints

syllables (Odden, personal communication). As we will see, it is also necessary to separate these functions in Kɔnni, and *CONTOUR, *TONELESS, *SPREAD, and *FLOAT (or *(T)) are the actual constraints.

There is, however, an additional distinction to be made with respect to *(T) and *SPREAD. Since their referents are tones, there is a potential distinction between High and Low tones in these constraints, and this distinction will turn out to be relevant. So (464b) is actually a family of constraints.

(465)   *(T) = *(H), *(L)
        *SPREAD = *H-SPREAD, *L-SPREAD

The distinction is crucial, as we shall see. High tones spread, but Low tones do not. Low tones can remain floating, but High tones do not. Our initial statement of optimization of association in (464), then, gives the constraints in (466).

(466) a. *CONTOUR: every TBU is linked to not more than one tone
      b. *TONELESS: every TBU is linked to at least one tone
      c. *(H): every High tone is linked to at least one TBU
      d. *(L): every Low tone is linked to at least one TBU
      e. *H-SPREAD: every High tone is linked to not more than one TBU
      f. *L-SPREAD: every Low tone is linked to not more than one TBU

These will be introduced at the appropriate times. We will also see later that *CONTOUR must also be split into more than one constraint, depending on position in the word and the type of contour.

Before our first tableau, we must consider another constraint that keeps tones from wandering in unrestrained fashion, and helps keep morpheme edges distinct. This will be MAX(ASSOC).

(467) **MAX(ASSOC)**: an association line in the input will have a correspondent in the output

The effect of this constraint is to keep lexical tones associated to the TBUs which sponsor them. The idea is that tones are generally pre-linked in the input, and these pre-linkings are maintained in the output. It is not only that association lines are not deleted and tones set afloat, but that a tone associated to a particular TBU in the input will also be associated to that particular TBU in the output. Let us examine a simple tableau to see this in operation. In the next and in all following tableaus, morpheme boundaries are marked with a hyphen, not only for the segmental material, but between tones as well.

(468) tǎŋ 'stone' with MAX(ASSOC) >> *CONTOUR

	UR	L -H | | tan-ŋ	MAX(ASSOC)	*CONTOUR
☞ a.		L H \ / taŋ		*
b.		L H | taŋ	*!	
c.		L H | taŋ	*!	

In (468), the Low tone is sponsored by the noun stem tan^6 and so must associate to its sponsoring TBU by MAX(ASSOC). Likewise, the High tone is sponsored by the suffix -ŋ and must associate to the syllable containing its sponsoring TBU. In the winning candidate (468a), MAX(ASSOC) is unviolated when both High and Low tones associate to the single TBU of the word. Since (468a) has a contour tone, it is evident that MAX(ASSOC) outranks *CONTOUR. In candidate (468b), the High tone is not associated to its sponsoring TBU, and in candidate (468c), the Low tone is not associated to the syllable taŋ containing its sponsoring TBU either.

The interpretation of MAX(ASSOC) when it is associated to a segment which is not a TBU by itself in the output deserves further discussion. The suffix -ŋ is not a TBU in either the input or the output, so I will interpret MAX(ASSOC) as preserving an association line which is linked to a segment in the input and the TBU to which that segment belongs in the output.

The constraints *(H) and *(L) are both violated by the losing candidates in (468), and might themselves force acceptance of the winning candidate, but there is no way to tell from tǎŋ what ranking they should have with respect to each other or to *CONTOUR. The next tableau shows that they do in fact need to have separate rankings, and so using them to determine the winning candidate in (468) would have been inappropriate. The downstep in líá!ká is a result of a floating Low tone.

---

[6]The actual stem is *tan*, as seen in the plural *tan-a*. But when the suffix -ŋ is added to *tan*, the result is *taŋ*. See section 4.3.2 for details.

6.2 Basic tonal constraints

(469) líá!ká 'the axe' shows *(H) >>*(L)

	UR HL-H | | lıa-ka	*(H)	Max(Assoc)	*Contour	*(L)
☞ a.	H L H \ | l ıa k a				*
b.	H L H \/ | l ıa k a			*!+	
c.	H L H | |/ l ıa k a			*!	
d.	H L H | | l ıa k a	*!	*		
e.	H L H | \ l ıa k a	*!	*		*
f.	H L H | | l ıa k a	*!	*		

+This and candidate (469c), in a more detailed analysis, are actually ruled out by*HLH (section 6.2.2).

The winning candidate (469a) violates only the constraint *(L). Other possible candidates violate other constraints, which must therefore be ranked higher than *(L). Candidates (469b and c) have contours and so violate *Contour, while candidates (469d, e, and f) all have some violation of Max(Assoc). Candidates (469d and e) have the High tone associated to the input suffix floating in output, and candidate (469f) has the High tone which is associated to the noun stem in the input floating in the output. We will see, however, that *(H) outranks Max(Assoc), and so it is the violation of *(H) which is fatal.

In (469), the constraint *(H) is violated whenever Max(Assoc) is, and in this tableau, their effects cannot be distinguished. To separate out the effects of these, we will look at a tableau in which a floating High tone is present in underlying representation. The associative morpheme for third person is a floating High tone, as shown by the fact that all possessed nouns in third person begin with a High tone (see sections 6.1.5 and 6.3.6). I assume that although the floating High in this case is outside of a word and is part of a phrase, the *(H) constraint is the same one as is relevant within words.

One other constraint is needed to rule out a possible candidate in (471). As noted, no TBU in Kɔnni may have more than two tones associated with it, and cross-linguistically, it is not a common occurrence for a TBU to have three tones, though such are not unknown. This can be formalized as the constraint in (470).

(470) *TRIPLE-T: three or more tones may not be associated to a single TBU

With this in place, we are ready to present the tableau in (471).

(471) ʊ̀ tá!ŋ́ 'his stone' shows *TRIPLE-T, *(H) >> MAX(ASSOC)

	UR L H L - H | | | ʊ tan -ŋ	*TRIPLE-T	*(H)	MAX (ASSOC)	*CONTOUR	*(L)
☞ a.	L H L H | \ / ʊ tan			*	*	*
b.	L H L H | | / ʊ tan		*!		*	
c.	L H L H | | / ʊ tan		*!	*	*	
d.	L H L H | \ | / ʊ tan	*!			*	

The winning candidate (471a) violates a majority of the constraints in the tableau, including MAX(ASSOC) by the delinking of the Low tone of 'stone'. However, it does not violate *(H), as candidates (471b and c) do. This establishes that it is more crucial for a High tone to associate than for an underlying Low tone to associate to its sponsor. A candidate in which the tones HLH are all associated to *taŋ* is ruled out by the constraint *TRIPLE-T. Other failed

6.2.2 More complex constraints—*HLH, etc.

The losing candidate in (471d) also has the configuration HLH which is practically unknown in Kɔnni (generalization 451b) and never occurs within a word, even if spread over three separate syllables. Rather, when morphemes concatenate that would have produced such a HLH sequence, the result is H!HH.

One plausible reason for the lack of phonetic HLH can be traced to the nature of communication. A language must have "texture" to it, i.e., a variation in whatever parameters are relevant. However, these parameters must not vary so rapidly that it is perceptually difficult to parse the information present, nor articulatorily difficult to produce.[7] In a tonal language, this implies avoidance of two extremes, both a totally "flat" pitch extending over some domain, and too rapid an alternation between Highs and Lows. Graphically, either situation below is not desirable.

(472) a. _____

b. ⁻ ⁻ ⁻ ⁻ ⁻
    _ _ _ _ _

This situation translates into two types of constraints in OT. A constant Low tone such as in (472a) is prohibited in Kɔnni by a constraint requiring at least one High tone per word, to be discussed in section 6.3.1.2 (also, see footnote 16 in chapter 6 commenting on the asymmetry of allowing all-High-toned words while disallowing all-Low-toned ones). The ill-formedness of (472b), a constant alternation between High and Low tones, is instantiated in Kɔnni by the fact that there is never a HLH sequence on TBUs, while HLLH is allowed.

---

[7]The notion of perceptual or articulatory "difficulty" has been notoriously hard to translate into rigorous terms, especially since many sounds or sequences that are considered "difficult" by speakers of one language are common in another. As a native English speaker, the labial-velar stops of Kɔnni were difficult for me to make and perceive accurately for some time, and listening to a Buli speaker, it was obvious that he had major difficulties trying to pronounce English "squirrel." Nonetheless, the recent attempt to quantify "difficulty" in terms of articulatory effort made by Kirchner (1998) may lead to more exact methods to be rigorous about the whole topic.

(473) *HLH = no Low can be singly associated between two High tones:

The citation form of the constraint, *HLH, is shorthand for the fuller representation of the forbidden configuration at the right of (473). The precise form of this constraint is proposed tentatively; there may be another configuration that would be as adequate. The crucial prohibition is the *association* of a single Low tone when surrounded by Highs. Though this constraint is ranked quite highly, it is violated in a few specific cases in Kɔnni (see sections 6.4.1.2 and 6.4.2.2), so is not undominated.

The absence of a constraint symmetric to *HLH is notable, i.e., there is no *LHL, and cross-linguistically, there seem to be plenty of cases where one prominent syllable is surrounded by nonprominent ones. Speculatively, this could be due to the greater salience of peaks relative to valleys, or that the marked tone of the language may be flanked by unmarked tones, but not the reverse.

As mentioned, the result of concatenating morphemes with HLH tones is H!HH, not HH!H. In the output, it is the rightmost High which has spread left.[8] A constraint against rightward spreading is evidently active.

(474) *R-SPREAD: a tone must not be associated both to its sponsoring TBU and to a TBU to its right

This constraint depends, of course, on being able to correctly identify the sponsoring TBU of a particular tone. As we shall see below, in practice this presents no problem. In Kɔnni, this constraint may be violated in the specific case of noun-adjective complexes (section 6.3.5) and tones of verbs (section 6.4.1), so it will not be top-ranked.

The constraint mentioned previously against spreading must be mentioned at this point as well, that is, *H-SPREAD, which prohibits any spreading of a High tone. Since the High here is multiply linked, then *H-SPREAD must be ranked below *HLH.

---

[8]In Cahill (1992a), I proposed a second type of High-spread which spread a High tone leftward one syllable across words. This was largely on the basis of the form kàgbá wún!ná 'this is a bowl', where the High on kàgbá was assumed to be a result of spreading (in other contexts 'bowl' is all Low-toned, as in kàgbà kààní 'one bowl'). However, I now believe the final High on kàgbá to be inserted to give a High tone on a nominal (section 6.3.1.2). Longer words which have two word-final Lows but have a High elsewhere (e.g., kpàgàsúŋkpàgà wún!ná 'this is a fish (sp.)') show that the HLH context is necessary for leftward High-spreading.

6.2 Basic tonal constraints

(475) ná!pɔ́ríŋ 'calf (leg)' shows *HLH >> *H-SPREAD, *(L)

UR H L- H
  | | |
  napɔr -ŋ
	*(H)	*HLH	*R-SPREAD	*H-SPREAD	*(L)

☞ a. H L H
  | / |
  napɔrɩŋ
				*	*

b. H L H
  |\ |
  napɔrɩŋ
		*!		*	*

c. H L H
  | | |
  napɔrɩŋ
	*!				

Candidate (475c), though perfectly satisfying a one-to-one matching between tones and TBUs, is nevertheless rejected because it violates *HLH. Candidate (475b) is rejected because its spreading of High is rightward, leaving candidate (475a) as optimal.

The constraint *(H), though playing no role in the candidates listed in (475), since there is no floating High, is included to visually demonstrate its ranking above *H-SPREAD. In the initial discussion of constraints in section 6.2, it was pointed out that both *(H) and *H-SPREAD could be stated as parts of a more generalized constraint, 1TBU/High: every High is linked to exactly one TBU (see 465). The question was raised there whether it was possible to have the one constraint covering both situations. Though *(H) is undominated, *H-SPREAD can be violated, and so we see that *(H) and *H-SPREAD must be ranked differently, and thus we cannot conflate the two constraints into 1TBU/High for Kɔnni. The relative rankings of *HLH and R-SPREAD cannot be established from this tableau, but are supported in (569).

Ranking of *HLH with respect to MAX(ASSOC) can be established by examining the form *jɔ́rɔ́ŋ !káání* 'one ladder' (476).

(476) jɔ́rɔ́ŋ !káání 'one ladder' shows *HLH > > Max(Assoc)

UR H -H L H 　　│　│　　│ │ 　　jɔrɔ-ŋ　kaanı	*HLH	*R- Spread	Max (Assoc)	*H- Spread	*(L)
☞ a.　H H L H 　　　│ │　／│ 　　　jɔrɔŋ　kaanı			*	*	*
b.　　H　H L H 　　　│　／\ │ 　　　jɔrɔŋ　kaanı	*!	*	*	*	
c.　　H H　L H 　　　│ │　│ │ 　　　jɔrɔŋ　kaanı		*!			

Again, candidate (476c) violates the highly-ranked *HLH, and candidate (476b) violates *R-Spread. Candidate (476a), though violating Max(Assoc), is the optimal candidate, showing that *HLH is more highly ranked.

The rankings we have motivated thus far, then, are:

(477) *Triple-T, *(H), *HLH > > Max(Assoc) > > *Contour, *(L)
　　　*HLH > > *H-Spread

So far we have not established a ranking among the first three constraints, but we will see later that of these, only *Triple-T and *(H) are undominated in Kɔnni. The ranking of *R-Spread is problematic. I have tentatively ranked it at the same level as *HLH; we will see later that it does outrank *(L) and other constraints.

6.2.3 Tone on epenthetic vowels

An epenthetic vowel, inserted to prevent undesirable consonant clusters and maintain optimal syllables, must bear some tone, and the tone which surfaces depends on the surrounding tones. With verbs, the grammatical tonal melody determines the tone of the final epenthetic *I*, but in nouns the situation is slightly more complex. In some cases there are more tones than syllables in the underlying representation so that the constraints on tone mapping can assign a tone which is underlying to the epenthetic vowel. In other cases, no such "surplus" tone is available, and a tone must

6.2 Basic tonal constraints

be either inserted or spread. A tone on epenthetic vowels is generally Low, but is High in one context.

The status of a vowel as epenthetic in (478) is based on alternations in the noun paradigm. (The epenthetic vowels are bolded in the data below.) In the first set of data, an epenthetic vowel occurs in each word, but there is a tone already available for association to that vowel (strictly speaking, to the syllable of which that epenthetic vowel is the nucleus). In (478a), the tone comes from the suffix -ŋ́, and in (478b), the tone is present in the stem.

(478) Tone on epenthetic vowels I
    a. bììsíŋ   'breast'
        bòllɔ̀gíŋ   'armpit'
        tígíŋ   'house'

    b. yíí!gísí   'trees (sp.)'   yíí!gíŋ   'tree (sp.)' (cf. yíík!ká 'the tree (sp.)')
        bɔ́!líká   'the ball'   bɔ́lì   'ball'
        nááchígí!síří 'the ankle'   nááchígí!síŋ 'ankle' (cf. nááchígísà 'ankles')
        káwún!tíří   'the corn (maize)'   káwún!tíŋ   'corn'   (cf. káwúntà 'corn (PL)')

The tones in nouns from (478a) are represented in input and output in (479). This is the simplest case, in which the number of TBUs and tones match exactly.

(479) a. bììsíŋ   'breast'
         L H   L H
         | | | |
        bııs -ŋ → bıısıŋ

    b. tígíŋ   'house'
       H H   H H
       | | | |
     tig -ŋ → tigiŋ

In contrast, in (478b), the tones are available to associate to the epenthetic vowel, but the *HLH constraint comes into play, similar to the cases in the previous section. The tones in a sample noun from (478b) are presented in the tableau in (480).

(480) nááchígí!síŋ 'ankle'

	UR H H H L-H
	       | | | |
	    naachıgıs -ŋ
		*HLH	*R-Spread	Max
				(Assoc)
					*(L)

☞ a.	H H H L H | | | | naa chı gı sıŋ				*
b.	H H H L H | | | \\\| naa chı gı sıŋ	*!			
c.	H H H L H | | | | naa chı gı sıŋ	*!		*	

Candidate (480a) violates *(L) by having a floating Low tone, but none of the other constraints. Candidates (480b and c) and any others which have the Low associated between two Highs fatally violate *HLH. One way to satisfy *HLH would be to delete the final High tone altogether, but this would violate the undominated Max(H) constraint, discussed in section 6.3.3. Let us examine another closely related form.

(481) nááchígí!sírí 'the ankle'

	UR H H H L-H
	       | | | |
	    naachıgıs -rı
		*HLH	*R-Spread	*(L)

☞ a.	H H H L H | | | /| naa chı gı sırı			*
b.	H H H L H | | | | | naa chı gı sı rı	*!		
c.	H H H L H | | |\\ | naa chı gı sı rı		*!	*

The tableau in (481) differs from that in (480) in that a High tone has spread. The winning candidate (481a) violates no constraints except *(L). Candidate (481b), while preserving a one-to-one matching of tone to syllable,

6.2 Basic tonal constraints

has a Low associated between two Highs, fatally violating *HLH, and candidate (481c) has the High tone spreading from the left rather than the right. The tone on the epenthetic vowels thus far is accounted for with constraints already in place.

For other nouns, there is no tone readily available to associate to the epenthetic vowel, and a tone must be inserted to match the inserted vowel. In the nouns in (482a) and (482b), the epenthetic vowels are Low toned, but in (482c), they are High toned.

(482) Tone on epenthetic vowels II
    a. Low-toned epenthetic vowels
        bììsìrí   'the breast'
        kònchìàgìrí 'the cornstalk'
        bùllɔ̀gìtí   'armpits'
        hàgìtí   'barks, shells'
        ɲìgìsí   'bush partridges (sp.)'
        kpàjìgìsí   'warts'

    b. Low-toned epenthetic vowels in borrowed words
        bɔ́lì   'ball'
        síméntì   'cement'
        wɔ́fìsì   'office'
        sìpánì   'spanner, wrench'
        sìkúlì   'school'
        sɔ́kìsì   'socks'
        mílìkì   'milk'

    c. High-toned epenthetic vowels
        tígírí   'the house'
        búllɔ́gírí   'the bag'
        kpáánίká   'the dance (sp.)'
        wáríkú   'the block'
        zàmpúgítí 'hedgehogs'
        yúgítí   'nights'
        kúgúsí   'trees (sp.)'
        gbígbágísí 'trees (sp.)'

In (482a and b) we note that an epenthetic vowel has a Low tone when a High or Low tone is to the left or right, as long as there is either one Low or a word boundary adjacent to the syllable containing the epenthetic vowel. When the epenthetic location has High tones on both left and right, as in

(482c), then the epenthetic vowel is High-toned. The more general case seems to be that a Low tone is inserted when needed, and we will see in section 6.3.1 that toneless noun stems receive a Low tone as the default. In OT terms, it is more optimal to insert a Low tone than to insert a High tone, and this brings into play the DEP family of constraints prohibiting insertion. Note that the parentheses around the H and L below have nothing to do with floating tones, unlike the use of parentheses in *(L) and *(H).

(483) **DEP(H):** a High tone in the output must have a correspondent in the input
      DEP(L): a Low tone in the output must have a correspondent in the input

Since inserting a Low tone is better than inserting a High one, DEP(H) must outrank DEP(L). We will see these in action again in the discussion of polarity in section 6.3.3. We also reintroduce the undominated *L-SPREAD first noted in (466f).

(484) ***L-SPREAD:** every Low tone is linked to not more than one TBU

(485) bììsìrí 'the breast' *TONELESS, *L-SPREAD, *H-SPREAD, DEP(H) >> DEP(L)

	UR L -H | | bɪɪs-rɪ	*TONE-LESS	*L-SPREAD	*H-SPREAD	DEP(H)	DEP(L)
☞ a.	L L H | | | bɪɪ sɪ rɪ					*
b.	L H H | | | bɪɪ sɪ rɪ				*!	
c.	L H |\ | bɪɪ sɪ rɪ		*!			
d.	L H | /| bɪɪ sɪ rɪ			*!		
e.	L H | | bɪɪ sɪ rɪ	*!				

6.2 Basic tonal constraints

The winning candidate (485a) violates no constraints except DEP(L) by inserting a Low tone. Candidate (485b) is worse, by inserting a High tone. Candidates (485c and d) both are bad by spreading a tone, (485c) being especially bad by spreading it rightward. Finally, candidate (485e) is ruled out since Kɔnni does not permit toneless syllables. Candidates (485a and c) are phonetically identical, and the choice between them, depending on the relative rankings of *L-SPREAD and DEP(L), cannot be made solely on the basis of this tableau. However, we note that in the borrowed words in (482b), there is an opportunity for the High tones preceding the epenthetic vowel to spread, and they do not. In those cases a tone has clearly been inserted rather than spread, and I posit the same is happening in the tableau in (485).

The epenthetic vowel in at least some of the borrowed words has possibly been lexicalized and no longer behaves as synchronically epenthetic. This is the case for bɔ́lɪ̀ 'ball', as shown by the definite form bɔ́!lɪ́ká 'the ball'. If the I in bɔ́lɪ̀ were synchronically epenthetic, then the input form would have a High tone from the noun stem bɔ́l- and a High tone from the suffix -ká. Since the epenthetic vowel is between two High tones, it should also be High, following the pattern in (482c) and giving the unattested *bɔ́lɪ́ká. Its tonal behavior in retaining the Low tone, however, shows that this Low, historically epenthetic, has become lexicalized.[9]

The last pattern of tone on epenthetic vowels is when the epenthetic vowel surfaces with a High tone, as in (482c). This only happens when the epenthetic vowel occurs between two High-toned TBUs. In tígírí 'the house', for example, the underlying tones are a High from the noun stem tíg- and a High from the suffix -rí. The constraints already in place give the correct phonetic output, but with an indeterminacy in the structure.

---

[9] Alternatively, if one assumes a HL input tone for English 'ball', then the vowel may or may not be epenthetic.

(486) tígírí 'the house'

UR H -H | | tig -ri	*Toneless	*HLH	*R-Spread	*H-Spread	Dep(H)	Dep(L)
☞ a. H H H | | | ti gi ri					*	
b. H H | / | ti gi ri				*		
c. H H |\ | ti gi ri			*!	*		
d. H L H | | | ti gi ri		*!				*
e. H L H | / | ti gi ri				*		*!
f. H H | | ti gi ri	*!					

Both candidates (486a and b) are marked as winning; each violates only one constraint. There is no data at hand to determine the ranking of *H-Spread and Dep(H), and it would be difficult to find such data, given that (486a and b) are phonetically identical, as any other relevant forms would also be. The same indeterminacy in structure will also be encountered in the discussion of polarity in section 6.3.3 (see the tableau in 500) and for the same reasons.[10] However, other candidates are clearly ruled out by various constraints. While candidate (486b) is a possible winner, candidate (486c) loses by spreading the High to the right rather than to the left. Candidate (486d) inserts a Low tone and loses by violating *HLH. Candidate (486e) is well formed and identical to (486b) in structure, except for the Low tone it has inserted. Inserting the Low violates Dep(L), a constraint which is low

[10]Actually, if constraints are regarded as universal, then the OCP, though ranked low to the point of virtual invisibility in Kɔnni, would still be present and would rule in favor of candidate (486b), since the OCP would penalize two adjacent High tones. Then (486b) would win by consistency with the larger theory and not by any evidence from within Kɔnni itself.

ranked but which makes the difference here. Candidate (486f) also loses, since a TBU must have a tone in Kɔnni.

On the basis of these patterns, we can identify some vowels as epenthetic even when alternations with and without the vowel in question are not available, e.g., *dèmbíŋ* 'man', *dèmbìké* 'the man'. The epenthetic *i* is High toned when the High from the indefinite suffix *-ŋ́* is available for association with the final syllable. But when no tone is available to associate with *i*, then a Low is inserted, as in *bìisìrí* 'the breast' in (485). If there were two Lows in the noun stem, this could account for the tonal pattern in the definite *dèmbìké*, but in the indefinite, two Lows in the noun stem would predict the unattested *dèmbǐŋ with a rising tone on the final syllable, the result of the stem Low and the suffixal High, as in fact occurs in words like *dààkpăŋ* 'bachelor'.

6.3 Nominals

6.3.1 Simple singulars, plurals, definites

In this section I consider noncompound single nouns. In Kɔnni, disyllabic nouns which are apparently identical in tone can turn out to have quite different underlying tone patterns, as evidenced by their different behavior in various tonal contexts. The solution is positing toneless noun stems. These stems do have a High tone in citation form, and an insertion mechanism is proposed for this.

6.3.1.1 Toneless noun stems

Disyllabic nouns in Kɔnni illustrate a variety of tonal patterns when placed in various contexts. For example, nouns which have the same LH surface tones in citation form behave quite differently in different tonal environments. If underlying High and Low tones were mapped one-to-one onto syllables, there would be of course only four possible tone patterns: HH, HL, LH, LL. However, the real situation is more complex; there are at least eight actual tonal behaviors of disyllabic nouns. Much of the complexity comes from the fact that some of these nouns have toneless roots and/or no suffix in singular form.

Consider the four disyllabic nouns in (487), extracted from appendix A, which all have the same LH tonal pattern in citation form but show different behavior in different tonal contexts. ("Ø" indicates a syllable unspecified for tone.) While I have not put all nouns in my database through these tonal frames, it appears that all but the 'hat' pattern below are fairly common, as indicated by the approximate counts in the last column.

(487)
	UR	Citation	'One X'	'His/her X'	Count
a. 'fish'	LH	zàsíŋ	zàsíŋ !káání	ʋ̀ zá!síŋ	35
b. 'louse'	ØH	kpìbíŋ	kpìbíŋ !káání	ʋ̀ kpíbíŋ	10
c. 'hat'	LØ	kàgbá	kàgbà kàànì	ʋ̀ kágbà[11]	3
d. 'woman'	ØØ	hɔ̀gú	hɔ̀gú !káání	ʋ̀ hɔ́gʋ̀	12

In citation form, all nouns have the same tone pattern, but in the forms 'one X', 'hat' is differentiated from the other words. The last column, 'his/her X', distinguishes the other three from each other.

Note that the nouns of (487a and b) end in -ŋ, as do approximately eighty percent of Kɔnni nouns. This -ŋ contributes the High tone of the second syllable. In contrast, the nouns in (487c and d) end in a vowel, and I posit that these have no tone lexically on the second syllable. The other dichotomy comes between (487a and c), which I analyze as having a lexical Low tone contributed by the root, and (487b and d) which I analyze as having a toneless root.[12]

The pattern for *zasŋ* 'fish' is exactly as we would expect for a noun with LH present lexically. The downstep in the 'his/her X' column is placed as expected, between the High of the suffix and the High of the first syllable that is the realization of the associative morpheme. But for *kpibiŋ* 'louse', there is no downstep in the 'his X' column as would be expected if there were a lexical Low tone. The conclusion is that the Low which shows up in the citation form is not present in the underlying form, but is added as a default. In 'his/her louse', there is a High from the associative construction and a High from the suffix available to associate to the two syllables of *kpibiŋ*, and no Low need be inserted.

The nouns 'hat' and 'woman' have no -ŋ suffix and so any High in forms of these words cannot be the contribution of that suffix. If there were a lexical High as part of the root, it would show up consistently in the same position in the word, similar to the Highs in *máásà* 'a cake' or *tá!síŋ*

---

[11]For this particular word, there is considerable variation among speakers. Amadu's citation form has all Low tones, while Tahiru's forms in tone frames have tones identical to those of *zasŋ* 'fish', as in (487a). In the discussion above, I have taken the tones in forms as pronounced by Abdulai Sikpaare, who is recognized among Kɔnni speakers as an outstanding speaker.

[12]The related Gur languages Mooré and Dagaare have also been analyzed as having the cognate noun stem of 'woman' as underlyingly toneless. For Mooré, the cognate word is *págá* (Kenstowicz, Nikiema, and Ourso 1988), and for Dagaare it is *pɔ́gɔ́* (Anttila and Bodomo 1997). With the limited data available for all languages in question, it has not been possible to identify any toneless cognates corresponding to the Kɔnni 'louse' class of words.

6.3 Nominals

'headpan'. Instead, a High tone shows up in different positions in these words, and not at all in 'one hat'. As I will discuss below, the High tone in the nouns for which there is no lexical High is the result of a phrasal constraint inserting a High. The lack of a lexical High in 'hat' and 'woman' explains why there is only one High, on the initial syllable of the noun, in 'his/her hat, his/her woman'. The High comes from the floating High associative marker, and that is the only High in these phrases.

Another piece of evidence that the High tone on hɔ̀gú 'woman' is not lexical but inserted, and that 'woman' is lexically toneless, is the tonal pattern of the noun stem when followed by an adjective, such as hɔ̀gù-kpí!íŋ 'big woman', hɔ̀gù-bìàká 'the bad woman', hɔ̀gù-sɔ́bílí-kpí!íŋ 'big black woman' (see more examples in appendix D). In all of these, the noun stem hɔgʋ is totally Low-toned. There is a High tone in the word, but it occurs on the adjective.[13]

The basic tone patterns of singular disyllabic nouns, then, fall into a pattern based on whether their stem is High, Low, or toneless, and whether or not they have the common High-toned -ŋ singular suffix.

(488)   With -ŋ (H)   Without -ŋ (Ø)

stem H	HH	jɔ́rɔ́ŋ	'ladder'	HL	máásà	'a cake'
stem L	LH	zàsíŋ	'fish'	LØ	kàgbá	'hat'
stem Ø	ØH	kpìbíŋ	'louse'	ØØ	hɔ̀gú	'woman'

The form máásà 'a cake' is the only word in the second column for which I posit an underlying tone on the second syllable. This is on the basis of its tonal behavior. The form máá!sá wún!ná 'this is a cake' shows that there must be a lexical Low in the second syllable of máásà, rather than being an inserted Low. Recall that an epenthetic vowel with no tone will be pronounced as High when between two Highs, and we would expect the unattested *máásá wún!ná if the second syllable were underlyingly toneless. Other disyllabic tone patterns, such as for tá!síŋ 'headpan' and nìmbúà 'sibling' involve more than one lexical tone in the noun stem.

The word kpìbíŋ 'louse' has a posited High tone, which is sponsored by the -ŋ suffix. Since I have posited a toneless noun stem for this, the appearance of the Low tone on the first syllable must be accounted for. The crux of the matter is that it is better to insert a Low default tone than it is to insert a High default or to spread the lexical High tone. The undominated constraint *TONELESS is active here.

---

[13] Kenstowicz, Nikiema, and Ourso (1988) use a similar pattern of Low tone on 'woman' to argue for its tonelessness in Mooré.

(489) kpìbíŋ 'louse' shows *Toneless, *H-Spread, Dep(H) >> Dep(L)

UR -H | kpibi-ŋ	*Toneless	*H-Spread	Max (Assoc)	Dep(H)	Dep(L)
☞ a. L H | | kpibiŋ					*
b. H H | | kpibiŋ				*!	
c. H L | | kpibiŋ			*!		*
d. H /| kpibiŋ		*!			
e. H | kpibiŋ	*!				

The constraint Max(Assoc) is important here for retaining the lexical tone on the correct syllable, that is, favoring the correct *kpìbíŋ* in (489) over the incorrect **kpíbìŋ*. Since the underlying High tone is sponsored by the -ŋ suffix, Max(Assoc) motivates the High to stay on the syllable containing the sponsoring TBU, in this case, the final syllable.[14]

A conclusion from this section is that disyllabic nouns may have stems which are High, Low, or toneless. The Low or toneless noun stems must have a High tone inserted when in citation form, and to that matter we now turn.

---

[14] Also relevant is the constraint High-Rt, illustrated in the tableau in (494), which says that a High tone aligns with the right edge of its prosodic domain. This outranks Low-Rt, giving the result that High tones end up on right edges of words in preference to Low tones. However, here the Max(Assoc) constraint is sufficient also to rule out a reasonable candidate.

6.3.1.2 H-Present

No noun (or other word, to my knowledge) in Kɔnni is pronounced with all Low tones.[15] Neither of the nouns kàgbá 'hat' nor hɔ̀gú 'woman' has an underlying High tone present in the forms I have posited, yet they both surface in citation form with a High tone on the second syllable. At times kagba shows up as all Low toned, as in kàgbà kààní 'one hat' or ŋ̀ wó kàgbà 'I lack (a) hat', but there is a High tone present somewhere in the utterance. Actually, the relevant domain over which a High is required may be a smaller unit than an utterance, perhaps a phrasal unit, but certainly larger than the word. The toneless nouns are rare enough that a variety of syntactic constructions is not available; so I tentatively leave the domain as the utterance. Related to the discussion about the tonal texture of an utterance in section 6.2.2, we see that in Kɔnni, an utterance must have a High tone somewhere. If there is none in underlying representation, one is inserted. This is the only situation where High insertion unambiguously takes place.

(490) **H-Present:** there must be at least one High tone present in an utterance.

There is cross-linguistic evidence for some form of this constraint in a variety of languages. In Mixtec of San Miguel El Grande, in Mexico (Goldsmith 1990, from data in Pike 1948), there are no words which are all Low toned. The Mooré and Dagaare languages of West Africa have a similar pattern: in disyllabic nouns, HH, HL, and LH are attested, but not LL (Kenstowicz, Nikiema, and Ourso 1988, Anttila and Bodomo 1997). All these were reported before the advent of Optimality Theory. Finally, for North Kyungsang Korean (Kim 1997), a constraint STEMH (all stems must contain a High tone) is proposed, similar to what I am proposing here. In all these languages a "flat" texture of Lows is not tolerated.[16]

We will see how this constraint operates in single words first. When a High tone is inserted, here DEP(H) is violated and must therefore be outranked by other constraints which rule out the alternate candidates below. The word kàgbá is posited to have a Low tone since there is always a

---

[15]This is absolutely true of the speech of Sikpaare. However, as noted in footnote 11, Amadu actually pronounces kagba with all Low tones in citation form. Amadu has also given six other nouns with all Low tones. Half of these are names of birds. I will take the forms of Sikpaare, the official town crier, to analyze.

[16]It is interesting that there is an asymmetry in High and Low tones. There is often a High tone required in a word, but I know of no language in which a Low tone is required. Languages tolerate words with all High tones, but not words with all Low tones. Explaining this asymmetry is a subject for further research.

Low present in any context (see appendix A), unlike the noun stems I have posited as toneless.

(491) kàgbá 'hat' H-Present >> Dep(H)

	UR L | kagba	H-Present	*R-Spread	Max(Assoc)	Dep(H)
☞ a.	L H | | kagba				*
b.	H L | | kagba			*!	*
c.	L L | | kagba	*!			
d.	L |\ kagba	*!	*		

The winning candidate (491a) violates Dep(H) by inserting a High, but no other constraints. Candidate (491b) has the same tones as (491a) but in the reverse order. It loses because its lexical Low tone is not associated to its sponsoring TBU.[17] Candidates (491c and d) lose by not having a High tone present, with candidate (491d) also violating *R-Spread and the undominated *L-Spread as well.

As previously mentioned, the word *kagba* sometimes surfaces as all Low toned, as in kàgbà kàání 'one hat' or ŋ́ wó kàgbà 'I lack (a) hat', but a High tone is present somewhere in the utterance.

The noun hɔ̀gú 'woman' brings up another complication. I have analyzed it as toneless, partly because of its tonal behavior in ù hɔ́gù 'his woman'. Supporting this is the fact that in compounds, the stem for 'woman' does not have a High tone, e.g., hɔ̀gùkpǎŋ 'spinster', hɔ̀gùlíà 'girl'. Analysts for other Gur languages have also analyzed the cognate noun for 'woman' as toneless on the basis of similar evidence (see footnote 144). In related Gur languages, the noun has a High-toned suffix, analyzed as underlyingly High in Dagbani (Hyman 1993) and Mooré (Kenstowicz et

---

[17]This would not be a violation of a Linearity constraint (which prohibits elements from being ordered differently in the output than in the input), since the High is not present in the input and so has no underlying sequence with respect to the Low.

6.3 Nominals

al. 1988) and as an inserted High in Dagaare (Anttila and Bodomo 1997). Historically and comparatively, then, 'woman' has a High tone on its second syllable. However, in these other languages, the second vowel is a suffix, and in Kɔnni, there is no suffix and no underlying High tone.

The complication comes in the fact that of the two toneless syllables of *hɔ̀gʊ́*, it is the second that receives the High tone, not the first. This could be regarded as merely a historical relic, and it is probably connected with the historical roots, but I propose that there is also a synchronic phonological principle at work here that extends beyond this particular class of words, and this is that floating tones tend to dock to the right rather than to the left.

As pointed out in Cahill (2000), there is a cross-linguistic tendency for tones which spread or dock to do so in a rightward direction. In Mixtec of Mexico (analyzed by Goldsmith 1990 and Tranel 1996, both based on data in Pike 1948), some nouns have a suffixal High tone which is underlyingly unassociated. This tone shows its effects on a following word, if one is present. Lango of Uganda (Clifton 1975) has a similar phenomenon. Clements and Ford's (1979) second tonal association convention, according to which T_1 rather than T_2 will spread to the free vowel V_2 in the configuration in (492), also illustrates the pervasiveness of rightward spreading. This is exemplified by Hausa borrowings into Nupe (Hyman and Schuh 1974). Hyman and Schuh also make the claim that spreading in African languages is always rightward. This is too strong a claim, since we have seen leftward spreading in Kɔnni, and it also exists in other languages. However, in Bantu languages, the phenomena of tone "doubling," tone shift, and tone spread are generally rightward as well (Odden 1995 and references therein).

(492) Clements and Ford's (1979) second tonal association convention

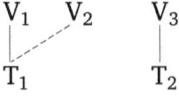

Though there seems to be a cross-linguistic tendency for tones in general to spread rightward, there is a much stronger tendency for floating tones to dock to the right.[18] In the Kɔnni cases presented here, a constraint dealing

---

[18]Chumbow and Nguendjio (1991) do, however, give data from several constructions in Bangwa which all have floating tones docking to the left. Some of these constructions have heads to the left, as the associative construction and some verbal aspect markers, but some do not. It seems that in Bangwa, and perhaps the entire Mbam-Nkam subgroup (Hyman and Tadadjeu 1976), other factors override tones associating rightward.

only with floating tones would be sufficient. However, there is a connection between directionality of both spreading and docking of tones. With this in mind, I propose a constraint that includes both of these situations.

(493) ALIGN TONE-RIGHT: ALIGN (TONE, PROSDOM-R): align a tone to the right edge of its prosodic domain(TONE-RT)

The effect of this constraint aligns any tone to the right edge of its particular domain. This would include the cases of docking a floating tone, spreading a linked tone, or shifting the position of a tone. In the cases considered in this section, the domain of the constraint would include a single noun. (In section 6.3.6, it will also apply to the second noun of an associative noun phrase.) Of course, other conflicting constraints prevent a tone from being realized on the last TBU in most cases. For example, LINEARITY, which preserves the serial ordering of elements and penalizes metathesis, would prevent a tone in question from skipping over intervening tones to dock on the last TBU, and constraints against contour tones, toneless TBUs, etc. also come into play here.

This does not completely solve the problem, however. In my analysis of *hɔ̀gú* 'woman', both the High and Low tones are inserted. To get the proper sequencing, we must split the TONE-RT constraint into its components with High and Low tones. In Kɔnni, we have seen nominal suffixes are generally High toned, and the tendency from this and historical factors is that the end of a word is quite likely to be High toned. So the constraint dealing with High tone, HIGH-RT, will be ranked higher than LOW-RT, and indeed the latter will be ranked very low.

(494) hɔ̀gú 'woman' HIGH-RT >> LOW-RT also *H-SPREAD >> DEP(L)

UR hɔgʊ	H-PRESENT	*H-SPREAD	DEP(H)	HIGH-RT	DEP(L)	LOW-RT
☞ a. L H | | hɔgʊ			*		*	*
b. H L | | hɔgʊ			*	*!	*	
c. L L | | hɔgʊ	*!					
d. L |\ hɔgʊ	*!					
e. H |\ hɔgʊ		*!	*			

The winning candidate (494a) violates a number of constraints, but none fatally. Candidate (494b) is ruled out by having the inserted Low tone at the right. Candidates (494c and d) are ruled out by not having a High tone present at all, and candidate (494e) shows it is better to insert a Low tone than to spread a High.

The exact ranking of HIGH-RT cannot be determined from this tableau, other than that it is higher than LOW-RT. I have ranked it fairly low in the above tableau, since it is clear that there are many cases in Kɔnni in which it is massively violated. We shall see a more restricted version of this which applies only to verbs in section 6.4.1, and this version will be undominated.

6.3.2 The -sI suffix

Though most nominal suffixes are unambiguously High toned, some cases of the noun class 3 plural suffix -sI are not. The data below is extracted from appendix B and shows that while most cases of -sI are High toned, some have Low tone. Out of 120 words from noun class 3 in appendix B, eighteen have Low tone on the suffix -sI. All eighteen of these are listed in (495), along with a selection of "normal" High toned suffix nouns. All the nouns that Amadu pronounces with all Low tones except one are also in this list. The words in (495) are arranged in order of increasing number of syllables, and like tones are grouped together. After considering and rejecting an account based on systematic phonological differences, I propose a historical explanation for this pattern, which has resulted in what appear to be arbitrary subclasses in present-day Kɔnni.

(495) Nouns

	Singular	Singular + definite	Plural	Plural + definite
a. Low-toned -sI				
'axe'	líǃáŋ	líáǃká	líásì	líáǃsísì
'fruit (sp.)'	jíǃíŋ	jíǃíká	jíísì	jíǃsísí
'bath sponge'	gbàrà	gbàrìká	gbàrìsì	
'bird (sp.)'	mùlè	mùlìké	mùlìsì	
'hat, straw'	kàgbà (Am.)	kàgbàká	kàgbàsì	
'whydah (bird)'	jùlà	jùlìká	jùlìsì	jùlìsìsí
'parrot'	dààkúǃáŋ	dààkúáǃká	dààkúásí	
'flying ant'	yàyúǃóŋ	yàyúóǃké	yàyúósì	
'ditch'	fùáǃlíŋ	fùàlíŋǃká	fùàlísì	
'bird (sp.)'	tíǃtíì	tíǃtíǃká	tíǃtíísì	
headpan'	'táǃsíŋ	tásíǃká	tásísì	tásíǃsísí
'cat'	gááǃlúǃúŋ	gááǃlúúǃké	gááǃlúúsì	
'sleeping mat'	kàlìŋà	kàlìŋká	kàlìnsì	
'weaverbird'	gàɲìàrà	gàɲìàrìká	gàɲìàrìsì	
'Twi language'	kàmbòŋíŋ	kàmbòŋké	kàmbònsì	
'tree (sp.)'	káíŋkúǃóŋ	káíŋkúóǃké	káíŋkúósì	
'chicken (sp.)'	gbíŋgbíǃŋíŋ	gbíŋgbíŋǃké	gbíŋgbínsì	
'tomato'	kàmánǃtúǃóŋ	kàmánǃtúóǃké	kàmánǃtúósì	
b. High-toned -sI				
'chicken'	kpíáŋ	kpíáká	kpíásí	
'animal, herd'	dɔ̌ŋ	dɔ̀kká	dɔ̀ŋìsí	
'cobra, spitting'	jììŋ	jììká	jììsí	jììsísí
'squirrel (sp.)'	chíǃíŋ	chííǃká	chííǃsí	chííǃsísí
'ball'	bɔ́lì	bɔ́ǃlíká	bɔ́ǃlísí	
'dove'	ŋmáríŋ	ŋmáríká	ŋmárísí	
'bird'	némǃbíŋ	némǃbíké	némǃbísí	
'donkey'	bùníŋ	bùŋká	bùnsí	
'dwarf'	kékíríŋ	kékíríké	kékírísí	
'bowl'	kúrúbâ	kúrúbáǃká	kúrúbáǃsí	
'capsule (medicine)'	túpáyà	túpáǃyáká	túpáǃyásí	
'fly, tsetse'	kákpáǃríŋ	kákpáǃríká	kákpáǃrísí	
'tree (sp.)'	chúnǃchúlí	chúnǃchúlíké	chúnǃchúlísí	

6.3 Nominals

Nouns	Singular	Singular + definite	Plural	Plural + definite
'English (lg. or man)'	bàtúú!líŋ	bàtúú!líké	bàtúú!lísí	bàtúú!lísísí
'fish (sp.)'	púɲí!lú!ŋ̀	púɲí!lúŋ!ké	púɲí!lún!sí	púɲí!lún!sísí
'mussel'	káláŋbí!áŋ	káláŋbíá!ká	káláŋbíá!sí	
'well-being'	bùkáátà	bùkáá!tíká	bùkáá!tísí	
'cattle egret'	kpàlìgìnántìà	kpàlìgìnán!tíáká	kpàlìgìnán!tíásí	
'fish (sp.)'	kpàgàsóŋkpàgà	kpàgàsóŋkpàkká	kpàgàsóŋkpàgàsí	

One characteristic that the Low -*sI* nouns have in common is that the noun stems without exception end with a Low tone. This is shown either by a surface Low if the noun ends in a vowel, or a downstepped High if the noun ends in -*ŋ* in citation form. This also corresponds to a Low tone or a downstep before the singular definite suffix -*ká/-ké*.

Having a stem-final Low tone, however, is a necessary but not sufficient condition for having a Low -*sI*. Many nouns with a High -*sI* also have stem-final Low tones and even identical tone patterns to the Low -*sI* nouns, as seen in (496).

(496) HL stems	-sì	'axe'	lí!áŋ	líásì
	-sí	'squirrel (sp.)'	chí!íŋ	chíí!sí
	-sì	'headpan'	tá!síŋ	tásísì
	-sí	'bird'	ném!bíŋ	ném!bísí
HHL stems	-sì	'chicken (sp.)'	gbíŋgbí!ɲíŋ	gbíŋgbínsì
	-sí	'fly, tsetse'	kákpá!ríŋ	kákpá!rísí

The presence of a Low-toned -*sI* is thus not fully predictable from the tone of the noun stem, although its absence is predictable. If the noun stem ends with a High tone, then there will not be a Low-toned -*sI*. This unpredictable tone will be considered lexical, and so I propose that these eighteen nouns with Low-toned -*sI* have this Low on -*sI* in the lexicon rather than the normal High-toned suffix.

I believe a reasonable explanation for the source of this Low -*sI* is historical and involves borrowed words. Recall that in borrowed words which had word-final consonants in the source language, that an epenthetic *I* was added (section 5.5) and that if an epenthetic vowel is word final, it receives an inserted Low tone (section 6.2.3). This is the obvious case with *sɔ́kìsì* 'socks', in which the word-final -*s* becomes -*sì* with a Low tone. A similar and easily traceable borrowed word is *kàmán!túósì* 'tomatoes', which derives from the English (and originally from the New

World language Nahuatl), possibly Buli *kàmāntòs* 'tomato' (Kröger's dictionary explicitly states it as a borrowing).[19] The Buli word-final -s had an epenthetic -*I* added in Kɔnni, with Low tone, and this was interpreted as the noun class 3 plural suffix. Not all the Low -*sɪ* words can be connected with any other language, though I find cognates for 'axe', 'sleeping mat', 'Twi', 'chicken (sp.)' in Kröger's Buli dictionary and a possible cognate for 'parrot' in Twi and Hausa.

We note that the plural definite suffix in nouns with Low-toned -*sɪ* has the normal High tone, e.g., *líásì* 'axes', *líá!sísí* 'the axes'. This shows the plural definite is not an exact reduplicate of the plural suffix, since the tones are different.

The result of the historical processes is that there is a small group of nouns of noun class 3 which have an idiosyncratically toned suffix, a plural -*sì* with a lexical Low tone rather than the usual High.

6.3.3 Class 1 tone polarity[20]

Though all other nominal suffixes are High toned, the noun class 1 plural suffix is consistently opposite in tone to the preceding tone. In this section I show that this unusual tonal behavior must be explained by a morpheme-specific constraint. Before specifically showing how to account for these forms within an OT approach, I will review three other researchers' approaches to "polar" suffixes in Gur languages.

In previous studies of nouns in Gur languages, it has been noted that in many or most nouns, the nominal suffix has a tone opposite to that of the noun stem. In Mooré, for example, disyllabic nouns have one of the patterns LH, HL, or HH but never LL. Kenstowicz, Nikiema, and Ourso (1988) analyze this and a similar pattern in Lama by hypothesizing that all suffixes have a lexical High tone, and the stems are either High, Low, or toneless. An underlying /L-H/ sequence surfaces as an unchanged [LH], a /H-H/ sequence changes to [HL] by a version of Meeusen's rule (dissimilation, I presume as a consequence of the OCP), and a /Ø-H/ changes to [H-H] as a result of spreading the only High tone present. So in Kenstowicz et al.'s analysis of Mooré,

---

[19]An alternative would be to view "tomato" and the other words as being inherited through the common ancestor of Buli and Kɔnni, and indeed Gur, since a similar form occurs in the Gur language Dagbani. This would entail, however, that tomatoes were known in the area before or at the time that Buli and Kɔnni diverged as separate languages. Since tomatoes are native to the New World and were only brought across the Atlantic with European explorers, the earliest opportunity for this would have been in the 1500s. If the two languages were distinct at that time, as I suspect, then the genetic hypothesis is untenable.

[20]The bulk of the analysis in this section was published as Cahill (1998b), though there have been some modifications made to that analysis.

6.3 Nominals

the apparent tonal polarity is actually an epiphenomenon, the result of other processes. Hyman (1993) proposes a similar analysis for Dagbani.

One aspect of this analysis is common to Kɔnni. As argued above, suffixes on most nouns in Kɔnni are High toned. This was shown not by a detailed analysis of alternations as in Mooré, but by the fact that these suffixes do not alternate or show any polarity; they show up as High toned in almost all cases. (On the basis of these languages, at least, it seems possible that nominal suffixes were High toned in proto-Gur, or at least the branch which contains Kɔnni, Mooré, and Lama.)

The plurals of noun class 1 in Kɔnni however, behave in a way inconsistent with the idea that they are High toned. These are exemplified by the forms in (497), extracted from appendix B. The suffix on the plural form is either -a or -e, depending on vowel harmony, and this suffix is *not* surface High toned, but exhibits tonal polarity, surfacing with a tone opposite to the previous stem tone.

(497)

Singular	Plural	Root tone	Plural suffix tone	
tăŋ	tàná	L	H	'stone/s'
síŋ	sía	H	L	'fish/es (sp.)'
wíŋ	wíè	H	L	'face mark/s'
bìisíŋ	bììsá	L	H	'breast/s'
yìsíŋ	yìsé	L	H	'antelope'
tígíŋ	tígè	H	L	'house/s'
sìkpááŋ	sìkpárà	LH	L	'heart/s'

The general Mooré analysis using underlying High tones for the suffixes cannot be applied to Kɔnni. As shown in (497), the -ŋ singular suffix is High toned. If the plural suffix -a/-e is also High, we would expect the same tonal patterns in the singular as in the plural, but instead we find two distinct patterns in the singular and plural. The singular always ends in a High tone, but the plural ends in a tone opposite to the last tone of the noun stem. Furthermore, the plurals of this noun class are the only ones which act in this manner.

So for this particular morpheme of Kɔnni, we do have an apparent polar-toned suffix, in contrast with Mooré in which most nouns have an apparent polar suffix. In Mooré, these nouns and the nouns which did not exhibit polarity can be analyzed with the same set of rules to give a unified, nonpolar account. In Kɔnni, most nouns do *not* have any apparent polarity; the polar suffix is the exceptional one. As long as we are limited to the constraints presently in place, positing a lexical High tone to account for these is unworkable, since this would lead to the same behavior as the other suffixes, which are definitely High toned.

While the Kɔnni plural suffix cannot be High toned underlyingly, neither can it be Low toned underlyingly within the system of constraints discussed thus far. Since the suffix often surfaces as Low, a lexical Low tone on the "polar" suffix is a hypothesis worth exploring. In this scenario, the suffix is Low but changes to High because a High tone is necessary in a word (H-Present). However, this runs into problems in the case of *tànáhá* 'the stones'. This word is divided into morphemes as *tàn-á-há*. If the plural suffix *-a* is underlyingly Low toned, there is now no motivation for it to change to High, since a High is already present in the definite suffix *-há*. A Low tone for the "polar" suffix in the general system proposed thus far is therefore unsupported.[21] In our present system of constraints, then, neither High nor Low for a lexical tone of the noun class 1 plural suffix is sufficient to account for the facts. The last representation-based solution available is that the suffixes of noun class 1 in Kɔnni are toneless.

Anttila and Bodomo (1997, 2000) discuss a polarity phenomenon in Dagaare very similar to that of Mooré. However, in their analysis, all nominal suffixes in Dagaare are underlyingly toneless. For disyllabic nouns, they have the same tone patterns as Mooré did: LH, HL, and HH. If the root is toneless, Anttila and Bodomo's analysis inserts a default H, which spreads to both syllables, giving surface HH. If the root has a lexical tone, the OCP acting as a specific constraint ensures that the inserted tone is not identical to the root tone but is opposite, giving surface LH and HL. It may be possible to re-analyze Mooré in the same way, with toneless suffixes. Kenstowicz et al. (1988) had rejected the insertion of High tones for Mooré on the grounds that Pulleyblank (1986) had shown that the default in a Low-High tonal system is typically Low not High. More recently, however, Clark (1990) and Creissels and Grégoire (1993) have analyzed Igbo and Manding, respectively, as having a High tone as the default.

---

[21]If the possibility of levels in OT is entertained (as in McCarthy and Prince 1993, Kiparsky 2000), where one ranking of constraints applies at one morphological level and another ranking at the next level, one might consider *tànáhá* as being generated in two levels: first [tàn-á], then [tàná-há]. It would be in level 1 that H-Present would force the insertion of a High, without considering the additional High-toned suffix which is added at a later level. However, the case of *hɔ̀gú* in compounds would seem to negate this possibility. Consider the word *hɔ̀gù-kpàn-ní* 'the spinster', literally 'the woman-single'. The morphological bracketing would be [[[hɔ̀gù][kpàn]]nʃ], with the compounding of the lexical items done before the definite suffix [-nʃ] is added. The word *hɔ̀gú* in isolation has the High tone inserted because of H-Present (see tableau in 494), but in this compound it has no High. The constraint H-Present thus applies to the entire word (or longer utterance) and not to any hypothetical previous level. Thus, if there are any levels in Kɔnni, this phenomenon does not apply to them.

6.3 Nominals

Unlike Anttila and Bodomo's account of Dagaare, the Low tone is clearly the default in Kɔnni. But we need to explore the possibility of the class 1 plural suffix being toneless, and within this hypothesis, to determine if the surface tone on this suffix can be predicted from principles and constraints already in place. Though some forms can be so accounted for, not all of them can, and other constraints will be needed.

Consider the two plurals *tíg-è* 'houses' and *tàn-á* 'stones' with the assumption of a toneless suffix and the constraints already in place for Kɔnni. In *tíg-è*, if the noun stem has an underlying High and the suffix is toneless, the constraints will force an insertion of a Low tone on the suffix (better to insert a Low than to spread a High or insert a High). In *tàn-á*, if the noun stem has a Low tone and the suffix is toneless, a High will be inserted on the suffix to satisfy H-PRESENT. The same analysis works for longer words as well. Relevant cases would include *búllɔ́gà* 'bags' and *dàmpàlá* 'bench' (lit., 'logs'). In *búllɔ́gà*, a Low is inserted on the suffix to contrast with the previous Highs, and in *dàmpàlá*, a High is inserted to contrast with the previous Lows. No nouns of greater length are known in this noun class.

There are at least two sets of data, however, which are problematic for this approach and show that other factors must be considered. The first set includes forms like the previously mentioned *tàn-á-há* 'the stones', in which there seems to be no motivation from H-PRESENT to insert a High tone on a plural suffix *-a*, since the word already has a High tone in it from *-há*. The second set includes words like *jágâ* 'shades', in which a Low tone has been added to the two lexical Highs of the stem; there is no motivation from *TONELESS to insert a tone on a toneless suffix, since the final TBU would already have a tone available. I will examine these more closely.

In forms like *tànáhá* 'the stones', the plural suffix *-a* has a High tone, but the definite suffix *-ha* is also High. If the motivation for inserting the High on *-a* is that a High tone must be present in a noun (H-PRESENT), it should not work in these definite plural cases, since there is already a lexical High present in the definite suffix. If H-PRESENT does not force insertion of a High, I see two other possibilities to rescue the toneless analysis within the present system of constraints.

The first is that, for *tànáhá*, the toneless second syllable receives its High tone by spreading from the suffix *-há*, as in (498a). This seems promising: the spreading in Kɔnni we have seen thus far is right-to-left, and High tone is the tone that spreads, rather than Low. However, a second possibility, that of an inserted polar tone, also exists, as in (498b). In this case, the *-a* receives an inserted tone which has the value of High from polarity to the preceding stem tone, and the *-há* has a lexical High. As we will see, it is impossible to decide between these two phonetically identical representations for this word.

(498) Possible sources of High tone on *tànáhá* 'the stones'

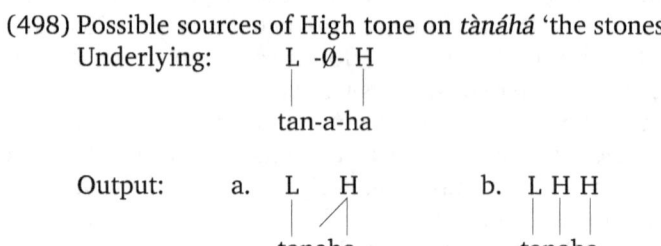

However, it is possible to show that at least some words must have an inserted tone for the polar suffix. This is clear in the case of words like *jágâ* 'shades', which as a member of noun class 1 has the plural suffix *-a* (singular *jág-íŋ*). The word *jágâ* was argued in section 6.1.6 to have two lexical High tones, with the second High combined with a Low to make a falling tone on the second syllable. This is tonally similar to *sîà* 'fishes (sp.)' from (497), in that these both have falling tones on the last TBU of the word. In *sîà* this is visually obscured by the fact that the falling tone is spread over a diphthong (recall that the TBU in Kɔnni is the syllable rather than the mora). Other polysyllabic cases such as *bítîè* 'chins', *kpìbîè* 'lice', and *dààgbúgê* 'stumps' also exist. Of these, let us consider *sîà* as a concrete representative of this class of words.

With the syllable as TBU, the solution of inserting a tone motivated by *Toneless will not work. The stem of *sîà* has a High tone, shown not only by the plural form here, but by the definite form *sínní* (see appendix B for all forms). When the suffix *-a* is added to the stem *sɪ-*, it combines with that stem to form one syllable; there is no phonetic distinction between the polymorphemic diphthong here and one produced from diphthongization of monomorphemic long mid vowels. If the TBU already has a tone on it, there is no reason from the constraints already discussed to insert another. In fact, *Contour would prevent that, and the result would be the unattested **sîá*.

The forms up to this point may all be accounted for by inserting a tone opposite to the last noun stem tone, not from any constraint discussed thus far, but by a different process. However, the set of words like *yíímà* 'arrows' shows a simple insertion will not work. The citation and definite singular form of 'arrow' (*yí!íŋ* and *yíí!rí*) show by the downstep that the root *yɪɪ* must have a HL underlying tone. But this is exactly the tone that appears on the plural form *yíímà*, with no modification. If there were an obligatory inserted polar tone, this tone would need to be High in this

6.3 Nominals

case to contrast with the final Low in the root, and we would expect that stem-final Low to float, with the unattested result *yíí!má.

A more satisfactory approach in terms of the Optimality Theory worldview comes when we reexamine the surface forms of noun class 1 plurals and note the surface generalization that the last tone of the plural suffix is opposite to the one before. This is true whether there is an inserted tone on the suffix (as in *tàná, tígè, jágâ*), a possibly spread tone (as in *tànáhá*), the last tone of the word is an underlying tone of the root (as in *yíímà*), or the polar tone is floating as in *bítíé!hé*. So rather than have an inserted tone as a necessary part of the suffix, we will have a surface-true POLAR constraint. If it is necessary to insert other tones, they will follow from the interaction of POLAR and other constraints, but if the underlying representation already satisfies the POLAR constraint, it remains as is.

(499) **POLAR:** in a noun class 1 plural, the last tone of the plural is opposite in value to the immediately preceding tone.

This definition of POLAR is crucial to account for all the data in an OT framework. I discuss how a morpheme-specific OCP constraint differs from this after (509). Previously, I defined "the plural" as noun stem + plural suffix, but not including any plural definite suffix that may be present.

In *tàn-á-há* 'the stones', POLAR forces the -*a* suffix to have a High tone.

(500) tàn-á-há 'the stones' POLAR >> *H-SPREAD, DEP(H)

	UR L -Ø- H | | tan-a-ha	POLAR	*H-SPREAD	DEP(H)	DEP(L)
☞ a.	L H H | | | tanaha			*	
☞ b.	L H | ／| tanaha		*		
c.	L L H | | | tanaha	*!			*

The ambiguity in the tableau in (500) as to the winning candidate comes from the indeterminacy of the ranking of *H-SPREAD and DEP(H). As already noted, this is inherently difficult to establish, since a multiply linked single

High and two Highs are phonetically indistinguishable. This is unfortunate, since they are the very constraints that would decide between candidates (500a and b). The issue amounts to whether it is better to spread a High onto an empty TBU or insert a new High. Both cases are known to occur elsewhere: a High is inserted to prevent a noun from being all Low toned, and a High can spread if the alternative is a [HLH] configuration. From the wider theory of OT, we can say that a very low-ranked OCP would rule out (500a) in favor of (500b) (see footnote 138), but there is no evidence from within Kɔnni that would decide the issue.

The tableau for *jágâ* 'shades', however, representing nouns which have a falling tone on the last syllable by insertion of a Low tone, gives unambiguous results. This crucially uses the constraint MAX(H), hitherto undefined, which forbids the deletion of High tones.

(501) **MAX(H):** a High tone in the input has a correspondent in the output

(502) *jágâ* 'shades' shows POLAR, MAX(H) >> *CONTOUR

	UR HH-Ø | jag -a	POLAR	MAX(H)	*CONTOUR	DEP(L)
☞ a.	H H L | |/ jaga			*	*
b.	H L | | jaga		*!		*
c.	H L |\\| jaga		*!	*	*
d.	H H | | jaga	*!			

In (502), the HH tonal pattern of the root associates to the root and also to the final syllable of the word including the plural suffix. With a HL pattern word finally, the winning candidate (502a) satisfies POLAR and violates only the lower-ranked *CONTOUR. Candidates (502b and c) delete a High tone and so are ruled out by MAX(H). Candidate (502d) retains all its lexical tones, but violates POLAR.

6.3 Nominals

Words like *bítîè* 'chins' also have a falling tone to end the word, but this word-final Low is lexical, not inserted. This is shown by the singular forms *bítí!éŋ* 'chin' and *bítíé!rí* 'the chin', in which the High tone of the suffix sets the final Low of the stem afloat, causing downstep. This form is also accounted for by this approach.

(503) *bítîè* 'chins' shows MAX(H) >> *CONTOUR

	UR H H L-Ø
	   | |
	   bitie-e
		POLAR	MAX(H)	*CONTOUR	DEP(L)

☞ a.	H HL | |/ bi tie			*	
b.	H HLH | |/ bi tie			*	*!
c.	H L | | bi tie		*!		
	H H | | bi tie	*!			

The winning candidate (503a) violates *CONTOUR but no other constraints listed. Candidate (503b) is quite similar to (503a) but differs (and loses) by the insertion of a High tone. Candidate (503c) has deleted an input tone and so loses. Candidate (503d) is the only one which violates POLAR, and it loses for that reason.

Another type of noun we must account for is one in which a Low polar tone is inserted, but ends up floating and causing downstep, as in *jú!ráhá* 'the chests' or *jágá!há* 'the shades', which would have the configurations shown in (504).

(504) Input   Output

a.   H   H   H L H
     | | → | /|
     ɲʊ -ra -ha   ɲʊ ra ha   ɲʊ́!ráhá 'the chests'

b.   HH   -H   H H L H
     | | → | | /
     jag -a -ha   ja ga ha   jágá!há 'the shades'

In these, in what sense is the polar tone "the tone of the plural," as POLAR refers to it? The inserted polar tone is not associated to anything, let alone the plural morpheme. I take the "tone of the plural" to mean the last tone of a plural noun which precedes a tone contributed by a morpheme which follows the plural morpheme, whether it be the plural definite morpheme or another word altogether. So in forms like ɲʊ́!ráhá or jágá!há, there is a polar tone and POLAR is satisfied even when the polar tone is floating.[22]

(505) jágá!há 'the shades'

	UR HH -Ø-H | | jag -a -ha	MAX(H)	POLAR	*HLH	*CONTOUR	*(L)
☞ a.	H H L H | | | ja ga ha					*
b.	H H LH | | |/ ja ga ha			*!	*	
c.	H L H | /| ja ga ha	*!				*
d.	H H L | | | ja ga ha	*!	*			

The winning candidate (505a) violates only *(L) of the constraints listed. Candidate (505b) violates *HLH by having a Low tone associated

---

[22]It is also possible that Output-Output tonal correspondences could be invoked to account for the presence of the Polar tone when it is floating.

6.3 Nominals

between Highs. Candidates (505c and d) lose by deleting one of the input High tones. Candidate (505d) is the only one which violates POLAR, by not having a polar tone which precedes the definite suffix *-ha*.

Up to this point, POLAR has never been violated, but one small but regular set of data shows that it can be overridden by another constraint. Four nouns in my data (506) have a stem which ends in a vowel, and that vowel is Low toned. In the plural, the suffix adds a high tone. However, when the definite plural suffix is added to that, the polar tone is apparently gone altogether. The latter two examples have a mixed noun class and exhibit noun class 1 morphology only in the plural.

(506) | Plural | Plural definite | |
|---|---|---|
| sìsìé | sìsìèhé | 'grass cutters' |
| jùá | jùàhá | 'tails' |
| nìá | nìàhá | 'rains' |
| bìé | bìèhé | 'goats' |

The factor that overrides POLAR in these forms is a prohibition against word-internal contours, which we formalize as the following:

(507) *CONT-INT: contour tones within a word are prohibited

*CONT-INT is violated only in one highly specific case examined in section 6.3.9. With this constraint in place, we present the tableau for *bìèhé* 'the goats'.

(508) bìèhé 'the goats'

	UR L -Ø-H
	   | |
	  bi-e -he
		*CONT-INT	POLAR	*CONTOUR

☞ a.	L H | | bie he		*	
b.	LH H |/ | bie he	*!		*

Winning candidate (508a) violates POLAR by not having any identifiable tone of the plural suffix *-e* as opposite to the Low stem tone. The final tone is indeed opposite to the preceding tone, but this final tone has its source in the definite suffix, not the plural suffix. However, candidate (508b) (*bìéhé), which unambiguously has a polar tone on the suffix, has a tonal configuration of a word-internal contour which is almost unknown in Kɔnni.[23] This fatally violates *CONT-INT.

Alternative analyses which do not incorporate a POLAR constraint either fail or are less adequate for one reason or another. An underlying High or Low for the plural suffix, along with the OCP, was not attractive, since the OCP is not active as a general constraint for either High or Low tones in Kɔnni. However, a version of the OCP restricted to this particular morpheme might be made to work. Let us assume first, that the noun class 1 plural suffix is lexically High, as are other nominal suffixes in Kɔnni, and second, that Kɔnni has a version of the OCP which disallows adjacent High tones when the second High is on the plural suffix.

(509) (hypothetical)
 OCP_{NC1}: the noun class 1 plural cannot have a High tone if the preceding tone is also high

With this very specific form of the OCP in hand, the Highs on the plural suffixes of *tàn-á* 'stones' and *tàn-á-há* 'the stones' are accounted for straightforwardly as being the lexical tones. In *múg-à* 'rivers' the lexical High on -a is disallowed by the OCP. This OCP would have to be more highly ranked than MAX(H) in order for the lexical High tone to be deleted. We have not seen any tonal deletions at all thus far in Kɔnni, and this is cause for caution in accepting this analysis. However, the real complication comes in the form *bítìè* 'chins'. Here the noun stem has a HHL lexical tone, as seen in the citation and singular definite forms *bítí!éŋ* 'chin' and *bítíé!rí* 'the chin'. A lexical High for the plural would be adjacent to the stem Low and so be allowed by the OCP. The result would be a HHLH for 'chins', with expected association as in (510).

(510) H H L H
       | \ /
       b i t i e

The above configuration would be pronounced as **bítí!é*, which is not the attested form. This tonal configuration, while not common, is attested in Kɔnni, as shown by the verb in *ǹ dágá!á !júókú* 'I am showing the room', taken from appendix F. As far as is known, MAX(H) is undominated; there are

---

[23]The only known forms with word-internal contours are discussed in section 6.3.9.

no deletions of High tones in Kɔnni. So the combination of having a lexical High for the noun class 1 plural and an OCP$_{NC1}$ constraint is unworkable.

The phenomenon of Kɔnni polarity is particularly suited to OT, since it illustrates a "conspiracy." The surface phenomenon is expressed in the constraint POLAR, but this polar tone may be an inserted one, an underlying one, or possibly even a spread tone. A rule-based account would need several separate rules to account for this, almost certainly based on some version of the OCP, and involve insertion of a polar tone with later deletions in some cases.

6.3.4 Derived nouns

Most gerundive nouns derived from verbs have a Low tone on any pre-final syllable and a High on the final syllable which comes from the -ŋ suffix, as (511) shows. For each of the nouns in (511), there is a corresponding verb which is identical to the noun in all respects but that of tone and the final -ŋ (with the single exception of *wɔgɪ* 'to fight' corresponding to *wàgíŋ* 'fighting', to be discussed further below).

(511) pɔ̀gìlíŋ   'holding'   wàgíŋ   'fighting'
      bàlíŋ   'talking'   sìbíŋ   'knowing'
      lɔ̀bìríŋ   'hiding'   dùàgíŋ   'lying down'
      jʋ̀ʋ́síŋ   'asking, request'   chààríŋ   'winnowing'
      chìsìmíŋ   'sneeze'   chùùríŋ   'diarrhea'
      dɔ̀míŋ   'thunder (shaking)' ɲìgìsíŋ   'lightning (flashing)'
      gèrèntíŋ   'burp'   gìríŋ   'fence (surrounding)'
      kɔ̀síŋ   'cough'   hàgìríŋ   'strength (stronging)'
      làmíŋ   'taste'   nàtíŋ   'split'
      ŋmììgíŋ   'weakness'   gàlìmíŋ   'blaming'
      ɲʋ̀ʋ̀gíŋ   'smell'   pʋ̀ʋ̀síŋ   'whisper'
      sɔ̀bíŋ   'writing'   sɔ̀bíŋ   'excreting'
      tààríŋ   'plastering'   tùùríŋ   'marking, line'
      tʋ̀ʋ̀líŋ   'headpad'

Since verbs have no underlying tone in Kɔnni, the tonal patterns on these is explained by the simple addition of the singular nominalizing suffix -*ŋ*, with High tone, to the toneless stem. Default Low tones are inserted on the toneless syllables. This pattern can be accounted for by the constraints already in place, and the tableau for these will look like that for a noun stem which is underlyingly toneless, such as *kpìbíŋ* in (489).

There are, however, a handful of derived nouns which do not have the above LH or LLH tonal pattern, but have a stem tone which begins with a

High tone. All of the cases in my data are listed in (512). In light of our previous analysis, we analyze the patterns in (512a) as having a HL stem tone, and those in (512b) as having a H stem tone.

(512) a. láá!líŋ 'playing' chú!níŋ 'walk'
      káá!síŋ 'sitting place' dúá!síŋ 'lying-down place'
      túú!líŋ 'heat'

   b. chúáríŋ 'taboo' búlíŋ 'well'
      páálíŋ 'swamp' péríŋ 'button'
      sígíŋ 'reincarnated one'

There is nothing irregular about the tone of the corresponding verbs; they follow the normal verb tonal patterns. There are at least two ways to account for these patterns. One possibility is that these nouns are not derived at all, but are underlyingly nouns, and the corresponding verbs are derived by back-formation from the nouns. Another possibility is that these forms are a historical remnant of a period when verbs did have contrastive tone. Some comparative data helps us decide that the latter alternative is more attractive.

Only a few of these forms can be compared with the Buli forms found in Kröger (1992). Buli has a noun cognate with *túú!líŋ* 'heat', but with a HH tone. Similarly, the cognate noun of *búlíŋ* 'well' has LL tone. Buli also has verbs corresponding to the derived nouns *dúá!síŋ* 'lying-down place', *túú!líŋ* 'heat', *búlíŋ* 'well', and *péríŋ* 'button' in (512). Verbs in Buli are underlyingly toneless as they are in Kɔnni.

If nouns were the basic forms in the case at hand, we would expect a better match with tones than is evidenced with the two forms for 'heat' and 'well' (though a systematic reconstruction of the tones of Proto-Buli-Kɔnni has not yet been done).

I propose that the second scenario is more likely, that Proto-Gur had contrastive tone on verbs, that there was a nominalizing process in Proto-Gur, and that some of the nouns derived from verbs at that stage became frozen in form and today in Buli and Kɔnni exist as separate lexical items rather than synchronically derived forms. Though neither Buli nor Kɔnni has contrastive tone on verbs, many other Gur languages do. These include at least Dagaare (Bodomo 1997), Dagbani (Olawsky 1996), Kasem (Awedoba 1993), Supyire (Carlson 1994), Cɛfɔ (Winkelmann 1998), Kusuntu (Kleinewillinghöfer 1999), Samoma (Kedrebéogo 1997), Nootre (von Roncador 1999), Mbelime (Rietkerk 1999), Pana (Beyer 1999), and Konkomba (Steele and Weed 1966). This last reference has enough Konkomba cognates listed to be useful, and Adams Bodomo (personal communication) has also kindly supplied cognates from Dagaare, as follows:

(513)

	Kɔnni noun (from (512)	Kɔnni verb	Konkomba verb	Dagaare verb	
a.	chʊ́!nɪ́ŋ	chʊm-	chùúm	chéŋ~chéɲí	'walk'
	káá!sɪ́ŋ	ka-, kas-, kal-	kǎl		'sit'
	dʊ́á!sɪ́ŋ	dʊa	dùóm		'lie-down'
	tʊ́ʊ́!lɪ́ŋ	tʊʊl-		túlì	'be hot'
	láá!lɪ́ŋ	laal-		láárì	'to laugh, play'
b.	páálɪ́ŋ	paal-	púú	pààlì	'flow'
	búlɪ́ŋ	bul-		búlí	'ooze up'
	pérɪ́ŋ	per-		pìrì	'button, fasten'
	sígɪ́ŋ	sig-		sígí	'reincarnate, be named after'

Note that all the Konkomba verbs have a High tone somewhere in them, and there is a correspondence between the rising tone on the Konkomba verbs in (513a) and the H!H tone on the Kɔnni nouns. The sole Konkomba verb which has only High tone corresponds to a different pattern in Kɔnni. For the Dagaare verbs, the set in (513a) has a predominant HL pattern[24] and those in (513b) have either HH or LL patterns. (It is also interesting that both of the LL verbs are *p*-initial, which I have proposed elsewhere are borrowed into Kɔnni.) This evidence is hardly enough to be conclusive, but it is suggestive that such systematic correspondences can be drawn up.

For this reason, I tentatively propose that the nouns in (512) which do not have Low-toned stems are not synchronically derived from verbs, but were derived at an earlier stage of the language, a stage in which verbs had a tonal contrast. These nouns were then frozen in form and relexicalized so that at present Kɔnni these nouns and the verbs from which they were originally derived constitute two separate lexical entries. Besides the comparative evidence, the internal evidence in Kɔnni of the different vowels in *wɔgɪ* 'to fight' corresponding to *wàgɪ́ŋ* 'fighting', mentioned at the beginning of this section, shows that these are now separate forms lexically.

---

[24]The exception is *chéŋ ~ chéɲí* 'walk'. In light of the Kɔnni and Konkomba citation forms, and others which could be cited (Buli *cheŋ*, Kusaal *tɪn*, Birifor *chɪn*), it seems likely that the original form was monosyllabic, and the present Dagaare disyllabic variation with the monosyllabic form is the innovation.

6.3.5 Adjectival extensions

Just as nouns have contrastive tone, adjectival extensions to noun stems contrast in lexical tone, as seen in (514), taken from the list of noun-adjective forms in appendix D.

(514) LH   jà-kùúŋ   'old thing'   jà-yèèlíŋ   'white thing'
     HLH   jà-kpí!íŋ   'big thing'   jà-háá!líŋ   'new thing'
     H   jà-wɔ́ŋ   'long thing'   jè-góbíŋ   'short thing'

Adjectives have the same suffixes as noun stems. All of the words in (514) have the singular indefinite -ŋ suffix with accompanying High tone.

Adjectives which are derived from verbs, however, generally do not have a contrast in tone but, as in the case of derived nouns discussed in the preceding section, have all Low tones on the stem and a final High which has its source in the -ŋ suffix. These are illustrated after the Low-toned jà- 'thing' to avoid any perturbations due to High spreading. (Recall that Low tones do not spread in Kɔnni, so this is a neutral environment.)

(515) Adjectives derived from verbs: LH or LLH tone pattern
     jè-chììkíŋ   'carried thing'   jà-dùnsíŋ   'heavy thing'
     jà-sùùlìkíŋ   'filled (full) thing'   jà-hàgìríŋ   'strong thing'
     jà-vììníŋ   'good thing'   jà-chùùsìkíŋ   'spoiled thing'
     jà-tùáŋ   'bitter thing'   jà-nànsíŋ   'sweet thing'
     jà-fùùsìkíŋ   'inflated thing'   jà-bɔ̀bìkíŋ   'tied/wrapped thing', etc.

However, just as most derived nouns followed a single tonal pattern, but there was a significant number of nouns with other tonal patterns, so there are five adjectives in my data which clearly do not follow the pattern in (515), but have a H!H in the adjective. In terms of our analysis of downstep as a floating Low and a suffixal -ŋ, the adjective stems in these cases have either HL or HHL as the tonal pattern.

(516) Derived adjectives: HL or HHL adjectival stem
     jà-kú!kíŋ   'dried thing'   jà-bíí!kíŋ   'ripe thing'
     jà-sún!íŋ   'cool thing'   jè-díí!kíŋ   'eaten things'
     jè-dígín!tíŋ   'dirty thing'

As in the case of the derived nouns with anomalous tone in the preceding section, I will assume these adjectives also have their source in verbs

6.3 Nominals

with a particular tonal pattern in an earlier stage of the language, and that these adjectival forms have been lexicalized over time so they have a separate lexical entry from the verb that was originally their source. This is supported by cognates in (517) for all of the above from Konkomba (Steele and Weed 1966).

(517)
Kɔnni adjective	Kɔnni verb	Konkomba verb	
-kú!kíŋ	kʊ	ŋkúùn	'dry'
-bíí!kíŋ	bi	pʷìr̥	'be ripe'
-sún!síŋ	sʊnsɪ	ñsūòn[25]	'be cool'
-díí!kíŋ	di	jîm	'eat'
-dígín!tíŋ	diginti	tījɔ̄ntì	'be dirty'

Note that all the Konkomba verbs have a High-Low (or Mid-Low or Mid-Mid-Low) pattern, while the Kɔnni adjectives all have a HL or HHL stem. Though this is not the place for a reconstruction of Proto-Gur tone, it seems that the tonal pattern of these derived adjectives in Kɔnni reflects the tonal pattern of verbs in the parent language of Konkomba and Kɔnni.

We have seen that some noun stems are best treated as underlyingly toneless, but in the case of adjectives, there are none with behavior that would lead us to posit toneless adjectives. Toneless adjectives would show up with a Low tone on the stem by default, and High from the suffix, yielding patterns like the hypothetical -bàbáŋ when following a Low-toned noun stem. When following a High-toned stem, however, we would expect the High from either the noun or the suffix to spread, or a High to be inserted, as in the tableau in (486), and this would yield -bábáŋ, with all High tones. There is no adjective which has this type of behavior; if there is a Low tone in the adjective in one form, this Low remains in other forms of the paradigm, though often as downstep. The conclusion is that no adjective stems, at least in my data, are underlyingly toneless.

---

[25] The word-final nasal in Konkomba indicates that the previous vowels are nasalized, rather than a phonetic nasal consonant.

(518) "small": two forms

		Singular	Singular definite	Plural	Noun stem
a. L	'small bone'	kɔ̀b-bíŋ		kɔ̀b-bìsí	kɔ̀b-
	'small cleared area'	kɔ́g-ꜜbíŋ			kɔ́g-
	'small cutlass'	kàrɛ́ntìà-bíŋ			kàrɛ́ntìà-
	'small father'	chòm-bíŋ		chòm-bìsí	chɔ̀N-
	'small hat'	kàgbàà-bíŋ	kàgbàà-bìké	kàgbàà-bìsí	kàgbàà-
	'small lizard'	gòráá-ꜜbíŋ		gòráá-ꜜbísí	gòráá-
	'small shea tree'	téꜜbíŋ		téꜜ-bísí	táá-
	'small thing'	jè-bíŋ	jè-bìké	ɲìm-bìsí	jàà-/ɲìN-
	'small tin can'	kɔ́ŋkòm-bíŋ		kɔ́ŋkòm-bìsí	kɔ́ŋkɔ̀N-
	'small woman'	hɔ̀gù-bíŋ	hɔ̀gù-bìké	hɔ̀gù-bìsí	hɔ̀gù-
b. HL	'small broom'	súm-bíꜜlŋ		súm-bísì	súN-
	'small chicken'	kpìè-bíꜜlŋ	kpìè-bíꜜlké	kpìè-bísì	kpìà-
	'small dog'	gbè-bíꜜlŋ	gbè-bíꜜlké	gbè-bísì	gbàà-
	'small farm'	kúó-bíꜜlŋ	kúó-bíꜜlké	kúó-bísì	kúá-
	'small horse'	dùùm-bíꜜlŋ			dùùN
	'small river'	múgú-bíꜜlŋ	múgú-bíꜜlké	múgú-bísì	múgú-
	'small (junior) wife'	hɔ̀gù-bíꜜlŋ			hɔ̀gù-

6.3 Nominals

The adjectival form translated 'small' which attaches to noun stems actually has two forms which differ only in tone but have different historical sources. Note the difference in tonal patterns in (518a and b). The singular definite suffix and the plural suffix mark all of these, both in (518a and b), as belonging to noun class 3. Again assuming that the final High tone of the words is due to suffixal -ŋ́, the forms in (518a) can be analyzed as having a Low tone for the stem and those in (518b) as having a HL tone for the stem. The ratios of the number of forms in (518a) to the number in (518b) approximates the ratio in my data: the (518a) forms are more common, but (518b) forms are far from rare. There seems to be no correlation between any phonological shape of a noun and which form of 'small' it takes. Changes in vowels between the 'small' form and the stated noun stem are due to ATR spread from the adjective.

Note that both Low-toned and High-toned noun stems occur with both forms of 'small'. Note also that the plural forms in (518b) have the Low-toned form of the plural suffix -sì, while the forms in (518a) have the High-toned form -sí. Besides the difference in tones, these forms are shown to be distinct by other lines of evidence. It seems that a noun stem will select a particular form of 'small' to conjoin with; matching a noun with the other form will be incorrect. Amadu once pronounced the wrong form, *kɔ̀b-bí!ŋ́ rather than the correct kɔ̀b-bǐŋ 'small bone'. He immediately corrected himself. Also, there is one pair of words above which differs only in the form of 'small' which is chosen, but this makes a difference in meaning. These are hɔ̀gù-bǐŋ, which is the normal construction for 'small woman', and hɔ̀gù-bí!ŋ́, which is a specific relational term 'small (junior) wife' for a junior wife in a polygynous marriage.

There are two adjectival forms in Buli which seem to be cognates, but in that language they have segmental differences. The forms are *biik* (def. *biika*, pl *bisa*) and *bilik* (def. *bilika*, pl *bilisa*). Kröger (1992) notes that the latter is used only with a restricted set of nouns (e.g., *pò-bìlī* 'junior wife'). Tonally, these both have a rising tone when following a Low-toned noun and in that way resemble the forms in (518a). There is, however, another Buli candidate to serve as a model for the initially High-toned forms in (518b). This is *bíík* 'child' (def. *bííká*, pl *bísá*). A reasonable possibility is that Kɔnni, as the more innovative language, merged the first two adjectives completely, giving the pattern in (518a), and adopted the noun *bíík* 'child' as an adjectival form, giving the forms in (518b).

The direction of High-tone spreading within noun-adjective complexes is from left to right, from the noun stem into the adjective. This is unlike the case in other environments in Kɔnni, in which an underlying HLH configuration yields surface H!HH, but there is no spreading at all if there is more than one Low tone between Highs (section 6.2.2). In the specific case of noun-adjective, however, this direction of spreading is reversed. The only other case that I am aware of in Kɔnni in which there is rightward spreading is into preverbal particles.

(519) H-spread from noun into adjective
    a. tígí-yéé!líŋ   'white house' (cf. jà-yèèlíŋ 'white thing')
    b. tígí-kú!úŋ   'old house' (cf. tìk-kùúŋ 'old village')
    c. jɔ́rɔ́-dún!síŋ   'heavy ladder' (cf. jà-dùnsíŋ 'heavy thing')
    d. tígí-yéélí-!bíŋ   'small white house'

The underlying and surface forms of *jɔ́rɔ́-dún!síŋ* 'heavy ladder' and *tígí-yéélí-!bíŋ* 'small white house' are given in (520), with underlying tones above the syllables they are sponsored by.

(520) H-spread from noun into adjective

    a. H H- L   H   H H   L H
        | | | | → | |\ |
        jɔrɔ-dʊns-ŋ   jɔrɔ-dʊnsɪŋ   jɔ́rɔ́-dún!síŋ 'heavy ladder'

    b. H   -L   -L-H   H   H L H
        | | | | → | /|\ |
        tigi-yɛɛlɪ-bi-ŋ   tigi-yɛɛlɪ-biŋ   tígí-yéélí-!bíŋ 'small white house'

Previously, we have seen the common cases in which there is leftward High spreading in the HLH context, in a variety of contexts (section 6.2.2). If that happened here, we would expect the downstep in a different place for (520a), as in the unattested **jɔ́rɔ́-dún!síŋ*. Not only does the High spread rightward through one Low tone, but in the case of *tígí-yéélí-!bíŋ* 'small white house', the High from the noun stem *tígí* spreads through both Low-toned syllables of *yɛɛlɪ*. I have represented the output of (520b) with only one floating Low tone which causes downstep; at this point I assume that more than one identical floating tone would be collapsed into one, though it would not change the analysis significantly if two or more floating Lows were present.

A High tone will also spread from an adjective into another adjective, again rightward. The example in (521c) shows that a High may spread from an adjective through another adjective, into a third adjective, and the last example (521d) shows that if adjectives are not preceded by a High tone, those adjectives may be Low toned.

6.3 Nominals

(521) H-spread from adjective into adjective
    a. hɔ̀gʊ̀-sɔ́bɩ́lɩ́-bɩ́!áŋ   'bad black woman'
       (cf. jà-bìáŋ 'bad thing')
    b. jà-wɔ́gʊ́-vɩ́ɩ́ŋ!ká   'the good long thing'
       (cf. jà-vɩ̀ɩ̀ŋká 'the good thing')
    c. hɔ̀gʊ̀-sɔ́bɩ́lɩ́-bɩ́-bɩ́á!ká   'the small bad black woman'
       (cf. jè-bǐŋ 'small thing')
    d. hɔ̀gʊ̀-ŋmìm-bì-vɩ̀ɩ̀ŋká   'the small good red woman'

The hypothesized inputs and outputs for the forms in (521a–c) are shown in (522), with underlying tones lined up above their sponsoring TBUs. Note that *hɔgʊ* 'woman' is toneless in the input.

(522) H-spread from adjective into adjective

a.   -H HL - L- H   L L H HL H
       | | | | → | | | /\ /
    hɔgʊ-sɔbɩl -bɩa-ŋ   hɔgʊ-sɔbɩlɩ-bɩaŋ   'bad black woman'

b.   L -H - L -H   L H L H
       | | | | → | /|\ |
    ja-wɔgʊ vɩɩŋ-ka   ja-wɔgʊ-vɩɩŋka   'the good long thing'

c.   -HHL -L -L- H   L L H H L H
       | | | | | → | | | /\ |
    hɔgʊ-sɔbɩl- bi-bɩa-ka   hɔgʊ-sɔbɩlɩ-bi-bɩaka   'the small bad black woman'

In the configurations in (520) and (522), the High of the noun stem or adjective has spread until it reaches a Low before a High, which produces a downstepped High in the last syllable of all the above. The number of Low tones between this High and the final syllable seems irrelevant; there are cases above with one, two, or three input Low tones (in 522b, a, and c).

The adjective -*sɔ́bɩ́!lɩ́ŋ* 'black' is shown to have a HHL root by the downstep after the two High tones when it occurs as the last adjective in a complex.

(523) jà-sɔ́bɩ́!lɩ́ŋ   'black thing'
     jà-sɔ́bɩ́lɩ́-!ká   'the black thing'

A disyllabic Low-toned adjective seems to block this spreading of High, as in *yèèlì* in (524a), but two monosyllabic Low-toned adjectives do not, as in -*bí-bíá-* in (524b).

(524) a. jà-háálí-yèèlì-kpí!íŋ 'new white big thing' (cf. jà-háá!líŋ 'new thing')
      b. hɔ̀gù-sɔ́bílí-bí-bíá-!ká the small bad black woman'

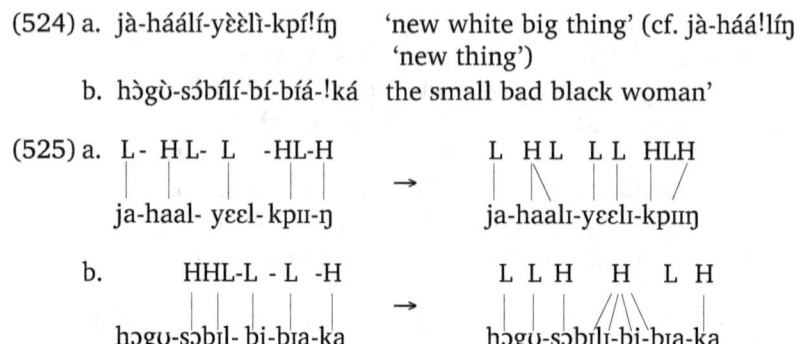

Accounting for this pattern with constraints poses some obvious challenges. This rightward spreading is limited to adjectives, and a relevant constraint must make reference to "adjective." This is done in (526).

(526) *HL$_{adj}$: a Low tone cannot be associated to an adjective when preceded by a High tone (shorthand for *HL)

$$\overset{\text{*HL}}{\underset{X_{adj}}{|}}$$

This is a descriptive constraint which is morphologically restricted and thus idiosyncratic: it has no phonetically based motivation. As far as I know, it is undominated. Let us take two cases as representative, the first being *hɔ̀gù-sɔ́bílí-bí-bíá-!ká* 'the small bad black woman' from (524b). The adjective -*sɔ́bílí* has a HHL lexical tone, as shown by the downstep in the citation form *jà-sɔ́bí!líŋ* 'black thing'. The other adjectives -*bi* and -*bɪa* are lexically Low toned.

(527) hɔ̀gù-sɔ́bílí-bí-bíá-!ká 'the small bad black woman'

	UR	*HL$_{adj}$	M$_{AX}$ (A$_{SSOC}$)	*H-S$_{PREAD}$	*(L)
	HHL -L -L -H | | | | | hɔgu-sɔbɪl -bi -bɪa-ka				
☞ a.	H H L H | //\\ | hɔ̀gù-sɔbɪlɪ-bi-bɪa-ka		**	***	*
b.	HHL L L H | || | | | | hɔ̀gù-sɔbɪlɪ-bi-bɪa-ka	*!			
c.	HH LL L H | |\\ | | | hɔ̀gù-sɔbɪlɪ-bi-bɪa-ka	*!		*	*

6.3 Nominals

Candidate (527a) wins because, unlike the other candidates, there is no Low tone in an adjective preceded by a High. In candidate (527b), the last syllable of -sɔbılı has a Low tone preceded by a High. In candidate (527c), the adjective -bi also has a Low preceded by a High.

The next form in this context we will examine is tígí-yéé!líŋ 'white house' from (519a). In this form a High tone spreads into the adjective -yéé!líŋ. Here there is a High tone on the tonal tier directly preceding the -yɛɛlı- adjective in tígí-yéé!líŋ.

(528) tígí-yéé!lí-ŋ 'white house'

	UR H- L -H | | | tig-yɛɛl-ŋ	*HL$_{adj}$	*HLH	MAX (ASSOC)	*H-SPREAD	*(L)
☞ a.	H L H /|\ | tigi-yɛɛlŋ			*	**	*
b.	H L H /| | | tigi-yɛɛlŋ	*!	*		*	
c.	H L H | /| | tigi-yɛɛlŋ	*!	*			
d.	H L H |\ /| tigi-yɛɛlŋ			*	**	*

Candidate (528a) is the winner, although it violates MAX(ASSOC) by delinking the lexical Low tone, *H-SPREAD twice by spreading a High tone two TBUs and also has a floating Low tone. Candidates (528b and c) both fatally violate *HL$_{adj}$. The violation in (528b) is obvious, but in (528c) less so. The constraint *HL$_{adj}$ is violated when a Low tone associated to an adjective is preceded by a High tone. The two conditions are that the Low is linked to an adjective, and on the tonal tier, that Low is preceded by a High. In (528c), even though the Low is linked to the last syllable of the noun, it is also linked to the adjective. Furthermore, on the tonal tier, this Low is preceded by a High, so the conditions are met for a violation of *HL$_{adj}$. Candidate (528d) is not the one pronounced, but in the tableau in (528) it is tied with the winning candidate (528a). It is possible that the constraint *HL$_{adj}$ should actually be expressed as forbidding a *lower* tone in the adjective than in the noun immediately preceding. Then the HL sequence would be prohibited, as is already the case, but also a H!H sequence across the morpheme boundary would be prohibited. If not, another constraint would be needed to rule out (528d).

Finally, the form jà-háálí-yèèlì-kpí!íŋ 'new white big thing' is problematic because the High tone does not spread throughout the adjectives. The morphemes that we will focus on are háálí- 'new' and yèèlì- 'white'. The final vowels in these are epenthetic, (see section 5.5 for discussion). In jà-háá!líŋ 'new thing', we see by the downstep that 'new' has a lexical High-Low tone, and in jà-yèèlíŋ 'white thing' we see that 'white' has a lexical Low tone, and these are the forms in the input in (529).

(529) jà-háálí-yèèlì-kpí!íŋ 'new white big thing'

	UR L -HL -L - HL-H | | | | | ja-haal-yɛɛl-kpıı -ŋ	*HL$_{adj}$	M$_{AX}$ (A$_{SSOC}$)	*H- S$_{PREAD}$	*(L)
☞ a.	L H L LL HLH | \\ | | \/ ja-haalı-yɛɛlı -kpııŋ			*	**
b.	L H L LL HLH | | | | | \/ ja-haalı-yɛɛlı -kpııŋ	*!			*
c.	L H LL HLH | //\\ \/ ja-haalı-yɛɛlı -kpııŋ		*	**!*	*

The optimal form is (529a), though the question arises of its violating *HL$_{adj}$. There is a High followed by a Low associated to an adjective, which may seem to violate *HL$_{adj}$, but the floating tone originally from -haal- is between the two, so the Low associated to the adjective is not adjacent to the High and thus does not violate *HL$_{adj}$. Candidate (529b) loses since the Low associated to -haalı- is immediately preceded by a High, also on -haalı-. Were it not for the floating Low, (529c) would be optimal. However, as it is, (529c) violates *H-S$_{PREAD}$ more than (529a) and so loses.

6.3.6 Associative noun phrases

An associative (or genitive or possessive) noun phrase in Kɔnni consists of two adjacent nouns, where the first is the possessor (or dependent) noun, and the second is the possessed (or head) noun. As seen in the data below,

6.3 Nominals

repeated from (458) and (459), when the dependent noun in an associative noun phrase is third person, whether singular or plural, pronoun or full noun, the head noun always begins with a High tone. This shows the presence of a grammatical High tone for this construction, which I analyze as an underlying floating High between the two nouns.

(530) a.

	1st	2nd	3rd	3rd nonhuman	
Singular	ǹ dàáŋ	fī dàáŋ	ʊ̀ **dá**!áŋ	kà **dá**!áŋ	'my, etc. stick'
Plural	tī dàáŋ	nī dàáŋ	bà **dá**!áŋ	à **dá**!áŋ	

b.
tăŋ	ʊ̀ **tá**!**ŋ́**	'stone, his/her stone'
kàgbá	ʊ̀ **kág**bà	'hat, his/her hat'
dàmpàlá	ʊ̀ **dám**!pálá	'bench, his/her bench'

c. bʊ̀áwá **dá**!**áŋ** 'child's stick' (bʊ̀àwá 'the child', dàáŋ 'stick')

bʊ̀á **kár**èǹtìà 'child's cutlass' (bʊ̀á 'child', kàréǹtìà 'cutlass')

chʊ̀rú **dám**!pálá 'husband's bench' (chʊ̀rú 'husband', dàmpàlá 'bench')

In the broader African context, the associative morpheme consisting entirely of tone arose historically from a morpheme which had segmental as well as tonal content. This morpheme occurred between the possessed and possessor nouns, in conformity with Greenberg's word-order universals (Greenberg 1966). When the segmental content, often a vowel, was lost, the tonal effect remained behind (see discussion in Welmers 1963). A more extensive list of associative noun phrases is found in appendix E.

A floating High tone in Kɔnni is prohibited by the constraint *(H) (see 466), and this constraint is undominated. A floating High tone can be eliminated by one of two strategies: deleting it or associating it to a TBU. In Kɔnni, elimination of a High tone never occurs and is ruled out formally by the constraint MAX(H), introduced in section 6.3.2. The only alternative left is to associate this floating High tone, and then the question of direction of docking arises.

In Kɔnni, the second noun is always the one to receive the High tone that marks the associative construction. In Cahill (2000), I list twenty-nine languages with associative tone and show that unless there is some marked circumstance such as a toneless syllable, in all these languages the associative tone docks either to the rightmost noun or to the head noun (which can be the same noun, as in the case of Kɔnni). There is no language I have seen in which the associative tone normally docks leftward to the dependent noun. As a result of this, I proposed two constraints: HEAD-PROMINENCE and TONE-RIGHT, which, taken together with constraints against floating tones, determine the direction of docking of the floating associative tone. As we have previously seen, in Kɔnni there is often leftward spreading of a High, so presumably the relevant constraint forcing docking of the High rightward would be HEAD-PROMINENCE, based on Cahill (2000).

(531) **HEAD-PROMINENCE (HEAD-PROM):** if a portion of a phrase is not identical with its underlying representation, the head of the phrase will increase in phonetic prominence.[26]

In terms of the tones discussed here, High tones are considered more "prominent" than Low tones, and this prominence may be related to the other asymmetries of High and Low tones, e.g., the constraint *HLH exists but not *LHL, and a Low rather than a High is the default tone for insertion. In this light, "prominence" must be understood as comparing input and output forms with respect to High tones. If an output has more High tones than its corresponding input form, it is "more prominent." With these constraints in place, we present the tableau illustrating a basic associative noun phrase.

---

[26]The effects of this constraint go beyond associative morphemes. For other examples of phonetic prominence of heads of phrases, see Cahill (2000). Also, since in current syntactic theory prepositions are heads of prepositional phrases, but prepositions are rarely phonetically prominent, the constraint should be qualified to exclude prepositional phrases.

6.3 Nominals

(532) ù zá!síŋ 'his/her fish' (cf. zàsíŋ 'fish')

	UR: L H L -H
	    | | |
	   ʊ zas -ŋ
		*(H)	Max(H)	Head-Prom	*HLH	*(L)

☞ a.	L H L H | \\ / ʊ zasıŋ					*
b.	L H L H | | | ʊ zasıŋ	*!			*	
c.	L L H | | | ʊ zasıŋ		*!			
d.	L H L H |/ | | ʊ zasıŋ			*!	*	
e.	L H L H | | |/ ʊ zasıŋ				*!	

The winning candidate (532a) violates only the low-ranked constraint *(L), while satisfying the others listed. Candidate (532b) loses by having the High tone remain floating and so violating *(H). Candidate (532c) loses by deleting the High tone altogether. Candidate (532d) loses by having the associative High tone dock to the dependent rather than the head noun. Finally, candidate (532e) loses by having a Low associated between two High tones, and so violating *HLH. Both candidates (532b and d) also violate *HLH, but the undominated constraints they violate outrank *HLH, and so in the interpretation of the tableau, *HLH is not the constraint that incurs the fatal violation. However, if these undominated constraints were not present, or ranked lower, *HLH would still rule out these candidates. This raises the possibility that what appears to be a fatal violation in a tableau is not actually the fatal one if we had a fuller understanding of the constraints active in a language.

The constraints in place can also account for the toneless nouns and noun stems discussed in section 6.3.1, such as *kpìbíŋ* 'louse', *kàgbá* 'hat', and *hɔ̀gú* 'woman'. The word *kpìbíŋ* 'louse' was argued in section 6.3.1 to have a toneless stem, though the suffix -ŋ contributes an underlying High tone. In citation form, the Low on the first syllable is inserted as a default (see tableau in

489). The associative construction is consistent with and provides additional support for this tonelessness. Since *(H) is never violated, the remainder of the tableaus in this section will not list this constraint or candidates which violate it.

(533) ù kpíbíŋ 'louse' (cf. kpìbíŋ 'louse')

	L H -H | | u kpibi-ŋ	Max(H)	Head-Prom	*H-Spread	Dep(L)
☞ a.	L H H | | | u kpibiŋ				
b.	L L H | | | u kpibiŋ	*!			
c.	L H L H | \ | u kpibiŋ				*!
d.	L H | /| u kpibiŋ	*!		*	
e.	LH L H |/ | | u kpibiŋ		*!		

The winning candidate (533a) violates no listed constraints. Candidate (533b) loses by deleting the High associative tone. Candidate (533c) loses by inserting a Low tone. Candidate (533d), phonetically identical to (533a), still loses by deleting the associative High tone. Candidate (533e) loses by not associating the High to the head noun.

Candidate (533d) is interesting in that it is phonetically identical to the winning candidate (533a) but by the constraints in place, it is definitely ruled out. Unlike approaches such as Optimal Domains Theory (Cassimjee and Kisseberth 1998, Cole and Kisseberth 1994), in the approach here association lines are crucial.

Another noun which I analyze as partially toneless is *kàgbá* 'hat', which has a single Low tone, but whose High in citation form is inserted to satisfy H-Present in (491).

6.3 Nominals

(534) ʊ̀ kágbà 'his hat' (cf. kàgbá 'hat') MAX(H), HEAD-PROM >> MAX(ASSOC)

	L H L | | ʊ kagba	MAX(H)	HEAD-PROM	H-PRESENT	MAX (ASSOC)	DEP(H)	DEP(L)
☞ a.	L H L | | | ʊ kagba				*		
b.	L L H | | | ʊ kagba	*!				*	
c.	L L L | | | ʊ kagba	*!		*!			*
	L H L L |/ | | ʊ kagba		*!				*

Candidate (534a) wins, even though it violates MAX(ASSOC) by having the Low tone on the right of *kagba* instead of the left. In candidate (534b), I assume the associative High tone has been deleted, and the High at the end of *kagba* has been inserted as it was in the citation form of the noun. The additional phonetically identical candidate ʊ̀ kàgbá, with the High having its source in the associative morpheme, would be ruled out by a LINEARITY constraint forbidding metathesis, which never occurs in Kɔnni. Candidate (534c), which deletes the High tone, loses both by deletion of the High and by the absence of a High tone. Candidate (534d) loses by associating the High to the pronoun rather than the head noun.

The other toneless noun is *hɔ̀gʊ́* 'woman', which I analyze in (494) as having no underlying tones at all. If so, the question arises as to the High associative tone docks to the first rather than the second syllable. The reason, I presume, is that a floating tone when docking will not "skip" over a nearby available TBU in favor of one more distant from its starting position. This would involve issues of adjacency which are not fully resolved in my mind, and the formulation of the relevant constraint is worth more research. I tentatively propose:

(535) **NOSKIP:** a floating autosegment will dock to the nearest available TBU

(536) ù hɔ́gù 'his wife' (cf. hɔ̀gú 'woman, wife') NoSkip, Head-ProM
>> High-Rt

L H | ʊ hɔgʊ	NoSkip	Head-Prom	High-Rt	*H-Spread	Dep(L)
☞ a. L H L | | | ʊ hɔgʊ			*		*
b. L L H | | | ʊ hɔgʊ	*!				*
c. L H | |\ ʊ hɔgʊ			*	*!	
LH L L |/ | | ʊ hɔgʊ	*!				**

Candidate (536a) violates High-Rt, which would pressure the High tone to be realized on the rightmost syllable of *hɔgʊ*. This constraint was crucial in determining the relative positions of the tones in the citation form *hɔ̀gú*, in which both the Low and High were inserted. However, here the High is not inserted, but is present in the input. Furthermore, it has a specific position with respect to the head noun; it precedes it. It docks to the nearest available TBU: the first syllable. In candidate (536b), the associative High tone ignores the immediately adjacent syllable to dock on the last syllable, fatally violating NoSkip. Candidate (536c) also violates High-Rt even though it has a High tone in the rightmost syllable. But the High is not totally aligned to the right, since it also is associated to the first syllable. Since both (536a and c) violate High-Rt, then the decisive constraint is one which is ranked lower, in this case *H-Spread. Comparing (536a and c), we see it is better to insert a Low than to spread the High tone. Finally, candidate (536d) loses by associating the High to the nonhead pronoun.

At least two other situations illustrate the interaction of the associative High tone with other constraints we have discussed. The first is the associative noun phrase *níígʲé kɔ́bà* 'cows' bones', with two nouns rather than the pronoun + noun construction for which we have seen several tableaus. Both nouns in this phrase are members of noun class 1, with the plural suffixes subject to the Polar constraint, here repeated from (499).

6.3 Nominals

(537) POLAR: in a noun class 1 plural, the last tone of the plural is opposite in polarity to the immediately preceding tone.

In the citation forms *nííg-è* 'cows' and *kɔ̀b-á* 'bones', the tonal polarity of the suffixes is clearly seen, but in the associative construction, the situation is less clear. We see from the second downstep in *kpá!áŋ kɔ́!bíŋ* 'guinea fowl's bone', as well as the citation form *kɔ̀bíŋ,* that the noun stem *kɔ̀b-* has a Low tone; otherwise there would be no downstep in *kɔ́!bíŋ* when the High associative tone docks to it. The plural suffixes of both 'cows' and 'bones' are underlyingly toneless, as discussed in section 6.3.3.

(538) nííg!é kɔ́bà 'cows' bones'

	H H L | | niige kɔba	Head-Prom	*HLH	*R-Spread	Polar	*H-Spread	Dep (H)	Dep (L)
☞ a.	H L H L | ╱ | | niige kɔba					*		*
b.	H L H L | | | | niige kɔba		*!					*
c.	H H L H | | | | niige kɔba		*!		*		*	
d.	H H L |\ | | niige kɔba			*!	*	*		
e.	H H L L | | | | niige kɔba	*!			*			*

The application of POLAR and HEAD-PROM to the candidates in (538), especially the winning candidate (538a), is worth closer inspection. The phrasing of HEAD-PROM is such that if there is any change from input to output, the head noun must increase in prominence. What statement this is making about any other part of the phrase is less clear. Here I will take the position that if the head noun increases in prominence, HEAD-PROM is satisfied, no matter what another part of the phrase does. Since the head noun *kɔba* 'bones' has only a Low tone in the input, any candidate in which it has a High tone will satisfy HEAD-PROM, as do candidates (538a–d). As for POLAR, in candidates (538a–d), POLAR is satisfied by the head noun kɔba, with either a LH or HL tone, and candidates (538b–d) clearly do or do not satisfy it, but there is some question about candidate (538a) with respect to this constraint. The matter of an inserted, floating tone satisfying the POLAR constraint was discussed after (504). Briefly, POLAR is satisfied in noun class 1 plural forms when the last tone preceding any tone contributed by a morpheme which follows the plural morpheme is polar to the previous tone. In (505), this morpheme following the plural morpheme was the plural definite suffix; here it is the following word. So candidate (538a) satisfies POLAR by inserting the Low tone, even though this Low is not associated to the segmental part of the plural morpheme. Candidate (538b) straightforwardly satisfies POLAR, but fatally violates the higher-ranked *HLH, as does candidate (538c). Candidate (538d) is especially bad in that it violates not only POLAR, which would be enough to eliminate it, but also the even higher-ranked *R-SPREAD. Finally, candidate (538e) straightforwardly and fatally violates HEAD-PROM.

Another example shows not only the interactions with POLAR and *HLH, but also the need to have a constraint which has the effect of deleting extra floating Low tones. This is chùrú dám!pálá 'husband's logs'[27] (cf. chùrú 'husband', dàmpàlá 'logs'). Recall that a [HLLH] sequence of tones is allowed, but not HLH. Here I will extend the idea of HLLH tones, all of which are associated, to a sequence in which one of the Low tones may be floating and suggest that this, too, is allowed. If so, then a tonal sequence which triggers the leftward High-spreading so common in Kɔnni must not have two Low tones, even if one of them is floating. The situation arises since dàmpàlá was shown in (463) to have two underlying Low tones, while bùrìmíŋ 'oryx' has one. When the High associative morpheme docks to the input form dàmpàlá, it replaces the first Low, which could be viewed as being set afloat, as in the incorrect (539a). However, this configuration with two Lows would be allowed in Kɔnni, and gives no motivation for the High to spread, as it does, giving the correct (539b). I conclude that one of the Low tones is deleted, giving only one floating Low, rather than two as in (539c).

---

[27]The term dàmpàlá, which I gloss as 'logs' here to emphasize the plural nature of the noun, is glossed elsewhere as 'bench'. It refers to a low platform with several narrow logs placed in parallel to form a resting place.

6.3 Nominals

(539) a. H L L H
          | | | |
          *dam pa la

b. H L   H
    | \ /|
    dam pa la

c. H L L   H
    | \ /|
    *dam pa la

I propose, then, a constraint which disallows floating Low tones when adjacent to another Low tone, whether that other Low is floating or not.

(540) *(L)L: a floating Low tone is not allowed adjacent to another Low tone[28]

*(L)L, in combination with constraints saying it is better to delete a Low than to insert a High, has much the same effect as the Stray Erasure conventions of derivational phonology. These other constraints, of course, are DEP(H), which we have already seen, forbidding insertion of a High tone, and MAX(L), which forbids deleting a Low tone. The related MAX(H), forbidding the deletion of a High, has already been active in several tableaus and is undominated in Kɔnni. However, MAX(L) is new.

(541) MAX(L): a Low tone in the input must have a correspondent in the output

Like hɔ̀gú 'woman, wife', chʋ̀rú is underlyingly toneless and receives both its tones by insertion. Since the various possibilities for hɔ̀gú have already been presented in tableau form in (494), and chʋ̀rú has an identical analysis, all the candidates in the tableau in (542) will have the correct output for chʋ̀rú, and none of the constraints will be marked as applying to it. The word dàmpàlá, as a plural of noun class 1, is subject to the POLAR constraint.

---

[28]Alternatively, one could merely have a constraint that says in essence, that a tone which has no phonetic implementation or effect is not allowed to be present in the output.

(542) chùrú dàm!pálá 'husband's logs' *(L)L >> DEP(H)

		H L L-Ø | | chùrú dampal-a	*(L)L	HEAD- PROM	*HLH	POLAR	DEP (H)	*H- SPREAD	MAX (L)
☞	a.	H L H | /| chùrú dampala					*	*	*
	b.	H LL H | /| chùrú dampala	*!				*	*	
	c.	H L L H | | | chùrú dampala	*!				*		
	d.	L LH | || chùrú dampala		*!			*		
	e.	H LH | || chùrú dampala			*!		*		*
	f.	H LL | || chùrú dampala				*!			
	g.	H L H LH \ | / chùrú dampala					**!		

The winning candidate (542a) has added a High tone to avoid violation of POLAR, but violating DEP(H) in the process. It has also deleted one of the Lows, violating MAX(L), and spread a High, violating *H-SPREAD. However, all other candidates violate higher-ranked constraints. Candidate (542b) violates *(L)L by having two floating Low tones. Candidate (542c) also violates *(L)L by having a floating Low adjacent to an associated Low. Candidate (542d) violates HEAD-PROM by not having the High associate to the head noun (and on the interpretation that the High is deleted, also violates MAX(H)). Candidate (542e) loses by violating *HLH. Candidate (542f) fatally violates POLAR by not having a polar tone on the plural suffix -a. The last candidate (542g) would have a pronunciation *chùrú dám!pá!lá*. Two downsteps within a word is unusual, but attested. The fatal violation comes because (542g) violates DEP(H) twice by inserting two High tones, rather than

6.3 Nominals

violating it once as in candidate (542a). We see here that it is necessary to delete a Low tone in this set of circumstances.[29]

In most associative constructions with pronouns, the pronominal tone is Low, as in (536), for example. However, with a few nouns, the pronoun is always High.

(543) 1s ń !náá 'my mother'   ń !chúá 'my father'
      1p tí !náá 'our mother'   tí !chúá 'our father'
      2s fí !náá 'your mother'   fí !chúá 'your father'

This happens only with a few nouns, with all first-person and second-person singular pronouns. Interestingly, these are the same nouns which have altogether different forms when possessed by all third-person pronouns and second-person plural (and the ones in my data are all kinship terms, which may be relevant).

(544) 2p   nì nǔŋ 'your(PL) mother'   nì chɔ̌ŋ 'your(PL) father'
      3s   ù nûŋ   'his mother'   ò chɔ̂ŋ   'his father'
      3p   bà nûŋ 'their mother'   bà chɔ̂ŋ 'their father'
      3s nh kà nûŋ 'its mother'   kà chɔ̂ŋ 'its father'
      3p nh à nûŋ   'their mother'   à chɔ̂ŋ   'their father'

In terms of autosegmental representation, the nouns in (544) have a single Low tone in the noun stem, and the final ŋ in these is not the suffixal -ŋ of most citation nouns, but part of the noun stem. This is shown by both its morphological and tonal behavior. Morphologically, the singular definite article simply adds on to the forms above, yielding nuŋwo 'the mother' and chɔŋwa 'the father'. If the final ŋ were the singular suffix, it would be replaced by the definite suffix, yielding the unattested *nuwo and *chɔwa. Tonally, the suffixal -ŋ is always High toned, but in the associative forms it is Low.[30] The nouns nuŋ 'mother' and chɔŋ 'father' will be analyzed as having a Low stem tone, similar to kagba 'hat'. In constructions where the noun tone is rising, as in nì nǔŋ 'your(PL) mother', the High tone at the right is supplied to meet the demands of the constraints H-PRESENT and H-RT, as with kàgbá (see tableau in 491). In the third-person associative constructions where the tone is falling, the Low tone is lexical and the High tone is from the High tone associative morpheme, as in ò kágbà (see the tableau in 534).

---

[29]In another set of circumstances, with multiple particles, it seems that a floating Low may remain present in the output. See section 6.4.2.2 for discussion.

[30]If the falling tone were H!H instead of HL, this would support the suffixal -ŋ but it is not.

The forms in (543) are less straightforward. They are marked in that this is one of only two situations in which the subject or possessive pronouns are High toned, the other being the conditional (section 6.5). I will propose that these nouns have a High-Low-High tone pattern, with the Low lexically pre-linked to the noun.

(545) Underlying forms for 'mother' and 'father'

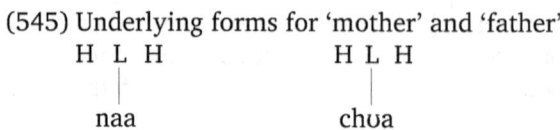

The prelinking of the Low tone is, I propose, what distinguishes the tonal pattern of ŋ̀ !náá 'my mother' from that of constructions such as ŋ̀ gú!úŋ 'my rope' which also has a HLH underlying pattern for the noun tone (cf. gú!úŋ 'rope'). (Whether the second High of naa must be floating is secondary to the pre-linking of the Low and the first High being floating.) I further propose that the pronouns for first-person singular and plural, and second-person singular, are lexically toneless. In this case, the toneless pronoun provides a convenient docking place for the floating High in front of the noun. In this scenario, it is the markedness of the noun that is the source of the unusual pattern, not the pronoun.[31] This is supported by the fact that it is only this small group of nouns which gives a High tone to the possessor pronoun; with all other nouns, the pronoun is Low toned, as in ǹ tígírí 'my house', m̀ bʋ́á 'my child', etc. The proposed representations of input and output are illustrated in (546).

(546) ń !náá 'my mother'

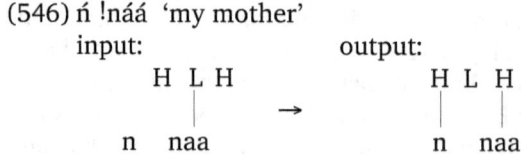

Of course, the same tonal pattern of a floating High in front of a noun also occurs with the third-person associative constructions, but in these cases, the pronoun is always Low toned. For this reason, I propose that these third-person pronouns have a lexical Low tone. Then the floating High, given an even choice of whether to dock left or right, docks right to the head noun. But in ń !náá 'my mother', the floating tone docks to the

---

[31] An alternate expression for 'our father' for at least one speaker is tí chɔ̌ŋ rather than the more common tí !chʋ́á. That the pronoun is low when this form of the noun is used would support the idea that it is the noun that gives rise to the exceptionality of the tonal pattern in tí !chʋ́á, not the pronoun.

6.3 Nominals

toneless TBU which is available. Interestingly, in Dagbani, another related Gur language with tonal similarities to Kɔnni, all third-person possessive pronouns are High toned (Issah 1993). In Dagbani, it seems very likely that the third-person pronoun, like the first and second, are underlyingly toneless, in contrast to Kɔnni, where their different behavior presses us to propose different underlying representations. A tableau for ń !náá 'my mother' is shown in (547). Though none of the candidates listed violates *(H), since the posited floating High tones all dock, it is included in the tableau as a reminder that it is this constraint (together with MAX(H)) which forces association of the floating High tone.

(547) ń !náá 'my mother' *TONELESS >> MAX(ASSOC)

H L H | N naa	*TONELESS	*(H)	*HLH	MAX (ASSOC)	DEP(L)

☞ a. H L H
       | |
       n   naa
				*	

b. L HL H
     | \ /
     n naa
				*	*!

c.   H L H
        \ /
     n naa
	*!			*	

d. H LH
     | ||
     n naa
			*!		

Winning candidate (547a) violates MAX(ASSOC) by not having the lexical Low tone associated. Candidate (547b) has the same violation, but also an additional violation of DEP(L) by inserting a Low tone, and this proves fatal here. Candidate (547c) also violates MAX(ASSOC), but the fatal violation comes by leaving the pronoun toneless, and candidate (547d) loses by having a HLH configuration. In short, we see that it is better to have the floating High dock to the pronoun than to insert a default Low tone. For comparison, a tableau for ŋ̀ gú!úŋ 'my rope' is shown in (548). The noun 'rope' has the same HLH tones in input as 'mother' in (547); the difference is that there is no pre-linking of the second tone, the Low, in 'rope'.

(548) ŋ̀ gú!úŋ 'my rope' MAX(ASSOC) >> DEP(L)

H L-H | | N guu -ŋ	*TONELESS	*HLH	MAX(ASSOC)	DEP(L)

☞ a. L H L H
  | \ /
  ŋ   guuŋ
				*

b. H L H
   | |
   ŋ   guuŋ
			*!	

c. H L H
    \ /
   ŋ   guuŋ
	*!			

d. H   L H
   | | |
   ŋ   guuŋ
		*!		*

The winning candidate (548a) violates only DEP(L) by inserting a Low tone on the pronoun. Candidate (548b) loses by a fatal violation of MAX(ASSOC). Candidate (548c) loses by leaving the pronoun toneless, and candidate (548d) loses by having a HLH sequence.

6.3.7 Compound nouns

Common compound nouns may consist of either a noun-noun sequence or a noun-adjective sequence. There are possibly other types of compounds, but they are rare and perhaps do not exist as distinct categories. The noun-adjective compounds are labeled as compounds mainly on the basis of their lexicalized change of meaning from the composition of their components, e.g., ɲùɲɲìŋká 'fruit', which is literally 'things that have come out'. These compounds have the same tonal patterns as ordinary noun-adjective complexes and so will not be discussed separately in this section. What will be discussed is noun-noun compounds. A list of such compound nouns, arranged by noun class, is found in appendix C.

As previously mentioned in section 2.1.4, compound nouns differ from the associative noun construction, in which two nouns are also abutted, in two ways I am aware of. First, in associative noun constructions, each noun possesses its own suffix. However, in compound nouns, only the last noun has a suffix; the first (and any other) nouns manifest only their stems. Second,

6.3 Nominals

associative constructions always have a High tone on the first syllable of the second noun and any subsequent noun, but in compound nouns, the second noun's first syllable is High toned only if lexically so or as a result of the usual tonal processes discussed in section 6.1. The differences are illustrated in the minimal pairs in (549). The first member of each pair is a compound and the second an associative noun phrase; both use the same noun stems.

(549) compounds versus associative noun phrases (repeated from (65))
    a. hánǐì-nŭŋ   'mother-in-law' cf. há!nííŋ 'in-law', nŭŋ 'mother'
        há!níín nûŋ   'in-law's mother'

    b. hààgìn-tììsí   'bush-trees' cf. hààgíŋ 'bush', tììsí 'trees'
        hààgín tíí!sí   'bush's trees'

Note that the first of each pair, the compound, has a Low tone beginning the second noun, while the second of each pair, the associative noun phrase, has a High tone beginning the second noun. Also note the lack of the *-N* suffix in the compound in (549a).[32] Additional examples of compounds are given in (550).

(550) Compounds (selected from appendix C)

	Singular	Singular definite	Plural
'arrow' (bow-nail) cf. tɔ̆n 'war, bow', yí!íŋ 'nail, arrow'	tɔ̀n-yí!íŋ	tɔ̀nyíí!ní	tɔ̀nyíímà
'cheekbone' (cheek-shea nut) cf. kààmíŋ 'cheek', kpíŋ 'shea nut'	kààŋ-kpíŋ	kààŋkpínní	kààŋkpíè
'larynx' (voice-flute) cf. lɔ̀líŋ 'voice', wííŋ 'flute'	lɔ̀lù-wííŋ	lɔ̀lùwííkú	lɔ̀lùwíítɪ̀[33]
'pupil of eye' (eye-dwarf) cf. níŋ 'eye', kékíríŋ 'dwarf'	níŋ-kékíríŋ	níŋkékíríké	níŋkékírísí

---

[32] I am not certain why there is a nasal (presumably the suffix) present in the first noun of the compound in (549b). It may be that Amadu was coining a compound and gave more emphasis to tonal qualities in marking it as a compound than the suffixal morphology.

[33] The *i* of the stem of *lɔlŋ* assimilates to the following *w* as *u*.

'toenail'   ná-!yíbíŋ   ná!yíbíkú   ná!yíbítí
(leg-scratching)
cf. náŋ 'leg', yìbíŋ
'scratching'

'catfish (sp.)'   ɲáám-bún-!dááŋ ɲáámbún!dáásí ɲáámbún!dáákú
(water-donkey-male)
cf. ɲááŋ 'water',
bún!íŋ 'donkey',
-rááŋ 'male'

Compound nouns can be accounted for with the constraints already in place. Here we examine two as samples. First is ɔ̀lʊ̀-wííŋ 'larynx' in (551) and then ná-!yíbíŋ 'toenail' in (552).

(551) ɔ̀lʊ̀-wííŋ 'larynx'

	*Toneless	Max(Assoc)	Dep(L)
L H-H | || ɔl wII-ŋ			
☞ a. L L H H | | | | ɔlʊ wIIŋ			*
b. L H H | | | ɔlʊ wIIŋ		*!	
c. L H H | | | ɔlʊ wIIŋ	*!		

The winning candidate (551a) violates Dep(L) by inserting a default Low. Candidate (551b) inserts no tones and spreads the three lexical tones out over the three lexical syllables, but loses by having the High of wííŋ associated to a TBU other than its sponsoring one, fatally violating Max(Assoc). Candidate (551c) loses by having a toneless syllable.

(552) ná-!yíbíŋ 'toenail'

	*HLH	Max(Assoc)
H L -H | | | na yıbı-ŋ		

☞ a. H L H
    | /|
    na yıbıŋ
		*

b. H LH
   | | |
   na yıbıŋ
	*!	

The winning candidate (552a) violates Max(Assoc) by not having its Low tone associated with its sponsor, but the other candidate (552b) violates the higher-ranked *HLH. Other candidates are possible, but one can recognize a pattern we have seen before, in the tableaus in (475) and (476).[34]

The main point is that once the suffixal tone is stripped off the first noun of a compound, the compound acts exactly like any other noun with a single stem.

6.3.8 Postnominal modifiers

There are several types of postnominal modifiers in Kɔnni, sketched in section 1.2.4. These include quantifiers such as *mana* 'all', deictics such as *gee* 'this', and the locative particle *ma/me*. For these modifiers, the main task is to determine their underlying tone pattern; then these words also fit neatly into the pattern of constraints which has been established. I will examine these three as representative of the genre.

The modifier *mana* 'all' seems to act much like *hɔ̀gú* 'woman', which has been postulated as toneless. It is LH in citation form and as the subject of a sentence but HL when following a noun. The final High in citation and subject form is forced by the H-Present and High-Rt constraints. The HL tone when following a noun means that it may be possible to treat *mana* as a type of noun, since it exhibits behavior characteristic of nouns, including what appears to be the initial High tone characteristic of the associative construction when following a noun or a third-person pronoun.

---

[34]It would be helpful to also examine the same HLH tonal input but with the Low ending the first noun, i.e., HL#H in addition to the H#LH above. But such a form is not available in my data, though HL#LH forms remain as in the input, e.g., *hánìì-chɔ́ŋ* 'father-in-law'.

(553) a. màná 'all'
　　b. nì màná 'you(PL) all'
　　c. bà mánà 'all of them'
　　d. bùnsí mánà 'all the donkeys'
　　e. níí!gé mánà 'all the cows' (cf. níígè 'cows')
　　f. màná !bɔ́bá mìŋ 'all are tying'
　　g. tì màná !bɔ́bá mìŋ 'all of us ("we all") are tying'
　　h. bà mánà bɔ̀bá mìŋ 'all of them ("they all") are tying'[35]

It is also possible that *mana* has a single lexical Low tone, as in the case of *kagba*. The analysis and tableaus work out equally well whether *mana* is totally toneless or has a single Low tone. Unfortunately, *mana* does not occur in the syntactic contexts (e.g., 'one X', see 487) that would provide the distinction between the two possibilities, and we must live with the indeterminacy.

In contrast, *gee* 'this, these' is LH in citation and consistently !H after nouns, supporting the notion that it is LH lexically. The definite article is required before *gee*.[36] Since all definite articles are High toned, this means that there is no context in which the preceding noun ends with a Low tone before *gee*, which I predict would yield *gèé*.

(554) a. gèé 'this'
　　b. hɔ̀wwá !géé 'this woman'
　　c. náá!gíbú !géé 'this cow'
　　d. níí!géhé !géé 'these cows'
　　e. ɲí!náhá !géé 'these teeth'
　　f. ù kɔ́bá!há !géé 'these his bones'

In contrast to both of these, the locative particle *ma/me* (the vowel depends on ATR vowel harmony with the preceding noun) takes on the tone of the preceding noun. Depending on context, this particle may be translated as 'at, in, on, by'.

---

[35]The tonal differences in *bɔba* 'tying' are due to the subject pronoun and are discussed in section 6.4.1.

[36]There are some forms in my data which do not appear to use a definite article, such as *níí!géé !géé* 'these cows'. However, the long [ee] on *níí!géé* as well as the tone indicate that this is actually a shortened form of *níí!géhé* with the definite article *-hé* added to the plural *níígè*.

6.3 Nominals

(555) a. tígím mé   'at house'
b. tígírí mé   'at the house'
c. tígírí !géé mé   'at this house'
d. háá!gím má   'in the bush'
e. bìnní má   'at the year (= "last year")'
f. kpàlá má   'in calabash'
g. tígè mè   'at houses'
h. níígè mè   'by cows'
i. wɔ́fìsì mà   'at office'
j. ɲʊ̀m má   'at market' (cf. ɲʊ̌ŋ 'market')
k. bìŋkpìàm má   'on shoulder' (cf. bìŋkpìáŋ 'shoulder')
l. kúrúbá mà   'in the bowl' (cf. kúrúbâ 'bowl')
m. kàgbà má   'by the hat' (cf. kàgbá 'hat')

Since *ma/me* always receives its tone from the preceding noun, I consider it to be underlyingly toneless. In the first nine examples in (555), where there is the same number of tones as syllables in the noun, the *ma/me* would receive its tone by spreading from the previous noun, as in *tígím mé* 'at house' and *tígè mè* 'at houses'.[37]

(556) a. H H → H H
    | | | |\
    tigim me   tigim me

b. H L → H L
    | | | |\
    tige me   tige me

The next three examples (555j–l) are crucial in that the last tone on the noun is opposite the tone on *ma*. But in citation form, all these nouns have a contour tone on the final syllable (*ɲʊ̌ŋ* 'market', *bìŋkpìáŋ* 'shoulder', *kúrúbâ* 'bowl'). Here, the last tone of the noun surfaces on the *ma* particle, as shown in the representations in (557).

(557) a. LH → L H
    | | |
    ɲʊm ma   ɲʊm ma

---

[37]As in two previous cases, the possibility of tone insertion here rather than spreading is ruled out only by the theory-internal positing of a low-ranked OCP that would prefer spreading to identical adjacent tones.

b. L   L H   L   L   H
    | | | | | |
    bɪŋkpɪam ma → bɪŋkpɪam ma

c. H H H L   H H H   L
    | | | | | | | |
    kʊrʊba ma   →   kʊrʊba ma

This tonal behavior is consistent with *ma/me* being a suffix, a part of the word, with one-to-one mapping of tones to TBUs. If it were an independent word, we would expect the unattested *ɲŭm má*, with the LH mapping onto the noun and the *ma* having the same tone as the last in the noun, as in the first nine examples in (555). The tonal behavior of (555m) is also consistent with this. Recall that *kagba* was posited as LØ underlyingly (see 487), with the final High tone added to satisfy H-PRESENT. If *kagba-ma* were all one word with only one Low tone underlying, a High tone on the last syllable would be consistent with the previous analysis, to satisfy H-PRESENT and HIGH-RT.

However, the fact that suffixes are present on nouns, and even that the post-nominal modifier *gee* precedes *ma/me*, is in favor of its being a separate word. A reasonable position is that *ma/me* is a clitic, a word which functions as a separate word syntactically, but is phonologically attached to the end of the noun phrase. It shares in ATR harmony and tone spread as if it were attached to the previous word.[38]

6.3.9 Nonfinal contours

Though the prohibition against word-internal tone contours in Kɔnni is almost absolute, there are a few words in which a word-internal contour appears. These are limited to five words in my data, all of which are noun class 5 plural indefinite nouns. In the following data, note that only the plural indefinite forms have this rising tone within a nonfinal syllable of the word.

---

[38]Data not in my corpus but desirable to elicit would be "at woman" and "at straw hat," with *hɔgʊ-ma* and *kagba-ma,* since these are posited to be toneless on one or both syllables.

6.3 Nominals

(558)

	Singular	Singular definite	Plural indefinite	Plural definite
'chief'	nàáŋ	nààŋwá	**nàá!líŋ**	nààlí!bá
'father' (1st/2nd pers)	chừá	chừàwá	**chừà!líŋ**	chừàlí!bá
'friend'	zừá	zừàwá	**zừà!líŋ**	zừààlí!bá
'husband'	chừrú	chừrừwá	**chŭl!líŋ**	chừllí!bá
'sibling-in-law'	chǐí	chǐìwá	**chǐí!líŋ**	chǐìlí!bá

One of the forms, chŭl!líŋ 'husbands' (with short ʊ, but the rising tone continuing into the coda l) has a variant chừrú!líŋ based on the singular, and the rising tone in this particular word could be viewed as a result of elision of the second syllable with tone remaining. However, the rest cannot be so explained. What they all have in common, except 'husbands', is that they are monosyllabic nouns with a rising tone on a long vowel in the singular (and all, even 'husbands', have bimoraic first syllables). They also all take the -!líŋ plural suffix (not all nouns in class 5 have the same suffix). This suffix is unique in Kɔnni in that it always has a downstep preceding it, and therefore also always has a High preceding. This circumstance leads us to suspect that this High tone has its source in the suffix itself, and the fact that all the singular forms have rising tones is not related. (In fact, the word-final rising tones in the singulars can be attributed to the power of the H-PRESENT constraint.) Attributing this High to the suffix would give a representation of input and output such as the following.

(559) L -HL -H   L H L H
       | | | →   \\/ /
       zʊa -lɪ -ŋ   zʊa lɪŋ   zừá!líŋ

The -ŋ is separated from the -lɪ part of the suffix on the basis of the plural definites, in which the -ŋ is replaced by -bá. Also, some plurals do have a simple -ŋ to mark the plural form, and this contributes a High tone, such as lí!áŋ 'daughters' (cf. lìà 'daughter'). This leaves the -lɪ suffix with a HL underlying tone. In the plural definite forms such a tone acts in a perfectly regular manner when combined with the High-toned plural definite suffix -bá.

(560) L -HL -H   L HLH
       | | | → | |/
       zʊa -lɪ -ba   zʊa lɪba   zừàlí!bá

Why the plural indefinite behaves in such an anomalous manner is still unknown. It would be consistent with the example of other nouns for it to have a H!H contour on the final syllable, which would preserve all the tones, such as in *chìrí!ŋ́* 'a tree (sp.)'. What we may conclude is that for noun class 5, the H!H contour on a final syllable is disallowed.

6.4 Verbal tone

Some Gur languages have a contrast in verbs on the basis of their tonal behavior. For example Crouch (1985) posits two verb classes for Vagla on the basis of their differing tonal patterns in several contexts. Other Gur languages which have a tonal contrast in verbs include at least Dagaare (Bodomo 1997), Dagbani (Olawsky 1996), Kasem (Awedoba 1993), Supyire (Carlson 1994), Konkomba (Steele and Weed 1966), and Ncam (Bassar; Cox 1998). In Kɔnni, on the other hand, all verbs exhibit the same tonal behavior in all contexts that I have examined. The only differences in behavior relate to the number of syllables in the verb, and even these are predictable.

6.4.1 Aspectual tone

The claim in this study is that Kɔnni verbs have no lexical tone. This is shown by the constant melody imposed on verb stems of various syllables by the tense/aspect/mood used. For some, the subject person makes a difference in the tonal pattern, and for others the tonal pattern is constant no matter which person is subject. These will be illustrated for Imperfective, Perfective, Future, Future Imperfective, Imperative, and Imperative Imperfective. These are all exemplified in greater length in appendix F.

When I say that verbs have no "lexical tone," I mean that no verb is distinguished from another by tone alone, and tone is not contrastive for verbs in the way it is for nouns. However, a tonal melody is assigned as part of the morphology. A verb of Imperfective aspect has a different tonal pattern than the same verb in its Future form. The tone of the aspects and tenses, therefore, is part of the input to the phonology and is shown as such on the tableaus in this section.

Kɔnni is far from unique among Gur languages in having tonal melodies corresponding to a particular tense, aspect, or mood. If a Gur phonology or grammar covers tone in any detail, it will generally have a discussion of such patterns in that language. Works which provide at least some mention of variation in verbal tone include Steele and Weed (1966) for Konkomba,

6.4 Verbal tone

Kröger (1992) for Buli, Crouch (1985) for Vagla, Bergman, Gray, and Gray (1969) for Tampulma, Hunt and Hunt (1981) for Hanga, Cox (1998) for Ncam, Crouch (1994) for Dɛg, and Carlson (1994) for Supyire.

6.4.1.1 Imperfective aspect

The imperfective aspect indicates an action or state which is continuing, incomplete, or in progress at the time referred to. A basic distinction in Kɔnni is between actions that are in progress and those that are completed; the indicative mood, imperative mood, and future tense all have subdivisions based on imperfective versus unmarked. The simple imperfective as outlined in this section may refer to either the past or the present; the context makes it clear which is referred to. A literal gloss would be something like 'they laughing'. Legitimate translations can thus be either 'they are laughing' or 'they were laughing', depending on the larger context. In this section, for brevity I gloss the simple imperfective as English present progressive 'they are laughing'. The imperfective aspect which is combined with future and with imperative will be considered below.

The simple imperfective is one of the aspects in Kɔnni which varies in tonal behavior according to the subject pronoun. As noted in section 2.4 and illustrated in (561) and (562), the first- and second-person subject pronouns take one pattern, and the third-person subject pronouns take another. For the sake of brevity in the following discussion, first-person singular and third-person singular will be given as illustrative of both patterns. The *mìŋ* particle is an affirmation marker.

(561) Imperfective
  ǹ síǃá mìŋ 'I am bathing.' tì síǃá mìŋ 'We are bathing.'
  síǃá mìŋ 'You are bathing.' nì síǃá mìŋ 'You(PL) are bathing.'
  ʋ̀ sìá mìŋ 'S/he is bathing.' bà sìá mìŋ 'They are bathing.'

As seen in the following examples of verbs with varying syllable counts (CVCVC- is the maximal stem in Kɔnni), the pattern on the verb, including the suffix -*a*/-*e,* is LH or LLH for third person, and HǃH or HHǃH for first person.

(562) Imperfective: third- and first-person subjects
  a. ʋ̀ là-á mìŋ 'S/he is laughing.'
   ʋ̀ kpàt-á mìŋ 'S/he is finishing.'
   ʋ̀ sùlìs-é mìŋ 'S/he is polishing.'

b. ǹ lá-!á mìŋ   'I am laughing.'
   ŋ̀m kpát-!á mìŋ   'I am finishing.'
   ǹ súlís-!é mìŋ   'I am polishing.'

Considering the third person first, the most obvious analysis would give the -a/-e suffix a lexical High tone, as with most nominal suffixes. The verb stem would have a Low tone for this aspect, as evidenced by the form làá 'laughing'. The analysis of a Low inserted by default is ruled out by this form, since there is no motivation to insert a default Low tone on a TBU which already has a tone. The presence of downstep in the first person forms also shows that a Low is present. This Low tone is a grammatical one, present in the input, since it is part of the morphology marking imperfective aspect. The configuration of third-person imperfective aspect, then, would be the following, illustrated for one- and three-syllable verbs.

(563) Imperfective: L on verb stem

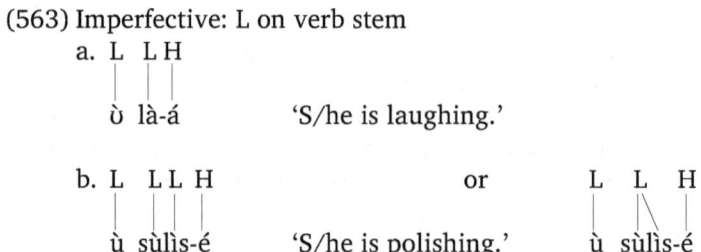

The Low tone on the second syllable of sùlìs-é in (563b) could be a result of either an inserted Low, as shown, or spreading from the previous Low. From the constraints established thus far, we have seen *H-SPREAD, but have not dealt with the corresponding *L-SPREAD, let alone its ranking with respect to DEP(L). For this reason, we do not know if it is better in the general case to insert a Low tone than to spread one (see discussion based on 482 and 485). However, in the specific case of verbs, a key observation is that all syllables of a verb up to the final one have the same tone. This is not only true for the Low tones of the third-person imperfective aspect, but also for the High tones of the first-person imperfective and, as we shall see as the section unfolds, for all verb aspects and tenses (see summary in 592). A constraint having the force of enforcing a uniform tone for the verb stem is at work here. This is specific for verbs. I propose a constraint of the ALIGN family to account for these.

(564) ALIGN(T,Rt; Verb,Rt): align the right edge of a tone to the right edge of a verb (ALIGN-Verb-Rt)

6.4 Verbal tone

This constraint is specific to verbs; nouns do not have the same kind of behavior. Also, this constraint can be gradiently violated, with more violations incurred for the greater distance a tone is from the right edge (or rightmost TBU) of the verb. To satisfy this constraint, a tone must be associated to the final syllable of the verb. A floating tone will be defined as violating it once; it obviously violates it, but just as obviously cannot be assigned any meaningful "distance" away from the rightmost TBU. Any associated tone may violate it more than once, depending on the distance from the final syllable. Taken together with *TONELESS and the MAX(T) constraints, this constraint can account for the rightward spreading of High tones in verbs. It also is consistent with the presence of all the Low tones in the third-person imperfective forms.

With these constraints in place, plus one more, the forms can be accounted for. This additional constraint is needed as a general prohibition in Kɔnni and will also play an active role in the imperative forms. Recall that the only tonal contour allowed on a single mora in Kɔnni is a HL falling tone. A constraint prohibiting rising tones on single moras is as follows.[39]

(565) ***LH-μ:** a rising tone is not allowed on a single mora

This constraint is never violated in Kɔnni. Also, on the basis of the discussion in section 6.3.6, the third-person pronoun is assumed to have a lexical Low tone, but nothing crucial here hinges on that assumption.

The winning candidate (566a) violates ALIGN-Verb-Rt once, since the Low tone is not associated to the last syllable, but is only one syllable away from it. Candidate (566b) is phonetically identical to (566a), but inserting the extra Low tone leads to more violations of ALIGN-Verb-Rt than (566a) has. The first Low in (566b) is two TBUs away from the final syllable (two violations) and the second Low is one TBU away from the final syllable (one additional violation). Candidate (566c) has a rising tone on the final short vowel, violating the undominated *LH-μ. Candidate (566d) takes the High tone of the suffix and associates it to the second syllable, thus achieving a one-to-one, left-to-right mapping of tones; however, ALIGN-Verb-Rt is violated three times, once for the High which is not aligned to the rightmost edge, and twice for the Low which is two TBUs from the right edge. Similarly, candidate (566e) incurs more violations of ALIGN-Verb-Rt than winning candidate (566a).

---

[39]We shall also see the need for a constraint *H!H-μ, prohibiting a H!H contour on a single mora. These two constraints could conceivably be combined as a single one, something like HL-μ, saying only HL falling contours are allowed on short vowels.

(566) ù sùlìs-é 's/he is polishing' *LH-μ >> Align-Verb-Rt

	L　H │ sulis -e	*LH-μ	Align- Verb-Rt	*H-Spread	*L-Spread	Dep(L)
☞ a.	L　　H │\　│ su li se		*		*	
b.	L L H │ │ │ su li se		**!*			*
c.	L　H /│\│ su li se	*!			*	
d.	L H L │ │ │ su li se		**!*			*
e.	L H │ │\ su li se		**!	*		

The first-person subject forms in (562b) add another complexity. As repeated from (562), the first-person forms have either a H!H or HH!H tone pattern on the verb.

(567) Imperfective: first-person subjects
  ǹ lá-!á mìŋ 'I am laughing.'
  ŋ̀m kpát-!á mìŋ 'I am finishing.'
  ǹ súlís-!é mìŋ 'I am polishing.'

This pattern translates into a HLH set of tones. The LH was already present in the third-person forms, the High from the suffix and the Low from the verb stem. The additional High tone is clearly a result of the first-person subject, but nothing we have seen indicates that the pronouns in themselves ever have a High tone, and in fact, one of the claims in the discussion in section 6.3.7 was that the first-person pronoun was toneless. I propose therefore that there are two allomorphs of the imperfective tonal morpheme, that the choice of tonal morpheme for the imperfective aspect is sensitive to which person is subject, so that the input tone for forms in which first person is subject is HLH, including the suffixal High.

6.4 Verbal tone

The question in such a representation is why in a HLH tonal configuration, the surface result is HH!H rather than the H!HH, since we have seen several examples of such. One possibility could be that the morphemic representation simply supplies the number of High tones which matches the syllables in the verb stem, whether one or two. However, it would be preferable to have a uniform representation for the morpheme. If so, then the High tone has spread rightward rather than in the leftward direction we have seen in a number of contexts before. The only other case of rightward High tone spreading we have seen was in the case of noun-adjective complexes, in which a High from a noun stem or adjective could spread into an adjective. However, these cases differ in that the adjectives had an underlying tonal specification, while the verbs here do not. The ALIGN-Verb-Rt constraint which we introduced in (564) is the motivation for this pattern: verbs have a consistent tone on all syllables up to the last one.

One more constraint is needed at this point and further on. For every H!H tone we have seen, it has been on either a long vowel or a vowel-nasal sequence (e.g., *ʊ̀ bʊ́!á* 'his/her child', *ʊ̀ tá!ŋ* 'his/her stone'). Though a falling tone HL can occur on a short vowel (e.g., *kʊ́rʊ́bâ* 'bowl'), the H!H fall evidently cannot. The reason for this is quite likely perceptual; a H!H on a short vowel is too slight a difference in too short a time to perceive reliably. Here I present a simple descriptive constraint.

(568) ***H!H-µ:** a H!H contour is not allowed on a monomoraic sequence

This constraint is undominated in Kɔnni.[40] We can now examine the tableau for a sample imperfective form, concentrating on the verb alone.

---

[40]As noted, this may well be combined with *LH-µ into one constraint HL-µ, saying only HL falling contours are allowed on short vowels.

(569) ǹ súlís-!é mìŋ 'I am polishing' ALIGN-Verb-Rt >> *R-SPREAD
also *H!H-μ >> ALIGN-Verb-Rt

HL -H | sulis -e	*H!H-μ	*HLH	ALIGN-Verb-Rt	*R-SPREAD	*H-SPREAD
☞ a. H L H | \ | su li se			**	*	*
b. H L H | / | su li se			***!		*
c. H L H | | | su li se		*!	***		
d. H L H / | \ / su li se	*!		*	*	*

In the winning candidate (569a), ALIGN-Verb-Rt is violated twice, once by the floating Low not being aligned to the rightmost TBU of the verb, and once by the spread High tone which in spite of spreading is still not associated with the rightmost TBU of the verb. This tableau shows indirectly that ALIGN-Verb-Rt outranks *R-SPREAD; if the rankings were reversed, then candidate (569b) would win, which it does not. Candidate (569b) is worse than (569a) in that it has three violations of ALIGN-Verb-Rt rather than the two violations of candidate (569a). The first High of the verb is two TBUs away from the right edge, violating it twice, and the floating Low is not associated with the right edge, violating it once more. Candidate (569c) straightforwardly loses by violating *HLH, though it also has three violations of ALIGN-Verb-Rt, which would cause it to lose even in the absence of *HLH. Candidate (569d) fulfills the requirements of ALIGN-Verb-Rt more completely than any other candidate, but fatally violates *H!H-μ by having a H!H contour on a short vowel. The above tableau through transitivity also offers support for *HLH outranking *R-SPREAD.

Transitive forms of the imperfective, that is, when the verb has a direct object following it, have the additional complexity that they add length to the final vowel of the verb, as shown in the forms in (570b and c). This lengthened vowel is an allomorph of the imperfective when in a transitive

6.4 Verbal tone

context.[41] (As we shall see, the perfective aspect also has separate allomorphs for transitive and intransitive.)

(570) Imperfective transitive sentences
    a. ǹ dí!é ɲìndìkké   'I am eating food.'
       ù dìé ɲìndìkké   'S/he is eating food.'

    b. ŋ̀m kpátá!á !júókú   'I am finishing the room.'
       ɲ kpàtáá !júókú   'S/he is finishing the room.'

    c. ǹ súlísé!é gbíábí!kú 'I am polishing the door.'
       ù sùlìséé gbíábí!kʊ   'S/he is polishing the door.'

The reason the forms in (570a) do not lengthen the final suffixal vowel is the prohibition against triple vowels in Kɔnni (*VVV, discussed in section 5.7.2). In (570a), the first vowel is the stem vowel and the second is the Imperfective suffix. In the consonant-final stems in (570b and c), the suffixal vowel after the consonant may be lengthened with no adverse consequences.

Another pattern to notice in (570) is the effect the final High tone of the verb has on the following noun. In (570a), the noun begins with two Low tones and is pronounced as such, and in (570c) the underlying word-initial High tones of the noun also surface. However, in (570b) the noun in citation form has a LH pattern *(jùòkú)*, and this after the High of the verb yields an input HLH tone sequence which unsurprisingly surfaces as the usual H!HH.

In the tableau in (571) we concentrate on the tonal pattern of the verb itself. The "V" in the input indicates the extra vowel length which is part of the morphology of the transitive imperfective aspect.

---

[41]One may wonder whether the presence of any postverbal word causes lengthening, or whether lengthening is limited to transitive clauses. There is no lengthening of the verb when followed by the affirmation marker *mìŋ*, as in *ò kpàtá mìŋ* 's/he is finishing', or by another verb, as in *ù sùgùr-é súgùr-è mìŋ* 's/he is washing (repeatedly)'. Other postverbal components such as locatives, adverbials, and benefactives are syntactically identical to verbs and noun phrases. I conclude that the presence of a direct object is the factor that causes lengthening in the affirmative imperfective aspect.

(571) ǹ súlísé!é gbíábí!kú 'I am polishing the door'

HL -H | sulis -eV	*H!H-μ	*HLH	Align-Verb-Rt	*H-Spread

☞ a. H L H
    / | \ /
    su li see
			*	*

b. HL H
   | \ |
   su li see
			**!	*

c. H LH
   | / |
   su li see
			**!*	*

d. H L H
   | | |
   su li see
		*!	***	

e. H L LH
   | | ||
   su li see
			**!*	

f. H L H
   | | \ |
   su li see
			**!	

The optimal candidate (571a) is identical to the failed candidate (571d), except that here the form has a long final vowel, which is capable of bearing the H!H contour. The candidate in (571a) satisfies Align-Verb-Rt better than any other candidate, with no violations of higher-ranked constraints. Candidate (571b) loses by not satisfying Align-Verb-Rt as well as (571a) does; the High has not spread as far. Candidate (571c) violates Align-Verb-Rt even more. Candidate (571d) loses by violating the highly-ranked *HLH. Candidates (571e and f) are phonetically identical, but both lose by multiple violations of Align-Verb-Rt.

6.4.1.2 Perfective aspect

The perfective aspect in Kɔnni denotes a completed action. As with the imperfective, the time of reference may be either in the past or present, with legitimate translations being either "had done X" or "has done X," depending on the context. Here I gloss these with the English present

6.4 Verbal tone

perfect 'has done X'. The tone of the perfective, like the imperfective, depends on the subject pronoun. Again, the third person has a different tone pattern than the first and second persons. The second-person singular form in (572) has a null pronoun.

(572) Perfective
    ǹ sí!yá   'I have bathed.'   tì sí!yá   'We have bathed.'
    sí!yá   'You have bathed.'   nì sí!yá   'You (PL) have bathed.'
    ù sìyá   'S/he has bathed.'   bà sìyá   'They have bathed.'

As with the imperfective, the first- and third-person singular subject forms will be given to illustrate the patterns above. If no object is present, the affirmative marker *mìŋ* is often but not obligatorily present, as in *ǹ sí!yá mìŋ* 'I have bathed'. I will give forms omitting this particle.

As seen in the forms in (573) using verbs of different syllable counts, the pattern on the verb is a High-toned suffix *-yá/-yé*, giving a LH, LLH, or LLLH tone on the verb for third-person forms and a H!H, HH!H, or HHH!H tone for the first-person forms, quite similar to the imperfective forms.

(573) Perfective: third- and first-person subjects, intransitive
    a. ù là-yá   'S/he has laughed.'
       ù kpàtì-yá   'S/he has finished.'
       ù sùlìsì-yé   'S/he has polished.'

    b. ǹ lá-!yá   'I have laughed.'
       ŋm kpátí-!yá   'I have finished.'
       ǹ súlísí-!yé   'I have polished.'

The analysis is also similar to the imperfective forms. The difference for the intransitive forms is that there is a *-yA* suffix instead of an *-A* suffix, with an epenthetic vowel inserted when needed between the final C of the root and the *-yA*.

(574) ǹ súlísí-!yé 'I have polished'

HL -H | sulis -yA	*H!H-μ	*HLH	Align-Verb-Rt	*H-Spread
☞ a. H L H / | \ | su li si ye			**	
b. H L H | |\ | su li si ye		*!	****	
c. H L H |\ /| su li si ye			***!	
d. H L H / | \ \// su li si ye	*!			

The winning candidate (574a) violates ALIGN-Verb-Rt twice by having neither the Low nor the initial High tone aligned to the right of the verb. Candidate (574b) violates it four times by having the Low one TBU away from the right, and the initial High three TBUs away. This in itself is enough to cause it to lose, but in addition, (574b) violates the higher-ranked constraint *HLH, as defined in (473). Candidate (574c) loses by violating ALIGN-Verb-Rt more than the winning candidate does. Candidate (574d), with a H!H contour on the final syllable, loses in violating *H!H-μ because that final syllable does not contain a long vowel.

For transitive forms, the perfective suffix is -wá/-wó instead of the -yá/-yé suffix used for intransitive forms.

(575) Perfective: first- and third-person subjects, transitive forms
    a. ǹ lá!wá bòàwá   'I have laughed (at) the child.'
       ù làwá !búáwá   'She has laughed (at) the child.'

    b. ŋm̀ kpátú!wá jùóŋ   'I have finished a room.'
       ù kpàtùwá !júóŋ   'S/he has finished a room.'

    c. ǹ súlísú!wó gbíá!bíŋ   'I have polished a door.'
       ù sùlìsùwó gbíá!bíŋ   'S/he has polished a door.'

6.4 Verbal tone

The tonal pattern on the verb itself can be accounted for by the same means as above; the tones are identical to the ones on the intransitive forms with the only change being that the transitive perfective suffix is -wá/-wó rather than the intransitive -yá/-yé. However, one surprising pattern emerges in the preceding and other data with this construction. The verb ends with High tone. With the third-person subjects, a following noun which is LH in citation surfaces unsurprisingly as !HH, a result of HLH → H!HH. However, with first person the following LH noun surfaces with that same LH intact rather than as H!HH. In the following pitch tracings, note especially the level tone on !búáwá in the first tracing and the rising tone on bùàwá in the second.

(576) Pitch traces for ù làwá !búáwá and ǹ lá!wá bùàwá

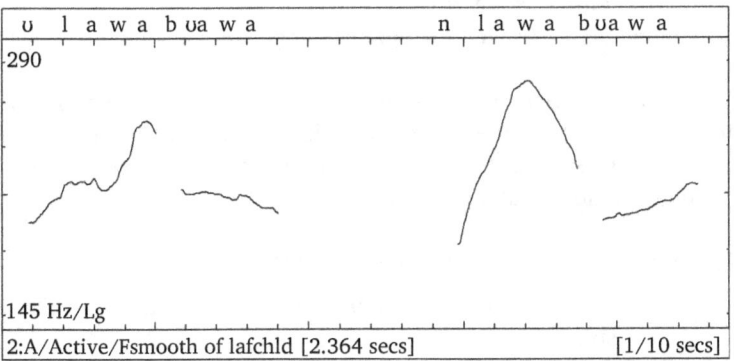

This is the first case of a phonetic [HLH] we have seen; it is specific to the first person and to the transitive perfective aspect. Recall that in the transitive imperfective, a LH noun following the verb would always surface as !HH, whether first- or third-person subject (see (570) and the discussion following it). To account for the LH pattern of the noun in the first-person transitive perfective, either there has to be a different tonal representation for first person than third, or a new constraint or constraints will need to be introduced which are specific to first-person transitive perfective. At this point, there is no argument or data that I am aware of which would decide the point.

6.4.1.3 Future tense

The future tense is self-explanatory; it refers to a time in the future. This tense has the future particle nàN preceding the verb, but also has a consistent High tone on the verb, no matter what person is subject.

(577) Future
    ǹ nàn síí 'I will bathe.'   tì nàn síí 'We will bathe.'
    nán síí 'You will bathe.'   ní nàn síí 'You(PL) will bathe.'
    ʋ̀ nàn síí 'S/he will bathe.'   bà nàn síí 'They will bathe.'

There is, however, one tonal anomaly. The second-person singular has a High tone on the future particle *nan.* This is also the only person in which the subject pronoun is not overt. For all subject pronouns, the pattern on the verb itself is completely regular in that the verb has a High tone on all syllables, regardless of the number of syllables.

(578) Future
    ʋ̀ nàn láá   'S/he will laugh.'
    ʋ̀ nàŋ kpátí   'S/he will finish.'
    ù nàn súlísí   'S/he will polish.'

I posit a Low tone on the future particle *nàN,* and a single High tone for the future tense which applies to the verb itself. The constraint ALIGN-Verb-Rt forces the tone to align to the right. There is no other tone present, so the High tone extends all along the verb.

(579) ù nèn súlísí 's/he will polish' ALIGN-Verb-Rt >> *H-SPREAD

H sulisi	ALIGN-Verb-Rt	*H-SPREAD	DEP(L)
☞ a. H / | \ su li si		*	
b. H L L | | | su li si	*!**		**
c. H L | | \ su li si	*!*		*
d. L L H | | | su li si	*!**		**

Candidate (579a) violates no constraints listed but *H-SPREAD. Other candidates have fatal violations of ALIGN-Verb-Rt. Candidate (579b) has

6.4 Verbal tone

three violations, once by the Low and twice by the initial High, which is two TBUs away from the right edge of the verb. Candidate (579c) has one less violation of ALIGN-Verb-Rt by spreading Low, so the Low tone does not violate the constraint, but the High still does twice. Candidate (d) violates ALIGN-Verb-Rt in a manner similar to (579b).

6.4.1.4 Future imperfective

Whereas the simple future tense denotes an action in the future, the future imperfective denotes a future action that is continuing: "I will be Xing" rather than "I will X." For this, the usual imperfective verbal suffix is present, but also a High-toned preverbal particle *dí* which has no direct translation into English.

(580) Future imperfective
ǹ nàn dí sí!á 'I will be bathing.'   tí nàn dí sí!á 'We will be bathing.'
nán dí sí!á 'You will be bathing.'   ní nàn dí sí!á 'You(PL) will be bathing.'
ù nàn dí sí!á 'S/he will be bathing.'   bà nàn dí sí!á 'They will be bathing.'

As with the future, the *naN* future particle is High toned with the second-person singular and Low toned with all other subject pronouns. The tonal pattern on the verb itself is constant across all subject pronouns.

(581) Future imperfective intransitive
ù nàn dí lá!á   'S/he will be laughing.'
ù nàn dí kpá!tá   'S/he will be finishing.'
ù nèn dí súlí!sé   'S/he will be polishing.'

The tone on the verb itself is identical to that in the imperfective first-person intransitive, exemplified in (562b). The constraints already in place will account for the pattern, and the tableau in (582) is identical to (569) except for the words surrounding the verb in (569).

(582) ù nèn dí súlí!sé 's/he will be polishing'

HL -H | sulis -e	*H!H-μ	*HLH	Align-Verb-Rt	*H-Spread
☞ a. H L H | \ | su li se			**	*
b. H L H | / | su li se			***!	*
c. H L H | | | su li se		*!	***	
d. H L H / | \/ su li se	*!		*	*

In the winning candidate (582a), Align-Verb-Rt is violated twice, once by the floating Low not being aligned to the rightmost TBU of the verb, and once by the spread High tone which in spite of spreading is still not associated with the rightmost TBU of the verb. Candidate (582b) is worse, by having three violations of Align-Verb-Rt rather than the two violations of candidate (582a). The first High of the verb is two TBUs away from the right edge, violating it twice, and the floating Low is not associated with the right edge, violating it once. Either one of these is enough to make it a losing candidate. Candidate (582c) straightforwardly loses by violating *HLH, though it also has three violations of Align-Verb-Rt, which would cause it to lose even in the absence of *HLH. Candidate (582d) fulfills the requirements of Align-Verb-Rt more completely than any other candidate, but fatally violates *H!H-(by having a H!H contour on a short vowel.

The future imperfective transitive tonal pattern on the verb is identical to the first-person imperfective transitive in (570): a H!H, HH!H, or HHH!H, depending on the number of syllables in the verb.

(583) Future imperfective transitive
    ù nàn dí lá!á !búáwá   'S/he will be laughing (at) the child.'
    ù nàn dí kpátá!á !júókú   'S/he will be finishing a room.'
    ù nèn dí súlísé!á gbíá!bíŋ   'S/he will be polishing a door.'

6.4 Verbal tone

This pattern is accounted for by the same means as the imperfective intransitive forms above. See the tableau in (571) for the relevant constraints and violations.

The future imperfective forms do have one anomaly as compared to the simple imperfective forms. This is the presence of an [a] as what appears to be the final vowel of the verb. It is invariably [a]; it occurs even after [+ATR] verbs such as *ù nèn dí súlísé!á gbíá!bíŋ* 's/he will be polishing a door' (see other examples in appendix F)[42] and before +ATR nouns as in *ù nàn dí chógísá!á !bólíŋ* 's/he will be fetching fire'. This extra [a] does not occur with monosyllabic verbs, which already have two vowels in the imperfective aspect: a lexical stem vowel and the /-A/ imperfect suffix (e.g., *di-e* in the sentence *ù nèn dí dí!é !sááŋ* 's/he will be eating porridge', not **ù nèn dí dí!éá !sááŋ*). The fact that the [a] does not occur with monosyllabic verbs seems to mark it as part of the verb, since a sequence of three vowels within a word is prohibited by the undominated constraint *VVV, but three vowels across a word boundary are permitted (see discussion in section 5.7). In this scenario, the shortening of the extra vowel is accounted for. However, the mismatch of ATR marks this [a] as a separate word from the verb. At this point I leave the question open, but tentatively treat the vowel as part of the verb.

6.4.1.5 Imperative

The imperative is not used as frequently in Kɔnni as it is in English. The bare command is not as polite, and in most cases the indirect 'that you learn' *(dí !fí búgúrí)* would be used in preference to the more direct *bùgùrí* 'learn!'. Nonetheless, here I examine the direct imperative form. This consists of the bare verb, with any epenthetic vowel needed at the end and a long vowel for CV verb stems. As a direct command, the second-person plural pronoun may be used to give a command to a group. This merely adds the pronoun *nì/nì* 'you(PL)' to the forms in (584), with no change to the tone of the verb.

(584) Imperative
    làá   'laugh!'
    kpàtí   'finish!'
    sùlìsí 'polish!'

From the examples above, with LH rise, LH, and LLH, it is clear that there is a LH melody over the imperative forms. One possibility is that the High tone is supplied by a vocalic suffix with no features except High

---

[42]In faster speech, the aspectual vowel assimilates to the [a], as in *ù nèn dí súlísá!á gbíá!bíŋ*.

tone, but there is no need to multiply entities in this way here. In (585) I present a tableau for the last form: *sùlìsí* 'polish!'.

(585) sùlìsí 'polish!' *LH-μ >> ALIGN-Verb-Rt

LH sulisi	*LH-μ	ALIGN-Verb-Rt	*H-SPREAD

☞ a.   L   H
     | \ |
     su li si
		*	

b.   L L H
      | | |
      su li si
		**!*	

c.   L   H
       / | \ |
       su li si
	*!		

L   H
      | | \
      su li si
		**!	*

The winning candidate (585a) violates only ALIGN-Verb-Rt, and that only once, by failing to have the Low tone aligned to the final syllable. Candidate (585b) is phonetically identical, but has multiple violations of ALIGN-Verb-Rt and so fails. Candidate (585c), in which ALIGN-Verb-Rt is fully satisfied, violates the undominated *LH-μ by having a rising tone on the short word-final vowel. Candidate (585d), which would be an ideal candidate in most cases, loses by multiple violations of the morphologically specific ALIGN-Verb-Rt.

6.4.1.6 *Imperative imperfective*

The imperative imperfective is used to urge someone to continue doing something, or to do something in a continuous rather than punctilear fashion. The High-toned suffix *-má/-mé* is attached to the verb stem, which otherwise has Low tone throughout.

(586) Imperative imperfective
    là-má   'be laughing!'
    kpàtì-má   'be finishing!'
    sùlìsì-mé   'be polishing!'

6.4 Verbal tone

This tonal pattern is identical to the simple imperative and is accounted for in precisely the same way. The tableau in (587) is quite similar to (585).

(587) sùlìsìmé 'be polishing!'

L -H │ sulisi-me	*LH-μ	Align-Verb-Rt	*H-Spread

☞ a.   L   H
   / │ \   │
   su li si me
		*	

b. L L L H
   │ │ │ │
   su li si me
		!**	

c.   L   H
   / / │ \ │
   su li si me
	*!		

d. L   H
  │ / │ \
  su li si me
		**!*	*

The winning candidate (587a) violates Align-Verb-Rt only once, while (587b and d) have multiple violations. Candidate (587c) satisfies Align-Verb-Rt but has a rising tone on the last syllable, violating *LH-μ.

6.4.1.7 Indirect imperative

As mentioned, a more polite method of request is literally, "that you X." This can also be used with other pronouns, having the force of "I/he/they/etc. should X." This aspect may be termed "indirect imperative," or perhaps "hortative." In imperfect aspect, it has the -má/-mé suffix, as can the imperative.

When a syllabic nasal follows another syllable, that nasal is desyllabified, as in the first-person examples in (588a). The hyphenated -n there is phonologically attached to the preceding word, in the same syllable, but syntactically a separate word, as with all pronouns.

(588) Indirect Imperative, with /di/ 'eat'
    a. dí-n !díí   dí-n !dí-mé   'that I eat, I should eat'
    b. dí tí !díí   dí tí !dí-mé   'that we eat, we should eat'

c. dí !fí díí   dí !fí dí-mé   'that you eat, you should eat'
d. dí !ní díí   dí !ní dí-mé   'that you(PL) eat, you(PL) should eat'
e. dú-!ú díí   dú-!ú dí-mé   'that s/he eat, s/he should eat'
f. dí !bé díí   dí !bé dí-mé   'that they eat, they should eat'

First person has a different tonal pattern than second or third person in (588); note the position of the downstep (!) after the pronoun in first-person forms but before the pronoun in second- and third-person forms. First- and third-person singulars are taken as representative of the two patterns, with a variety of verbs in (589).

(589)   1s subject   3s subject
     a. dín !síé   dú!ú síé   'I, s/he should dance.'
        dín !sé-mé   dú!ú sé-mé   'I, s/he should be dancing.'

     b. dín !tíírí   dú!ú tíírí   'I, s/he should stretch.'
        dín !tíírí-má   dú!ú tíírí-má   'I, s/he should be stretching.'

     c. dím !búgúrí   dú!ú búgúrí   'I, s/he should learn.'
        dím !búgúrí-má   dú!ú búgúrí-má   'I, s/he should be learning.'

On each of these, the verb has all High tones, and there is a downstep present in the whole phrase, but the location of the downstep is after the first-person pronoun but before the third-person pronoun.

One foundational question here is whether the input tone on the verb should be represented with a High tone alone or with a Low-High. The tone on the verb is always High, but there is always a downstep present, indicating a Low tone. When discussing tone on pronouns, it was shown that a reasonable analysis of possessive pronouns was that third-person pronouns were lexically Low toned, but first-person pronouns were toneless. (Second-person singulars also grouped with first person in that context, but do not here.) If so, then the downstep in first-person forms above must be derived from the verbal tone melody. Furthermore, these are semantically and morphologically imperatives, and the imperatives we have examined in the previous sections clearly have a LH melody. For these reasons, I assume a LH melody for the indirect imperative aspect.

The most straightforward pattern to account for is the one with *dí tí! búgúrí* 'we should learn', as follows:

6.4 Verbal tone

(590) dí tí! búgúrí 'we should learn'

	H LH | dɪ tɪ bʊgʊrɪ	*HLH	*R-Spread	*(L)
☞ a.	H L H | \ / |\ dɪ tɪ bʊgʊrɪ		*	*
b.	H L H | / |\ | dɪ tɪ bʊgʊrɪ	*!		
c.	H L H | \ | |\ dɪ tɪ bʊgʊrɪ	*!		
d.	H L H / | \ / | dɪ tɪ bʊgʊrɪ		*!*	
☹* e.	H L H | / |\ \ dɪ tɪ bʊgʊrɪ			

In the winning candidate (590a), no high-ranking constraints are violated. In both (590b and c), there is a single Low associated between two High tones, violating *HLH. Finally, candidate (590d) loses by having the High spread rightward rather than leftward. Candidate (590e) is not optimal, but cannot be ruled out by any of the constraints listed. This is related to the interaction of tones within preverbal particles. A High tone spreads rightward one TBU into a particle. This is not a general pattern of Kɔnni; it does not happen between a verb and noun, for example ŋ̀ wó àlíbɛ́sà 'I lack onion' and other examples from appendix A. Additional constraints would be necessary to force rightward spreading of a High across particles only, which would take us into the still largely uncharted area of phrasal tonology.

(591) dím! búgúrí 'I should learn'

	H LH	*HLH	*R-Spread	*(L)
	| dɪ m bʊgʊrɪ			
☞ a.	H L H | /|\\ dɪm bʊgʊrɪ			*
b.	H L H | |\\ | dɪm bʊgʊrɪ	*!		
c.	H L H | | |\\ dɪm bʊgʊrɪ	*!		
d.	H L H | \\ /| dɪm bʊgʊrɪ		*!	

The candidates in (591) win and lose for precisely the same reasons as they do in (590), with the exception that both the winning candidate and candidate (591d) violate *R-Spread once less in (591) than they do in (590), since there is one less TBU in the relevant domain. The forms represented by dʊ́!ʊ́ búgúrí 's/he should learn' have the additional complication that there are two Low tones between the Highs.

The utterances dí!bá búgúrí 'they should learn' and dʊ́!ʊ́ búgúrí 's/he should learn' differ from the utterances in the preceding tableaus in that the pronouns ba and ʊ in these are posited to have Low tones underlyingly rather than be toneless as the first-person pronouns are. In these cases, the High tone does not spread from the left, but from the right.

6.4.1.8 Summary

A summary of the intransitive patterns on the tense/aspect/moods discussed in this section is given below.

(592) Tone of intransitive verb aspects—summary
    a. Imperfective
        ʊ̀ là-á mìŋ   'S/he is laughing.'   ǹ lá-!á mìŋ   'I am laughing.'
        ʊ̀ kpàt-á mìŋ 'S/he is finishing.'   ŋ̀m kpát-!á mìŋ 'I am finishing.'
        ʊ̀ sùlìs-é mìŋ 'S/he is polishing.'   ǹ súlís-!é mìŋ 'I am polishing.'

b. Perfective
ù là-yá	'S/he has laughed.'	ǹ lá-!yá	'I have laughed.'
ù kpàtì-yá	'S/he has finished.'	ŋ̀m kpátí!yá	'I have finished.'
ù sùlìsì-yé	'S/he has polished.'	ǹ súlísí-!yé	'I have polished.'

c. Future
ù nàn láá	'S/he will laugh.'
ù nàŋ kpátí	'S/he will finish.'
ù nàn súlísí	'S/he will polish.'

d. Future imperfective
ù nàn dí lá-!á	'S/he will be laughing.'
ù nàn dí kpát-!á	'S/he will be finishing.'
ù nàn dí súlís-!é	'S/he will be polishing.'

e. Imperative
làá	'laugh!'
kpàtí	'finish!'
sùlìsí	'polish!'

f. Imperative imperfective L on verb stem
là-má	'be laughing!'
kpàtì-má	'be finishi!ng'
sùlìsì-mé	'be polishing!'

g. Indirect imperative
dín !síé	'I should dance.'	dú!ú síé	'S/he should dance.'
dín !tíírí	'I should stretch.'	dó!ó tíírí	'S/he should stretch.'
dím !búgúrí	'I should learn.'	dó!ó búgúrí	'S/he should learn.'

h. Indirect imperative imperfective
dín !sé-mé	'I should be dancing.'
dú!ú sé-mé	'S/he should be dancing.'
dín !tíírí-má	'I should be stretching.'
dó!ó tíírí-má	'S/he should be stretching.'
dím !búgúrí-má	'I should be learning.'
dó!ó búgúrí-má	'S/he should be learning.'

6.4.2 Preverbal particles

Preverbal particles include, besides the future marker previously mentioned, the negative marker *ká*, future negative *kááN*, and the marker *tíN* 'was, would' with invariant High tone. Markers for which the tone is either High or Low according to context are *waa* 'at that time', *ya* 'still', *ŋaaN* 'had been', *vп* 'again', *ko* 'just'. (Glosses are rather free, based on English translation of the entire sentence in which they are found.) All these preverbal particles occur after the subject noun phrase, whether a simple pronoun or a multiword noun phrase, as in (593), in which tone is omitted because the quality of recording did not permit accurate transcription.

(593) be dembisi dı   ko   nyıŋ
       3p men   then just come.out
      'Their men then just came out.'

The object for study here is interaction of tones across nonlexical words. My aim is only to lay out patterns, argue for the underlying tones of several particles, and point out briefly how the utterances do or do not conform to the patterns and constraints we have already seen. The data given here is the tip of the iceberg of phrasal tonology, the bulk of which must await more in-depth analysis. For additional examples, see appendix G.

6.4.2.1 Single preverbal particles

The negative marker *ká/ké*, the future negative *kááN*, and the marker *tíN* 'was, would' all have High tone in whatever context they are in. This is shown by the examples in (594), where there are a variety of contexts. The future negative *kááN* is much more restricted in its application than the others, and therefore fewer examples are given.

(594) Tonal patterns with *ká/ké*, *kááN*, and *tíN*

a. ù yè **ké** dígè   'S/he is still not cooking.'
   ù tíŋ **ká** bɔ́bà   'S/he was not tying.'
   ù **ká** yí!yá   'S/he has not given.'
   ŋ̀ **ká** gárà   'I am not going.'
   ù **ká** chíí !záá   'S/he did not carry millet.'
   ǹ yá **!ká** mía   'I am still not building.'

b. ŋ̀ **káán** dígí   'I will not cook.'
   ù **káán** lán !jítí   'S/he will not taste soup.'
   ù **káán** dí dí!gé   'S/he will not be cooking.'

c. ù **tín** yá bɔ̀bá mìŋ   'S/he was still tying.'
   ù **tíŋ** wáá !dí!é mìŋ   'S/he was then eating.'
   ǹ **tím** bɔ́bá!á mìŋ   'S/he was tying.'

6.4 Verbal tone

    ǹ **tíŋ** ká mîà   'S/he was not building.'
    ù **tín** yé !ké dígé!é   'S/he was not still cooking.'

These particles will appear in the following discussion and data, but since they are invariably High toned, they are assumed to be lexically High toned. I will not discuss them further, except in relation to other particles. The particles which have variable tone will be the main focus of this section.

Sample sentences showing variation in the tone of *ya* 'still, yet' are in (595). Note by comparing (595a and b) that after the third-person pronoun, *ya* is Low toned, but after the first-person pronoun, *ya* is High toned. This is reminiscent of the imperfective and perfective aspects in which the verb had a High tone after the first-person pronoun. Furthermore, if there is another preverbal particle with High tone preceding *ya*, as in (595c), then *ya* is also High. However, if the High-toned particle comes after *ya*, as in (595d), then the *ya* may still be Low toned. The tone on the verb itself in (595) is identical to the tone it would have without the *ya*, a LH on positive statements, and HL on negative statements (with *ká* 'NEG'). Finally, the presence of a downstep in (595e) indicates that *ya* has a Low tone, rather than being lexically toneless.

(595) Tonal patterns with *ya* 'still'
    a. ù **yà** bɔ̀bá mìŋ   'S/he is still tying.'
    b. ǹ **yá** !bɔ́bá mìŋ   'I am still tying.'
    c. ù tín **yá** !bɔ́bá mìŋ 'S/he was still tying.'
    d. ù **yà** ká mîà   'S/he is still not building.'
    e. ǹ **yá** !ká mîà   'I am still not building.'

In summary, *ya* is High toned only when there is a High toned word preceding it, including the first-person singular pronoun.

From its behavior in (595), it appears that *ya* has an underlying Low tone. If there is a High-toned word to its left, that High spreads to *ya*, and the dissociated Low causes a downstep as in (595e) between *yá* and *ká*. If *ya* had no underlying Low tone, we would expect a simple HH sequence of *yá* and *ká*. Another aspect of the behavior of *ya* is noteworthy: the rightward direction of the spreading of High onto the *ya*.

The particle *waa* is a temporal deictic which can be translated "now" or "then," depending on the context. In general, it means "at the time being talked about." There are two patterns to explain with *waa*, as seen in the data in (596). First, like *ya* in (595), its tone varies with context, being High when preceded by a High-toned word, including the first person pronoun. Second, unlike *ya*, a verb following *waa* will have an initial High tone, whether downstepped or not. For example, compare (595a) with (596a).

(596) Tonal patterns with *waa* 'now, then'
    a. ù **wàà** bɔ́!bá mìŋ   'S/he is now tying.' (cf. ù bɔ̀bá mìŋ)
    b. ŋ̀ **wáá** !bɔ́!bá mìŋ   'I am now tying.' (cf. m̀ bɔ́!bá mìŋ)
    c. ù tíŋ **wáá** !dígé mìŋ   'S/he was then cooking.' (cf. ù tín dí!gé mìŋ)
    d. ǹ tíŋ **wáá** !dígé mìŋ   'I was then cooking.' (cf. ǹ tín dí!gé mìŋ)
    e. ù ká **wáá** !mí!á   'S/he is not now building.' (cf. ù ká mîa)

As with *ya* in (595), *waa* itself has a High tone only when following a High-toned word, including the first-person singular pronoun. When following the Low-toned third-person pronoun in (595a), *waa* is Low toned. Just as I proposed *ya* to have an underlying Low tone, I propose *waa* to have an underlying Low tone. This is because of the presence of downstep in (596b) as compared to (596a). If *waa* were toneless, we would not expect a downstep between *waa* and the verb *bɔ́!bá* in (596b); there would merely be two High tones abutting. However, the verbs after *waa* always have a word-initial High tone, quite unlike the forms with *ya* in (595). In the light of this pattern, it is likely that waa also has a High tone as well as a Low, giving it a LH lexical tone.

The particle *ŋaaN* is translated 'has been' or 'had been', depending on the time reference. It is another particle whose tone varies with context, as illustrated in (597).

(597) Tonal patterns with *ŋaaN* 'has/had been'
    a. ŋ̀ **ŋáám** !mía mìŋ   'I have been building.'
    b. ù **ŋààm** mîa mìŋ   'S/he has been building.'
    c. ŋ̀ **ŋáám** !bɔ́!bá mìŋ   'I have been tying.'
    d. ù **ŋààm** bɔ́!bá mìŋ   'S/he has been tying.'
    e. ŋ̀ **ŋáán** !súgú!ré mìŋ   'I have been washing.'
    f. ù **ŋààn** súgú!ré mìŋ   'S/he has been washing.'

As with *waa* and *ya*, *ŋaaN* has a High tone only when following a High-toned word, including the first-person singular pronoun. It follows the patterns of these other particles in that a High tone on *ŋaaN* results in a downstep between it and the verb following, as in (597a, c, and e). The presence of downstep in (597a and c) indicates the presence of a Low tone in *ŋaaN*. As with *waa*, a verb following *ŋaaN* always has a High tone, so I assume a LH lexical tone for *ŋaaN*.

The particles *ko* 'just', *woN* 'already', and *vɪɪ* 'again' exhibit the same tonal behavior as the particles *waa* and *ŋaaN* which have been analyzed as having LH lexical tone. They are Low toned when preceded by a Low

6.4 Verbal tone

tone, but High toned when preceded by a High-toned word, including the first-person pronoun. A verb following these particles always begins with a High tone, even when without the particle it would begin with a Low tone, as in (598b), (599b), and (600b).

(598) Tonal patterns with *ko* 'just'
    a. ŋ̀ **kó** !bɔ́bá!á mìŋ   'I am just tying.'
    b. ù **kò** bɔ́bá!á mìŋ   'S/he is just tying.' (cf. ù bɔ̀bá!á mìŋ 's/he is tying')
    c. ù tíŋ **kó** !dá!gá mìŋ   'S/he was just showing.'

(599) Tonal patterns with *woN* 'already'
    a. ŋ̀ **wón** !dá!gá mìŋ   'I am already showing.'
    b. ù **wòn** dá!gá mìŋ   'S/he is already showing.'
    c. ù tíŋ **wón** !dí!é mìŋ   'S/he was already eating.'

(600) Tonal patterns with *vıı* 'again'
    a. m̀ **víí** !dá!gá mìŋ   'I am again showing.'
    b. ù **vìì** dá!gá mìŋ   'S/he is again showing.'
    c. ù ká **víí** !dígè   'S/he is not again cooking.'

To sum up, all the particles except *ya* have similar tonal behaviors and can be accounted for by positing a LH lexical tone pattern. The particle *ya*, in contrast, is posited to have only a Low tone in the lexicon.

6.4.2.2 Interaction of preverbal particles

The High tone which has spread from the left in the preceding examples spreads only one particle to the right. This is shown when we have two of the Low-toned particles following a High-toned word. In these cases, there is a free variation in pronunciation.

(601) a. ù tíŋ **ŋáán** yè dí!gé mìŋ   'S/he had been still cooking.'
       ù tíŋ **ŋáán** !yé dí!gé mìŋ

    b. ù tíŋ **wáá** kò dá!gá mìŋ   'S/he was then just showing.'
       ù tíŋ **wáá** !kó dá!gá mìŋ
    c. ù tín **yé** kò dá!gá mìŋ   'S/he was still just showing.'
       ù tín **yé** !kó dá!gá mìŋ

d. ù ká **wáá** vìì dá!gá   'S/he is not now again showing.'
ù ká **wáá** !vìì dá!gá

Also note that as a result of this one-word spreading of High, that there is now a phonetic HLH sequence in (601). This is now the second case of [HLH] we have seen, the first being the perfective transitive forms with first-person subjects (see 575, 576). Those were an idiosyncratic form tied into a particular morphosyntactic context, but the situation here is a more general one. The particles in (601) which have surfaced with High tone as a result of spreading *(ŋáán, wáá, yé)* have an underlying Low tone, and this might be profitably looked at with a level-based approach to OT, as in Kiparsky (2000).

In the utterance *ù tín yé kò dá!gá* 's/he was still just showing' from (601c), the two possible pronunciations from the same input are shown in (602).

(602) a. H   L   LH   L H   H (L)   L   H L H
         | | | | | | →   \ | | |/
         tin ye ko daga   tín yé kò dá!gá

    b. H   L   LH   L H   H (LL)   H L H
        | | | | | | →   \   / / /
        tin ye ko daga   tín yé   !kó dá!gá

I assume the Low tone shown as floating (enclosed in parentheses in 602a) is present in output form. Certainly, there are input Lows from both ye and ko; the question is the representation of the output. If the floating Low is not present, then there is a clear violation of *HLH. If the floating Low is present, then *HLH is not violated. Whether both Lows in parentheses in (602b) are present, or whether only one is, is unanswerable; the main point is that there is at least one floating Low present to account for the downstep at that position.

The spread of a High tone to the following particle has a "ripple effect," delinking the tone on that second particle and displacing the entire string of tones from their sponsoring morphemes. This can be seen most clearly in a case such as *ù tíŋ ŋáán yè dí!gé mìŋ* 's/he had been still cooking', from (601a). Note that the same sequence of tones is present in input as in output, with the exception of one Low.

(603) a.
```
    L  H  LH  L  LH   L         L   H      L H L H L
    |  |  |   |  ||   |    →    |   /\     | \ / |
    ʊ  tiŋ ŋaan ye dige miŋ      ʊ̀  tíŋ ŋáán  yè  dí!gé mìŋ
```

b.
```
    L  H  LH  L  LH   L         L   H     L   H L H L
    |  |  |   |  ||   |    →    |   /\    |   /\ / |
    ʊ  tiŋ ŋaan ye dige miŋ      ʊ̀  tíŋ ŋáán  !yé  dí!gé mìŋ
```

The input tones which I have posited in the discussion above are given to the left in (603). Except for the two input Low tones I have in bold being collapsed into one Low in the output, all input tones are present in the output, merely shifted.

The formal OT analysis of this I must leave to the future. Some of the features needed to account for these patterns will be a constraint or constraints which spread a High tone one and only one TBU to the right only on particles. This does not happen with other lexical categories. For example, with the input ŋ̀ wó àlìbɛ́sà 'I lack onion', the High from the verb wó does not spread to the noun àlìbɛ́sà. Thus the constraint(s) needed to account for particles must refer specifically to particles or perhaps nonlexical morphemes. This is quite likely the same constraint or constraints needed to account for the rightward spreading of High in the tableau in (590), with the indirect imperative dí tí !búgúrí 'we should learn'.

6.5 Tone on conditionals

Though Gur phonologies which cover tone in any detail comment on different tone patterns on verbs due to various aspects, few go beyond that to more diverse grammatical conditionings of tone. In this work, I present only one of what I suspect are several syntactic functions of tone in Kɔnni. This is the change of normally Low tone on a subject pronoun to High when it is the subject of a dependent conditional clause. After discussing tonal differences when a pronoun is subject of the conditional clause, I will also mention the pattern when a noun is subject. The imperfective aspect is used here to illustrate this pattern, because it is one of the aspects in which the subject pronoun makes a difference in the grammatical tone on the verb. A more complete discussion would include conditional with other aspects.

There is a pause between a conditional clause and the following one, and the tone is reset, with no influence of one clause on the other, thus in (604b–d) I only give the first conditional clause. Note the difference in pronoun tone in a declarative sentence versus in a conditional clause.

(604) First-person pattern
    a. ŋ̀ gárá!á !ɲúŋ   'I am going to market.'
       tì gárá!á !ɲúŋ   'We are going to market.'

    b. máŋ gáráà ɲŭŋ…   'if I am going to market…'
       tí gáráà ɲŭŋ…   'if we are going to market…'

Third-person pattern
    c. ù gàráá !ɲúŋ   'S/he is going to market.'
       bà gàráá !ɲúŋ   'They are going to market.'

    d. ú gáráà ɲŭŋ…   'if s/he is going to market…'
       bá gáráà ɲŭŋ…   'if they are going to market…'

In (604a and b), with first-person subject, the first syllable of the verb is High whether conditional or not. In the nonconditional (604a) the subject pronoun is Low, while in the conditional (604b) the subject pronoun is High. From (604b), we can see that the High conditional tone has replaced the normal Low tone on the pronoun, rather than being added to it. This is because of the lack of downstep between *tí* and *gáráà*. Were a Low tone preserved, the downstep would be present between them. I conclude that a High tone marking conditional is part of the input to the phonology of such a clause. Note that the tone on the verb itself also changes from [HH!H] in (604a) to [HHL] in (604b).

The third-person data in (604c and d) shows similar effects: first, that the tone on the subject pronoun changes to High in the conditional and second, that the normal LH melody of the imperfective in third person is replaced by a HHL melody. The High tone on the first syllable of the verb is not a result of spreading from the High-toned pronoun. If it were, and the LH tones of the verb were preserved, then the tone on the verb would be [HH!H] rather than [HHL]. The High tone on the last syllable of the verb would also result in the !H on the noun *ɲuŋ* following, rather than the actual rising tone. It seems, then, that a conditional construction alters the basic tonal melody of the verb in that construction.

The subject person makes a difference in the normal imperfective pattern; first- and third-person subjects cause different tonal patterns, as seen in (604a and c). However, in the conditional, this tonal distinction is neutralized; the tonal patterns in (604b and d) are the same. Therefore, there is one tonal melody for the conditional, independent of the subject pronoun. I have indicated this above as phonetic [HHL], but in light of verbal melodies crowding to the right, I propose a simple HL for the melody, mapped as follows:

6.5 Tone on conditionals

(605) H   H L L H
     | /\ | \/   ú gáráà ɲʊ̌ŋ... 'if s/he is going to market...'
     ʊ g a r a a ɲʊŋ

The normal imperfective aspect tone is discussed and a tableau (567) is given in section 6.4.1.1. A tableau is given in (606) for the verb in (605). The High tone on the pronoun is assumed present in input and thus not represented in the tableau.

(606) ú gáráà ɲʊ̌ŋ... if s/he is going to market...'

HL garaa	Align-Verb-Rt	*Cont-Int	*R-Spread	*H-Spread	*(L)
☞ a. H L |\ | garaa			*	*	
b. H L | | garaa	*!				
c. H L |/| garaa	*!	*!			
d. H L /\ garaa	*!		*	*	*

As easily seen, the major constraint which shapes the output is Align-Verb-Rt, which wants all tones of a verb to be aligned with the rightmost TBU. In the winning candidate (606a), this is done, but in none of the others. Candidate (606b) is otherwise optimal, but the others have additional defects. Candidate (606c) has a nonfinal contour, violating *Cont-Int. The ranking of this with respect to Align-Verb-Rt is unknown; a violation of either is enough to eliminate a candidate. Candidate (606d) has the final Low floating, and this not only violates the low-ranked *(L), but more importantly, also violates Align-Verb-Rt, since the Low is not associated to the final TBU of the verb.

When nouns are the subject of a conditional clause, the particle *dí* is inserted, as in (607), with the verb being High toned, at least in the imperfect aspect.

(607) a. ɲúá!há **dí** vííná, ǹ nàn dáá   'If the yams are good, I will buy.'
    b. níí!gé **dí** kíéŋ, ǹ nàn chígí   'If cows are coming, I will run.'

The particle *dí* 'if' in conditional clauses closely resembles the subordinating conjunction *dì* 'that' which introduces a relative clause, but differs in tone, as seen in (608).

(608) a. dààwá **dí** !kêŋ...   'if the man comes...'
    b. dààwá **!dí** kén!néwó   'the man **who** came...'

Though the surface forms of both cases of *dí* are High toned, the downstep before the *dí* in (608b) indicates that it is underlyingly Low toned.

6.6 Yes/no question intonation

The only intonational pattern for which I have systematic data is polar (yes/no) questions. A fuller study of intonation, including possibilities of attitudes and emphasis affecting pitch, must wait for another occasion. Polar questions, as mentioned in section 1.2.2, are syntactically exactly the same as the corresponding statements. The phonetic difference is that in questions, the initial pitch as well as the pitch over the entire utterance is higher, and the last segment, whether vowel or nasal, is lengthened and has a slow fall in pitch. This contrasts with English, in which the polar question "You're going to the park?" has a rise in pitch at the end. A sample is given in the display in (609). Note the higher pitch and lengthened and falling tone on the last syllable.

(609) Waveforms and pitch traces for
    A. tì díè sààbʊ 'we are eating porridge'

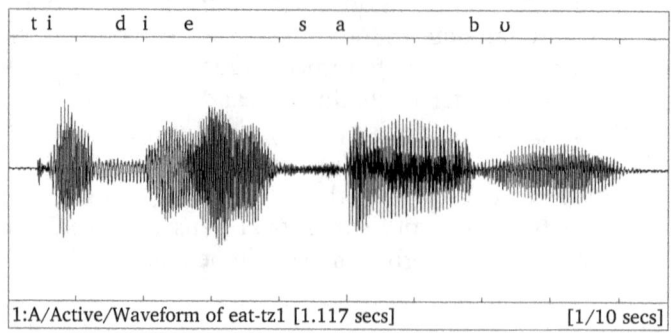

6.6 Yes/no question intonation

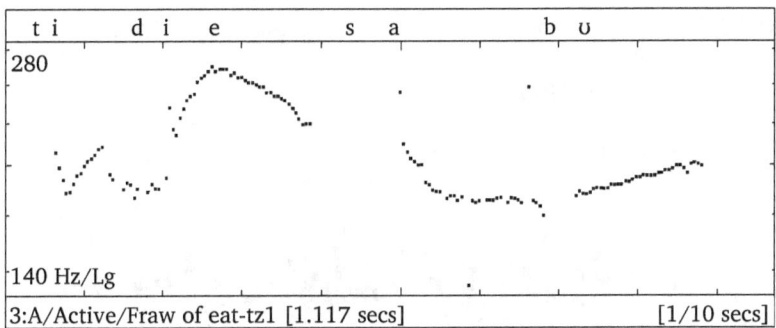

B. nì díè sààbúù 'are you(PL) eating porridge?'

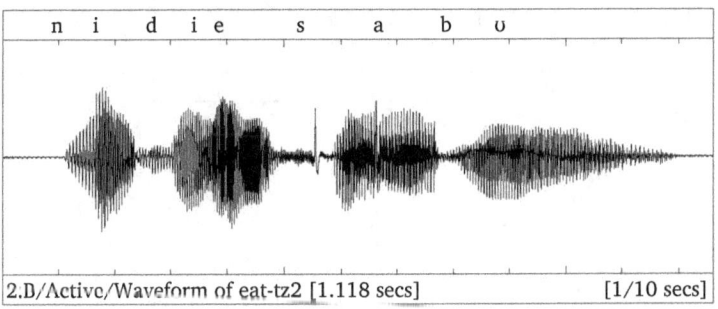

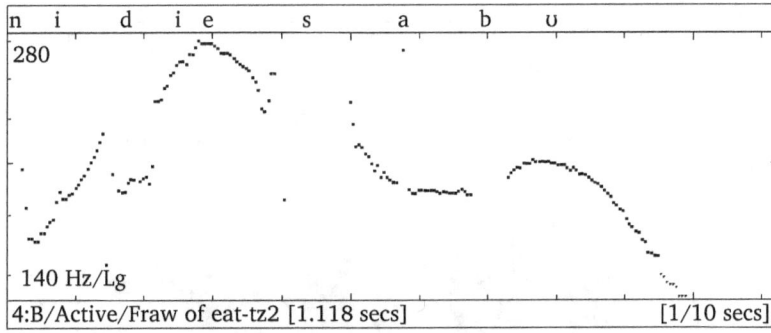

Besides the distinction between statement and question, Amadu was also able to consistently produce a difference in intonation between a polar question in which the speaker expresses little emotion and one in which he or she expresses surprise or shock. The "surprise question" has both a higher pitch in general and also a greater difference in pitch between High and Low, as exemplified in (610).

(610) Waveforms and pitch traces for nì díè sààbʊ̀ʊ̀ 'are you(PL) eating porridge?'
A. normal intonation

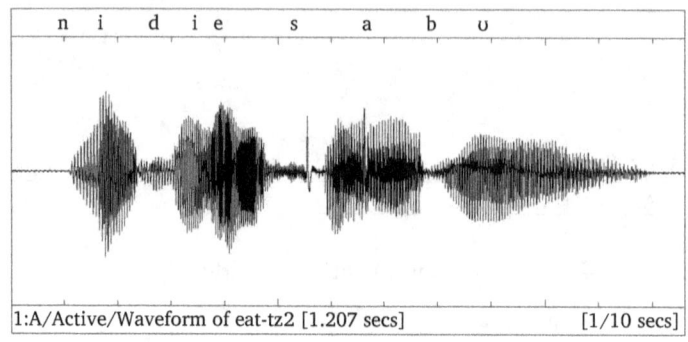

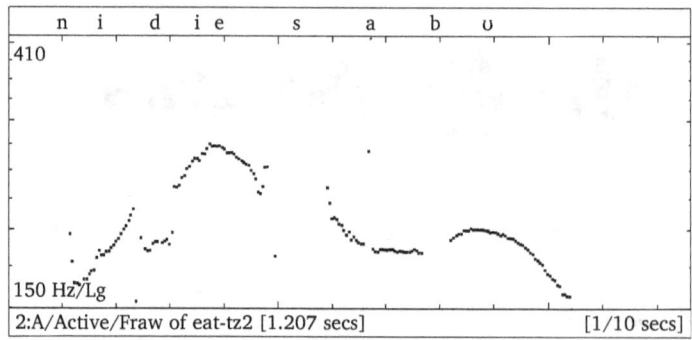

B. "surprise" intonation

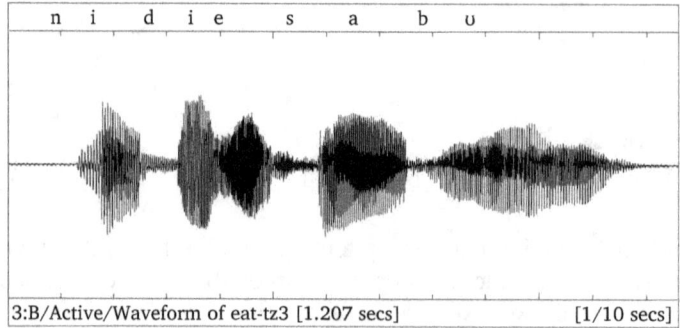

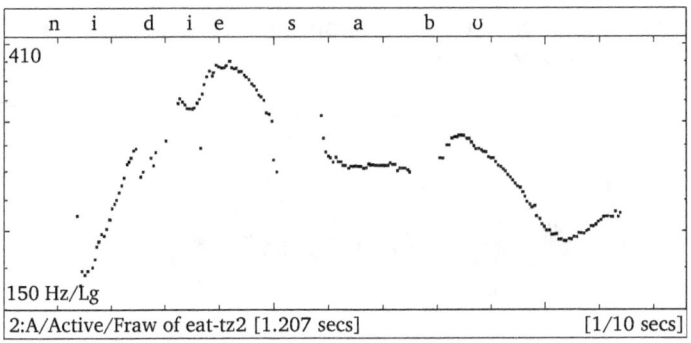

6.7 A note on stress

In this phonology, I have not mentioned stress as a relevant quality of words. Most Gur phonological descriptions do not discuss stress. In Dagaare, claims have been made that phonological stress is intimately tied into the tonal system (Anttila and Bodomo 1996, 2000). They write that stress occurs on the penultimate syllable of Dagaare, which then attracts tone. This is based also on Kennedy's (1966) concept of "primary" and "secondary" syllables. However, all the examples they give are disyllabic, and they do not consider the possibility that the relevant quality is the word-initial position rather than stress. Carlson (1994) mentions stressed syllables in Supyire and ties several phonological processes into them. What he labels as stressed syllables are always the initial syllables of roots also. Kröger (1992) says stress does not play an important role in Buli phonology. He writes that the "articulatory energy" of initial syllables is generally greater than subsequent ones in polysyllabic verbs and nouns, and also follows predictable patterns in compounds. This sounds very much like a predictable phonetic pattern.

In Kɔnni, there do not seem to be any phonetic correlates of stress (vowel length, amplitude) which are significant and independent of tone. To illustrate, CECIL graphs for waveform, pitch, and amplitude of kùlí 'tortoise' and kùléhé 'the tortoises' are shown in (611).

(611) Waveform, pitch track, and amplitude for
A. kùléhé 'the tortoises'

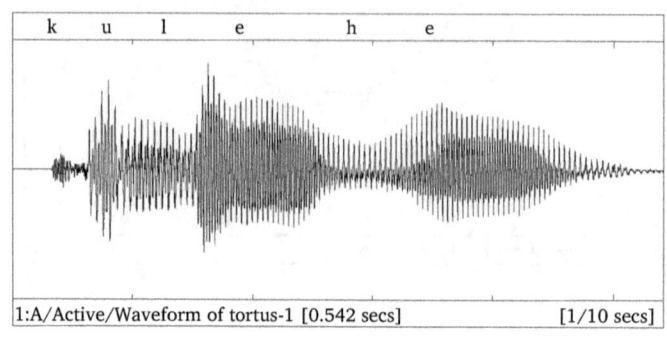
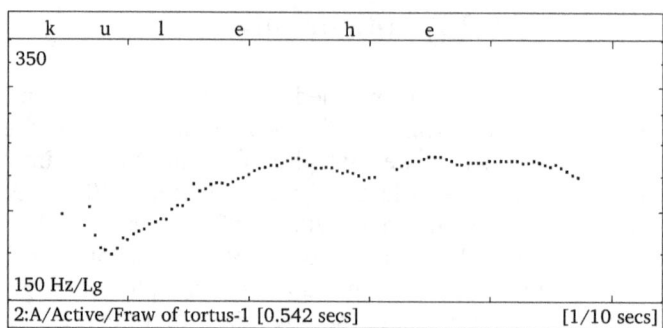
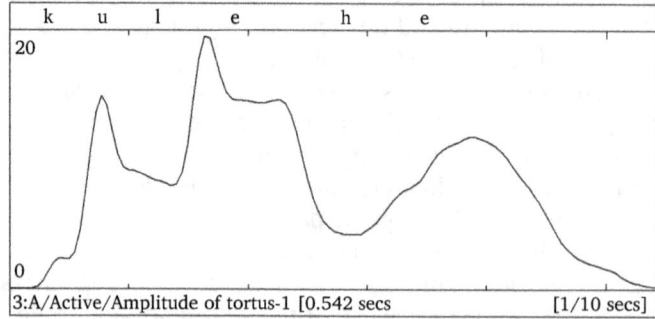

6.7 A note on stress

B. kùlí 'tortoise'

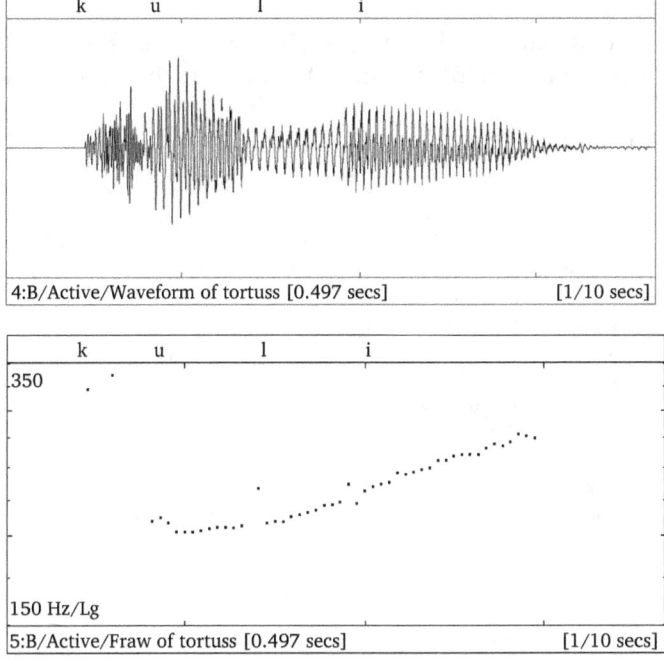

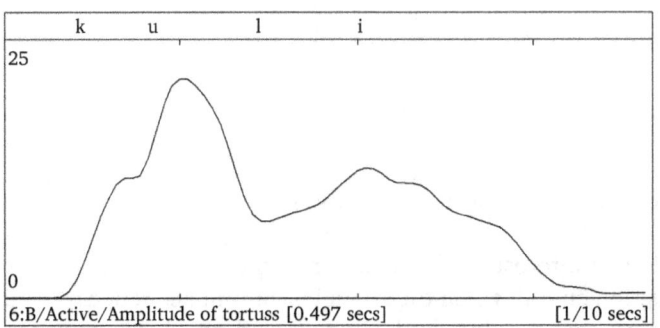

Note that while the first two syllables in both words (spoken in isolation in the same recording session) are LH, in A the second syllable has greater amplitude, while in B the first syllable has greater amplitude. If "articulatory energy" is what the other Gur writers are referring to when they speak of "stress," then this does not seem to be consistent in Kɔnni. Though more research undoubtedly needs to be done in this area, it appears that stress is not phonologically contrastive or distinctive in Kɔnni.

6.8 Concluding remarks

The following diagram gives the rankings of constraints as established in this chapter. The constraints in (612b) cannot be related to the ones in (612a).[43]

(612) Ranking of tonal contraints
   a.

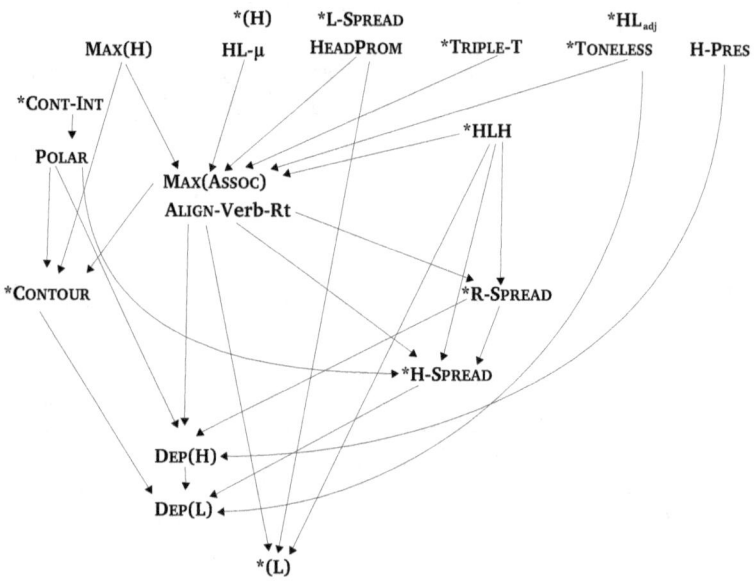

   b. NoSkip >> High-Rt >> Low-Rt

Of particular interest in this chapter is the direction of spreading of High tones. In general, when there is a HLH input sequence, the output is H!HH, where there is leftward High spreading. This happens within words and across words. However, in the specific morphological contexts of a verb and of an adjective, there is rightward High spreading. As usual in such cases, the more specific context takes precedence over the more general one, and the morphologically specific constraint Align-Verb-Rt is ranked more highly than the more general *R-Spread.

---

[43]The constraint HL-μ in (612) conflates *H!H-μ and *LH-μ.

6.8 Concluding remarks

Another matter which is not yet fully resolved is the matter of the interaction of floating Low tones with *HLH. When *dàmpàlá* 'logs' is in an associative construction with initial floating High tone, the result of the HLLH input tones is *dám!pálá,* with the two Low tones on the noun being either both set afloat or possibly one deleted (see 539 and 542), and High spreads leftward. However, when a series of preverbal particles such as *ù tíŋ wáá kò dágà mìŋ* 's/he was then just showing' also has input tones HLLH (/*tíŋ wàà kò dágà/*), the first High spreads rightward, and there remains a HLH phonetic sequence. The difference between the two quite probably has to do with phrasal phonology, but the details remain elusive.

7

Conclusion

In this chapter, I sum up some of the most interesting patterns of data, some of the theoretical implications of the Kɔnni data, and I give a tableau to illustrate as full a range of constraints as possible which apply to one sample form. The tableau focuses not just on one area such as consonantal assimilation, but on all areas in this work which apply to one Kɔnni word.

7.1 Data highlights

Some of what I consider the most interesting phenomena of Kɔnni will connect directly to theoretical issues, some will not. There is a caveat here to the reader: I may have omitted in this section what other researchers may consider interesting, so any reader looking here first will not find a complete catalogue of phonological phenomena in Kɔnni. Furthermore, some data is interesting because it is unusual, other data is interesting because it has some significance to current theoretical concerns; the latter will overlap with the theory highlights section.

One interesting morphological pattern is the agentive nouns which are derived from verbs: they have both a reduplicative CV prefix and a suffix (section 2.1.3). The high vowel of the prefix varies according to both the stem vowel and, if the stem is a glide, according to the place of the glide (section 5.6). The suffixal /r/ of the agentive nouns is involved in a dissimilation pattern (section 4.4).

Another point of interest concerns pronouns. There are at least three different classes of person/number splits, discussed in section 2.4, from which the following is repeated.

(613) Construction   Person/number split
      Imperfective and perfective aspects   3 versus non-3
      Indirect imperative   1 versus non-1
      'father/mother' possessor   2s/1 versus 2p and 3

To conclude these most general comments, I note that verbs in Kɔnni are much less specified in the lexicon than nouns. While all consonants may be verb initial, the consonants of C_2 or, if present, C_3 are extremely restricted (section 3.3.3). The vowels are even more restricted. There is only one distinctive vowel in a Kɔnni verb, in the initial syllable; any others after that are /I/ or, as a result of harmony, [U] (see sections 3.3.3 and 5.4.1). Tone is not contrastive on verbs but is completely predictable as a result of their tense and aspect (section 6.4.1).

7.1.1 Consonants

The fact that some word-initial consonantal contrasts were missing before certain vowels is attributed to historical processes in section 4.1.1. Some patterns in phonology may not be the result of synchronic processes or constraints at all, but merely historic relics. The phenomena of *g*-deletion and *n*-deletion, which occur only in certain noun classes (sections 4.3.1 and 4.3.2), were also shown to be the result of historical patterns, leading to this highly idiosyncratic synchronic pattern.

Kɔnni has a fairly normal pattern of nasal place assimilation, with the exception that a nasal before a labial-velar KP is [ŋKP] within a word, and [ŋmKP] across a word. This pattern has not been previously documented in any language to my knowledge.

The behavior of /r/ in various suffixes is quite varied. In one inflectional suffix, /r/ totally assimilates to a preceding sonorant (section 4.2.4). However, in a derivational suffix, /r/ dissimilates to [t] when preceded by a liquid, but in a lexical suffix dissimilates to [d] (section 4.4).

7.1.2 Vowels

One interesting phonetic observation is the large degree of overlap in F_1 and F_2 values for the vowels [ɪ, i] and [ʊ, o], discussed in section 5.1.3. This has implications not only for the difficulty of an outsider hearing the

7.1 Data highlights

distinctions between these, but also points the way to a possible merger of vowels in the future.

The ATR-based vowel harmony system within words has two features worthy of note, both discussed in section 5.2.1. First is the systematic alternation of [a ~ e ~ o] in suffixes, with [o] occurring only when directly following [u] or [w]. Second is the spread of ATR from an adjective one and only one syllable into the preceding noun stem.

Across words, particles agree with the "nearest" lexical item in ATR, but when a particle occurs between two lexical items of opposite values of ATR, the syntactic construction is what determines what is "nearest." This syntax/phonology interface is discussed in section 5.2.2.

Long mid vowels diphthongize (discussed in section 5.3), with V_1 always being a high vowel and V_2 being the same [a ~ e ~ o] alternation we saw in suffixes.

There must be agreement of high vowels in [dorsal] across [dorsal] consonants, and agreement of [coronal] across [coronal] consonants when the input vowels are /a/ and a [coronal] vowel. The different conditions on these two agreements preclude merging these as a unified phenomenon, but they are obviously closely related. These are discussed in sections 5.4.1 and 5.4.2.

With vowels in hiatus, sometimes the first vowel totally assimilates to the second, and sometimes there is no assimilation at all. The difference lies in the syntactic construction involved, and this syntax/phonology interface is discussed in section 5.9.

7.1.3 Tones

The fact of a H!H tonal contour on a single tone-bearing unit is virtually undocumented in the tonal literature, but is not uncommon in Kɔnni (section 6.1.1, also footnote 1 in chapter 6) and may turn out to be not uncommon once more areal tonal studies are done.

Disyllabic nouns with a citation LH tone pattern have four different behavioral patterns and so must have one of four distinct underlying tonal representations to account for differences in perturbational patterns.

While nouns, adjectives, and at least some particles have contrastive lexical tone, verbs take their tone entirely from the grammatical construction in which they occur; verbs have no underlying tone in Kɔnni (section 6.4).

It seems that there is a requirement that an utterance (or perhaps phrase) have at least one High tone.

The phenomenon of tonal polarity has been reported before, but in Kɔnni such polarity is limited to a single morpheme, the noun class 1 plural suffix (section 6.3.3) and so does not reflect a general phonological pattern in the language.

7.2 Theoretical highlights

Since theories change over time, it is quite possible that some of the phenomena listed below may not be of as much theoretical interest some years from now as they are today. Nonetheless, a good portion of these deal with phenomena which are not straightforward and so should present points of interest and challenge to any phonological theory in the foreseeable future.

7.2.1 Optimality Theory

Several constraints referring to a specific lexical category or even a particular noun class or specific morpheme are active in Kɔnni (sections 4.3.1, 4.3.2, 5.2.1.2, 5.7.2, 6.3.3, 6.4.1.1). In light of the claim that constraints are universal, these constraints must be seen as falsifying this claim. A particular morpheme is a property of a particular language, and a constraint referring to that morpheme does not have the possibility of applying to another language; it cannot be universal.

As noted in sections 4.2.1 and 4.6.3, one particular set of constraints may adequately account for a form, but when a larger corpus is examined, other constraints are then necessary. But then the second set of constraints is adequate to account for the first set of data. Does this render the first set of constraints superfluous, nonexistent? Or does this merely lend extra "strength" to the nonoptimality of the failed candidates? In the current state of OT, with no agreed-upon set of constraints, this must be regarded as an unsettled question.

Optimality Theory has been described as the theory that thrives on exceptions, but as discussed in section 5.10, room must be made for true exceptions, as those in section 5.7.2.

7.2.2 Consonants

The variable nasal place assimilation referred to above ([ŋKP] within a word, [ŋmKP] across a word) challenges our views of how to represent labial-velars and possibly multiply-articulated consonants in general (section 4.2.1.2). There is no straightforward phonological analysis of how to represent the difference between the two. A phonetically based

7.2 Theoretical highlights

representation can describe the difference, but even so cannot explain why there is this systematic difference.

The alternation of the noun class 1 plural suffix between [-a] in some cases and [-ra] in those preceded by /aa/ or /ʊʊ/ is accounted for not by straightforward epenthesis of [r], but a replacement of the middle vowel in an illicit VVV sequence by the least marked consonant, [r] (section 4.5.2). This type of analysis is, as far as I know, unique in the literature.

A true case of consonantal epenthesis occurs when [ʔ] is inserted before vowel-initial nouns in some cases. This supports the notion that a glottal place is even more unmarked than coronal (section 4.5.2).

In the coronal phonology, we need to refer to the morphological classes of lexical item versus derivational suffix versus inflectional suffix to account for the different ways an input /n-r/ sequence is resolved (sections 4.2.4 and 4.4).

7.2.3 Vowels

The fact that the [closed] feature accounts for the intricate phenomena of vowel harmony and diphthongization better than the traditional [high] and [low] features is good evidence that [closed] rather than these or other alternatives is a more adequate feature to represent vowel height (sections 5.2.1 and 5.3).

There are several phenomena in the vowel system of Kɔnni which relate to issues of adjacency. In the [a ~ e ~ o] suffixal alternation, the [o] alternate occurs only when adjacent to [u] or [w]. In terms of features, the vocalic [dorsal] spreads only to a placeless adjacent vowel (section 5.2.1). However, when both input vowels are high, [dorsal] may spread from one vowel to another across a consonant, but the consonant must also be [dorsal] (section 5.4.1). In yet another pattern, [coronal] may spread from one vowel to another across a [coronal] consonant, but the first vowel must be the placeless /a/ (section 5.4.2).

Issues of the representation of geminate vowels are found in a few areas. Diphthongization, discussed in section 5.3, is a challenge in that theories based on CV phonology assert that a long vowel is represented by a single melodic set of features linked to two V-slots. However, diphthongization must treat each vowel as a separate unit. Related to this is the centralization of front vowels before ŋ, which may only apply to the second V-slot of a long vowel, again forcing a view of a long vowel as two distinct units. However, the inalterability of [aa] as compared to the extreme malleability of input [a] (sections 5.1.1, 5.1.2, 5.4.2, 5.7.2) reinforces the traditional view of geminate vowels as having a distinct representation.

The connection between phonology and syntax appears not once, but twice in Kɔnni, both times in relation to vowels. The first is in ATR harmony across words, in which a particle agrees in ATR with the "nearest" lexical item. However, when a particle is trapped between lexical items of opposite values of ATR, it is the syntactic construction which determines the value that particle will take. Previous approaches to the syntax/phonology interface have used either a direct reference to the syntactic tree or an indirect construction of prosodic phrases. Neither of these approaches will work with the Kɔnni ATR situation and a new approach based on the nonstructural notion of theta-marking is proposed in section 5.2.2. In the second case of a phonology/syntax interface, whether total assimilation of vowels occurs in hiatus situations depends on the syntax as well. In this situation, a direct reference to the syntactic structure accounts for the patterns (section 5.9.2). So two distinct patterns of syntax/phonology interaction are found in Kɔnni.

The epenthetic vowel in Kɔnni is [I], but the maximally underspecified vowel is /a/. This is in contrast to theories which say that the epenthetic vowel is the maximally underspecified vowel (section 5.5).

7.2.4 Tones

As mentioned, disyllabic nouns with a citation LH tone pattern actually must have one of four distinct underlying tonal representations to account for differences in perturbational patterns. Toneless nouns are necessary in this set.

(614)		UR	Citation	'One X'	'His/her X'
a.	'fish'	LH	zàsíŋ	zàsíŋ !káání	ʊ̀ zá!síŋ
b.	'louse'	ØH	kpìbíŋ	kpìbíŋ !káání	ʊ̀ kpíbíŋ
c.	'hat'	LØ	kàgbá	kàgbà kààní	ʊ̀ kágbà
d.	'woman'	ØØ	hɔ̀gú	hɔ̀gú !káání	ʊ̀ hɔ́gʊ̀

Also, there is no doubt that, unlike some Bantu languages, a lexical Low tone is necessary in Kɔnni to account for many tonal phenomena, including the frequent occurrence of downstep.

7.3 A "complete" tableau

In the course of this work, only one particular phenomenon or pattern was examined at a time. This is, of course, an eminently practical matter;

7.3 A "complete" tableau

to give all reasonable output candidates for all the inputs and give constraints by which the optimal candidate is selected is extremely unwieldy, given that there could be multiple candidates concerning each of the areas of vowel assimilation, consonantal assimilation, tone spreading, etc.

However, I believe it might be instructive to conclude with one form and all the constraints which apply to it, whether faithfulness or well-formedness constraints. Somewhat arbitrarily, I have chosen the form núán!ní 'the floor pounder'. This has citation form núá!mɨ́ŋ and plural form núámà. While there is no form that can exemplify all the patterns discussed in this work, núán!ní exhibits several: nasal place assimilation, total assimilation of suffixal /r/, diphthongization, agreement of suffix in ATR value, and downstep. The input representation will have the tones marked as the morphemes are listed in the lexicon. Candidates (615b–e) are nonoptimal because of deficiencies in the vowels, candidates (615f–j) because of the consonants, and candidates (615k–n) because of the tones.

(615) nóán!ní 'the floor pounder'

HL -H / nOOm-rI	*[VV]$_{mid}$	DEP (ATR)	HI DIPH	MAX[cl]	MAX(H)	*[son]r	*HLH	IDENT [son]	MAX(L)	DEP (V$_{CL-CL}$)	DEP [cl]
☞ a. nóán!ní											
b. nɔ́ɔ́n!ní	*!										
c. nɔ́án!ní			*!								
d. nóɔ́n!ní		*!									*!
e. núón!ní											
f. nóán!rí						*!					
g. nóám!rí						*!					
h. nóán!dí								*!			
i. nóán!tí								*!			
j. nóá!mírí										*!	
k. HL H | | nóánmí							*!				
l. H L H | | | nóánnì							*!				
m. H H | | nóánmí					*!						
n. H L | | nóánnì									*!		

7.3 A "complete" tableau

The constraints listed in (615) are only the ones which eliminate one or more of the candidates in this particular tableau; others are obviously active in Kɔnni. Candidate (615a), the winning candidate, violates none of the constraints listed (though it would violate other lower-ranked constraints such as *(L)). Candidate (615b) loses by maintaining a long mid vowel. Candidate (615c) loses since V_1 of the diphthong is not a high vowel, as well as by deleting a [closed] feature, while 615d) loses by adding a [closed] feature. Candidate (615e) and any other candidate which has an ATR vowel loses by inserting an ATR. Candidates (615f and g) lose by having a sonorant-r sequence. Candidates (615h and i) lose by changing the [sonorant] value of the input /r/. Candidate (615j) loses by inserting a vowel, which is acceptable for other forms but eliminates the candidate here. Candidates (615k and l) lose by having a Low tone associated between two High tones. Candidate (615m) loses by deleting a Low tone, and (615n) by deleting a High tone.

The fourteen candidates listed are only the tip of the iceberg, of course. In the tableau in (615) I have divided the candidates into those violating vocalic-based, consonantal-based, and tonal-based constraints only, with the candidates violating constraints applying to one area all being optimal with regard to the other areas. If I were to consider all the candidates based on the above violations of constraints, there would be 4 x 5 x 4 = 80 candidates to consider, rather than the fourteen I have listed. Adding just two more candidates, for example ones having ATR on the first syllable and on the last syllable, would raise the candidate permutations to 120. This is merely a concrete demonstration of the number of candidates which would need to be considered which are reasonably close to the optimal one. This sample form was a relatively short disyllabic one; the permutations and number of reasonable candidates would multiply exponentially with longer words, to say nothing of phrases, clauses, and entire utterances.

This exercise only serves to illustrate the fact that the human mind, which can handle all these complexities in real time processing, whether in this or any theory of phonology, is a marvelously intricate and (though the word has been used to the point of abuse in recent years) awesome creation.

Appendix A

Perturbation of target nouns in tone frames

The aim here is to give nouns of various lengths in tone frames that will provide a Low tone before and after the target noun and a High tone before and after. This goal is not entirely met, since the frame 'his/her X' has a floating High and not strictly a Low tone immediately preceding the target noun. Only one example is given of each tone class, but if there are fewer than five examples in my data, the number of examples is given.[1] Nouns are given in citation forms as well as in frames, and the proposed underlying tone of each noun is listed as well as the surface tone. Since most citation forms of nouns end with the singular suffix /-ŋ́/, I separate the High tone from the noun stem tone by a hyphen in my proposed underlying tones. A High which, in my analysis, is inserted to maintain the constraint of a High tone in a noun is not listed in my proposed underlying tones.

The frames
'this is X'   'one X'
'I lack X'   'his/her X'

---

[1] I have not put all nouns in my database in these frames, so presumably considering more nouns will expand the "rare" patterns somewhat.

One-syllable nouns

1. súŋ   'broom'   súŋ wún!ná   súŋ !káání
   H-H   ŋ̀ wó súŋ   ù súŋ
2. tăŋ   'stone'   tăŋ wún!ná   tăŋ !káání
   L-H   ŋ̀ wó !táŋ   ù tá!ŋ (H-!H on single syllable)
3. bùá   'child'   bùá wún!ná   bùá !káání
   L   (4 examples)   ŋ̀ wó !bùá   ù búà

Two-syllable nouns

1. jɔ́rɔ́ŋ   'ladder'   jɔ́rɔ́ŋ wún!ná   jɔ́rɔ́ŋ !káání
   H-H   ŋ̀ wó jɔ́rɔ́ŋ   ù jɔ́rɔ́ŋ
2. hɔ̀gú   'woman'   hɔ̀gú wún!ná   hɔ̀gú !káání
   Ø   ŋ̀ wó !hɔ́gú   ù hɔ́gù
3. kpìbíŋ   'louse'   kpìbíŋ wún!ná   kpìbíŋ !káání
   Ø-H   ŋ̀ wó kpíbíŋ   ù kpíbíŋ
4. zàsíŋ   'fish'   zàsíŋ wún!ná   zàsíŋ !káání
   L-H   ŋ̀ wó !zásíŋ   ù zá!síŋ
5. kàgbá   'hat'   kàgbá wún!ná   kàgbà !kààní
   L (3 examples)   ŋ̀ wó kàgbà   ù kágbà
6. náá!gíŋ   'cow'   náá!gíŋ wún!ná   náá!gíŋ !kààní
   HLHL?   ŋ̀ wó náá!gíŋ   ù náá!gíŋ
7. tá!síŋ   'headpan'   tá!síŋ wún!ná   tá!síŋ !káání
   HL-H (3 examples)   ŋ̀ wó tá!síŋ   ù tá!síŋ
8. máásà   'a cake'   máá!sá wún!ná   máásà kààní
   HL (2 examples)   ŋ̀ wó máásà   ù máásà
9. nìmbúà   'sibling'   nìmbú!á wún!ná   nìmbúà kààní
   Ø-HL (1 example)   ŋ̀ wó nímbúà   ù nímbúà
10. gùrá!áŋ   'lizard'   gùrá!áŋ wún!ná   gùrá!áŋ kààní
    ØHL-H (1 example)   ŋ̀ wó !gúrá!áŋ   ù gúrá!áŋ

Three-syllable nouns

1. wásígá   'dried porridge'   wásígá wún!ná   wásígá !káání
   HHH   ŋ̀ wó wásígá   ù wásígá
2. bùrìmíŋ   'bush donkey'   bùrìmíŋ wún!ná   bùrìmíŋ !káání
   L-H (4 examples)   ŋ̀ wó !búrímíŋ   ù bú!rímíŋ
3. dàmpàlá   'bench'   dàmpàlá wún!ná   dàmpàlá !káání
   LLH   ŋ̀ wó dàmpàlá   ù dám!pálá
4. kùkwábíŋ   'feather'   kùkwábíŋ wún!ná   kùkwábíŋ !káání
   ØH-H   ŋ̀ wó !kúkwábíŋ   ù kúkwábíŋ
5. ná!pɔ́ríŋ   'calf (leg)'   ná!pɔ́ríŋ wún!ná   ná!pɔ́ríŋ !káání
   HL-H (4 examples)   ŋ̀ wó ná!pɔ́ríŋ   ù ná!pɔ́ríŋ

6. kúrúbâ   'pot'   kúrúbá !wún!ná   kúrúbá kààní
   HHHL (4 examples)   ŋ̀ wó kúrúbâ   ù kúrúbâ
7. táɲéé!líŋ   'ash'   táɲéé!líŋ !wún!ná   táɲéé!líŋ kààní
   HHL-H (2 examples)   ŋ̀ wó táɲéé!líŋ   ù táɲéé!líŋ
8. kàréntìà   'cutlass'   kàrén!tíá wún!ná   kàréntìà kààní
   ØHL   ŋ̀ wó !kàréntìà   ù kàréntìà
9. káláŋgbí!áŋ   'mussel'   káláŋgbí!áŋ !wún!ná káláŋgbí!áŋ kààní
   HHHL-H (1 example)   ŋ̀ wó káláŋgbí!áŋ   ù káláŋgbí!áŋ

Four-syllable nouns
1. àlìbésà   'onion'   àlìbé!sá wún!ná   àlìbésà káání
   LLHL   ŋ̀ wó àlìbélsà   ù á!líbélsà
2. kàmbùntáá!míŋ 'papaya'   kàmbùntáá!míŋ wún!ná kàmbùntáá!míŋ !kààní
   LLHL-H (1   (lit.,   ŋ̀ wó kàmbùntáá!míŋ ù kám!búntáá!míŋ
   example)   'Ashanti
                   shea nut')

Five-syllable noun
1. sìgìlínsìgì   'hiccups'   sìgìlín!sígí wún!ná sìgìlínsìgì káání
   LLHLL (2 examples)   ŋ̀ wó sìgìlínsìgì   ù sígílínsìgì

Appendix B

Nouns, plurals, and definite articles

There are occasional gaps in the following data. I have left these as is, though in most cases the pattern is clear enough so the missing data could easily be predicted. The nouns here are not all the data I have, but my criterion for inclusion of a word here was that I had at least three of the four categories (with the exception of noun class 4, where mass nouns often have no plural). Also, although I have a separate section for compound nouns, I have included here nouns that I suspect to be historically compound because of the mix of ATR vowels, but have no clue as to the meaning of the individual components.

Noun class 1 (108 words)

Nouns	Singular	Sg + Art	Plural	Pl + Art
'ankle'	nááchígí!síŋ	nááchígí!síri	nááchígísà	—
'anklebone'	bògòrìtàŋ	bògòrìtànní	bògòrìtànà	bògòrìtànáhá
'arrow'	tònyí!líŋ	tònyí!lní	tònyífmà	—
'axe handle'	léékúŋ	léékúnní	léékúò	—
'bachelor'	dààkpàŋ	dààkpànní	dààkpànà	dààkpànáhá
'back of head'	kpààŋ	kpààrí	kpàrá	kpàráhá
'bag'	búllɔ́gíŋ	búllɔ́gírí	búllɔ́gà	búllɔ́!gáhá
'bat'	jìnjáámíŋ	jìnjáánní	jìnjáámá	jìnjáámáhá
'beans, bambara'	sììmíŋ	sììmí	sììmé	sììméhé
'beans, small'	túŋ	túmní	túò	túó!hé
'bee'	síébíŋ	síébírí	síébíè	síébíé!hé
'bone'	kɔ̀bíŋ	—	kɔ̀bá	—
'breast'	bììsíŋ	bììsíri	bììsá	bììsáhá
'bush'	hààgíŋ	hààgírí	—	—
'butterfly'	kpánjábíŋ	kpánjábírí	kpánjábà	kpánjá!báhá
'castanets'	chàmíŋ	chànní	chàmá	—
'cheek'	kààmíŋ	kààní	kààmá	kààmáhá
'chest'	ɲóóŋ	ɲóórí	ɲórà	ɲó!ráhá
'chin'	bítíéŋ	bítíérí	bítíè	bítíé!hé
'cloud'	nììmààŋ	nììmààrí	nììmàrá	—
'cock, rough-feathered'	kpàráátúŋ	kpàráátúnní	kpàráátúò	kpàráátúó!hé
'cooking place'	kúgíŋ	kúgúrí	kúgè	—
'cooking room'	jùòdìkkíŋ	jùòdìkkírí	jùòdìkké	jùòdìkkéhé
'corn (maize)'	káwón!tíŋ	káwón!tírí	káwóntà	—

Nouns, plurals, and definite articles

Nouns	Singular	Sg + Art	Plural	Pl + Art
'cornstalk'	kònchiàgíŋ	kònchiàgìrí	kònchiàgá	—
'crop (of bird)'	kágí!líŋ	kágí!lí	kágílà	kágí!láhá
'day'	dàáŋ	dàárí	dàrá	dàráhá
'drum (fordancing)'	tàmpáŋ	—	tàmpáná	—
'drum (2-headed)'	gìŋgáŋ	gìŋgànní	gìŋgáná	—
'duck'	gbìɲóáŋ	gbìɲùàrí	gbìɲɔ̀rá	—
'egg'	gílí	gílí	gílà	gí!láhá
'elder'	jàkùòŋ	jàkùòrí	ɲìŋkùrá	ɲìŋkùráhá
'face mark'	wíŋ	wínní	wíɛ̀	wíɛ́!hé
'fetish, neck'	sámíŋ	sámí	sámà	—
'fish (sp.)'	síŋ	sínní	sìà	sìá!há
'fish (sp.)'	kpàágíŋ	kpàágìrí	kpàágá	kpàágáhá
'fish trap'	sògóŋ	—	sògá	—
'floor pounder'	nóá!míŋ	nóán!ní	nóámà	—
'floor pounding stick'	lùlí	lùllí	lùlè	díé!hé
'forehead'	dííŋ	díírí	díè	díé!hé
'frog'	yàníŋ	yàní	yàná	yànáhá
'fruit of tree (sp.)'	kìŋkàmòòmíŋ	kìŋkàmòònní	kìŋkàmòòmá	kìŋkàmòòmáhá
'gecko'	chòó!síŋ	chòósí!rí	chòósá	chòó!sáhá
'grasscutter (animal)'	sìsíŋ	sìsìnní	sìsìé	sìsìéhé
'grasshopper'	sàŋkpààŋ	sàŋkpààrí	sàŋkpàrá	sàŋkpàráhá
'grinding stone, lower'	nííŋ	núrí	nâ	nâ!há
'gullet (of fowl)'	làŋkòòsíŋ	làŋkòòsìrí	làŋkòòsé	làŋkòòséhé
'hawk'	kpàlìgíŋ	kpàlìgìrí	kpàlìgá	kpàlìgáhá

Nouns	Singular	Sg + Art	Plural	Pl + Art
'heart'	sìkpááŋ	sìkpáárí	sìkpàrà	sìkpáꜜráhá
'hive'	pìmpàrìmíŋ	pìmpàrìmní	pìmpàrìmá	—
'hoe'	kòóŋ	kòòrí	kòrá	kòráhá
'hole for seed'	bànlàgíŋ	bànlàgírí	bànlàgá	bànlàgáhá
'hole in tree'	yùlí	yùlí	yùlé	yùléhé
'house'	tígíŋ	tígírí	tígè	tíꜜgéhé
'hyena'	gbàànchòóŋ	gbààncòòrí	gbààncòrá	gbààncòráhá
'jigger'	bɔ̀bìlíŋ	bɔ̀bìlírí	bɔ̀bìlá	bɔ̀bìláhá
'knee'	dùŋ	dùnní	dùné	dùnéhé
'land'	gààŋ	gààrí	gàrá	—
'land god'	tàŋgbáŋ	tàŋgbánní	tàŋgbánà	—
'lion'	gbégímíŋ	gbégínní	gbégímé	gbégíméhé
'liver'	wùùbíŋ	wùùbírí	wùùbé	—
'lizard (sp.)'	síŋgétígíŋ	síŋgétígírí	síŋgétígé	síŋgétígéhé
'lizard (sp.)'	wóꜜtágbáŋ	wótágbànní	wótágbàná	wótágbànáhá
'log'	dàmpàlí	dàmpàlí	dàmpàlá	dàmpàláhá
'louse'	kpìbíŋ	kpìbínní	kpìbíè	kpìbíéhé
'maggot'	zɔ̀nzɔ́ŋ	zɔ̀nzɔ́nní	zɔ̀nzɔ́à	zɔ̀nzóáꜜhá
'mouse'	hàŋkòóŋ	hàŋkòòrí	hàŋkòrá	hàŋkòráhá
'mouth'	nóáŋ	nóárí	nóà	nóáꜜhá
'nail, arrow'	yíꜜlíŋ	yíꜜlrí	yíꜜmà	yíꜜlmáhá
'name'	sààŋ	sààrí	sàrá	sàráhá
'occiput'	kpááŋ	kpààrí	kpàrá	kpàráhá
'okra'	ŋmááꜜníŋ	—	ŋmáànà	ŋmááꜜnáhá
'penis'	kɔ̀lí	kɔ̀lí	kɔ̀lá	—

Nouns, plurals, and definite articles 443

Nouns	Singular	Sg + Art	Plural	Pl + Art
'pestle'	tàndúŋ	tàndúnní	tàndúò	tàndúó!hé
'pigeon'	nìŋmàríŋ	—	nìŋmàrá	—
'place'	jígíŋ	jígírí	jígê	—
'porcupine'	sààmíŋ	sàànní	sààmá	—
'pot, big'	bùmbóŋ	bùmbònní	bùmbúó	—
'pot, eating'	tímbálí	tímbállí	tímbálà	—
'pot, water'	kpágíŋ	kpágírí	kpágà	—
'problem'	wííŋ	wíírí	wíà	wíá!há
'rat'	dàyúóŋ	dàyúòrí	dàyúrá	dàyúráhá
'river'	múgúŋ	múgúrí	múgà	mú!gáhá
'scrotum'	yɔ̀límíŋ	yɔ̀límí	yɔ̀límá	—
'seed'	bíŋ	bínní	bíê	bíé!hé
'shade'	jágíŋ	jágírí	jágà	jágá!há
'shea fruit'	táá!míŋ	táán!ní	táámà	táá!máhá
'shea nut (whole)'	kpíŋ	kpínní	kpíê	—
'sheep'	yísíŋ	—	yísè	yí!séhé
'sitting place'	káá!síŋ	káá!sírí	káásà	káá!sáhá
'skink'	kpáá!jálíŋ	kpáá!jállí	kpáá!jálá	—
'sore'	kùjààgíŋ	kùjààgírí	kùjààgá	—
'soup leaves (sp.)'	bànyùògíŋ	bànyùògírí	bànyùògá	bànyùògáhá
'sparrow'	gìnníŋ	gìnní	gìmê	gìméhé
'spear'	tímíŋ	tímí	tímè	—
'stone'	tâŋ	tànní	tàná	tànáhá
'stump'	dàagbúgíŋ	dàagbúgírí	dàagbúgè	dàagbúgé!hé
'tail'	jùŋ	jùnní	jùà	jùàhá

Nouns	Singular	Sg + Art	Plural	Pl + Art
'termite hill (sp.)'	tógóŋ	túgórí	tógá	túgá!há
'toad'	bùntòóŋ	bòntòòrí	bùntòrá	bùntòráhá
'tooth'	ɲíŋ	ɲínní	ɲínà	—
'tortoise'	kùlí	kùlí	kùlè	kùléhé
'tree (sp.)'	ɲòóŋ	ɲòórí	ɲòrá	ɲòráhá
'tree(sp.)'	vá!hálí	vá!hálí	vá!hálá	vá!háláhá
'tribal scar'	bèŋ	bènní	bènè	bènéhé
'vagina'	tààgíŋ	tààgírí	tààgá	tààgáhá
'yam'	ɲóŋ	ɲónní	ɲóà	ɲóá!há
'year'	bìŋ	bìnní	bìná	bìnáhá

Noun class 2 (58 words)

'armpit'	bùllɔ́ŋ	bùllɔ́kkú	bùllɔ̀gìtí	
'baboon'	fááŋ	fáákú	fáátí	fáátítí
'bark, shell'	hàŋ	hàkkú	hàgìtí	
'basket (sp.)'	jík!kɔ́ríŋ	jík!kɔ́rúkú	jík!kɔ́ttí	
'boat'	háá!ríŋ	háá!rúkú	háá!rítí	
'building, multistory'	kòsíŋ	kòsùkú	kòsìtí	
'calabash, water'	kùòlíŋ	kùòlùkú	kùòlìtí	
'centipede'	nàkpàchìyí!ŋ	nàkpàchìyí!kú	nàkpàchìyí!tí	
'clothes'	gàríŋ	gàrúkú	gàttí	
'cockroach'	làálíŋ	làálókú	làálítí	làálìtí
'courtyard'	gbààŋ	gbààkú	gbààtí	gbààtìtí
'crocodile'	yíbíŋ	yíbókú	yíbítí	

Nouns, plurals, and definite articles

Nouns	Singular	Sg + Art	Plural	Pl + Art
'door'	gbiá!bíŋ	gbiábʊ́!kú	gbiábíti	gbiábí!títi
'earthworm'	gbáráŋ	gbáráku	gbáráti	gbáráti̋ti̋
'farm'	kóáŋ	kóákű	kóáti̋	kóáti̋ti̋
'farmed area'[1]	kɔ́!ŋ	kɔ̋k!kú	kɔ̋gíti̋	
'fence'	gìríŋ	gìrókú	gìríti̋	gìrítíti̋
'fiber, rope'	bɔ̀ŋ	bɔ̀kkó	bɔ̀gíti̋	
'fingernail'	nú!yíbíŋ	nú!yíbɔ̀kú	nú!yíbíti̋	
'fish (sp.)'	gígá!ríŋ	gígá!rókú	gígá!ríti̋	gígá!rítíti̋
'fish (sp.)'	mìmáaŋ	mìmáakú	mìmáatí	mìmáatíti̋
'frog (sp.)'	kàmbá!ló!ŋ	kàmbá!lók!kú	kàmbá!ló!gíti̋	kàmbá!ló!gítíti̋
'ghost'	kógó!tí̋	kógó!kó[2]	kógó!ti̋	
'grass, thatch'	hòòŋ	hòòkɛ́	hòòti̋	hòòtíti̋
'hawk'	kpíf!líŋ	kpíf!lókú	kpíf!líti̋	kpíf!lítíti̋
'hedgehog'	zàmpʊ́ŋ	zàmpókkú	zàmpógíti̋	zàmpógítíti̋
'hog, bush'	dòaŋ	dòákú	dòati̋	dòátíti̋
'hole'	vɔ́ríŋ	vɔ́rókú	vɔ́ttí	
'inside'	sòŋ	sòkó	sòti̋	sòtíti̋
'jackal'	jòlú!ŋ	jòlú!kó	jòlúti̋	
'kite, black'	kpé!jusíŋ	kpé!jusùkú	kpé!jusíti̋	
'leaf'	vááŋ	váákű	vááti̋	vááti̋ti̋
'lizard, monitor'	yúóŋ	yúókú	yúótí	yúótíti̋
'lung'	zùzùgùŋ	zùzùkkú	zùzugíti̋	

[1]This term refers to an area which has been previously farmed, but has not been used for some time.
[2]Alternatively, kók!kú.

Nouns	Singular	Sg + Art	Plural	Pl + Art
'market'	ɲɔ̀ŋ	ɲɔ̀kkú	ɲògítí	
'middle'	sɔ́n!sɔ́ŋ	sɔ́n!sɔ́kkú	sɔ́n!sɔ́gítí	
'moon'	chííŋ	chííkú	chííti	chíítítí
'night'	yóŋ	yókkú	yógítí	yógítítí
'path'	siéŋ	siékú	siétí	
'pit'	gúólúlŋ	gúólúlkú	gúólti	
'rain'	nììŋ	nììkú	nììtí	
'scorpion'	chiàkòríŋ	chiàkòrókú	chiàkòttí	chiàkòttítí
'seat, inside'	kólríŋ	kólrúkú	kólrítí	
'shoulder'	gbìŋkpiáŋ	gbìŋkpiákú	gbìŋkpiàtí	
'skin, book'	gbáŋ́ŋ	gbáŋkú	gbántí	
'snail'	kpóŋkpáwòlìjáágù	kpóŋkpáwòlìjáá!gókú	kpóŋkpáwòlìjáá!gótí	
'speech, language'	báliŋ	bálikú	báltí	
'spleen?'	yábìlìáŋ	yábìlìákú	yábìlìàtí	
'spoon'	dììsíŋ	dììsòkú	dììsìtí	
'termite hill (sp.)'	kpèchúóŋ	kpèchúókú	kpèchúóti	kpèchúótítí
'tongue'	jìlélŋ	jìlélkú	jìlétí	
'turtle'	lèèlíŋ	lèèlùkú	lèèltí	
'viper'	bùasíŋ	bùasòkú	bùasìtí	
'voice, throat, larynx'	lòlíŋ	lòlòkú	lòltí	
'vulture'	zùúŋ	zùúkú	zùtí	zùtítí
'wing'	chòbíŋ	chòbòkú	chòbtí	
'wood'	dááŋ	dáákú	dáàtí	dààtítí
'worm'	gbáríáíŋ	gbáríákú	gbáríátí	gbáríátítí

Noun class 3 (120 words)

Nouns	Singular	Sg + Art	Plural	Pl + Art
'arm'	núúŋ	núúké	núúsí	
'animal, herd'	dɔ̀ŋ	dɔ̀kká	dɔ̀ŋìsí	
'antelope (oribi)'	wàlíŋ	wàlíká	wàlìsí	wàlìsísí
'axe'	líˈáŋ	líˈká	líásí	líáˈsísí
'back'	kòáŋ	kòáká	kòàsí	kòàsísí
'ball'	bɔ́lì	bɔ́ˈlíká	bɔ́ˈlísí	
'barrel, drum'	áŋˈkórá	áŋˈkóríká	áŋˈkórísí	
'basket'	kpáríŋ	kpáríká	kpárísí	
'bath sponge'	gbàrà	gbàrìká	gbàrìsì	
'bell'	bímbélíníŋ	bímbélíŋké	bímbélínsí	
'bird'	némˈbíŋ	némˈbíké	némˈbísí	
'bird (sp.)'	tíˈléŋkpì	tíˈléŋˈkpíké	tíˈléŋˈkpísí	
'bird (sp.)'	tíˈtíí	tíˈtíˈká	tíˈtíísí	
'bird (sp.)'	mùlè	mùlké	mùlìsì	
'bowl'	kóróbâ	kóróbáˈká	kóróbáˈsí	
'button'	péríŋ	péríké	pérísí	
'capsule (medicine)'	túpáyà	túpáˈyáká	túpáˈyásí	
'cat'	gáálˈlúˈúŋ	gáálˈhúˈké	gáálˈlúúsì	
'catfish'	gbíŋ	gbììká	gbììsí	
'cattle egret'	kpàlìgìnántìà	kpàlìgìnánˈtíáká	kpàlìgìnánˈtíásí	
'chicken'	kpíáŋ	kpíáká	kpíásí	
'chicken (sp.)'	gbíŋgbíˈŋíŋ	gbíŋgbíŋˈké	gbíŋgbínsì	
'cobra, spitting'	jííŋ	jììká	jììsí	jììsísí
'cookpot'	kóróbâ	kóróbáˈká		

Appendix B

Nouns	Singular	Sg + Art	Plural	Pl + Art
'dance (sp.)'	kpááná	kpáánká	kpáánsí	
'ditch'	fòà!líŋ	fòàl!ká	fòàlísí	
'dog'	gbààŋ	gbààká	gbààsí	
'donkey'	bòŋŋ	bòŋká	bòŋsí	
'dove'	ŋmáríŋ	ŋmárīká	ŋmárísí	
'drum (sp.)'	gòròmànsàà	gòròmànsààká	gòròmànsààsí	
'dwarf'	kékíríŋ	kékíríké	kékírísí	
'English (Ig. or man)'	bàtúú!líŋ	bàtúú!líké	bàtúú!lísí	bàtúú!lísísí
'entrance through wall'	kpàŋvólí	kpàŋvólíké	kpàŋvólísí	
'fish (sp.)'	kánj!láŋ	kánj!láŋká	kánj!lánsí	kánj!lánsísí
'fish (sp.)'	kpàgàsòŋkpàgà	kpàgàsòŋkpàkká	kpàgàsòŋkpàgìsí	
'fish (sp.)'	nàntìkùlìmíŋ	nàntìkùlìŋké	nàntìkùlìnsí	
'fish (sp.)'	púŋú!lú!ŋ	púŋú!lúŋ!ké	púŋú!lúŋ!sí	púŋú!lúŋ!sísí
'fish (sp.)'	tótóríŋ	tótórīká	tótórísí	tótórísísí
'fish (sp.)'	yìrìŋ	yìrìké	yìrìsí	
'flute'	wííŋ	wííká	wíísí	
'fly'	nánjóóŋ	nánjóóká	nánjóósí	nánjóósísí
'fly, tsetse'	kákpá!ríŋ	kákpá!ríká	kákpá!rísí	
'flying ant'	yàyú!òŋ	yàyú!òká	yàyú!òsi	
'fruit (sp.)'	jí!líŋ	jí!líká	jí!sí	jí!sí
'funeral song'	hápé	hápéké	hápésí	
'grass blade'	mànchíŋ	mànchíké	mànchísí	
'ground, bare'	gbàntálíŋ	gbàntálíká	gbàntálísí	
'hat'	sɪbúbúŋ	sɪbúbúké	sɪbúbúsí	sɪbúbúsísí

Nouns, plurals, and definite articles 449

Nouns	Singular	Sg + Art	Plural	Pl + Art
'hat, straw'	kàgbà (Am.) kàgbá (Abd.)	kàgbàká	kàgbàsì	
'headpan'	tálsíŋ	tásíꜝká	tásísí	tásíꜝsísí
'head scarf'	bɔ́bíŋ	bɔ́bíká	bɔ́bísí	bɔ́bísísí
'intestine, large'	wútúlíŋ	wútúlíꜝké	wútúlísí	
'knife'	jíbíŋ	jíbíká	jíbísí	jíbísísí
'knife, small'	bàríŋ	bàríká	bàrísí	
'lamp'	pópólí	pópólíké	pópólísí	pópólísísí
'leg'	náŋ	náŋká	nágísí	
'lizard'	gùráꜝláŋ	gùráꜝlká		
'man'	dèmbíŋ	dèmbìké	dèmbìsí	dèmbìsísí
'Mamprusi'	gbàŋwááŋ	gbàŋwááká	gbàŋwáásí	
'monkey'	ŋmààmíŋ	ŋmààŋká	ŋmàànsí	ŋmàànsísí
'mosquito'	dòmíŋ	dòŋká	dònsí	dònsísí
'mussel'	kálángbíꜝláŋ	kálángbíáꜝlká	kálángbíáꜝlsí	
'owl'	kpìtímíŋ	kpìtìŋké	kpìtìnsí	
'parrot'	dàakùláŋ	dàakùáꜝlká	dàakùásì	
'partridge (sp.)'	ɲíŋ	ɲìkká	ɲìgìsí	ɲìgìsísí
'person'	vúóŋ	vúóké	vúósí	vúósísí
'pot'	gbìéŋ	gbìéké	gbìésí	gbìésísí
'pot (sp.)'	chóáŋ	chóáká	chóásí	
'puddle'	chúnchúúríŋ	chúnchúúríké	chúnchúúrísí	
'rabbit'	sóáꜝmíŋ	sóánꜝká	sóánꜝsí	sóánꜝsísí
'rope, drum'	gáꜝníŋ	gáŋꜝká	gáꜝnsí	
'sack'	bɔ̀ɔ̀rà	bɔ̀ɔ̀ríká	bɔ̀ɔ̀rísí	bɔ̀ɔ̀rìsísí

Nouns		Singular	Sg + Art	Plural	Pl + Art
'sleeping mat'		kálìŋà	kálìŋká	kálìnsí	tìasísí
'sleeping mat'		tìàŋ	tìàká	tìàsí	
'smock'		tógò	tógóké	tóːgósí	
'squirrel, forest'		bágábá	bágábáká	bágábásí	bágábásí
'squirrel (sp.)'		chíɪ́ŋ	chíɪ̌ːká	chíɪ̌ːsí	chíɪ̌ːsísí
'swamp'		páálíŋ	páálíká	páálísí	
'swallow (bird)'		jàŋkpálááːrɪ́ŋ	jàŋkpálááːrɪ́ká	jàŋkpálááːrísí	
'sweet potato ball (Hs)'		fóórá	fóóríká	fóórísí	
'tomato'		kàmánːtúːóŋ	kàmánːtúːóké	kàmánːtúóòsì	
'town, village'		tĭŋ	tikká	tigìsí	
'trap'		cháchábí	cháchábíká	cháchábísí	
'tree'		tĭːŋ	tĭːká	tĭːsí	
'tree (sp.)'		bíɲɪ̌ːlíŋíŋ	bíɲɪ̌ːlíŋké	bíɲɪ̌ːlínsí	
'tree (sp.)'		chírɪ̌ːŋ	chírɪ̌ːká	chírɪ̌ːsí	
'tree (sp.)'		kálíŋkúːóŋ	kálíŋkúóːké	kálíŋkúóòsì	
'tree (sp.)'		káɲárǐŋ	káɲárǐká	káɲárísí	
'tree (sp.)'		kŏŋ	kŏkká	kŏgúsí	
'tree (sp.)'		kpàlíŋ	kpàlíká	kpàlísí	
'tree (sp.)'		kpègílíŋ	kpègílké	kpègílísí	kpègílísísí
'tree (sp.)'		mómógílíŋ	mómógílíká	mómógílísí	
'tree (sp.)'		ɲírŕŋ	ɲírká	ɲírsí	
'tree (sp.)'		pàmááliŋ	pàmááliká	pàmáálíslí	
'tree (sp.)'		pónǐŋ	pónké	pónsí	
'tree (sp.)'		sěŋ	sěkké	sěgìsí	

Nouns, plurals, and definite articles

Nouns	Singular	Sg + Art	Plural	Pl + Art
'tree (sp.)'	yíꜝgíŋ	yíꜝlká	yíꜝgísí	
'tree (sp.)'	chúnꜝchúlí	chúnꜝcɔ́ulké	chúnꜝchúlísí	
'tree (sp.)'	gbígbáŋ	gbígbáꜝká	gbígbágísí	
'tree (sp.)'	hààríŋ	hààríká	hààrísí	hààrísísí
'tree (sp.)'	jíꜝlŋ	jíꜝlká	jíꜝlsí	
'tree, baobab'	tùòŋ	tùòké	tùòsí	tùòsísí
'tree, dawadawa'	dùòŋ	dùòká	dùòsí	dùòsísí
'tree, kapok'	gòmíŋ	gòŋká	gòŋsí	gònsísí
'tree, shea'	táꜝláŋ	táꜝlká	táꜝlsí	táaꜝlsísí
'tree, thorn'	hángóŋ	hángóké	hángósí	
'Twi language'	kàmbòŋíŋ	kàmbòŋké	kàmbònsì	
'vein'	gílíŋ	gílíká	gílísí	
'waist, bottom'	chìáŋ	chìáká	chìásí	chìásísí
'wall'	páŋ	pákká	págísí	
'wart'	kpàjíŋ	kpàjìlká	kpàjígísí	
'water drum (head)'	gáríwá	gáríwáká	gáríwásí	
'weaver-bird'	gàɲìàrà	gàɲìàríká	gàɲìàrìsí	
'well'	búlíŋ	búlíꜝká	búlísí	búlísísí
'well-being'	bùkáátà	bùkááꜝtíká	bùkááꜝtísí	
'white beans' (Twi)	àdùwá	àdùwáká	àdùwásí	
'white man' (Hausa)	nàsáárá	nàsááríká	nàsáárísí	
'whydah, pin-tailed'	jùlà	jùlíká	jùlìsí	jùlìsísí
'window'	tókóró	tókórōké	tókórósí	tókórósísí

451

Noun class 4 (33 words - as mass nouns, many of these have no plural form)

Nouns	Singular	Sg + Art	Plural	Pl + Art
'alcohol'	dááŋ	dáábú	dáátí	dáátítí
'anger'	sìɲíŋíꜝríŋ	sìɲíŋíꜝlbú		
'ash'	táɲééꜝlíŋ	táɲééꜝlíbú	táɲééꜝlíꜝtí	
'blood'	zíŋ	zímbú	zíntí	zíntítí
'broom'	sóŋ	sómbú	sóntí	sóntítí
'fight'	wàgíŋ	wàgíbú	wàgítí	
'fire'	bòlíŋ	bòlíbú		
'fish'	zàsíŋ	zàsíbú	zàsítí	
'flour'	zóŋ	zómbú	zóntí	zóntítí
'funeral, death'	kǔŋ	kùmbú	kùntí	kùntítí
'heat'	tóóꜝlíŋ	tóóꜝlíbú		
'hunger'	kóŋ	kómbú	kóntí	kóntítí
'jealousy'	níɲmááꜝríŋ	níɲmááꜝríbú		
'lightning'	ɲìgìsíŋ	ɲìgìsíbú		
'meat'	nɔ̀ŋ	nɔ̀mbú	nɔ̀ntí	nɔ̀ntítí
'medicine'	tíŋ	tííbú	tíítí	tíítítí
'net'	níŋ	nííbú	níítí	níítítí
'oil'	kpááŋ	kpáábú	kpáátí	kpáátítí
'peanut'	sìŋkpááŋ	sìŋkpáábú	sìŋkpáátí	sìŋkpáátítí
'playing'	láálꜝíŋ	láálꜝíbú	láálꜝítí	
'porridge'	sààŋ	sààbú	sààtí	sààtítí
'roan antelope'	káŋ	kámbú	kágítí	kágítítí
'sand'	támꜝbúsíŋ	támꜝbúsíbú	támꜝbúsítí	támꜝbúsítítí
'sleep'	gbíꜝlíŋ	gbíꜝlíbú	gbíꜝítí	gbíꜝítítí

Nouns, plurals, and definite articles 453

Nouns	Singular	Sg + Art	Plural	Pl + Art
'smell'	ɲòògíŋ	ɲòògìbú		
'sweat'	wàlíŋ	wàlíbú		
'taboo'	chóáríŋ	chóáríbʋ́		
'thing'	jááŋ	jàábú	ɲìntí	ɲìntítí
'thunder'	dɔ̀míŋ	dɔ̀mbú		
'war, bow'	tɔ̀ŋ	tɔ̀mbú	tɔ̀ntí	
'water'	ɲááŋ	ɲáábú	ɲááti	ɲáátítí
'weakness'	ŋmììgíŋ	ŋmììgíbú		
'wind'	bìlɔ̀gìsíŋ	bìlɔ̀gìsíbú		

Noun class 5 (18 words)

Nouns	Singular	Sg + Art	Plural	Pl + Art
'burier (for humans)'	chíí!bú	chíí!búwá	chíí!bíŋ	chííbí!ríŋ
'chief'	nááŋ	nààŋwá	náá!líŋ	nààl!bá
'child'	bòá	bòàwá	bàllí	bàllí
'daughter'	lá	lá!wá	lí!àŋ	
'father (1st/2nd pers)'	chʋá	chʋàwá	chʋá!líŋ	chʋàl!bá
'father (3rd person)'	chɔ̀ŋ	chɔ̀ŋwá	chʋá!líŋ	chʋàl!bá
'friend'	zʋá	zʋàwá	zʋà!líŋ	zʋàl!bá
'husband'	chʋ̀rʋ́	chʋ̀rʋ̀wá	chʋ̀l!líŋ	chʋ̀llí!bá
'in-law (older)'	há!níŋ	há!níwá	hánfí!líŋ	hánfí!líbá
'mother (1st/2nd pers)'	náá	nàáwá	níí!líŋ	níí!bé
'mother (3rd person)'	núŋ	núŋ!wó	níí!líŋ	níí!bé
'sibling, older'	mʋ́	míí!wá	míí!líŋ	míí!bá
'sibling-in-law'	chíí	chììwá	chíí!líŋ	chíí!bá

Appendix B

Nouns	Singular	Sg + Art	Plural	Pl + Art
'sister'	táá	táá!wá	táá!líŋ	táálí!bá
'stranger'	cháánù	chááŋ!wá	cháá!níŋ	
'woman'	hɔ̀gṹ	hɔ̀wwá	hũ̀àŋ	hṹàbá

agentives (samples only; many more could be generated)
| 'buyer' | dìdàárú | dìdàárùwá | dìdàáríŋ | |
| 'cook' | dìdigìrú | didigìrúwó | dìdigìríŋ | |

Mixed classes (43 words, labeled by singular/plural morphology)

		Singular	Sg + Art	Plural	Pl + Art
2/1	'block'	wáríŋ	wárkú	wárà	
	'goat'	bííŋ	bìikú	bìé	bìèhé
	'guinea fowl'	kpá!áŋ	kpáá!kú	kpíínè	kpíí!néhé
	'rain'	nííŋ	nĩĩkú	nĩã́	nĩàhá
	'room'	jùóŋ	jùòkú	jùné	jùnéhé
3/1	'antelope'	yísíŋ	yísìké	yìsé	yìséhé
	'ant, driver'	pìŋjíŋ	pìŋké	pìŋé	pìŋéhé
	'fish (sp.)'	yɔ̀bìlíŋ	yɔ̀bìlíká	yɔ̀bìlá	yɔ̀bìláhá
	'guess'	támà	táŋ!ká	támà	tá!máhá
	'guinea worm'	pìllíŋ	pìlliké	pìllé	pììléhé
	'kapok fruit'	gòŋgùmíŋ	gòŋgùŋká	gòŋgùmá	
	'millipede'	nàntàkògìlíŋ	nàntàkògìliké	nàntàkògìlé	
	'potato, Frafra'	yɛ́!síŋ	yɛ́!sìká	yɛ́sà	
	'shoe'	nũ̀ríŋ	nũ̀rìká	nũ̀rá	
	'tree, tamarind'	wú!síŋ	wú!síké	wúsè	wú!séhé

Nouns, plurals, and definite articles

Nouns	Singular		Sg + Art	Plural	Pl + Art
4/1	bùuní	'boundary'	bùuníŋ	bùumbú	bùuné
	náá!gí	'cow'	náá!gíŋ	náágí!bú	níígè
	ní	'eye'	níŋ	nímbú	nínè
	wú!lú	'genet'	wú!lúŋ	wúúm!bú	wúú!néhé
	dùu	'horse'	dùuŋ	dùumbú	dùunéhé
	gú!lú	'rope'	gú!lúŋ	gúúm!bú	gúúnéhé
1/2, 4	sómí	'fish (sp.)'	sómíŋ	sónní	sóntí
	nónógó!ŋ	'fish, electric'	nónógó!ŋ	nónógòn!ní	nónógò!tí
3/2, 4	yìsí	'antelope (sp.)'	yìsíŋ	yìsìké	yìsìtí
	yɪ̀bí	'cane'	yɪ̀bíŋ	yɪ̀bíká	yɪ̀bítí
	sìbì	'hartebeest'	sìbìŋ	sìbìká	sìbìtí
	àlìbɛ́sà	'onion' (Hausa)	àlìbɛ́sà	àlìbɛ́!sìká	àlìbɛ́!sítí
	zùú	'vulture'	zùúŋ	zùúké	zúútí
1/3	gbárgí	'cripple'	gbárgíŋ	gbárgírí	gbárgísí
	kpɛ́lí!gí	'magpie'	kpɛ́lí!gíŋ	kpɛ́lígí!rí	kpɛ́lígí!sí
	bòrìmí	'oryx'	bòrìmíŋ	bòrìnní	bòrìnsísí
	kpàjí	'tick'	kpàjíŋ	kpàjìnní	kpàjìgísí
	tàngóó	'trash heap'	tàngóóŋ	tàngóórí	tàngóósí
2/3	mìí	'ant, biting'	mìíŋ	mììkú	mììsí
	yí	'blindness'	yí	yí!kú	yíísísí
	chíà	'chair'	chíàŋ	chíá!kú	chíá!sísí
	gìlíngáá!lá	'crow, pied'	gìlíngáá!láŋ	gìlíngáá!kú	gìlíngáá!sí
	kpàálí	'handle'	kpàálíŋ	kpààlíkú	kpààlísí
	sàŋkpàrí	'navel'	sàŋkpàríŋ	sàŋkpàríkú	sàŋkpàrìsí
	kpìlí	'thigh'	kpìlíŋ	kpìllíkú	kpìllísísí

4/3	'termite'	tíálíŋ	tíálíbʊ́	tíálísí	
5/3	'blind person'	yîì	yíí!wá	yíí!sí	yíí!sísí
3/1/5	'ancestor'	kpììlíŋ	kpììlìké	kpììlé	kpììlìbé

Appendix C

Compound nouns

Compounds with 2 nouns

Noun class 1	Singular	Sg + Art	Plural	Pl + Art
'arrow' (bow-nail)	tɔ̀nyɩ́ˈlɩ́ŋ	tɔ̀nyɩ́ˈlní	tɔ̀nyɩ́ímà	
cf. tɔ̀ŋ 'war, bow', yɩ́ˈlɩ́ŋ 'nail, arrow'				
'cheekbone' (cheek-shea nut)	kààŋkpíŋ	kààŋkpínní	kààŋkpîê	kààŋkpíéˈhé
cf. kàámíŋ 'cheek', kpíŋ 'shea nut'				
'hail' (rain-stone)	nìitǎŋ		nìitǎná	
cf. níŋ 'rain', tǎŋ 'stone'				
'nipple' (breast-mouth)	bìisìnóáŋ	bìisìnóárí	bìisìnóá	
cf. bìisíŋ 'breast', nóáŋ 'mouth'				
'papaya' (Ashanti shea nut)	kàmbʊ̀ntááˈmíŋ	kàmbʊ̀ntáánˈní	kàmbʊ̀ntáámà	kàmbʊ̀ntááˈmáhá
cf. kàmbɔ́ŋ 'Ashanti', tááˈmíŋ 'shea nut'				
'stump' (wood-??)	dààgbúgíŋ	dààgbúgírí	dààgbúgê	dààgbúˈgéhé
cf. dááŋ 'wood, stick'				
'tamarind fruit' (tamarind-seed)	wúsɩ́bíŋ	wúsɩ́bínní	wúsɩ́bîê	wúsɩ́bíéˈhé
cf. wúsíŋ 'tamarind tree', bíŋ 'seed'				
'testicle' (scrotum-seed)	yɔ̀lìmbíŋ	yɔ̀lìmbínní	yɔ̀lìmbîê	yɔ̀lìmbíéˈhé
cf. yɔ̀lìmíŋ 'scrotum', bíŋ 'seed'				

Noun class 2				
'anus' (waist-??)	chìàfííŋ	chìàfííkú	chìàfíítí	
cf. chìáŋ 'waist'				
'colon' (intestine-female)	wútúlíníˈlíŋ	wútúlíníˈlkú	wútúlíníˈtí	
cf. wútúlíŋ 'intestine', -nˈlíŋ 'female'				

Compound nouns

	Singular	Sg + Art	Plural	Pl + Art
'inner corner of eye' (eye-hole) cf. níŋ 'eye', vɔ́ríŋ 'hole'	nímvɔ́ríŋ		nímvɔ́ttí	
'larynx' (voice-flute) cf. lɔ̀líŋ 'voice', wííŋ 'flute'	lɔ̀lìwííŋ	lɔ̀lìwíkó	lɔ̀lìwíítí	lɔ̀lìwíítttí
'nose front' (nose-male) cf. mìsí 'nose', -ràáŋ 'male'	mìrààŋ	mìrààkó	mìrààtí	
'toenail' (leg-scratching) cf. náŋ 'leg', yíbíŋ 'scratching'	ná!yíbíŋ	ná!yíbíkó	ná!yíbítí	
'tree (sp.)' (oil-leaf) cf. kpááŋ 'oil', vááŋ 'leaf'	kpáámvááŋ	kpáámváákó	kpáámváátí	

Noun class 3

	Singular	Sg + Art	Plural	Pl + Art
'Achilles tendon' (leg-vein) cf. náŋ 'leg', gílíŋ 'vein'	nágílíŋ	nágílíká	nágílísí	
'alcohol pot' (alcohol-pot) cf. dááŋ 'alcohol', chúáŋ 'pot (sp.)'	dááchúáŋ	dááchúáká	dááchúásí	
'back of knee' (knee-??) cf. dúŋ 'knee'	dùŋgólíŋ	dùŋgólíké	dùŋgólísí	
'bark' (tree-shell) cf. tííŋ 'tree', hǎŋ 'shell'	tììhǎŋ		tììhàgìtí	
'brother-in-law' (sibling.in.law-man) cf. chí 'sibling.in.law', dèmbíŋ 'man'	chììdèmbìŋ	chììdèmbìké	chììdèmbìsí	
'dung beetle' (feces-IDEO) cf. bìntí 'feces'	bìndúdù̀	bìndú!dúké	bìndú!dúsí	bìndú!dúsísí

	Singular	Sg + Art	Plural	Pl + Art
'father-in-law' (in.law-man)	hánìidèmbĩŋ	hánìidèmbìké		hánìidèmbìsí
cf. hánìi 'in-law', dèmbĩŋ 'man'				
'leopard' (bush-dog)	hàŋgbààŋ	hàŋgbààká	hàŋgbààsí	
cf. hààgĩŋ 'bush', gbààŋ 'dog'				
'nim tree' (white.man-tree)	nàsàràtĩĩŋ	nàsàràtìıká	nàsàràtĩisí	
cf. nàsárá 'white man', tĩŋ 'tree'				
'pupil of eye' (eye-dwarf)	nĩŋkékírĩŋ	nĩŋkékírìké	nĩŋkékírìsí	
cf. nĩŋ 'eye', kékírĩŋ 'dwarf'				
'tree (sp.)' (monkey-dawadawa.tree)	ŋmààndʋ̀ʋ̀ŋ	ŋmààndʋ̀ʋ̀ká	ŋmààndʋ̀ʋ̀sí	
cf. ŋmààmĩŋ 'monkey', dʋ̀ʋ̀ŋ 'dawadawa tree'				

Noun class 4

	Singular	Sg + Art	Plural	Pl + Art
'breast milk' (breast-water)	bììsìɲááŋ			
cf. bììsĩŋ 'breast', ɲááŋ 'water'				

Noun class 5

	Singular	Sg + Art	Plural	Pl + Art
'father-in-law' (in.law-father)	hánììchɔ̀ŋ	hánììchɔ̀ŋwá	hánììchʋ̀à!lĩŋ	hánììchʋ̀àlí!bá
cf. há!nĩĩŋ 'in-law (older)', chɔ̀ŋ 'father'				
'fisher' (lake-cutter)	gbágíchíárʋ̀	—		
cf. gbágĩŋ 'lake', cha 'cut'				
'groom' (woman-marryer)	hɔ̀gʋ́fààrìtú	—		
cf. hɔ̀gʋ́ 'woman, wife', faarı 'marry a wife'				

Compound nouns

	Singular	Sg + Art	Plural	Pl + Art
'hoodless cobra' (toad-swallower) cf. bóntòòɲ 'toad', ɲu 'to swallow'	bóntòòɲìirú	—		
'mother-in-law' (in.law-mother) cf. há!nííŋ 'in-law (older)', nũŋ 'mother'	hánììnùŋ	hánììnùŋwó	há!nínílíŋ	há!nínílíbé
'mud ball, for building' (dirt-child) cf. tàntí 'dirt', bùá 'child'	tàmbùá	tàmbàlí		
'sister-in-law' (sibling.in.law-woman) cf. chíí 'sibling-in-law', hògú 'woman'	chììhògú	chììhòwwá	chììhòòbá	chììhòòbáhá

Mixed noun class

	Singular	Sg + Art	Plural	Pl + Art
'bushbuck' (bush-goat) cf. hààgíŋ 'bush', bíiŋ 'goat'	hàmbìíŋ	hàmbììké	hàmbìé	hàmbìèhé
'kingfisher' (water-remover) cf. ɲááŋ 'water', liiri 'remove'	ɲáálíí(rí)tù	ɲáálíí!túké	ɲáálíí(rí)!tíŋ	

Compounds with 3 nouns

	Singular	Sg + Art	Plural	Pl + Art
'catfish (sp.)' (water-donkey-male) cf. ɲááŋ 'water', bún!líŋ 'donkey', -rààŋ 'male'	ɲáámbún!dááŋ	ɲáámbún!dáákó	ɲáámbún!dáásí	
'cock (sp.)' (??-male-??) cf. kpíáŋ 'chicken', -rààŋ 'male'	kpàráátúŋ	kpàráátúnní	kpàráátúò	kpàráátúó!hé

	Singular	**Sg + Art**	**Plural**
'lip' (mouth-skin-leaf)	núágbámvááŋ	núágbámváákú	núágbámváátí
cf. núáŋ 'mouth', gbáŋ́ŋ 'skin', vááŋ 'leaf'			
'woodpecker' (wood-cutter-IDEO)	dààchìaròkɔ̀kɔ́	dààchìaròkɔ̀kɔ́ká	dààchìaròkɔ̀kɔ́sí
cf. dááŋ 'wood, stick', -chìarú 'cutter'			

Appendix D

Noun-adjective complexes

The noun-adjective complexes below are grouped together when possible, generally by the noun modified, except in the case of 'small X', for which I have many examples. Within each section, the glosses are alphabetized.

Single adjective

	SG	SG.DEF	PL	PL.DEF
'bad thing'	jà-bìáŋ	jà-bìàkú	ɲìm-bìàtí	ɲìm-bìàtítí
'big thing'	jà-kpíˈíɲ	jà-kpííˈká	ɲìŋ-kpíímà	ɲìŋ-kpííˈmáhá
'black thing'	jà-sɔ́bíˈlíɲ	jà-sɔ́bílí-ˈká	ɲìn-sɔ́bílà	ɲìn-sɔ́bíˈláhá
'long/tall thing'	jà-wɔ́ŋ	jà-wɔ́kkú	ɲìŋ-wɔ́gítí	ɲìŋ-wɔ́gótítí
'new thing'	jà-hááˈlíɲ	jà-háálíˈká	ɲìŋ-háálà	ɲìŋ-hááˈláhá
'old thing'	jà-kòóŋ	jà-kòòrí	ɲìŋ-kòrá	ɲìŋ-kòráhá
'red thing'	jà-ŋmìníɲ	jà-ŋmìká	ɲìŋ-ŋmìná	ɲìŋ-ŋmìnáhá
'short thing'	jè-góbíŋ	jè-góbírí	ɲìŋ-góbè	ɲìŋ-góˈbéhé
'small thing'	jè-bǐŋ	jè-bìké	ɲìm-bìsí	ɲìm-bìsísí
'white thing'	jà-yèèlíɲ	jà-yèèlìká	ɲìn-yèèlá	ɲìn-yèèláhá
'black teeth'			ɲín-sɔ́bílà	
'bad woman'	hɔ̀gù-bìáŋ	hɔ̀gù-bìàká	hɔ̀gù-bìàtí	hɔ̀gù-bìàtítí
'big woman'	hɔ̀gù-kpíˈíŋ ~hɔ̀k-kpíˈíŋ	hɔ̀gù-kpííˈká ~hɔ̀k-kpííˈká	hɔ̀gù-kpíímà	hɔ̀gù-kpííˈmábá ~hɔ̀k-kpííˈmábá
'black woman'	hɔ̀gù-sɔ́bíˈlíŋ	hɔ̀gù-sɔ́bílíˈká	hɔ̀gù-sɔ́bílà	hɔ̀gù-sɔ́bíˈlá-há
'red woman'	hɔ̀gù-ŋmìníŋ			

	SG	SG.DEF	PL	PL.DEF
'small woman'	hɔ̀gù-bǐŋ	hɔ̀gù-bìké	hɔ̀gù-bìsí	
'black house'	tígí-sɔ́bí!líŋ		tígí-sɔ́bílà	
'large house'	tígí-kpí!íŋ		tígí-kpíímà	
'new house'	tígí-háá!líŋ			
'old house'	tígí-kú!úŋ			
'small house'	tígí-bí!ŋ		tígí-bísì	
'white house'	tígí-yéé!líŋ		tígí-yéélà	
'bad village'	tìg-bìáŋ			
'large village'	tìk-kpí!íŋ			
'new village'	tìk-háá!líŋ			
'old village'	tìk-kùúŋ		tìk-kùrá	
'small village'	tìg-bǐŋ			
'small axe'	lé-!bíŋ		lé-!bísí	
'small baboon'	fé-bí!ŋ́		fé-bísì	
'small basket (sp.)'	jíkɔ̀rì-bǐŋ		jíkkɔ̀rì-bìsí	
'small bone'	kɔ̀b-bǐŋ		kɔ̀b-bìsí	
'small broom'	súm-bí!ŋ́			
'small chicken'	kpìè-bí!ŋ́	kpìè-bí!ké	kpìè-bísì	
'small child'	bùò-bǐŋ		bàllì-bìsí	
'small cleared area'	kɔ́g-!bíŋ			
'small cow'	né-!bíŋ	né-!bíké	né-!bísí	
'small cutlass'	kàréntìà-bǐŋ			
'small dog'	gbè-bí!ŋ́	gbè-bí!ké	gbè-bísì	
'small farm'	kúó-bí!ŋ́	kúó-bí!ké	kúó-bísì	
'small father'	chòm-bǐŋ		chòm-bìsí	
'small hat'	kàgbàà-bǐŋ	kàgbàà-bìké	kàgbàà-bìsí	
'small hoe'	kù-bǐŋ		kù-bìsí	
'small horse'	dùùm-bí!ŋ́			
'small house'	tígí-bí!ŋ́		tígí-bísì	
'small lizard'	gùráá-!bíŋ		gùráá-!bísí	
'small market'	ɲù-bǐŋ		ɲù-bìsí	
'small meat'	nòm-bǐŋ		nòm-bìsí	
'small place'	jígí-bí!ŋ́			
'small bowl'	kúrúbé-!bíŋ		kúrúbé-!bísí	
'small river'	múgú-bí!ŋ́	múgú-bí!ké	múgú-bísì	
'small roan antelope'	kágí-bí!ŋ́			
'small shea tree'	té!bíŋ		té!-bísí	
'small stick'	dàà-bí!ŋ́	dàà-bí!ké	dàà-bísì	

Noun-adjective complexes

	SG	SG.DEF	PL	PL.DEF
'small tail'	jù-bĭŋ		jù-bìsí	
'small tin can'	kɔ́ŋkòm-bĭŋ		kɔ́kòm-bìsí	
'small toad'	bùntù-bĭŋ		bùntù-bìsí	
'small tree'	tìì-bí!ŋ́			
'small waist'	chè-bí!ŋ́		chè-bísì	
'small (junior) wife'	hɔ̀gù-bùò-bĭŋ			
'small (junior) wife'	hɔ̀gù-bí!ŋ́			
'small woman'	hɔ̀gù-bĭŋ	hɔ̀gù-bìké	hɔ̀gù-bìsí	
'small yam'	ɲú-bí!ŋ́		ɲú-bísì	

Adjectives derived from verbs

	SG	SG.DEF	PL	PL.DEF
'bitter thing'	jà-tùáŋ	jà-tùàká	ɲìn-tùàtí	ɲìn-tùàtítí
'carried thing'	jè-chììkíŋ	jè-chììkìrí	ɲìn-chììké	ɲìn-chììkéhé
'cool thing'	jà-fiàlìkíŋ	jà-fiàlìkìrí	ɲìm-fiàlìká	ɲìm-fiàlìkáhá
'cool/wet thing'	jà-sún!síŋ	jà-súnsí!ká	ɲìn-súnsà	ɲìn-sún!sáhá
'dirty thing'	jè-dígín!tíŋ	jè-dígíntí!ká	ɲìn-dígíntà	ɲìn-dígín!táhá
'dried thing'	jà-kú!kíŋ	jà-kú!kírí	ɲìŋ-kúkà	ɲìŋ-kú!káhá
'full thing'	jè-sùùlìkíŋ	jè-sùùlìkìrí	ɲìn-sùùlìké	
'good thing'	jà-vììníŋ	jà-vììŋká	ɲìm-vììná	ɲìm-vììnáhá
'heavy ladder'	jɔ́rɔ́-dún!síŋ ~jɔ́d-dún!síŋ	jɔ́rɔ́-dúnsí!ká	jɔ́rɔ́-dúnsà	
'heavy thing'	jà-dùnsíŋ	jà-dùnsìká	ɲìn-dùnsá	ɲìn-dùnsáhá
'inflated thing'	jà-fùòsìkíŋ	jà-fùòsìkìrí	ɲìm-fùòsìká	ɲìm-fùòsìkáhá
'opened thing'	jà-yùòrìkíŋ	jà-yùòrìkìrí	ɲìn-yùòrìké	ɲìn-yùòrìkéhé
'planted thing, seed'	jà-bùríŋ	jà-bùrìbú		
'ripe thing'	jà-bíí!kíŋ	jà-bíí!kírí	ɲìm-bííkè	ɲìm-bíí!kéhé
'round thing'	jà-gìlìgìkíŋ	jà-gìlìgìkìrí	ɲìŋ-gìlìgìké	ɲìŋ-gìlìgìkéhé
'spoiled thing'	jà-chùòsìkíŋ	jà-chùòsìkìrí	ɲìn-chùòsìká	ɲìn-chùòsìkáhá
'spoken thing' ('language')	jà-bàlìkíŋ	jà-bàlìkìrí	ɲìm-bàlìká	ɲìm-bàlìkáhá
'strong thing'	jà-hàgìríŋ	jà-hàgìrìká	ɲìŋ-hàgìrá	ɲìŋ-hàgìráhá
'sweet thing'	jà-nànsíŋ	jà-nànsìká	ɲìn-nànsá	ɲìn-nànsáhá
'swollen thing'	jà-mɔ̀rìkíŋ	jà-mɔ̀rìkìrí	ɲìm-mɔ̀rìká	ɲìm-mɔ̀rìkáhá
'tied thing'	jè-gbìŋkíŋ	jè-gbìŋkìrí	ɲìŋ-gbìŋké	ɲìŋ-gbìŋkéhé
'tied/wrapped thing'	jà-bɔ̀bìkíŋ	jà-bɔ̀bìkìrí	ɲìm-bɔ̀bìká	
'washed thing'	jè-sùgùrìkíŋ	jè-sùgùrìkìrí	ɲìn-sùgùrìké	ɲìn-sùgùrìkéhé

	SG	SG.DEF	PL	PL.DEF
'sweet mouth'[1]	núá-!nánsíŋ			
'sweet soup'			jì-nànsá	
'sweet meat'	nɔ̀n-nànsíŋ			
'sweet yam'	ɲú-!nánsíŋ			
'sweet house'	tígí-!nánsíŋ			
'sweet village'	tìgì-nànsíŋ			
'sweet song'	yílí-!nánsíŋ			
'swept house'	tígí-sáárí!kíŋ			
'swept place'	jígí-sáárí!kíŋ	jígí-sáárí!kírí	jígí-sááríkà	jígí-sáárí!káhá
'swept room'	jùò-sààrìkíŋ			
'swept yard'	gbà-sààrìkíŋ			
'corn seed'			káwúm!búrá	
'millet seed'	záá-bú!ríŋ		záá-búrà	
'peanut seed'	sìŋkpáá-!búríŋ		sìŋkpáá-!búrá	
'eaten things'[2]	jè-díí!kíŋ	jè-díí!kírí	ɲìn-dííkè	ɲìn-díí!kéhé
'cooking thing, pot'	jà-dìkkíŋ		ɲìn-dìkké	
'cooking room'	jùò-dìkkíŋ	jùò-dìkkìrí	jùò-dìkké	jùò-dìkkéhé
'cooking place'	jígí-dík!kíŋ	jígí-dík!kírí	jígí-díkkè	jígí-dík!kéhé
'worn hat'	kàgbà-bùbùkíŋ			

Two adjectives

	SG	SG.DEF	PL
'small white thing'	jà-yèèlì-bǐŋ		ɲìn-yèèlì-bìsí
'small black thing'	jà-sɔ́bílí-!bíŋ		ɲìn-sɔ́bílí-!bísí
'big white thing'	jà-yèèlì-kpí!íŋ		ɲìn-yèèlì-kpíímà
'big black thing'	jà-sɔ́bílí-kpí!íŋ	jà-sɔ́bílí-kpíí!ká	ɲìn-sɔ́bílí-kpíímà
'good big thing'	jà-vììŋ-kpí!íŋ	jà-vììŋ-kpíí!ká	
'good long thing'		jà-wɔ́gú-vííŋ!ká	
'old white thing'		jà-kù-yèèlìká	
'old black thing'	jà-kù-sɔ́bí!líŋ		
'long white thing'	jà-yèèlì-wɔ́ŋ	jà-yèèlì-wɔ́kkú	ɲìn-yèèlì-wɔ́gítí
'new white thing'		jà-háálí-!yéélíká	
'big black woman'	hɔ̀gù-sɔ́bílí-kpí!íŋ	hɔ̀gù-sɔ́bílí-kpíí!ká	
'bad black woman'	hɔ̀gù-sɔ́bílí-bí!áŋ		
'small black stone'	tàn-sɔ́bílí-!bíŋ		tàn-sɔ́bílí-!bísí
'big black stone'	tàn-sɔ́bílí-kpí!íŋ		tàn-sɔ́bílí-kpíímà
'small white stone'	tàn-yèèlì-bǐŋ		tàn-yèèlì-bìsí
'big white stone'	tàn-yèèlì-kpí!íŋ		tàn-yèèlì-kpíímà

---

[1] The derived adjective glossed 'sweet' here, after normal Ghanaian English usage, generally means "good-tasting." The idiom 'you have a sweet mouth', however, means "you speak well." With 'village' or 'house', it means "peaceful."

[2] The word for 'food' differs from this only tonally, with forms *jè-dìkíŋ, jè-dìkìrí, ɲìndìké, ɲìn-dìkéhé*. Presumably the two are related, with 'food' possibly being a frozen form.

Noun-adjective complexes

	SG	SG.DEF	PL
'small white house'	tígí-yééli-!bíŋ		tígí-yééli-!bísí
'big white house'	tígí-yééli-kpí!íŋ		tígí-yééli-kpíímà
'small black house'	tígí-sɔ́bílí-!bíŋ		tígí-sɔ́bílí-!bísí
'big black house'	tígí-sɔ́bílí-kpí!íŋ		tígí-sɔ́bílí-kpíímà
'small white cow'	ná-yèèli-bìŋ		ná-yèèli-bìsí
'big white cow'	ná-yèèli-kpí!íŋ		ná-yèèli-kpíímà
'small black cow'	ná-sɔ́bílí-!bíŋ		ná-sɔ́bílí-!bísí
'big black cow'	ná-sɔ́bílí-kpí!íŋ		ná-sɔ́bílí-kpíímà

Derived adjectives

'big spoiled thing'	jà-kpíí-!chúúsí!kíŋ	
(alternate order)		jà-chúúsí-kpíí!ká
'cool white thing'		jà-fíálí-!yééliká
'cool/wet old thing'		jà-súnsí-!kúúrí
'cool/wet white thing'		jà-súnsí-!yééliká
'new spoiled thing'	jà-háálí-!chúúsí!kíŋ	
'old spoiled thing'	jà-kú-chúúsí!kíŋ	

Three adjectives

	SG	SG.DEF
'big white spoiled thing'	jà-yèèlì- kpíí-!chúúsí!kíŋ	
'new white big thing'	jà-háálí-yèèlì-kpí!íŋ	jà-háálí-yèèlì-kpíí!ká
'old white big thing'		jà-kù-yèèlì-kpíí!ká
'old white spoiled thing'	jà-kù-yèèlì-chùùsí!kíŋ	
'big bad black woman'		hɔ̀gù-sɔ́bílí-kpíí-bíá!ká
'small bad black woman'		hɔ̀gù-sɔ́bílí-bí-bíá!ká
'small good red woman'		hɔ̀gù-ŋmìm-bì-vììŋká

Four adjectives (unnatural)

'the old red big bad thing'	jà-kù-ŋmìŋ-kpíí-!bíáká

Appendix E

Associative noun phrases

Two nouns

'bush's trees'	hààgíŋ tíí!sí	(hààgíŋ 'bush', tììsí 'trees')
'bowl's bottom'	kórúbá !chí!áŋ	(kórúbá 'bowl', chíáŋ 'waist, bottom')
'bowl's handles'	kórúbá !núúsí	(kórúbá 'bowl', núúsí 'arms')
'bowl's opening'	kórúbá !núáŋ	(kórúbá 'bowl', núáŋ 'mouth')
'child's cutlass'	búá káréntìà	(búá 'child', káréntìà 'cutlass')
'child's knife'	búá jí!bíŋ	(búá 'child', jíbíŋ 'knife')
'child's stick'	bùàwá dá!áŋ	(bùàwá 'the child', dááŋ 'stick')
'cow's father'	náá!gíŋ chɔ́ŋ	(náá!gíŋ 'cow', chɔ́ŋ 'father')
'cow's leg'	náá!gíŋ náŋ	(náá!gíŋ 'cow', náŋ 'leg')
'cow's stick'	náá!gíŋ dá!áŋ	(náá!gíŋ 'cow', dááŋ 'stick')
'cows' bones'	níg!é kɔ́bà	(níg!è 'cows', kɔ̀bá 'bones')
'cows' tick'	níg!é kpá!jíŋ	(níg!è 'cows', kpájíŋ 'tick')
'cows' ticks'	níg!é kpá!jígísí	(níg!è 'cows', kpájígísí 'ticks')
'crop's inside'	kágílí sú!ŋ	(kágílí 'the crop (of bird)', súŋ 'inside')
'dance's beginning'	gìlìnsìèlé pí!líŋ	(gìlìnsìèlé 'dance (sp.)', pìlíŋ 'beginning')
'dog's mother'	gbáàŋ núŋ	(gbááŋ 'dog', núŋ 'mother (3s)')
'fish's child'	kpàgàsúŋkpàgà búá!wá	(kpàgàsúŋkpàgà 'fish (sp.)', bùàwá 'the child')
'fish's fruit'	kpàgàsúŋkpàgà kíŋkàmòòmá	(kpàgàsúŋkpàgà 'fish (sp.)', kíŋkàmòòmá 'fruit (sp.)')
'fish's tail'	kpàgàsúŋkpàgà jú!ŋ	(kpàgàsúŋkpàgà 'fish (sp.)', júŋ 'tail')
'fishes' children'	sí!á bállí	(sìà 'fishes (sp.)', bállí 'children')
'guinea fowl's bone'	kpá!áŋ kɔ́!bíŋ	(kpá!áŋ 'guinea fowl', kɔ̀bíŋ 'bone')
'guinea fowl's bones'	kpá!áŋ kɔ́bà	(kpá!áŋ 'guinea fowl', kɔ̀bá 'bones')
'guinea fowl's gullet'	kpáá!kú láŋ!kóósíŋ	(kpáá!kú 'the guinea fowl', láŋkòòsíŋ 'gullet')
'guinea fowls' gullets'	kpíí!né láŋ!kóósé	(kpíínè 'guinea fowls', láŋkòòsé 'gullets')

'guinea fowls' bones'	kpíílné kòbà	(kpíínè 'guinea fowls', kòbá 'bones')
'husband's bench'	chùrú dám!pálá	(chùrú 'husband', dàm!pàlá 'bench')
'husband's guin. fowl'	chùrú kpá!láŋ	(chùrú 'husband', kpá!láŋ 'guinea fowl')
'husband's louse'	chùrú kpíbíŋ	(chùrú 'husband', kpíbíŋ 'louse')
'lightning'	nííŋ bó!líŋ	(nííŋ 'rain', bòlíŋ 'fire')
'man's dance (sp.)'	dàawá gílìnsìèlé	(dàawá 'the man', gílìnsìèlè 'dance (sp.)')
'man's egret'	dàawá kpá!lìgínántìà	(dàawá 'the man', kpàlìgínántìà 'egret')
'man's fish'	dàawá zá!sìŋ	(dàawá 'the man', zàsìŋ 'fish')
'man's fish (sp.)'	dàawá nántìkùlìmíŋ	(dàawá 'the man', nàntìkùlìmíŋ 'fish (sp.)')
'man's hat'	dàawá kágbà	(dàawá 'the man', kàgbá 'hat')
'man's hawk'	dàawá kpá!líǵíŋ	(dàawá 'the man', kpàlígíŋ 'hawk')
'man's louse'	dàawá kpíbíŋ	(dàawá 'the man', kpíbíŋ 'louse')
'man's navel'	dàawá sáŋ!kpáríŋ	(dàawá 'the man', sàŋkpàríŋ 'navel')
'man's wife'	dàawá hɔ́gʊ̀	(dàawá 'the man', hɔ̀gʊ́ 'wife, woman')
'woman's porridge'	hɔ̀wwá sáá!bú	(hɔ̀wwá 'the woman', sààbú 'the porridge')
'woman's red beans'	hɔ̀wwá !páwáágá	(hɔ̀wwá 'the woman', pàwààgá 'red beans')

Three nouns[1]

'my friend's husband'	ń zóá chùrú	(zóá 'friend', chùrú 'husband')
'her friend's husband'	ʊ̀ zóʟá chùrú	(zóá 'friend', chùrú 'husband')
'my friend's wife'	ń zóá hɔ́gʊ̀	(zóá 'friend', hɔ̀gʊ́ 'woman')
'his friend's wife'	ʊ̀ zóʟá hɔ́gʊ̀	(zóá 'friend', hɔ̀gʊ́ 'woman')
'her husband's dance'	ʊ̀ chʊ́lrʊ́ gílìnsìèlè	(chùrú 'husband', gílìnsìèlé 'dance')
'his wife's stringy soup'	ʊ̀ hɔ̀gʊ́ !jí!sàálá	(hɔ̀gʊ 'woman', jí-sàálá 'stringy soup')
'Ali's sibling's child'	àlí tá!lá bʊ́!á	(àlí Alí, táà 'sibling', bʊ́á 'child')

---

[1] Commas in vernacular indicate a slight pause.

'man's hoe's handle'   dààwá kù!ún léékúŋ   (dààwá 'the man', kùúŋ 'hoe', léékúŋ 'handle')
'man's hoe's handle'   dààwá kùú!rí léékúŋ   (dààwá 'the man', kùùrí 'the hoe', léékúŋ 'handle')
'man's wife's beans'   dààwá hɔ́gù̀, pá!wáágá   (dààwá 'the man', hɔ̀gú 'woman', pàwáágá 'beans')
                       ~dààwá hɔ́!gú pá!wáágá
'woman's duck's gullet' hɔ̀wwá gbí!ɲúárí láŋ!kóósíŋ (hɔ̀wwá 'the woman', gbìɲùàrí 'the duck', làŋkòòsíŋ 'gullet')

Four nominals

'his father's farm's path'   ó chɔ́ŋ !kúán síéŋ
(i.e., path to his father's farm) (cf. ó chɔ́ŋ 'his father', kúáŋ 'farm', síéŋ 'path')

Appendix F

Verb aspects

For each aspect, a full set of pronoun subject forms is given to illustrate whether the subject pronoun makes a difference in the tonal pattern or not. Thereafter, only the third-person singular is given, or if person makes a difference, then first- and third-person singular subjects are given as illustrative.

Imperfective

These forms may be glossed as either past or present progressive in English; for economy of space I have glossed these as the present progressive only.

Imperfective intransitive

Various subject pronouns
ǹ sí!á mìŋ	'I am bathing'		tì sí!á mìŋ	'we are bathing'
sí!á mìŋ	'you are bathing'		nì sí!á mìŋ	'you(PL) are bathing'
ù siá mìŋ	's/he is bathing'		bà siá mìŋ	'they are bathing'

CV stem
ǹ dí!é mìŋ	'I am eating'		ù ɖié mìŋ	's/he is eating'
ɲ̀ gbí!á mìŋ	'I am touching'		ù gbiá mìŋ	's/he is touching'
ǹ lá!á mìŋ	'I am laughing'		ù laá mìŋ	's/he is laughing'
m̀ mí!á mìŋ	'I am building'		ù miá mìŋ	's/he is building'
ǹ sí!é mìŋ	'I am dancing'		ù sié mìŋ	's/he is dancing'
ǹ tú!ó mìŋ	'I am digging'		ù tuó mìŋ	's/he is digging'

CVC, CVN, or CVVC stem
m̀ bɔ́!bá mìŋ	'I am tying'		ù bɔ̀bá mìŋ	's/he is tying'
ǹ dá!gá mìŋ	'I am showing'		ù dàgá mìŋ	's/he is showing'
ǹ dí!gé mìŋ	'I am cooking'		ù digé mìŋ	's/he is cooking'
ǹ dù!má mìŋ	'I am biting'		ù dùmá mìŋ	's/he is biting'
ŋ̀m kpá!tá mìŋ	'I am finishing'		ù kpàt-á mìŋ	's/he is finishing'
ǹ lá!má mìŋ	'I am tasting'		ù lamá mìŋ	's/he is tasting'
ǹ tí!rá mìŋ	'I am stretching'		ù tĩrá mìŋ	's/he is stretching'

Verb aspects

CVCVC stem

ǹ chɔ́gǃsá mìŋ	'I am fetching'	ò chɔ̀gìsá mìŋ	's/he is fetching'
ŋ̀ gálǃmá mìŋ	'I am blaming'	ù gàlìmá mìŋ	's/he is blaming'
ŋ̀m̀ kpámǃsá mìŋ	'I am folding'	ò kpàmìsá mìŋ	's/he is folding'
ǹ súgúǃré mìŋ	'I am washing'	ù sùgùré mìŋ	's/he is washing'
ǹ súlǃsé mìŋ	'I am polishing'	ù sùlìsé mìŋ	's/he is polishing'

Imperfective transitive

CV stem

ǹ dǃǃé ɲìndìkké	'I am eating food'	ù dìé ɲìndìkké	's/he is eating food'
ŋ̀m̀ gbǃǃá ǃchíftí	'I am touching (the) load'	ù gbìá ǃchíftí	's/he is touching (the) load'
ǹ láǃá ǃbúáwá	'I am laughing (at) the child'	ù làá ǃbúáwá	's/he is laughing (at) the child'
m̀ míǃá ǃjúóŋ	'I am building a room'	ò mìá ǃjúóŋ	's/he is building a room'
ǹ síǃé gìlìnsìèlè	'I am dancing the *gilinsiele*'	ù sìé gìlìnsìèlé	's/he is dancing the *gilinsiele*'
ǹ túǃó ǃvɔ́rìŋ	'I am digging a hole'	ù tùó ǃvɔ́rìŋ	's/he is digging a hole'

CVC, CVN, or CVVC stem

m̀ bɔ̀báǃá ǃdáátí	'I am tying sticks'	ò bɔ̀báá ǃdáátí	's/he is tying sticks'
ǹ dágáǃá ǃjúókú	'I am showing the room'	ù dàgáá ǃjúókú	's/he is showing the room'
ǹ dígéǃé ɲùà	'I am cooking yams'	ù dìgéé ɲùà	's/he is cooking yams'
ǹ dómáǃá ǃnɔ́mbú	'I am biting meat'	kà dùmáá ǃgbááká	'it is biting the dog'
ŋ̀m̀ kpátáǃá ǃjúókú	'I am finishing the room'	ù kpàtáá ǃjúókú	's/he is finishing the room'
ǹ lámáǃá ǃjítí	'I am tasting soup'	ù làmáá ǃjítí	's/he is tasting soup'
ǹ tííráǃá ǃwó nàŋ	'I am stretching his/her leg'	ù tììráá ǃwó nàŋ	's/he is stretching his/her leg'

CVCVC stem

ǹ chɔ̀gúsá!á !bólíŋ	'I am fetching fire'	ù chɔ̀gúsáá !bólíŋ	's/he is fetching fire'
ŋ̀ gálímá!á gáárú	'I am blaming (the) thief'	ù gàlímáá gáárú	's/he is blaming (the) thief'
ŋ̀m̀ kpámíśá!á gbáníŋ	'I am folding skin'	ù kpàmìsáá gbáníŋ	's/he is folding skin'
ǹ súgúré!é !gáttí	'I am washing clothes'	ù sùgúréé !gáttí	's/he is washing clothes'
ǹ súlísé!é gbíábí!kú	'I am polishing the door'	ù sùlíséé gbíábí!kú	's/he is polishing the door'

Perfective

Perfective intransitive

Various subject pronouns

ǹ sí!yá	'I have bathed'	tí sí!yá	'we have bathed'
sí!yá	'you have bathed'	ní sí!yá	'you(PL) have bathed'
ù síyá	's/he has bathed'	bà sìyá	'they have bathed'

CV stem

ǹ dí!yé	'I have eaten'	ù diyé	's/he has eaten'
ŋ̀m̀ gbí!yá	'I have touched'	ù gbìyá	's/he has touched'
ǹ lá!yá	'I have laughed'	ù làyá	'she has laughed'
m̀ mí!yá	'I have built'	ò mìyá	's/he has built'
ǹ sé!yé	'I have danced'	ú sèyé	's/he has danced'
ǹ tú!yé	'I have dug'	ú tùyé	's/he has dug'[1]

---

[1] Phonetically [tʷìyé].

Verb aspects

CVN stem

ǹ dóṇ!yá	'I have bitten'	ù dòŋyá	's/he has bitten'
ǹ lán!yá	'I have tasted'	ù lànyá	's/he has tasted'

CVC or CVVC stem

m̀ bɔ̀bí!yá	'I have tied'	ù bɔ̀bìyá	's/he has tied'
ǹ dágí!yá	'I have showed'	ù dàgìyá	's/he has showed'
ǹ dígí!yé	'I have cooked'	ù dìgìyé	's/he has cooked'
ŋ̀m̀ kpátí!yá	'I have finished'	ù kpàtìyá	's/he has finished'
ǹ tíírí!yá	'I have stretched'	ù tììrìyá	's/he has stretched'

CVCVC stem

ǹ chɔ́gísí!yá	'I have fetched'	ù chɔ̀gìsìyá	's/he has fetched'
ŋ̀ gálín!yá	'I have blamed'	ù gàlìnyá	's/he has blamed'
ŋ̀m̀ kpámísí!yá	'I have folded'	ù kpàmìsìyá	's/he has folded'
ǹ súgúrí!yé	'I have washed'	ù sùgùrìyá	's/he has washed'
ǹ súlísí!yé	'I have polished'	ù sùlìsìyé	's/he has polished'

Perfective transitive

CV stem

ǹ sú!wá ɲááŋ	'I have bathed (with) water'	ù sùwá ɲááŋ	's/he has bathed (with) water'
ǹ dú!wó sàáŋ	'I have eaten porridge'	ù dùwó !sááŋ	's/he has eaten porridge'
ŋ̀m̀ gbú!wá !tííŋ	'I have touched a tree'	ù gbùwá !tííŋ	's/he has touched a tree'
ǹ lá!wá bòàwá	'I have laughed (at) the child'	ù làwá !bòàwá	'she has laughed (at) the child'
m̀ mó!wá jùóŋ	'I have built a room'	ù mòwá !jùóŋ	's/he has built a room'

ǹ sé!wó gílìnsièlé   'I have danced the *gilinsiele*'   ù sèwó gílìnsièlé   's/he has danced the *gilinsiele*'
ǹ tú!wó vɔ́ríŋ   'I have dug a hole'   ù tùwó vɔ́ríŋ   's/he has dug a hole'

CVN stem
ǹ dóŋ!wá nɔ̀mbú   'I have bitten the meat'   kà dòŋwá !gbáaká   'it has bitten the dog'
ǹ láŋ!wá jítí   'I have tasted soup'   ù làŋwá !jíì   's/he has tasted soup'

CVC or CVVC stem
m̀ bɔ́bú!wá dáàtí   'I have tied sticks'   ù bɔ̀bùwá !dáàtí   's/he has tied sticks'
ǹ dágú!wá jùòkú   'I have showed the room'   ù dàgùwá !jùòkú   's/he has showed the room'
ǹ dígí!wó ɲúà   'I have cooked yams'   ù dìgùwó ɲùà   's/he has cooked yams'
ŋm̀ kpátú!wá jùòŋ   'I have finished a room'   ù kpàtùwá !jùòŋ   's/he has finished a room'
ǹ tííró!wá ù náŋ   'I have stretched his/her leg'   ù tììròwá !ú náŋ   's/he has stretched his/her leg'

CVCVC stem
ǹ chágísú!wá bólíŋ   'I have fetched fire'   ù chàgìsùwá !bólíŋ   's/he has fetched fire'
ŋ̀ gálíŋ!wá gáárú   'I have blamed a thief'   ù gàlìŋwá gáárú   's/he has blamed a thief'
ŋm̀ kpámísú!wá gbáníŋ   'I have folded a skin'   ù kpàmìsùwá gbáníŋ   's/he has folded a skin'
ǹ súgúrú!wó gáttí   'I have washed clothes'   ù sùgùrùwó !gáttí   's/he has washed clothes'
ǹ súlísú!wó gbíá!bíŋ   'I have polished a door'   ù sùlìsùwó gbíá!bíŋ   's/he has polished a door'

Future

Future intransitive

Various subject pronouns
ǹ nàn síí 'I will bathe'
nán síí 'you will bathe'
ù nàn síí 's/he will bathe'

tì nàn síí 'we will bathe'
nì nàn síí 'you(PL) will bathe'
bà nàn síí 'they will bathe'

CV stem
ù nèn díí 's/he will eat'
ò nàŋ gbíí 's/he will touch'[2]
ù nàn láá 's/he will laugh'

ù nàm míí 's/he will build'
ù nèn síé 's/he will dance'
ù nèn túó 's/he will dig'

CVN stem
ò nàn láŋ 's/he will taste'

kè nèn dúŋ 'it will bite'

CVC stem
ò nàm bɔ́bí 's/he will tie'
ò nàn dágí 's/he will show'
ù nèn dígí 's/he will cook'

ò nàŋ kpátí 's/he will finish'
ò nàn tííí 's/he will stretch'

---

[2] Also pronounced ò nàŋm gbíí; likewise all the nasals in this section which I have transcribed with ŋ before [KP] have an alternate pronunciation ŋm in faster speech.

CVCVC stem
ù nàn chɔ́gísí   's/he will fetch'   ù nèn súgúrí   's/he will wash'
ù nàn gálíŋ   's/he will blame'   ù nen súlísí   's/he will polish'
ù nàŋ kpámísí   's/he will fold'

Future transitive

CV stem
ù nèn díí ǃsááŋ   's/he will eat porridge'   ò nàm mɨ́ɨ́ ǃjúóŋ   's/he will build a room'
ù nàŋ gbíí ǃtííká   's/he will touch the tree' ù nèn sɨ́é gìlìnsìèlé   's/he will dance the *gìlìnsìèlé*'
ù nàn láá ǃbúáwá   's/he will laugh (at) the child' ù nèn túó vɔ́ríŋ   's/he will dig a hole'

CVN stem
ù nàn lán ǃjítí   's/he will taste soup'   kè nèn dúŋ gbááká   'it will bite the dog'

CVC stem
ò nàm bɔ́bɨ́ ǃdáátí 's/he will tie sticks'   ò nàŋ kpátí ǃjúókú   's/he will finish the room'
ù nàn dágí ǃjúókú   's/he will show the room'   ò nàn tíírí ǃò náŋ   's/he will stretch his/her arm'
ù nèn dígí ɲúà   's/he will cook yams'

CVCVC stem
ù nàn chɔ́gísí ǃbólíŋ 's/he will fetch fire'   ù nèn súgúrí ǃgáttí   's/he will wash clothes'
ù nàn gálíŋ gáárú   's/he will blame a thief' ù nen súlísí gbiáǃbíŋ   's/he will polish a door'
ù nàŋ kpámísí gbánin 's/he will fold a skin'

Future imperfective

Future imperfective intransitive

Various subject pronouns
ǹ nàn dɪ́ sɪ́!à   'I will be bathing'
nán dɪ́ sɪ́!à   'you will be bathing'
ù nàn dɪ́ sɪ́!à   's/he will be bathing'
tɪ̀ nàn dɪ́ sɪ́!à   'we will be bathing'
nì nàn dɪ́ sɪ́!à   'you(PL) will be bathing'
bà nàn dɪ́ sɪ́!à   'they will be bathing'

CV stem
ù nèn dɪ́ dɪ́!é   's/he will be eating'
ù nàn dɪ́ gbɪ́!á   's/he will be touching'
ù nàn dɪ́ lá!á   's/he will be laughing'
ù nàn dɪ́ mɪ́!á   's/he will be building'
ù nèn dɪ́ sɪ́!é   's/he will be dancing'
ù nèn dɪ́ tú!ó   's/he will be digging'

CVN stem
ù nàn dɪ́ dú!má   's/he will be biting'
ù nàn dɪ́ lá!má   's/he will be tasting'

CVC stem
ù nàn dɪ́ bɔ́!bá   's/he will be tying'
ù nàn dɪ́ dá!gá   's/he will be showing'
ù nèn dɪ́ dɪ́!gé   's/he will be cooking'
ù nàn dɪ́ kpá!tɪ́   's/he will be finishing'
ù nàn dɪ́ tɪ́!rɪ́   's/he will be stretching'

CVCVC stem
ù nàn dɪ́ chɔ́gɪ́!sá   's/he will be fetching'
ù nàn dɪ́gálɪ́!má   's/he will be blaming'
ù nàn dɪ́ kpámɪ́!sá   's/he will be folding'
ù nèn dɪ́ súgù!ré   's/he will be washing'
ù nèn dɪ́ súlɪ́!sé   's/he will be polishing'

Future imperfective transitive

CV stem

ù nèn dí dí!é !sáán̄	's/he will be eating porridge'	ù nàn dí mí!á !júón̄	's/he will be building a room'
ù nàn dí gbí!á tíīká	's/he will be touching a tree'	ù nèn dí sí!é gìlìnsìèlé	's/he will be dancing the gilinsiele'
ò nàn dí lá!á !búáwá	's/he will be laughing (at) the child'	ù nèn dí tú!ó vɔ́rín̄	's/he will be digging a hole'

CVN stem

kà nàn dí dímá!á !gbááká	'it will be biting a dog'	ù nàn dí lámá!á !jítí	's/he will be tasting soup'

CVC stem

ù nàn dí bɔ́bá!á !dáátí	's/he will be tying sticks'	ù nàn dí kpátá!á !júókú	's/he will be finishing a room'
ù nàn dí dágá!á !júókú	's/he will be showing a room'	ù nàn dí tífrá!á !ó nán̄	's/he will be stretching his/her leg'
ù nèn dí dígélá ɲúā	's/he will be cooking yams'		

Verb aspects

CVCVC stem

ù nàn dí chɔ́gìsá!á !bólíŋ 's/he will be fetching fire' ù nèn dí súlísé!á gbíá!bíŋ 's/he will be polishing a door'³

ù nàn dí gálímá!á gáárú 's/he will be blaming a thief' ù nèn dí súgúré!á gáttí 's/he will be washing clothes'

ù nàn dí kpámísá!á gbáníŋ 's/he will be folding a skin'

Imperative

Imperative intransitive

CV stem

sɨ́	'bathe!'		mɨ́	'build!'
dɨ́	'eat!'		sɛ́	'dance!'
gbɨ́	'touch!'		tùú	'dig!'
làá	'laugh!'			

CVN stem

dǔŋ 'bite!'⁴ lǎŋ 'taste!'

---

³In faster speech, the aspectual vowel assimilates to the [a], as in *ù nèn dí súlísá!á gbíá!bíŋ*.
⁴This form is never heard in actual conversation; it would be extremely rude.

CVC stem
bɔ̀bí   'tie!'
dìgí   'cook!'
tììrí   'stretch!'

CVCVC stem
chɔ̀gìsí   'fetch!'
sùgùrí   'wash!'   dàgí   'show!'
                                kpàtí   'finish!'

                                kpàmìsí   'fold!'
                                sùlìsí   'polish!'

Imperative imperfective

Imperative imperfective intransitive

CV stem
dìmé   'be eating!'
làmá   'be laughing!'
sìmé   'be dancing!'   gbìmá   'be touching!'
                                 mìmá   'be building!'
                                 tùmé   'be digging!'

CVN stem
dòmmá   'be biting!'
             (see fn. 183)   làmmá   'be tasting!'

CVC stem
bɔ̀bìmá ~ bɔ̀mmá   'be tying!'
dìgìmé   'be cooking!'
tììrìmá   'be stretching!'   dàgìmá   'be showing!'
                                 kpàtìmá   'be finishing!'

Verb aspects

CVCVC stem		
chɔ̀gìsìmá	'be fetching!'	kpàmìsìmá 'be folding!'
sùgùrìmá	'be washing!'	sùlìsìmé 'be polishing!'

Iterative

Note that the semantics of this construction varies with the verb.

Imperfective

ù mìà mí!á mìŋ	's/he is building (several things)'	ù pùò pú!ó mìŋ	's/he is dividing (into groups)'
ò bɔ̀bà bɔ́!bá mìŋ	's/he is tying (several things)'	ù pìlì pí!lé mìŋ	's/he is roofing (several houses)'
ù bùgùrà búgú!rá mìŋ	's/he is learning (several things)'	ù sùgùrè súgú!ré mìŋ	's/he is washing (several things)'

Perfective/neutral

ù mìí !mìí mìŋ	's/he built (several times)'	ù púó !púó mìŋ	's/he divided (several times)'
ò bɔ̀bú !bɔ́bí mìŋ[5]	's/he tied (several things)'	ù pìlí !pílí mìŋ	's/he roofed (several houses)'
ù sùgùrí !súgúrí mìŋ	's/he washed (several things)'	ò búgùrí !búgúrí mìŋ	's/he learned (several things)'

---

[5] Or ò bɔ̀b !bɔ́bí mìŋ in casual speech.

Future

ù nàm mɨ́ !mɨ̂	's/he will build (several times)'	ù nàm púó !púò	's/he will divide (several times)'
ù nàŋ gáá !gáà (hààgíŋ)	's/he will go (several times) (to bush)'	ù nàn chɨ́sɨ̀n !chôŋ	's/he will walk (several times)'
ù nàm bɔ́bʊ́ !bɔ́bɨ̂	's/he will tie (into groups)'	ù nàm pɨ́lɨ́ !pɨ́lɨ́	's/he will roof (several times)'
ù nàn chɨ́sɨ̀n !chɨ́sɨ̀ŋ	's/he will sneeze (several times)'	ù nàn súgúrí !súgúrî	's/he will wash (several times)'
ù nàŋ kpégírí !kpégírí	's/he will break (several times)'		

Future Imperfective

ù nàn dɨ́ mɨ́là !mɨ́lá	's/he will be building (several things)'	ù nàn dɨ́ dɨ́!é !dɨ́!é	's/he will be eating (several times)'
ù nàn dɨ́ nɨ́gá!á !ngá!á	's/he will be beating (several times)'	ù nàn dɨ́ gʊ́rà!á !gʊ́rá!á	's/he will be sleeping (several times)'
ù nàn dɨ́ súgúré!é súgúré!é	's/he will be washing (several things)'	ù nàn dɨ́ chɨ́sɨ́má!á !chɨ́sɨ́má!á	's/he will be sneezing (several times)'

Appendix G

Preverbal particles

Single particles

Tonal patterns with *ká/ké* 'NEG'

ŋ̀ **ká** mã̀	'I am not building'	ù **ká** mã̀	's/he is not building'
ŋ̀ **ká** gárà	'I am not going'	ù **ké** dígè	's/he is not cooking'
ù **ká** bɔ́bà	's/he is not tying'	ù **ká** yí!yá	's/he has not given'
ù **ká** chíí !záá	's/he did not carry millet'		

Tonal patterns with *kááN* 'NEG.FUT' (same pattern with all pronouns)

ù **káán** díí	's/he will not eat'	ù **káán** dígí	's/he will not cook'
ù **káán** súgúrí	's/he will not wash'	ù **káán** lán !jítí	's/he will not taste soup'
ù **káán** dí dí!gé	's/he will not be cooking'		

Tonal patterns with *tíN* 'was, would'

ǹ **tín** sí!á mìŋ	'I was still dancing'	ù **tín** sí!á mìŋ	's/he was still dancing'
ǹ **tín** bɔ́!bá mìŋ	'I was tying'	ù **tín** bɔ́!bá mìŋ	's/he was tying'
ǹ **tín** súgú!ré mìŋ	'I was washing'	ù **tín** súgú!ré mìŋ	's/he was washing'

Tonal patterns with *ya* 'still'

ǹ **yé** !síé mìŋ	'I am still dancing'	ù **yè** sìé mìŋ	's/he is still dancing'
ǹ **yá** !bɔ́bá mìŋ	'I am still tying'	ù **yà** bɔ́bá mìŋ	's/he is still tying'
ǹ **yé** sùgùré mìŋ	'I am still washing'	ù **yè** sùgùré mìŋ	's/he is still washing'

Tonal patterns with *waa* 'now, then'

ŋ̀ **wáá** !sí!é mìŋ	'I am now dancing'	ù **wàà** sí!é mìŋ	's/he is now dancing'
ŋ̀ **wáá** !bɔ́!bá mìŋ	'I am now tying'	ù **wàà** bɔ́!bá mìŋ	's/he is now tying'
ŋ̀ **wáá** !súgú!ré mìŋ	'I am now washing'	ù **wàà** súgú!ré mìŋ	's/he is now washing'

Tonal patterns with *ŋaaN* 'has/had been'

ŋ̀ **ŋáám** !míá mìŋ	'I have been building'	ù **ŋààm** mîâ mìŋ	's/he has been building'
ŋ̀ **ŋáám** !bɔ́!bá mìŋ	'I have been tying'	ù **ŋààm** bɔ́!bá mìŋ	's/he has been tying'
ŋ̀ **ŋáán** !súgú!ré mìŋ	'I have been washing'	ù **ŋààn** súgú!ré mìŋ	's/he has been washing'
ŋ̀ **ŋááŋ** !ké dígé!é	'I have not been cooking'	ù **ŋààŋ** ké dígé!é	's/he has not been cooking'

Tonal patterns with *ko* 'just'

ŋ̀ **kó** !bɔ́!bá mìŋ	'I am just tying'	ù **kò** bɔ́!bá mìŋ	's/he is just tying'

Tonal patterns with *woN* 'already'

ǹ **wón** !dí!é mìŋ	'I am already eating'	ù **wòn** dí!é mìŋ	's/he is already eating'
ŋ̀ **wón** !dá!gá mìŋ	'I am already showing'	ù **wòn** dá!gá mìŋ	's/he is already showing'
ŋ̀ **wóm** !búgú!rá mìŋ	'I am already learning'	ù **wòn** búgú!rá mìŋ	's/he is already showing'
ŋ̀ **wón** dìì mìŋ	'I already ate'	ù **wón** dìì mìŋ	's/he already ate'
ŋ̀ **wón** dàgì mìŋ	'I already showed'	ù **wón** dàgì mìŋ	's/he already showed'
ŋ̀ **wón** bùgùrì mìŋ	'I already showed'	ù **wón** bùgùrì mìŋ	's/he already showed'

Tonal patterns with *vīī* 'again'

ǹ **vīī** ˈmˈlá mìŋ	'I am again building'	ò **vīī** mˈlá mìŋ	's/he is again building'
ǹ **vīī** ˈdáˈgá mìŋ	'I am again showing'	ò **vīī** dáˈgá mìŋ	's/he is again showing'
ǹ **vīī** ˈsùgùˈré mìŋ	'I am again washing'	ò **vīī** sùgùˈré mìŋ	's/he is again washing'
ǹ **vīī** dìgì mìŋ	'I again cooked'	ǹ **vīī** sùgùrì mìŋ	'I again washed'

Interaction of 2 particles

tín ya

ǹ **tín yá** ˈmíá mìŋ	'I was still building'	ù **tín yá** ˈmíá mìŋ	's/he was still building'
ǹ **tín yé** ˈdígé mìŋ	'I was still cooking'[1]	ù **tín yé** ˈdígé mìŋ	's/he was still cooking'
ǹ **tín yé** sùgùré mìŋ	'I was still washing'	ù **tín yé** sùgùré mìŋ	's/he was still washing'

tíŋ waa

ǹ **tíŋ wáá** ˈmíá mìŋ	'I was then building'	ù **tíŋ wáá** ˈmíá mìŋ	's/he was then building'
ǹ **tíŋ wáá** ˈdígé mìŋ	'I was then cooking'	ù **tíŋ wáá** ˈdígé mìŋ	's/he was then cooking'
ǹ **tíŋ wáá** ˈsùgùré mìŋ	'I was then washing'	ù **tíŋ wáá** ˈsùgùré mìŋ	's/he was then washing'

tíŋ won

ù **tíŋ wón** ˈdíˈlé mìŋ	's/he was already eating'

---

[1] In the utterance *ǹ tín yé ˈdígé mìŋ*, the bolded syllable is phonetically slightly lower than the following, though both are marked High in the transcription. This could be due to the lowering effect of the voiced stops on either side of the vowel, but it is also possible that there is some variation in the utterance where the first syllable of *dígé* is actually Low, as in the three-particle utterances.

tíŋ ŋaaN
ǹ **tíŋ ŋááŋ** !gbí!mé mìŋ 'I had been tying'   ù **tíŋ ŋááŋ** !gbí!mé mìŋ 's/he had been tying'

tíŋ ko
ù **tíŋ kó** !dá!gá mìŋ 's/he was just showing'

waa woN
ò **wáá wòn** dágà mìŋ 's/he is already now showing'   ŋ̀ **wáá wòn** dágà mìŋ 'I was then already showing'

Interaction of three particles

Note: the third particle varies freely in tone between L and !H.

tíŋ waa ko
ù **tíŋ wáá !kó** dí!é mìŋ 's/he was then just eating'   ù **tíŋ wáá kò** dá!gá mìŋ 's/he was then just showing'
ù **tíŋ wáá kò** bógò!rá mìŋ 's/he was then just learning'

tín ya ko
ù **tín yé kò** dá!gá mìŋ 's/he was still just showing'

tíŋ ŋaan ya
ù **tíŋ ŋááń !yé** dí!gé mìŋ 's/he had been still cooking'   ù **tíŋ ŋááń yà** bɔ́!bá mìŋ 's/he had been still tying'

ká waa vii
ù **ká wáá vìì** mí!á 's/he is not now again building'
ù **ká wáá !víí** súgù!ré 's/he is not now again washing' (~vìì)
ù **ká wáá !víí** dá!gá 's/he is not now again showing' (~vìì)

References

Note: "ROA" below is the Rutgers Optimality Archive, found at http://roa.rutgers.edu/.

Aaron, Uche. 1996/1997. Grammaticization of the verb 'say' to future tense in Obolo. *Journal of West African Languages* 26(2):87–93.

Abaglo, P., and Diana Archangeli. 1989. Language particular underspecification: Gengbe /e/ and Yoruba /i/. *Linguistic Inquiry* 20:457–480.

Akanlig-Pare, George. 1997. Tonal structure of Buli phonological nouns. *Gur Papers/Cahiers Voltaïques* 2:63–67. Universität Bayreuth.

Akanlig-Pare, George, and Michael Kenstowicz. 2003. Studies in Buli Grammar. *MIT Working Papers on Endangered and Less Familiar Languages* 4:1–34.

Akinlabi, Akinbiyi. 1994. Alignment constraints in ATR harmony. *Proceedings of the 5th Annual Conference of the Formal Linguistics Society of Mid-America. Studies in the Linguistic Sciences* 24:1–18.

Akinlabi, Akinbiyi, ed. 1995. *Theoretical approaches to African linguistics. Proceedings of the 25th Annual Conference on African Linguistics.* Trenton, N.J.: Africa World Press, Inc.

Akinlabi, Akinbiyi. 1995. Featural affixation. In Akinlabi, 217–238.

Akinlabi, Akinbiyi. 1996. Featural affixation. *Journal of Linguistics* 32:239–289.

Alderete, John. 1997. Dissimilation as local conjunction. *Proceedings of the North East Linguistics Society* 27:17–32.

Anderson, Stephen R. 1976. On the description of multiply-articulated consonants. *Journal of Phonetics* 4:17–27.

Anttila, Arto. 1995. How to derive variation from grammar. Paper presented at the International Workshop on Language Variation and Linguistic theory, University of Nijmegen, Netherlands [also ROA-63-0000].

Anttila, Arto, and Adams Bodomo. 1996. Stress and tone in Dagaare. ms. Stanford University [also ROA-169-1296].

Anttila, Arto, and Adams Bodomo. 2000. Tonal polarity in Dagaare. In Vicki Carstens and Frederick Parkinson, *Advances in African Linguistics: Proceedings of the 28th Annual Conference on African Linguistics, Cornell University,* 119–134. Trenton, N.J.: Africa World Press.

Archangeli, Diana. 1997. Optimality Theory: An introduction to phonology in the 1990s. In Archangeli and Langendoen, 1–32.

Archangeli, Diana. 1999. Lexical irregularity in OT: DOT vs. variable constraint ranking. Paper presented at Linguistic Society of America, Los Angeles, January 1999.

Archangeli, Diana, and D. Terence Langendoen, eds. 1997. *Optimality Theory: An Overview.* Malden, Mass.: Blackwell.

Archangeli, Diana, Laura Moll, and Kazutoshi Ohno. 1998. Why not *NC. Paper presented at Chicago Linguistic Society meeting.

Archangeli, Diana, and Douglas Pulleyblank. 1994. *Grounded phonology.* Cambridge, Mass.: MIT Press.

Awedoba, A. K. 1993. *Kasem studies Part 1: Phonetics and phonology.* Research Review, Supplement No. 7. Legon: Institute of African Studies, University of Ghana.

Baker, Mark. 1989. Object sharing and projection in serial verb constructions. *Linguistic Inquiry* 20:513–553.

Beacham, Charles G. 1968. The phonology and morphology of Yom. Ph.D. dissertation. Hartford Seminary Foundation.

Beckman, Jill. 1997. Positional faithfulness, positional neutralisation, and Shona vowel harmony. *Phonology* 14:1–46.

Beckman, Jill N., Laura Walsh Dickey, and Suzanne Urbanczyk, eds. 1995. *Papers in Optimality Theory.* UMOP 18. Amherst, Mass.: GLSA.

Bendor-Samuel, John. 1971. Niger-Congo: Gur. In T. A. Sebeok, *Linguistics in sub-Saharan Africa, Current Trends in Linguistics* 7, 141–178.

Bergman, Richard, Ian Gray, and Claire Gray. 1969. *The phonology of Tampulma.* Collected Field Notes 9. Legon: The Institute of African Studies, University of Ghana.

Beyer, Klaus. 1999. La morphologie du verbe in pana. Paper presented at 2nd Colloquium on Gur Languages, Cotonou, Benin, March 29–April 1, 1999.

Bickmore, Lee. 1996. Bantu tone spreading and displacement as alignment and minimal misalignment. ROA-161-1196.

Black, H. Andrew. 1991. The phonology of the velar glide in Axininca Campa. *Phonology* 8:183–217.

Blass, Regina, ed. 1975. *Sisaala-English/English-Sisaala dictionary*. Tamale: Ghana Institute of Linguistics, Literacy, and Bible Translation.

Bodomo, Adams. 1997. *The structure of Dagaare*. Stanford, Calif.: CSLI Publications.

Bodomo, Adams. 1998. Serial verb constructions as complex predicates: Evidence from Dagaare and Akan. In Ian Maddieson and Thomas J. Hinnebusch, *Language history and linguistic description in Africa. Trends in African Linguistics 2, Proceedings of 1995 ACAL, UCLA*, 195–204. Trenton, N.J.: Africa World Press.

Bradshaw, Mary. 1995. Tone on Verbs in Suma. In Akinlabi, 255–272.

Browman, C. P., and L. Goldstein. 1989. Articulatory gestures as phonological units. *Phonology* 6:201–251.

Browman, C. P., and L. Goldstein. 1990. Tiers in articulatory phonology, with some implications for casual speech. In J. Kingston and M. E. Beckman, *Papers in laboratory phonology I: Between the grammar and physics of speech*, 341–376. Cambridge: Cambridge University Press.

Browman, C. P., and L. Goldstein. 1992. Articulatory phonology: An overview. *Phonetica* 49:155–180.

Burzio, Luigi. 1996. Surface constraints versus underlying representations. In Jaques Durand and Bernard Laks, *Current trends in phonology: Models and methods*, Salford, Manchester: European Studies Research Institute.

Byrd, Dani. 1994. Articulatory timing in English consonant sequences. Ph.D. dissertation. UCLA; distributed as UCLA Working Papers in Phonetics 82.

Cahill, Michael. 1985. An autosegmental analysis of Akan nasality and tone. M.A. thesis substitute. University of Texas, Arlington.

Cahill, Michael. 1992a. *A preliminary phonology of the Kɔnni language*. Collected Field Notes 20. Legon: The Institute of African Studies, University of Ghana.

Cahill, Michael. 1992b. The case of the missing Kɔnni 'p'. *Journal of West African Languages* 21(1):15–24.

Cahill, Michael. 1993. Preliminary X-Bar syntax analysis of Kɔnni. ms.

Cahill, Michael. 1994. Diphthongization and underspecification in Kɔnni. *UTA Working Papers in Linguistics* 1:109–126.

Cahill, Michael. 1995a. A reconstruction of the consonants of proto-Buli/Kɔnni. ms. OSU.

Cahill, Michael. 1995b. A reconstruction of the vowels of proto-Buli/Kɔnni. ms. OSU.

Cahill, Michael. 1996. ATR harmony in Kɔnni. *Papers in Phonology: OSU Working Papers in Linguistics* 48:13–30.

Cahill, Michael. 1997a. The phonology of labio–velar stops. *Gur Papers/Cahiers Voltaïques* 2:69–80.
Cahill, Michael. 1997b. Towards reconstruction of the noun class system of proto–Buli-Kɔnni. class handout. OSU.
Cahill, Michael. 1998a. Nasal assimilation and labial-velar geometry. In Ian Maddieson and Thomas J. Hinnebusch, *Language history and linguistic description in Africa. Trends in African Linguistics* 2:127–136. Proceedings of 1995 ACAL, UCLA. Trenton, N.J.: Africa World Press.
Cahill, Michael. 1998b. Tonal polarity in Kɔnni nouns: An Optimal Theoretical account. *OSU Working Papers in Linguistics* 51:19–58.
Cahill, Michael. 1999a. Review of Bodomo, Adams. The structure of Dagaare. *Notes on Linguistics* 2(2):28–32.
Cahill, Michael. 1999b. Triple splits from proto-Buli-Kɔnni. *OSU Working Papers in Linguistics, Historical Linguistics* 52:41–50.
Cahill, Michael. 1999c. Diphthongization in Kɔnni: A feature geometry account. *Journal of African Languages and Linguistics* 20:21–39.
Cahill, Michael. 1999d. Aspects of the phonology of labial-velar stops. *Studies in African Linguistics* 28:155–184.
Cahill, Michael. 2000. Tonal associative morphemes in Optimality Theory. *OSU Working Papers in Linguistics* 53:31–70.
Cahill, Michael, and Frederick Parkinson. 1997. Partial class behavior and Feature Geometry: Remarks on Feature Class Theory. *Proceedings of NELS* 27:79–91.
Callow, John. 1965. *Collected field reports on the phonology of Kasem*. Collected Field Notes 1. Legon: The Institute of African Studies, University of Ghana.
Carlson, Katy. 1997. Sonority and reduplication in Nakanai and Nuxalk (Bella Coola). ms. UMass, Amherst. ROA-230-1197.
Carlson, Robert. 1983. Downstep in Supyire. *Studies in African Linguistics* 14:35–45.
Carlson, Robert. 1994. *A grammar of Supyire*. New York: Mouton de Gruyter.
Carlson, Robert, with Kafano Sanogo. 1992. *Dictionannaire supyire-français avec index français-supyire*. Bamako: SIL.
Casali, Roderic F. 1988. Some phonological processes in Nawuri. M.A. thesis. University of Texas, Arlington.
Casali, Roderic F. 1995. An overview of the Nawuri verbal system. *Journal of West African Languages* 25(1):63–86.
Casali, Roderic F. 1997. Vowel elision in hiatus contexts: Which vowel goes? *Language* 73(3):493–533.
Casali, Roderic F. 1998. Predicting ATR activity. Paper presented at 34th Chicago Linguistic Society.

Cassimjee, Farida, and Charles Kisseberth. 1998. Optimal Domains Theory and Bantu tonology: A case study from Isixhosa and Shingazidja. In Hyman and Kisseberth, 33–132 [also ROA-176-0297].

Chomsky, Noam, and Morris Halle. 1968. *The sound pattern of English.* New York: Harper and Row.

Chumbow, Beban S., and Emile G. Nguendjio. 1991. Floating tones in Bangwa. *Journal of West African Languages* 21(1):3–14.

Clark, Mary. 1990. *The tonal system of Igbo.* Dordrecht: Foris.

Clements, George N. 1981. Akan vowel harmony: A nonlinear analysis. In George Clements, *Harvard Studies in Phonology 2*. Bloomington: Indiana University Linguistics Club.

Clements, George N. 1985. The geometry of phonological features. *Phonology* 2:225–252.

Clements, George N. 1990. The role of the sonority cycle in core syllabification. In John Kingston and Mary Beckman, *Papers in laboratory phonology 1: Between the grammar and physics of speech*, 283–333. Cambridge: Cambridge University Press.

Clements, George N. 1991. Place of articulation in consonants and vowels: A unified theory. *Working Papers of the Cornell Phonetics Laboratory* 5:77–123.

Clements, George N. 1998. Affricates as internally unsequenced stops. Paper presented at the Workshop on Syllable Structure and Gesture Timing, Ohio State University.

Clements, George N., and K. C. Ford. 1979. Kikuyu tone shift and its synchronic consequences. *Linguistic Inquiry* 10:179–210.

Clements, George N., and Elizabeth V. Hume. 1995. The internal organization of speech sounds. In Goldsmith, 245–306.

Clifton, John M. 1975. Nonsegmental tone in Lango. *Proceedings of the Sixth Conference on African Linguistics.* OSU Working Papers in Linguistics 20:99–105.

Cole, Jennifer, and Charles W. Kisseberth. 1994. An Optimal Domains Theory of Harmony. *Studies in the Linguistic Sciences* 24:101–114.

Connell, Bruce. 1994. The structure of labial-velar stops. *Journal of Phonetics* 22:441–476.

Cook, Thomas. 1969. Efik. In Elizabeth Dunstan, *Twelve Nigerian Languages*, 35–46. New York: Africana Publishing.

Cox, Monica. 1998. Description grammaticale du ncam (bassar), langue gurma du Togo et du Ghana. Thèse de diplome. Ecole Pratique des Hautes Etudes, Paris.

Creissels, Denis, and Claire Grégoire. 1993. La notion de ton marqué dans l'analyse d'une opposition tonale binaire: Le cas du mandingue. *Journal of African Languages and Linguistics* 14(2):107–154.

Crouch, Marjorie. 1985. A note on syllable and tone in Vagla verbs. *Journal of West African Languages* 15(2):29–40.

Crouch, Marjorie. 1994. *Phonology of Dɛg.* Tamale: Ghana Institute of Linguistics, Literacy, and Bible Translation.

Crouch, Marjorie, and Patricia Herbert, eds. 1981. *Vagla-English/English-Vagla dictionary.* Tamale: Ghana Institute of Linguistics, Literacy, and Bible Translation.

Crouch, Marjorie, and Nancy Smiles. 1966. *The phonology of Vagla.* Collected Field Notes 4. Legon: The Institute of African Studies, University of Ghana.

Crystal, David. 2003. *A dictionary of linguistics and phonetics,* fifth edition. Cambridge, Mass.: Basil Blackwell.

Cutler, Anne. 1995. Spoken word recognition and production. In Joanne L. Miller and Peter D. Eimes, *Speech, language, and communication,* 97–136. Academic Press.

Dakubu, M. E. Kropp. 1997. Oti-Volta vowel harmony and Dagbani. *Gur Papers/Cahiers Voltaïques* 2:81–88.

Dimmendaal, Gerrit. 1983. *The Turkana language.* Dordrecht: Foris.

Dolphyne, Florence Abena. 1988. *The Akan (Twi-Fante) language: Its sound systems and tonal structure.* Accra: Ghana Universities Press.

Donegan, Patricia J. 1978. *On the natural phonology of vowels.* Ph.D. dissertation. Ohio State University. Reprinted as OSU Working Papers in Linguistics 23.

Eberhard, David. 2003. Mamainde tone: An optimality account of plateauing, floating tones, and toneless syllables in an amazonian language. ROA 615-0903.

Eisner, Jason. 1997. What constraints should OT allow? Paper presented at the Linguistic Society of America, Chicago. ROA-204-0797.

Essien, Okon E. 1990 *A grammar of the Ibibio language.* Ibadan: University Press.

Ferguson, Charles A., Larry M. Hyman, and John J. Ohala, eds. 1975. *Nasálfest: Papers from a symposium on nasals and nasalization.* Stanford, Calif.: Language Universal Project, Stanford University.

Flemming, Edward. 1995. Auditory representations in phonology. Ph.D. dissertation. UCLA.

Foley, William A. 1975. Some rules involving nasals and their implications. In Ferguson, Hyman, and Ohala, 213–230.

Foley, William. 1991. *The Yimas language of New Guinea.* Stanford, Calif.: Stanford University Press.

Fougeron, Cécile, and Patricia A. Keating. 1995. Articulatory strengthening in prosodic domain-initial position. *UCLA Working Papers in Phonetics* 92:61–87.

Fountain, Amy V. 1998. An Optimality Theory approach to Navajo prefixal syllables. Ph.D. dissertation. University of Arizona.

Garber, Ann E. 1987. A tonal analysis of Senufo: Sucite dialect. Ph.D. dissertation. University of Illinois at Urbana-Champaign.

Goldsmith, John. 1976. Autosegmental phonology. Ph.D. dissertation. MIT.

Goldsmith, John. 1984. Meussen's Rule. In M. Aronoff and R. Oehrle, *Language sound structure*, 245–249. Cambridge, Mass.: MIT Press.

Goldsmith, John. 1990. *Autosegmental and metrical phonology*. Cambridge, Mass.: Basil Blackwell.

Goldsmith, John, ed. 1995. *The handbook of phonological theory*. Cambridge, Mass.: Basil Blackwell.

Goldsmith, John. 1997. Review of Steven Bird. Computational phonology: A constraint-based account. *Phonology* 14:133–141.

Golston, Chris. 1996. Direct Optimality Theory: Representation as pure markedness. *Language* 72:713–748.

Greenberg, Joseph. 1966. Some universals of grammar with particular reference to the order of meaningful elements. In Joseph Greenberg, *Universals of Language*, second edition, 73–113. 245–249. Cambridge, Mass.: MIT Press.

Guy, Gregory R. 1997. Violable is variable: Optimality Theory and linguistic variation. *Language Variation and Change* 9:333–347.

Haegeman, Lilianc. 1991. *Introduction to Government and Binding Theory*. Cambridge, Mass.: Blackwell.

Hammond, Mike. 1995. There is no lexicon! ROA-43-0195.

Harris, J. 1969. *Spanish phonology*. Cambridge, Mass.: MIT Press.

Hayes, Bruce. 1986a. Assimilation as spreading in Toba Batak. *Linguistic Inquiry* 17(3):467–499.

Hayes, Bruce. 1986b. Inalterability in CV phonology. *Language* 62:321–351

Hayes, Bruce. 1990. Diphthongisation and coindexing. *Phonology* 7:31–72.

Hayes, Bruce. 1999. Phonetically-driven phonology: The role of Optimality Theory and inductive grounding. In Michael Darnell, Edith Moravscik, Michael Noonan, Frederick Newmeyer, and Kathleen Wheatly (eds.), *Functionalism and formalism in linguistics, I: General papers*, 243–285. Amsterdam: John Benjamins [also ROA-158-1196].

Hayes, Bruce, and Tanya Stivers. 1996. The phonetics of post-nasal voicing. ms. UCLA.

Heine, Bernd, and Mechthild Reh. 1984. *Grammaticalization and renalysis in African languages*. Hamburg: Helmut Buske.

Hess, Susan. 1992. Assimilatory effects in a vowel harmony language: An acoustic analysis of Advanced Tongue Root in Akan. *Journal of Phonetics* 20:475–492.

Hopper, Paul J., and Elizabeth Closs Traugott. 1993. *Grammaticalization.* New York: Cambridge University Press.

Hsu, Chai-Shune. 1996. A phonetically-based Optimality-Theoretic account of consonant reduction in Taiwanese. *UCLA Working Papers in Phonetics* 92:1–44.

Hualde, J. I., and J. Cole. 1997. Two views on phonological alternations. Paper presented at Mid-Continental Workshop on Phonology III, University of Indiana.

Hubbard, Kathleen. 1998. Quantity or quality? Characteristics and typology of vowel length. Paper presented at Linguistic Society of America, New York City.

Hulst, Harry van der, and Jeroen van de Weijer. 1995. Vowel harmony. In Goldsmith, 495–534.

Hume, Elizabeth. 1992. Front vowels, coronal consonants and their interaction in non-linear phonology. Ph.D. dissertation. Cornell University.

Hume, Elizabeth. 1998. The role of perceptibility in consonant/consonant metathesis. In Susan Blake, Eun-Sook Kim, and Kimary Shahin, *WCCFL XVII Proceedings, CSLI,* 293–307.

Hunt, Geoffrey R., and Rosemary H. Hunt. 1981. *A phonology of the Hanga language.* Collected Field Notes 18. Legon: The Institute of African Studies, University of Ghana.

Hyman, Larry M. 1993. Structure preservation and postlexical tonology in Dagbani. In Sharon Hargus and Ellen M. Kaisse, *Studies in lexical phonology,* 235–254. San Diego: Academic Press.

Hyman, Larry. 1999. The limits of phonetic determinism in phonology: *NC revisited. Paper given at Linguistic Society of America, Los Angeles, January 1999.

Hyman, Larry M., and Charles Kisseberth, eds. 1998. *Theoretical aspects of Bantu tone.* Stanford, Calif.: CSLI Publications.

Hyman, Larry M., and Russell G. Schuh. 1974. Universals of tone rules: Evidence from West Africa. *Linguistic Inquiry* 5:81–115.

Hyman, Larry M., and M. Tadadjeu. 1976. Floating tones in Mbam-Nkam. In Larry M. Hyman, *Studies in Bantu Tonology,* 57–111. Southern California Occasional Papers in Linguistics.

Inkelas, Sharon. 1994. The consequences of optimization for underspecification. ROA-40-1294.

Inkelas, Sharon, C. Orhan Orgun, and Cheryl Zoll. 1996. Exceptions and static phonological patterns: Cophonologies vs. prespecification. ROA-124-0496.

Inkelas, Sharon, and Draga Zec. 1995. Syntax-phonology interface. In Goldsmith, 535–549.

Inouye, S. 1995. Trills, taps and stops in contrast and variation. Ph.D. dissertation. UCLA.

Issah, Dawuni. 1993. Some tonal processes and tone representation in Dagbani. M.A. thesis. University of Texas, Arlington.

Itô, Junko, Yoshihisa Kitagawa, and Armin Mester. 1996. Prosodic faithfulness and correspondence: Evidence from a Japanese argot. *Journal of East Asian Languages* 5:217–294.

Itô, Junko, and R. Armin Mester. 1995. Japanese phonology. In Goldsmith, 817–838.

Jakobson, Roman, Gunnar Fant, and Morris Halle. 1952. *Preliminaries to speech analysis*. Cambridge, Mass.: MIT Press.

Jenewari, Charles. 1973. Vowel harmony in Kalabari Ijo. *Research Notes from the Department of Linguistics and Nigerian Languages* 6:59–78. University of Ibadan.

Jiang-King, Ping. 1998. An Optimality account of tone-vowel interaction in Northern Min. Ph.D. dissertation. Chinese University of Hong Kong.

Johnson, Keith. 1997. *Acoustic and auditory phonetics*. Cambridge, Mass.: Blackwell.

Jones, Peggy. 1987. *The phonology of Dilo*. Collected Field Notes 19 (misprinted as #18). Legon: The Institute of African Studies, University of Ghana.

Jordan, Dean. 1980. *A phonology of Nafaanra*. Collected Field Notes 17. Legon: The Institute of African Studies, University of Ghana.

Joseph, Brian, and Arnold Zwicky, eds. 1990. *When verbs collide: Papers from the 1990 Ohio State Mini-Conference on Serial Verbs*. OSU Working Papers in Linguistics 39.

Jun, Jongho. 1995. Perceptual and articulatory factors in place assimilation: An Optimality Theoretic approach. Ph.D. dissertation. UCLA.

Jun, Sun-Ah. 1993. The phonetics and phonology of Korean prosody. Ph.D. dissertation. Ohio State University.

Kage, René. 1999. *Optimality Theory*. Cambridge: Cambridge University Press.

Kaise, Ellen. M. 1985. *Connected speech: The interaction of syntax and phonology*. Orlando, Fla.: Academic Press.

Kang, Hyeon-Seok. 1997. Phonological variation in glides and diphthongs of Seoul Korean: Its synchrony and diachrony. Ph.D. dissertation. Ohio State University.

Kaun, Abigail. 1995. The typology of rounding harmony: An Optimal Theoretical approach. Ph.D. dissertation. UCLA.

Kebikaza, Kezié Koyenzi. 1994. Les tons du verb kabiyé dans les formes de l'inaccompli. In Thomas Geider and Raimund Kastenholtz, *Sprachen und Sprachzeugnisse in Afrika. Eine Sammlung philologischer Beiträge*,

Wilhelm J. G. Möhlig zum 60. Geburtstag zugeeignet, 263–279. Köln: Rüdiger Köppe Verlag.

Kedrebéogo, Gérard. 1997. Tone in Samoma. *Gur Papers/Cahiers Voltaïques* 2:97–108.

Kennedy, Jack. 1966. *The phonology of Dagaari*. Collected Field Notes 6. Legon: The Institute of African Studies, University of Ghana.

Kenstowicz, Michael. 1994. *Phonology in generative grammar*. Cambridge, Mass.: Blackwell.

Kenstowicz, Michael, Emmanuel Nikiema, and Meterwa Ourso. 1988. Tonal polarity in two Gur languages. *Studies in the Linguistic Sciences* 18(1):77–103.

Kilpatrick, Eileen. 1985. Bongo phonology. *Occasional Papers in the Study of Sudanese Languages* 4:1–62. Juba: Summer Institute of Linguistics, Institute of Regional Languages, and the University of Juba.

Kim, No-Ju. 1997. Tone, segments, and their interaction in North Kyung-Sang Korean. Ph.D. dissertation. Ohio State University.

Kinda, Jules. 1997. Les tons du mòoré et leur incidence sur les segments. *Gur Papers/Cahiers Voltaïques* 2:109–116.

Kiparsky, Paul. 1994. An optimality-theoretic perspective on variable rules. Paper presented at NWAVE 23. Stanford University.

Kiparsky, Paul. 2000. Opacity and cyclicity. *The Linguistic Review* 17:351–365.

Kirchner, Robert. 1998. An effort-based approach to consonant lenition. Ph.D. dissertation. UCLA.

Kleinewillinghöfer, Ulrich. 1999. The verb in Kusuntu. Paper presented at 2nd Colloquium on Gur Languages, Cotonou, Benin, March 29–April 1, 1999.

Kröger, Franz. 1992. *Buli-English dictionary*. Münster: Lit Verlag.

Kuch, Lawrence. 1993. *The phonology of Birifor*. Collected Field Notes 21. Legon: The Institute of African Studies, University of Ghana.

Ladefoged, Peter. 1964. *A phonetic study of West African languages*. West African Language Monographs 1. Cambridge: Cambridge University Press.

Ladefoged, Peter, and Ian Maddieson. 1996. *The sounds of the world's languages*. Cambridge, Mass.: Blackwell.

Lahiri, Aditi, and Vincent Evers. 1991. Palatalization and coronality. In Paradis and Prunet, 79–100.

Langdon, Margaret A., and Mary J. Breeze, eds. 1981. *Konkomba-English/English-Konkomba dictionary*. Tamale: Ghana Institute of Linguistics, Literacy, and Bible Translation.

Leben, Will. 1973. Suprasegmental phonology. Ph.D. dissertation. MIT.

Lébikaza, Kézié Koyenzi. 1999. *Grammaire kabiyè: une analyse systématique.* Köln: Rüdiger Köppe Verlag.
Lehiste, Ilse. 1970. *Suprasegmentals.* Cambridge, Mass.: MIT Press.
Lombardi, Linda. 1990. The non-linear organization of the affricate. *Natural Language and Linguistic Theory* 8:375–425.
Lombardi, Linda. 1998a. Coronal epenthesis and markedness. ROA-245-0298.
Lombardi, Linda. 1998b. Restrictions on direction of voicing assimilation: An OT account. ROA 246-0298.
Lombardi, Linda. 1998c. Evidence for MaxFeature constraints from Japanese. ROA-247-0298.
Lombardi, Linda. 1999. Positional faithfulness and voicing assimilation in Optimality Theory. *Natural Language and Linguistic Theory* 17:267–302.
Lombardi, Linda. 2001. Why place and voice are different: Constraint-specific alternations in Optimality Theory. In Linda Lombardi, *Segmental phonology in Optimality Theory,* 13–45. New York: Cambridge University Press [also ROA-105-0000].
Lombardi, Linda. 2002. Coronal epenthesis and markedness. *Phonology* 19:219–252.
Maddieson, Ian. 1978. Universals of tone. In Joseph H. Greenberg, *Universals of human language,* 2: Phonology, 335–366. Stanford, Calif., Stanford University Press.
Maddieson, Ian. 1984. *Patterns of sounds.* Cambridge: Cambridge University Press.
Maddieson, Ian. 1993a. Investigating Ewe articulations with electromagnetic articulography. *Forshungsberichte des Instituts für Phonetik und Sprachliche Kommunikation der Universität München* 31:181–214.
Maddieson, Ian. 1993b. Investigating Ewe articulations with electromagnetic articulography. *UCLA Working Papers in Phonetics* 85:22–53.
Maddieson, Ian. 1996. Phonetic universals. *UCLA Working Papers in Phonetics* 92:160–178.
Maddieson, Ian. 1997. Phonetic universals. In William J. Hardcastle and John Laver, *The handbook of phonetic sciences,* 619–639. Cambridge, Mass.: Blackwell.
Maddieson, Ian. 1998. Collapsing vowel harmony and doubly-articulated fricatives: Two myths about the Avatime phonological system. In Ian Maddieson and Thomas J. Hinnebusch, *Language history and linguistic description in Africa,* 155–166. Papers from the 26th Annual Conference on African Linguistics at UCLA 1995. Trenton, N.J.: Africa World Press.
Makashay, Matthew J. 1998. Dynamic invariance in auditory neural map formation. ms. Ohio State University.

Manessy, Gabriel. 1975. *Les langues oti-volta.* LACITO 15. Paris: SELAF.
Manessy, Gabriel. 1979. *Contribution à la classification généologique des langes voltaïques. Le group proto-central. Langues et civilisations à tradition orale 37.* Paris: SELAF.
McCarthy, John. 1981. A prosodic theory of nonconcatenative morphology. *Linguistic Inquiry* 12:373–418.
McCarthy, John. 1988. Feature geometry and dependency: A review. *Phonetica* 43:84–108.
McCarthy, John. 2002. *A thematic guide to Optimality Theory.* Cambridge: Cambridge University Press.
McCarthy, John, and Alan Prince. 1993. Prosodic morphology I. RuCCS TR-3, Rutgers University [also ROA-482-1201].
McCarthy, John, and Alan Prince. 1994. The emergence of the unmarked: Optimality in prosodic morphology. NELS 24:333-379 [also ROA-13-0594].
McCarthy, John, and Alan Prince. 1995. Faithfulness and reduplicative identity. In Beckman, Dickey, and Urbanczyk, 249–384 [also ROA-60-0000].
McCarthy, John, and Alison Taub. 1992. Review of Paradis and Prunet (eds.) 1991. *Phonology* 9:363–370.
McCord, Michael S. 1989. Acoustical and autosegmental analyses of the Mayogo vowel system. M.A. thesis. University of Texas, Arlington.
Melançon, L., and André Prost. 1971. *Dictionnaire buli-français.* Dakar: Publication du Départment de Linguistique Générale et de langues Négro-Africaines de la Faculté des Lettres et Sciences Humaines.
Miller-Ockhuizen, Amanda L. 1998. Towards a unified decompositional analysis of Khoisan lexical tone. In M. Schladt, *Language, identity, and conceptualization among the Khoisan.* Quellen zur Khoisan Forshung 15. Köln: Rüdiger Köppe Verlag [also ROA-203-0697].
Mills, Elizabeth. 1984. *Senoufo phonology: Discourse to syllable.* SIL Publications in Linguistics 72. Dallas: Summer Institute of Linguistics and the University of Texas at Arlington.
Myers, Scott. 1987. Tone and the structure of words in Shona. Ph.D. dissertation. University of Massachusetts, Amherst.
Myers, Scott, and Troi Carleton. 1996. Tonal transfer in Chichewa. *Phonology* 13:39–72.
Naba, Jean-Claude. 1994. *Le gulmancema: essai de systématisation; phonologie, tonologie, morphophonologie nominale, système verbal* (= Version rév. Phil. Diss. 1992, Univ. Bayreuth). (Grammatische Analysen afrikanischer Sprachen; Bd. 3.) Köln: Rüdiger Köppe Verlag.
Naden, Tony. 1986. Première note sur le Kɔnni. *Journal of West African Languages* 16(2):76–112.

Naden, Tony. 1988. The Gur languages. In M. E. Kropp-Dakubu, *The languages of Ghana*, 12–49. London: Kegan Paul Institute.

Naden, Tony. 1989. Gur. In John Bendor-Samuel and Rhonda L. Hartell, *The Niger-Congo languages*, 140–168. New York: SIL/University Press of America.

Nagi, Naomi, and William Reynolds. 1997. Optimality Theory and variable word-final deletion in Faetar. *Language Variation and Change* 9:37–55.

Napoli, Donna Jo, and Marina Nespor. 1979. The syntax of word-initial consonant gemination in Italian. *Language* 55:812–841.

Nespor, Marina, and Irene Vogel. 1986. *Prosodic phonology.* Dordrecht: Foris.

Neukom, Lukas. 1995. Description grammaticale du nateni (Bénin): Système verbal, classification nominale, phrases complexes, textes. *Arbeiten des Seminars für Allgemeine Sprachwissenschaft (ASAS)* 14. Zurich: Universität Zürich.

Newman, Paul. 1968. Ideophones from a syntactic point of view. *Journal of West African Languages* 5:107–118.

Ní Chiosáin, Máire, and Jaye Padgett. 1997. Markedness, segment realisation, and locality in spreading. Report No. LRC-97-01, Linguistics Research Center, University of California, Santa Cruz [also ROA-188-0497].

Nicole, Jacques. 1998. Les classes nominales dans les langues voltaïques. ms. SIL, Togo.

Nikiema, Norbert, and Jules Kinda, eds. 1994. *Moor gom-biis no-tuur gulsg sebre - Dictionnaire orthographique du moore.* Version provisoire. Sous la direction de Norbert Nikiema avec la collaboration de Jules Kinda. 2 tomes. Sous-Commission Nationale du Moore (ed.); Ouagadougou: Sous-Commission Nationale du Moore.

Noske, Manuela. 1996. [ATR] harmony in Turkana. *Studies in African Linguistics* 25(1):61–99.

Odden, David. 1981. Problems in tone assignment in Shona. Ph.D. dissertation. University of Illinois, Champaign-Urbana.

Odden, David. 1982. Tonal phenomena in KiShambaa. *Studies in African Linguistics* 13:177–208.

Odden, David. 1987. Kimatuumbi phrasal phonology. *Phonology* 4:13–36.

Odden, David. 1990a. C-command or edges in Makonde. *Phonology* 7:163–169.

Odden, David. 1990b. Tone in the Makonde dialects: Chimaraba. *Studies in African Linguistics* 21(1):61–105.

Odden, David. 1994. Adjacency parameters in phonology. *Language* 70:289–330.

Odden, David. 1995. Tone: African languages. In Goldsmith, 444–475.

Odden, David. 1996. *The phonology and morphology of Kimatuumbi*. New York: Oxford University Press.
Odden, David. 1998. Principles of tone assignment in Tanzanian Yao. In Hyman and Kisseberth, 265–314.
Ohala, John J. 1975. Phonetic explanations for nasal sound patterns. In Ferguson, Hyman, and Ohala, 289–316.
Ohala, John J., and Manjari Ohala. 1993. The phonetics of nasal phonology: Theorems and data. In Marie K. Huffman and Rena A. Krakow, *Nasals, nasalization, and the velum. Phonetics and Phonology* 5:225–249. San Diego, Calif.: Academic Press.
Olawsky, Knut J. 1996. *An introduction to Dagbani phonology*. Arbeiten des Sonderforschungsbereichs 282, Nr. 76. Düsseldorf: Heinrich-Heine-Universität.
Ouoba, Bendi Benoît et al., eds. 1994. *Mi gulimancéma leni mi bonpienma tínàa - Dictionnaire bilingue gulimancéma-français, lexique français-gulmancéma*. Publ. par la Sous-Commission Nationale du Gulmancéma. Réd. dir. par B. B. Ouoba. Fada N'Gurma, Ouagadougou: Sous-Commission Nationale du Gulmancéma.
Ourso, Méterwa. 1989. Lama phonology and morphology. Ph.D. dissertation. University of Illinois, Urbana-Champaign.
Padgett, Jaye. 1996. Partial class behavior and nasal place assimilation. *Proceedings of the Southwestern Optimality Theory Workshop 1995*. Coyote Working Papers in Linguistics, 145–183. University of Arizona Tucson.
Paradis, Carol, and Jean-François Prunet. 1991. Introduction: Asymmetry and invisibility in consonant articulations. In Paradis and Prunet, 1–28.
Paradis, Carole, and Jean-François Prunet, eds. 1991. *The special status of coronals: Internal and external evidence*. New York: Academic Press.
Parkinson, Frederick. 1996a. The Incremental Constriction Model for the description of vowel height. *OSU Working Papers in Linguistics* 48:149–182.
Parkinson, Frederick. 1996b. The representation of vowel height in phonology. Ph.D. dissertation. Ohio State University.
Pater, Joe. 1996. *NC. *Proceedings of NELS* 26:227–239. Amherst, Mass.: GLSA.
Pater, Joe. 1999. Austronesian nasal substitution and other NC effects. In René Kager, Harry van der Hulst, and Wim Zonneveld, *The prosody-morphology interface*, 310–343. New York: Cambridge University Press [also ROA-160-1196].

Payne, David. 1981. *The phonology and morphology of Axininca Campa.* Summer Institute of Linguistics Publications in Linguistics 66. Dallas: Summer Institute of Linguistics and the University of Texas at Arlington.

Perlmutter, David. 1995. Phonological quantity and multiple asssociation. In Goldsmith, 307–317.

Peterson, Thomas H. 1971. Mooré structure: A generative analysis of the tonal system and aspects of the syntax. Ph.D. dissertation. UCLA.

Pierrehumbert, Janet. 1993. Dissimilarity in the Arabic verbal roots. *Proceedings of the North East Linguistics Society* 23:367–381. Amherst, Mass.: GLSA.

Pike, Kenneth. 1948. *Tone languages: A technique for determining the number and type of pitch contrasts in a language, with studies in tonemic substitution and fusion.* University of Michigan Publications in Linguistics 4. Ann Arbor: University of Michigan Press.

Pike, Kenneth L., and Charles C. Fries. 1949. Coexistent phonemic systems. *Language* 25:25–50.

Poletto, Robert. 1996. Base-identity effects in Runyankore reduplication. *OSU Working Papers in Linguistics* 48:183–210.

Poletto, Robert. 1998a. Syntax and tone in Runyankore. *OSU Working Papers in Linguistics* 51:95–146.

Poletto, Robert. 1998b. Constraints on tonal association in Olusamia: An Optimality Theoretic account. In Hyman and Kisseberth, 331–364.

Poulter, Todd. 1984. Buli phonology. ms. Tamale: Ghana Institute of Linguistics, Literacy, and Bible Translation.

Price, Norman. 1989. *Notes on Mada phonology.* Language Data, Africa Series, Publication 23. Dallas: Summer Institute of Linguistics.

Prince, Alan, and Paul Smolensky. 1993. Optimality Theory: Constraint interaction in Generative Grammar. RuCCS TR-2, Rutgers University, now ROA-537-0802.

Pulleyblank, Douglas. 1986. *Tone in lexical phonology.* Dordrecht: Reidel.

Pulleyblank, Douglas. 1997. Optimality Theory and features. In Diane Archangeli and D. Terence Langendoen, *Optimality Theory: An overview,* 59–101. Malden, Mass.: Blackwell.

Rennison, John. 1997. *Koromfe.* Routledge Descriptive Grammars. London: Routledge.

Reynolds, W. 1994. Variation and Optimality Theory. Ph.D. dissertation. University of Pennsylvania.

Reynolds, William T. 1997. Post-high tone shift in Venda nominals. ROA-194-0597.

Rialland, Annie. 1981. Le système tonal du gurma. *Journal of African Languages and Linguistics* 3:39–64.

Rialland, Annie. 1983. Le système tonal du moba comparé à celui du gurma. In J. Kaye, H. Koopman, D. Sportiche, and A. Dugas, *Current Approaches to African Linguistics* 2:217–237. Dordrecht: Foris.

Rice, Keren. 1999. Featural markedness in phonology: Variation, Part II. *Glot International* 4(8):3–7.

Rietkerk, Dieke. 1999. The Mbelime verb system. Paper presented at Second Colloquium on Gur Languages, Cotonou, Benin, March 29–April 1, 1999.

Roberts-Kohno, R. Ruth. 1998. Empty root nodes in Kikamba: Conflicting evidence and theoretical implications. In Ian Maddieson and Thomas J. Hinnebusch, *Language history and linguistic description in Africa*, 185–194. Papers from the 26th Annual Conference on African Linguistics at UCLA in 1995. Trenton, N.J.: Africa World Press.

Rosendall, Heidi James. 1992. *A phonological study of the Gwari lects*. Language Data, African Series 24. Dallas: Summer Institute of Linguistics.

Rosenthall, Samuel. 1994. Vowel/glide alternations in a theory of constraint interaction. Ph.D. dissertation. University of Massachusetts, Amherst.

Rubach, Jerzy. 1994. Affricates as strident stops in Polish. *Linguistic Inquiry* 25:119–143.

Russell, Jann Maree. 1985. Moba phonology. M.A. thesis. Macquarie University, Sydney.

Russell, Kevin. 1995. Morphemes and candidates in Optimality Theory. ROA-44-0195.

Russell, Kevin. 1997. Optimality Theory and morphology. In Archangeli and Langendoen, 102–133.

Ryder, Mary Ellen. 1987. An autosegmental treatment of nasal assimilation to labial-velars. CLS 23:2. Parasession on Autosegmental and Metrical Phonology, 253–265.

Sagey, Elizabeth. 1990. *The representation of features in non-linear phonology*. New York: Garland Press.

Schaefer, Robert. 1975. *The phonology of Frafra*. Collected Field Notes 15. Legon: The Institute of African Studies, University of Ghana.

Schane, Sanford A. 1973. *Generative phonology*. Englewood Cliffs, N.J.: Prentice-Hall.

Schane, Sanford A. 1984. The fundamentals of particle phonology. *Phonology* 1:129–155.

Schane, Sanford A. 1995. Diphthongization in particle phonology. In Goldsmith, 586–608.

Schein, Barry, and Donca Steriade. 1986. On geminates. *Linguistic Inquiry* 17:691–744.

Schröeder, Helga, and Martin Schröeder. 1987. Vowel harmony in Toposa. Juba, Sudan. ms. Summer Institute of Linguistics.

Selkirk, Elisabeth. 1986. On derived domains in sentence phonology. *Phonology* 3:371–405.

Shaw, Patricia A. 1991. Consonant harmony systems: The special status of coronal harmony. In Paradis and Prunet, 125–158.

Smolensky, Paul. 1993. Harmony, markedness, and phonological activity. ROA-37-1094.

Snider, Keith. 1984. Vowel harmony and the consonant *l* in Chumburung. *Studies in African Languages* 15(1):47–57.

Snider, Keith. 1990. Tonal upstep in Krachi: Evidence for a register tier. *Language* 66:453–474.

Snider, Keith. 1999. *The geometry and features of tone.* Summer Institute of Linguistics and the University of Texas at Arlington Publications in Linguistics 133. Dallas.

Somé, Penou-Achille. 1998. L'influence des consonnes sur les tons en dagara, langue voltaïque du Burkina Faso. *Studies in African Linguistics* 27:3–47.

Spencer, Andrew. 1991. *Morphological theory.* Cambridge, Mass.: Blackwell.

Spratt, David, and Nancy Spratt. 1968. *The phonology of Kusal.* Collected Field Notes 10. Legon: The Institute of African Studies, University of Ghana.

Steele, Mary, and Gretchen Weed. 1966. *The phonology of Konkomba.* Collected Field Notes 3. Legon: The Institute of African Studies, University of Ghana.

Steriade, Donca. 1993. Closure, release, and nasal contours. In Marie K. Huffman and Rena A. Krakow, *Nasals, nasalization, and the velum,* 401–470. San Diego: Academic Press.

Steriade, Donca. 1994. Positional neutralization and the expression of contrast. ms. UCLA.

Steriade, Donca. 1995a. Underspecification and markedness. In Goldsmith, 114–174.

Steriade, Donca. 1995b. Licensing retroflexion. ms. UCLA.

Steriade, Donca. 1997. Licensing laryngeal features. ms. UCLA.

Suh, Kyunghoon. 1998. Diphthong formation in Optimality Theory. In Benjamin Bruening, *MIT Working Papers in Linguistics* 31:415–428. Proceedings of the 8th Student Conference in Linguistics.

Suzuki, Keiichiro. 1998. A typological investigation of dissimilation. Ph.D. dissertation. University of Arizona.

Swadesh, Mauricio, Evangelina Arana, John T. Bendor-Samuel, and W. A. A. Wilson. 1966. A preliminary glottochronology of Gur languages. *Journal of West African Languages* 3(2):27–65.

Toupin, Michael. 1995. *The phonology of Sisaale-Pasaale*. Collected Field Notes 22. Legon: The Institute of African Studies, University of Ghana.
Toupin, Michael. 1997. A grammar of Sisaala-Pasaale. ms. Tamale: Ghana Institute of Linguistics, Literacy, and Bible Translation.
Tranel, Bernard. 1996. Rules vs. constraints: A case study. Paper presented at conference on Current Trends in Phonology: Models and Methods, Royamont, France. ROA-72-0000.
Vago, Robert M., and Harry Leder. 1987. On the autosegmental analysis of vowel harmony in Turkana. In David Odden, *Current approaches to African linguistics* 4:383–396. Dordrecht: Foris.
Vance, Timothy J. 1987. *An introduction to Japanese phonology*. Albany, N.Y.: State University of New York Press.
von Roncador, M. 1999. Remarques sur la morphologie verbale du nootré. Paper presented at Second Colloquium on Gur Languages, Cotonou, Benin, March 29–April 1, 1999.
Walsh-Dickey, Laura. 1997. The phonology of liquids. Ph.D. dissertation. University of Massachusetts, Amherst.
Ward, Ida C. 1933. *The phonetic and tonal structure of Efik*. Cambridge: W. Heffer and Sons.
Welmers, William. 1963. Associative *a* and *ka* in Niger-Congo. Language 39:432-447.
Welmers, William E. 1973. *African language structures*. Berkeley: University of California Press.
Wichser, Magdalena. 1994. Description grammaticale du kar, langue senoufo du Burkina Faso. Thèse Diplôme de l'Ecole Pratique des Hautes Etudes. Paris.
Wilson, W. A. A., and John Bendor-Samuel. 1969. The phonology of the nominal in Dagbani. *Linguistics* 52:56–82.
Winkelmann, Kerstin. 1998. *Die Sprache der Cɛfɔ von Daramandugu*. Berichte des Sonderforschungsbereichs 269. Frankfurt am Main.
Woock, Edith Bavin, and Michael Noonan. 1979. Vowel harmony in Lango. CLS 15:20–29.
Yip, Moira. 1996. Feet, tonal reduction, and speech rate at the word and phrase level in Chinese. ROA-159-1196.
Yip, Moira. 2002. *Tone*. New York: Cambridge University Press.
Zubritskaya, Katya. 1997. Mechanism of sound change in Optimality Theory. *Language Variation and Change* 9:121–148.

Subject Index

A

adjacency issues 93, 104, 126, 130, 145, 149ff., 170, 186, 204ff.
adjectives
    ATR harmony 187ff.
    morphology 45
    tone 356ff.
agentive nouns
    morphology 50ff.
    prefix vowel 275
article, definite 71, also under determiner
Articulatory Phonology 114
aspect 59ff.
    imperfective 60, 387, 399, 402
    perfective 62, 394
    future 21, 397, 399
    imperative 64, 401, 402
    "imperfective II" 65
    indirect imperative 403
    "neutral" 67
aspiration 100
assimilation (see also "ATR harmony")
    consonantal 103ff.
        nasal place 105ff.
        /r/, total 123ff.
        voicing 129
    vowel
        across coronals 250ff.
        across /g/ 244ff.
        before [ŋ] 258ff.
        to glide 254ff.
        total, across hiatus 288ff.

associative construction and tone 364ff.
ATR harmony
    across words 205ff.
    active value of, 190ff.
    syntax and 218
    within words 185ff.

B

Buli 3

C

c-command 221
centralization of vowels 258ff.
clause structure 9ff.
[closed] feature 191, 230, 231ff., 235ff.
conditionals 413
consonants
    aspiration 100
    assimilation 103ff.
    contrast justification 98
    deletion 136ff.
    duration 102ff.
    epenthesis 161ff.
    inventory 8, 97
    labialization 135
    lenition 117
    palatalization 135
    prevoicing 101
    weakening 117
co-occurrences of phonemes 78ff.

Correspondence Theory 25ff.

D

deletion, consonantal 136ff.
  of /g/ 136ff.
  of /n/ 141ff.
demonstratives 71
determiners 71ff.
dialects 3–4
diphthongization 226ff.
dissimilation (also see polarity, tonal)
  of /r/ 144ff.
  word-class dependent 144ff.
distribution of phonemes 86
  word finally 87
  root vs. affix 88
  consonant clusters 92
  co-occurrences of phonemes 78ff.
duration
  consonant 102ff.
  nasals 115
  vowels 179ff.

E

elision (see "deletion")
epenthesis
  consonantal
    glottal stop 161ff., 164ff.
    /r/ 162ff., 167ff.
  tone 335
  vowel
    identity of epenthetic vowel 270
    interconsonantal 263ff., 272ff.
    word-final 262
    tone on 324ff.

F

Feature Geometry 31ff., 112, 230
formants 181ff.
frequency of phonemes 76

G

Gur languages 3ff.

H

historical factors 4, 39, 68–69, 89, 99, 125, 134, 138, 342, 354, 359, 365,

I

interrogatives 11
  polar questions 11, 416
  content questions 12
intonation
  polar question 11, 416
  "surprise question" 417

L

labialization 135
labialvelars
  nasal assimilation 111ff.
lenition of consonants 117ff.
levels of OT 287
locatives 63, 383

M

Mampruli 3ff.
minimal size of nouns and verbs 95
modifiers 70
  demonstratives 71
  numbers 71
  tone 381ff.
monovalent features 191, 192
morphology
  noun classes 36ff.
  adjectives 45ff.
  compound nouns 55
  derived nouns 48ff.
  derived adjectives 52ff.
  derived verbs 68
  verbal aspect 58ff.

N

nasals
  assimilation of place 105ff.
nouns
  agentive 50
  compound 51, 54, 378
  derived 48ff., 353ff.
  tone 331ff.
  toneless 331ff.

Subject Index

morpheme-specific phonology 136ff., 141ff., 342ff.
noun phrase
   associative 364ff.
   syntax 15ff.
numbers 71, 289

O

obliques 23
Optimality Theory 25ff.
   constraint types 27ff.
   exceptions 301
   optionality 134
   tone analyses 304
   typology 27
   variable rankings 134

P

palatalization 135
particles, preverbal
   syntax 21ff.
   ATR harmony 209ff.
phonemes
   frequency 76ff.
   co-occurrences 78ff.
   distribution 86ff.
phonetics
   aspiration 100
   duration, consonant 102ff.
   duration, vowels 179ff.
   formants 181ff.
   prevoicing 101
polarity, tone 342ff.
prevoicing 101
privative features (see "monovalent features")
pronouns 13ff., 73
   different divisions 73

Q

questions (see "interrogatives")

R

/r/
   assimilation, total 123
   dissimilation 144ff.
   separate phoneme 119ff.
   replacement of V with /r/ 169ff.

reduplication 20, 37, 50ff., 66, 275ff.
Rutgers Optimality Archive 25

S

specification of features 302ff.
speech rate 300
stress 419ff.
syllables
   minimality 95
   noun and verb structure 89
   types 93
   as tone bearing unit 307ff.
syntax-phonology interface 165, 205ff., 218, 295ff.

T

tone
   adjectives 356ff.
   associative NP 364
   compound nouns 378
   conditionals 413ff.
   contours, nonfinal 384
   derived nouns 353ff.
   distribution in words 306
   downstep 312
   epenthesis 335
   epenthetic vowels 324 ff.
   floating 312, 313, 365ff.
   inventory 8, 305ff.
   morphemic 313ff.
   nouns 331ff.
   nominal suffixes 310ff., 339
   OCP 314ff.
   polarity 342ff.
   postnominal modifiers 381ff.
   preverbal particles 407ff.
   tone-bearing unit 307ff.
   toneless nouns 331
   verbal aspect 386ff.
typology
   rightward tone spread 337
   H-present 335
   epenthetic vowels 270

V

verb phrase
   syntax 18ff.
   preverbal particles 21, 407ff.
verbal extensors 69ff.

voicing assimilation 129
vowels
(see assimilation)
   agentive nouns 275
   across /g/ 244ff.
   across coronals 250ff.
   backing before [ŋ] 258
   to glide 254ff.
   total, in hiatus 288ff.
   ATR harmony 184ff.
   contrast justification 177ff.
   diphthongization 226ff.
   duration 179ff.
   epenthesis 262ff.
   formant measurements 181ff.
   height features 191ff.
   inventory 8, 175
   shortening 278ff.

W

weakening of consonants 117
word order 9ff.

Index of Constraints

(listed when defined, discussed, or causing fatal violations in tableaus)

A

*aa]-Adj 283
AGR[ATR] 196, 203, 204, 242
ALIGN[ATR]μ 193, 194, 249
ALIGN[ATR]$_{UTT}$ 213, 216, 225
ALIGN TONE-RIGHT 338
ALIGN H-Right (=High-RT) 338, 339
ALIGN L-Right (=Low-RT) 338, 339
ALIGN-Verb-Rt 388, 390, 392, 394, 396, 398, 400, 402, 403, 415
*[+ant]$_{fric}$[−ant]$_{vow}$ (= *[+ant][−ant]) 135, 136
ATR-AGR( ) 224
ATR/[closed] 202, 203, 237, 238, 243

C

C[αvoi]C[-αvoi] (CC±voi) 130, 132, 133
*C$_{dors}$V$_{cor}$ 253
C$_{iPL}$C$_{iPL}$ 93
[closed]/PLACE 202, 203, 268, 269
*CLOSING 236, 237
CODACOND 130, 134, 140, 156, 274
*Complex (= *Comp) 252, 253, 256, 257
*CONT-INT 351, 415
*CONTOUR 317, 319
*[cor][cor] 170
*[cor]ŋ 260, 261

*Cpl$_i$Cpl$_j$ 108, 110, 272, 273

D

DEP[ATR] 193, 194, 195, 197, 203, 205, 213, 214, 432
DEP[closed] (= DEP[cl]) 202, 203, 205, 235, 237, 238, 239, 240, 242, 243, 432
DEP[+cont] 166, 168
DEP[−cont] 166, 167
DEP[Cor] 164, 166, 167, 202, 203, 205, 268
DEP[Dors] 87, 164, 202, 203, 205, 261, 268, 269, 271, 276
DEP(H) 328, 334, 374
DEP(L) 328, 330, 368, 377
DEP[Lab] 164
DEP[nas] 127, 153, 173
DEP[Phar] 164, 167
DEP(V) 132, 133, 156, 267
DEP(V$_{∅CL}$) 269, 274, 276, 277, 278
DEP(V$_{CL}$) 269, 276, 277, 278
DEP(VCL-CL) 269, 432
[dors]-AGR 204, 205, 213
*[dors]SHARE 260, 261

515

F

Faith[aa] 201, 217, 225, 253, 283
*F$_i$F$_j$ 105

G

Generalized OCP 150
*g$_{NC2/3}$ 140, 173

H

*(H) 317, 319, 320, 367
Head-Prom 366, 367, 368, 369, 370, 371, 374
HiDiph 241, 242, 243, 282, 432
High-Rt (see "Align H-Right")
*H!H-μ 391, 392, 394, 396, 400
*HL$_{adj}$ 362, 363, 364
*HLH 321, 323, 324, 326, 330, 350, 367, 371, 374, 377, 378, 381, 392, 394, 396, 400, 405, 406, 432
H-Present 335, 336, 339, 369
*H-Spread 317, 328, 334, 339, 364, 370

I

ICC[F] 104
Ident[ant]$_C$ 135, 136
Ident[ATR]$_{LEX}$ 197, 198, 211, 212, 214, 216, 217, 225
Ident[ant]$_V$ 135,136
Ident[cont] 118,119
Ident[F] 159
    Ident[F]$_{LEX}$ 159
    Ident[F]$_{PART}$ 159
    Ident[F]$_{DER}$ 159
    Ident[F]-WI 292, 293, 294, 298
Ident[nas] 127, 173
    Ident[nas]$_{DER}$ 159
    Ident[nas]$_{LEX}$ 160
Ident[son] 127, 128, 129, 131, 132, 160, 173, 432
    Ident[son]$_{LEX}$ 123,
    Ident[son]$_{STEM}$ 153, 154, 155
Ident[voi] 118, 119, 173
    Ident[voi]$_{LEX}$ 153, 154, 155, 157, 159, 160
IDOnsLar 131, 132, 133

L

*(L) 317,
Lazy 104
*LH-μ 389, 390, 402, 403
*(L)L 373, 374
Low-Rt (see "Align L-Right")
*L-Spread 317, 328
*[liq]V[liq] 126,129
*[liquid]V[liquid] (= *[liq]V[liq]) 155, 156

M

Max(Assoc) 317, 318, 334, 336, 378, 380
Max[ATR] 193, 194,196, 198, 200, 201, 204, 211, 212, 213, 214, 216, 217, 225, 249, 294, 298
Max-BR[pl] 276, 277
Max(C) 110, 119, 132,133, 140, 144, 267, 269, 274
Max[cl] 235, 237, 238, 239, 240, 242, 243, 282, 432
Max[cor]$_V$ 254, 256
Max[Cpl] 109, 174
    Max[Cpl]$_{rel}$ 109, 110,128, 160, 174
Max[dors] 272
Max[H] 348, 349, 350, 367, 368, 369, 432
Max[L] 373, 432
Max[lab] 87
    Max[lab]$_V$ 256
MaxLex 281, 282
MaxMS 281, 282, 294
Max[nas] 110, 132
Max[place]$_G$ 255, 256, 257
Max[pl]$_{OBST}$ 108, 133,134, 174
Max[pl]$_{NAS}$ 108, 174
Max(S) 168, 235, 282, 293, 294

N

*]$_{N\text{-}Adj}$[ATR 199, 200, 249, 283
*n$_{NC1}$ 143, 144, 173
NoGap 193, 194, 195, 213, 253
NonFinal[dors] 271
NoSkip 369, 370
*NVr 126, 128, 160
ŋ// 86ff., 267, 269, 271

O

OCP (see also GOCP) 149, 352
ONS-lex 165,166, 295

P

[phar]-edge] 166, 168,170
POLAR 347, 348, 349, 374

R

[rhotic]V[rhotic] (= *rVr) 152, 153, 155
*rr 154, 155
*R-SPREAD 322, 323, 324, 326, 328, 405, 406

S

*[son]d 158, 159
*[son]r 126,128,129, 160,173, 432

T

*TONELESS 317, 328, 330, 334, 377, 378, 380
*TRIPLE-T 320

V

*VCV$_{[cor]}$ 252, 253
*VDV 118,119, 156, 157, 168
*V$_{Fi}$#V$_{Fj}$ 292, 293, 294, 298
VG-AGR 255, 256, 257, 274, 278
VgV-AGR 247, 249, 271
*VV$_{mid}$ 235, 237, 240, 242, 282, 432
*VVV 168,170, 281, 282

W

WEAK 104

X

XP-distinct 298

SIL International and
The University of Texas at Arlington
Publications in Linguistics
Recent Publications

140. **The phonology of Mono**, by Kenneth S. Olson. 2005.
139. **Language and life: Essays in memory of Kenneth L. Pike**, ed. by Mary Ruth Wise, Thomas N. Headland, and Ruth M. Brend. 2003.
138. **Case and agreement in Abaza**, by Brian O'Herin. 2002.
137. **Pragmatics of persuasive discourse of Spanish television advertising**, by Karol J. Hardin. 2001.
136. **Quiegolani Zapotec syntax: A Principles and Parameters account**, by Cheryl A. Black. 2000.
135. **A grammar of Sochiapan Chinantec: Studies in Chinantec languages 6**, by David Paul Foris. 2001.
134. **A reference grammar of the Northern Embera languages: Studies in the languages of Colombia 7**, by Charles Arthur Mortensen. 1999.
133. **The geometry and features of tone**, by Keither Snider. 1999.
132. **Desano grammar: Studies in the languages of Colombia 6**, by Marion Miller. 1999.
131. **The structure of evidential categories in Wanka Quechua**, by Rick Floyd. 1999.
130. **Cubeo grammar: Studies in the languages of Colombia 5**, by Nancy L. Morse and Michael B. Maxwell. 1999.
129. **Aspects of Zaiwa prosody: An autosegmental account**, by Mark W. Wannemacher. 1998.
128. **Tense and aspect in Obolo grammar and discourse**, by Uche Aaron. 1998.
127. **Case grammar applied**, by Walter A. Cook, S.J. 1998.
126. **The Dong language in Guizhou Province, China**, by Long Yaohong and Zheng Guoqiao, translated from Chinese by D. Norman Geary. 1998.
125. **Vietnamese classifiers in narrative texts**, by Karen Ann Daley. 1998.
124. **Comparative Kadai: The Tai branch**, ed. by Jerold A. Edmondson and David B. Solnit. 1997.

For further information or a full listing of SIL publications contact:

International Academic Bookstore
SIL International
7500 W. Camp Wisdom Road
Dallas, TX 75236-5699

Voice: 972-708-7404
Fax: 972-708-7363
E-mail: academic_books@sil.org
Internet: http://www.ethnologue.com

www.ingramcontent.com/pod-product-compliance
Lightning Source LLC
Chambersburg PA
CBHW071231300426
44116CB00008B/994